THE LIFE OF JESUS

AMS PRESS

NEW YORK

THE LIFE OF JESUS

by

MAURICE GOGUEL

Docteur ès Lettres, Docteur en Théologie
D.D. (St. Andrews)
Directeur d'études at the École des Hautes Études (Sorbonne)
Professor at the Faculté libre de Théologie
Protestante (Paris)

TRANSLATED BY

OLIVE WYON

NEW YORK
THE MACMILLAN COMPANY
1933

Library of Congress Cataloging in Publication Data

Goguel, Maurice, 1880-1955.
   The life of Jesus.

   Translation of the 1st v. of a trilogy entitled
Jésus et les origines du christianisme; the 2d v.
has title: The birth of Christianity.
   Reprint of the 1933 ed. published by Macmillan,
New York.
   Bibliography: p.
   Includes index.
   1. Jesus Christ—Biography. 2. Bible. N.T.—
Biography. I. Title.
BT301.G65   1976   232.9'01 [B]   75-41114
ISBN 0-404-14546-9

Reprinted from an original copy in the collections
of the Ohio State University Libraries

From the edition of 1933, New York
First AMS edition published in 1976
Manufactured in the United States of America

AMS PRESS INC.
NEW YORK, N.Y.

PREFACE

THIS book is an historical work. Although it deals with a question which is of immediate interest for the Christian faith, I have not felt at liberty to treat it with a different method than that which is accepted by historians in general, the only method by which it is possible to establish the reality of the facts of the past. In considering the historical aspect of the problem of Jesus, I do not deny that convinced Christians have a perfect right to look at the question from a different angle, and to regard Jesus from the point of view of his spiritual and religious significance.

But this book is a work of religious history, and I have tried to understand the religious sentiments and ideas with which it confronts us. In so doing, however, I do not feel that I have departed from the historical method any more than the historians of art, who do not confine themselves to a mere catalogue of the works which they are studying, but try to understand them from the aesthetic point of view.

The twofold nature of the problem of Jesus explains why it is that most of those who have dealt with it have satisfied neither the historians nor the devout, and that very often they have displeased both at the same time. For nineteen centuries the prophecy which was pronounced by the aged Simeon over the infant Jesus, "he shall be a sign which shall be spoken against" (Luke ii. 34), has never ceased to be fulfilled. This attempt of mine will meet the same fate. Some will charge me with failing to make sufficient use of the critical method because I have used the psychological method. Others will blame me for having tried to apply the historical method to a problem which, from their point of view, is not amenable to criticism. They are pained, and, indeed, scandalized, by what they regard as a lack of respect for the Christian tradition. I hope that the representatives of both schools of thought will at least admit the honesty and sincerity of my effort.

Is it necessary to say that I have the most profound respect for all forms of the Christian faith, even for those which are furthest from my own point of view? If I have been obliged, in many instances, and on essential points, to formulate conclusions which contradict the traditional beliefs, and may even wound the convictions of many people, may I say that I have done this out of respect for what I believe to be the truth, and never in order to hurt the feelings of those whose convictions I do not share. If, in spite of the fact that I have been very watchful on this point, some expressions may have escaped me which may shock any Christian believer, Catholic or Protestant, I crave pardon in advance.

In undertaking to retrace the origin of Christianity, to describe what Jesus was, what he did, and what he thought, to relate the story of his life (to the extent in which the documents at our disposal render this possible), and to show how the Christian Church was the direct outcome of his life and his teaching—I do not deny that I am acting audaciously. For about a century, and with special intensity for the past twenty or twenty-five years, criticism has submitted the Gospel tradition to a process of merciless analysis, which has reduced the tradition to such a fragmentary condition that to many historians it has seemed impossible to combine these fragments into a coherent whole. In all that concerns the life of Jesus, many critics—who have no desire to use the scientific historical method in order to attack Christianity—are, if not actually sceptical, at least absolutely agnostic in their outlook. They believe that every attempt to reconstruct the story of his life, or even to sketch in the main lines of the narrative, is doomed to failure. Further on (in Chapter VII) you will find the reasons which I have given to show that, far from sharing this feeling, I feel that the moment has come to tackle the problem of Jesus afresh with a method based on the results attained by the criticism of the Gospels during the past thirty years.

In a second volume I hope to be able to show how that faith in and attachment to Jesus which he had implanted in the hearts of his disciples, after a temporary eclipse at the moment of the Passion, reappeared in them as the affirmation of the resurrection of their master, and how on the foundation of this faith the Christian Church was founded and its doctrine developed.

The way in which the story of Jesus is presented in this first volume is directly conditioned by the present state of historical science. My effort has been directed towards the reconstruction of the main lines of the development of the Gospel narrative. In my opinion this is the point at which, at the present moment, it is most necessary to clear the way. This volume, which is already larger than I wished it to be, would have grown beyond measure if I had undertaken a systematic explanation of the tradition as a whole. I have preferred to confine my efforts to those elements which have seemed to me the most useful for helping me to disengage the framework of the life of Jesus. My ambition has been to give a sketch of the life of Jesus which might perhaps be open to development and enrichment, but in which my successors would find nothing to omit. In order to avoid all misunderstanding, I state quite frankly that I do not reject en bloc as legendary all the elements in the tradition of the Gospel history which I have not used.

It has not always been possible to register at all points, with that absolute precision which might be desired, the degree of certitude, or of probability, for the solutions which I have adopted. In formulating them I have not always been able to avoid sounding rather dogmatic. I have tried, however, to distinguish between those conclusions which seemed to me to be well established and those which are only more or less probable conjectures. Further, it has seemed to me that in the present state of the question it would be more interesting to mark definitely the position which I have adopted in these matters than to use such careful and guarded language that the final impression on the mind of the reader would be hazy and blurred.

In view of the aim of this work I have not deemed it necessary to give a complete analysis of the Gospel records, nor even of those which I have actually used. However carefully such a process is carried out, to some extent it always betrays the original. I have assumed that I have the right to think that my readers will have by them either the Greek Testament itself or a good translation, which they will consult in order to follow the discussions in the following chapters.

A book of this kind is based upon a mass of detailed researches, for in the Gospel tradition there is no point, however small or trivial it may appear, which may not provoke endless discussion. In order not to weary the reader, I have refrained from giving all the documentation which I could have given to justify my point of view, nor have I discussed all the theories which I do not accept. So far as technical discussions are concerned, it has seemed best to confine myself rigidly to the necessary minimum. On a certain number of points I have referred those who wish for further information to my earlier works. I hope that it will be realized that I have also examined with care the other questions to which I have proposed solutions.

I owe much to the critics of the nineteenth and the twentieth centuries. The notes in which I refer to the works of various scholars do not give any adequate idea of the extent of this debt. It is greater than I have been able to indicate, and, indeed, greater than I myself can altogether realize.

The solution of a problem like that of the life of Jesus can never be the work of one individual, nor of a single generation. I shall feel amply rewarded for my efforts if, profiting by the work of my predecessors, I have been able to offer a contribution which those who come after me will be able to utilize, in order to do better work and to carry the subject further than I have been able to do.

AUTHOR'S NOTE

THE four Gospels are mentioned under the names of Matthew, Mark, Luke, and John, for the sake of convenience; this does not mean, however, that the present writer accepts the traditional views on the authorship of the Gospels.

When an asterisk is placed after a reference it shows that the passage in question occurs in one or two other Gospels.

For the study of the problems raised by the Gospel narrative the most convenient edition of the New Testament is that of EBERHARD NESTLE (*Novum Testamentum graece cum apparatu critico cuvavit* + D. EBERHARD NESTLE, *Editionem tertiam decimam novis curis elaboravit*, ERWIN NESTLE, Stuttgart, 1927). The critical apparatus of this edition, although valuable, does not dispense the reader from having recourse to works which are fuller and more complete, of which the most important is the complete edition of TISCHENDORF (*editio octava critica major*, Leipzig, 1869–1872), until the appearance of the edition of this fundamental work which is being prepared by a group of English scholars.

A *Synopsis* is an indispensable tool for the student. The best is that of ALBERT HUCK, *Synopse der drei ersten Evangelien, Anhang: Die Johannesparallelen*,[8] Tübingen, 1931.

May I venture to recommend the version of the New Testament which I have published in collaboration with my colleague HENRI MONNIER and a group of exegetes (*Le Nouveau Testament, traduction nouvelle d'après les meilleurs textes avec introductions et notes sous la direction de* MAURICE GOGUEL *et* HENRI MONNIER, Paris, Payot, 1929).

The manuscripts and versions of the New Testament are mentioned according to the system of Gregory, which is now universally adopted. The *Novum Testamentum* of NESTLE and the *Synopse* of HUCK both give the table with the usual *sigla*.

The works of FLAVIUS JOSEPHUS (*A. J.* = *Antiquities*, *G. J.* = *Jewish War*, *V.* = *Vita*, *Hal.* = *Halôsis* [the Slavonic version of the *Jewish War*)] are quoted according to the traditional division, supplemented by the indication of the paragraphs of the edition of NIESE (the same arrangement is followed in the edition issued by THACKERAY).

TRANSLATOR'S NOTE

THE author has read this translation in proof; he has introduced a certain number of changes into the text and the notes for the English edition. Substantially, however, this work is a full and unabridged translation of the *Vie de Jésus* which first appeared in March 1932.

The quotations from the Bible have been rendered from the Authorised Version.

In *The Christ-passage from Josephus*, on pages 84 and 85, the translator has followed the rendering given by G. R. S. MEAD, in *The Gnostic John the Baptizer*, pp. 106–107. (J. M. Watkins, 1924.)

In the passages quoted from the *Book of Enoch* the version used is that of DR. R. H. CHARLES (*The Book of Enoch* or *I Enoch*, pp. 85–88 and 124–125 (in part). Translated from the Editor's Ethiopic Text. Clarendon Press. 1912.)

OLIVE WYON

LONDON,
March 1933

CONTENTS

CHAPTER II

CHAPTER III

PAGE

THE PAULINE EVIDENCE   105

CHAPTER IV

PAGE

THE GOSPELS

CHAPTER V

THE GOSPEL TRADITION 162

CHAPTER VI

CHAPTER XII

THE FIRST PART OF THE GALILEAN MINISTRY

CHAPTER XIII

THE CRISIS IN GALILEE

CHAPTER XIV

THE JERUSALEM MINISTRY   400

CHAPTER XV

THE DAY OF THE LAST SUPPER OF JESUS AND THE DATE OF HIS DEATH   429

CHAPTER XVI

THE LAST EVENING IN THE LIFE OF JESUS 438

CHAPTER XVII

THE STORY OF THE PASSION 463

CHAPTER XXI

THE GOSPEL

BIBLIOGRAPHICAL NOTES

I. Works of a General Character. Reviews

BAUER = WALTER BAUER, *Griechisch-deutsches Wörterbuch zu den Schriften des Neuen Testaments*, Giessen, 1928.

D.A.C.L. = *Dictionnaire d'archéologie chrétienne et de liturgie*, publié par Dom F. CABROL et Dom H. LECLERCQ, Paris, 1907 ss.

Congrès = *Congrès d'histoire du christianisme. Jubilé Alfred Loisy*, Paris, Amsterdam, 1928.

HENNECKE, *Neut. Ap.* = *Neutestamentliche Apokryphen in Verbindung mit Fachgelehrten in deutscher Uebersetzung herausgegeben, Zweite Auflage*, Tübingen, 1924.

HENNECKE, *Hndb. z. d. neut. Ap.* = *Handbuch zu den neutestamentlichen Apokryphen in Verbindung mit Fachgelehrten herausgegeben*, Tübingen, 1904.

LICHTENBERGER, *Encyclopédie* = *Encyclopédie des sciences religieuses*, Paris, 1877–1882.

P.G. = MIGNE, *Patrologie grecque*.

R.E. = *Realencyclopädie für protestantische Theologie und Kirche begründet von* HERZOG, *in dritter Auflage herausgegeben von* HAUCK, Leipzig, 1896–1913.

R.G.G.[1] et *R.G.G.*[2] = *Die Religion in Geschichte und Gegenwart herausgegeben von* F. M. SCHIELE, Tübingen, 1909–1913. *Zweite Auflage herausgegeben von* H. GUNKEL *und* L. ZSCHARNACK, Tübingen, 1926 ss.

R.h. = *Revue historique*.

R.h.l.r. = *Revue d'histoire et de littérature religieuses*.

R.h.p.r. = *Revue d'histoire et de philosophie religieuses*.

R.h.r. = *Revue de l'histoire des religions*.

S.B.A. = *Sitzungsberichte der preussischen Akademie der Wissenschaften, Philosophisch-historische Klasse*.

Schriften = *Die Schriften des Neuen Testaments neu übersetzt und für die Gegenwart erklärt in erster und zweiter Auflage herausgegeben von* JOHANNES WEISS, *in dritter Auflage herausgegeben von* W. BOUSSET *und* W. HEITMUELLER, Göttingen, 1917–1918.

T.R. = *Theologische Rundschau*.

T.U. = *Texte und Untersuchungen*.

II. Works Frequently Quoted

ABEL: VINCENT et ABEL.

BAUER, *L.J. nt. Ap.* = *Das Leben Jesu im Zeitalter der neutestamentlichen Apokryphen*, Tübingen, 1909.

BERTRAM, *Leidensgeschichte* = *Die Leidensgeschichte Jesu und der Christuskult*, Göttingen, 1922.

B

BRANDT, *Ev. Gesch.* = *Die evangelische Geschichte und der Ursprung des Christentums*, Leipzig, 1893.

BULTMANN, *Syn. Trad.* = *Geschichte der synoptischen Tradition*, Göttingen, 1921, ²1931.

COUCHOUD, *Le mystère* = *Le mystère de Jésus*, Paris, 1924.

DALMAN, *Itin.* = *Les itinéraires de Jésus*, *Trad.* JACQUES MARTY, Paris, 1930.

DIBELIUS, *Formgeschichte* = *Die Formgeschichte des Evangeliums*, Tübingen, 1919.

EISLER = *IHΣOYΣ BAΣIΛEYΣ OY BAΣIΛEYΣAΣ*, Heidelberg, 1928–1930.

FULDA, *Das Kreuz* = *Das Kreuz und die Kreuzigung*, Breslau, 1878.

MAURICE GOGUEL, *Eucharistie* = *L'eucharistie des origines à Justin Martyr*, Paris, 1910.

MAURICE GOGUEL, *Sources* = *Les sources du récit johannique de la passion*, Paris, 1910.

MAURICE GOGUEL, *Intr.* = *Introduction au Nouveau Testament*, Paris, 1922 ss.

MAURICE GOGUEL, *J. de N.* = *Jésus de Nazareth, Mythe ou Histoire?* Paris, 1925.

MAURICE GOGUEL, *Jean-Baptiste* = *Au seuil de l'Évangile. Jean-Baptiste*, Paris, 1928.

HOLL, *Ges. Aufs.* = *Gesammelte Aufsätze zur Kirchengeschichte, II, Der Osten, III, Der Westen*, Tübingen, 1928.

JÜLICHER = *Die Gleichnissreden Jesu*, Freiburg im Breisgau, Tübingen, Leipzig, *I*², 1899, *II*, 1899.

KEIM = *Die Geschichte Jesu von Nazara*, Zurich, 1869–1872.

KLAUSNER = *Jesus of Nazareth, his Life, Times, and Teaching, translated by* H. DANBY, London, New York, 1927.

KUNDSIN = *Topologische Ueberlieferungsstoffe im Johannesevangelium*, Göttingen, 1925.

LINCK, *De antiquissimis* = *De antiquissimis quae ad Jesum Christum spectant testimoniis*, Giessen, 1913.

LOISY, *Syn.* = *Les Évangiles synoptiques*, Ceffonds, 1907–1908.

MERX = *Die vier kanonischen Evangelien nach ihrem aeltesten bekannten Text*, Berlin, 1897–1911.

ED. MEYER = *Ursprung und Anfänge des Christentums*, Berlin, Stuttgart, 1921–1923.

MOULTON-MILLIGAN = *The Vocabulary of the Greek Testament*, London, New York, 1914–1929.

REINACH, C. M. R., = *Cultes, mythes et religions*, Paris, 1905–1923.

RENAN = *Vie de Jésus*, Paris, 1863.

J. RÉVILLE, *Q. E.* = *Le quatrième Évangile*, Paris, 1901.

SCHÜRER = *Geschichte des jüdischen Volkes im Zeitalter Jesu Christi*,[3] Leipzig, 1898–1910.

SCHWEITZER, = *Geschichte der Leben-Jesu-Forschung*,[2] Tübingen, 1913. (seconde édition de *Von Reimarus zu Wrede*, Tübingen, 1906). Unless otherwise stated, I quote from the second edition. English translation: *The Quest of the Historical Jesus*, 1910.

SCHWARTZ, *I. II. III. IV = Aporien im vierten Evangelium, Nachr. der kgl. Ges. der Wiss. z. Göttingen, Phil.-hist. Kl.*, *I*, 1907, *II, III, IV*, 1908.

STRACK = *Jesus, die Haeretiker und die Christen nach den aeltesten jüdischen Angaben*, Leipzig, 1910.

STRACK-BILLERBECK = *Kommentar zum Neuen Testament aus Talmud und Midrasch*, München, 1922–1928.

VINCENT ET ABEL—*Jérusalem, Recherches de topographie, d'archéologie et d'histoire*, Paris, 1912 ss. (quoted, as required, under the names of one author or the other).

JOH. WEISS, *Aelt. Ev. = Das aelteste Evangelium*, Göttingen, 1903.

WELLHAUSEN, *Mt. = Das Evangelium Matthaei*, Berlin, 1904.

WELLHAUSEN, *Mc. = Das Evangelium Marci*, Berlin, 1903.

WELLHAUSEN, *Lc. = Das Evangelium Lucae*, Berlin, 1904.

WELLHAUSEN, *Einl.*[1] = *Einleitung in die drei ersten Evangelien*, Berlin, 1905.

WELLHAUSEN, *Einl.*[2] = *Einleitung in die drei ersten Evangelien, Zweite Auflage*, Berlin, 1911.

THE LIFE OF JESUS

CHAPTER I

THE LIFE OF JESUS IN RESEARCH

ALBERT SCHWEITZER, referring to *Lives of Jesus* of the imaginative type, once said: "When you have read two or three of them you have read them all!"[1] We might say exactly the same thing about the *Lives* written by Catholics, conservative Protestants, Liberals, Rationalists, and the exponents of the myth theory. It seems as though all the historians who attempt to portray the life of Jesus were condemned to turn round and round within the same circle of ideas, as though they were compelled to choose from a very limited number of combinations.

But although an historical survey of the *Lives of Jesus*[2] may seem somewhat monotonous, the subject is one of very real interest. First of all, it is the history of nineteen centuries of Christianity and its opponents, for every kind of theological system, every form of piety, and even every attack on Christianity, is reflected in an interpretation of the facts of the Gospel story. It is also the history of a long and patient effort. At first sight this movement appears to be confused and disorderly; it is often arrested by periods of stagnation, and by curious reactionary phases; if, however, it is observed from a sufficiently detached point of view, it becomes evident that it bears the marks of unceasing progress[3]; thus, very gradually,

[1] SCHWEITZER: *Geschichte der Leben-Jesu-Forschung*[2], Tübingen, 1913, p. 358.
[2] In ZÖCKLER, art. *Jesus-Christus, R.E.*, IX, pp. 1–43, and in SCHWEITZER there is a great deal of bibliographical information, although it is far from being complete, and, so far as Catholic works are concerned, in the encyclopaedia *Le Christ*, published by the Abbés BARDY and TRICOT, Paris, 1932. (So far as the works of non-Catholics are concerned, the information in this encyclopaedia leaves much to be desired.)
[3] It is true that even in the twentieth century books have been issued which might have been written two or three centuries earlier, as, for instance, harmonies like that of ALEXANDRE WESTPHAL (*Jésus de Nazareth*, Lausanne, 1914) or those of P. P. LAGRANGE and LAVERGNE (*Synopsis evangelica*, Paris, Barcelona, 1926; *Synopse des quatre Évangiles*, Paris, 1927). This is merely an instance of survival.

an historical problem emerges from a religious and theological problem, and the questions which this raises have been formulated in such a way that they are gradually brought into closer harmony with the character and the data of the actual documents.

I. The Problem of the Life of Jesus before the Eighteenth Century

The problem of the life of Jesus did not become an historical problem until after the eighteenth century. From the sixteenth century until that time, Christian people, Protestants as well as Catholics, believed that the teaching of Jesus was in absolute harmony with the teaching of their respective Churches, and they believed that in the four Gospels they possessed a very reliable narrative of the story of their Lord. Their one idea was so to harmonize and paraphrase the four accounts of the evangelists that they might be given in a form suitable to the mentality of the faithful. This endeavour gave rise to various "Harmonies" of the Gospels, and also to works in which the Gospel story is paraphrased in order to make it easier to understand.

The first Harmony of this kind was that of Tatian. Written first of all in Greek, or possibly directly in Syriac—even yet this point has not been definitely settled—the *Diatessaron* seems to have been the first form in which the Christians of Syria possessed the Gospel in their own tongue. This book was in use for a long time, in spite of repeated efforts to reintroduce the separate Gospels.

Tatian's service to the Churches of Syria had no counterpart in the Christian communities which spoke Greek or Latin. The tendency towards concentration which, about the middle of the second century, had already set aside the four Gospels, which were destined to form part of the New Testament Canon, did not lead to the final triumph of one of these Gospels, or to their fusion with each other. The existence of four parallel but distinct narratives forms one of the paradoxes of the history of the Canon of the New Testament. The explanation lies in the fact that at that time the Church was forced to defend her position against the attacks of the followers of Marcion, the Gnostics, and the Montanists. The Church erected an insuperable barrier against the attacks of the heretics by taking the evangelical literature which was then in use and crystallizing it, thus transforming an actual custom into a binding tradition. This transformation took place during the third quarter of the second century. It ended with Irenaeus and the Muratorian Canon. From that time the harmonizing process could no longer touch the Gospels; all it could do in the way of development was to supply a sort of commentary on their text.

The most important work of this kind was that of the Reformed theologian Andrew Osiander. This book was published at Basle in 1537, under a title which needs no explanation: *Greek and Latin Gospel Harmony in four books, in which the Gospel story is combined according to the four Evangelists, in such a way that no word of any one of them is omitted, no foreign word added, the order of none of them is disturbed, and nothing is displaced, in which, however, the whole is marked by letters and signs which permit one to see at a first glance the points peculiar to each evangelist, those which he has in common with the others, and with which of them.*[1]

In order to carry through a programme of this kind the writer was obliged to admit that where a word or an action of Jesus was reported two or three times in a slightly altered form, or was perhaps placed in a slightly different order, Jesus must have said the same thing or accomplished the same action two or three times over.[2]

[1] Harmoniae evangelicae libri IV graece et latine in quibus evangelica historia ex quatuor evangelistis ita in unum est contexta, ut nullius verbum ullum omissum, nihil alienum immixtum, nullius ordo turbatus, nihil non suo loco positum, omnia vero litteris et notis ita distincta sint ut quid cujusque evangelistae proprium, quid cum aliis et cum quibus commune sit, primo statim aspectu deprehendere queas.

[2] Thus, to give one instance only, some have held that Jesus cleansed the Temple on three separate occasions: (i) at the beginning of his ministry, according to John; (ii) on the day of his Triumphal Entry into Jerusalem, according to Matthew and Luke; and (iii) on the day after the Triumphal Entry, according to Mark. CALVIN, in his *Commentarii in harmoniam ex Matthaeo, Marco et Luca compositam* (1555) (on Matt. xx. 29, *Opera Calvini*, 45, col. 560), characterizes Osiander's method as superficial; at the same time, Calvin himself also made similar combinations regarding, for instance, the genealogies of Jesus given by Matthew and by Luke.

The rigour of the principle laid down by Osiander was slightly modified by following writers, as, for instance, in the *Harmonia quatuor evangelistarum* by the Lutheran Martin Chemnitz[1] and in a series of harmonies which were published during the seventeenth century and at the beginning of the eighteenth, among which the most well-known are those by Father Bernard of Montereuil, the Calvinistic theologian Leclerc, and Nicolas Toinard.[2]

These works prepared the way for the transition from the problem of the Gospel Harmony to that of the synopsis[3]; the aim of the latter is no longer how to combine the four accounts into one, but to study their relation with each other.

The *Lives of Jesus* which appeared before the eighteenth century are still less scientific than the Harmonies. They are literary compositions, sometimes poems, designed for edification and instruction. It is sufficient to mention the *Historiae evangelicae libri quatuor* by the Spanish priest Juvencus (towards 300), an epic poem in more than three thousand verses; the paraphrase of the Fourth Gospel by Nonnus of Panopolis (towards 400), who, before his conversion, had written a poem in honour of the mysteries of Bacchus, the *Paschale Carmen* in verse, and the *Opus paschale* in prose, of Caelius Sedulius, which dates from the second half of the fifth century.

For the Middle Ages we may mention the following: in the thirteenth century there is the *Vita Christi* by St. Bonaventura; in the fourteenth century the *Vita Jesu Christi a*

---

[1] Continued and published after his death by his disciple, POLYCARPE LEYSER (1593–1611); completed and issued in a second edition by J. GERHARD (1652).

[2] P. BERNARD DE MONTEREUIL: *La Vie du Sauveur du monde, Jésus-Christ, tirée du texte des IV Évangiles réduit en un corps d'histoire*, Paris, 1639. J. CLERICUS: *Harmonia evangelica cui subjecta est historia Christi ex quatuor Evangeliis concinnata*, Amsterdam, 1699. NICOLAS TOINARD: *Evangeliorum harmonia graeco-latina*, Paris, 1707.

[3] The term synopsis was created by GRIESBACH (*Synopsis evangeliorum Matthaei, Marci, et Lucae*, Halle, 1774–1776; [2]1797, [3]1809, [4]1822). In the second edition the Johannine parallels are added for the account of the Passion. The order followed is now that of Matthew, and now that of Mark. It would be useless to enumerate all the synopses which have been published.

quatu or evangeliiset scriptoribus orthodoxis concinnata by the Strasbourg monk, Ludolph of Saxony;[1] and the *De Gestis Domini* of Simon of Cascia.

The first *Life of Jesus* of modern times, that of the Jesuit Father Jerome Xavier, nephew of Saint François Xavier, was composed in Portuguese in 1602, and translated into the Persian language by a native of Lahore[2] in order to give to the Mongol King Akbar (1542–1605) a favourable idea of the doctrine preached by the missionaries. This *Life of Jesus* was translated into Latin by the Reformed theologian Louis de Dieu[3] in order to show what liberties the Jesuit missionaries had taken with the text.

Sometimes these *Lives of Jesus* appeared in dramatic form. This was the case, for example, in the Χριστὸς πάσχων (eleventh century), a tragedy in 2,640 verses on the death and resurrection of Jesus, and in the French mystery plays of the Middle Ages. Finally, we ought to mention the Bible narratives of the Middle Ages which hold the balance fairly evenly between paraphrase and translation.

Even after the birth of the science of historical criticism people still went on harmonizing and paraphrasing the Gospels. This kind of literature, conceived from a point of view which science had outgrown, is not always entirely devoid of value. It is impossible to deny the literary value of some of these *Lives of Jesus*, and we can only pity those whose minds are so closed to spiritual things that they cannot appreciate that which this or that author has put of his own soul into a work which may be entirely devoid of scientific value. In such works we often find valuable material on archaeology, geography, and history, as well as illuminating glimpses of the setting of the Gospel narrative. They also contain remarks of real value

[1] This work was extremely popular at the end of the fifteenth and the beginning of the sixteenth century. It has been translated into French, Catalan, Portuguese, and Castilian. In French, fourteen editions were published between 1502 and 1534; it was also reprinted at Lyons in 1641, 1642, and 1644. Cf. Lucien Febvre: *Les origines de la réforme française*, *R.h.*, CLXI, 1929, p. 47, n. 1.

[2] And later in Latin.

[3] *Historia Christi persice conscripta simulque multis modis contaminata a* Hieronymo Xavier *jatine reddita et animadvertationibus notata a* Ludovico de Dieu, Lugduni Batavorum, 1639.

on points of method, and criticisms of certain obscurities and errors which have escaped the notice of the authors of several *Lives of Jesus*.[1]

II. The Birth of Criticism

Two conditions must be fulfilled before the life of Jesus can be treated as a problem of history. The first is this: all pre-conceived dogmatic ideas of the Person and Work of Christ must be entirely ruled out of court; and the second: the question of the sources must be ventilated; that is to say, the problems of the composition of the Gospels, of their relation to each other, of their character and of their documentary value, must be studied with care. In the eighteenth century, at least in certain circles, the first condition was fulfilled to some extent, sufficiently at least to allow the critical studies of the life of Jesus to enjoy a period of initial success. But the literary criticism of the Gospels was still in such an elementary state that the work which had been done in the eighteenth century had to be done all over again in the nineteenth century.

[1] Of these *Lives of Jesus* we will quote as examples, among the Catholic works, those of SEPP (1843–1846) (German), VEUILLOT (1864), SCHEGG (1874) (German), LE CAMUS (1883), P. DIDON (1891), FILLION (1922), F. KLEIN (1931), LEBRETON (1931), LEPIN (in the *Encyclopaedia*, "*Christ*," 1932); among those written by Protestants, those of NEANDER (1837) (German), RIGGENBACH (1858) (German), ELLICOTT (1860) (English), DE PRESSENSÉ (1865), SCHAFF (1865) (English), FARRAR (1874) (English), BOVON (1893), WABNITZ (1904–1906). HENRI MONNIER: *Dictionnaire encyclopédique de la Bible de* A. WESTPHAL (art. *Jésus-Christ*, I, Paris, 1932). The wide knowledge of the literature of the Talmud gives a peculiar value to the work of WABNITZ. A special place among Catholic *Lives of Jesus* must be assigned to the recent works of P. P. DE GRANDMAISON (*Jésus-Christ, sa personne, son message, ses preuves*, Paris, 1928) and LAGRANGE (*L'Évangile de Jésus-Christ*, Paris, 1928). The former book is not a *Life of Jesus* in the literal sense of the word: one might search it in vain for a connected narrative of the facts of the life of Jesus. It is also rather a dogmatic than an historical work. P. de Grandmaison begins with the Catholic doctrine of Jesus Christ and tries to show that this has been in no way shaken by the theories and negations of modern historians. P. Lagrange, for his part, confines his efforts to a commentary on the Gospel narrative.

Biblical criticism, prepared by the admirable work of Richard Simon, was born when the influence of the English Deists, of Voltaire, of the Encyclopedists and of Holbach in France, of the Rationalism of the Enlightenment in Germany, had liberated the minds of men—or of some among them—from the yoke of dogma. Voltaire in particular, with a very sure instinct, knew how to place his finger on the weak spots in the traditional conception of the story of Jesus. What he says, for instance, about the witness of Josephus to Jesus reveals a very penetrating critical sense.

The honour, however, of having produced the first essay in systematic criticism of the story of Jesus belongs to Germany. This was the work of a professor of Oriental languages at Hamburg, Hermann Samuel Reimarus (1694–1768).[1] He was not free from dogmatic bias. The manuscript of 4,000 pages which he left behind him at his death, and which is preserved in the Library of Hamburg, is an apology for Natural Religion. He took up the study of the Gospel story in order to prove that ecclesiastical Christianity had no right to claim for itself the life and the teaching of Jesus. Between 1774 and 1778 Lessing published seven portions of the work of Reimarus under the title of *Fragmente des wolfenbüttelschen Ungenannten*. The last two fragments deal with the life of Jesus and are called: *The Story of the Resurrection* and *The Aims of Jesus and of His Disciples*. In the latter study Reimarus argues that, fundamentally, Jesus always remained a Jew. In using the terms "the Kingdom of God" and the "Messiah" he was simply following the usage of the Jews of his own day. The idea of founding a new religion was quite foreign to him. What he wanted to do was to re-establish Jewish national independence, to place himself at the head of his people as "Son of God," that is to say, as the Messianic King, for in his mind the expression "Son of God" had no metaphysical significance. On two different occasions he thought he was on the verge of realizing his programme: first of all when he sent out the Twelve on their mission, and secondly, when he made the Triumphal Entry into Jerusalem, revealing himself as the Coming One, the Expected King, acclaimed by the Hosannas of his own followers, and when, as Master, he cast out

[1] On Reimarus, see SCHWEITZER, pp. 13–26.

those who sold and bought in the Temple, in the very teeth of the scribes and the Pharisees. But this second attempt of Jesus provoked a violent reaction, and in the struggle which ensued Jesus perished. His disciples, who at first were utterly stunned by the blow, recovered their self-control, and, in order to avoid returning to the laborious and difficult life which they had led before Jesus had dazzled their vision with his hopes of the Messianic Kingdom, they imagined the idea of a Second Coming of the Messiah, guaranteed by a resurrection which they invented, and created the idea of a spiritual redemption by his death, which, instead of the defeat which it was in reality, was thus transformed into the pledge of a new hope.

There are two significant points in this daring interpretation of the Gospel story. The first is this: that Reimarus laid great emphasis upon the hopes of the future which Jesus had painted in glowing colours for his disciples; and the second: that Reimarus was the first to recognize the capital importance of the development from Jesus to the Church. No thinker followed up the thought of Reimarus on either of these points, and for a long time after his death the problems which he had raised fell into oblivion. This may have been due to the fact that his solutions were considered too arbitrary and superficial. It was not until Ferdinand Christian Baur came upon the scene that the problem of Jesus and the Church was raised once more, and then only in a very general way, for Baur's attention was directed far more towards the interpretation of Apostolic Christianity than towards the interpretation of Jesus[1]; even at the present time criticism does not attach sufficient importance to this question: How did Christianity issue from the work and teaching of Jesus? On the other hand, the problem of eschatology had to wait until nearly the year 1890 before it again occupied the attention of Christian scholars.

[1] BAUR only touched the problem of Jesus incidentally, as, for instance, in a controversial work directed against UHLHORN (*Die Tübinger Schule und ihre Stellung zur Gegenwart*, Tübingen, 1859, ²1860, especially pp. 30 f.); he has not dealt with this subject in any work of the same rank as his *Paulus der Apostel Jesu Christi*, Stuttgart, 1845 (revised by ZELLER)², Leipzig, 1866–1867. The *Kritische Untersuchungen über die Kanonischen Evangelien*, Tübingen, 1847, only deals with the literary problem of the Gospels.

The "fragments" of Reimarus made a great sensation and gave much offence. John Solomon Semler published a refutation of these ideas[1] in which, without taking up the question in all its bearings, he discussed some of the statements of Reimarus and claimed that the material images borrowed by Jesus from Judaism should be interpreted in a spiritual sense.

The ideas of Reimarus did not influence the movement which ensued, either positively or negatively. They are more like a prologue than a beginning. The work of the Rationalists, which extended from the middle of the eighteenth century until towards 1830, developed independently of the ideas of Reimarus. Without touching the dogmatic conception of the person of Jesus, the Rationalists tried to link together the different events in his life by making some of them explain the others. The older form of Rationalism, without, on that account, claiming to eliminate the idea of miracle altogether, tried to explain certain facts which are reported as miraculous by natural causes. It was only in a second phase, with the famous Paulus, that the ultimate consequences of this principle were evolved. But the Rational school lacks the historical sense. For it Jesus is a modern man, a moralist, a master of wisdom, in whom religion and reason are harmoniously combined.[2] The man who represents Rationalism most fully is Heinrich Eberhard Gottlob Paulus (1761–1851),[3] who, with the exception of the Virgin Birth, eliminated all the miracles from the Gospel story by showing that the disciples attributed supernatural causes to facts which they had not fully understood. For instance, they believed that Jesus stilled the storm, but

---

[1] *Beantwortung der Fragmente eines Ungenannten insbesondern vom Zwecke Jesu und seiner Jünger*, Halle, 1779.

[2] Among the principal Rationalists we may mention HESS (1741–1828), REINHARD (1753–1812), and in a certain sense also HERDER (1744–1803), who, however, differs from the others in this, that he does not try to modernize Jesus, and that in writing on these questions he displays a spirit of intuition and taste which is absent from the majority of the older Rationalists.

[3] *Philologisch-kritisches und historisches Kommentar über die drei ersten Evangelien*, Lübeck, 1800, ²1804. *Das Leben Jesu als Grundlage einer reinen Geschichte des Urchristentums*, Heidelberg, 1828. *Exegetisches Handbuch über die drei ersten Evangelien*, Heidelberg, 1830–1833.

the real explanation is this: at the very moment when the disciples roused Jesus from sleep, the ship doubled a promontory and sailed into a zone of calm water, protected from the fury of the wind.[1]

In certain respects Schleiermacher's position was the very opposite of Rationalism. His *Life of Jesus*, however, which was published after his death (based on his first course of University lectures)[2], Reminds us of the Rationalist school in its ideas, in this sense, that its tone is dogmatic rather than historical. It is based mainly upon the Fourth Gospel. The Rationalists pictured Jesus as the apostle of a reasonable and modern religion, whereas Schleiermacher discovered the Christ of his own theological position in the Gospel narrative.

At the close of the eighteenth century another type of the *Life of Jesus* appeared: the imaginative biography, which, in order to supplement the principles of history, had recourse to the imagination, sometimes by pretending to utilize documents which had been rediscovered in some mysterious way. In such instances the literary fiction sometimes borders on deceit.

The first of these imaginative *Lives*, which served as models, and to a large extent also as sources for those which followed, are the works of Karl Friedrich Bahrdt (1741–1792)[3] and of Karl Heinrich Venturini (1768–1849)[4]. According to these two writers Jesus belonged to the sect of the Essenes, and had been systematically instructed and prepared by the masters of this Order in order to detach the Jews from their material

---

[1] We might also mention as Rationalist *Lives of Jesus* those of KARL-AUGUST HASE (1800–1890) (*Das Leben Jesu zunächst für akademische Studien*, Leipzig, 1829) and of CHRISTOPH-FRIEDRICH VON AMMON (1766–1850) (*Geschichte des Leben Jesu mit steter Rücksicht auf die vorhandenen Quellen*, Leipzig, 1842–1847).

[2] He gave this course for the first time in 1819 and for the last time in 1832. SCHLEIERMACHER's *Life of Jesus* was compiled from notes taken at this last course of lectures and published by RÜTENICK (*Das Leben Jesu*, Berlin, 1864).

[3] *Ausführung des Plans und Zwecks Jesu in Briefen an Wahrheit suchenden Lesern*, Berlin, 1784–1792 (11 vols.).

[4] *Natürliche Geschichte des grossen Propheten von Nazareth*, Bethleem (Copenhagen), 1800–1802,[2] 1806 (4 vols.). The work has appeared without the name of the author.

form of Messianism. Aided by supernumaries behind the scenes, in the course of his ministry he achieved a series of actions ingeniously manipulated in order to make people believe that he possessed a supernatural power. The Resurrection was a clever piece of dramatic production. Jesus, taken down from the cross in an unconscious condition, was tended in a cave by some Essene physicians, and then was able to show himself from time to time to those who believed that he had died.[1]

More recently Nicholas Notowitch[2] has asserted that before he began his ministry Jesus spent six years in India among some Buddhist priests. In support of this theory he invoked the aid of some alleged manuscripts found in a convent in Tibet, manuscripts which, in the opinion of specialists, either never existed at all or, if they did, were pure forgeries.

Just as unconvincing as the Buddhist documents is the letter of the Egyptian doctor Benan, published in Germany in 1910; according to this document Egyptian priests at the temple at Heliopolis gave Jesus a regular training before they sent him out to preach in his native land.[3]

Alongside of these imaginative *Lives of Jesus* there should also be mentioned (separately), the account of the Passion of Christ according to the visions of Anne Catherine Emmerich;

---

[1] For various reasons we can add to the group of imaginative *Lives of Jesus* the works of SALVADOR (*Jésus-Christ, sa doctrine*, Paris, 1838, 2 vols.), GFÖRER (*Kritische Geschichte des Urchristentums*, Stuttgart, 1831–1838), of GHILLANY (under the pseudonym of RICHARD VON DER ALM) (*Theologische Briefe an Gebildeten deutscher Nation*, 1863), LUDWIG NOACK (*Aus der Jordanwiege nach Golgotha*, Mannheim, 1870), P. DE RÉGLA (Dr. P. A. DESJARDINS) (*Jésus de Nazareth*, Paris, 1891), PIERRE NAHOR (ÉMILIE LEROU) (*Hiésous*, Paris, 1903), E. BOSC (*La Vie ésotérique de Jésus Christ et les origines orientales du christianisme*, Paris, 1902), etc.

[2] *La Vie inconnue de Jésus-Christ*, Paris, 1894.

[3] *Ein Jugendfreund Jesu, Brief des aegyptischen Arztes Benan aus der Zeit Domitians* hrg. von ERNST EDLER VON DER PLANITZ, Berlin, 1910. The entire non-authenticity of the letter of Benan has been shown quite conclusively by C. SCHMIDT (*Der Benanbrief, Eine moderne Leben-Jesu-Fälschung des Herrn Edler von der Planitz aufgedeckt, T.U.*, 44, 1, Leipzig, 1921). Cf. also JÜLICHER and FASCHER, art. *Benanbrief und aehnliche Leben-Jesu Fälschungen, R.G.G.*[2], I, cols. 886–888.

she saw these visions between the years 1820 and 1823, and she also received the stigmata.[1] These visions raise a problem in psychology, not one of history or of criticism.

The *Lives of Jesus* of the imaginative type belong rather to imaginative literature than to the sphere of history. The one purpose they serve is that they reveal the inadequacy of the documents; this leads some critics to believe that it is impossible to write a *Life of Jesus* at all.

III. FROM STRAUSS TO THE END OF THE NINETEENTH CENTURY

The *Life of Jesus* by David Friedrich Strauss (1808–1874)[2] was published in 1835. This is an important date in the history of the *Lives of Jesus*. Strauss believed that religion was based not upon facts but upon ideas. He held that ideas could play their part without manifesting themselves as visible phenomena. In consequence, he argued, it matters very little whether the Gospel records, in which religious ideas are expressed, are historical or not. Thus Strauss came to the criticism of the *Life of Jesus* with an absolutely open mind, both from the religious and from the theological point of view. At this point the myth idea crept in, the important element in which was not the affirmation of non-reality but the idea that a supposed fact may be simply the symbolical expression of a higher truth. So far as tradition was concerned Strauss was freer than his predecessors; this was due to his point of view. But the slight

[1] There are numerous editions of this book. The best are those of BRENTANO, Sulzbach, 1834, and of SCHMÖGER, Regensburg, 1858–1860, ²1879.

[2] *Leben Jesu kritisch bearbeitet*, Tübingen, 1835–1836 (the second volume appeared in 1835), ³1838–1839, ⁴1840. In the third edition Strauss made considerable concessions to his opponents. He seems to have done this in the hope that it would make it possible for him to be nominated to a chair in theology in the Faculty of Theology at Zurich; when, owing to the pressure of public opinion, his nomination was revoked, Strauss withdrew all the concessions which he had made. *The Life of Jesus* by STRAUSS was translated by LITTRÉ (Paris, 1839, ³1864). Cf. *Streitschriften zur Verteidigung meiner Schrift über das Leben Jesu und zur Charakteristik der gegenwärtigen Theologie*, Tübingen, 1837. On Strauss consult TH. ZIEGLER, art. *Strauss*, *R.E.*, XIX, pp. 76–92; SCHWEITZER, pp. 69–123, which contains a wealth of bibliographical information.

importance which he attached to facts exposed him to the temptation of slipping almost unconsciously into the "myth" interpretation. Another peculiarity of the *Life of Jesus* by Strauss (and this was also the reason why it was an epoch-making book) is this: before him, and often after him, the framework of the life of Jesus was made up of an arbitrary combination of data drawn from the Synoptic Gospels and also from the Fourth Gospel; Strauss, however, saw that the difference between the Synoptic Gospels and the Fourth Gospel created a dilemma; he found his own solution by deciding in favour of the Synoptic Gospels.

The *Life of Jesus* by Strauss caused a great commotion. The long controversy which resulted from it[1] raged round three principal points: the myth theory, the relation between Jesus and the Christ, and the question of the literary composition of the Gospels. Ultimately the discussion of the third and last point was by far the most important of the three in its bearing on the development of the problem as a whole.

One of the weak points in the system of Strauss was that he had no definite theory about the composition of the Gospels and the relative value of the witness of each of them; his adversaries, on the other hand, were no better armed than he was himself. It almost looks as though there were a tacit recognition of the fact that no progress at all would be possible until this all-important question was settled; hence, for nearly thirty years the energies of the critics were devoted very largely to the study of the actual text of the Gospels. Between 1835 and 1863, that is to say, between Strauss and Renan, there took place that enormous labour upon the Gospels which is recalled by the names of Weiss, Wilke, Reuss, Albert Réville, of Baur and his disciples, to whom we must add, in

[1] The spirit of this controversy was extremely violent; one of the pamphlets which was written against Strauss, by Pastor Eschenmayer, is called: *Der Ischariotismus unserer Tage*, Tübingen, 1835. To the honour of traditional theology we must note the fact that when Neander was consulted by the Prussian Government with a view to prohibiting the circulation of the book, Neander asked the Government not to suppress it by an edict, saying that the only way to defend the sacred interests of the Church was to refute the arguments it contained. (Schweitzer, p. 104. English edition, p. 102 (trans.).)

the following period, the names of Weiszäcker, Holtzmann, and Bernhard Weiss.[1]

The *Vie de Jésus* which Renan wrote in Syria, and published on his return to Europe,[2] caused a still greater sensation than that of Strauss, and elicited a host of replies. Schweitzer says humorously: "Whoever wore a soutane and could wield a pen, charged against Renan, the bishops leading the van,"[3] and the representatives of the Catholic Church were not the only champions who entered the lists.[4]

Owing to its literary qualities, Renan's *Vie de Jésus* (the first *Vie de Jésus* to appear in a Catholic country) reached an enormous public. Renan's book is as easy to read as that of Strauss is difficult; consequently it was read by hosts of people who were neither initiated into nor even prepared for exegetical research. This fact was rather a hindrance to the progress of

[1] On these works, see *Intr.*, I, pp. 67 ff., II, pp. 24 ff.

[2] This book was published on June 24, 1863, and in that year it ran into ten editions. Three others (the thirteenth, considerably revised) appeared in 1864. A popular abridged edition, which came out in 1864, ran into fifteen editions that year. H. GIRARD and H. MONCEL (*Bibliographie des œuvres de Ernest Renan*, Paris, 1923, pp. 84–93) give a list (up to 1923) of 205 editions in French and 216 in other languages. The *Vie de Jésus* by Renan has been translated into German, English, Danish, Spanish, Esperanto, Greek, Dutch, Hungarian, Italian, Portuguese, Russian, Swedish, and Czech.

[3] A. SCHWEITZER: *The Quest of the Historical Jesus*, p. 188.

[4] SCHWEITZER (pp. 647–651) has compiled a list (composed from books in the Library at Strasbourg, thus certainly incomplete, and one that does not contain articles and reviews in various journals) of eighty-five books or pamphlets whose publication was caused by the *Vie de Jésus* by Renan. Among the Catholic publications there are: FREPPEL: *Examen critique de la Vie de Jésus de M. Renan*, Paris, 1864; GRATRY: *Jésus-Christ. Réponse à M. Renan*, Paris, 1864. Among the Protestant works of a conservative order: BEYSCHLAG: *Ueber das Leben Jesu von Renan*, Berlin, 1864; N. ROUSSEL: *Les deux Jésus, celui de M. Renan et celui de l'Évangile*, Paris, 1864; and especially E. DE PRESSENSÉ: *Jésus-Christ, son temps, sa vie, son œuvre*, Paris, 1865. Among the others: COLANI: *Examen de la Vie de Jésus de M. Renan*, Strasbourg, Paris, 1864 (extract from the *Revue de Théologie*); HAVET: *Jésus dans l'histoire, Examen de la Vie de Jésus de M. Renan*, Paris, 1863 (extract from the *Revue des Deux-Mondes*); A. RÉVILLE: *La Vie de Jésus de M. Renan devant les orthodoxes et devant la critique*, Paris, Rotterdam, 1864; SCHERER: *La Vie de Jésus* (an article appearing in *Le Temps* and reproduced in *Mélanges d'histoire religieuse*, Paris, 1864, pp. 61–137).

these studies. There are certain questions—to which the life of Jesus belongs—which gain by being discussed at leisure by specialists, and to some extent by being brought as far forward as possible, before they come out into the full glare of publicity. Renan's *Vie de Jésus*, owing to the profound excitement which it caused (as can be well understood), has perhaps compromised, or at least delayed, the critical education of the French public which the *Revue de Strasbourg* had just begun.

A great deal has been said, and rightly, of the literary charm of Renan's book. The *Vie de Jésus*, as a work of art, has survived, and will long outlive works of a scientific kind. But its literary merits have been exaggerated,[1] for although there is great charm of style in the book, this is too often spoilt by lack of taste. In the words of Schweitzer: "the gentle Jesus, the beautiful Maries, the fair Galilean women who form the escort of the 'charming carpenter,' might have simply stepped out of the windows of one of the ecclesiastical art shops on the Place Saint-Sulpice."[2] Too often the glamour of the style conceals vagueness of thought and of historical construction. Colani was possibly not altogether wrong when he said: "M. Renan thinks too much of beauty and not enough of the truth."[3] The final effect of the book as a whole is fugitive and intangible. What Renan puts forward with one hand he takes away with the other. His critical position is uncertain. The discourses of the Fourth Gospel are rejected, but the setting is retained, apart from any theory to justify such treatment of the subject, and it is impossible to escape the impression that Renan used the Fourth Gospel simply in order to balance his story. Jesus is presented as a kind of gentle dreamer who wanders through the countryside of Galilee smiling at life,

---

[1] Some authors have some adverse criticisms to make about the style of the *Vie de Jésus*. MARCEL PROUST (*Pour un ami*, *Revue de Paris*, November 15, 1920, p. 171) calls the *Vie de Jésus* of Renan "une espèce de Belle Hélène du christianisme" ("a kind of Beautiful Helen in Christianity") ; and MARIE LENÉRU (*Journal*, *Revue de France*, July 1, 1921, p. 61) says that the tone of the *Vie de Jésus* "a l'abondance ecclésiastique, le débit facile et fleuri d'un curé beau diseur et un peu fat !" ("has the clerical fluency, the easy and flowery utterance of a curé who is a fine talker and a bit of a cockscomb !").
[2] A. SCHWEITZER: *The Quest of the Historical Jesus*, p. 182 (Eng. trans.).
[3] *Revue de théologie*, I, 1863, p. 378, n. 1.

whom his followers draw into a sombre drama which turns him into a wonder-worker, and a candidate for the Messiahship, and brings him to his death. The birth of Christianity was not due to any creative impulse given by him, but to the passion of an unbalanced visionary who gave the world the story of a God who rose again.

Renan's work did, however, achieve one thing, and it was this: he brought forward the problem of the life of Jesus in such a way that henceforward it was impossible to withdraw it from this leading position.

Among the appreciations of the work of Renan, that of Edmond Scherer[1] is singularly penetrating; it anticipates views which were only to be developed fifty years later, and on that account it is worth quoting one or two passages. He says that there are two ways of conceiving what a *Life of Jesus* should be. "Perhaps science would be most worthy of its name, in this respect, if it were to confess that a proper biography is impossible." We ought to confine ourselves to "grouping under certain heads all that an intelligent criticism can say about the Gospels. This would give rise to a series of dissertations rather than to a *Vie de Jésus*, but we would then have a work which even by its very gaps would make us see and feel both the actual situation and the state of this problem."

Renan's efforts, however, were directed mainly towards the reproduction—not so much of the documents themselves, as of the impression which they made upon his mind. He gives us his own personal interpretation; the intuition of the artist supplements the scarcity of the historical material. "The public," Scherer remarks, "does not like doubt; it resigns itself with difficulty to that supreme form of science which is to know that one knows nothing" (pp. 86–89).

From the attitude of Scherer it is interesting to pass on to that of the great exegete of Strasbourg: Edward Reuss. It is characteristic of his work that in the whole vast field of Biblical research covered by Reuss there is no *Life of Jesus*. This was due to the fact that Reuss felt that the absence of a real connexion between the facts reported in the Gospels constituted an insuperable obstacle to the construction of a *Life*

[1] The *Vie de Jésus* in *Mélanges d'histoire religieuse*, pp. 61–137.

of Jesus;[1] this allows us to conclude that Colani was expressing the general feeling of the school of Strasbourg when he wrote in his *Review*: "We opened M. Renan's book with sympathetic curiosity. We closed it with a sense of keen disappointment. It did not contain what we hoped to find in its pages." [2]

Although, at the moment when Renan's *Vie de Jésus* was published, the critics of the Strasbourg school could judge that it was the work of a writer more concerned with art than with criticism, and one who was insufficiently aware of the complexity of the problems involved, it was not long before people saw that the situation was quite different; it was the progress realized by the study of the Gospels which gave rise to the feeling—possibly prematurely—that the moment had come to make a fresh attempt on the lines laid down by Strauss. Actually, Renan's *Vie de Jésus* was followed by several others, which may be characterized by the somewhat infelicitous but inevitable term used by Schweitzer, as "liberal" in tendency.[3]

[1] See the characteristic passages of Reuss which have been quoted in my work entitled: *Critique et histoire. A propos de la Vie de Jésus*, Paris, 1928, pp. 20 ff. "In the circle of the intimate friends of Reuss, we learn from A. Causse (*La Bible de Reuss et la renaissance des études d'histoire religieuse en France, R.h.p.r.*, IX, 1929, p. 27, n. 64), people did not speak very kindly of Renan," and he quotes a passage from a letter of Scherer to Reuss of March 22, 1886, which passes a very severe criticism on the author of the *Vie de Jésus*. "We are assured, he says, that Reuss quoted it more than once with great approval."

[2] *La Vie de Jésus de M. Renan, Revue de théologie*, II, 1864, p. 57.

[3] Among them we will name, without pretending in any way to give a complete list, the second *Life of Jesus* by Strauss (*Das Leben Jesu für das deutsche Volk bearbeitet*, Leipzig, 1864, translated into French by Nefftzer and Dolfus, Paris, 1864. Cf. *Der Christus des Glaubens und der Jesus der Geschichte*, Berlin, 1865, against the *Life of Jesus* by Schleiermacher, published in 1864), the works of Daniel Schenkel (*Das Charakterbild Jesu*, Wiesbaden, 1864, 4[1873]), of Keim (*Die Geschichte Jesu von Nazara in ihrem Verhältniss mit dem Gesamtleben seines Volkes frei untersucht und ausführlich erzählt*, Zurich, 1869–1872, 3 vols.; *Geschichte Jesu nach den Ergebnissen heutiger Wissenschaft für weitere Kreise übersichtlich erzählt*, Zurich, 1872, 4[1875]), the second *Life of Jesus* by Karl Hase (*Geschichte Jesu nach akademischen Vorlesungen*, Leipzig, 1876), the works of Sabatier (*Essai sur les sources de la Vie de Jésus*, Paris, 1866; article *Jésus-Christ* in the *Encyclopédie* of Lichtenberger, VII, Paris, 1880, pp. 341–401), of B. Weiss (*Das Leben*

These works are very varied in character. In all the questions concerned (Synoptic or Johannine setting, Messianic consciousness, the essential content of the thought of Jesus, the eschatological question) we meet samples of every kind of critical and theological opinion, from one extreme to the other. All these *Lives of Jesus*, however, possess a certain family likeness: they present the problem in the same way; and the majority, and above all the older ones, tend to modernize Jesus, and to make him the type of the religious man. Many of these works eliminate or spiritualize the eschatological statements reported in the Gospels, and finally, and possibly this is the most typical fact of all, they all try to make up for the insufficient connexion between the facts recorded in the Gospels

Jesu, Berlin, Stuttgart, 1882, ³1884), of W. BEYSCHLAG (*Das Leben Jesu*, Halle, 1885–1886, ³1893), of E. STAPFER (*Jésus-Christ avant son ministère*, Paris, 1896; *Jésus-Christ pendant son ministère*, Paris, 1897, ²1899; *La mort et la résurrection de Jésus-Christ*, Paris, 1898), of ALBERT RÉVILLE (*Jésus de Nazareth, Études critiques sur les antécédents de l'histoire évangélique et la Vie de Jésus*, Paris, 1897, ²1906), of OSKAR HOLTZMANN (*Das Leben Jesu*, Tübingen, 1901. Cf. *War Jesu Ekstatiker?* Tübingen, 1903), of R. OTTO (*Leben und Wirken Jesu nach historisch-kritische Auffassung*, Göttingen, 1902), of K. FURRER (*Das Leben Jesu Christi*, Leipzig, 1902, ²1905), of P. W. SCHMIDT (*Die Geschichte Jesu*, Tübingen, 1899–1904), of LOISY (*Les Évangiles synoptiques*, Ceffonds, 1909, I, pp. 203–253. This part of the Introduction was published separately in *Jésus et la tradition évangélique*, Paris, 1910), of C. PIEPENBRING (*Jésus historique*, Paris, 1909, ²Strasbourg, Paris, 1922), of HEITMÜLLER (*Jesus*, Tübingen, 1913), of WERNLE (*Jesus*, Tübingen, 1916), of LEPSIUS (*Das Leben Jesu*, Potsdam, 1918), of JOSEPH KLAUSNER (*Jesus of Nazareth, His Life, Times, and Teaching*, translated from the original Hebrew by H. DANBY², London, New York, 1925, ²1927. The original Hebrew was published in Jerusalem in 1922; it came out in a German translation in 1930), of CASE (*Jesus, a New Biography*, Chicago, 1927), of HEADLAM (*The Life and Teaching of Jesus the Christ*, London, 1923; *Jesus Christ in History and Faith*, London, 1925). A special place should be reserved for works like those of MAURENBRECHER (*Von Nazareth zu Golgotha*, Berlin, Schönebergs, 1909) or of KAUTSKY (*Der Ursprung des Christentums*, Stuttgart, 1908), which regard the movement which Jesus inspired as a social movement, or that of R. EISLER *ΙΗΣΟΥΣ ΒΑΣΙΛΕΥΣ ΟΥ ΒΑΣΙΛΕΥΣΑΣ*, Heidelberg, 1928–1930), who regards it mainly as a political movement, of which in the New Testament writings we have only an altered picture, due to the work of men of a quietist tendency. For a discussion of Eisler's theories we venture to refer the reader to our own articles : *Jésus et le messianisme politique*, *R.h.*, CLXII, 1929, pp. 217–267, and *Les théories de M. Robert Eisler*, *R.h.p.r.*, X, 1930, pp. 177–190.

by having recourse to the method of psychological reconstruction and interpretation.[1]

It is not saying too much to speak of a consensus of criticism of the *Lives of Jesus* at the end of the nineteenth and the beginning of the twentieth century.

IV. THE PROBLEM OF THE LIFE OF JESUS IN THE TWENTIETH CENTURY

At the present time there seems very little left of the ideas upon which critics seemed to be agreed a quarter of a century ago. Even the most decided opponents of mythical theories seem to agree to-day only about the fact of the condemnation

[1] We ought at least to mention the attempts which have been made in various quarters to treat the problem of Jesus from the point of view of psychology, psycho-pathology, and, more recently, of psycho-analysis. As types of the first kind we may mention the works of LOOSTEN (*Jesus Christus vom Standpunkt des Psychiaters*, Bamberg, 1905), RASMUSSEN (*Jesus, eine vergleichende psychopathologische Studie*, Leipzig, 1905), of BINET-SANGLÉ (*La Folie de Jésus*, Paris, 1910, ff.), of SCHAEFFER (*Jesus in psychiatrischer Beleuchtung*, Berlin, 1910). (For these works as a whole, cf. SCHWEITZER: *Die psychiatrische Beurteilung Jesu, Darstellung und Kritik*, Tübingen, 1913.) Of ST. HALL (*Jesus the Christ in the Light of Psychology*, New York, 1917), of W. E. BUNDY (*The Psychic Health of Jesus*, New York, 1922), of C. A. BERNOUILLI (*Jesus wie sie ihn sahen, Eine Deutung der drei ersten Evangelien*, Basel, 1928). As types of the second kind of work we may mention BERGUER: *Quelques traits de la Vie de Jésus au point de vue psychologique et psychanalytique*, Geneva, Paris, 1920. Cf. C. JOURNET: *Quelques réflexions sur la Vie de Jésus au point de vue psychologique et psychanalytique de M. G. Berguer*, Geneva, 1920; LOMBARD: *De quelques points de méthode à propos de la Vie de Jésus de M. G. Berguer*, Rev. de théol. et de philos., 1922, pp. 34–67; and my own observations in *R.h.p.r.*, I, 1921, pp. 269–276. Without denying the services that psychology can render to historians of the life of Jesus, we must always remember that the psychological interpretation cannot be employed until after the facts have been established on a solid basis; also we should remember the great difference there is, in habits of thought and feeling, between a Palestinian of the first century and people of the present day. We should also take into account the following remarks of WEIDEL (*Jesu Persönlichkeit. Eine Charakterstudie*, Halle, 1913, p. 83): "Perhaps the true point of view would consist in reversing the usual opinion of medical men: The man of genius is the only true man, who exhausts all the possibilities of human nature, whereas 'normal' human beings remain deeply imbedded in the animal side of their nature."

of Jesus as the result of an obscure Messianic movement.[1]
We have travelled a long way from the point of view of Renan
who wrote in 1849 (before his travels in Syria had revealed
Jesus to him): "If we try to put down all that the Gospels
contain of actual fact, we could scarcely obtain one page of
history about Jesus."[2] Where Renan speaks of one page,
certain critics of the present day would only speak of one line.

There are several reasons for this change.[3] At the close of
the nineteenth century, the theory of the two sources, known
as the "Two-Document Hypothesis," elaborated and defined
down to the minutest detail by sixty years of labour, was so
generally victorious that criticism was able to turn to a new
problem, that of the composition of the Gospel of Mark, and
the analysis of the sources on which it is based. The question
was not new, but from 1900 onwards it came to the fore as
a question of first-rate importance, and the studies of Wrede,
Johannes Weiss, and Wellhausen[4] established the fact that the
work of the earliest evangelist was not written as a whole, but
that it consisted of a collection of incidents which seem to
have existed independently before they were grouped in a
setting constructed under the influence of certain theological
ideas. This shook, if it did not destroy, the essential premises
upon which all the previous *Lives of Jesus* were based, from
those of the Rationalists to that of Oskar Holtzmann, that is
to say, the idea of the direct value of the Marcan narrative,
more or less completed or corrected by data drawn from
Matthew, Luke, and even from John.

[1] In this respect it is very interesting to compare what Loisy thought in
1907–1910 (*Syn.*, I, pp. 174–253) with what he wrote in 1922 (*La passion
de Marduk*, *R.h.l.r.*, 1922, p. 297; *La légende de Jésus*, id., 1922, pp. 433–476).
[2] *Les historiens critiques de la Vie de Jésus*, La liberté de penser, III, 1849, p. 468,
quoted by J. POMMIER: *La pensée religieuse de Renan*, Paris, 1925, p. 200.
This article was altered a good deal by Renan when he re-issued it in
1857 in the *Études d'histoire religieuse*. On this point, see POMMIER (already
quoted), pp. 202 ff.
[3] MAURICE GOGUEL: *L'orientation de la science du Nouveau Testament*, *R.h.r.*,
XCVI, 1927, pp. 324 ff.
[4] W. WREDE: *Das Messiasgeheimniss in den Evangelien*, Göttingen, 1901.
JOHANNES WEISS, *Das aelteste Evangelium*, Göttingen, 1903. J. WELLHAUSEN:
Das Evangelium Marci, Berlin, 1903; *Das Evangelium Matthaei*, Berlin, 1904;
Das Evangelium Lucae, Berlin, 1904; *Einleitung in die drei ersten Evangelien*,
Berlin, 1905, ²1911.

At the same time, the Johannine problem also was renewed by the works of Schwartz, Wellhausen, and others,[1] which showed that the composition of the Fourth Gospel was more complex than had been hitherto believed, and that the theological character of the work did not exclude the utilization of historical traditions by its author. This meant that the distinction drawn between an historical and a theological book disappeared, and it became clear that the Gospels—the Synoptics as well as the Fourth Gospel—are, properly speaking, neither religious books nor histories, but religious books composed in the historical form, and with the utilization of materials which are, and may be, historical. This means that the dilemma: the Synoptics or the Fourth Gospel? which, from Strauss onwards, had dominated the problem of the life of Jesus, no longer existed, and it appeared that the difference between the Synoptics and the Fourth Gospel was one of degree rather than of nature. This conclusion has made the whole problem of the life of Jesus far more complicated, since the documents at our disposal are no longer of direct use, and above all because both the framework and the setting of the life of Jesus are entirely lacking.

On the other hand, towards the close of the nineteenth century an essential element in the traditional conception of the life of Jesus was rendered problematic by the development of the study of the problem of eschatology. Whereas, for a a long time, eschatology had been practically eliminated from the thought of Jesus,[2] a large number of authors following Weiffenbach in Germany, and Wabnitz in France,[3] have been led to think that the eschatological statements of Jesus should be taken quite literally. Finally, the popularity of Albert Ritschl's theology during the last twenty years of the nine-

---

[1] On this literature, see *Intr.*, II, pp. 52 ff.

[2] Some regard the eschatological statements reported in the Gospels as non-authentic (for instance, COLANI: *Jésus-Christ et les croyances messianiques de son temps*, Strasbourg, 1864), others interpret them in a purely spiritual sense (VOLKMAR: *Jesus Nazarenus und die erste christliche Zeit*, Zurich, 1882), or they explain them as an instance of adaptation of style to Jewish ideas (HAUPT: *Die eschatologischen Aussagen Jesu in den synoptischen Evangelien*, Berlin, 1895).

[3] WEIFFENBACH: *Der Wiederkunftsgedanke Jesu*, Leipzig, 1873. WABNITZ: *L'idéal messianique de Jésus*, Montauban, 1878.

teenth century—in which the idea of the Church or the Christian community, identified in practice with the Kingdom of God preached by Jesus, occupied a central position, has called forth various studies on the idea of the Kingdom of God, notably that of Johannes Weiss,[1] which have shown that in the thought of Jesus this Kingdom was not an ideal society called to a process of progressive development, but an entirely new economy which God will realize by a cosmic cataclysm in which the present world will disappear.

At the moment when the ideas which we have just reviewed began to influence men's minds a concerted attack was directed against traditional conceptions, with rare dialectical power, by Albert Schweitzer.[2] Although he rendered homage to the labour and the scientific value of the critics of the nineteenth century, he argued that their combined effort had led simply to failure, and, generalizing this conclusion, Schweitzer declared that Jesus could not be understood from the historical point of view at all; in his opinion, every effort to reconstruct his life in the sphere of history led inevitably to a series of insoluble antinomies.

A dozen years later a new school arose, full of ardour—its name cannot be translated into French (or English)—the *formgeschichtliche Schule*, which, from a slightly different point of view, renewed the contention that any and every attempt to construct a *Life of Jesus* was impossible.[3] Less original than it believes itself to be, and than it says it is, this school has at least had the merit of welding all kinds of scattered ideas into a coherent whole, and of drawing very definite conclusions from them, which may be thus summarized:

(i) The setting of the Gospel narratives is artificial, the

---

[1] JOH. WEISS: *Die Predigt Jesu vom Reiche Gottes*, Göttingen, 1892, ²1900.

[2] ALBERT SCHWEITZER: *Von Reimarus zu Wrede*, Tübingen, 1906 (first edition of his *Geschichte der Leben-Jesu-Forschung*).

[3] MAURICE GOGUEL: *Une nouvelle école de critique évangélique, la form- und traditionsgeschichtliche Schule*, R.h.r., XCIV, 1926, pp. 114–160. MARTIN DIBELIUS: *Zur Formgeschichte der Evangelien, T.R.*, 1929, pp. 155–216. These two articles contain all the bibliographical material necessary for information about this new school.

transitions in them are schematic, and due to an editor's hand; they are not organically connected, and they only conceal the fact that the Gospel narrative was originally formed of a multiplicity of isolated elements separate from each other.[1]

(ii) The Gospels are not historical documents. They were neither composed nor preserved in order to make known the Jesus who lived and taught in Galilee and in Judaea and who died at Jerusalem. They are religious documents which represent what Jesus was for the faith and piety of the circles in which they were composed.

(iii) The different forms under which the material of the Gospel story has been presented shows that they have been elaborated in view of the differing functions of the life of the Church; they are so closely adapted to this purpose that it would be foolish to imagine that it would be possible to discover an historical kernel within them.

The logical consequence of these theses would be to render it impossible to write a *Life of Jesus* of any kind at all, and actually the protagonists of the *formgeschichtliche Schule* maintain that henceforth it is impossible to construct a *Life of Jesus*. "We can no longer know the character of Jesus, his life, or his personality," writes Bultmann, ". . . there is not one of his words which we can regard as purely authentic."[2] And again "In my opinion we can sum up what can be known of the life and personality of Jesus as simply nothing."[3] And Bertram for his part says: "The figure of Jesus is not directly accessible to history. It is futile to try to place him within a process of historical development . . . ; not what he was, but what he is, is all that is revealed to the believer; the historian must be content with this statement."[4]

It would be easy to show by various quotations that

---

[1] This argument has been developed by KARL LUDWIG SCHMIDT (*Die Rahmen der Geschichte Jesu*, Berlin, 1919). The critics of the new school regard the book by K. L. Schmidt as having opened a new era in the science of history. They forget that similar ideas have often been expressed for many years past, especially by Reuss. It is, of course, true that these critics have not always drawn the conclusions they should have drawn from these ideas.
[2] *Die Erforschung der synoptischen Evangelien*, Göttingen, 1925, p. 33.
[3] *Jesus*, Berlin, 1926, p. 12.
[4] *Neues Testament und historische Methode*, Tübingen, 1928, p. 41.

scepticism, or at least agnosticism, in all that concerns the history of Jesus is a state of mind which is very widespread, although it is not always expressed so explicitly as by the representatives of the *formgeschichtliche Schule*. Nothing shows this more clearly than the fact that two eminent Catholic exegetes, Father L. de Grandmaison and Father M. J. Lagrange,[1] have renounced the idea of giving a sketch of the *Life of Jesus*. Father Grandmaison does this by simply ignoring the problem altogether. Father Lagrange says explicitly: "I have definitely given up the idea of giving a *Life of Jesus* to the public according to the classical formula, in order that the four Gospels may speak more clearly for themselves." They do not provide enough material to write a history of Jesus "in the way in which a modern writer would write the life of Caesar Augustus or of the Cardinal Richelieu." And again: "They form the only *Life of Jesus* which can be written; all we have to do is to understand them."[2]

Thus the immense labour of research which has been expended upon the life of Jesus from the days of Reimarus to the *formgeschichtliche Schule* seems to have ended in nothing but a confession of impotence. Then must criticism, after having exhausted the possibilities which have been offered to it, simply declare that it has failed? Or should we rather regard this confession of impotence as the expression of a passing mood of weariness and discouragement? We will try to see, in another chapter, whether perhaps this defeat, or, if one will, this apparent failure, may be due to certain errors of appreciation and to the failure to make a sufficiently clear distinction between a religious problem and an historical problem; this has led to the demand for history to give a certitude which it cannot give, for a certainty which actually adheres only to religious intuition and to faith. Let us note one fact which gives us the right to ask this question: it is this: Albert Schweitzer declares that it is impossible to give an historical account of Jesus from the point of view of what he calls thoroughgoing eschatology, yet he

[1] See above, p. 42, n. 1.
[2] P. VI. Cf. MGR. BATIFFOL (*Les origines évangéliques, à propos de trois livres français, Le Correspondant*, December 25, 1928, p. 809), who expresses some misgiving about the concessions which Père Lagrange has made to criticism.

has written a sketch of the history and of the thought of Jesus;[1] Rudolf Bultmann, again, takes the same point of view, and, as we have seen, has expressed his mind very plainly on the subject, yet he too has found it possible to draw up an outline of the thought and teaching of Jesus.[2] Such inconsistency seems incompatible with such vigorous intellects as these; hence we are led to enquire whether the radical scepticism against which they instinctively react may not be a conclusion drawn from the development of some, but not all, the factors which constitute the problem as a whole.

However that may be, the deficiency of the historians explains certain facts which characterize modern books about Jesus. First of all there is the fact of the abundance of imaginative works, for this is the only way we can describe certain books in which the authors make Jesus the mouthpiece of their own theories.[3] Then there is the vogue of the myth theory,[4] which has been a regular phenomenon for the past twenty-five years; it looks as though a whole host of literary men and of philosophers were advancing in good order to take possession of the territory abandoned by the historians in their retreat.

V. Theories of Non-Historicity

It was not until the eighteenth century that the idea that possibly Jesus never existed at all made a timid appearance with "some disciples of Bolingbroke, more ingenious than learnéd," who, according to Voltaire (who, however, brushes

[1] *Das Messianitäts- und Leidensgeheimnis, Eine Skizze des Lebens Jesu,* Tübingen, 1901. Cf. *Geschichte,* pp. 390–433.

[2] *Jesus.*

[3] Thus BARBUSSE (*Jésus,* Paris, 1927. Cf. *Les Judas de Jésus,* Paris, 1927) represents Jesus as the prophet of a social revolution with Communist tendencies, and ÉTIENNE GIRAN (*Le jardin plein de sources,* I. *L'Évangile retrouvé,* Paris, 1927) pictures him as the herald of an entirely "spiritual" religion freed from the fetters of dogma.

[4] For the history of these theories, see my book: *Jésus de Nazareth, mythe ou histoire?* Paris, 1925, pp. 9–32. SCHWEITZER, pp. 498–564. A. DREWS: *Die Leugnung der Geschichtlichkeit Jesu in Vergangenheit und Gegenwart,* Karlsruhe, 1926. WINDISCH: *Das Problem der Geschichtlichkeit Jesu, T.R.,* I, 1929, pp. 226–288. II, 1930, pp. 207–252.

aside their view very decidedly), held that the obscurities and contradictions in the Gospel tradition gave them the right to deny the existence of Jesus.[1] These ideas, which the disciples of Bolingbroke did not venture to express in writing, were made public at the close of the eighteenth century by Volney and Dupuis.[2] For these writers Jesus was neither a man nor a god; they claimed that he really represented a solar deity like the divinities which men have worshipped down the ages. After enjoying a certain vogue—proved by the numerous editions of the work of Dupuis and the abridged edition which he himself issued—these ideas fell into complete oblivion.

Neither in his first nor in his second *Life of Jesus* did Strauss cast any doubt upon the actual existence of Jesus. His myth theory, however, did prepare the way for the negations which were to follow.

The first author of the nineteenth century to pronounce definitely against the actual existence of Jesus was Bruno Bauer. Starting from the study of the Synoptic Gospels and their relation to each other, from the year 1841 he took his own stand, in opposition to that of his master, Ferdinand Christian Baur, and announced that he believed in the priority of the Gospel of Mark,[3] explaining the characteristics of the other narratives by what he called the creative power of the Gospels, and the action of dogmatic and theological preconceptions. Ten years later,[4] he argued that the factor which had caused the evolution of the tradition had also determined its birth. Mark, the primitive evangelist, thus became a creative figure, and his work was conceived as the expression of the faith of

---

[1] *Dieu et les hommes*, édition de Kehl, XXXIII, pp. 273 ff.

[2] VOLNEY: *Les ruines ou Méditations sur les révolutions des Empires*, Paris, 1791, [2]1808. DUPUIS: *L'origine de tous les cultes ou la religion universelle* (3 vols. and 1 atlas), Paris, year III (1794). *Abrégé de l'origine de tous les cultes*, Paris, year VII (1798). The ideas of Dupuis were challenged in a light but very efficacious way by J. B. PÉRÈS, a former Oratorian, who had been professor of mathematics and physics at Lyons, then deputy for the Imperial *procureur* at Agen and Librarian in that town (d. 1840). Pérès published, at first anonymously (Paris, 1827), then under his own name, in several editions, a pamphlet called: *Comme quoi Napoléon n'a jamais existé*, in which he applied the method of Dupuis to the story of Napoleon.

[3] *Kritik der evangelischen Geschichte des Johannes*, Bremen, 1840. *Kritik der evangelischen Geschichte der Synoptiker*, Leipzig, 1841–1842.

[4] *Kritik der Evangelien*, Berlin, 1850–1851.

the early Christians, while Jesus was nothing more than a fictitious character, the product, not the creator of Christianity. When Bruno Bauer had arrived at this conclusion he had to propose an explanation of the genesis of Christianity which could take the place of the one which he had renounced. This he presented in a book entitled *Christ and the Caesars*,[1] in which he argued that Christianity was born at the beginning of the second century, through the confluence of the different currents of thought which issued from Judaea, Greece, and Rome.

Bruno Bauer, who early in his career was obliged to give up the work of theological teaching in which he had first made his name, remained an isolated phenomenon. His ideas had very little influence; at a later date, the critics of the radical Dutch school and certain exponents of the myth theory developed arguments which were very similar to his own; all this took place quite independently, however, without any knowledge of Bauer's theories. It was only later that the Dutch radicals discovered that he was the forerunner of their ideas.

The radical Dutch school[2] directed its efforts first of all towards the criticism of the Pauline Epistles, dating as late as the second century. The conclusions which they have drawn from this argument in connexion with the problem of Jesus have been developed with increasing force by critics like Pierson, Matthes, Naber, Van Loon, and for a time at least by Loman, and, later, by Bolland. The reasons which have made them decide against the existence of Jesus are mainly negative. They make a good deal of the uncertainty of the Gospel tradition, the absence of all external evidence, and think that they can thus justify, not merely the scepticism which believes it impossible to gain any positive conception about the life of Jesus, but also the actual denial of his existence. But from

[1] *Christus und die Cäsaren. Der Ursprung des Christentums aus dem römischen Heidentum*, Berlin, 1877. On Bruno Bauer, see M. KEGEL: *Bruno Bauer und seine Theorie über die Entstehung des Christentums*, Leipzig, 1908.
[2] For information about this school the reader is referred to the somewhat biassed work entitled: *Die holländische radikale Kritik des Neuen Testaments*, G. A. VAN DEN BERGH VAN EYSINGA, Jena, 1912.

their own point of view they have not given any coherent explanation of the origin of Christianity and of the formation of the Gospel tradition, or at least they have merely evolved theories which are based very largely on conjecture. This explains why the Dutch school has exercised so little influence outside the land of its birth.[1]

The defenders of the Dutch radical school are fond of complaining[2] that a veritable conspiracy of silence has been organized against them. It is a fact that their theories have not spread very far outside Holland. The discussion of this question was only taken up at all seriously at the beginning of the twentieth century, partly, perhaps, owing to the noisy campaign conducted in Germany by Arthur Drews, but mainly under the influence of the breakdown of traditional ideas on the life of Jesus which occurred at that moment.

Certainly a great gulf exists between these two statements: "Jesus cannot be explained from the point of view of history; it is impossible to know his life definitely and in detail," and, "He never existed at all." Loisy and Guignebert, whose views on the question of definite historical knowledge about Jesus are extreme, have ranged themselves quite decidedly against the myth theory of Dr. Couchoud.[3] Bultmann and Bertram have taken up quite as definite a position. Bultmann writes, for instance: "There is no foundation at all for any doubt of the actual existence of Jesus; indeed, the idea of his historicity does not need to be defended."[4] When, however, we look at

---

[1] The influence of the Dutch school of thought is, however, visible in the anonymous work entitled: *Antiqua Mater, Study of Christian Origins,* London, 1887. The author (EDWIN JOHNSON) does not discover any traces of Christianity until towards the year 150, in Justin Martyr; he thinks that Christianity was born in the Jewish communities of the Dispersion, and that the story of Jesus is a mystery which may be compared with that of Dionysius.

[2] See, for example, DREWS: *Die Leugnung,* pp. 71 ff.

[3] LOISY: *Revue critique,* 1924, pp. 447 ff. GUIGNEBERT: *Le problème de Jésus,* Paris, 1914. *R.h.r.,* XCIV, pp. 215-244. *Le Jésus de l'histoire* in *Jésus et la conscience moderne,* Paris, 1928, pp. 7-28.

[4] BULTMANN: *Jesus,* p. 16. BERTRAM: *Hat Jesus gelebt? Eine Auseinandersetzung mit A. Drews, Z. f. den evangelischen Religionsunterricht,* XXXVIII, 1927, pp. 113-124. *Das Problem der Geschichtlichkeit Jesu und seine Bedeutung für die christliche Mission, Z. f. Missionskunde und Religionswissenschaft,* 1927, pp. 193-206.

the matter from a rather exterior and detached point of view, there would seem to be a less deep gulf between the ideas of men like Couchoud and Loisy than between those of Bruno Bauer and Holtzmann.

Recent theories about the non-historicity of Jesus present a less united front than would appear at the first glance. They agree in scarcely anything save in that which they deny, and to some extent in the arguments by which they try to justify these negations. It would be quite interesting to refute them by opposing one theory against another. For some, like Robertson,[1] Bolland,[2] and to some extent also Arthur Drews,[3] the legend of Jesus is simply the reappearance of an ancient Semitic cult which was preserved, in a more or less hidden manner alongside of and on the fringe of the religion of Israel and of Judaism. According to this theory Jesus is merely a new form of a divinity called Joshua, which was probably connected with the Adonis of Syria and the Tammuz of Babylonia. Others, like William Benjamin Smith[4] and G. T. Sadler,[5] think that Christianity is simply the transformation of the Jewish Gnostic sect of the

---

[1] *Christianity and Mythology*, London, 1900, 1910. *A Short History of Christianity*, London, 1902. *Pagan Christs. Study in Comparative Theology*, London, 1902, 1911. *The Historical Jesus, A Survey of Positions*, London, 1916. *The Jesus Problem, A Restatement of the Myth Theory*, London, 1917.

[2] BOLLAND: *De evangelische Jozua*, Leyden, 1907. *Het Evangelien*, Leyden, 1909, 1910. This theory has been taken up afresh by NIEMOJEWSKI (*Gott Jesu im Lichte fremder und eigener Forschung*, München, 1910. *Das werdende Dogma vom Leben Jesu*, Jena, 1910) and FUHRMANN (*Der Astralmythus von Christus*, 1912).

[3] A. DREWS: *Die Christusmythe*, Jena, 1909, ²1910; 2nd part, Jena, 1911; new edition, Jena, 1924, translated into French by R. STAHL, Paris, 1926. *Die Petruslegende*, Frankfurt-am-Main, 1910. *Das Marksevangelium als Zeugnis gegen die Geschichtlichkeit Jesu*, Jena, 1921, 1928. *Die Entstehung des Christentums aus dem Gnostizismus*, Jena, 1924. *Die Marienmythe*, Jena, 1928. Drews combines the theory of a pre-Christian Jesus with an astral interpretation of the Gospel tradition.

[4] *Der vorchristliche Jesus*, Giessen, 1906; Jena, 1911. *Ecce Deus, Die vorchristliche Lehre des reingöttlichen Jesus*, Jena, 1911. *The pre-Christian Jesus*, Am. Journ. of Theology, 1911, pp. 258 ff.

[5] *Has Jesus Christ Lived on Earth?* London, 1914. *Behind the New Testament*, London, 1921.

Nazarenes or Nasoraeans in which a protecting divinity was worshipped.[1]

According to pan-Babylonians like Jensen[2] and Zimmern[3] the story of Jesus was the product of the transformation of the myth of Gilgamesh, of that hero, half-human and half-divine, who set out in search of immortality.

Albert Kalthoff has given a Marxist interpretation of the birth of Christianity and of the Gospel tradition. In his view Christianity arose as the result of contact between the oppressed Roman proletariat and the Messianic hopes of the Jews.[4]

Arthur Drews, who for several years has carried on a systematic campaign of writing and lecturing, has certainly done most to popularize the theory of non-historicity. To a large extent his system lacks originality and even coherence; it is a sort of potpourri of all the arguments, which, from very different points of view, have been advanced against the historicity of the Christian tradition. The system of Drews was suggested to him by considerations of a philosophical order. In his book, *Die Religion als Selbstbewusstsein Gottes* (1906, [2]1925) he advanced the theory that the cult of Jesus was a relic of superstition which ought to be purged out of religion. It seemed to him that the system of Benjamin Smith was fitted to usher in the reform which he desired to see realized, thus he welcomed it with enthusiasm, combining the theory of a pre-Christian Jesus with that of an astral system renewed from Dupuis and Volney, adding some considerations of his own, especially that of an unforeseen connexion between Christ the Lamb of God (*Agnus Dei*) and the Vedic god, *Agni*. Later

---

[1] The root N S R expresses the idea of protection.

[2] *Das Gilgameschepos in der Weltliteratur*, I, Strasbourg, 1904. *Moses, Jesus, Paulus, Drei Varianten des babylonischen Gilgamesch, Eine Anklage wider die Theologie, ein Appel an die Laien*, Frankfurt-am-Main, 1906, 1909. *Hat der Jesus der Evangelien gelebt?* Frankfurt-am-Main, 1910. In addition Jensen admits an astral interpretation of the Gospel tradition.

[3] *Zum Streite um den Christusmythe. Das babylonische Material in seinen Hauptpunkten dargestellt*, Berlin, 1910. Zimmern thinks that the Gospel legend may have been influenced by the worship of Marduk, Mithra, and Tammouz.

[4] *Das Christusproblem, Grundlinien zu einer Sozialtheologie*, Leipzig, 1902, 1903. *Die Entstehung des Christentums*, Leipzig, 1904. *Was wissen wir von Jesus?* Berlin, 1904.

he had to include in his system the interpretation—to say the least, surprising—which Hermann Raschke[1] has given of the Gospel of Mark, which claims that the second Gospel is a work of Marciqn, explaining that the stories it contains are a series of etymologies of the names of places.

In France, after the passing vogue of the theories of Volney and Dupuis, until quite recently, the arguments of non-historicity have found very few supporters. It is quite possible that the systems of Bruno Bauer and of the radical Dutch school have simply been ignored outright, because no one knew anything about them, or, perhaps (and this comes to the same thing in the end), they have been known only by a few specialists, who, regarding them as fantastic speculations without any weight behind them, have judged it superfluous to mention them. Even when the contradictory lectures of Berlin were translated into French,[2] they remained almost unnoticed.[3] The question has, however, been raised in France quite apart from all Dutch, German, or English publications. Salomon Reinach,[4] without definitely pronouncing in favour of the non-historicity of Jesus, has dealt again and again with the difficulties which seemed to him to cast a doubt upon the actual story of the Passion, especially the absence of non-Christian evidence, in particular the lack of an authentic report from Pilate to Tiberius, and also the influence of the prophecies on the Gospel narrative. Later he became convinced that the Passion was an historical fact, and pronounced himself in favour of the argument proposed by Eisler.[5]

In 1923 Robert Stahl argued that the personality of Jesus was entirely mythical, in a book which, partly perhaps because

---

[1] *Die Werkstatt der Markusevangelisten. Eine neue Evangelientheorie*, Jena, 1924. Cf. *Lieux et routes de Jésus d'après l'Évangile selon Marc*, Congrès, I, pp. 188–201.

[2] A. LIPMAN: *Jésus a-t-il existé?* Paris, 1912.

[3] The same can be said for the books of L. GANEVAL (*Jésus dans l'histoire n'a jamais vécu*, Paris, 1875) and MOUTIER-ROUSSEL (*Le Christ a-t-il existé?* Paris, 1922.

[4] *Orpheus*, Paris, 1919. *Le verset 17 du Psaume*, XXII, C. M. R., II, pp. 437–442. *A propos de la curiosité de Tibère*, C. M. R., III, pp. 16–23. *Bossuet et l'argument des prophéties*, C. M. R., IV, pp. 174–180. *Simon de Cyrène*, C. M. R., IV, pp. 181–188, etc.

[5] "*Aux clous de la croix*," Congrès, I, pp. 114–116.

of its ill-chosen title, has not attracted much attention.[1] Stahl considers the most ancient Christian document to be Chapter xii in the Revelation of John, in which there is mentioned a Messiah who was taken up to heaven directly after his birth. This he regards as the act of the birth of Christianity. The purely Apocalyptic Messiah in question he considers was first of all symbolized in the Fourth Gospel, and then made concrete in the Synoptic Gospels; Paul or pseudo-Paul only came later on.

To Dr. P. L. Couchoud belongs the honour of having brought the question of the historical existence of Jesus before the public at large[2] in a small book whose literary merits have gained it a large number of readers. The theory of Couchoud stands out from those of his predecessors on more than one point, especially in this: that instead of setting aside the Pauline evidence as non-authentic, or as an interpolation, he has tried to call in its aid to support his system.[3] Essentially the theory of Couchoud is a sociological interpretation of Christianity.[4] Behind the story of its origin there is not an

---

[1] R. STAHL: Le document 70, Strasbourg, Paris, 1923. GEORGE BRANDÈS (Die Jesussage, translated by EDWIN MAGNUS, Berlin, 1925) also places the Christ of the Apocalypse at the starting-point of the development of the Christian tradition.

[2] In two articles (L'énigme de Jésus; Le mystère de Jésus) published in the Mercure de France on March 1, 1923, and March 1, 1924, then reproduced with some additions in Le mystère de Jésus, Paris, 1924. Cf. MAURICE GOGUEL, J. de N., L. DE GRANDMAISON: Jésus dans l'histoire et dans le mystère, Paris, 1925.

[3] He has been followed on this point by P. ALFARIC: Le Jésus de Paul, R.h.r., LXCV, 1927, pp. 256–286, and Congrès, II, pp. 70–99. La plus ancienne vie de Jésus, l'évangile selon Marc, Paris, 1929. Pour comprendre la vie de Jésus. Examen critique de l'évangile selon Marc, Paris, 1929. Cf. my article La relation du dernier repas de Jésus dans 1 Cor. xi et la tradition historique chez l'apôtre Paul, R. h. p. r., X, 1930, pp. 61–89.

[4] The sociological method has also been applied to the problem of Christianity by Albert Bayet and Edouard Dujardin. BAYET (Les morales de l'évangile, Paris, 1927) points out that the Gospels contain different moral conceptions; this he explains by saying that they are the reflections of different currents of thought, which, he argues, proves that Christianity does not, as is generally believed, spring from one source (on the theory of Bayet see my remarks, R.h.p.r., VII, 1927, pp. 468–472, and those of P. HUBY: Laïcisme contre l'Évangile. M. Albert Bayet exégète, Études, 1928, t. 194, pp. 294–313). DUJARDIN (Le Dieu Jésus, Essai sur les origines et la

individual fact, or a personality, but a social fact, a collective mystical experience, in a word, a mystery, which expresses itself in a divine story revealed in a supernatural manner, which at the same time justifies this history. The high spirituality of the primitive myth was gradually effaced, and Jesus was gradually humanized. It was in the Gospel of Mark that his transfer to the human plane was definitely realized.

formation de la légende évangélique, Paris, 1927) argues that the legend of the Gospel should be explained and interpreted in the same way as those of Mithra, Attis, or Osiris, that it is only the reflection, in the form of a myth, of a rite observed in a very ancient mystery which was practised on the fringe of Judaism. But he weakens his argument very much by saying that in the year 29 of our era this mystery took on new life when Jesus offered himself up voluntarily as a human sacrifice.

CHAPTER II

NON-CHRISTIAN SOURCES OF THE GOSPEL STORY

THE study of the sources of the story of Jesus, the examination and discussion of the problems which they raise, and the theories with which they are connected, would fill many volumes. I do not propose to treat these questions in an exhaustive manner, if indeed it would ever be possible to do so; my aim is simply this: I wish to define my own position concerning the problems which are raised by these questions. At the same time I will try to justify my point of view, especially with regard to those questions which have been so much to the fore of late years, questions which still cause a great deal of controversy at the present time.

The sources which relate to the story of Jesus may be divided into two groups: in the first there is a connexion with Christianity and in the second there is none. At first sight the second group[1] might appear to be the more reliable of the two, since it cannot be suspected of having been influenced by the faith of the Christians. We shall see that some of these sources have been influenced by anti-Christian apologetic.

In point of fact, all that can be gathered from the second group—(that is, from sources which are sufficiently early to be regarded as reliable)—is this: that a person did once exist whose name was Jesus or Christ, and that he was crucified in Palestine during the reign of Tiberius. No further details are given.

1. THE JEWISH SOURCES

i. *The Tradition in the Talmud*[2]

The references to Jesus and his disciples in the Talmudic tradition are in direct opposition to the claims of the Christian

---

[1] The Roman texts relating to Jesus have been collected and studied by K. LINCK: *De antiquissimis quae ad Jesum Nazarenum spectant testimoniis.*

[2] H. LAIBLE: *Jesus Christus im Thalmud*, Leipzig, 1891 (English version with additions by DALMAN and STREETER: *Jesus Christ in the Talmud, Midrash, Zohar, and the Liturgy of the Synagogue*, Cambridge, 1893), 1900 (with Dalman's additions to the English edition). SAMUEL KRAUSS: *Das Leben Jesu nach jüdischen Quellen*, Berlin, 1902. A. MEYER: *Jesus im Talmud* in

tradition.[1] It is difficult to assign any independent historical value to this evidence. Klausner, who thinks that the Talmud, in its most primitive sections,[2] has preserved some direct memories of Jesus, considers that their ultimate value is very slight. In order to explain this fact he observes that the authorities of the Talmud scarcely mention any facts belonging to the period of the second Temple. He points out that we would know scarcely anything about the Maccabean revolt if we had been restricted to the accounts in the Talmud. It is not surprising that this tradition should not tell us any more about Jesus. He lived in that stormy period when the conflict had begun with the Roman Procurators; attention was concentrated on events which seemed more important; thus he passed through Jewish history almost unnoticed. When Christianity had become powerful the memories of Jesus in Jewish circles had become very vague and indefinite. All that can be said to remain definitely of that which the Tannaïm say about Jesus, amounts, in the opinion of Klausner, to this: Jesus practised magic, poured scorn on the words of the wise men, led the people astray, and claimed that he had not come to take something away from the Law, but to add something to it. On the eve of the Passover he was hung on a charge of heresy and of leading the people astray. His disciples, who numbered five, cured sick people in his name.

The historical interest of the witness of the most ancient Rabbis lies in the fact that although they are writing against the Christian tradition they do not deny it, but they interpret it in a manner which would lead to the destruction of the basis of the Christian faith.[3]

HENNECKE: *Hndb. z. d. neut. Ap.*, pp. 47–71. R. T. HERFORD: *Christianity in Talmud and Midrash*, London, 1903. H.-L. STRACK: *Jesus, die Häretiker und die Christen nach den aeltesten jüdischen Angaben*, Leipzig, 1910 (a full bibliography). KLAUSNER, pp. 18–54.

[1] See especially S. KRAUSS: *L. J. n. jüd. Qu.*, pp. 152–155.

[2] KLAUSNER lays down the principle that it is only the traditions of the *Tannaïm* (the doctors of the first two centuries of our era) which can contain historical elements, and that those of the *Amoraïm* (doctors of the third, fourth, and fifth centuries) are devoid of value.

[3] KLAUSNER (p. 20) declares that the essentially historical value of the references in the Talmud is to make it quite clear that there is no reason at all to doubt the existence of Jesus.

The most definite and circumstantial passage in the Talmud is the *Baraïta* which is preserved in the treatise *Sanhedrin* (43*a*) of the Talmud of Babylon. Klausner declares that it has "more historical value" than the others;[1] this is what it says: "On the eve of the Passover Jesus of Nazareth was hung. During forty days a herald went before him crying aloud: 'He ought to be stoned because he has practised magic, has led Israel astray and caused them to rise in rebellion. Let him who has something to say in his defence come forward and declare it.' But no one came forward, and he was hung on the eve of the Passover. . . ."

There is one contradictory statement in this passage. Jesus is sentenced to be stoned, but finally he is hung.[2] According to *Sanhedrin*, 7, 4, stoning is the punishment of those who have practised magic, seduced the people, and led them into idolatry. To say that Jesus was condemned to death by stoning is an attempt to justify his condemnation from the Jewish point of view, but the fact that Jesus was crucified was too firmly fixed by tradition for the Talmudic writers to go so far as to say that he was stoned. The contradictory element in this narrative is the same as that in the Gospel story which attributes to the Jews the initiative of the revolt against Jesus, and reports that the condemnation and execution were carried out by the Romans. This coincidence proves that the tradition of the Talmud depends upon the Christian tradition.

The Gospel narratives give the impression that the trial of Jesus was carried through with a haste which proves that the condemnation had been decided in advance, and that in reality it was not a legal trial at all, but a judicial murder. By saying that forty days elapsed between the sentence and the execution, not only was plenty of time left for the defence of the accused, but also it gave them every opportunity to

[1] See KLAUSNER (p. 27) and STRACK (p. 1.18*). A *baraïta* is a tradition from the *Tannaïm*, but not included in the *Mishna*, which is the ancient part of the Talmud.

[2] It would be possible, it is true, to try to solve this difficulty by pointing out that according to a regulation in the work *Sanhedrin* (6, 4) the bodies of those who had been stoned should also be hung. Nevertheless, it would still seem curious that the *baraïta* should not mention the actual execution, but only the act which followed it.

appear; thus this is the reply of the *Baraïta* to this accusation.[1]
It is the defence of those who condemned Jesus to death.

We might say the same about the accusation of having practised
magic with which Jesus is charged, here and elsewhere.[2] "The
Talmud," says Klausner, "does not deny that Jesus did signs
and wonders, but it explains them as acts of sorcery" (p. 275).
Very judiciously he points out the striking analogy between
this interpretation and that of the Pharisees, who, in order
to weaken his influence over the people (according to
Mark iii. 22*), accused Jesus of casting out demons by
Beelzebub, the prince of the demons.

We know the Talmudic tradition (cf. *Aboda Zara*, 40d), which
calls Jesus Ben-Pandîrā or Panthera, a tradition which,
according to Klausner (p. 23), is really ancient, and belongs
to the time of Rabbi Eliezer ben Hyrcanus and Rabbi Yish-
mael, that is, possibly to the end of the first or the beginning
of the second Christian century.[3] Although a funeral urn of
an archer named Tiberius Julius Abdes Pantera, who came
from Sidon, has been discovered, and this soldier belonged to
a cohort which was transferred to the Rhine in the year A.D. 9,
after having been in a garrison in Palestine,[4] it would be rash
to conjecture that Jesus was the son of a Roman soldier. This

[1] The criminal procedure described in *Sanhedrin* could only be carried
out with difficulty. Probably it was thus conceived in order to show that
the *Sanhedrin* did not pronounce a sentence lightly.

[2] For instance, *Bab. Sabbath*, 104 b (STRACK, p. 29*); *Bab. Sanhedrin*, 107b
(STRACK, p. 33*), etc. JUSTIN MARTYR (*Dial. c. Tryphon*, c. 69) proves that
the Jews regarded Jesus as a magician.

[3] This story passed from Jewish polemics into the arguments used by the
pagans. Celsus makes a great deal of it (*Origen C. Celsum*, I, 32, 33, 69).
The name of Ben-Panthera seemed to be so imbedded in the tradition
that the Christian apologists felt the need to explain it. EPIPHANIUS (*Haer.*,
78, 7) makes Panthera, the grandfather of Jesus, the father of Joseph and
of Cleopas. Others, like ANDREW OF CRETE (vii, viii f.) (*Oratio in circum-
cisionem Domini*, P.G., 97, c. 916), JOHN OF DAMASCUS (d. 754) (*De fide
orthodoxa*, IV, 14; P.G., 94, c. 1156), the monk EPIPHANIUS (towards 800)
(*Vita Mariae*, P.G., 120, c. 190) represents him as a common ancestor of
Mary and of Joseph.

[4] This monument, which was found at Bingerbrück, is preserved in the
museum at Kreuznach. See EISLER, pl. XLV.

story is simply intended to counter the tradition of the supernatural birth of Jesus. Klausner (pp. 23 ff.) considers that this
is proved quite clearly by the very choice of the name Ben-
Panthera which he holds to be simply a transposition of
υἱός τῆς παρθένου (son of the virgin), a term used by the
Christians. This opinion can be maintained in spite of the
objection of Eisler (II, p. 350), who remarks that the word
did not pass from Greek into Aramaic.[1] This fact is in reality
favourable to Klausner's interpretation, because if υἱός τῆς
παρθένου has been transformed into Ben-Panthera, without
knowing the meaning of the word, it was only natural that
people should have tried to explain it. Eisler also thinks
(II, p. 351) (and this is an idea which should be noted, and
could very well be combined with that of Klausner) that the
aim of making Jesus the son of a Roman soldier was in order
to destroy the tradition that he was a descendant of the House
of David. The formation of this legend may have been facilitated by a coarse anachronism which identified Mary the
mother of Jesus with Miriam bath-Bilga, the daughter of a
priest who had left Judaism in order to marry a soldier in
the Seleucid army.[2]

In the Talmud, therefore, all we can discover are some modified reflections of the Christian tradition; it would be futile
to attempt to draw from it the least hint which might be useful
from the historical point of view. The only interest in its

[1] EISLER (II, p. 352) thinks that the origin of the name which the Greek
sources give under the form πανθήρα, but the Jewish sources in the form
Pandera is the story of the hero of Troy, Pandaros, the traitor who, in
spite of the truce, shot an arrow at Menelaus (*Iliad*, V, 88–126). The proofs
brought forward by Eisler to show that Ben-Panthera was a Jewish word
of opprobrium, meaning a new Pandaros, are very weak. It is impossible to
accept the theory that this name was given to Jesus because his entry into
Jerusalem as King of the Jews had broken the peace which existed between
the Jews and the Romans since the days of Varus, and that it set in motion
the events which led finally to the destruction of Jerusalem. First of all
Eisler has not proved that the action of Jesus was directed against the
Romans, and, even if things had happened as he says they did, the initiative
of the conflict was not taken by Jesus but by Pilate with his incessant
provocations (the affair of the standards, for instance).

[2] *T. Sukka*, IV, 28. *B. Sukka*, Berlin, 56 b. *J. Sukka*, V, 7 (EISLER, II,
p. 351).

evidence lies in the fact that, at least in a certain sense, it confirms the witness of the Gospels.

More daring still is Eisler's hypothesis which he has defended with all his resources of great learning, and also with great powers of imagination. He claims that some reliable data, entirely independent of the Gospel tradition, may be found in books of an earlier date, or in their sources, as for instance in the *Toledoth Jeshu* or in the *Josippon*, which have, however, been mutilated, rendered unrecognizable, and almost entirely suppressed by being censored by Christians. It cannot be denied that this process has been exercised very severely in Jewish writings, but can it have caused the disappearance of ancient data which were independent of the Gospel tradition? or of some controversial points directed against Christianity, its traditions and its history? This is a question which cannot be answered with any certainty. If it could be proved that the former solution were the right one, it does not follow that the lost evidence could be found and reconstituted, and still less that the explanation which Eisler finds so attractive could be retained.[1]

ii. *Flavius Josephus*

The earliest testimony to Jesus on the non-Christian side, if it were authentic, would be that of the Jewish historian, Flavius Josephus.[2]

Josephus, son of Matthias, was born in Jerusalem in the year A.D. 37 or 38; he belonged to an eminent priestly family, and he received an extensive education. He prided himself on the fact that he had examined the doctrines of the Pharisees, the Sadducees,

---

[1] On this see my article *R.h.*, CLXII, 1929, pp. 217 ff.

[2] The best versions of the works of Josephus are those of B. Niese (Berlin, 1885–1895) and of Thackeray (with an English translation, London and New York, 1926 ff.). An excellent French translation has begun to appear under the direction of Th. Reinach (*Œuvres complètes de Flavius Josèphe traduites en français*, Paris, 1900 ff.). An edition of *Against Apion*, prepared by Theodore Reinach, appeared in the *Collection des universités de France* in 1930. Of the abundant literature relating to Josephus it is sufficient to mention here: Schürer, I, pp. 74–106 (with a good bibliography); R. Laqueur: *Josephus*, Giessen, 1920; Eisler, I, pp. xxxv–xliv; Thackeray, I, pp. i–xvi; Th. Reinach: *C. Apion*, pp. i–vii.

and the Essenes very closely; he also tells us that he lived three years in the desert with a hermit named Banus. When he returned to Jerusalem at the age of nineteen he joined the Pharisee party; in these circles he rose to such eminence that at the age of twenty-six he was sent to Rome to treat for the release of certain Jewish priests who had been taken to Rome as captives; owing to the support of the Jewish actor Alityrus and the Empress Poppea this mission was successful. It is not impossible that this visit marked the beginning of the intrigues which were finally to make him a protégé of the Imperial House. On his return to Jerusalem in 66 he claims that he tried to oppose the war party. However, when the rupture with the Romans was complete he received an important command in Galilee. After the fall of Jotapata in 67 he was made prisoner, but he was able to mitigate his lot and gain the favour of Vespasian by announcing to him that he would become Emperor. When, two years later, this prophecy was fulfilled, Josephus was set free; henceforth he bore the name of Flavius. During the last campaign and the siege of Jerusalem he did not leave Titus. Then he went to Rome, where he lived under the protection of the Emperors, and devoted himself to historical and literary work. In all probability his death occurred during the first decade of the second century.

The works of Josephus which have been preserved are the following:

(i) Περὶ τοῦ Ἰουδαϊκοῦ πολέμου (*History of the Jewish War*), in seven books; this was written first of all in Aramaic, shortly after the fall of Jerusalem, and was rendered into Greek before 79 (*G.J.I.*, 1, ¶ 3). Eisler (I, pp. 247 ff.) thinks that the first edition was also translated into Greek under the title of Περὶ ἁλώτεως or Περὶ ἁλώσεως Ἱεροσολύμων (*On the Captivity* (of the author), or *On the Taking of Jerusalem*) and that it is the text of this first edition which has been preserved in the Slavonic version (see further on, pp. 61 ff.). Although we regard this theory with many reservations, it is convenient to designate the text given in the Slavonic version by the term *Halôsis*.

(ii) Ἰουδαικὴ ἀργαιολογία (*Antiquities*), in twenty books; finished in 93 or 94, re-published after the year 100.

(iii) Βίος (*Autobiography*), written after 100, as a rejoinder to the history of the Jewish revolt by Justus of Tiberias. Josephus endeavours to prove that he did not instigate the rebellion, as his adversary says he did, but that, on the contrary, he did all in his power to prevent it.

(iv) Περὶ ἀρχαιότητος Ἰουδαίων (*On the Antiquity of the Jews*). This work is known by the title of *Contra Apionem*, though this name was not the one given to it by Josephus. It consists of an apology for Judaism, in two books, composed after 93.

In the Greek text of the *Antiquities* there are two passages in which Jesus is mentioned:

XVIII, 3, 3, ¶¶ 63-64. About the same time came Jesus, a wise man, if indeed we should call him a man. For he was a doer of miracles and the master of men who receive the truth with joy. And he attracted to himself many of the Jews and many Greeks. He was the Christ, and, when after his denunciation by our leading citizens, Pilate condemned him to be crucified, those who had cared for him previously did not cease to do so, for he appeared three days afterwards, risen from the dead, just as the prophets of the Lord had announced this and many other marvels concerning him. And the group which is called that of the Christians has not yet disappeared.

XX, 9, 1, ¶ 200: Ananias called a Sanhedrin together, brought before it James, the brother of Jesus who was called the Christ, and certain others . . . and he caused them to be stoned.

This second passage raises questions which are less complicated than those raised by the first; hence it will be best to begin our examination of the evidence offered by Josephus with this passage. Origen quotes it three times, twice (*Contra Celsum*, I, 47, II, 13), without indicating in which book of Josephus it occurs, and once (*In Mt.*, t. X, ch. 17 on Mt. 13, 55, *Lommatzsch*, III, p. 46), saying that it occurs in the *Antiquities*. Eusebius quotes it literally (*Eccl. Hist.*, II, 23, 22), but, some lines earlier (*Eccl. Hist.* II, 23, 20), he gives another passage which he attributes equally to Josephus, and which represents the destruction of Jerusalem as the chastisement for the crime committed towards James the Just. This passage cannot be found in the works of Josephus which we possess, and it is certainly of Christian origin. Schürer (I, p. 581) concludes from this that the passage from Book XX is also suspect, and that it also is an interpolation. To us this view seems exaggerated. To say that Christians might be tempted to interpolate certain passages into the writings of Josephus, and even to admit that sometimes they may have done so, does not mean that the manuscript text of his works, in its present condition, was altered by the Christians every time that he mentions Christianity. Further, the difference between the expression: "Jesus surnamed the Christ," and the similar phrase (which is certainly of Christian origin): "he was the Christ" of Book XVIII, is too great to give us the right to judge that it can only have been written by a Christian.

The question of the authenticity of the passage in Book XVIII falls into a quite different category.[1] The passage occurs in the three manuscripts which we possess, but none of these goes back further than the eleventh century. Eusebius (*Eccl. Hist.*, I, 11, 7; *Dem. ev.*, III, 3, 105–106) knew it,[2] but Origen appears to have been unaware of its existence. For if he had read it in the text of the *Antiquities* which he used, could he have said that Josephus did not believe in Jesus as the Christ?[3] From the point of view of external criticism, therefore, it seems very probable that this passage has been either expanded or modified by Christian writers, and this conclusion is confirmed still more strongly by the fact that it seems to have existed in another form.[4]

The arguments from internal evidence are still more searching. If Josephus had actually said about Jesus: "if we ought to call him a man," and, "he was the Christ," if he had really mentioned the resurrection on the third day, the miracles, and the fulfilment of prophecy, he would have been a Christian.[5]

[1] The questions raised by this problem are discussed very fully by EISLER, I, pp. 1–88.
[2] S. ZEITLIN (*The Christ Passage in Josephus*, *The Jewish Quarterly Review, New Series*, XVIII, 1928, pp. 237–240) even thinks that he himself wrote it. The argument which he uses is this: that in this passage the Christians are called a race ($\phi \tilde{v} \lambda o v$), a term which Eusebius also uses, but which was not in current use as a description of the Christians. In my opinion this argument carries no weight.
[3] καίτοι γε ἀπιστῶν τῷ 'Ιησοῦ ὡς Χριστῷ (*C. Celsum*, I, 47).
[4] In an apocryphal dialogue about a religious discussion at the court of the Sassanids we read: "Josephus spoke of Christ as a just and good man, manifested by grace divine by means of miracles and signs, and who did a great deal of good to many people" (BRATKE: *Das sogenannte Religionsgespräch am Hofe der Sassaniden*, *T.U.*, 43, Leipzig, 1899, p. 36).
[5] However, although it has been challenged, from the time of the sixteenth century, especially by Osiander, the entire authenticity of this passage is still defended by critics of the first rank like BURKITT (*Josephus and Christ*,

The text bears obvious marks of a Christian writer, but is it a wholesale fabrication? or has the interpolator confined his efforts to adapting and altering a passage which, in the original, said something different from that which he wished it would say?

Schürer (I, pp. 547 f.) has tried to support the argument in favour of the absolute non-authenticity of the passage by saying that if we remove the expressions and phrases whose origin is manifestly Christian the residue is entirely insignificant. This argument proves nothing, for the interpolator has been able to mutilate the text in the process of expanding it.

Norden[1] had observed, in support of the same argument, that the story of the government of Pilate in Book XVIII of the *Antiquities* is constituted by a series of troubles which arose amongst the Jews, the leading idea of the whole being suggested by the words θόρυβος and θορυβεῖν. This scheme is interrupted by ¶¶ 63–64 which deal with Jesus. If this section were removed the series of "troubles" would be restored. Thus Norden concludes that these paragraphs were added at a later date. Corssen[2] objects that Norden's theory about the record of Pilate's government is very artificial. Although ¶ 62 deals with a difficulty which occurred at Jerusalem, and which concerned the Jews very directly (the question of the aqueduct), ¶¶ 65–80 deal with the scandal about Mundus and Paulina which took place at Rome, and was of no interest to the Jews, at least there is no hint of any aspect of this story which could have been of interest to them;[3] then, from the last words in ¶ 80 to ¶ 84 there is a narrative of events which would interest no one save Jews living in Rome. Hence this construction is altogether artificial, and it would not be difficult to imagine that in the original text

---

Theol. Tidschrift, 1913, pp. 135–144) and HARNACK (*Der jüdische Geschichtsschreiber Josephus und Jesus Christus, Internationale Monatschrift für Wissenschaft, Kunst und Technik*, 1913, pp. 1037–1068).

[1] NORDEN: *Josephus und Tacitus über Jesus Christus und messianische Prophetie. N. Jahrbuch f. d. klass. Altertum und die deutsche Litteratur*, 1913, pp. 637–668.

[2] *Die Zeugnisse des Tacitus und Pseudo-Josephus über Christus, Z.N.T.W.*, XV, 1914, p. 129.

[3] We might suppose, it is true, that the affair of Mundus and Paulina would irritate Tiberius and set him against Oriental religions in general, but this is not stated. Cf. *Œuvres de Flav. Josèphe*, IV, p. 148, n. 1.

the story of Jesus also was presented as a θόρυβος, and that it was the adaptation by the Christian writer which has caused this word to drop out. Corssen has observed further that there are in the text of ¶¶ 63–64 a certain number of expressions which are certainly in the style of Josephus, and that it would be difficult to understand how this could proceed from the hand of a Christian writer, even if he had made great efforts to imitate the style of Josephus.[1]

The hypothesis of adaptation, which is rendered very likely by this consideration, is confirmed by the fact that in Book XX, in a passage whose authenticity, as we have seen, there is no valid reason to doubt, there is the mention of "James the brother of Jesus surnamed the Christ." This phrase implies that Jesus has already been named, and that the surname "Christ" has been explained.

Is it possible to make a conjectural reconstruction of the original text of Josephus? Certain scholars, like Thomas Reinach and Eisler, have claimed that this would be possible. Reinach's emendation consists merely in omitting from the traditional text the words which cannot have been written by Josephus;[2] Eisler, who is more daring, has made an attempt to discover the words which the Christian redactor has omitted.[3]

[1] For instance, "to receive with pleasure," "the first among us," "a wise man." This latter expression agrees perfectly with the tendency of Josephus to represent movements like those of the Pharisees, Sadducees, and Essenes as though they were schools of philosophical thought. The idea of Greeks becoming followers of Jesus can hardly have been inspired by the Gospel tradition (CORSSEN, *Z.N.T.W.*, XV, 1914, pp. 132 ff.). The line of argument indicated by Corssen has been taken up and developed further by EISLER, I, pp. 46–83.

[2] Emended text by T. REINACH (*Josèphe sur Jésus, Revue des Études juives*, XXXV, 1897, pp. 13–14): "At this epoch there appeared Jesus, called the Christ, an able man (for he was a worker of miracles) who preached to people who were eager for something new, and he led astray many of the Jews and also many Greeks. Although Pilate, when he was denounced by some of the chief people among us, condemned him to be crucified, those who loved him (or whom he had deceived) from the beginning did not cease to be attached to him, and to-day the sect is still in existence, which, calling itself after him, is entitled the Christians."

[3] Emended text by EISLER (I, p. 873): "About that time a man named Jesus was the cause of fresh troubles. He was a wise man and energetic, if indeed he can be described as a man at all, for he was one of the most remarkable of men, and his own disciples called him a son of God, who

It is obvious that the cautious method of Reinach cannot reconstitute the original text, for there is no reason to believe that the Christian editor merely expanded the original text; the method of Eisler is curiously arbitrary. Even though it might be possible to discover what Josephus did not say, it is certainly impossible to discover what the Christian editor omitted, or even to say with any certainty at what point the omission took place.

Even if we admit the authenticity of the text of the passage in Book XX of the *Jewish Antiquities*, and something at least of that of Book XVIII, the brevity and the very summary nature of the allusions of Josephus to Jesus are striking.[1] There is another fact, however, which seems still more amazing, and that is, that Josephus does not allude in any way to the Christian movement, although it is impossible to suppose that he knew nothing about it; it is also very strange that he scarcely mentions the Messianism which occupied such a prominent position in Jewish history during the first century. The explanation of this silence lies in the character of Josephus and in the aim of his work. He wished to flatter the Romans and to get into their good graces, so he omitted anything which might offend or disquiet them. How, indeed, could he speak of the Messianists, and in particular of that group of them which bore the name of "Christian," without saying that the object of their ardent hope was the destruction of all earthly empires, on the ruins of which the Kingdom of the

is said to have worked miracles such as no other man has yet achieved. . . . He was a master, who did great things for those people who joyfully receive that which is unusual. . . . He led astray many of the Jews and also many Greeks and was regarded by them as the Christ. . . . Further, after Pilate had condemned Jesus to be crucified (having been charged with crime by some of the first men among us), those who had loved (or admired) him before did not cease to stir up trouble. They thought that after he had been dead for three days, he once more appeared among them alive, and they believed that the Prophet of the Lord had foretold this and many other marvels regarding him. And still the clan of those who are called Christians after him has not been stamped out."

[1] The summary nature of the evidence of Josephus is, however, less astonishing when we remember, as H. WINDISCH (*T.R.*, 1929, p. 278) points out, that Josephus does not name a doctor like Hillel, and makes no allusion to the Jewish heretical schools.

Messiah was to be established?[1] Since he felt it impossible to mention Christianity shorn of its Messianic element, Josephus preferred to be silent, in order that he might not expose Judaism to the accusation of a compromising connexion with a movement which was already hateful in the eyes of the ruling classes, to which, as Corssen has suggested (*Z.N.T.W.*, XV, 1914, p. 135), during his first visit to Rome, Josephus may have called the attention of the court of Nero.[2]

APPENDIX.—THE EVIDENCE OF THE SLAVONIC VERSION OF THE JEWISH WAR[3]

In 1906 Alexander Berendts gave to the world the text of certain fragments which are of interest to the history of Christianity, which are peculiar to the Slavonic version of

[1] Nor is there any question of Messianism in what Josephus says about John the Baptist in *A.J.*, XVIII, 5, 2 ¶¶ 117–119.

[2] The reasons which explain the silence (or the discretion) of Josephus, also explain the fact that, according to PHOTIUS (cod. 13), Justus of Tiberias, author of a *Chronicle* and a *History of the Jewish War*, written at the same time and in the same spirit as the works of Josephus, does not mention Jesus or Christianity either. So far as Philo is concerned, the fact that he makes no mention of the Gospel is sufficiently explained when we recall the fact that most probably he died very soon after the year 40 of our era, and there is nothing to prove that Christianity had been taken to Alexandria before that date.

[3] A. BERENDTS: *Die Zeugnisse vom Christentum im slavischen "de Bello Judaico" des Josephus* (*T.U.*, XIV, 4), Leipzig, 1906. A. BERENDTS and K. GRASS: *Flavius Josephus vom Jüdischen Kriege nach der slavischen Uebersetzung deutsch herausgegeben und mit dem griechischen Text verglichen*, Dorpat, 1924–1927 (*Acta et Commentationes Universitatis Dorpatensis, B. Humaniora*). There is a German text and translation of the principal passages in EISLER. French translation by SALOMON REINACH: *Jean-Baptiste et Jésus suivant Josèphe. Compte rendu critique du Jésus Basileus de R. Eisler*, Paris, 1929 (extract from the *Revue des études juives*), pp. 132–136. This translation has been reproduced as an appendix to Vol. VII of the *Œuvres de Fl. Josèphe*, translated into French, Paris, 1932. There is an English translation by THACKERAY as an appendix to his edition III, pp. 635–658 (with an indication, pp. 659–660, of the passages in the Greek text which have no equivalent in the Slavonic version); EISLER gives a bibliography and a complete history of all the works and discussions relating to the Slavonic version of Josephus. We would refer the reader to the two articles which we have written on this question: *R.h.*, CLXII, 1929, pp. 217–267, and *R.h.p.r.*, X, 1930, pp. 177–190.

the *Jewish War*. Although they were published in Russia for the first time in 1866–1869, and then again in 1879, and were noticed by Bonwetsch in 1893, they did not attract the attention of Western scholars. Berendts considered them authentic, and thought that the Slavonic version had been based on the Hebrew or Aramaic edition, which preceded the Greek edition, in which Josephus would not have thought it fitting to reproduce them. This theory was vigorously opposed by critics like Schürer, Harnack, and Jean Réville, and the arguments by which they supported the complete non-authenticity of the passages peculiar to the Slavonic version, or, as it is more convenient to call it, the *Halôsis*, seemed so conclusive that, although some writers like Seeberg, Frey, and Goethals declared themselves convinced of the authenticity of this version, or at least of the antiquity of the text, the question was regarded as settled as soon as it was propounded. Robert Eisler reopened the question in 1926 with a series of communications to various learned societies, and he has devoted an important work to the defence of the authenticity of the Slavonic version in which he only admits that there have been certain Christian interpolations; he made use of these by supplementing them, with the help of other non-Christian documents which he managed to discover in order to construct an entirely new conception of the Gospel story. The admission of a considerable amount of interpolation is not the only modification that Eisler has imposed upon the theory of Berendts. He has also recognized that the theory of a translation made directly from the Hebrew or the Aramaic into Slavonic is untenable. In his opinion the Slavonic version was made in Lithuania between 1250 and 1260, on the basis of a Greek edition of the *Halôsis*, and he thinks that if the passages peculiar to it are not in the Greek text, and that even sometimes they seriously contradict it, this is because the Greek edition which we possess has been seriously altered by the Christian censor. Although, in this new form, the theory of the authenticity of the Slavonic fragments avoids some of the objections which made the theory of Berendts untenable, there are still, in our opinion, sufficient reasons against this theory to make us pronounce, without hesitation, against the authenticity of these passages, and it is impossible to avoid the conclusion that we are here dealing with evidence—in itself very interesting—relating to Jewish anti-Christian controversies.[1]

In order to show, even in a brief and arbitrary way, the reasons which have led us to this conclusion we must give first of all the two principal passages in the text of the *Halôsis* which refer to Jesus.[2]

II, ¶ 174: At that time also a man came forward—if even it is fitting to call him man (simply). His nature as well as his form were a man's, but his showing forth was more than (that) of a man. His works, that is to say, were godly and he wrought wonder deeds, amazing and full of power. *Therefore it is not possible for me to call him a man (simply).* But again, looking at the existence he shared with all, I would also not call him an angel. And all that he wrought through some kind of invisible power, he wrought by word and command. Some said of him that "our first Law-giver (Moses) has risen from the dead and shows forth many cures and arts." But others supposed (less definitely) that he is sent by God. Now he opposed himself in much to the Law, and did not observe the Sabbath according to ancestral custom. Yet, on the other hand, he did nothing reprehensible nor any crime, but by word solely he effected everything.[3] And many from the folk followed him and received his teachings. And many souls became wavering, supposing that thereby the Jewish tribe would free themselves from the Romans' hands. Now it was his custom often to stop on the Mount

---

[1] Before we could use these passages from this point of view we would need to be quite certain at what period and in what setting they were written. It is not certain whether it is possible to find a solution to these questions.

[2] We are using here, slightly adapted in order to bring it into closer harmony with the German translation by EISLER (II, p. 297), the translation given by SALOMON REINACH (pp. 134 ff.). We print in italics the words which Eisler regards as interpolations. In order to examine the problem thoroughly it would be necessary to consider all the passages which refer to John the Baptist (according to II, ¶ 110, and according to II, ¶ 168). I have done this elsewhere (*Jean-Baptiste*, pp. 20–33). We ought also to examine the passage which reports the troubles stirred up in Galilee by the disciples of Jesus after the death of Agrippa I. For the discussion of this last passage, to which the threefold evidence of Tacitus, Josephus (Greek), and the Christian tradition is opposed, and which assumes that Cuspius Fadus and Tiberius Alexander exercised the functions of Procurator in common, I would refer the reader to my article in the *Revue historique*.

[3] Reinach takes this to mean that he did not perform magical incantations or make passes with his hands.

of Olives, facing the city. And there also he avouched his cures to the people.

And there gathered themselves to him of servants a hundred and fifty, but of the folk a multitude. But when they saw his power, that he accomplished everything that he would by word, they urged him that he should enter the city and cut down the Roman soldiers and Pilate, and rule over us. But that one scorned it.[1] And thereafter when knowledge of it came to the Jewish leaders, they gathered together with the high priest and spoke: "We are powerless and weak to withstand the Romans. But as withal the bow is bent,[2] we will go and tell Pilate what we have heard, and we will be without distress, lest if he hear it from others, we be robbed of our substance, and ourselves be put to the sword and our children ruined." And they went and told it to Pilate.

And he sent, and had·many of the people cut down. And he had that wonder-doer brought up. And when he had instituted a trial concerning him he perceived that he is a doer of good, but not an evil-doer, nor a revolutionary, nor one who aimed at power, and let him free. He had, you should know, healed his dying wife. And he went to his accustomed place and wrought the accustomed works. And as again more folk gathered themselves together around him, then did he win glory through his works more than all.

The teachers of the Law were (therefore) envenomed with envy and gave 30 talents to Pilate, in order that he should put him to death. And he, after he had taken the money, gave them consent that they should themselves carry out their purpose, and they took and crucified him according to the ancestral law.[3]

---

[1] The Roumanian version has "but his spirit was not disposed to that." Reinach believes that here the text is corrupt and that something has fallen out.

[2] The meaning seems to be: "The matter is started; nothing can stop it"; evidently what the text means is that Pilate, in crushing the revolt, will not make any distinction between the innocent and the guilty and will lay the blame upon the authorities. S. REINACH renders: "Since the bent bow menaces us all," and thinks this is a Scriptural phrase (Ps. ii. 2; Zech. ix. 13). This interpretation introduces an element into the text which does not exist.

[3] S. REINACH translates thus: "In accordance with the law of the Emperors" (Roumanian text). The Roumanian text (EISLER, I, pp. 430–461) is an apocryphal account of Nicodemus contained in a manuscript belonging to the Rabbi Moses Gaster of London and translated by him for Eisler. In this account, which is fairly full, some fragments have been inserted which are given as coming from Josephus and which recur in the *Halôsis*. Chapter 18 corresponds to the fragment which follows *Hal.*, II, ¶ 174

According to V, ¶ 195[1]: Above the inscription was suspended another in the same characters, saying: Jesus the king did not reign, but he was crucified *by the Jews* because he had predicted the destruction of the city and the ruin of the Temple.

One remark must be made about the position of the fragment about Jesus on the Mount of Olives.[2] It is inserted between two incidents: the affair of the standards and the affair of the aqueduct, both of which were actions of Pilate which provoked great resentment among the Jews; Josephus also, although he supported the Roman cause, could not help feeling with his own people in this matter. The Greek text suggests a very close connexion between the two episodes. In the Slavonic version, however, the material inserted between these two fragments is quite different in character. It also mentions, it is true, some massacres of the Jews, but in this instance Pilate does not provoke the trouble; he simply confines his efforts to taking measures which, from his point of view, were inevitable. The coherent character of the Greek text does not reappear in the Slavonic version; this fact alone is sufficient to cast suspicion on the passages which appear in the latter version only.

It is quite clear that these passages refer to Jesus, although he is not actually named. Eisler (II, pp. 354 ff.) does not

(excepting that the healing of the wife of Pilate is not mentioned), but only to the point where it is said that Jesus having been set free the doctors of the Law were eaten up with envy (the beginning of Chapter 19); then comes a long account of the trial of Jesus, which is an elaborate paraphrase of the traditional account in the Gospels (Chapters 19–29, seven pages in Eisler's book); at the close Pilate declares: "His people, the Jews, say that he aspires to be King, and it is for this that I have condemned him to death, but first of all you must bind him and scourge him." The Roumanian text adds that, according to others, the Jews gave Pilate thirty talents in order to bribe him to destroy Jesus. Under these conditions it is very rash to use the words "after the usage of the Emperors" to correct the Slavonic text; on this point Eisler is more discreet than Reinach.

[1] After the mention of the pillars which bore the inscription (in Greek and in Latin, according to the Greek text; also in Hebrew, according to the Slavonic version) which forbade foreigners to enter the sanctuary.

[2] SEEBERG (*Eine neue Quelle zur Geschichte des Urchristentums* in *Von Christus und dem Christentum*, Leipzig, 1908, p. 53) has some useful observations on this subject.

think that the absence of the name is due to the censor who wished to eliminate an insulting term—Jesus Ben-Panthera—for it would have been possible to omit whatever might hurt the feelings of the Christians, and yet leave the name of Jesus in the text. He imagines that the person who omitted the name of Jesus is the Jewish owner of the Greek manuscript whence the Slavonic version is derived, the reason being that he wished to avoid difficulties with the censor. But the fear of the censor would have led not merely to the suppression of the name of Jesus, but of the whole passage; now no one can read this passage without seeing instantly that it is an attempt to tell the story of Jesus. Further, the absence of a proper name is not an isolated fact. In *Hal.*, II, ¶ 220, Jesus is not named; he is simply called, "worker of miracles." Nor is John the Baptist named in the two passages which refer to him (*Hal.*, II, ¶ 110 and ¶ 168). Thus we are here dealing with something systematic.

Some explanation is needed, and this is the conclusion at which I have arrived: the author of the fragment wished to insert things which he believed concerning Jesus which he could not say directly because he neither wished nor dared to contradict the Christian tradition openly.[1] The narrative in the Slavonic version is based upon the Christian tradition.[2] The idea that Jesus might be Moses risen from the dead arises out of the interpretation of the Sermon on the Mount as the legislation of the New Covenant, with the addition, also, of the Gospel narratives, according to which people were asking whether Jesus might not be a prophet risen from the dead (Mark vi. 14–16), Mark viii. 27–28*), and the episode of the Transfiguration in which he talks with Moses (Mark ix. 2–8*).[3] The idea that the followers of Jesus wanted to urge him on to deliver his people from the yoke of Rome comes from John vi. 15, in which it is said that the people wanted to take

---

[1] This is the reason which prevents me from believing, as I did at first, that the passages from the Slavonic version are Christian in origin. See the article: *Le témoignage de la version slave de la Guerre juive de Josèphe sur la mort et la résurrection de Jésus*, R.h.r., XCIII, 1926, pp. 22–43, in which I have summarized the remarks which I made in a discussion which followed the first communication of Eisler to the *Société Ernest Renan*.

[2] I have tried to show this in detail: *R.h.r.*, XCIII, 1926, pp. 29–38.

[3] This comparison between Moses and Jesus was frequent. Cf. John i. 17.

Jesus and make him king.[1] The council meeting of the Jewish authorities, which precedes the decision to denounce him to Pilate, is merely a paraphrase of John xi. 47–48.

In my opinion, to infer from the Slavonic fragment that its author did not know anything about the Galilean ministry of Jesus because he narrates only the circumstances which led Pilate to crucify him, or have him crucified, is an untenable position.

The idea that Jesus was denounced to Pilate by the Jewish authorities, an idea which is developed to the point of buying from the Jews Pilate's consent to the death of Jesus, and the admission of the innocence of Jesus by the Procurator, are elements which come from the Gospel tradition in the secondary form given to them by apologetics.

The healing of the wife of Pilate, the thirty talents, an obvious transference of the thirty pieces of silver paid to Judas, are details which do not need to be noted specially; finally the execution of Jesus by the Jews is an idea which often occurs in the more secondary forms of the Gospel tradition, especially in the Gospel of Peter.[2]

Even if we admit the interpolations which Eisler believes he has discovered, sufficient signs still remain of the dependence of this narrative upon the Christian tradition. Thus the Slavonic narrative does not bear the marks of independent evidence. If a person who possesses first-hand information is relating the facts he knows, he does not weave into his narrative elements drawn from a tradition which actually contradicts his own statements.

But is it legitimate to admit that the text is interpolated? We do not believe so. Certainly it is not absolutely coherent; but the hypothesis of alteration is not the only theory which might explain its character. The dual nature of the sources (the Christian tradition and anti-Christian controversy) in itself makes this quite evident.

From a comprehensive point of view, on the whole this passage is favourable to Jesus. Even if we hold that the early phrases have been either interpolated or recast, if they do

[1] Cf. also Acts i. 6, where the disciples enquire of the Risen Christ when he will restore the Kingdom to Israel.

[2] W. Bauer: *L.J. nt. Ap.*, pp. 199, s. 478.

not actually affirm the idea of the divinity of Jesus, at least they clearly imply it, and the fact remains that Jesus accomplished miracles by his word, without having recourse to any magical process; that the impression he produces is such that the people regard him either as Moses who has reappeared on the earth, or as a messenger of God; that, urged to place himself at the head of an insurrectionary movement, he refuses, and that finally, if the Jewish authorities sacrifice him, it is because they believe that the enterprise to which his followers wish to drive him is a rash one, and they insist on avoiding being involved in the repercussions of a movement destined to certain defeat.

It is because the general tenor of these passages seems favourable towards Jesus that, at first sight, we were inclined to regard them as a development of Christian legend. Since, however, from this point of view it is impossible to give a satisfying explanation for the absence of the name of Jesus, we ought to add that there is nothing in this passage which represents Jesus as Saviour, nothing which refers to the virgin birth, nor to the resurrection. The theory of a pastiche in which the point of view of Josephus was remembered, and his style imitated, is obviously untenable. Anyone who reads this passage thinking to find in it an exact picture of what really happened, would imagine that Jesus possessed a miraculous power which would have allowed him to have made some attempt to liberate his nation from the yoke of Rome. Instead of doing so, however, and in spite of the urgent requests of his followers, he refused, and in spite of his lack of courage, he perished a victim to the Roman system of oppression, without even having the glory of being considered a martyr in a sacred cause. These considerations lead inevitably to the conclusion that actually Jesus was only an impostor, a timid and unhappy individual; hence there is no need for us to regard him as a divine personage, or a prophet, to expect anything of him or to venerate his memory. The tendency of the passage therefore is distinctly anti-Christian; it avoids gross calumnies, it is true, but its general drift is quite clear. The picture presented in the Slavonic fragment is based too closely on the Christian tradition to have been of a kind to make the Christians abandon their faith; thus we can only conclude that it was conceived with a view of hindering Jews from becoming converted to Christianity.

From these considerations, therefore, we can see the reason for the lack of unity in this passage, without finding it necessary to have recourse to any theory of interpolation. The author has blended his own inventions with ideas borrowed from the Christian tradition in such a way that he manages to insinuate what he dare not say openly for fear of the censor. It is therefore impossible to attribute this passage to Josephus, or to admit that it has any documentary value as evidence. It is simply a fragment of Jewish apologetic and nothing more.

The passage which relates to the inscription in the Temple, said to have commemorated the crucifixion of Jesus, only needs a very brief notice. Eisler regards this inscription as a reply of the Jewish authorities to the inscription on the Cross, which they regarded as an insult to their nation; in order to hold this view, however, he is obliged to consider the incident as it is reported by John; the Johannine story, however, is only a secondary development of historical data supplied by Mark in a more sober and restrained manner. There are also further and more serious objections. An inscription would not have borne the word "Jesus" by itself, a name which was in fairly wide use, but "Jesus, son of Joseph," or "Jesus the carpenter," or "Jesus of Nazareth," in any case there would have been some more precise designation. Hence there is no evidence of an eye-witness behind *Halôsis*, V, 195. Further, the words "crucified by the Jews" show very clearly that the Slavonic version depends very closely on the Christian tradition, and even on a secondary form of this tradition. Eisler tries to escape from this conclusion by saying that the intervention of the Romans was not mentioned because in the person of Jesus it was important to make it quite clear that he was not a Messianic impostor, accepted by the authorities, that is to say that Judaism itself had been condemned, but that Jesus had been rejected by the Jews. Eisler considers these words "by the Jews" as a Christian interpolation. From the point of view of criticism this is untenable. We have no right to eliminate a clause in a passage which, as it has been transmitted to us is perfectly homogeneous, simply because it constitutes a decisive objection to the authenticity of a text which we desire to be authentic.[1]

Hence we may sum up thus: the passages which belong to the Slavonic version are neither authentic nor historical. They may be of some interest for the history of the development of legend, and for that of Jewish apologetic; for the story of Jesus they are of no value whatsoever.

II. Pagan Sources

i. *Thallus the Samaritan*[2]

The first non-Christian author who, so far as we know, has alluded, if not to Jesus, at least to the Gospel tradition, is Thallus, concerning whom Julius Africanus thus expresses himself:[3] Τοῦτο τὸ σκότος ἔκλειψιν τοῦ ἡλίου Θαλλος ἀποκαλεῖ ἐν τρίτῃ τῶν ἱστωριῶν, ὡς ἐμοὶ δοκεῖ ἀλόγως. "Thallus, in the third book of his history, calls this darkness an eclipse of the sun, but in my opinion he is wrong." The reference is to the darkness which, according to the story in the Gospels, accompanied the death of Jesus; thus Thallus explains this mysterious darkness as an eclipse of the sun. Julius Africanus was opposed to this view; in his mind the darkness was not a natural phenomenon, but a miracle. If

---

[1] In my opinion no useful purpose would be served by discussing the last passage in which Jesus is mentioned (after V, ¶ 214); it refers to the resurrection and the veil of the Temple. It is enough to note that it is added after the description of the sanctuary, and is thus placed after a passage in which there has been a mention of persecutions of the Christians during the period which followed the death of Agrippa I (II, ¶ 221), whereas its normal position would have been after the place in which the crucifixion is mentioned. If the author had been using an historical tradition he would have placed this detail in the period to which it belonged. The position of this fragment betrays the hand of an interpolator who here introduces fragments which he wants to add to the text wherever it gives him an opportunity to do so.

[2] Eisler, II, pp. 138 ff. Cf. Maurice Goguel: *Un nouveau témoignage non-chrétien sur la tradition évangélique d'après M. Eisler, R.h.r.,* XCVIII, 1928, pp. 1–12.

[3] C. Müller: *Fragmenta historicorum graecorum,* Paris, 1841–1870, III, pp. 517 ff. This fragment has been preserved by the Byzantine chronicler George the Syncellus. It is curious that no exegete has given any attention to this text, although it has been reproduced by Schürer, III, p. 369.

Thallus had been writing simply as a chronographer who mentions an eclipse which occurred in the fifteenth year of the reign of Tiberius, Julius Africanus would not have said that he was mistaken, but he would have used his evidence to confirm the Christian tradition.[1] Thus Thallus interpreted a fact that Christian tradition presented as miraculous as a natural phenomenon. This proves that he knew this tradition.

Eusebius[2] reports that Thallus had written a history in three books which covered the period from the fall of Troy to the 167th Olympiad (112-109 B.C.). The text of Eusebius must certainly have been altered, since we know that Thallus mentioned a fact which belonged to the fifteenth year of Tiberius. Adopting a conjecture of Carl Müller, Eisler proposes to correct $\rho\xi\zeta$ (167th) to $\sigma\zeta$ (207th) (A.D. 49-52).[3] The theory is attractive, but, since we only possess the *Chronicle of Eusebius* in an Armenian version we cannot be sure whether the alteration has taken place in the Greek text and not in the Armenian version, or at the moment of the passage from the Greek to the Armenian. One thing only is certain, and this is that Thallus wrote after 29 (the fifteenth year of Tiberius) and before 221 (the date at which his work was used by Julius Africanus).

Some passages in Thallus which have been preserved by various writers reveal an author eager to combine the legends and traditions of the East with those of Greece.[4]

Now Müller, Schürer, Christ,[5] and later, Eisler, identify this Thallus with that freedman of Tiberius, of Samaritan origin,

---

[1] Just as ORIGEN (*C. Celsum*, II, 33, 59) and EUSEBIUS (*Chronique*, éd. KARST, Leipzig, 1911, p. 213) invokes that of Phlegon of Sardis.

[2] *Chronique*, éd. KARST, p. 125.

[3] The ρ is supposed to have been substituted for an σ and the ξ is said to be a dittograph for the ζ. The reading $\sigma\xi\zeta = 267$ (289-292 A.D.) is impossible, since Julius Africanus, who has used Thallus, ends his *Chronicle* in the year 221.

[4] SCHÜRER, III, p. 369. W. CHRIST: *Geschichte der griechischen Literatur*, München, 1905, p. 705.

[5] These authors have not perceived the interest which the evidence of Thallus possesses for the history of the Christian tradition. In consequence the identification which they propose cannot be suspected of having been imagined to meet the needs of the case.

mentioned by Josephus,[1] who lent a large sum of money to Agrippa shortly before the latter became King of Judaea. The name of Thallus is not so common that we might consider it rash to identify the person named by Josephus with the author of the *Chronicle* used by Julius Africanus and Eusebius. Freed by Tiberius, being in a condition to lend a large sum to Agrippa, at that time Thallus could not have been a very young man. We are still within the range of possibility if we conjecture that he may have lived some fifteen or twenty years after the master who had set him free; this would place the probable *terminus ad quem* of his death about the year 60. As there is no reason to think that Thallus would have waited till the last months of his life to write his *Chronicle*, it would seem that it may have been written during the middle of the first century of our era,[2] at Rome. Now, as we have seen, Thallus was offering the usual interpretation given by the Christians concerning the darkness which accompanied the death of Jesus. This shows that this detail was known in Rome, in the middle of the first century, in a circle near to the Imperial House. A small detail of this kind could not have been preserved and transmitted save within the setting of a narrative of the Passion.

Eisler (who was the first to perceive the interest of the evidence of Thallus) has thus brought to light two facts of great importance: (i) the Gospel tradition, or at least the traditional story of the Passion, was known in Rome in non-Christian circles towards the middle of the first century; (ii) the enemies of Christianity tried to destroy this Christian tradition by giving a natural interpretation to the facts which it reported.

---

[1] *A.J.*, XVIII, 6, 4, ¶ 167. It is true that Thallus is only a conjecture which all the editors of Josephus (with the exception of Niese) have adopted since the eighteenth century. The manuscripts, with one exception (E, which also does not contain the text, but simply a summary of the *Antiquities*), read ἄλλος Σαμαρεύς. E only has Σαμαρεύς, which is a correction intended to eliminate an obscure passage. No other Samaritan being mentioned in the pages which precede it, and the name of Thallus being verified by the inscriptions for the servants of the house of Claudius, the correction of ἄλλος into θάλλος seems most natural.

[2] SALOMON REINACH (*Jean-Baptiste et Jésus suivant Josèphe*, p. 122) admits that he wrote verse 52.

ii. *Pliny the Younger*

The first Latin passage in which Christ is mentioned dates from 110; this is the letter in which Pliny the Younger, who was then Governor of Bithynia, consults Trajan about the line of action he should take with regard to the Christians.[1] He states that the enquiries he has made have convinced him that Christianity is merely a crude superstition. There is only one point to note in what he says about the practices of the Christians. He says that they assemble themselves together regularly on a certain day, and sing "a hymn to Christ as to a god" (*carmen Christo quasi deo dicere*). This passage is clear evidence that Christ was worshipped, but it does not tell us plainly exactly what the Christians thought about him. The expression *Christo quasi deo* seems to indicate that, in Pliny's opinion, Christ was not a god like those which other men worshipped. May we not conclude that the fact which distinguished Christ from all other "gods" was that he had lived upon the earth?

The passage from Pliny is not a piece of independent evidence of the Christian tradition, because it was after having examined Christians about their beliefs that Pliny tells Trajan what he has discovered.

iii. *Tacitus*

The evidence from Tacitus is more explicit:

"In order to destroy the rumour (which accused him of having set fire to Rome) he (Nero) invented a charge of guilt, and inflicted the most appalling tortures on those who were hated on account of their abominations, and who were called Christians by the multitude. This name comes to them from Christ, whom the Procurator Pontius Pilate, under the rule of Tiberius, had handed over to the torture. Repressed for the moment, this detestable superstition

---

[1] *Ep.*, X, 96. The authenticity of this passage, which has sometimes been challenged since Semler, is now usually accepted, although it may very well contain some Christian interpolations, which, however, do not affect the subject with which we are dealing at all. See GUIGNEBERT, *Tertullien*, Paris, 1901, pp. 77–90. MAURICE GOGUEL: *L'Eucharistie des origines à Justin Martyr*, Paris, 1910, pp. 259–263. E. C. BABUT: *Remarques sur les deux lettres de Pline et de Trajan relatives aux chrétiens de Bithynie*, R.h.l.r., 1910, pp. 289–307.

broke out anew, no longer simply in Judaea, where the evil arose, but at Rome, into which there flows all that is horrible and shameful in the whole world, and finds many people to support it."[1]

The authenticity of this passage, which is contested only by Hochart and Drews,[2] is admitted by all philologists. It contains two different statements. First of all, a mention of the persecution of Nero, which reflects the sentiments of Tacitus and of his contemporaries towards the Christians, then some remarks about the Christ, which may be drawn from a documentary source, because there is not a word like *dicunt* or *ferunt* which would justify us in believing that Tacitus was speaking from hearsay. Some authors have thought that in this instance the historian was utilizing information which he had procured from a Christian source;[3] but this view breaks down when we note that the leading idea in this mention of Christianity is the fact that the Christian movement, suppressed by the execution of its founder, did not reawaken until a little before the year 64; in any case this idea cannot be of Christian origin. Neither can Tacitus have procured his information from a Jewish source. What he actually says about the "detestable superstition" which reawakens simultaneously both in Judaea and in Rome, a little before the year 64, does not distinguish between the two forms of Messianism which were represented by Christianity and by Judaism. The words "not only in Judaea" can only refer to the outbreak of nationalism which provoked the Jewish revolt and the Jewish war.[4] Further, a Jewish document would never have represented Judaism as united with Christianity, nor would it ever have called Jesus "the Christ."

---

[1] *Annales*, XV, 44. We follow here the translation by H. GOELZER.

[2] HOCHART: *Études au sujet de la persécution des chrétiens sous Néron*, Paris, 1885, p. viii; *De l'authenticité des Annales et des Histoires de Tacite*, Bordeaux, 1890; *Nouvelles considérations au sujet des Annales et des Histoires de Tacite*, Paris, 1894. DREWS: *Die Christusmythe*, I, p. 179.

[3] E. MEYER (*Ursprung und Anfänge des Christentums*, Berlin, Stuttgart, 1921–1923, I, p. 209, n. i; III, p. 505) and CICHORIUS (quoted by NORDEN: *N. Jahrb.*, 1913, pp. 651 ff.) think that Tacitus is alluding to the article in the creed "he suffered under Pontius Pilate," or that he is making use of information gathered in the course of his administration in Asia.

[4] CORSSEN: *Z.N.T.W.*, XIV, 1913, p. 123.

Thus Tacitus is evidently quoting from a pagan source. May we infer that Tacitus had consulted the Imperial archives for an official report of the trial of Jesus? The hypothesis is simply mentioned as a reminder, for it is very doubtful whether an official report about the death of Jesus[1] was ever sent to Rome, and, even if this document had ever existed, Tacitus would scarcely have been able to make use of it, since the archives of the Emperor were secret, and there is nothing to justify us in supposing that an exception to the general rule would have been made in favour of the historian.[2]

Harnack thinks that Tacitus had made use of the *Jewish Antiquities*. The fact that he did use the *Jewish War* is not a final argument in support of this hypothesis. Tacitus could not neglect a document as important as the narrative of the war by Josephus, but it seems very unlikely that Tacitus, who had the most profound contempt for Judaism, would have searched the *Antiquities* to find something to complete his narrative of the fire of Rome. The differences between the passage in Josephus and that in Tacitus are too great to allow us to suppose that the one might have been the source of the other. Josephus says that the death of Jesus did not cause the faith of his disciples to break down; according to Tacitus Christianity vanished for a time after the death of its founder. The attitude of Josephus towards Christianity is, on the whole, favourable;[3] that of Tacitus is wholly contemptuous. Finally, Tacitus appears to take the word "Christ" as a proper name, while Josephus knows that the leader of the sect was called Jesus, and that the word Christ represented the dignity which he claimed to possess.

Goetz[4] suggests that Tacitus obtained his information about Christianity from his friend Pliny the Younger. The point of view of the two men is the same. On the other hand, while they were agreed in regarding it as a pure superstition, Pliny considers this superstition innocent; whereas Tacitus seems

[1] See later, pp. 99 ff.

[2] TACITUS: *Histoires*, IV, 40. Cf. PH. FABIA: *Les sources de Tacite*, Paris, 1893, pp. 324 ff.

[3] Assuming of course that we admit the authenticity of the passage *A.J.*, XVIII, 3, 3, ¶¶ 63–64, as Harnack does.

[4] *Die ursprüngliche Fassung der Stelle Ant.*, XVIII, 3, 3, *und ihr Verhältniss zu Tacitus, Ann.*, XV, 44, *Z.N.T.W.*, XIV, 1913, pp. 295 ff.

to have been influenced by the charges laid at the door of the Christians, and he describes their superstition as "detestable."

Monsignor Batiffol[1] has suggested that Tacitus might have borrowed his paragraph about the Christians from the *Histories* of Pliny the Elder. This is a conjecture which, by its very nature, cannot be verified, and is in consequence without interest. But one fact seems to us to be certain, and that is this: that Tacitus knew a document which was neither Jewish nor Christian, but pagan, which connected Christianity with the Christ who was crucified under Pontius Pilate. It is not necessary to emphasize the importance of this statement.

iv. *Suetonius*

In his *Life of Nero* (16), Suetonius mentions the persecution of the Christians, but without saying anything about him whose name they bore. In his *Life of Claudius* (25, 4) he speaks incidentally of the expulsion of the Jews from Rome: "*Judaeos impulsore Chresto assidue tumultuantes Roma expulit.*"[2] "He expelled from Rome the Jews who, under the influence of Chrestos, did not cease to agitate." Is Chrestos[3] an unknown Jewish agitator who stirred up trouble in the Jewish colony at Rome?[4]

---

[1] *Orpheus et l'Évangile*, Paris, 1910, pp. 46 ff.

[2] The book of Acts (xviii. 2) alludes to this expulsion of the Jews. We have further evidence in the works of the historian Paulus Orosius, according to which the measure in question was put into force in the ninth year of the reign of Claudius, possibly in 49 (VII, 6, 15). Orosius appeals to the authority of Josephus, but either the reference he gives has become confused in transmission, or he is alluding to some passage in Josephus which has not been preserved.

[3] LINCK (*De antiquissimis*, p. 106, n. 2) gives a list of more than eighty inscriptions in which this name occurs.

[4] EISLER (I, pp. 132 ff.), who understands the text of Suetonius in this sense, thinks that this Chrestos was none other than Simon Magus who may have gone to Rome and given himself out to be the Christ, Jesus *redivivus*. Simon Peter is said to have opposed him. It is assumed that it was the quarrels and discussions between the partisans of the two Simons, as well as between the Messianist Jews and those who were sceptical, which caused the decree of expulsion to be issued by Claudius. Even merely to discuss this hypothesis we would need to have a confidence in the romance of the *Clementines* which it does not deserve.

Or, since the Christians seem to have been called Χρηστιανοί at Rome and not Χριστιανοί,[1] can it be that the Jewish circles in Rome had been agitated by the preaching of the Gospel, and that Suetonius, who only viewed the matter from the point of view of a detached outsider, may have thought that this "Chrestos" about whom they disputed was actually in Rome at that time? The nature of the passage forbids us to draw from it any certain conclusions in answer to our questions. In any case, the fact that Suetonius names Chrestos as a person who was known, without adding to his name *quodam* or *aliquo*, seems to favour the second interpretation. If Suetonius really believed that Jesus had come to Rome in the reign of Claudius, this shows how little the Romans thought of the traditions to which the Christians referred.

5. Conclusion

Thus the testimony of the Latin authors to Jesus does not amount to very much, and, if we except the evidence of Tacitus, all it does is to reveal the existence of groups of believers bearing the name of Christ. It is quite natural that this material should be so scanty. The importance assumed by Christianity later on makes it very easy for us to fall into an error in perspective. Because the birth of Christianity was the most pregnant fact in the whole history of the first century, we find it difficult to realize that its contemporaries did not see its importance. We forget that, for a Pliny or a Tacitus or a Suetonius, and, indeed, for the whole of Roman society in the first century, Christianity was merely a contemptible Eastern superstition. It was ignored, save when it proved the occasion of political and social ferment. It is from this point of view alone that the Latin authors speak of it, and it is natural that they should not take the trouble to collect and

---

[1] In Tacitus (*Annals*, XV, 44) the *codex Mediceus* has the form *Chrestianos*; in the only three passages in the New Testament where the word "Christians" occurs (Acts xi. 26, xxvi. 28; 1 Pet. iv. 16) the original text of ℵ has Χρηστιανοί, that of Manuscript B Χριστιανοί. The form Χρηστιανοι is frequently found in inscriptions (Linck: *De antiquissimus*, pp. 78 ff.). Cf. also Justin, I, Ap. 4. Tertullian: *Apol.* 3. *Ad nationes*, 13. Lactantius: *Div. Inst.*, IV, 7.

examine the real or fictitious traditions to which those whom they regarded as agitators referred.

Windisch[1] has remarked that the relative silence of Roman authors regarding Jesus is not without parallels. Herodotus speaks similarly of the religion of the Persians without any mention of Zoroaster. Dion Cassius (69, 12–14) gives an account of the Jewish revolt under Hadrian without mentioning the name of Bar Cochba, and apart from Philostratus we would scarcely have known the name of Apollonius of Tyana.

Thus the evidence of the Latin authors is mainly negative; that of Tacitus, it is true, constitutes a serious objection to the theory of non-historicity; but the evidence supplied by the other writers does not yield any material for the enrichment of our knowledge of the life of Jesus which we possess in the Christian tradition.

APPENDIX.—THE "ACTA PILATI"[2]

From time to time, both the friends and enemies of Christianity have invoked the authority of a report addressed by Pilate to Tiberius, that is to say, of an official account of the charges against Jesus and of his sentence; but sometimes they have referred to the text of a book whose existence they have merely supposed to be true, and sometimes they have been deceived by false information.

Is it certain that the Procurator of Judaea, after he had passed a capital sentence upon an "alien" (that is to say, on a person who did not possess the status of Roman citizenship), would have sent in an account of this fact to Rome, and that a detailed report of the trial and the sentence of Jesus would thus have found a place in the Imperial archives? Salomon

---

[1] *T.R.*, 1929, p. 278.

[2] R. A. LIPSIUS: *Die Pilatusakten*, Kiel, 1871, ²1886. HARNACK: *Gesch. der altchrstl. Litt. bis Eusebius*, Leipzig, 1893–1904, II, i, pp. 604–612. BARDEN-HEWER: *Gesch. der altkirchl. Litt.*, I, Freiburg im Breisgau, 1902, pp. 409–411. A. STUELKEN: *Pilatusakten* in HENNECKE: *Neut. Ap.*, pp. 77 ff., and *Handb. z. d. neut. Ap.*, pp. 143–153. S. REINACH: *A propos de la curiosité de Tibère*, *C.M.R.*, III, p. 161. EISLER, I, pp. 128 ff.; II, pp. 327 ff.

Reinach and Eisler claim that this is so. The matter is, however, far from certain, and it is very possible that in the eyes of Pilate the verdict passed on Jesus and his execution were simply an administrative act incurred in the discharge of the duty of policing Palestine, of which he was not in any way bound to render an account. The anxiety of the Procurators to prevent their administration from being considered either weak or brutal, according to circumstances, would lead them to exercise a certain reserve in their reports to Rome. Where a man like Pilate was concerned, we must also take into account the fact that he would be very anxious to hide his fraudulent and brutal transactions from the authorities. Philo[1] has preserved for us the accusation against Pilate by Agrippa; in it the Procurator is accused, among other things, of having put to death, time after time, and regularly, people whose sentence was illegal (τοὺς ἀκρίτους καὶ ἐπαλλήλους φόνους).

Can we think that, in the case of each of these judicial murders, Pilate would send a report to Rome? It would doubtless be going too far to affirm that there may be no mention of Jesus of any kind in the Imperial archives, but the existence at Rome of a report concerning the death of Jesus cannot be affirmed *a priori*, and it remains at least very problematical.

The first mention of such a report appears towards the middle of the second century in the *Apology* of Justin Martyr. In order to support what he says about the miracles and the Passion of Jesus, Justin refers his readers to the "acts of that which took place under Pontius Pilate."[2] He does not express himself so clearly that we can be sure that he is himself acquainted with the document of which he speaks. He believes in its existence, and thinks that the Emperors to whom he addresses his remarks first of all may also have knowledge of it. Justin Martyr, in his view of the story of the Passion, follows the tradition of the Gospels, according to which the Jews took the initiative in bringing charges against Jesus, Pilate having only, after a certain resistance, yielded to their urgency. Now it is not at all certain that this is the true view

---

[1] *Legatio ad Cajum*, 38 (Éd. MANGEY, II, p. 590).
[2] JUSTIN, I, *Ap.*, 35, 9; 48, 3. Cf. 38, 7.

of his case, since the trial and the execution were Roman. Therefore it is clear that Justin possessed no other documentary evidence than that which the Gospels contained, and that he was so entirely persuaded that they gave an exact record of the facts, that he boldly conjectured the existence of a Roman document which would give the account of these facts in the same manner.

After Justin, Tertullian[1] speaks of a report which Pilate is supposed to have addressed to the Emperor; he thinks it was less a narrative of facts than a veritable apology for the Christian religion, which Pilate, "already a Christian in his conscience" (*jam pro sua conscientia christianus*), is supposed to have addressed to the Emperor, and as a result of which Tiberius is said to have asked the Senate that the divinity of Christ might be officially recognized. Such a document could only have been the work of a Christian writer.[2]

Had Tertullian such a document actually in his hands? or was he speaking from hearsay and conjecture? This second hypothesis seems the more likely, if we take into account the fact that in 5, 27, Tiberius is represented as having pronounced personally in favour of Christianity, and as having persisted in this attitude in spite of the refusal of the Senate to follow his suggestion; whereas in 21, 24, it is simply stated that the Caesars would have believed in Christ if they could have been Christians and Caesars at the same time. There is a difference between these two references which could not be explained if Tertullian were referring to a document which he actually had before his eyes.

Alongside of the acts, letters, or reports of Pilate which are of Christian origin there was another kind of *Acts of Pilate*, that of which Eusebius speaks (*Eccl. Hist.*, IX, 5, i) as "full

---

[1] TERTULLIAN: *Apologeticum*, 21, 24. Cf. 5, 21.

[2] EUSEBIUS (*Eccl. Hist.*, II, 2) quotes the passage from Tertullian, but does not seem to have known the document of which he speaks. Later there came into existence a whole literature called *Acta Pilati*, which, especially in the form which it assumed in the Gospel of Nicodemus, enjoyed a great vogue in the Middle Ages. This literature does not seem to have been earlier than the fourth century, although it may have been based on some far older material.

of blasphemies against Christ." They were published by order
of Maximinus Daïa, and measures were taken to ensure their
having the largest possible publicity.[1] It is usually admitted
that these acts of Maximinus Daïa were simply a piece of
controversial propaganda, merely a reply to the *Acta Pilati* of
the Christians, and, like them, destitute of all historical value.
Eusebius, who was already of this opinion, justifies this view
by an argument which until then had seemed irresistible. He
recalls that according to the testimony of Josephus[2] Tiberius
sent Pilate as Procurator to Judaea in the twelfth year of his
reign (August 19, 25–August 18, 26), and that this magistrate
remained in exercise of his duties almost until the death of
the Emperor (March 16, 37). Pilate would thus have governed
Judaea from the beginning of 26 to the end of 36 or the
beginning of 37. Now the Acts of Maximinus Daïa place the
crucifixion of Jesus under the fourth consulate of Tiberius, the
seventh year of his reign, probably at the Passover of the year
21. "Now it is shown," says Eusebius, "that at this epoch
Pilate was no longer governor of Judaea, if we are to believe
the testimony of Josephus" ($\epsilon\ddot{\iota}$ $\gamma\epsilon$ $\tau\hat{\omega}$ 'Ιωσήπῳ μάρτυρι
χρῆσθαι δέον. *Eccl. Hist.*, I, 9, 3–4). Eisler thinks that in
order to discredit the "Acts" which the Imperial Government
had just issued, the date of the death of Jesus was falsified
by Christian apologists, who altered the manuscript of Josephus
in this sense. He does not, however, explain how it was that
no enemy of the Christians arose to denounce such a shocking
forgery and to produce older manuscripts which would have
thrown the Christians into confusion. Are we to suppose that
they alone possessed the works of Josephus and that no one
outside their ranks had ever read him?

Eisler interprets the words: "if we are to believe the testimony of Josephus," which Eusebius employs in this sense, that
although he referred to them, he may have had the feeling
that the manuscripts which he used were not very reliable
evidence. Eusebius expresses himself in terms which show that
for him the evidence of Josephus is quite definite. The phrase
on which Eisler lays so much stress is, therefore, very likely
an ironical point addressed to the author and the defenders

---

[1] The schoolmasters were ordered to make their children read it.
[2] JOSEPHUS, *A.J.*, XVIII, 2, 2, ¶¶ 33–35. Cf. iv, 2, ¶ 89.

of the *Acta Pilati* of Maximinus Daïa. "You are trusting in a document," he says, "which contradicts decisive evidence, you are thus obliged to admit its falsity, at least to the extent that while denying the evidence you would not go so far as to reject the witness of Josephus." To us, therefore, it seems quite arbitrary to correct the text of the *Antiquities*, XVIII, 2, 2, 35; iv, 2, 89, as Eisler does, in such a way as to give to the government of the predecessor of Pilate, Gratus, a length of four years instead of eleven ($\overline{IA}$ corrected to $\overline{\Delta}$), and to that of Pilate himself a period of nineteen years instead of ten ($\overline{IZ}$ instead of $\overline{I}$).[1]

Eisler produces another argument in support of the date given by the Acts of Maximinus Daïa for the death of Jesus. How could the Imperial administration, he asks, give a false date in a document which it had published, since it possessed the actual records of the trial? Would it not have been highly imprudent to insert a date, whose falsity could easily be proved, in a document which was intended to confound the Christians? This argument would carry great weight if it could be proved that in the year 314 Maximinus Daïa had confined himself to publishing the records of the trial of Jesus which had been preserved in the Imperial archives; but the existence of such a record is, as we have seen, a very unlikely hypothesis. Further, extracts from the archives would not have been sufficiently popular in character for them to be read in the schools.

One point, however, remains to be explained, and this is the origin of the date 21 given for the death of Jesus. The question is raised under conditions which make it impossible to give a completely convincing reply. We are dealing with a document which we do not know, and of which we know nothing about the materials of which it is composed. All we can do is to hazard a guess of this kind: The polemic against Christ was not born in 314, at the date when Maximinus Daïa issued the anti-Christian *Acts of Pilate*; before this epoch controversialists must have tried to oppose the *Acts of Pilate*

---

[1] Here I will merely mention as a reminder the reason which will be discussed in Chapter VII, which lead us to assign positive value to the chronological data provided by the Gospels, data which do not agree with Eisler's system.

invoked by Justin and Tertullian, and very certainly by many others, with some other arguments. Just as the author of the Christian *Acta Pilati* of the fifth century has made use of older material, it is also possible that the pagan *Acta* of 314 were compiled with the help of earlier documents, and that among these there may have been some which, belonging to a period when the Gospels were not as widely known as they were destined to become later on, implied a different chronology from theirs. There have been traditions which assumed that Jesus died under the rule of Claudius, that is to say ten years later than the date indicated in the Gospels;[1] it is therefore possible—though we can say nothing certain in this respect— that there may have been documents in which the date of his death may have been fixed a little less than ten years before the date given by them.[2]

[1] For example, the letter of Pilate contained in the *Acta Petri et Pauli* is addressed to Claudius. We will return to these traditions farther on (pp. 230 ff.).

[2] EISLER (II, pp. 321 ff.) thinks that the record of the trial of Jesus ought to contain, in the order for the arrest issued by Pilate, some description of Jesus. He thinks that this must have existed, but as an addition to the epistle of Lentulus, an apocryphal work which is certainly not earlier than the thirteenth century. The portrait which it gives of Jesus is not at all consistent. Alongside of details which suggest the idea of his beauty there are others which tend to represent him as ugly, weakly, and even deformed. Eisler thinks that these latter traits belong to the authentic description and that the former were added by Christians who could not bear to think of Jesus as ugly. The contradictory nature of these statements is obvious, but it can be explained in a far more simple and satisfactory way than by Eisler's theory: it may be due to the fact that in the Church there existed side by side two conceptions, both inspired by theological ideas, which represented Jesus, on the one hand, as the ideal type of humanity, and on the other, as having taken upon himself all the defects, deformations, and miseries of humanity. On this point see BRAUN: *La description de l'aspect physique de Jésus par Josèphe, d'après les théories de M. Robert Eisler, Revue Biblique*, 1931, pp. 343–363, 519–543.

CHAPTER III

THE PAULINE EVIDENCE

I. THE PAULINE EPISTLES

No literary evidence about Jesus is earlier than that contained in the Epistles of the Apostle Paul.[1] In the eyes of many readers, the fact that these letters were collected into a series towards the end of the first century, and, half a century later, were incorporated into the Canon of the New Testament, to some extent changed their character. Instead of realizing that Paul's letters were the spontaneous overflow of a sensitive, vital personality, who gave free course to his emotions, to his enthusiasm and his indignation alike, men saw in them nothing but theological treatises.

The Pauline Epistles are not literary works in the usual sense of the word; that is to say, they were not written to supplement the writer's direct activity, when it could not be exercised on account of distance. They were not written for an indefinite public without regard for time or place. They are, however, far more valuable than those private letters which the study of the papyri has unearthed, because they supplement, not the simple and banal conversation of everyday life, but the work of preaching and teaching.

In the Epistles we find the reflection of an activity, which, at a very early date, diffused Christianity throughout one part of the eastern basin of the Mediterranean, and of a system of thought which fixed the setting within which Christian doctrine was developed. In order to understand these letters we need to forget the halo which has surrounded them for the last eighteen hundred years, a halo whose glorification makes

---

[1] They were composed between the years 50 and 58, according to the conclusions which I have stated in my *Introduction*, IV, 1 and 2. I would refer the reader to this work for all critical questions raised by the Epistles. I would simply remind the reader that I regard the following Epistles as authentic (I give them in the order in which I believe them to have been written): 1 and 2 Thessalonians, Philippians, 1 and 2 Corinthians (a compilation of fragments from at least six different letters), Galatians, Romans, Colossians, Philemon.

them unnatural. We must regard them not as a species of encyclical letters, but as incidental writings, hastily improvised between journeys, dictated in the evening after a day devoted to manual labour, or to preaching, or to both at once, by a man overburdened with fatigue and the cares of the churches, forced to meet all kinds of unexpected emergencies as best he may: to clear up a misunderstanding, to give instruction or warning to some individual or group, to answer questions which have been put to him. Each letter was written to meet some particular situation; if that were to disappear, the letter would lose its interest. Paul never wrote with an eye to the future; he was writing simply for the present. In the Early Church there is no trace of any custom of the regular reading of his letters. They were read aloud at the meetings of the faithful, perhaps from time to time they were reread as long as the question which had called them forth was occupying men's minds;[1] then they were placed among the records, though without any special care for their preservation; for when, between 90 and 100, people began to collect Paul's letters, it was discovered that several of them had been lost, and even the manuscripts of several of those which had been preserved, especially those of the letters to the Corinthians, were in rather bad condition.

Therefore we must not expect to find a complete statement of Paul's faith and theology in his Epistles. We do not find in them all he knew or all he believed. Written for people whom he himself had taught, they assume what his readers know already; very often they are based on allusions to instruction already given by the Apostle, and to the tradition common to primitive Christianity.

Paul bears a twofold witness to Jesus: first of all by his theology, and then by what we can gather from his letters in the form of quotations, or simple memories of words of Jesus, or allusions to certain facts in his life.

[1] Sometimes a letter received from the Apostle would be communicated to a neighbouring church. In Col. iv. 16 Paul recommends that his letter should also be read in the Church at Laodicea, and also that at Colossae the letter to the Church of Laodicea should be read.

II. THE THEOLOGY OF PAUL

Paul possessed a vigorous and systematic intellect, but his teaching was not dominated by philosophical considerations. He preached a Gospel; he did not teach a doctrine. Conscious that he was the bearer of a message of salvation, he did not wish to teach men, but, by rescuing them from death and perdition, to make them new creatures, members of the new humanity whose head was Christ, the second Adam, and thus to throw open to them the gate of the heavenly kingdom. These are religious affirmations, drawn directly from his own experience, and they are the main topic of his letters.[1] These affirmations, however, presuppose a conception which needs to be briefly stated in order to emphasize the points at which Pauline theology had been influenced and even determined by an historical tradition about Jesus.

The setting of this conception comes from Judaism. The world is dominated by sin and death, that is to say, it is under the control of demoniac powers, archangels or angels which have rebelled against God, whose head is Satan. By the sin of Adam the whole of humanity has been involved in the revolt of the demons, and it would be destined to die if God in His infinite love had not decided to save it. To Paul the initiative of redemption comes from God; it is a pure result of His grace (1 Thess. ii. 12, v. 9; 1 Cor. i. 9; 2 Cor. v. 18, viii. 9; Rom. viii. 28–39, ix. 24, xi. 32).[2]

Paul feels that his calling as an Apostle and as a Christian is the work of grace. "It is by the grace of God," he writes, "that I am what I am" (1 Cor. xv. 10). He feels that at the moment of his conversion he experienced something for which his previous life had not prepared him, that its normal course had been completely altered, that he had been gripped and constrained by some power outside himself. And it was this power which had seized him which had made him a missionary (1 Cor. ix. 16–17; 2 Cor. xii. 9; Phil. iii. 12).

The originality of Paulinism in relation to Judaism consists

---

[1] On this point see my study entitled *Paulinisme et Johannisme* in *Trois études sur la pensée religieuse du christianisme primitif*, Paris, 1931, pp. 43 ff.

[2] For the idea of grace see G. P. WETTER: *Charis, Ein Beitrag zur Geschichte des aeltesten Christentums*, Leipzig, 1913.

in the fact that it substitutes the idea of grace for that of merit and the observance of the law. It is by the Cross of Christ that God achieved His purpose, which is the salvation of men. In Pauline theology the necessity of the Cross is not sufficiently explained by the desire to safeguard the holiness of God, for Pharisaism insisted just as much on the omnipotence as on the holiness of God. If Paul does not make grace the direct and immediate cause of salvation, it is because he felt the necessity laid upon him to explain the death of Christ. That is the origin of his doctrine of redemption.

In order that salvation may be attained two things are required. When man appears before the tribunal of God it is necessary that he should be pronounced just; on the other hand, he needs to be delivered from the evil forces which dominate him. Justification and redemption correspond to these two needs. However close may be the relation between the two, in the thought of Paul they are still distinct, and are related to two different elements in the work of Christ. Justification is achieved by his death and his resurrection; redemption will only be realized by his glorious return at the end of the age. Justification has been achieved, redemption is still a matter of hope in the future (Rom. viii. 24), for the demoniac powers are still alive and active. The triumph of Christ at the end of the world, and by this the achievement of salvation are, however, assured, for, in principle, Jesus has gained the victory over the demons to which humanity is subject, although he has not yet annihilated them (2 Thess. ii. 8; 1 Cor. xv. 24; Col. ii. 15).

The fact that Paul lays far more emphasis upon justification than upon redemption ought not to lead us to conclude that the latter is only the consequence of the former. Justification takes place within the sphere of history, redemption lies in a realm outside history. All the effort of the missionary—and Paul is a missionary first and foremost—is directed towards persuading the individual sinner to accept justification. Once this point has been gained, everything else will flow from it, for, from the point of view of the individual, redemption appears to be a direct result of justification, and the Spirit whom the justified person receives is the firstfruits and the pledge of this fact (Rom. v. 10, viii. 23 ff., 31 ff.; Gal. iv. 6).

The present world, dominated by evil powers and characterized by sin, impotence, and death, is destined to perish. In its place there will arise a new world into which the faithful are introduced by justification; this will be the heavenly world[1] in which God and Christ are supreme. The time which will have to elapse (and which Paul believes will be short) between the death of Christ and his return is an interim period, in which, if we may thus express it, the two economies overlap. The first still exists because of the forces which dominate it; it is said that they will perish (1 Cor. ii. 6, xv. 24–26), never that they have perished. The second exists already, because by his resurrection Christ has become the head of a new humanity, and because those who are united to him by faith and who have received the earnest of the Spirit also belong to this new world, and have become new beings, new creatures.

Three facts dominate this present world: subjection to the forces of sin which condemn it to death, the promise which God has made to Abraham, and the Law which He promulgated through Moses. From each of these points of view the cycle is closed by the appearance of Christ. Through the Incarnation sin is conquered, and the faithful regain life (1 Cor. xv. 22; Rom. v. 17); the promise made to Abraham is accomplished (2 Cor. i. 20; Gal. iii. 16); and finally Christ is the end of the Law (Rom. x. 4; cf. Gal. iii. 21–iv, 5).

The Pauline Christ who accomplishes the work of salvation is a personality who is both human and superhuman, not God (the term is not used by Paul), but Son of God. Here the idea, which was to develop later, of the union of the two natures in the person of Christ is not present. The idea is rather that of a divine being who becomes man (Phil. ii. 5–11; cf. 2 Cor. iv. 4; Col. i. 15 ff.), it is the idea therefore of a being whose history unfolds in successive phases, first of all heavenly, then human, and then finally divine.

At a point in time fixed by God Jesus is born of the House of David, in the heart of the Jewish people (Gal. iv. 4; Rom.

[1] This does not mean that this world is, or will be, realized in heaven, but that it is the Kingdom of Him who is in heaven, that is, of God.

i. 3); he was perfectly holy (2 Cor. v. 21; Rom. v. 17–19; Phil. ii. 8). If Paul speaks sometimes of Christ as having the appearance of a man (Phil. ii. 7; Rom. viii. 3), it would be quite wrong to suggest that this idea is in any way related to docetism. In speaking of "appearance" Paul does not deny that Jesus differs from ordinary human beings, but he does not mean to say that he is not of the same nature as they are, with, of course, the one exception of sin.[1]

All that is essential in the work of Christ is summed up in his death on the Cross. The Cross is the essence of the wisdom and the power of God, of salvation, of the preaching of the Apostle (1 Cor. i. 17 ff.; Gal. v. 11, vi. 12–14; Phil. iii. 18; Rom. iv. 25, v. 10). When the question is raised: but how does the Cross of Christ achieve the salvation of sinners? Paul has recourse to several systems of ideas in his reply. He compares the death of the Saviour with the sacrifice of the Paschal Lamb (1 Cor. v. 7), or he speaks of propitiation, that is to say, he appears to conceive the redemptive death in terms of the Levitical sacrifice (Rom. iii. 25). He also introduces the idea of the sacrifice as a ransom (Rom. vi. 17 f.; Gal. iii. 13). Most frequently, however, he develops the idea of the condemnation of sin in the flesh of Christ (Gal. iii. 13; 2 Cor. v. 21; Rom. viii. 3). The death of Christ is a punishment for sin; he submits to it because he has accepted his solidarity with sinful humanity. These various views strike us by their dissimilarity. It is impossible to weld them together into a logical and balanced doctrine. This is because Paulinism is not a systematic structure, but an attempt, or to put it more precisely, a series of attempts, to interpret one fact: the death of Christ, which constitutes the basic fact upon which the theology of redemption is based.

Apart from the resurrection, however, this death would remain inoperative. The resurrection is not merely a reparation granted to Christ, a recompense for his sacrifice, still less is it a consequence of his divine nature; it is an act of God, an act of veritable creation (1 Thess. i. 10; Gal. i. 1; 1 Cor. vi. 14, xv. 15; 2 Cor. iv. 14; Rom. iv. 24–25, etc.). Without the

[1] H. J. HOLTZMANN: *Neutestamentliche Theologie*[2], Tübingen, 1911, II, p. 80.

resurrection the sacrifice of Christ would be vain (1 Cor. xv. 14–17). It is this which renders justification possible (Rom. iv. 25). The resurrection is at the same time a glorification; it does not merely restore Christ to the state in which he was before he humbled himself, it places him in glory at the right hand of God, and confers upon him the name which is above every name, the supreme title of *Kurios* (Κυριος), "Lord," which gives him the right to receive the adoration of all the inhabitants of the universe. In his glorified existence Christ is spirit, he is even *the* Spirit in the absolute sense of the word. The formula "Christ the power of God" almost makes of him a mode of the divine action (Phil. ii. 11; 1 Cor. i. 24, xv. 45; 2 Cor. iii. 17; Rom. viii. 9–11, 34; Col. iii. 1).

The death and the resurrection of Christ modify his position both in relation to the demoniac beings and to those who are united to him. According to certain passages (Rom. viii. 37; Col. i. 18–20, ii. 15), Christ has gained a victory which makes all beings subject unto him; he re-establishes order in the universe. According to 1 Cor. xv. 24–26 this victory will not be completed until time comes to an end, and the hostile forces are annihilated. From one point of view the matter is considered in principle, and in the absolute sense, and from the other in its chronological development. The defeat of the Satanic powers does not mean that they have been destroyed, they still exist, they are able to fight and deliver a final attack on Christ, but they can no longer triumph; at the end of the age all the enemies of Christ, and last of all *Thanatos*[1] will be placed under his feet. "Then cometh the end, when He shall deliver up the kingdom to God, even the Father" (1 Cor. xv. 24–26).

Underlying the Pauline Christology we can clearly discern a system of ideas which is really the Jewish Messianic doctrine already permeated by certain elements of Hellenism. The element of originality in Pauline thought lies in this: that it has made a synthesis of this system and the life, death, and

---

[1] *Thanatos* does not mean the abstract power of death; it means he who causes death, that is, Satan himself. This identification is evident in Paul, although it is not expressed explicitly, as it is in Heb. ii. 14.

resurrection of Jesus. It is the interpretation of the historical fact of Jesus by the Messianic doctrine.

Couchoud and Alfaric[1] have tried to reduce Paulinism to its dogmatic element alone, suggesting that what we have taken for an historical tradition was simply the utilization of some scriptural themes. We shall see later on that it is impossible to explain the allusions in the Epistles to the facts of the life of Jesus, or the quotations of words uttered by him[2] in the way they propose. If their theory were right, Paul's conception of the causes of the death of Christ would be homogeneous. But this is not the case. According to 1 Cor. ii. 8, Christ dies crucified by the action of the ἄρχοντες, that is to say, of rebellious demons who have revolted against God.[3]

[1] COUCHOUD: Le mystère, pp. 77 ff. ALFARIC: Congrès, II, pp. 70–99. For a discussion of the theory of Couchoud see my book J. de N., pp. 97–171; for the ideas of Alfaric, the article entitled La relation du dernier repas de Jésus dans 1 Cor. xi. 23–25, et la tradition historique chez l'apôtre Paul, R.h.p.r., X, 1930, pp. 61–89.

[2] See further on pp. 119 ff.

[3] COUCHOUD (Le mystère, p. 132), followed by ALFARIC (Congrès, II, p. 94), has proposed to interpret this passage by the Ascension of Isaiah without taking into account the danger of commenting on a text by another which is a century older. He overlooks the fact that in the Pauline passage the archontes, thinking that they will prevent the plan of God, really collaborate with him by crucifying Christ, while in the Ascension of Isaiah the angels of the different heavens do not oppose the passage of the Well-Beloved who descends from heaven right down to Sheol, where he despoils the angel of death, simply because the Well-Beloved changes his appearance at each stage of his descent, and the angels do not perceive that he has descended from the upper heavens. Although certain interpreters (as, for instance, HEINRICI: Der erste Brief an die Korinther (MEYER, V, 8), Göttingen, 1896, p. 95. BACHMANN: Der erste Brief an die Korinther, Leipzig, 1905, p. 123) have thought that the archontes might be the political authorities, either Jewish or Roman, who pronounced sentence on Jesus, and although at one time we may have accepted this interpretation (Juifs et Romains dans l'histoire de la passion, R.h.r., LXII, 1910, pp. 169 ff.), it seems to us certain, with EVERLING (Paulinische Angelologie und Dämonologie, Göttingen, 1888, pp. 12 ff.), DIBELIUS (Die Geisterwelt im Glauben des Paulus, Göttingen, 1909, pp. 89 ff.), LIETZMANN (An die Korinther, Tübingen, 1923, p. 11), JOH. WEISS (Der erste Korintherbrief (MEYER, V, 9), Göttingen, 1910, p. 54), that the archontes are spiritual powers. We recognize in them those seventy angels to whom, according to Enoch, 89, 59, God has entrusted the government of the world. They direct the nations and inspire their acts. For this they are responsible, for, according to Enoch, 90, 22 ff., they will be judged. When he says that they crucified the Saviour, Paul is thinking

According to Rom. viii. 3 it is God who causes his death, because He treats him as though he himself were sin personified. According to 1 Thess. ii. 15, it was the Jews who killed Christ just as they killed the prophets, and as they are now persecuting the apostle and the believers. The co-existence of these three explanations, which it would be impossible to try to reconcile dialectically, shows that we are not dealing with the development of a myth or of a doctrine, but with the interpretation of a fact of history by means of this doctrine.

The same conclusion is reached, with still more evidence, if possible, when we examine the relation between the justification and the redemption of the sinner. The death of Christ is, in principle, the defeat of the demons to whom humanity is subject, but it does not put an end to their reign. Justification is the act by which God imputes to the sinner the righteousness of Christ, and thus admits him to the life of the Spirit which is the heavenly life. It is by faith that God justifies. Although faith contains an intellectual element, in the Pauline sense of the word it is something quite different from that relative certitude which can be experienced in connexion with realities which cannot be known directly by the intelligence nor by the senses; faith is supremely mystical union with Christ, a union through which the believer lays hold of all that there is in Christ for him. He who is joined to the Lord is one spirit with him (1 Cor. vi. 17). Paul declares that he is "crucified with Christ"; it is no longer he that lives but Christ who lives in him, and this abolition of the individual life leads to the view that in Christ all differences of race and sex and social position have been overcome (Gal. ii. 19–20, iii. 27, vi. 14; cf. Rom. vi. 3–11, viii. 29, xiv. 9; 2 Cor. iv. 10–11). This union with Christ means a complete break with the past. The believer becomes a new creature, a member of the new humanity, of which Christ, the second Adam, is the

of the crucifixion by men, in which he sees the working of demoniac forces, just as in the Fourth Gospel the treachery of Judas, the arrest, the trial, and the execution of Jesus are explained by the action of "the prince of this world" (14, 30). As a parallel we might also cite the *Ascension of Isaiah*, 11, 19 (Christian interpolation), in which the devil incites the Jews against the Well-Beloved in order to make them crucify him.

head.[1] The break with the carnal life is, however, not consummated immediately.[2] A laborious effort is needed to attain the fruits of the Spirit which should grow spontaneously out of a spiritual being. A struggle is necessary in order that the justified believer may escape from the law of the flesh, which in theory no longer exists for him (Gal. v. 13; Rom. vi. 15, viii. 7–8, etc.). This is because he has only received the first-fruits of the Spirit, a pledge of that which will not be actually realized till later (2 Cor. i. 22, v. 5; Rom. viii. 23). "By hope were we saved" (Rom. viii. 24) says Paul. It is only at the coming of the Lord that salvation will be fully attained, that the sons of God will be manifested, that the redemption of humanity and of the whole creation will be accomplished (1 Thess. iv. 13–18; Phil. iii. 20–21; 1 Cor. xv. 51–57; Rom. viii. 18–24).

It is true that alongside of this conception, before final salvation is attained (according to which, for the faithful at least, there will be a period of temporary annihilation in the grave), there is another, according to which redemption simply means the expansion (beyond the limits now imposed upon us by our earthly existence), of a life which exists here and now within the Christian, a life which death cannot touch (Phil. i. 20–23; 2 Cor. iv. 16, v. 10). The fact that these two points of view concerning the accomplishment of salvation exist, shows that in Paulinism a traditional theological system has been used to express new conceptions. The material borrowed from Judaism would not fit into the scheme prepared for it by Paul. The influence which the theology of his youth exerted over him hindered him from coining new formulas which were entirely coherent. It cannot be denied that his system does contain some inconsistencies which have not been overcome. The brevity which he attributed to the intermediate

[1] Paul thinks also that mystical union with Christ is realized in baptism (Rom. vi. 2–5; 1 Cor. xii. 12; Gal. iii. 27) and by the Eucharist (1 Cor. x. 16–17, xi. 17–34). On this point see MAURICE GOGUEL: *Eucharistie*, pp. 178–184. To the apostle mystical union through the Sacraments is parallel with mystical union by faith. The idea that there can be any opposition between faith and sacrament is quite foreign to his mind.

[2] Witness the place that the exhortations to sanctification occupy in the Pauline Epistles. See for instance Gal. v. 1–6, 10.

period which separates justification from redemption[1] does not alter the fact that they are separated, although they are so closely related that the one cannot be understood apart from the other. We can only explain their dissociation when we admit that there is a real dislocation in the Jewish doctrine of Messianic redemption. There is no equivalent for this in the history of Jewish eschatology. This is due to the fact that in the thought of Paul two quite dissimilar elements are associated: on the one hand a doctrine of Messianic redemption which the Apostle had retained from his Jewish education, and on the other, the certitude (which had so mysteriously invaded his soul on the road to Damascus), that this Jesus of Nazareth, whom he had regarded as accursed because he had been hung on a tree (Deut. xxi. 23), was risen, just as those who believed in him had said that he was alive in heavenly glory, and that his resurrection proclaimed that he was the Messiah and the Son of God.

But the synthesis of the doctrine of redemption and the idea of Jesus as the Messiah could not be fully realized immediately. There were elements in the work of the Messiah-Saviour for which it was impossible to find fulfilment in the life, death, and resurrection of Jesus of Nazareth. Briefly, these elements were those which proclaimed a triumphant Messiah who restores the sovereignty of God; Paul solved the difficulty by dividing the work of the Saviour into two parts, connecting those elements which were impossible to realize in the life, death, and resurrection of Jesus with the glorious return of Christ.[2] Hence the Pauline theology, that is to say, the most ancient form of Christianity to which we have direct access, witnesses to the existence of an historical tradition about Jesus without which it would be inexplicable.

---

[1] According to 1 Thess. iv. 15, and 1 Cor. xv. 51 f., Paul thinks that the return of Christ, that is to say the achievement of full redemption, will take place during his lifetime. In other passages, however (for instance, Phil. i. 19 f.; 2 Cor. iv. 16 f.), he seems to think that his death will precede the end of the present era.

[2] It is impossible not to be struck by the analogy which exists between this idea and the attitude adopted by Jesus, when, before the Sanhedrin, he announced his return on the clouds of heaven.

III. The Dependence of Paul on an Historical Tradition

Another definite proof of the fact that the Apostle Paul did depend upon previous historical tradition is the attitude which he adopted before and after his conversion.

From the narrative in the Book of the Acts, and even on the testimony of the Epistles,[1] we know that Paul had been previously a violent persecutor of the Christians. It is evident[2] that he must have come into touch with the disciples of the Carpenter of Nazareth during the period which immediately followed the drama of Calvary.[3] He was horribly scandalized to see them pinning their faith to a man upon whom rested the curse of God.[4] What he felt may be surmised from the formula which he himself was to coin at a later stage: "Christ crucified, to the Jews a stumbling-block" (1 Cor. i. 23; cf. Gal. v. 11). In his eyes Christians were blasphemers and sacreligious people; therefore the authorities ought to take action against them, and it was the duty of every loyal Jew to give the authorities all the help they could, and to inflame their zeal still further.

Thus the Cross dominated the period which preceded the conversion of Paul just as, later on, it would also dominate his Christian life. Paul the persecutor is thus a witness to the truth of the crucifixion. The date of this evidence gives it a position of special importance.

The attitude of Paul towards the Twelve, the brothers of the

---

[1] Acts vii. 58, viii. 1–3, ix. 1 ff.; 1 Cor. xv. 9; Gal. i. 13, 23; Phil. iii. 6. Cf. Acts xxii. 4–8, xxvi. 9–15; 1 Tim. i. 13.

[2] Certain authors, it is true, think that we may conclude from Paul's words in 2 Cor. v. 16 that he had actually seen Jesus himself. The hypothetical nature of the phrase, "Even if we have known Christ after the flesh," does not seem to me to authorize this conclusion. For the discussion of this passage see *Introduction*, IV, 1, pp. 77 ff.

[3] We reckon that Jesus must have died at the Passover of the year 28 (see p. 226 ff.). MEYER (III, pp. 171, 206), who follows an entirely different line of argument from that which we have followed, finally places the date of the death of Jesus in 27 or 28 and the conversion of Paul in 28 or 29.

[4] In virtue of this principle laid down in Deuteronomy (xxi. 23), which he quotes in Gal. iii. 13: "Cursed is everyone that hangeth on a tree."

Lord, and the Church at Jerusalem, also proves his dependence on historical tradition. Paul speaks incidentally of James and the other brothers of the Lord (Gal. i. 19; 1 Cor. ix. 5).[1] Drews,[2] it is true, has argued that the term "brethren of the Lord" means "a group of Christians distinguished by their piety." But if that were so, the brothers of the Lord could not be mentioned as constituting a special group of persons different from the Apostles. Alfaric,[3] arguing from the passage in Rom. viii. 29, where Christ is called the "firstborn among many brethren," claims that the term ought to be taken in a spiritual sense only; but if this term, "brothers of the Lord," were derived from the idea expressed in this passage, then it ought to be applied to all Christians. It is therefore impossible to interpret Gal. i. 19 and 1 Cor. ix. 5 otherwise than as a reference to the brothers of Jesus "after the flesh";[4] the fact that Paul knew them makes it very clear that he was in touch with an historical tradition. Paul claims for his apostolate an authority equal to that of the apostolate of the Twelve,[5] but in order to obtain recognition he had to be very insistent (Gal. ii. 1–10).[6] The energy and tenacity with which he insists upon his apostolic authority show that his claims must have seemed presumptuous and paradoxical to those who witnessed the controversy. The term "chiefest apostles" (οἱ ὑπερλίαν

[1] ALFARIC (Congrès, II, pp. 74 ff.) has argued against the authenticity of Gal. i. 19, but the arguments with which he tries to support his contention are very weak. Cf. R.h.p.r., X, 1930, p. 85, n. 26.

[2] DREWS: Le mythe de Jésus, pp. 143 ff.

[3] ALFARIC: Congrès, II, pp. 75 ff.

[4] The references would have the same validity if, as in Catholic exegesis, the phrase "brothers of Jesus" were taken to mean half-brothers (from a former marriage of Joseph), or cousins.

[5] Paul mentions Cephas (Peter) several times, for instance in 1 Cor. ix. 5, xv. 5. From Gal. i. 19, ii. 1–14, we see that he knew Peter and John personally. He also names James, but this was not the James the son of Zebedee, one of the Twelve, but the brother of Jesus, who from about the year 44 till his death in 62 was head of the Church in Jerusalem.

[6] ALFARIC (Congrès, II, pp. 76 ff.) considers that this equality with the Twelve which Paul claims he possesses proves that their witness was similar in kind to his own, and that in consequence they also only knew the Master by revelation. But Paul does not say that his witness is of the same nature as that of the Twelve; he says simply that he has the same authority. The struggles which Paul had to endure in order to establish this fact show that his position was entirely different from that of the Twelve.

ἀπόστολοι, 2 Cor. xi. 5, xii. 11), which he applies in derision
to those who opposed him, shows that they could pride
themselves on some advantage which he did not possess. His
claims could not be contested so far as Judaism was concerned
(Phil. iii. 4–6; 2 Cor. xi. 21–22), nor from the point of view
of visions and signs which he had received (2 Cor. xii. 1–12).
One text in the Epistle to the Galatians: "Whatsoever they
were, it maketh no matter to me" (ii. 6), shows that the claim
which was used to support the superiority of the Twelve
belonged to the past. Their claim must have been this—and
it was one Paul could not deny—that they had been witnesses
of the life of Jesus and the companions of his ministry. This
reflection illuminates the passage in 2 Cor. v. 16, where Paul
declares that henceforth to have known Christ after the flesh
is a matter of no interest or importance. This was an advantage
which the Twelve possessed, and which he did not possess,
and this is why he denies that it has any value.[1]

In spite of the opposition he encountered—(exaggerated by
the Tübingen school, though it did exist)—and the conflicts
which took place between him and the Apostles at Jerusalem,
who remained attached to Judaism and its practices, Paul
was fully conscious of the unity of Christianity (1 Cor. xv. 11).
In spite of his certainty that he possessed a revelation which
was full and sufficient (Gal. i. 1 ff.), he insisted on keeping in
touch with the Church of Jerusalem. The story of Gal. ii. 1–10
shows how much he valued the recognition of his apostolate
and of his preaching of the Gospel by the heads of the Church
in Jerusalem, and when the crises which took place in Galatia
and Corinth seemed to render uncertain that which seemed
to have been definitely settled at the conference of 44, he

[1] ALFARIC (Congrès, II, pp. 73 ff.) argues that we have the right to interpret
the Epistle to the Galatians by that of the Gospels which appeared later.
The Epistle, he says, only establishes the fact that Peter, James, and John
were important people in the Church at Jerusalem, and he thinks that it
was because of this that Mark made them direct disciples of Jesus. But if
that were so, then he would also have made James an apostle instead of
making him out as hostile to Jesus, or at least as sceptical of his mission.
The contrast between the attitude which the Gospels assign to the brothers
of the Lord and the part which they played in the Early Church prevents
us on this point from interpreting the Gospel tradition as the reflection of
the life of the Primitive Church.

insisted on going to Jerusalem himself, in order to get into touch with James once more, although he was quite aware to what dangers this proceeding would expose him (Rom. xv. 30–32 proves this up to the hilt). We can only understand the importance that Paul attached to these matters if we remember that in the action of Christ, to whom he owed the birth of his faith, Paul saw the extension and the consequence of the historical ministry of Jesus, to which the Christianity of the Twelve and of the Church of Jerusalem owed its origin.

IV. Paul and the Gospel Tradition

The very structure of the thought of Paul, his relations with the Church of Jerusalem, all that he says about the Twelve and the brothers of Jesus, his whole activity, both as a persecutor and then as a missionary, make the Apostle a witness to an historical tradition. Even if the Pauline evidence did not amount to more than this, it would establish the fact that in the very earliest documents which mention Jesus he is represented as an historical personage.

But Paul's knowledge was not limited to the bare fact that Jesus had lived upon the earth; he had a definite idea of the story of his life.[1] If we were to act upon a suggestion made by Renan, we would find, as he says, that there is sufficient material in the Epistles from which we might construct a "small *Life of Jesus*."[2] It is important for the historian to be able to state that the testimony of Paul confirms that of the Gospels, and confirms its reliability. Wishing to revive the memory of his preaching in Galatia Paul writes: "You, before whose eyes Christ crucified has been placarded" (Gal. iii. 1). This simple phrase proves that a picture of the death of Jesus, as vivid and as impressive as possible, had occupied a central

---

[1] The analysis and the discussion of the quotations and reminiscences of the words of Jesus and of the allusions to the facts of His life which occur in the Pauline Epistles has called forth a very large number of books and pamphlets. On this subject see my book; *L'Apôtre Paul et Jésus Christ*, Paris, 1904, pp. 71–84. Among the most important works which have appeared on this question during the last twenty-five years I would name: J. Weiss: *Paulus und Jesus*, Berlin, 1909, and P. Olaf Moe: *Paulus und die evangelische Geschichte*, Leipzig, 1912.

[2] *Histoire du peuple d'Israël*, V, Paris, 1893, pp. 415–416.

place in the preaching of Paul. Of all the details with which it was filled, one alone can be discovered in the Epistles, and that is that Jesus died by crucifixion. The Apostle would certainly not have spoken about the death of Jesus without having said who this person was whose sufferings were of such extraordinary importance, without having given some account of his character and of his life, without having reported some of his sayings. Of all this the Epistles only retain a few faint traces. From them we learn that Jesus is man, that he was born of a woman (Gal. iv. 4; cf. 1 Cor. xv. 21; Rom. v. 15), that he belonged to the race of Abraham (Gal. iii. 16; Rom. ix. 5), and to the family of David (Rom. i. 3). He lived under the Jewish Law (Gal. iv. 4; Rom. xv. 8) and died upon a cross (*passim*), and, like the prophets, he was a victim of the Jews (1 Thess. ii. 15). Before he died, at a last meal with his disciples, he distributed to them bread and wine, as his body and his blood, and invited them to repeat this rite (1 Cor. xi. 23–25). Finally Paul mentions the burial of Jesus (1 Cor. xv. 4) and bears witness to the tradition concerning his appearances after his resurrection. He knows also that Jesus had brothers, among whom he names James, and apostles, who were associated with his work, of whom he names two, Peter and John. Fairly numerous passages mention the moral character of Jesus, speaking, for instance, of his holiness, of his gentleness, of his love. It is better not to lay too much stress on these passages, however, for it is never possible to decide whether these passages refer to the historical Jesus or to the pre-existent and glorified Christ. The Apostle never gives any circumstantial details of time and place; the protagonists of the myth theory argue that such a doctrinaire biography can only be a myth. But myths are not usually so restrained, and, above all, the Epistles allude to, but do not narrate, the story of Jesus. We ought not to attach a great deal of importance to the absence of chronological data. Luke is the only evangelist who attempts to give any indications of this kind (iii. 1 ff.). Mark, Matthew, and John, who did not trouble about chronology at all, were nevertheless sure that they were telling a real story. Indirectly, it is true, they do furnish some chronological information when they tell us that it was Pilate who pronounced the sentence of death on Jesus. But, indirectly, Paul too provides us with chronological information when he says that Christ, three days after his resurrection from the dead, appeared unto Cephas, to James, then "to above five hundred brethren at once, of whom the greater part remain until now" (1 Cor. xv. 3 ff.). All these witnesses of the resurrection are the contemporaries of the Apostle. Thus the drama of the Passion took place during a period which was quite close to that in which he lived.[1]

The explanation which the mythologues have evolved from the scanty data supplied by Paul also shows the weakness of their position. They regard these data as the development and presentation of prophetic themes from the Old Testament. How then do they explain the fact that the passages from which they imagine Paul derived his information (that is, Isa. liii, Psa. xxii, and the Wisdom of Solomon ii. 19–20) are not mentioned by him?

Alfaric attaches great importance to the fact that in order to justify his preaching and his theology Paul does not appeal to the testimony of those who had heard Jesus, but "painfully deduces his proofs from archaic passages."[2] From this he concludes that the Twelve were no better informed than he was. In this line of argument there is a peculiar anachronism. Because the scriptural arguments of Paul seem to a modern to be lacking in validity, Alfaric thinks that he only made use of them because he could find nothing better. But in those days the argument from the Scriptures was the one which appeared the most decisive. It is sufficient to recall the part played by the prophecies in the writings of Justin Martyr.

As he is a witness to the facts of the life of Jesus, Paul is also a witness of the tradition which related to his words. There are three at least[3] which are explicitly quoted.

In 1 Cor. vii. 10, Paul writes: "But unto the married I give charge, yea, not I but the Lord, that the wife depart not

[1] We might add that the idea that Christ appeared in the fullness of time (Gal. iv. 4) is closely connected with Paul's feeling that he is living in the era which immediately precedes the end of the present age (1 Thess. iv. 15; 1 Cor. xv. 51).

[2] ALFARIC: *Congrès*, II, p. 88.

[3] The "word of the Lord" to which appeal is made in 1 Thess. iv. 15 is not taken into account here because it is not certain that it does not refer to some apocryphal work which we do not possess.

from her husband." The point of this passage is emphasized
by the fact that in the same chapter the Apostle declares that
in the case of virgins and those who are unmarried he had
"no commandment of the Lord" (vii. 25; cf. 40) and that
the instructions which he gives to Christians married to pagans[1]
are introduced by the words: "To the rest say I, not the
Lord" (vii. 12). The commandment of the Lord invoked in
vii. 10 is a saying of Jesus preserved in two slightly different
forms in Mark x. 11-12 and in Matt. v. 32. If the word of the
Lord were, as Couchoud[2] thinks it must have been, an inspired
saying, it would be surprising that on questions so important
as those relating to the marriage of persons belonging to
different religious communities, the Spirit did not produce
oracles which were necessary for the life of the Church.
Alfaric[3] thinks that in this verse the "word of the Lord"
means the teaching of the Old Testament; if this were so,
however, how is it that Paul does not quote the passages from
which he drew his inspiration? How is it that—knowing that
the Old Testament was considered a complete revelation of
the will of God, and that the methods of interpretation then
in vogue would make it possible to discover in its pages answers
to questions quite remote from the mind of its writers—Paul
did not find in the Old Testament instructions for the case
of virgins, and of married people belonging to different religious
communities?

In 1 Cor. ix. 14, in order to establish the right of those who
preach the Gospel to be supported by the Churches, Paul
says: "Even so did the Lord ordain that they which proclaim
the gospel should live of the gospel." Here, again, Alfaric
thinks we are dealing with a command in the Old Testament,
but he does not notice that in the preceding words Paul has
first of all invoked a rational argument (ix. 7), that he then
appeals to the Old Testament (ix. 8-13), and that the authority
of the Lord is added to these proofs, and constitutes a final
argument which closes the discussion. The word of Jesus to

---

[1] This means cases where only one of the two partners has become a
Christian, because Paul will not allow a Christian to marry otherwise than
ἐν κυρίῳ (1 Cor. vii. 39).

[2] COUCHOUD: Le mystère, p. 96.   [3] ALFARIC: Congrès, II, pp. 85 ff.

which Paul alludes seems to be that which is preserved in Luke x. 7, and Matt. x. 10.

The last quotation of the words of Jesus which is found in the Epistles of Paul is also the most important, and is the one which has provoked most discussion.

In 1 Cor. xi. 23–25, Paul writes: "For I received of the Lord that which also I delivered unto you, how that the Lord Jesus in the night in which he was betrayed[1] took bread; and when he had given thanks[2] he brake it and said, This is my body, which is for you: this do in remembrance of me. In like manner also the cup, after supper, saying, This cup is the new covenant in my blood: this do, as oft as ye drink it, in remembrance of me."[3]

With the exception of a few critics who belong more or less directly to the radical Dutch school[4] and of Drews,[5] until recently the authenticity of this passage was scarcely questioned, and the arguments which have been put forward against it have seemed weak even to those who defend the myth theory.[6]

[1] In order to avoid the risk of adding to the text something in translating it we render ἐν τῇ νυκτί ᾗ παρεδίδοτο by "the night in which he was given up" (livré), which may mean, "given up to die" (cf. Rom. iv. 25), but which might also mean the "night in which he was betrayed by Judas." The passage in xi. 23–25 is of such a kind that it is impossible not to see that it is an extract from the story of the Passion; the words "the night in which he was given up" would be, indeed, very poorly explained if we were to follow ALFARIC (Congrès, II, pp. 89 ff.) by the fact that the "betrayal of Jesus" is a work of darkness and could only take place at night.

[2] The act of thanksgiving which the Jews pronounced not only for the meal as a whole, but for each of the elements which composed it.

[3] If a comma is placed or omitted between "ye drink it" and "in remembrance of me," the meaning is changed. With the comma, it means that the sign (symbol) of the Last Supper should be repeated at every celebration of the Lord's Supper, and without it, every time we drink wine.

[4] Among these it is enough to name VOELTER: Paulus und seine Briefe, Strasbourg, 1905, pp. 40 ff.

[5] DREWS: Le mythe de Jésus, pp. 146 ff.

[6] COUCHOUD (Le mystère, pp. 141 ff.) and ALFARIC (Congrès, II, pp. 89 ff.) do not make much of this.

The theory of the interpolation of verses 23–25 was put forward by Loisy, in 1927, at least in the form of an hypothesis. [1] His arguments are extremely subjective in character, for he has evidently been guided exclusively by impressions when he says that the passage assumes a very rapid degeneration of the Supper of the Lord at Corinth, [2] and that, on the other hand, we ought to hesitate to think that the Christian mystery, as it is expressed in the Pauline conception of the Eucharist, was already constituted in 55 or 56. [3] We ought to add that this Christian mystery is attested by other passages in Paul's writings. Loisy admits this, and enquires whether these verses also may not be interpolations? But he has done so little to prove that they are interpolations that he has not even compiled a list of suspected passages. [4] However great may be our respect for Loisy, and the admiration to which his works entitle him, even from him we cannot accept a theory which is based merely on subjective impressions. Our opinion on the authenticity of certain passages ought not to be dependent on a conception of the development of Christianity; on the con-

[1] *Les origines de la cène eucharistique, Congrès*, I, pp. 77–95. For a detailed discussion of the theory of Loisy we would refer the reader to our article mentioned above.

[2] Loisy does not take into account the fact that at the moment when Paul was writing to the Corinthians the disorders connected with the Sacrament were not isolated, but that everything was in a state of upheaval in the Church at Corinth. Things took place then (as, for instance, the case of incest) which are the very negation of Christianity. To doubt these facts is to overlook or misunderstand the intense religious ferment of the first century, when changes took place far more swiftly than at other periods, it would mean being driven to deny the crisis at Corinth itself, that is to say, to do what Loisy is very careful to avoid doing—to support the argument against the authenticity of the Epistles to the Corinthians.

[3] We ought to remember the enormous swiftness of the religious and theological development in the first century. At the moment of the conversion of Paul, eighteen months after the death of Jesus, the worship of the Lord Christ had already been established.

[4] Note once again that ideas which are closely related to those which we find in 1 Cor. xi. 23–25, occur in 1 Cor. x. 1–5, and 14–22. Loisy says that these passages "offer to criticism the same conditions as those which surround the passage of instruction on the Communion Service" (p. 85). This is far too vague to be discussed. We will only remark that these sections are very closely related to the discussion on idolatry, that is to say, to one of the essential elements in the Corinthian crisis.

trary, our historical theory should depend on the teaching of the passages in question.

The text of 1 Cor. xi. 23–25 being recognized as authentic, its exact interpretation depends on two questions. What is the meaning of the formula which introduces this passage: "I have received of the Lord," and what is the relation between the narrative of Paul and that of Mark (xiv. 22–25)?

Many critics conclude from this introductory formula that Paul's narrative originated in a vision, but they are not agreed about the content of this vision. Some believe that the whole story of the Last Supper originated in this way;[1] others, who are less radical, think that by a sort of process of auto-suggestion Paul became able to contemplate in a vision the episode which has been thus preserved in the tradition;[2] others, again, believe that it was not the story of the Last Supper, but the knowledge of the sacramental character of the Eucharist, which arose out of a vision granted to Paul.[3] It has also been suggested that, by a daring process of condensation, in the vision on the road to Damascus Paul has summed up all that he knew of Christ.[4] All these theories are arbitrary, and if we admit that he had a vision it seems difficult to limit the content to certain elements in the narrative. The critics whose opinions we have just mentioned have come too swiftly to the conclusion that Paul was referring to a vision. When the Apostle expounds truths which have been communicated to him in a supernatural manner, that is, when they are "mysteries" in the sense in which he uses this word (for example 1 Cor. xv. 51; Rom. xi. 25), or supernatural revelations, he does not attempt to hide the fact. This simply reinforces the authority of his

---

[1] PERCY GARDNER: *The Origin of the Lord's Supper*, London, 1893, pp. 5 ff. COUCHOUD: *Le mystère*, pp. 146 ff. ALFARIC: *Congrès*, II, pp. 89 ff. This theory will be discussed later, pp. 444 ff.

[2] BOUSSET: *Schriften*, II, p. 131. This was also the opinion of LOISY before he had begun to doubt the authenticity of the passage (*Syn.*, II, p. 532, n. i. *Les mystères païens et le mystère chrétien*, Paris, 1919, pp. 284 ff.). He has expressed it again in the second edition of the latter work (pp. 276 ff.).

[3] PFLEIDERER: *Urchristentum²*, Berlin, 1902, I, p. 301. HAUPT: *Über die ursprüngliche Form und Bedeutung der Abendmahlsworte*, Halle, 1894, p. 12.

[4] LIETZMANN: *An die Korinther*, p. 58. HEITMÜLLER: *Zum Problem Paulus und Jesus, Z.N.T.W.*, XIII, 1912, p. 323. NORDEN: *Agnostos Theos*, Leipzig, Berlin, 1913, p. 289. E. MEYER, III, p. 174, n. 3.

statements. Why then, in 1 Cor. xi, does he refer so quietly to the authority of the command of which he is reminding the Corinthians? Why does he say: "I have received . . . I have transmitted," which places what he has transmitted and what he has received on exactly the same level?

However, the vision-hypothesis is not absolutely ruled out by these considerations. The question under discussion cannot be solved save by the examination of the character of the narrative and of its relations with other forms of the same tradition. We shall see later that Mark, although he wrote some fifteen years or less after 1 Cor. xi was written, gives an account of the Last Supper of Jesus which corresponds to a stage in the tradition much earlier than the Pauline passage because it was less influenced by liturgical practice.[1] This is a clear proof that Paul did not create the narrative which he gives, but that he owed the substance of it to tradition.[2]

In addition to actual quotations, there are in Paul a fairly large number of allusions to the words of Jesus,[3] sufficient to

[1] See pp. 446 ff.

[2] ALFARIC (*Congrès*, II, pp. 89 ff.) conceives the formation of the Pauline narrative, the source, according to him, of all the others, in the following manner. Originally the groups of Christians used to meet together simply for a meal where they renewed and strengthened their fellowship with one another. Under the influence of the Hellenic religions Paul turned this into a mystical liturgy in which the faithful fed upon their God; hence the idea that Jesus had instituted this meal because he alone could give his body to be eaten and his blood for drink, and he could not have done this until the moment when he was about to be delivered up to death. Since the idea of the death of Jesus came from Isa. liii, where the Servant of Yaweh, who is put to death, is compared with a sacrificed lamb, it was natural to ally the idea of the death of the Lord with the sacrifice of the Paschal lamb and to make the Eucharist the Passover of the New Covenant. This whole theory is entirely arbitrary. No one has any right to reconstitute the whole passage by postulating a non-Eucharistic *agapé* by taking away from the Pauline text that which gives to the Supper of the Lord its sacramental character. Further, the assimilation of Christ to the Paschal lamb is only suggested in 1 Cor. v. 7, and then only in an incidental manner, and, as we have pointed out already, Paul had several interpretations of the death of Christ. We should add that, as we shall see later (Chapter XV), the assimilation of the Communion to a Passover does not belong to the most primitive form of the tradition.

[3] Here are a few examples (the references in brackets are to those words of Jesus in the Gospels to which Paul alludes): 1 Thess. iv. 8 (Luke x. 16; Matt. x. 40); Gal. iv. 17 (Matt. xxiii. 13; Luke xi. 52); 1 Cor. iv. 12–13;

allow us at least to consider the hypothesis that Paul may have had in his hands an early form of the collection of sayings known as the *Logia*.[1]

Thus the Pauline Epistles furnish very clear evidence to the existence of an historical tradition concerning Jesus. The Apostle gives these hints in too scattered and fragmentary a way for us to be able to attempt to group them once more into a whole. This can be explained, first of all, by the very fact of the composition of the epistles themselves, and then also by the nature of the Apostle's concern; he did not take the trouble to tell the Gospel story because he was sure that his readers would know at least the elements of it; nor did he try to prove—(what no one doubted)—that Jesus had actually lived, but only that he was the Christ; for this the Jews refused to accept, while the pagans regarded it as "foolishness."

Appendix I.—The Non-Pauline Epistles in the New Testament

The non-Pauline Epistles of the New Testament (several among them, at least) were not composed until a period when the tradition concerning Jesus was fixed in the form which it possesses in the Synoptic Gospels. The majority of them make very slight references to this tradition.[2]

We find, fairly frequently, the idea that Christ has left his

Rom. xii. 14 (Matt. v. 44*); 1 Cor. v. 4 (Matt. xviii. 20); 1 Cor. xiii. 2 (Matt. xvii. 20; Mark xi. 23*); 1 Cor. xiii. 3 (Luke xii. 33; Mark x. 21*); 2 Cor. x. 1 (Matt. xi. 29); Rom. xiv. 14 (Matt. xv. 11). It is evident that in the search for allusions to words of Jesus people have sometimes gone too far. RESCH (*Der Paulinismus und die Logia Jesu*, *T.U.*, XII, Leipzig, 1904) finds no less than 925 allusions in the Epistles which we regard as authentic, and in addition 133 in the Epistle to the Ephesians, 100 in the Pastoral Epistles, and 64 in the Pauline discourses in the Acts. His method has been severely but rightly criticized by WREDE (*Goet. Gel. Anz.*, 1905, p. 849 f.) and by JÜLICHER (*Theol. Litzg.*, 1906, col. 42 ff.).

[1] This hypothesis is suggested by the fact that the words of Jesus to which Paul alludes are found far more frequently in the tradition of the Logia than in that of Mark.

[2] There is no allusion to the life and the words of Jesus in the Johannine Epistles; we cannot, however, doubt that the two first at least are closely connected with the Fourth Gospel and are probably by the same author.

followers an example which they ought to follow (Heb. xii.
1–2, xiii. 13 ff.; 1 Pet. ii. 21–23; Eph. v. 2), which presupposes not only that Jesus was a real person, but that it
was possible to have a clear idea of his life and character.
The idea of imitation also lies behind the passage in 1 Tim. vi.
13–14, where there is the mention of Christ Jesus "who witnessed a good confession before Pontius Pilate," for, as
Baldensperger[1] has pointed out, Christ is here presented as
the ideal to those of the faithful who had to give an account
of their faith before pagan tribunals.

Among the non-Pauline Epistles there are three which need
special consideration because of their importance: these are
the Epistle to the Hebrews and the two Epistles of Peter.

As Windisch[2] has remarked, the Christ of the Epistle to the
Hebrews seems to be a celestial being rather than a man who
had made a deep impression on those who knew him. His
story is presented in abstract terms, connected with the traditional type of the Messiah, and are borrowed from the Old
Testament, especially from the Psalms. The references to his
death seem to set it apart from all historical contingencies.[3]
But what we said about Pauline soteriology might be repeated
concerning the Christology of the Epistle to the Hebrews.
The sacrifice of Christ only purifies sinners because it was
the death of an actual man. The author of the Epistle insists
on certain details which show that a story of Jesus, and of his
death in particular, constitutes the foundation of his theology.
The manifestation of Christ took place at a recent date which
belongs to the last period in the history of the world (i. 2),
the message of Christ has been carried by those who had
originally received the teaching of Jesus (ii. 3). His sufferings
and his temptations are described in terms which make him

---

[1] "*Il a rendu témoignage sous Ponce-Pilate*," Strasbourg, Paris, 1922.

[2] WINDISCH: *Der Hebräerbrief*, Tübingen, 1913, p. 28.

[3] One single detail is given which is not noted in the Synoptic Gospels,
but only implied by John xix. 20, and one which is likewise extremely
likely to be true, this is that Jesus suffered "without the gate" (xiii. 12).
This detail is introduced for its symbolical significance, but we cannot
admit that it is an allegorical invention, for if it were it would not stand
alone.

the model of those who have to endure suffering and persecution (ii. 18, iv. 15, v. 8). The fate of Christ is regarded as
exactly comparable with that of every man who has to die
once, after which comes the Judgment (ix. 27–28).

In the First Epistle of Peter, if we except the idea of Christ as
the pattern for the faithful, there is no allusion to the facts of
the life of Jesus or to his death. The Gospel story is conceived
as the realization of a prophetic programme. The holiness of
Jesus is supported by Isa. liii. 9 (ii. 22), and in connexion
with his sufferings Isa. liii. 4 ff. is quoted (ii. 24); a scriptural
interpretation is substituted for the Gospel narrative.

The Second Epistle of Peter dates from an epoch when the
collection of the letters of Paul was in existence, and was
considered authoritative (iii. 15–16); Christianity and its
doctrine had then taken on its essential form and direction.
The writer alludes to the story of the Transfiguration as it is
reported by the Synoptists (i. 16–18) and in so doing he places
it definitely within the sphere of the Gospel tradition. This
does not prevent him from regarding the person and work
of Jesus from a wholly dogmatic point of view.

Regarded as a whole, the non-Pauline Epistles place us in the
presence of the same fact as the writings of Paul: that is, a
story which serves as a foundation for the development of a
doctrine. The further one goes from the origin, the more
important does the doctrine become, and it tends to substitute
itself for the story, of which originally it was the interpretation.

APPENDIX II.—THE REVELATION OF JOHN

The author of the book of Revelation knew the Gospel tradition.
Although he does not refer to it directly, his allusions to it in
the course of the book are sufficiently definite to leave us in no
doubt on the matter.[1]

The Christ of the Apocalypse, in spite of the name of Jesus

[1] See for instance iii. 3 (cf. Matt. xxiv; 43–44; Luke xii. 39–40), iii. 5 (cf.
Matt. x. 32; Luke xii. 8), xiii. 10 (cf. Matt. xxvi. 52), xxi. 6, xxii. 17 (cf.
John iv. 10 ff., vii. 37).

by which he is most frequently called, is a heavenly being. He is the Lord who is in the heavens, and whose return is awaited (i. 5 f., 13 f., iii. 11). The worship of Christ, which occupies such a large place in the book, is worship rendered to a celestial being.

But this celestial being has had a human history (i. 5, v. 9, xi. 8), and it is for this cause that he is Saviour. It is because the Lamb has been slain that he is worthy to open the seals of the book (v. 6). He is the One who was dead and is alive again (i. 18, ii. 8). The frequent mention of the "blood of the Lamb" (i. 5, v. 9, vii. 14, xii. 11) assumes a doctrine of redemption, which, like that of Paul and of the deutero-Pauline Epistles, is an interpretation of the drama of Calvary. Although there is no direct allusion to the story of the Passion in the book of Revelation, in order to realize the significance of this fact we need to remember the allegorical character of the book. The mere mention of the "Lamb that had been slain"[1] was sufficient for the readers to recall the remembrance of the Passion with sufficient vividness.

There are, on the other hand, certain pictures in the book of Revelation which are obviously mythical, in which there appears a Messiah entirely devoid of all human characteristics. In order to understand them and realize their significance we need to remember that the Revelation of John belongs to a species of literature which had been developed during the two centuries which preceded the Christian era, a literature which has its own rules, customs, and methods; the apocalyptic writers always made a great deal of use of the works of their predecessors, adopting the pictures which they had outlined, renewing them, touching them up—in a word, adapting them to new situations. This is the explanation of the incoherence, the doublets, the repetitions which we find in the Johannine Apocalypse.[2] We have to try to grasp the meaning of the

---

[1] The symbolism of the Lamb in Revelation is not connected with the idea of the Paschal Lamb. This is a fact which contradicts the theory of the mythologues who argue that the idea of the death of Christ is derived from the Passover ritual.

[2] For instance the juxtaposition of the three scenes of the seven seals (v, 1–8, 2), of the seven trumpets (viii, 2–11, 19), and the seven bowls (xv, 1–16, 21).

author through the medium of these dissimilar materials which literary analysis tries to unravel. We cannot attribute to the author directly all the ideas and all the sentiments which we find in the documents utilized and reproduced by him, without taking into account the corrections of detail which there are in them, and above all the indications which proceed from the general plan of the book.

This principle of interpretation ought to be applied in particular to the picture in chapter xii, in which Stahl and Couchoud[1] believe that they have discovered the idea of a purely ideal Christ. There appears in heaven a woman clothed with the sun, with the moon under her feet, and on her head a crown of twelve stars. She is on the eve of her confinement. A great and fiery dragon with seven heads and seven crowns, whose tail sweeps the heavens, and makes a third of the stars fall to the earth, stands opposite her, ready to devour the child which is to be born. He is to rule the nations with a rod of iron, that is to say, to be the Messiah; he is caught up into heaven to be with God, and the woman flees into the desert where she will be nourished for 1,260 days. Then there is a battle in heaven.[2] Michael and his angels cast down the dragon, which is the devil and Satan and his angels, on to the earth, and in heaven a voice proclaims the victory which has just been gained. The devil which has been defeated

---

[1] STAHL: *Le document 70*, pp. 6–14. COUCHOUD: *Le mystère*, pp. 149–151. On the book of Revelation, xii, see WELLHAUSEN: *Zur apokalyptischen Literatur* in *Skizzen und Vorarbeiten*, VI, Berlin, 1899, pp. 215–225. *Analyse der Offenbarung Johannis* in *Abh. der k. Ges. der Wiss. zu Göttingen, Phil.-hist. Kl.*, N.F., IX, 4, Berlin, 1907, pp. 18–21. HUGO GRESSMANN: *Der Messias*, Göttingen, 1929, pp. 389–392.

[2] It is not said who provoked this battle. We might conjecture that the dragon wanted to try to seize the child which had been caught up into heaven. However, this attempt would have been too essential a part of the drama to have been merely implied. GRESSMANN (*Der Messias*, p. 394) remarks that in the first part of verse 4 there is an element ("His tail draweth the third part of the stars of heaven") which, where it stands, plays no part in the story. He conjectures that originally verse 4a was connected with verses 7–12, and that the battle in heaven was caused by this assault on the heavenly powers. The fragment 4a 7–12 would come originally from a myth which was independent of the drama in which the woman is the central figure.

pursues the woman, who receives the wings of an eagle and flees into the desert, where she will be fed for a time, times, and half a time.[1] The earth comes to her assistance by swallowing up a river which the dragon had poured out in order to drown her. Then the devil departs to make war upon the other children of the woman, those who observe the commandments of God and are faithful to the testimony of Jesus, and he goes to the seacoast.[2]

This section of the book is certainly the adaptation of a much older apocalyptic fragment. The interest which is at first concentrated on the birth of the Messiah is transferred later on to the celestial song which celebrates the victory won over the dragon, further on to the destiny of the woman, and finally to that of the believers. The victory is gained, according to verses 7–9, by Michael and his angels, according to verse 11 by the martyrs. The two flights of the woman to the desert are manifestly a doublet. Whereas at the beginning the woman represents the mother of the Messiah, that is to say, probably the people of Israel,[3] at the close she is the mother of the faithful, that is, the Church. The part played by the Messiah is not the same from the beginning to the end of the story. He does not intervene in the assault delivered by Michael and his angels on the dragon, whereas it is he who gives victory to the martyrs.[4] His part is singularly restricted. It is not said how the child who will rule the nations with a rod of iron, after having escaped the dangers which threatened him at his birth, will fulfil his destiny. This shows that this section has not been introduced into the Apocalypse on account of what it says about the Messiah, and that, to use the expression of Gressmann,[5] the myth only received a Christian varnish at

[1] That is to say, during three years and a half, the equivalent of 1,260 days; the half of a week of years, the unit of time in apocalyptic calculations.
[2] This last feature serves to unite what has gone before with the picture which follows.
[3] Even if originally she was an astral personality, as LOISY argues in L'Apocalypse, Paris, 1923, p. 225.
[4] One must add that what is said in chapter xii about Satan being cast down is not related to the mention of the same fact in chapters xix–xx, portions of the book which there are good reasons for attributing to the author of the book of Revelation.
[5] GRESSMANN: Der Messias, p. 400.

the conclusion of the fragment. For the writer the main interest lies in the idea of the dragon who is cast down upon the earth. This refers to the persecuting Emperor. This explains to the faithful the sufferings which they have to endure. Having given this explanation, he did not think it necessary to reproduce the conclusion of the myth, in which, after he had reigned on the earth for a time, the dragon was finally destroyed.[1]

The adaptations which are obvious in chapter xii prove that the author was using some earlier material which was certainly Jewish.[2] It is, in fact, impossible to imagine that at the close of the first century a Christian would represent the Messiah as caught up into heaven immediately after his birth. The first document is a borrowed fragment; hence we cannot use it in describing the Christology of the author of the Revelation.

[1] GRESSMANN: *Der Messias*, p. 395.

[2] At the very least, in the form which the author of the book of the Revelation knew and used, for GRESSMANN (*Der Messias*, pp. 396 ff.), following BOUSSET, has shown that the myth was originally Egyptian. From the point of view which interests us, we do not need to enter into the previous history of the tradition used by the Christian Apocalyptic writer, nor do we want to know whether it is the result of the combination of two or even three different myths, or if the astral character of the picture is primitive, all of which GRESSMANN contests, for reasons which appear to be decisive.

CHAPTER IV

THE GOSPELS[1]

THE problem of the character and the documentary value of the Gospels is not presented to us, as we are so often led to think it is, in the form of a dilemma. We are not called to decide for or against one of the two following theories: (1) that the Gospel history as a whole, and in every part of it, is a literal and accurate account of all that took place; or (2) that we ought to reject it entirely, as a mere tissue of legend, which, even at the best, can serve no useful purpose save that of supplying material for the imagination or nourishment for the meditations of pious souls.

I. WHAT A GOSPEL IS

The word "Gospel" was current in Christian language before it was used to describe the stories of the life of Jesus. When Paul used it he meant the redemption of the sinful world by the death and resurrection of Jesus Christ, and the preaching of this message of salvation. It is both the "Gospel of God" (as, for instance, in Rom. i. 1), since God is the first author of salvation; the "Gospel of Jesus Christ" (as for instance in Rom. i. 9, and Phil. i. 27), since Christ is the content of the message; and the "Gospel of Paul" (e.g. 2 Cor. iv. 3), since he has received the commission to proclaim it. It is in this sense also that we meet the word in the Gospels (e.g. Mark i. 1, 14, 15, etc.).[2] The fact that the same word is used for the stories of the ministry of Jesus is because the life of Jesus, and, above all, his death and

[1] For further details we would refer the reader to our previous works: *Intr.*, I and II: *Une nouvelle école de critique évangélique. La form- und traditionsgeschichtliche Schule. R.h.r.*, XCIV, 1925, pp. 114–160.
[2] There are only two passages in which the word Gospel is put into the mouth of Jesus by Mark and by Matthew; Luke has no parallel to these passages. They are: Mark xiii. 10; Matt. xxiv. 14; Mark xiv. 9; Matt. xxvi. 13. In both cases the word means the future proclamation of the Gospel. The two sections in question do not seem to have been found in the primitive form of the Gospel of Mark. (Cf. *Intr.*, I, pp. 297 ff.)

his resurrection, were the foundation upon which the whole doctrine of salvation was based.[1]

The double meaning of the word "Gospel" still exists in the fact that at the present time it is still used to describe both the doctrine of Christianity and the original narrative of the life of Jesus.

The double meaning—both religious and historical—of the word "Gospel" already shows that the four accounts preserved in the New Testament are not meant to serve exclusively either a biographical or an historical purpose, but that their aim is also practical and definitely religious. Indeed, Luke and John both say plainly why they wrote their Gospels: Luke says he wrote it for Theophilus, in order that he "might know the certainty of those things in which he had been instructed" (Luke i. 4), while John says that he wrote his Gospel in order that his readers might know that "Jesus is the Christ, the Son of God, and that believing they might have life in his name" (John xx. 31).

The Gospels were written for Christians only. This is proved by what they assume their readers already know. Although it is true that they may have served to aid the memories of the first missionaries, there is an error in perspective in the passage in Papias,[2] who represents the Gospel of Mark as the transcription of the missionary message of Peter.

From the literary point of view the Gospel was created by Christianity. The analogies which some claim to have perceived between the Gospels and the Greek literature of "Memoirs" (ἀπομνημονεύματα)[3] and "Lives" (Βίοι) are very vague, and, since it is very unlikely that Mark at least would have known this literature, the resemblances which have been noted would be due to the fact that in both cases the writer is relating the life of a hero.[4]

---

[1] It is not clear whether Mark called his work a Gospel, or whether the name was given to it later on.

[2] Preserved by Eusebius: *Eccl. Hist.*, III, 39.

[3] We know that Justin described the Gospels as "Memoirs of the Apostles," ἀπομνημονεύματα τῶν ἀποστόλων (*I Ap.*, 66, 3). The choice of the word was made in order to explain the word "Gospel" by a term which his pagan readers could immediately understand.

[4] If we need to find prototypes to the Gospels we would discover them rather in certain narratives in the Old Testament, in which history is used as a source of religious teaching and edification.

Certain details are absent from the Gospels which are usually found in every biography—information about the family of the hero, about his childhood, a description of his actual appearance, and chronological data concerning his life. The Gospels were not written to introduce to their readers a person of whom they knew nothing. Look at the way in which Jesus is introduced in the Gospel of Mark: "In those days Jesus came from Nazareth in Galilee and was baptized in the Jordan by John" (i. 9). This is not the way in which an unknown person is introduced to the readers of a book. The Gospels formed part of the faith and theology—if this term is not too much of an anachronism—of the people among whom they appeared. They are religious works, in direct relation with the life of the Christian community. Between the Gospels and the life of the Church, with its varied activities in preaching, evangelizing, teaching, apologetics, and controversy, there has been both action and reaction; the Gospels have influenced the life of the Church, while at the same time they have been influenced by it.

II. The Development of the Gospel Literature

Although the Gospel of Mark is the earliest of these books in our possession, it is quite certain that it had been preceded by some written accounts, more or less fragmentary, of the Gospel tradition. These writings were the recollections of those who had known and loved Jesus and felt his influence; they recorded instances of the example which he had given, and some of his sayings, which they had treasured for their inspiration, and which they transmitted as a precious treasure to those who shared their faith.

It seems that Mark was the first to undertake the task of gathering these memoirs into a coherent narrative; previously they had been preserved in a spontaneous manner, without any attempt to put them into any kind of order. The fact that when Luke wrote his Gospel, fifteen or twenty years after Mark, several attempts at writing the Gospel story were already in existence (Luke i. 1), does not constitute an objection to this view, for a literature like that of the Gospels, which responds so manifestly to an actual need, would inevitably, once it had been born, develop with a singular intensity.

Luke knew several Gospels; the composition of the narratives of Matthew and of Luke almost simultaneously and independently of each other is significant, and it is very probable that several of the Apocryphal Gospels whose names we know, or of which we possess some fragments, like the Gospel of Peter, the Judaeo-Christian Gospels of the Hebrews, of the Ebionites or of the Twelve Apostles, and, perhaps, the Gospel of the Egyptians, appeared before the middle of the second century. After this date the development of the Gospel literature ceased. The four Gospels which were then most widely read—those of Matthew, Mark, Luke, and John—were placed in a category by themselves. The actual authority which they exerted in practice was elevated to the dignity of a principle, and the tendency to concentration which, normally, would have led to the choice of one of the Gospels which was most widely read, or to the combination of several,[1] was suddenly arrested.[2] After that there were no new Gospels, save those which were composed by the heretical sects, or fragmentary narratives, like some of the Gospels of the Infancy, certain stories of the Passion, which arose on the fringe of the canonical writings, not in order to replace them, but simply in order to embroider the material which they supplied.

At the same time another transformation was taking place, or, at least, was being completed. Originally the Gospels had been works which, if not anonymous, were at least impersonal. Possibly people knew, or thought they knew, who had composed them, but no one attached much importance to this knowledge. It was the content of the Gospels alone which gave them their value. No author is visible in Mark or in Matthew; in the third Gospel, although the narrative itself is just as impersonal, the author speaks directly in the preface addressed to Theophilus; the Fourth Gospel was originally an impersonal work, but the editors who have given it the

---

[1] As was the case in Syria with the *Diatessaron* of Tatian.

[2] This canonization of the Gospels arose by a sort of spontaneous reaction. It was the instinctive defence of the Church against the dangers by which it was threatened, the dangers of Marcionism, Gnosticism, and Montanism.

form which we know have suggested, by some added touches here and there, first of all, that it was based upon evidence of a peculiarly reliable kind, that of the disciple "whom Jesus loved"; that is to say, as they discreetly suggest, on the testimony of the Apostle John (xix. 35), and then that it was this disciple himself who actually wrote it (xxi. 25).

About the same time, or possibly a little later, in certain parts at least of the Gospel of Peter, the story is presented as that of an eyewitness, and Papias, in order to defend the Gospels of Mark and Matthew to which some doubtless preferred that of John, reports that the first is the work of a secretary of Peter, and that it is a faithful reproduction of the narratives of the apostle, while the second has been edited and compiled by the apostle Matthew.[1]

This process of development, which we see taking shape thus during the first half of the second century, ended with Irenaeus in the theory that a Gospel can only be authoritative if it is the work of an apostle.[2] The establishment of this principle definitely put an end to the period of the creation of Gospel literature.

III. The Composition of the Synoptic Gospels

The prolonged labour of criticism in the nineteenth century, which began with C. H. Weisse and C. G. Wilke in 1838[3] and ended with Wernle and Hawkins in 1899[4] led to results which we may regard as decisive, even though in some respects they may still need some further clarification. These results may be summed up thus:

[1] The fact that neither of these two Gospels corresponds to the definition given by Papias shows that he had to prove that they fulfilled the conditions necessary to make them authoritative.

[2] Or at least indirectly: this made it possible to preserve the Gospels of Mark and Luke, by placing them under the patronage of Peter and of Paul.

[3] C. H. Weisse: *Die evangelische Geschichte kritisch und philosophisch bearbeitet*, Leipzig, 1838. C. G. Wilke: *Der Urevangelist oder eine exegetische-kritische Untersuchung der Verwandschaftsverhältnisse der drei ersten Evangelien*, Dresden, Leipzig, 1838.

[4] Wernle: *Die synoptische Frage*, Freiburg im Breisgau, Leipzig, Tübingen, 1899. Hawkins: *Horae synopticae*, Oxford, 1899, ²1909.

(1) The Gospel of Mark is the oldest of the three Synoptic Gospels; it served as a source to two others;

(2) There is a second source for the literature of the Gospels, constituted by a collection of sayings of Jesus, the Logia, which probably contained a minimum of narrative setting;[1]

(3) The Gospels of Matthew and Luke are combinations of Mark and of the Logia, supplemented by certain written material or certain oral traditions used by both of them.[2]

Within the general framework of this theory, which is known as the Two-Document Hypothesis, several questions remain unanswered:

(1) Was the Gospel of Mark used by Matthew and Luke absolutely identical with the one we now possess? or did it differ at certain points? (Question of Proto-Mark.)

We think that save for certain slight alterations in detail which are brought out by textual rather than by literary criticism, there are two chief points at which the Gospel of Mark has been altered (apart from the very probable mutilation of its ending): the introduction of the cycle of Bethany and of the division into days in the narrative of the Jerusalem ministry, and, in chapter xiii, in the Synoptic Apocalypse (xiii. 14), the substitution of the announcement of the "abomination of desolation," that is to say, of the profanation of the Temple, for that of the siege of Jerusalem. It is also possible that certain sections from the Logia may not have been present in the Gospel of Mark in the state in which Luke knew it. Matthew seems to have had in his hands a revised copy of Mark, whereas Luke still used the primitive text.

[1] German critics call this document Q (initial letter of the word *Quelle*: source). We prefer to use the term already employed by Papias and to call this source the Logia (Λ).

[2] An English critic, B. H. STREETER (*The Four Gospels. A Study of Origins*, London, 1924, ²1927), has argued that behind the Synoptic Gospels there was, in addition to Mark and the Logia, a third document, Proto-Luke, which is supposed to have been a complete Gospel, composed of the combination of the Logia with special traditions. For the reasons which prevent us from accepting this theory, and for an interpretation of the facts mentioned by Streeter, see my article, *Luke and Mark*, in the *Harvard Theological Review*, XXV, 1933. See also the important work of W. BUSSMANN: *Synoptische Studien*, Halle, 1925–1931.

(2) What is the relation between the two sources of the Gospel tradition, the Logia and Mark? Wellhausen regards the Logia as secondary in relation to Mark, whereas Harnack, adopting an idea thrown out by Bernhard Weiss, but not developed by him, maintains that the editor of the second Gospel used the Logia as part of his source material. Streeter, finally, believes that the two documents are independent of each other. It seems to me that Harnack's theory ought to be accepted. Mark knew the Logia, and, in my opinion, assumed that his readers knew it too; that is why he only drew on it when he felt it absolutely necessary in describing the personality and the activity of Jesus.

(3) What is the exact nature of the Logia? For my own part, I regard it less as a literary source, constructed in logical form, than a collection which was continually being enlarged by the introduction of sayings of Jesus scattered through tradition. Hence the Logia themselves are also very varied. Matthew and Luke knew this collection in two different forms. We may also assign to the Logia not only the sections which are common to Matthew and Luke and which are absent from Mark, but also certain others which are only found either in Matthew or in Luke. It is not doubtful, for instance, that the Beatitudes, which appear both in Matthew and in Luke, come from the Logia, in spite of the differences in form and even in content which exist in the two passages as we know them. It is impossible, on the other hand, to assign the curses which follow the Beatitudes in Luke to a different origin from that of the Beatitudes themselves.

(4) Are there any other connexions between the Gospels of Matthew and Luke than those which are the result of their common dependence on Mark, the Logia, and, eventually, on other sources? This question has sometimes been answered by suggesting that Matthew was used by Luke, more rarely by the idea that Luke influenced Matthew. These two theories seem to us to be untenable, and this for two reasons. First of all, they do not explain the omission by the evangelist, who is regarded as the second, of a whole series of characteristic and important passages given by the first. Further, between

the two texts there are differences of arrangement which make it very improbable that there is any direct literary connexion between them.[1]

For a document like the Logia, which was continually growing, it is impossible to fix an exact date of composition; all we can do is to try to fix the date when it began.

If Paul, as is at least probable, was familiar with an early form of the Logia, the collection would have been begun before the year 50. The primitive kernel of the collection may be earlier still. One of the primary reasons for thinking this is the way in which the Lord's Prayer is introduced in Luke. The disciples of Jesus come to him and ask him to teach them a prayer, as John the Baptist taught his disciples (Luke xi. 1). This is far more probable than the teaching of the Lord's Prayer *ex professo*, in the course of an ordered discourse, as is reported by Matthew (vi. 9 ff.). Besides, the Christian tradition, so jealous to affirm the complete independence of Jesus in regard to John the Baptist, could not have imagined an incident in which he would follow an example given by his Forerunner.

The rhythmical form of certain sayings of Jesus and their lapidary style made it particularly easy to engrave them upon the memory. Possibly Jesus cast them in this form on purpose, in order that they might be easily retained. The fact that he may have had a habit of fixing certain sayings in the memory of his hearers may have been the germ of the formation of a collection of his discourses.

The Gospel of Mark, in its original form, seems to have been written at Rome during the years which immediately followed the capture and destruction of Jerusalem, approximately between 70 and 72. It was revised about ten years later, perhaps by the author himself.

The composition of the Gospel of Luke may be placed between

---

[1] Especially the fact that in one Gospel elements will be found scattered throughout the work which are grouped together in the other. Facts of this kind are evident, whether we accept the hypothesis that Matthew was the source of Luke or *vice versa*.

72 (the date of the composition of Mark) and 90, a date to which the composition of the Acts of the Apostles, the second book addressed to Theophilus, does not seem to be posterior. We may fix the date of the redaction of this work about the year 85.

The dependence of the Gospel of Matthew upon what we believe to be the second form of the Gospel of Mark gives as the date of composition the earliest that is possible, somewhere about the year 85. In my opinion it cannot be earlier than the year 90.

IV. THE PLAN OF MARK

In the first chapter of this book the reasons were stated which, from the beginning of the twentieth century, have given a foremost position to the critical analysis of the Gospel of Mark and research into the sources on which it is based.

Papias, in the fragment which Eusebius (*Eccl. Hist.*, III, 39) has preserved, says that Mark wrote "accurately, but not in order" (οὐ μέντοι τάξει). This looks as though the Bishop of Hierapolis wished to justify in advance the opinion which Eusebius would have to give about him when he declared, rather contemptuously, that he had "a very small mind." In the Gospel of Mark there are traces of an orderly plan, and unmistakable signs of care in composition. The divisions of the story are clearly defined. After a brief introduction, which includes the mention of John the Baptist, and of the baptism and temptation of Jesus (i. 1–13), the story of the Galilean Ministry proper begins, which extends from i. 14 to viii. 26. This terminates at the moment when Capernaum ceases to be the centre of the activity of Jesus. The section with which the second part of the Gospel opens, the Messianic Confession of Peter (viii. 27–30), is like the pivot around which the whole construction of the plan of Mark turns. This incident took place on heathen territory, outside the country of Palestine, and though, later on, we still sometimes find Jesus in Galilee, the evangelist makes it very clear that he is only there in passing. In the exact sense of the word the Galilean Ministry is over. Jesus is about to set his face to go up to Jerusalem.

At the same time his activity takes on new forms; he gives his teaching principally to his disciples, and this teaching deals not with the Kingdom of God but with the Son of Man, and the destiny which awaits him, according to the Scriptures (viii. 31–x. 52). With the arrival at Jerusalem a new period opens which is divided into two parts: the ministry in Jerusalem (xii. 1–xiii. 37) and the Passion (xiv. 1–xvi. 8).

The Galilean narrative is divided into a certain number of sections which reveal a careful plan. Some passages describe Jesus doing actions or giving teaching which attracts crowds and makes a favourable impression upon them, while others show him in conflict with the growing opposition of the Jewish authorities; the way in which these incidents alternate is too regular to be accidental. After each difficulty which Jesus meets the evangelist shows him intensifying his activity, or at least taking measures which will ensure its continuance. Thus, after a picture of the activity of Jesus, most of which is displayed within the framework of one day at Capernaum (i. 14–45), there comes a series of five conflicts, dealing with the forgiveness of sins, the publicans, fasting, and the Sabbath (ii. 1–iii. 6). This group of stories concludes with the picture of the Pharisees and the Herodians taking the resolve to compass the death of Jesus. The sections which follow (iii. 7–19) show Jesus undiscouraged by this hostility, continuing his ministry of healing, and preparing for the future by the institution of the apostolate. Then, in iii. 20–35, the evangelist lays emphasis anew mainly on the idea of hostility, by telling how the relatives of Jesus wanted to take him away on the pretext that he was mad, while the Pharisees accuse him of being possessed by the prince of the demons. Here he shows that the very essence of the ministry of Jesus is misunderstood. The evangelist feels the need to explain this defeat; he does this in the section of parables (iv. 1–34) which shows that only to the initiated is it given to know the mystery of the Kingdom of God, but that to those who are without all is presented in the form of parables, that "seeing they may see and not perceive, and hearing they may hear and not understand, lest at any time they should be converted" (iv. 11–12). This is the theory of the hardening of the heart by Providence. After this explanation there follow some striking miracles. Jesus

miraculously stills a storm while he is crossing the lake
(iv. 35–41); on the eastern shore he delivers a demoniac
possessed by a legion of demons (v. 1–20); and when he returns
to Galilee he cures a woman with an issue of blood and raises
to life the daughter of Jairus (v. 21–43). These amazing feats
do not produce a lasting impression. Immediately after these
things Jesus is rejected by his compatriots in his own town
of Nazareth in such a way that he is amazed at their unbelief
(vi. 1–6a). Once again Jesus is not discouraged, but he sends
the Twelve forth on their mission (vi. 6b–13). Two sections
follow (Herod's remarks about Jesus and the death of John
the Baptist (vi. 14–29) which form a kind of parenthesis, and
the Galilean period terminates with the double cycle of the
feeding of the crowds who had come to listen to his teaching
(vi. 31–viii. 26). The distribution of the bread, an anticipation
of the banquet which the elect will take with the Messiah in
the Kingdom of God, is something more than a miracle. In
the view of Mark it was a supreme attempt of Jesus to win
the people. His efforts failed; after the miraculous feeding
of the multitudes he was again in conflict with the scribes
and Pharisees. The failure of the Galilean ministry was
complete.

In the plan of the second part of the Gospel it is possible
to distinguish two main currents which are to some extent
contradictory. The one is defined by Peter's confession
(viii. 27–30), the threefold announcement of the coming
suffering, the death and the resurrection of the Son of Man
(viii. 31–32, ix. 30–32, x. 32–34), the prediction of the
sufferings awaiting the disciples (viii. 24–ix. 1), the transfiguration, and the conversation about the return of Elijah
(ix. 2–13); the other section is composed of various fragments
which have no direct relation to the idea of the sufferings of
the Son of Man; in this instance the material at the disposal
of the evangelist was not quite suitable for his purpose.

In the third part of the Gospel the scheme is perfectly
clear: Jesus enters Jerusalem as Messiah (xi. 1–11), asserts
his authority by driving the money-changers out of the Temple
(xi. 15–19), confutes those who ask him by what authority
he does these things (xi. 27–33), then, taking the offensive
himself, he passes sentence on the behaviour of the Jewish

people in the parable or allegory of the vineyard (xii. 1–12). After that Jesus replies victoriously to the captious questions which are put to him (xii. 13–34), and places his interlocutors in an awkward position by asking them in their turn about the Davidic descent of the Messiah (xii. 35–37). To conclude his public ministry he pronounces some severe strictures on the Pharisees (xii. 38–40).[1] Finally, there is some teaching addressed to the disciples only on questions relating to the future (prophecy of the destruction of the Temple, xiii. 1–4) and a long eschatological discourse: the Synoptic Apocalypse (xiii. 5–33).

In the last part—the Passion—the order of the narrative is directly determined by that of the facts.

The plan of Mark is both historical and geographical, since it follows the story of Jesus in its different elements and in its varied setting; it is also psychological, because it suggests the reasons which caused Jesus to leave Galilee for Judaea, and shows how his attitude and his teaching in the Temple lead the authorities to act against him. Finally, this plan is dogmatic, because it brings out the fulfilment of a providential programme in the story of Jesus, which culminates in the redemptive sacrifice of the Cross.[2]

Does this arrangement of the story, which seems to be a philosophical interpretation of the facts, correspond to the real development of the facts? or is this arrangement artificial?

[1] Here occurs the incident of the widow's mite (xii. 41–44), which could not be placed elsewhere since it took place in the Temple.

[2] A few observations will suffice to show that the schemes of Matthew and Luke are not of independent value but are the result of an adaptation of Mark's scheme, made necessary by the introduction of new material, and, later, especially in Matthew, by the desire to group together similar elements. The common sections are usually in the same order in Matthew and Luke as they are in Mark; Matthew and Luke never agree to give the facts in a different order from that of Mark. So far as Matthew is concerned, modifications of the order of Mark occur only in the narrative of the Galilean ministry (until the rejection of Jesus at Nazareth). In this part, as in the others, Luke follows exactly the thread of Mark's narrative, but he leaves it at two points (vi. 20–viii. 3. and ix. 51–xviii. 14), where he inserts, in two blocks, the greater part of the material which he adds to Mark, and then again takes up the thread of the narrative at the point where he had left it.

It is more than half a century since Reuss[1] pointed out the vague and arbitrary character of the connexion between the different parts of the Gospel narrative: "then," "after that," "in those days," "and he arrived." All these insignificant phrases simply string the facts together, but they do not establish any real co-ordination. The narrative is without order, but in quite a different sense from that in which Papias uses the expression.

As soon as we attempt to place the facts of the narrative in definite order we are confronted by great difficulties. A few instances will make this evident, and will show that it is impossible to construct a clear narrative from the design of the Gospel of Mark. When Peter, questioned by Jesus on the road to Caesarea Philippi, says to him, "Thou art the Christ," and Jesus forbids his disciples to tell this to anyone (viii. 29–30), Mark does not mean that the apostle is simply repeating teaching which he has received. He implies that his declaration was something entirely new. Even if, at most, the idea had been suggested to him, Peter has now grasped it in a fresh way.[2] It is this which makes it possible for Jesus to open up fresh views of the future to his disciples and to reveal to them the destiny which awaits him as Messiah. Thus this section marks something new, the recognition of Jesus as Messiah by his disciples, and the beginning of his teaching about the necessity of his sufferings. But the facts reported by Mark in the first part of the story contradict this view. Declarations of Jesus such as: "The Son of Man has power on earth to forgive sins" (ii. 10); "the Son of Man is Lord also of the Sabbath" (ii. 28), have no meaning unless they imply an assertion of Messianic authority; the healings of Jesus as they are conceived by Mark, the discussion of the charge levelled against Jesus that he expelled the demons by the power of Beelzebub, are Messianic manifestations. The evangelist was so convinced of this that in order to reconcile

---

[1] REUSS: *La Bible, Nouveau Testament. Première Partie, Histoire Évangélique*, Paris, 1876, p. 103.

[2] Matthew (xvi. 17) has made the narrative of Mark more detailed and developed, but has not essentially altered it, by making Jesus say to Peter: "Flesh and blood has not revealed this unto thee, but my Father which is in heaven."

them with the nature of Peter's Confession he created the theory of the secret of the Messiahship, and of the recognition of Jesus as Messiah by the demons, a theory whose artificial character is obvious, and which further contradicts the account given by the evangelist himself.[1]

So far as the idea of the death of Jesus is concerned, this comes out already in the saying of Jesus in the discussion about fasting: "The days will come when the bridegroom will be taken away from them; then will they fast in those days" (ii. 20), and it is no less evident in the report of the discussion between the Pharisees and the Herodians who "took counsel . . . how they might destroy him" (iii. 6).

In the second part of the Gospel, the three prophecies of the sufferings, absolutely doctrinaire summaries of the story of the Passion, are rather stereotyped in character, which raises doubts of their origin. It is difficult to understand how they could have been preserved, if (as the evangelist carefully explains to us after each of them), the disciples did not understand the words of Jesus, and did not dare to ask him what he meant.

We shall see further[2] that although Jesus may have known the dangers to which he was exposed in going up to Jerusalem, his entry into the Holy City did not bear the character of a march to death which is given to it in the Gospel tradition.

If, instead of considering the general plan of the Gospel, we examine the structure of each of the parts of which it is composed, we come to the same conclusions. Here, too, a few examples will suffice. The section ii. 1–iii, 6, in which are grouped together a series of five occasions on which Jesus was in conflict with the representatives of Jewish religious tradition, affords a very clear instance of the grouping of incidents according to their character.[3] There is another instance in the parables of iv. 1–34. The presence in vi. 14–29 of two sections

[1] This has been shown very well by WREDE (*Messiasgeheimnis*), although he has drawn inferences from this fact which are open to question.

[2] See later, pp. 398 ff.

[3] After these conflicts the Pharisees and the Herodians take counsel together to see how they may bring about the death of Jesus (iii. 6). This indication, which is not utilized in the later part of the narrative, shows that we are here confronted by a detached fragment of a tradition which differed from the Gospel of Mark.

(the perplexity of Herod when he hears rumours about Jesus and a retrospective account of the death of John the Baptist) which are on the fringe of the story, is no less characteristic. Finally, to confine our attention to the more outstanding facts, we should note that there seems something very obscure in the comings and goings of Jesus mentioned between vi. 30 and ix. 50. Either the evangelist has grouped a series of incidents which have no real connexion with each other, or there is an explanation of these comings and goings which he has not mentioned, or which he does not know; in any case, as it stands, his narrative is confused. In the second part of the Gospel there are two lines of narrative which converge, but do not combine. The one represents Jesus going up to Jerusalem to die; in the other the journey to Jerusalem is a triumphal Messianic progress, crowned by the solemn entry into Jerusalem.[1] In the last part of the Gospel Mark's narrative becomes very obscure owing to the swiftness with which the drama of the Passion is enacted, and also to the impossibility of understanding the legal character of the trial of Jesus solely from the data given in the text.

It would be easy to multiply observations of this kind. Those which we have given will suffice to show that the Gospel story as it is presented by Mark is, to some extent, an artificial construction. The historian therefore can only use his plan with great caution.[2]

---

[1] This is evident, for example, in the juxtaposition of the third prophecy of suffering (x. 32–34) and the request of the sons of Zebedee (x. 35–37), which suggest that Jesus was going up to Jerusalem that he might reign in glory.

[2] If the Gospel of Mark were, as COUCHOUD believes it to be (*Le Mystère*, pp. 35 ff.), a rendering of Pauline theology in narrative form, it would be impossible to understand its incoherencies. Without going so far as this, from Baur onwards it has often been suggested that the Gospel of Mark was written under the influence of Pauline theology. Without doubt, certain ideas of Paul do reappear in Mark, but the terminology is different, and it seems to be concerned with ideas common to primitive Christianity as a whole. One point of resemblance is more striking than all the others, and it is this: the affinity which seems to exist between the theory presented by Mark about the parables, in which Jesus said that he used them in order to prevent people who were not intended to understand the mystery of the Kingdom of God, from understanding them (Mark iv. 10–12, 33–34), and the idea (expounded in Rom. ix.–xi.) of the hardening of the heart of

V. The Arrangement of the Sections Peculiar to Matthew and Luke

Is it possible to reconstruct the life of Jesus by utilizing the sections peculiar to Matthew and Luke, at least those which come from the Logia? In my opinion it would not be impossible to arrive at fairly certain conclusions relating to the arrangement of the most ancient form of this collection,[1] but the purely didactic character of the sections of which they are composed[2] makes it very doubtful whether the first editor of this collection made any attempt, however slight, to reproduce the order and sequence of events.

Some writers have thought that the large section peculiar to Luke (ix. 51–xviii. 14) may preserve independent evidence of that part of the activity of Jesus which lay between the close of the Galilean ministry and the beginning of the ministry in Judaea. In this section Jesus seems to be continually moving on towards Jerusalem, but there is no well-marked geographical development, and the section as a whole is not homogeneous. It bears all the marks of a compilation. In ix. 51 it is said that Jesus sets his face to go up to Jerusalem because the time of his departure is near. The same note is repeated in xiii. 31 and xvii. 11, each time as though it had not already been mentioned that Jesus is going up to Jerusalem. Although in ix. 52 Jesus arrives at a Samaritan village, which means, therefore, that he has left Galilee, among the incidents which follow there are some which certainly,[3] and others

Israel by Providence. But there is a manifest difference between the two theories: in the Gospel the hardening of the hearts of those who listened to Jesus led to the drama of redemption; in the Epistle to the Romans the incredulity of Israel makes it possible to turn to the Gentiles. On the Paulinism of Mark, see *Intr.*, pp. 358–365. Martin Werner: *Der Einfluss paulinischer Theologie im Markusevangelium*, Giessen, 1925.

[1] On this question, see *Intr.*, I, pp. 226–250.

[2] In the Logia there are, properly speaking, very few actual incidents. Those which do occur have only been preserved in cases where they serve as a setting for the words of Jesus, as, for example, in the story of the centurion at Capernaum (Matt. viii. 5–13*) and the message of John the Baptist (Matt. xi. 2–6*).

[3] For example, xiii. 31–33: some Pharisees advise Jesus to leave Galilee because Herod wants to kill him.

probably,[1] must have taken place in Galilee. Incidents which
follow each other without any indication of a change of place
imply entirely different situations. Sometimes Jesus is speaking
to his disciples, or to people who are his usual listeners; at other
times to people who hear him occasionally; now he is speaking
in places which are the usual scene of his activity, and then
in districts where he is only a passing visitor. There is never
any transitional phrase to explain these changes of situation.
It is therefore impossible to use this section of Luke otherwise
than as a separate study of each isolated element of which it is
composed.

VI. The Fourth Gospel

In its present form the Fourth Gospel has certainly passed
through the hands of editors who have added two significant
items concerning the evidence upon which the narrative is
based (xix. 35) and the author of the book (xxi-24). The
editors have, however, certainly not confined their efforts
to the addition of these two verses. We must also assign
chapter xxi (which is in the nature of an appendix) to one
of them, the scenes in which the "beloved disciple" appears[2]
and perhaps still other elements. Further, by suppressing (in
some other scenes)[3] a proper name which originally must
have been there, and, in one instance, by indicating that
Jesus loved the disciple whose name is not mentioned,[4] he has
suggested—in a way which even to us is still transparent and
was still more so to the first readers of the Gospel—that the
"beloved disciple" was the Apostle John.

It is impossible that this apostle could have composed the
Fourth Gospel:

[1] For instance, x. 1–20: the sending of the Seventy. This section implies
that Jesus is not travelling but settled in some region where he is preaching.
This is evidently a doublet of the sending of the Twelve.
[2] That is to say, xiii. 23–26 (Jesus, in an aside, points out the traitor to the
beloved disciple), xix. 25–27 (Jesus confides his mother to his care),
xix. 31–37 (the thrust with the spear).
[3] i. 35–42 (call of the first disciples), xviii. 15–18, 25–27 (Peter's denial),
xx. 2–10 (visit to the sepulchre).
[4] xx. 2. But there is ὅν ἐφίλει ὁ Ἰησοῦς and not the expression ὅν ἠγάπα
which is found in the sections enumerated in n. 2.

(i) because this book at the very earliest dates from the last decade of the first century, and cannot therefore be the work of John, son of Zebedee, who died as a martyr in 44;[1]

(ii) because the theology of the Fourth Gospel represents a stage in the evolution of Christian thought which is later than Paulinism;

(iii) because the Fourth Gospel is not the work of one hand, but is a compilation of different elements.

Apart from editorial additions the Fourth Gospel is a work which gradually evolved. The story of the Raising of Lazarus must have existed in the shape of an independent narrative before it was included in the Gospel, since at the beginning of the story (xi. 2) the writer alludes to the episode of the anointing, which is only related in chapter xii, as though the incident were already familiar. Originally the Farewell Discourses ended at chapter xiv, whose closing words certainly sound like a definite conclusion. But both the story of the Raising of Lazarus and the discourse in chapters xv to xvii are so closely connected in ideas and in language with the rest of the Gospel that it is impossible not to assign them to the evangelist himself. Thus we may consider them as additions which he made later on.

The elements of which the narrative is composed are placed side by side rather than articulated into a whole. After a prologue, which is philosophical in character (i. 1–18), there comes a first story (which may be regarded as an introduction) relating to John the Baptist and to the testimony given by him to the Lamb of God who "taketh away the sin of the world." Following this testimony, several disciples of John the Baptist leave him in order to follow Jesus (i. 19–51). After these preliminary scenes, which take place at Bethany in Perea, Jesus, accompanied by his disciples, returns to Galilee, works his first miracle at Cana, and then goes down to Capernaum (ii. 1–12). As the Passover is near he goes up to Jerusalem. It is at this point that he drives the money-changers and merchants out of the Temple, and, at the request for a sign which would justify the authority which he has arrogated

[1] *Intr.*, II, pp. 92–102.

to himself, he replies with the saying about the Temple which will be destroyed and built up again in three days (ii. 13–25). Then comes the interview with Nicodemus who visits Jesus by night. John places in the mouth of Jesus a didactic exposition of the Gospel which makes us forget the occasion which called it forth, for the story ends without our learning whether Nicodemus is persuaded by what Jesus says to him, or whether he remains in his sceptical frame of mind (iii. 1–21).

After the conversation with Nicodemus comes the narrative of a second meeting with John the Baptist, at Enon near Salem in Judaea. John pays homage to Jesus; the latter, however, learning that his own disciples are baptizing more people than the Baptist, leaves Judaea, and returns to Galilee (iii. 22–iv. 3). Passing through Samaria he holds a conversation near Jacob's Well with a Samaritan woman who recognizes that he is a prophet; Jesus speaks of the living water, of the worship "in spirit and in truth," and declares the harvest is near. Several Samaritans believe in him (iv. 4–42).

Returning to Galilee, Jesus is not well received by his fellow-countrymen who want to see him work miracles like those which they had heard he had accomplished in Judaea (iv. 43–45). Then the evangelist tells the story of the healing of the child of an imperial official of Capernaum (iv. 46–54).

A festival (it is not said which) leads Jesus to go to Jerusalem, where he cures an impotent man at Bethesda. This cure, which was worked on the Sabbath Day, provokes discussions with the Jews (v. 1–47).

Returning to Galilee, about the time of the feast of the Passover, Jesus works the miracle of the feeding of the five thousand, which arouses such enthusiasm among those who took part that they wanted to take him by force and make him king. But he escapes from this ovation. The following day, in the synagogue at Capernaum, he gives a discourse on the Bread of Life which results in the alienation of a section of those who had followed him until that time. Peter, in the name of the Twelve, proclaims their attachment to Jesus (vi. 1–71).

The Feast of Tabernacles being near, the brothers of Jesus urge him to go to Jerusalem to manifest himself publicly. He refuses; then, after the departure of his brethren, he goes up to Jerusalem secretly (vii. 1–13). The teaching which he gives provokes controversy with the Jews, who desire to seize him, but he manages to elude them and to escape (vii. 14–viii. 59).[1]

Chapter ix contains the story of the healing of the man born blind, which, without any connecting link, follows the parable of the Good Shepherd (x. 1–21).

Then the narrative returns to the account of the public activity of Jesus at Jerusalem. On the Feast of the Dedication he declares that his works bear witness to him. The Jews wish to stone him, but he withdraws to Bethany in Perea, where John used to baptize his disciples (x. 22–42). He leaves his retreat on hearing of the illness of Lazarus, whom he raises to life again (xi. 1–44). On account of the excitement caused by the news of this miracle the Jews want to kill Jesus, and it is on this occasion that Caiaphas declares to the Sanhedrin that it is better that one man should die for the people (xi. 45–53). Threatened by his enemies Jesus withdraws into the desert of Ephraim (xi. 54–57).

With chapter xii a new section of the Gospel begins, the story of the Passion, in which the incidents are much more closely related to each other. The supper at Bethany and the anointing (xii. 1–11) are followed by the entry into Jerusalem (xii. 12–19); then comes a request from some Greeks who wish to see Jesus, a request to which Jesus replies indirectly by the announcement of his death (xii. 20–36); some reflexions of the evangelist on the unbelief of the Jews follow (xii. 37–43), which is completed by some declarations of Jesus himself (xii. 44–50). After this there is the story of the Last Supper, in the course of which Jesus washes the feet of his disciples, then announces the treachery of Judas, the dispersal of his followers and the denial of Peter (xiii. 1–38). These incidents are followed by the Farewell Discourses (xiv. 1–xvii. 26).

Then come the various parts of the story of the Passion: the arrest (xviii. 1–11), the Jewish trial and the denial of Peter (xviii. 12–27), the trial before Pilate (xviii. 28–xix. 16), the crucifixion (xix. 17–30), the thrust with the spear (xix. 31–37), and the burial (xix. 38–42).

---

[1] In vii. 53–viii. 11 is inserted the incident of the adulterous woman, which does not form part of the authentic text of the Gospel because it does not appear in the most ancient manuscripts.

Chapter xx forms the conclusion, with the stories of the resurrection. First of all Mary Magdalene finds the tomb empty and hastens to tell Peter and the other disciple about it (xx. 1–10); then Jesus shows himself to her (xx. 11–18). On the evening of the same day he shows himself to the apostles in the absence of Thomas (xx. 19–23), and eight days later he shows himself to them again, Thomas being present this time (xx. 24–29).

The Gospel finishes with a brief note in which the author declares that Jesus has accomplished many other miracles which are not narrated in this book, and that he himself has only written what he has in order that his readers may know that Jesus is the Christ, the Son of God, and that, believing, they might have life in his name (xx. 30–31).

In the appendix, which is constituted by chapter xxi, we find first of all the story of a manifestation of the Risen Lord on the shore of the Lake of Tiberias (xxi. 1–14); then the account of a conversation between Jesus and Peter, in which, three times in succession, he gives him a solemn charge to feed his sheep. In an appendix to this conversation the author shows that a saying of Jesus concerning the "beloved disciple" does not mean, as he thought it did, that the beloved disciple would not die (xxi. 15–23). Finally, the conclusion (in addition to the verse 24 of which we have already spoken) is formed by taking up with added emphasis one of the elements in the first conclusion (xx. 30): "There are also many other things which Jesus did, the which, if they should be written every one . . . even the world itself could not contain the books which should be written" (xxi. 25).

In arranging his narrative thus John had no intention of following any chronological or geographical order in the life of Jesus, for, although the mention of various festivals may seem to constitute a framework,[1] it is a framework which remains empty and unused, for the events which take place between the festivals—which constitute the skeleton of the narrative—almost amount to nothing.

Working on the assumption that the different episodes in

[1] The festivals are mentioned in stereotyped phrases which show the artificial character of the system. See ii. 13, v. 1, vi. 4, vii. 2, xi. 55.

the narrative are chosen to illustrate some dominant theme some critics have tried to discover a systematic plan in the Gospel. This theory has been developed with much ingenuity by critics like Holtzmann, Jean Réville, and Loisy. The interpretations which they propose sound quite probable if they are considered separately, but they contradict each other, and this shows that they are really artificial.

The following observations will help us to gain some idea of the plan of the Fourth Gospel.

(i) The idea of a progressive revelation during the ministry of Jesus is foreign to the mind of John. The declarations of John the Baptist already contain the whole essence of the Gospel. The Farewell Discourses of Jesus bear the promise of a future revelation which the disciples are not yet fit to receive, but no declarations more precise than the conversations with Nicodemus and the Samaritan woman. From the beginning of the book the principle of the necessity and the fruitfulness of the death of Christ is explicitly stated.

(ii) Further, in this book there is no idea of any development in the faith of the disciples[1] or of a growing hostility on the part of the Jews.[2]

(iii) The evangelist is not concerned with questions of narrative. His stories only contain a minimum of concrete features. The centre of gravity is not in the facts, but in the words to which they serve as the framework, and of which sometimes (the feeding of the multitudes, the healing of the man born blind, the raising of Lazarus) they are an allegorical expression. The only feature in the tradition about John which has been preserved in the incidents in chapter i relating to John the Baptist (evidently drawn from the same source as those in the Synoptic Gospels) is that which reports a testimony given by him to the Messiah.

(iv) Some elements which obviously belong to each other very closely are dissociated and separated by sections belonging

[1] From the beginning, at the word of John the Baptist, they leave their master to follow Jesus.
[2] According to John, Jesus dies at the time appointed for him by God; until that hour all the attempts of the Jews against him were futile (v. 18, vii. 19 ff., 30, 44, viii. 20, 59, x. 31, 39). Thus it is not an increase in the hatred of the Jews which provokes the final scene in the tragedy.

to a quite different tradition. The miracle at Cana (ii. 1-12) and that at Capernaum (iv. 43-54) which certainly belong to the same tradition[1] are separated by an incident which belongs to an earlier journey of Jesus to Jerusalem, to his visit to John the Baptist and his return by way of Samaria.

(v) The connexion between the incidents is most unsatisfactory. At the close of chapter v, for instance, Jesus is in Jerusalem. Without any conclusion or suggestion of a transition chapter vi begins thus: "After these things Jesus went over the Sea of Galilee, which is the Sea of Tiberias." Thus chapter vi is simply placed alongside of, but not connected with, chapter v.[2]

Chapter ix (the healing of the man born blind) falls into the same category. At the end of chapter viii we are told how on the last day of the Feast of Tabernacles, after an attempt had been made to arrest Jesus, he escapes in order to avoid being stoned. The narrative of chapter ix begins thus: "And as Jesus passed by he saw a man which was blind from his birth," with no explanation of the manner in which the dangers which threatened Jesus have been dispelled. Chapter ix ends with a word addressed by Jesus to the blind who think they can see. This shows that Jesus is surrounded by enemies. Chapter x opens—without any introduction—with the parable of the Good Shepherd, in which Jesus is speaking to his disciples.

These considerations lead us to believe that the Fourth Gospel is a collection of independent incidents,[3] selected in

---

[1] In ii. 1-12, and iv. 43-54, Cana is the centre of the activity of Jesus, and Capernaum takes a second place. The miracles mentioned in the two accounts are given as the first and the second, which proves that these two sections were written by someone who knew nothing of the miracles which had been worked in Jerusalem to which allusion is made in iv. 45. The matter introduced between the two Galilean fragments is composed of very dissimilar elements (cf. *Intr.*, II, pp. 271 ff.).

[2] It is, of course, true that some critics have suggested inverting the order of chapters v and vi, but this hypothesis is not supported by any reliable evidence. Also it would introduce another difficulty, for the connexion between chapter v and chapter vii would be no more satisfactory than that between chapter v and chapter vi.

[3] This independence is confirmed by the fact that often an idea which is expressed in an incident is expressed anew in a second incident and sometimes in a third without any allusion to what has already been said. This

order to throw light on various aspects of Christian truth. It is a series of meditations on the Gospel story, set in a framework composed of narratives relating to John the Baptist and the story of the Passion.

The attempt, therefore, to discover a history of the life of Jesus in the Johannine Gospel is due to a misunderstanding of the nature of this Gospel.

The historical value of John's narrative does not lie in its framework nor in its general construction, but in the traditional material which it has used. In my opinion, we can, to a very large extent, recognize and reconstruct the sources or some of the sources of the Gospel, in spite of alterations, adaptations, and additions which the evangelist introduced in order to make them useful for his purpose, which was that of the edification of his readers and the strengthening of their faith, not that of instruction in the actual facts of the life of Jesus, nor to satisfy an historical curiosity which did not exist when he wrote.

APPENDIX.—THE APOCRYPHAL GOSPELS

A priori the historian should recognize no difference between the Canonical and the Apocryphal Gospels. He must admit, however, that an actual difference between them does exist. The Apocryphal Gospels are of no direct use at all for the history of Jesus, but if we examine them carefully, tendencies which determine the development of the Gospel tradition will emerge enlarged and defined, as clearly as though they had been placed under a magnifying glass.

The Apocryphal Gospels fall into two groups: those which date from the period before the middle of the second century, that is to say before the canon of the four Gospels was complete, and those which were composed after that date. The former were, in certain circles, rivals of the Canonical Gospels. The others were either the gospels of certain sects, obvious adap-

can be seen in the following instances: the theme of the living water (iv. 4–42, vii. 37 ff.), of the idea of judgment (iii. 19, v. 22–30, viii. 16, xii. 31), Jesus the light of the world (viii. 12, ix. 1 ff.), the witness of Jesus and the witness rendered to him by God (iii. 11, 32, v. 31–39, viii. 13–18), etc.

tations of tradition to fit their own particular tenets, or embroideries on the main web of some sections of the Canonical Gospels; they did not wish to replace them, but rather to supplement them on points where they did not entirely satisfy either the curiosity or the imagination of the faithful (especially about the birth and childhood of Jesus and the story of the Passion). The Apocryphal Gospels of the former group are the only ones which are of any value at all; but only a few rare fragments of these have been preserved.

When we examine them closely we see that their source is the same as that of the tradition behind the Canonical Gospels, more or less altered and perverted by the influence of preconceived ideas, usually very easy to discern.

A few instances from the ancient Apocryphal Gospels will be sufficient to illustrate this point.[1]

A primary group is constituted by that which Saint Jerome calls the *hebraïcum* or the *evangelium hebraïcum*.[2] He says that he found a copy in the library at Caesarea and that he translated it from Aramaic into Greek and Latin for his own personal use. He quotes from it several times, but under different titles. If we compare the various passages in which he mentions it, and his testimony, with that which we know from other sources, and above all with the fragments which we possess[3] we see that to identify the Gospel of the Hebrews either—on the one hand, with the original of Matthew, or, on the other, with the Gospel of the Ebionites or of the Twelve Apostles and the Gospel of the Nazarenes—is only an ill-founded conjecture. Of the four documents of which he speaks Jerome had known only one, the Gospel of the Hebrews. The idea of an Aramaic

---

[1] On the Apocryphal Gospels, see *Neutest. Ap. und Handb. z. d. neutest. Ap.* PUECH: *Histoire de la littérature grecque chrétienne*, Paris, 1928, I, pp. 157–174. In these works the reader will find all the necessary bibliographical information.

[2] For this Gospel, or, rather, for this group of Gospels, see *Jean-Baptiste*, pp. 163–170.

[3] They have often been collected, especially by NESTLE (*Novi Testamenti graeci supplementum*, Leipzig, 1896, pp. 75–81), PREUSCHEN (*Antilegomena. Die Reste der ausserkanonischen Evangelien*, Giessen, 1901, pp. 2–11, German translation, pp. 106–112), and E. KLOSTERMANN (*Apokrypha II, Evangelien*, Bonn, 1904, in the *Kleine Texte* of LIETZMANN, No. 8).

original of Matthew is only a hypothesis suggested by the evidence of Papias,[1] evidence which should be regarded with great caution, and, if it has any value at all, it can only be applied to one of the sources of the First Gospel and not to this Gospel itself.[2] The Gospel of the Ebionites, or of the Twelve Apostles, which was used by the Christians who spoke Aramaic, must have had an original text in Greek.[3] The fragments which we know reveal an evident dependence upon the Synoptic Gospels and especially on that of Matthew. It seems to have been composed during the second half of the second century.

Origen attributed a certain authority to the Gospel of the Hebrews which was used equally by the Christians who spoke Aramaic but which, in contrast to the Gospel of the Ebionites or of the Twelve Apostles, was certainly composed in Aramaic.[4] On one single point, the word *mahar* (of the coming day) by which the word ἐπιούσιον (whose exact meaning is unknown, and which is generally rendered by "daily") is translated in the Lord's Prayer, suggests a conjecture that the Gospel of the Hebrews might contain, not something primitive referring to the Synoptic tradition, but a translation of an obscure Greek expression inspired by knowledge of Aramaic.[5] The Gospel of the Hebrews would necessarily have been of the Synoptic type if it were the original of Matthew. It was, however, shorter[6] than Matthew, although it contained several incidents which were not in the canonical Gospel. The Gospel of the Hebrews seems to have been written in the first half, possibly even at the beginning of the second century.

The Gospel of the Nazarenes, according to the works of

[1] "Matthew wrote in Hebrew (Aramaic) the words of the Lord, and each man interpreted them as he could." Passage preserved by EUSEBIUS (*Eccl. Hist.*, III, 39).

[2] *Intr.*, I, pp. 132 ff.

[3] Because of the substitution of ἐγκρίδης (fritters) for ἀκρίσης (locusts), in the account of John the Baptist.

[4] This comes from the fact that the Holy Spirit (the Hebrew word *rouah* is feminine) is represented as the mother of Jesus.

[5] We must also consider a possible hypothesis that the translation *mahar* may be a simple conjecture like all the other interpretations which have been made of ἐπιούσιον.

[6] According to the Stichometry of Nicephorus it had only 2,200 lines, whereas there were 2,500 in Matthew.

Schmidtke,[1] seems to have been simply a translation of the Gospel of Matthew, a rather free translation in the style of the Targums.

Only a few fragments remain of the Gospel of the Egyptians which may not have been composed until the second half of the second century; it seems to have been used in a group which had Gnostic tendencies; in spite of the very great obscurity of these fragments which remain it is possible to distinguish fairly clearly a decided tendency towards asceticism.

Among the Apocryphal Gospels Origen mentions the existence of a Gospel of Peter, but he gives no further indications which would enable us to describe it. Eusebius (*Eccl., Hist.* VI. xii. 2–6) reports that at the end of the second century Bishop Serapion of Antioch[2] discovered that the faithful belonging to a little church in his diocese, Rhossos, used this Gospel. At first he allowed them to continue this practice; then, having examined the Gospel more closely he discovered that it had a docetic tendency, and he forbade the Christians to read it. Eusebius, Jerome, and the decretal of Gelasian place the Gospel of Peter among those which should be rejected, but they give no precise description of it. In the winter of 1886–1887 there was discovered in the tomb of a monk at Akhmin in Upper Egypt a manuscript containing a fragment of a Gospel which critics were able to identify without any hesitation as that of Peter. The story is told by Peter in the name of the Twelve; he begins at the point where Jesus has just been condemned to death (by Herod and not by Pilate); he tells of the execution, the burial, and the resurrection of Jesus, and ends with an incomplete phrase which one might guess had served as an introduction to a narrative of the appearance of the Risen Lord on the shore of the Lake of Galilee, a story consequently very like that at the beginning of chapter xxi in John.

It is certain that the Gospel of Peter is based upon the Canonical Gospels, although it may not be impossible that on some point of detail the author may have used some secondary

---

[1] *Neue Fragmente und Untersuchungen zu den judenchristlichen Evangelien* (*T.U.*, III, R., VII, 1), Leipzig, 1911.

[2] Serapion was Bishop of Antioch from 190 to 211.

source, either written or oral. But he does not confine himself to the reproduction of the Canonical Gospels; he develops and transposes their narratives in such a way as to accentuate the tendency (more exclusively than they do) to throw the responsibility for the death of Jesus on the Jews.

The Gospel of Peter was probably composed during the first half of the second century.[1]

Several writings which date from the second and third centuries contain more or less precise allusions to the Gospel story conceived sometimes a little differently from those in the Canonical Gospels. One meets in them also quotations of sayings of Jesus of which some are variants of those which we find in the canonical tradition, and of which others have no equivalent. These are called the *Agrapha*.[2] Each must be judged separately on its own merits. When we consider, however (as we shall see in the next chapter), that tradition has acted not only as a force of preservation, but also as a force of transformation, adaptation, and even of creation, all sayings of this kind should be accepted with extreme caution, unless it can be proved that they are of comparatively early date. The sense of the necessity for this reserve is increased when we realize that each time that it is possible to verify a particular saying because a parallel canonical tradition is still in existence, we find that the extra-canonical data are only a tendentious perversion of the canonical data. This is enough for suspicion to be cast on the non-canonical tradition, and to make us decide that none but the material provided by the canonical Gospels can be used for the story of the life of Jesus.

[1] Among the Apocryphal Gospels we do not include either the *Diatessaron* of TATIAN or the *Gospel* of MARCION. The former work is only a combination of the canonical Gospels, while the second is an adaptation of the Gospel of Luke to Marcionite ideas. There may well be in both these works some elements which are not in the canonical Gospels, but they are no more important in proportion than the variants which belong to one manuscript or another, to manuscript D, for example.

[2] On the *Agrapha*, see among others: RESCH: *Agrapha. Ausserkanonische Evangelienfragmente* (*T.U.*, V, 4), Leipzig, 1889, ²1906. J. H. ROPES: *Die Sprüche Jesu die in den kanonischen Evangelien nicht überliefert sind* (*T.U.*, XIV, 2), Leipzig, 1898. *Neut. Ap.*, pp. 32 ff. A French translation of the principal *agrapha* is given by E. BESSON: *Les Logia agrapha. Paroles du Christ qui ne se trouvent pas dans les Évangiles canoniques*, Bihorel-lez-Rouen, 1923.

CHAPTER V

THE GOSPEL TRADITION

I. THE PROBLEM OF TRADITION

THE conclusions at which we arrived in the preceding chapter make it possible to formulate the problem which the Gospels present to the historian of the life of Jesus. He is not called upon to decide on their evidence as a whole, but to determine the value of each of the narratives which they contain, and, if possible, to get behind their present form to one which is older still. No incident can be judged on its merits alone, isolated from all those with which it is connected and without consideration for the stage of tradition to which it corresponds. This constitutes a factor of appreciation which is of the highest importance.

Perhaps before we try to estimate some of the general features in the development of the Gospel tradition it will be useful to define more closely the sense in which we use the expression "tradition."

Tradition, as distinguished from written literature, means the preservation and transmission of stories by word of mouth. Essentially it is in constant movement. Psychological study of the evidence shows to what a great extent, in reporting what they have seen and heard, men are prone to be influenced by their temperament, their prejudices, their feelings, and their passions. Even when they transmit a story, they do not play a purely passive part, but, at the least, they colour what they transmit to others with the reflection of their own personality. At each stage therefore a tradition is shaped and moulded into something different. Two opposing forces are at work within it: one which tends towards preservation, and another which tends to transform what it hears into something different. Hence in order to realize what constitutes the history of a tradition it is necessary to distinguish within it, as carefully as possible, the various stages through which it has passed, in order to be able to follow the transformations and perversions which have taken place in the narrative, and to be able to discern those which, even if not the most primitive, are at least the most ancient.

By primitive tradition we mean the earliest record of the events in question, that is, therefore, a record which, even if it does not correspond absolutely to what took place—for the direct evidence itself needs to be criticized—is at least very near to the facts.

A full and detailed history of the Gospel tradition would be a very lengthy work, needing the labours of several generations and the collaboration of critics, historians, psychologists, sociologists, and students of folklore. At present it is only possible to note some general features in its development by comparing the most ancient form of the tradition which we know (Mark) with the later forms (Matthew, Luke, John, and in certain instances the Apocryphal tradition).

However important the facts may be which we can thus bring to light, they do not permit us to lay down absolute general rules; even though we may supplement and illuminate the facts of the Gospel tradition by the aid of those which we find in other realms, we are still unable to construct what Martin Dibelius calls a *Biologie der Sage*.[1]

The Gospel tradition possesses certain features peculiar to itself[2] which do not belong, at least not in the same degree, to the traditions with which people have claimed they should be compared. Further, if we look into the matter very closely we see that, in the proper sense of the word, there are no laws of evolution in tradition but simply some facts of a more or less general character.[3]

[1] DIBELIUS: *Die Formgeschichte des Evangeliums*, Tübingen, 1919, p. 1. This idea, which has been suggested by the works of GUNKEL on the traditions of Genesis, was formulated for the first time by BOUSSET (*Kyrios Christos*, Göttingen, 1913, p. 41, n. 5; [2]1921, p. 33, n. 3).

[2] For instance, from the very beginning it was religious in scope and in interest, and then it became fixed in writing while it was still quite young, instead of waiting for centuries, as one often has to do in other cases.

[3] Possibly it will be useful to give an example at this point. The critics of the *formgeschichtliche Schule* claim to illuminate the evolution of the Gospel tradition by the laws of the evolution of epic legends which have been formulated by OLRIK (*Die epischen Gesetze der Volksdichtung*, *Z. f. deutsches Altertum*, 1909, pp. 1 ff.). One of these laws is that intensity is revealed by

The development of the Gospel tradition seems to be dominated by certain general tendencies, particularly by that of the grouping of incidents which were originally independent of one another. Sometimes, however, the evolution has been in the inverse order and cycles of tradition which were organic in character have been dissociated. Two instances from the Gospel of Mark will suffice to prove this point. The words with which (in Mark iii. 6) the series of conflicts between Jesus and the representatives of the Jewish religious tradition closes, reports a discussion of the Pharisees and the Herodians, who "took counsel together how they might kill him" (iii. 6). This certainly comes from a tradition in which the Galilean authorities are represented as directly influencing the course of events, and which Mark did not use again. The words "after six days" with which the story of the Transfiguration begins (ix. 2) shows that originally this episode was part of a series of stories enclosed within a compact chronological framework. Mark has not reproduced these narratives, at least not at this point.

To interpret the development of the Gospel tradition by the general laws which govern the evolution of popular traditions is a method which should only be used with great caution. Above all we should guard against the temptation of making conjectures based on these laws about facts which we have not directly observed.

The same care should be exercised in using the argument which claims that the development of the Gospel tradition

repetition (a double feeding of the multitudes in Mark and Matthew, a triple denial of Peter, triple prayer in Gethsemane, triple account of Paul's conversion in the book of the Acts, etc.). But other reasons may operate besides that of underlining the importance of an episode. The reason why Mark dealt with two stories of the feeding of the multitudes is probably because he was dealing with two parallel traditions and did not realize that he was here confronted with two pictures of the same incident. On the other hand, he may have given intensity to the scene in Gethsemane by repeating the triple prayer of Jesus, but Luke, who desires to attain the same end, uses quite different methods. He has suppressed the two last prayers of which he knew from Mark, but, by speaking of the "bloody sweat" and the intervention of the angel he placed the incident in the highest possible category.

is due to the influence of the cultus.[1] Those who follow this
line of argument try to explain something which is imperfectly
known by something which is absolutely unknown, for we
know nothing at all about the form of Christian worship which
was in use at the time when the Gospels were composed.
Further, although there certainly is some connexion between
the Gospel records and the cultus, we have no right to interpret this fact exclusively in the sense of the influence of the
cultus on the records; we must also take into account the
influence of the records—and, still more, of the facts which
they report—upon the cultus itself.

While there may be some use in comparing the Gospel tradition with certain similar traditions found in the Jewish and
Greek world, we must always remember that a comparison
is not an explanation, and an analogy is not the equivalent
of a genealogy. The form of certain aphorisms may have been
borrowed by Jesus from the Jewish *maschal* as it occurs in the
Wisdom literature, but this does not give us the right to
conclude that these aphorisms are actually derived from the
Jewish Wisdom literature. As for the analogies which have
been pointed out between the accounts of the miracles of the
New Testament and certain similar stories, Jewish or Greek,
they are striking, it is true, but their significance is nil, because
they are due simply to the nature of the facts.[2]

One method alone enables us to discern the real nature of
the development of the Gospel tradition, and that is to make
a careful analysis of the parallel narratives and then try to
discover the reason for the changes which have been introduced into the text. By means of this method it is possible to
disengage and bring to light certain general tendencies in the
development of the tradition.

[1] See the book by BERTRAM: *Die Leidensgeschichte Jesu und der Christuskult*,
Göttingen, 1922.
[2] The most interesting point which emerges from the comparative study
of these phenomnea is the existence of a common mental atmosphere.
In the light of these discoveries we realize that the miraculous incidents
in the Gospel story did not seem so amazing to the readers of those days
as they do to those of the twentieth century.

If we could complete this analysis with a synthesis something very valuable would have been accomplished. The *formgeschichtliche Schule* has tried to do this by classifying the Gospel stories in types corresponding to the diverse functions in the life of the Church, such as catechizing, preaching, moral exhortation, controversy, apologetics, etc. This school of thought suggests that it was the appearance and development of these diverse functions which determined the character of the corresponding stories.

This method, which at first sight looks attractive, proves to be very arbitrary. A complete classification of types is impossible;[1] it can only be done by making a series of abstractions which are based upon one simple formula. In reality, there are only what Dibelius has called mixed forms (*Mischformen*), that is to say, sections which combine the characteristic features of different types. While this is a legitimate and useful method of work, the classification of the material of the Gospel story in distinct types is dangerous and false if it claims to be the expression of the Gospel tradition, and is used as a method of reconstructing its history.

Even if it were legitimate to assume as a fact that there is a connexion between certain sections in the Gospel records, or certain groups of sections, and some particular function in the life of the Church, it would be wrong to conclude from this that the function has created the organ, that it was the needs of the work of catechizing, of preaching, or of public worship which determined the appearance of the material utilized by them which have given them their structure and their present shape. It is possible that in the cultus there may have been, not creation, but adaptation and utilization of some elements in the Gospel tradition for the needs of the life of the Church. If this be true, the material for the composition of the Gospels may have been influenced to some extent in its form by the uses to which they were put, but this does not

---

[1] We do not want to make capital out of the fact that those which have been proposed by Dibelius (*Formgeschichte*) on the one hand, and by Bultmann (*Geschichte der synoptischen Tradition*, Göttingen, 1921), [2]1931, on the other, are far from agreement with each other, for that might be explained by saying that at a first attempt it would be impossible to attain entirely satisfactory results.

explain the creation of the Gospels themselves. That this line
of argument is right is proved by the fact that this adaptation
was a gradual process. It is more complete in the later than
in the earlier forms of tradition. One example, taken from
amongst many, will be sufficient to prove this: Matthew, in
the instructions given by Jesus to the Twelve whom he is
sending out on their Mission, has preserved this exhortation:
"Go not into the way of the Gentiles, and into any city of the
Samaritans enter ye not" (Matt. x. 5). Neither Mark nor
Luke have preserved this injunction, which is not in agreement with the most primitive practice of the Early Church,
since missionary work in Samaria and pagan territory dates
from the very earliest days of Christianity. This principle is
not in harmony with the ideas of Matthew himself, who
records the instruction of Jesus to his disciples after he was
risen: "Go, make disciples of all the nations" (xxviii. 19).
Hence Matthew was here reproducing a very ancient element
in the tradition of the Logia without adapting it to the needs
of the Church of his day. Neither Mark nor Luke have recorded
this saying in their accounts of the sending of the Twelve on
their first Mission.

Comparison of the Gospel narratives may serve as a point of
departure for the whole work of research into the question of
the development of the Gospel tradition: but its results are
not permanent or satisfying. In the endeavour to distinguish
the historical elements in the Gospel story the method of
subtraction will not suffice; in other words, it is not enough
simply to eliminate details or episodes which have been added
later, such as, to take some rather crude examples, the dream
of Pilate's wife, or the scene of Pilate washing his hands in
order to throw the responsibility for the death of Jesus upon
the Jews (Matt. xxvii. 19, 24–25). The forces which determined
the development of the tradition did not begin to operate
only after the Gospel of Mark had been composed. We would
also need to eliminate the elements contained in the very
earliest record which are their product, and also—at least if
we wish to retain only that material of which we are absolutely
sure—those to which any suspicion of non-authenticity may
be attached.

II. The Development of the Tradition in the Synoptic Gospels

When we compare the three Synoptic Gospels with each other[1] we note certain modifications which have made the story more coherent, and sometimes more restrained, by the elimination of details which were considered superfluous or which had become unintelligible or devoid of interest for readers remote both in time and space from the setting of the Gospel story. For example, Matthew and Luke do not reproduce exactly what Mark says (iii. 6) about a consultation of the Pharisees and the Herodians against Jesus, a council which plays no part in the rest of the narrative. Matthew (xii. 14) modifies the statement by omitting the mention of the Herodians. Luke (vi. 11) transforms it still more by not mentioning the intention to kill Jesus; he says that they "communed one with another what they might do to Jesus."

Mark (iii. 22) reports the accusation brought against Jesus: that he cast our demons by Beelzebub, without telling the story of the healing of the demoniac. Matthew (xii. 22–23) and Luke (xi. 14) have filled in this gap, and the fact that the accounts they give are independent of each other prove that they have not reproduced a primitive form of the tradition which Mark is supposed to have mutilated, but that they have either created, or taken from some other source, the material they needed to make the story more convincing and logical.

Mark (xv. 2) and Matthew (xxvii. 11) represent Jesus being questioned by Pilate *ex abrupto*, without mentioning the accusa-

---

[1] With reference to this comparison we must note that if literary criticism has decided, in a way which can be considered conclusive, that the Gospel of Mark is earlier than those of Matthew and Luke, this does not mean that whenever a word or an incident is reported by all three evangelists the most ancient form is always found in Mark. One evangelist may have reproduced material from a very ancient source more correctly than another, who may have written some time before him. We ought also to take into account the fact that the Gospel of Mark, in its present form, has certainly been retouched several times by those who recopied it one after another. So far as the elements of the Logia reproduced by Matthew and by Luke are concerned, we may state that it is sometimes one and sometimes the other whose rendering is most ancient.

tions which have been brought against him. Luke (xxiii. 2) explicitly mentions these accusations.

Many of the corrections make the narrative clearer by replacing an ambiguous expression by one which is more precise. For instance: when Jesus arrives at the house of Peter's wife's mother, Mark says: "they tell him of her" (i. 30) which may mean that they asked him to do something for her or more simply, that they explained to him that she was ill and could not come out to welcome him. (Luke iv. 38) reads: "they besought him for her." In the incident of the feast given to the publicans, Mark (ii. 15) and Matthew (ix. 10) use an expression which leaves it uncertain whether the feast took place in the house of Levi or in that of Peter, where Jesus seems to have been staying. Luke (v. 29) says: "Levi made him a great feast in his own house."

In the story of Peter's denial, where we read in Mark (xiv. 70) and Luke (xxii. 59) that someone says to the apostle: "Thou art a Galilean," Matthew (xxvi. 73) adds: "for thy speech bewrayeth thee."

In the secondary Gospels details which are contradictory or difficult to understand have disappeared. In the section on the dangers of riches, Mark, after having enumerated the good things which the disciples will receive in compensation for those which they have renounced, adds these significant words: "with persecutions" (x. 30).[1] In Matthew and Luke these words are omitted.

Mark (xiv. 2) and Matthew (xxvi. 5) suggest that the Jews did not want to kill Jesus on the feast-day. Luke, quite rightly, evidently thought it strange that after this remark Jesus should die during the Passover festival, although nothing is said about the reason for the alteration in their plans. He therefore omits this detail.[2]

Obvious errors in previous accounts are sometimes sup-

[1] For the meaning of this phrase see my article: "*Avec des persécutions*," *R.h.p.r.*, VIII, 1928, pp. 264–277.
[2] He evidently knew the text of Mark because he has retained a relic which does not fit in with the context: "for they feared the people" (xxii. 2).

pressed. Mark (ii. 26) places the incident of the eating of the shewbread by David "under the high-priest Abiathar." According to Samuel xxi. 1–6, the incident took place in the time of Ahimelech, the father of Abiathar. Neither Luke nor Matthew have the words "under the high-priest Abiathar." Likewise they replace the inexact expression "king Herod" of Mark vi. 14 by the correct formula: "Herod the Tetrarch (Matt. xiv. 1; Luke ix. 17).

Other details have been omitted doubtless because they are regarded as deficient in interest. For instance, in the story of the stilling of the storm, Mark alone reports that Jesus was sleeping "in the hinder part of the ship . . . on a pillow" (iv. 38). He alone, in telling the story of Peter's denial, says that Peter was warming himself (xiv. 54).

Sometimes details have been omitted because they are no longer understood, or have lost their point, as, for example, the name of Boanerges given to James and John, according to Mark (iii. 17); the detail of the young man who fled naked at the moment that Jesus was arrested (Mark xiv. 51–52), and the names of Alexander and Rufus, sons of Simon of Cyrene (Mark xv. 21).

The fact that Matthew and Luke omit certain Aramaic terms which are found in Mark (v. 41, vii. 11, x. 51, xiv. 36) belongs to the same category.

In some instances details have been added in order to strengthen the story. Thus, according to Luke (xvii. 4) Jesus says that his disciples ought to pardon a man seven times a day if he repents seven times. Matthew (xviii. 21–22) does not speak of seven times but of seventy times seven. It is true that he is not speaking of offences committed upon the same day.[1] After his denial Peter "weeps," according to Mark (xiv. 72). According to Matthew (xxvi. 75) and Luke (xxii. 62) he "weeps bitterly." To the darkness and the rending of the veil of the Temple of which Mark speaks (xv. 33. 38) and Luke (xxiii. 44–45), Matthew (xxvii. 51–53) adds that there was an earthquake, that the rocks were rent, that

---

[1] The Gospel of the Nazarenes accentuates this point still further by combining Matthew and Luke. He speaks of forgiving seventy times seven in one day. (A fragment quoted by JEROME, *C. Pesl.*, III, 2.)

the graves were opened, and the dead that were in them arose.[1]

Luke dramatizes the dispute about precedence by placing it during the Last Supper (xxii. 24–30), whereas in Mark (x. 42–45) and in Matthew (xx. 25–28) it is an isolated incident.

We see sometimes how a saying serves as the point of departure for the construction of a story. Thus Luke (xxii. 27) reports the saying on service by placing it in the setting of a meal; this was not the case in Mark (x. 44) and Matthew (xx. 27). John goes further still, and transforms the saying into a gesture. Jesus takes upon himself the office of a servant by washing the feet of his disciples (John xiii. 4–11).

As the tradition developed it emphasized increasingly the importance of the teaching of Jesus. This was achieved in many ways; for example, by detaching certain sayings from the particular circumstances which had suggested them. The saying on divorce which in Mark (x. 11–12) and in Matthew (xix. 9) is a reply to the question: "What are the reasons which justify a man in repudiating his wife?" in the Sermon on the Mount (Matt. v. 32; Luke xvi. 18) has become a general axiom. The Lord's Prayer, which in Luke (xi. 1–4) is the response of Jesus to his disciples to their request for teaching on prayer, becomes a theoretical subject in Matthew (vi. 9–13).

Many of the modifications which we can discover are connected with the development of Christological ideas.[2]

In the conclusion of the story of Jesus walking upon the water Mark has: "and they were sore amazed in themselves beyond measure and wondered. For they considered not the miracle of the loaves, for their heart was hardened" (vi. 51–52). Matthew here introduces a definite Messianic confession: "Then they that were in the ship came and worshipped him, saying, Of a truth thou art the Son of God" (xiv. 33).

[1] It is by a development of the same kind that the Gospel of the Nazarenes (according to JEROME, *Ep.*, 120, 8 *ad Hedibiam*; in Matt. xxvii. 51) says that the *superliminare* (i.e. the lintel of the door) of the Temple, which was *mirae magnitudinis*, was broken.

[2] The most typical instance is that of the development of the account of the Baptism of Jesus. We have studied it in detail elsewhere (*Jean-Baptiste*, pp. 142 ff.).

In the story of the stilling of the storm the cry of distress which Mark reports: "Master! carest thou not that we perish?" (iv. 38) is changed by Matthew into a cry for help: "Lord! save us! we perish!" (viii. 25).

Mark's story contains many touches which attribute human emotion to Jesus. These are usually omitted by Matthew and Luke, as though their aim were to represent Jesus as always divinely serene and unmoved. In the story of the healing of the man with the withered hand Mark has this touch: "And when he had looked round about on them with anger, being grieved for the hardness of their hearts, he said . . ."(iii. 5). Matthew has: "then he saith" (xii. 13) and Luke: "and looking round about upon them all, he saith . . ." (vi. 10).

Mark represents Jesus as indignant with those who hinder the mothers from bringing their children to him; his attitude towards these little ones is full of human tenderness; he takes them in his arms (x. 13–16). These two features are absent from the record of Matthew and Luke.

Mark (xv. 34) and Matthew (xxvii. 46), place a cry of despair in the mouth of Jesus at the moment of death: "My God! My God! Why hast Thou forsaken Me?" Luke (xxiii. 46) replaces this with a word of confidence: "Father, into Thy hands I commend my spirit," and John by a word which may be interpreted as a cry of victory: "It is finished!"[1] (xix. 30).

Luke evidently thinks it impossible that the prayer of Jesus in Gethsemane should have no answer, so he introduces the angel who strengthens Jesus (xxii. 43). John does not wish to believe that Jesus ever suffered the Agony in Gethsemane, and he has transposed the incident. At the moment when the Passion is about to begin, Jesus says: "Now is my soul troubled, and what shall I say: 'Father save me from this hour?' but for this cause came I unto this hour! 'Father glorify Thy Name.' Then came there a voice from

---

[1] *Τετέλεσται* might mean, it is true, "It is the end = I am dying," but, on account of xix. 28 (Jesus, seeing that all was accomplished, and that the Scripture might be fulfilled, said "I thirst"), I believe that John means *τετέλεσται* in the sense of: "The redeeming work is accomplished."

heaven[1] saying, I have both glorified it and will glorify it again." And Jesus takes care to add: "This voice came not because of me, but for your sakes" (xii. 27-30). The precise form adopted in the Synoptic Gospels for the threefold prophecy of the sufferings, death and resurrection of the Son of Man (Mark viii. 31-32, ix. 30-32, x. 32-34) is also due to the influence of Christological ideas. Luke has preserved this saying: "For as the lightning, that lighteneth out of the one part under heaven, shineth unto the other part under heaven; so shall also the Son of Man be in his day. But first must he suffer many things, and be rejected of this generation" (xvii. 24-25). This is certainly older than the triple prophecy, since, in opposition to the ideas of primitive Christianity, suffering and rejection are mentioned, but not death, and there is no hint of the idea of resurrection.

The heightened emphasis upon the miraculous element, which is one of the most striking points in the development of the Gospel tradition, is a rather special form of the influence of Christological ideas.

Certain features which seem to indicate a limitation of the miraculous power of Jesus have been omitted. Thus Luke alone says at the beginning of the story of the healing of the paralytic: "The power of the Lord was present to heal" (v. 17), which implies that there were moments when Jesus was without this help.

The episode of Jesus at Nazareth terminates in Mark (vi. 5-6) with a phrase whose confused construction and fundamental inconsistency show that it contains an overloaded text: Καὶ οὐκ ἐδύνατο ἐκεῖ ποιῆσαι οὐδεμίαν δύναμιν, εἰ μὴ ὀλίγοις ἀρρώστοις ἐπιθεὶς τὰς χεῖρας ἐθεράπευσεν. Καὶ ἐθαύμασεν διὰ τὴν ἀπιστίαν αὐτῶν, that is to say, translating word for word: "and he could there do no miracle, save that having laid his hands on a few sick folk, he healed them; and he was amazed at their unbelief." In the parallel passage, Matthew has (xiii. 58): Καὶ οὐκ ἐποίησεν δυνάμεις πολλὰς διὰ τὴν ἀπιστίαν αὐτῶν, "and he could not work many miracles there because of their unbelief." The comparison between these two passages allows us to con-jecture that in its primitive form the episode may have con-

    [1] This is the incident of the angel in Luke in another form.

cluded thus: Καὶ οὐκ ἐδύνατο ἐκεῖ ποιῆσαι οὐδεμίαν δύναμιν διὰ τὴν ἀπιστίαν αὐτων, "and he could do no miracle there because of their unbelief." But to Mark, as to Matthew, it seemed impossible to imagine that Jesus was ever in a position in which it was impossible to work a miracle. Mark has introduced some incidents of healings due to the laying on of his hands, and, as the words διὰ τήν ἀπιστίαν "because of their unbelief" seemed to have no connexion with the rest of the passage, he has introduced, rather awkwardly, the words καὶ ἐθαύμασεν "and he was amazed." Matthew went further and confined himself to saying that Jesus did not work many miracles there, which implies that this was not because he could not, but because he judged it wiser not to do so.[1]

The story of the daughter of Jairus allows us to see the complete development of a story of this kind. In Mark, Jairus says to Jesus that his daughter is at the point of death (v. 23). While he is on the way to the house word is brought that she has died (v. 35). Jesus therefore did not set out in order to raise her from the dead. In Matthew (ix. 18) and Luke (viii. 42) the little girl has died when the father comes to ask for the help of Jesus, but this feature in the story cannot be primitive, since, in viii. 49 Luke says that while Jesus is on the road, the announcement is brought that she is dead.

It has often been noted that two accounts of healings in Mark have not been repeated in Matthew or Luke. These are the healing of a deaf-mute (vii. 31–37) and that of the blind man at Bethsaida (viii. 22–26). These two healings are highly specialized in character. Jesus does not act by words but by gestures, and there is something slow and laborious about them. It seems likely that because they were not in agreement with the idea of the direct and immediate power of the word of Jesus that the later evangelists left them out.

The conviction of the Christians that Jesus was the Messiah led them to conceive his history in terms of the fulfilment of prophecy and to search the Old Testament for all that could confirm this conviction and illustrate the connexion between the words of prophecy and the Gospel story. In several instances details have been introduced in order to show this agreement.

[1] MAURICE GOGUEL: Le rejet de Jésus à Nazareth, Z.N.T.W., XII, 1911, pp. 321–324.

We are here confronted with a fact which needs to be examined, and, owing to the arguments which have been founded on this fact by certain modern mythologues we must try to estimate its significance.[1]

In a number of incidents the agreement between the Gospel record and prophecy was only recognized later, at a stage which was clearly secondary in the development of the Christian tradition. Matthew in particular was very fond of discovering prophecies which anticipate the story of Jesus, and in a number of incidents he introduces quotations from the Old Testament where there are none in the parallel stories in Mark or Luke (for example: viii. 16–17, xii. 15–21, xiii. 10–15, 34, 35).

Above all, it was felt to be most important that in the story of the Passion there should be clear evidence of the fulfilment of prophecy. This testimony was discovered mainly in the Psalms, especially in the twenty-second Psalm. This Psalm describes the position of a just man, surrounded by enemies and cruelly ill-treated, who places all his trust in God. The Christians who read the Old Testament with the conviction that in it the story of Jesus was foreshadowed were not slow to recognize that what was said here could be applied with great force to Jesus, and they laid great stress on this coincidence, which, in their eyes, was providential.[2]

As the agreement between prophecy and history was only perceived later on, speaking generally, it was only gradually made more definite, and there are some cases in which it is possible to follow the progress of the process of assimilation, and to see how the agreement between prophecy and history, which had not been noticed originally, was gradually evolved by the addition of certain details, and, finally, emphasized and clinched by a quotation. A typical instance occurs in the

---

[1] On this point see *J. de N.*, pp. 196 ff. For the subject as a whole cf. F. NICOLARDOT: *Les procédés de rédaction des trois premiers évangélistes*, Paris, 1908, pp. 26–39. K. FEIGEL: *Der Einfluss des Weissagungsbeweises und anderer Motive auf die Leidensgeschichte*, Tübingen, 1910. K. WEIDEL: *Studien über den Einfluss des Weissagungsbeweises auf die evangelische Geschichte*, St. u. Kr, 1910, pp. 1–62, 163–194; 1912, pp. 169–286.

[2] They might equally well have quoted the passage in Plato (*Rep.*, pp. 362 ff.), where the just man is persecuted, ill-treated, and finally crucified, if they had known of it, and if the works of Plato had had the same value for them as the Old Testament.

case of the division of the garments of Jesus after he was crucified.[1] Here is another instance. Mark (xiv. 10–11) relates how Judas betrayed Jesus for money; Matthew, who had searched the Old Testament with great care for passages which would seem to be foreshadowings of the Gospel story, found these words in Zechariah xi. 12–13: "And I said unto them, If ye think good, give me my price; and if not, forbear. So they weighed for my price thirty pieces of silver. And the Lord said unto me, Cast it unto the potter: a goodly price that I was prised at of them. And I took the thirty pieces of silver, and cast them to the potter in the house of the Lord." In this passage, which he combines with a passage from Jeremiah which deals with the sale of a potter's field (xxxii. 6–15) Matthew sees a definite statement of the treachery of Judas, and he says decidedly (xxvi. 15) that the traitor had received thirty pieces of silver from the Sanhedrin, and tells how, after Jesus had been sentenced to death, Judas, full of remorse, took this money, and since the priests refused to take it back, he threw it down in the Temple. It was the price of blood, therefore it could not be placed in the sacred treasury. So it was decided to use it to buy the potter's field for the burial of strangers. And Matthew concludes his narrative thus: "Then was fulfilled that which was spoken by Jeremy the prophet,[2] saying, And they took the thirty pieces of silver, the price of him that was valued, whom they of the children of Israel did value; and gave them for the potter's field, as the Lord appointed me" (xxvii. 3–10).

On the other hand, there are instances where the details of the Gospel story have been actually created under the influence of prophecy.

The idea of the Virgin Birth, for instance, which we find in Matthew, arose, in part, from a passage in Isaiah vii. 14 (in the rendering of the Septuagint): "A virgin shall conceive and bear a son."[3]

The passage in Micah (v. 1) which says that the Messiah

[1] See pp. 536 ff.
[2] Actually the quotation which he makes is a combination of Jer. ii. 6–15 with Zech. xi. 12–13.
[3] This passage is quoted in Matt. i. 22. The Hebrew passage does not speak of a virgin but of a young woman. It does not refer to the Messiah.

will be born in Bethlehem of Judaea, has led to this result:
both Matthew and Luke, from differing points of view, which
cannot be reconciled with one another, have represented the
birth of Jesus as having taken place at Bethlehem (Matt. ii.
1–23; Luke ii. 1–39), whereas the primitive tradition represented him as a Galilean who came from Nazareth.

Sometimes the exegesis of prophecy has only caused the
modification of the additon of a detail. Thus Matthew (xxi.
15–17) relates how after the Cleansing of the Temple Jesus
welcomed an outburst of praise from some children. This
feature in the story was suggested by verse 3 in Psalm viii.:
"Out of the mouth of babes and sucklings hast thou ordained
strength," a verse which Matthew quotes.

The account of the mockery of Jesus on the Cross by the
passers-by (Mark xv. 29 ff.; Matt. xxvii. 39 ff.; Luke xxiii.
36–37) in its use of certain words[1] betrays the influence of
Psalm xxii. 8, and Matthew (xxvii. 43) has laid stress on this
element by introducing these words, which recall verse 9
of the same Psalm: "He trusted in God; let Him deliver
him now, if He will have him: for he said, I am the Son
of God."

We must, however, guard against the temptation of rushing
to a hasty conclusion in this matter, for there are instances in
which the influence of prophecy is not exerted on the narrative
but on the very gesture and words of Jesus himself. When we
remember that his mind was steeped in the language and
thought of the Old Testament, especially the Prophets and the
Psalms, and that he was full of the consciousness of being the
Messiah, it is not surprising that he should be inspired by
the Messianic programme which the Old Testament contains.
This may be the origin of the entry of Jesus into Jerusalem
(Mark xi. 1–10*) which he arranges in such a way that it
becomes the fulfilment of a prophecy of Zechariah (ix. 9).
Daniel vii. 13 seems to have served as a direct inspiration to
Jesus in his answer to the adjuration of the High Priest
(Mark xiv. 62*), and the only word from the Cross which
can be regarded as authentic consists of a verse from Psalm xxii.
(Mark xv. 34*).[2]

[1] Κινοῦντες τὰς κεφαλὰς (Mark xv. 29; Matt. xxvii. 39).
[2] On this point see Chapter XX.

When we compare the four Gospels with one another we perceive how, little by little, they were gradually adapted to the theological and ecclesiastical ideas of the Early Church, and the needs of its apologetic.

In the declaration of Jesus before the Sanhedrin, in place of the idea of a return upon the clouds of heaven, which occurs in Mark (xiv. 62) and Matthew (xxvi. 64), Luke (xxii. 69), writing at a moment when the expectation of the *parousia* was already fading, substitutes the idea of Jesus seated on the right hand of God, that is to say, the idea of the glorified Christ.

The alteration in the language of the announcement of the resurrection is quite typical. We know from Paul (1 Cor. xv. 4) that the phrase "rose on the third day" became a settled formula at a very early date. Thrice Mark uses a formula which was older still: "after three days" (viii. 31; ix. 31; x. 34), this might very well have meant originally "after a brief delay," though this rendering is not an equivalent. Matthew confirms this suggestion in the comment on Jonah: "For as Jonas was three days and three nights in the whale's belly, so shall the Son of Man be three days and three nights in the heart of the earth" (xii. 40). Matthew and Luke, reproducing the prophecy of the sufferings and the resurrection, substitute regularly "the third day" for "after three days," thus placing the prophecy of Jesus in harmony with the formula in which the faith of the Church had fixed it.[1]

The influence of the cultus is the explanation of the fact that in relating the Christian Eucharist to the Jewish Passover Feast, in spite of the most ancient tradition, the death of Jesus was said to have taken place on the fifteenth day of Nisan instead of on the fourteenth.[2]

The influence of apologetic has been very strong, especially on the accounts of the Passion and the Resurrection.[3] The

[1] However, in xxvii. 63, Matthew has the formula: "after three days."
[2] See Chapter XV.
[3] See on this point the suggestive studies of BALDENSPERGER: *Urchristliche Apologetik. Die aelteste Auferstehungskontroverse*, Strasbourg, 1909. *L'Apologétique et la primitive Église, et son influence sur la tradition des origines et du ministère galiléen de Jésus, Revue de Théologie et de Philosophie*, 1920, pp. 1–39.

difficulty which was created for the Christian missionary by the fact that Jesus had been condemned by a Roman judge— this Jesus whom the Christians represented as the Messenger of God—is shown by the way in which they try to modify or even omit all the elements in the story of the Passion which confuse this issue; this has caused a recasting of the whole story of the Passion, and has made Pilate a witness to the innocence of Jesus. So far as the accounts of the Resurrection are concerned, let us confine our attention to the instance of the guard placed at the door of the sepulchre (Matt. xxvii. 62–66; xxviii. 11–15), which is a characteristic example of an incident created by the imagination, certainly in all good faith, in order to reply to an objection raised by the Jews.

In the development of the Gospel tradition we note a very distinct tendency, if not to glorify the apostles, at least to eliminate or modify features in the story which show them in an unfavourable light. This tendency is closely connected with the part which they played in the development of the Church. For instance, where Mark, at the conclusion of the incident of Jesus walking on the water, speaks merely of a sort of stupor which possessed the disciples (vi. 51–52), Matthew (xiv. 33) says that they fell down before Jesus and declared that he was truly the Son of God.

After the conversation about the leaven of the Pharisees, where, according to Mark, Jesus asks his disciples: "How is that ye do not understand?" (Mark viii. 21) Matthew (xvi. 12) has: "Then they understood."

Luke does not repeat the reproaches which Jesus addressed to Peter when he protested against Jesus' prophecy of his sufferings, according to Mark (viii. 32–33) and Matthew (xvi. 22–23).

The request for the highest places in the Kingdom attributed by Mark to the sons of Zebedee (x. 35) is attributed by Matthew (xx. 20) to their mother, and entirely omitted by Luke.[1]

Tradition then is not merely an energy of passive preservation,

[1] It would be easy to show, especially by a study of the variants in the text of the Gospels, that similar phenomena were current throughout primitive Christianity.

it is something living; and it is of the essence of life to develop, to change, to adapt itself to varying situations.

The bearers of the tradition were men who were entirely free from all concern with or interest in questions of history or biography in the usual sense of the word; their whole habit of mind, the whole tendency of their interests and of their mentality, made them quite indifferent to the idea of historical accuracy, and very little able to judge on this point; the facts did not interest them so much as facts but as the revelation of a transcendent reality; hence we ought not to be surprised that, to some extent, tradition worked over and altered the material with which it had to deal. On the contrary, what might well surprise us is the fact that the Christian tradition did not subject the material to a more thorough transformation, by replacing the Gospel story with a myth which would have been an interpretation and explanation of the Christian faith at once more homogeneous, more direct, and more integral.

III. The Value Attached to the Tradition Concerning the Life of Jesus in Primitive Christianity

Primitive Christianity did not feel that it was directly connected with the earthly life of Jesus. The object of its faith and of its worship was not Jesus but the Christ. The first Christians were indifferent to the facts in the life of Jesus. Even if they were not quite so detached as the Apostle Paul proclaims himself to be, with a sort of sublime indifference, they too were not concerned to "know Christ after the flesh" (2 Cor. v. 16). It was enough for them to know Christ according to the spirit, and above all to wait for the Lord who was to return in glory. The faith of the primitive Church was not based upon the life of Jesus in which the Messiahship is represented so discreetly that it almost seems as though Jesus had hidden it intentionally. Primitive Christianity was based upon the Resurrection, through which the Messianic nature of Jesus had been manifested, while waiting for it to be victoriously proclaimed and imposed upon all by the *parousia*. Thus the gaze of the faithful was not directed to a figure in the past but towards the Lord whose glorious manifestation they expected in the future.

This explains why it was that for so long, during one or perhaps even two generations, people were satisfied to preserve fragmentary recollections of Jesus. The need for a connected account was not felt until the moment when, as the expectation of the speedy return of the Lord began to weaken, more and more importance began to be attached to the Messianic element in the life of Jesus.

The appearance of the Gospel of Mark was due to this transformation in Christianity, or, if this term seems too strong, to the displacement of its centre of gravity. People then felt the need to gather the traditions which related to the earthly life of Jesus into a unity, within a fixed framework, and to give to them both the coherence of a connected story and the character of a systematic explanation of the Messiahship of Jesus, and thus, indirectly, of Christianity itself. But this explanation was regarded from the transcendental point of view, not merely as immanent in history. This is why people were satisfied with an adaptation of the tradition and did not feel it necessary to recast and transform it entirely.

IV. CONCLUSION

The development of the tradition was neither casual nor accidental, and it was not determined merely by the play of imagination and by the carelessness with which the stories of the Gospel have been reproduced. It is the result of changes due to forces inherent in the tradition itself, which were operative long before the earliest Gospel had been compiled. From the very moment of the death of Jesus people were persuaded that he had worked an enormous number of miracles, and that he had lived, not as a human being, subject to the ordinary emotions and passions of men, but as a divine being.

When the mathematicians have determined by their calculations a certain number of points to a curve, they make what they call an extrapolation, that is to say, they prolong the line both before and behind. Can we do the same, and, after having admitted the character of the line which tradition has followed from Mark to John and even to the apocryphal accounts, try to reconstruct its evolution in the period for which the direct documents are of no avail? The idea is certainly attractive.

Admitting, for instance, that tradition has always tended to emphasize the miraculous element, we might ask whether the incident of Jesus walking on the water (Mark vi. 45–52) may not be the transformation of a quite natural incident? Is it possible that something like this took place: Jesus arrives with his disciples at a place of meeting agreed beforehand, and suddenly appears to them there when they thought he was still on the other side of the lake?[1]

But we cannot always argue like this. Though tradition may have intensified the miraculous element in the story of Jesus, it is not legitimate to jump to the conclusion that it introduced this element, and that it was not there originally as the explanation given by the first witnesses of facts, which, from the point of view which concerns us here, may or may not have been actually miraculous; this does not really matter greatly. In other words, because tradition may have increased the number of miracles in the Gospel story we have no right to conclude that at some particular time it contained none.

We might make similar remarks on many other points. Tradition, for example, has diminished or omitted all that was unfavourable to the apostles. It would be absurd to suppose that at the very beginning the record represented them as men without intelligence or character, understanding nothing of the aims and the thought of Jesus and having no real attachment to him at all.

The causes which determined these changes in the Gospel tradition are not those which determine its genesis.

It is therefore out of the question to attempt to reach the original reality, or at least the most ancient form of the tradition of the Gospel, by prolonging backwards the lines of which the comparison of the different accounts which we possess allows us to recognize some points. The creation and the transformation of a tradition are two quite different things, and, on the other hand, we have no proof that the development of the tradition has always taken place in the same direction.[2]

---

[1] This interpretation is given by JOHANNES WEISS: *Aelt. Ev.*, p. 221.

[2] The account of the baptism of Jesus is a typical example. It is based on a real fact, and has been constructed to explain the origin of the Messiahship of Jesus: Jesus is Messiah because at the moment of his baptism God anointed him with His Spirit, and adopted him as His Son (Mark). Matthew

It will never be possible to reconstruct the story otherwise than in a fragmentary and conjectural manner, and thus to resolve the problem of the life of Jesus. The principle laid down by the *traditionsgeschichtliche Schule* : that the Gospel stories ought to be considered from the point of view of the history of the tradition, is legitimate and necessary. By itself, however, it is inadequate.

immediately transforms the story by reducing it simply to the proclamation of his Messiahship, then John left it out altogether because it was incompatible with his Christological ideas. See on this point *Jean-Baptiste*, pp. 244 ff.

CHAPTER VI

PROBLEMS AND METHOD

I. HISTORY OR MYTH?

WAS Jesus a real person of flesh and blood, who lived in a particular place on this earth, and at a particular moment in time? Or is he a purely spiritual being, a symbol in which a group of men has expressed its aspirations and its dreams and translated its spiritual experiences, a myth by which a religious community has expressed its worship? This is the question with regard to which it is absolutely necessary to take up a position before we can determine in what way we are to interpret the Gospel records.

Many of the observations made in the preceding chapters, those, for instance, which deal with the Pauline testimony of Jesus, have already forced us to consider Jesus as a real person. Although the non-Christian evidence for Jesus is evidently not sufficient to enable us to construct the story of his life, if Jesus had never existed, evidence which is independent of the Christian tradition, like that of Josephus and Tacitus, would be impossible to explain.

The Talmudic tradition is important for this reason: it proves that the Jews, who bitterly opposed the Christians, never dreamed of arguing about the reality upon which their faith was based. The same remark may be made about the pagan opponents of Christianity, like Julian the Apostate, Celsus, or Porphyry,[1] who, although they borrowed a great deal of

---

[1] Of their works all that has been preserved is *De morte Peregrini* of LUCIAN, but we possess large extracts of the *True Discourse* by CELSUS (composed towards 180) in the *Contra Celsum* of ORIGEN, written towards 248 (cf. *Celsi ΑΛΗΘΗΣ ΛΟΓΟΣ excussit et restituere conatus est*, DR. OTTO GLÖCKNER, Bonn, 1924). On Celsus and his refutation by Origen we may consult among others, NEUMANN: art. *Celsus, R.E.*, III, pp. 772–775. DE FAYE: *Origène, sa vie, son œuvre, sa pensée*, I, Paris, 1923, pp. 138 ff. We know the arguments used by the unknown philosopher and by Porphyry (233–304) through the refutation of Macarius of Magnesia (towards 410), that of Julian the Apostate (331–363), through the refutation of Cyril of

material from the anti-Christian Jewish polemic,[1] never cast the slightest doubt on the reality of the Gospel story, but confined themselves to giving an interpretation which eliminated its miraculous and supernatural element. All that we know directly of this controversy does not go back, it is true, further than the second century, that is to say, it dates from a time when the Gospel tradition was already fixed, and when an enemy of Christianity could no longer have an exact idea of the conditions in which it first arose. But Christianity met with opposition from its very birth, especially from the man who was afterwards to be known as the Apostle Paul. How could the early enemies of the Church have possibly neglected to use an argument which would have utterly destroyed their claims if, in the eyes of all Jerusalem, it could have been proved that the story upon which their message was based was merely a fabrication? How was it that, if such an argument had been available, the controversialists of the second century did not take it up? and if it had been well founded, how is it that the Christians were able to refute it so completely that to-day not a trace of the controversy remains?

But on this point we are not reduced to conjectures, however well founded they may be. We know from the fragment of Thallus preserved by Julius Africanus that as early as the middle of the first century an enemy of Christianity did not deny the truth of what the Christians said about the darkness which accompanied the death of Jesus, but only argued that it was a natural phenomenon.

On the other hand, although controversial considerations had a strong influence on the development of the Christian tradition, we find nothing in the Gospels which suggests that directly or indirectly any argument had been advanced against the reality and historicity of the person of Jesus. In the stories of the appearances of the Risen Lord there are touches which

Alexandria. To this we must add the remark that the various apologies of the second century, those of Justin Martyr, Tatian, Aristides, Athenagoras, give us a very clear idea of the objections which the pagans brought against Christianity at that date.

[1] We know the anti-Christian Jewish controversy through the *Dialogue with the Jew Tryphon* by JUSTIN. The close relation between the Jewish and the pagan polemic has been made clear by W. BAUER, *L.J. nt. Ap.*, p. 454.

deliberately accentuate the material nature of his body; no evangelist ever felt the same need to prove the material nature of the body of Jesus during his active ministry.

The same remarks apply to the interpretation of the Passion given by certain Docetists. From the very beginning two statements existed side by side: Jesus is man and he is divine. This raised a problem which gave birth to the most varied theories until the moment when the orthodox doctrine was established. There were those which sacrificed one of the terms involved either by making Christ a simple human being, who was exalted to heaven after his resurrection, or by reducing the human element to such a point that it became a mere semblance. The latter was the doctrine of the Docetists of the second century, that of Cerinthus (if Cerinthus is not a purely legendary figure), in any case that of Marcion, of Basilides, and of the group whose ideas are reflected in the *Acta Johannis.* Basilides, according to Irenaeus (*Adv. Haer.*, I, 14. 4), taught that Simon of Cyrene did not merely carry the cross for Jesus but that he was miraculously substituted for him, and was crucified in his stead, bearing his likeness, while the true Jesus mingled with the crowd and smilingly watched the sufferings of his counterpart. It is evident that this is not a survival of a tradition older than the Gospel records, but simply a transposition of the material in order to reconcile the tradition, too firmly established to be denied, with the postulates of a particular form of Christology, which, by making Jesus a God only, could not admit that he had suffered or died.

May it not be, however, that the doctrine of the first century differed from that of the second? Jerome says that the blood of Christ had only just been shed in Judaea, and that the apostles were still living, when he met men who asserted that the body of Christ was merely a phantom.[1] Loisy[2] has rightly observed that in this passage, and in the context in which it occurs, there is so much hyperbole and inaccuracy that we must beware of interpreting it literally.

The Epistles of Ignatius[3] contain arguments against Docetism.

[1] *Adv. Luciferum*, 23.
[2] *De quelques arguments contre l'historicité de la passion*, R.h.l.r., 1913, p. 262.
[3] *Tral.*, 9. Cf. *Eph.* 7, 18. *Smyrn.*, 1, 2, 4. *Magn.*, 4.

The statement of Ignatius in which he asserts that "the Christ was truly born, that he ate and drank, that he was truly persecuted under Pontius Pilate, that verily he died and was verily raised from the dead," shows that the Bishop of Antioch was fighting against a Docetism which saw in the earthly life of Jesus nothing but a mere semblance. This theory was an interpretation and not a denial of the Gospel tradition. Thus, contrary to the suggestion of Salomon Reinach,[1] it was not the survival of an archaic conception which saw no value in the historic Jesus.

In order to leave no corner of this subject unexplored, we will examine the chief theories by which people have claimed that it is possible to explain the origin of Christianity other than by that of an historical Jesus.

It has been said that Christianity is a mystery religion. It is a doctrine of salvation which explains the redemption of the elect by the drama of a divine hero who dies and is raised from the dead, a drama which is both the prototype and the cause of the process through which the faithful soul must pass in order to die to things temporal and be born again unto life eternal. This being so, there is no plausible reason why we should not explain this religion just as we explain the other mystery religions which, at the time when it spread through the Hellenistic world, gathered a large number of followers into their fold. To explain the mysteries of Attis, Osiris, or Mithra, it is not necessary to suppose that Attis, Osiris, and Mithra were real persons whose story has been merely transformed into legend; there is no reason, so these critics argue, for not explaining Christianity like the other mystery religions, and hence no reason to suppose that Jesus was a real person.

This line of argument is an abuse of the process of reasoning by analogy, a form of reasoning which is only legitimate when the terms which are compared are really absolutely identical. Christianity, as it was constituted in the time of the Apostle Paul, is a mystery, in the sense that it implies a redemptive drama which is repeated symbolically for each member of the

[1] *Simon de Cyrène*, C.M.R., IV, pp. 181–188. Cf. the incisive criticism of LOISY: *R.h.l.r.*, 1913, pp. 269–270. Further on we will return to the incident of Simon of Cyrene. See pp. 530 ff.

faithful. But we do not truly define it if, taking into account the elements which it has in common with other religions, we overlook those which distinguish it from them, that is to say, the most essential elements of all. For, as Karl Holl has shown,[1] although Christianity conquered the other mystery religions with which it was in contact and came into conflict,[2] this was not due to the elements which it possessed in common with these forms of religion, but to that which distinguished it from them. Loisy, who, however, likes to use the term "Christian mystery," has rightly and justly insisted on the originality of Christianity compared with contemporary religions. "People may call Christianity a mystery religion if they wish, but it should be clearly understood that this mystery is unique in kind, and that it does not belong to the same category, that it is not of the same type as the heathen mysteries to which, however, it is compared, and from which to some extent it sprang."[3] To mention one point only, and a very important one: while the worshippers of Mithra, Attis, Osiris, or Adonis knew very well that the redemptive story of their divine hero was lost in the mists of such a fabulous antiquity that it possessed no reality, the Christians knew that their Christ had lived, not at the beginning, but at the end of time. His life, for them, belonged to recent history.

We should also note—and this is no less important—that although in one sense the story, or, if we prefer to call it so, the Gospel legend (for this name can be applied to the elaboration of the historical recollections concerning Jesus which adapted them to the needs of the Church), reflects the worship and the doctrine of the Christians, it ought not to be regarded as the product of this doctrine; it was the story which created the cultus, and not vice versa. If this were not the case we would not find these inconsistencies and this lack of connexion between the different elements in the Gospel story which modern criticism has brought to light, and which

---

[1] KARL HOLL: *Urchristentum und Religionsgeschichte, Ges. Aufs.*, II, pp. 1–32.
[2] There was no conflict between the other mystery religions. The fact that Christianity could not live in harmony with them shows that it possessed some element peculiar to itself.
[3] LOISY: *Les mystères païens et le mystère chrétien*[2], pp. 343 ff.

we shall have to mention very frequently in the following chapters. One typical instance will suffice. If there is one fact in the Gospel story which has been of capital importance for the doctrine of Christianity, it is, beyond all question, the death of Jesus. Now we shall see[1] that the story, as we have it in the Gospels, is not the unity it ought to be if it were (as the theory of non-historicity demands) a myth which had been superimposed upon the course of history. It is easy to perceive that the Gospel story arises out of the development and transformation of a tradition which was originally extremely simple, which had nothing of the cultual legend about it, since it was content to say that Pilate, after he had asked Jesus if he were the King of the Jews, gave the order that he should be crucified.

Many mythologues[2] have claimed that Christianity was merely the reappearance of an ancient Ephraimite mystery in which a solar deity is worshipped under the name of Joshua or Jesus.[3] It cannot be denied—and the New Testament confirms this in the clearest manner—that within the Christian community very early the name of Jesus came to be used as a divine name. But it was faith which made Jesus the heavenly Lord. It was the Resurrection which gave him this character.[4]

   The name of Jesus was in common use at the beginning of our era.[5] During the second and third centuries it became

[1] See Chapter XIX.
[2] ROBERTSON: *Short History*, p. 8. B. W. SMITH: *Der vorchr. Jesus*[3], p. 111. DREWS, pp. 45 ff.
[3] The two names are identical. Jesus (Jēschuā) is a shortened form of Joshua, which became current after the Exile. The LXX renders Joshua by 'Iησοῦς. In Zech. iii. 1–10 (cf. vi. 9–15) Joshua is regarded so little as the name of the Messiah, that it is the high priest Joshua who receives the promise of the coming of the Messiah.
[4] On this point see DEISSMANN: *Der Name Jesus*, in DEISSMANN and BELL: *Mysterium Christi*, Berlin, 1931, pp. 13–41.
[5] In the New Testament there are two persons bearing the name Jesus; they are Jesus-Barabbas (Matt. xxvii. 16–17, cf. p. 516, n. 1) and Jesus-Justus (Col. iv. 11), and one whose father was named Jesus, namely, the magician Bar-Jesus (Acts xiii. 6). The index of proper names in NIESE's edition of Josephus contains twenty persons bearing the name of Jesus, ten of whom lived in the first century. Let us note, in particular, among them, the Jesus, son of Ananias, who, in 62, prophesied the ruin of Jerusalem and of the Temple (JOSEPHUS, *G.J.*, VI, 5, 3, ¶¶ 300 ff.). Four high

more rare, and finally it disappeared; for reasons which are easy to understand. To the Jews it was so hateful that they would not give it to their children. The Christians, on the other hand, considered it too sacred to give to their children and felt it should be reserved for the Lord alone; it has been said that in the three passages in the New Testament which mention Jesus-Barabbas, Jesus surnamed Justus, and Bar-Jesus, a great number of scribes have either tried to alter the name of Jesus, or they have omitted it entirely[1]—the most typical instance is that which relates to Jesus-Barabbas—so utterly impossible did it seem to the Christians that the name of Jesus should be borne by others than their Lord. Among the Arabs on the contrary, where the same reasons did not exist to make them avoid the name of Jesus, the name of Isa is still fairly frequently used.

According to Christian tradition Jesus was sometimes mistaken for Elijah, for John the Baptist, or for some other ancient prophet who had reappeared on earth. It is never said that in him men saw Joshua *redivivus*. The assimilation of Jesus to Joshua is only found in passages (Barnabas, Justin, Eusebius),[2] which are certainly later than the epoch in which the historical tradition concerning Jesus arose.

B. Smith and Drews[3] appeal to the magic papyrus of the

priests bore the name of Jesus between 35 B.C. and A.D. 63 (SCHÜRER, I, pp. 216–220). Two inscriptions on graves in the neighbourhood of Jerusalem which date from the first century of our era bear the names *Jēschuā* and *Schimeon bar Jēschuā* respectively (CLERMONT-GANNEAU: *Archeological Researches*, I, pp. 437, 394). In a certain number of papyri, ostraca, and inscriptions, the name of Jesus is attested in the Diaspora of Egypt. (See the article 'Ιησοῦς in MOULTON-MILLIGAN and DEISSMANN.) One of the papyri is earlier than the Christian era (*P. Oxyr.*, 816). One of the inscriptions, that of Tell-el-Yahoudieh (funeral stele of Jesus, son of Phamis), belongs to the Augustan period (DEISSMANN, p. 21).

[1] The parallelism between Philem. 23–24 and Col. iv. 10–14, suggests that, in this Epistle, there was originally: "There salute thee Epaphras, my fellow-prisoner, Jesus surnamed Justus, Mark . . ." instead of "Epaphras, my fellow-prisoner in Christ Jesus, Mark" (ZAHN: *Einl. i. d. N.T.*, Leipzig, 1897, I, p. 319. AMLING: *Eine Konjektur im Philemonbrief*, *Z.N.T.W.*, X, 1909, pp. 261 ff. DEISSMANN, p. 31).

[2] DEISSMANN, p. 27.

[3] B. SMITH: *Der vorchristliche Jesus*, p. 37. DREWS, p. 61.

Bibliothèque Nationale, where the formula occurs: "I adjure thee by the God of the Hebrews, Jesus."[1] This papyrus, which is not earlier than the third century of our era, may very possibly reproduce a more ancient formula; nothing, however, justifies us in placing its date as far back as the mythologues would have us do. It contains a heathen formula[2] which simply proves that the name of Jesus was considered to have possessed great power, and this is sufficiently explained by the part played by exorcism in the name of Jesus in early Christianity.

It is true that, in Matt. i. 21, Joseph receives from the angel the command to give to the child who will be born of Mary the name of Jesus, "for he will save his people from their sins."[3] But this does not mean very much; it is simply one of those speculations, one might almost say one of those plays on words in connexion with proper names, which were much favoured in the ancient world, like the one we find, for instance, in the Epistle to Philemon (10–11) on the name of Onesimus.

The epithet of "Nazarene" or Nazoraean[4], still more than the name of Jesus, has been invoked by the mythologues in support of their hypothesis of a pre-Christianity. The name of Nazarene was not merely an epithet given to Jesus. It became a name for the Christians generally. Although in the West the terms "saints," "brothers," and then "Christians" were substituted for it, it still lived on in the East. No other instance is known where the followers of a religion are known by the name of the home of the founder of the religion. This argument, however, is not conclusive, for there are no absolute laws which

---

[1] Suppl. grec no 574, line 1549 ff. (K. PREISENDANZ: *Papyri graeci magici,* I, Leipzig, 1928, p. 170.)

[2] Pagan magical formulae were quite willing to use Jewish and Christian names (DEISSMANN: *Licht vom Osten*[2-3], Tübingen, 1909, p. 186), which does not prove, however, as REITZENSTEIN (*Poimandres,* Leipzig, 1904, pp. 15 ff.) suggests, that their authors really understood and knew Judaism and Christianity. DIETERICH (*Abraxas,* Leipzig, 1891, p. 203) quotes a magical passage in which Abraham, Isaac, and Jacob are taken to be names of the God of Israel.

[3] *Jesus* means, "God helps."

[4] On these two forms see later, pp. 194 ff.

determine the name given to a religion and to its followers. The special factors have to be taken into account in each case.

Salvatorelli[1] has argued that, in a number of passages where the expression "Jesus the Nazarene" occurs, the term Nazarene has only a geographical significance. When, for instance, in Mark i. 24, the demoniac says to Jesus: "What have we to do with thee, thou Jesus of Nazareth?" it looks as though the term expresses an important element in the personality of Jesus which strikes terror into the heart of the demons. "Jesus of Nazareth" seems to be the equivalent of "Jesus, Son of God Most High" which occurs in a similar passage (Mark v. 7). In Acts iii. 6; iv. 10, the formula "Jesus of Nazareth" is that by which the sick are healed and the demons expelled. The argument of Salvatorelli would have no force if we could prove that from the time of Jesus the formula "In the name of Jesus of Nazareth" was believed to have power to control the demons. Now the passages which contain it date from a time when the formulas "Jesus of Nazareth," "Jesus, Son of God Most High," "Jesus, Son of God," "Jesus Christ," "the Lord Jesus" are all equivalent and interchangeable. It would be useless to try to determine the exact significance of each of these elements, and false to hold that the simple words "In the name of Jesus," or "In the name of the Lord Jesus," were considered less efficacious than "In the name of Jesus of Nazareth." From all this we may conclude, therefore, that the phrase "of Nazareth" was simply used in order to distinguish one among the many who bore the name of Jesus.

Outside the New Testament and the Christian tradition there is no passage which states the existence in Galilee of a village called Nazareth.[2] Neither the Old Testament, nor Josephus, nor the Talmud mentions it; but we have no right to conclude from this silence, that, as Cheyne[3] thinks for instance, Nazareth is a geographical fiction. Josephus (*Vita*,

---

[1] SALVATORELLI: *Il significato di "Nazareno,"* Roma, 1911 (quoted by GUIGNEBERT: *La Vie cachée de Jésus*, Paris (1921), pp. 63 ff.).

[2] The fact that later on Nazareth became known, and that from the time of Constantine it was frequently visited by pilgrims, does not prove anything, for with holy places, as with relics, one always finds what one seeks.

[3] CHEYNE: art. *Nazareth, Enc. Bibl.*, III, cols. 3358–3362.

¶ 235) reports that in Galilee there were 204 villages and 15 fortified towns. Of these 219 localities we know very few, and, even if Josephus may have slightly exaggerated the number of places in Galilee, there is no doubt that there were many whose names were never mentioned in any record. Nazareth, a village of slight importance (cf. John i. 46) may have belonged to this section.[1]

The village of Nazareth existed, in any case at the close of the second or the beginning of the third century, and there is no indication that it was then of recent date.[2] Weinel[3] has rightly noted that those who imagined that they thought they could explain the term "of Nazareth" by a town which had never existed would have been in a very dangerous position so far as their enemies were concerned. Further, why would one have chosen as the "country" of Jesus a specifically Jewish village where, according to Epiphanius (xxx. 11) there was no church before the time of Constantine, and where Christians and Samaritans were forbidden to live? The fact that the Gospel tradition makes Jesus come from Nazareth is significant (Matt. xxi. 11; Mark i. 9; John i. 45; Acts x. 38). According to current Jewish ideas the Messiah was to be born at Bethlehem, the city of David. The traditions which are reproduced in the early chapters of Matthew and Luke are quite independent of each other. According to the first Gospel the family of Jesus, which lived at Bethlehem, after the flight into Egypt, went to Nazareth and settled there, in order to escape the hostility of Archelaus (Matt. ii. 13–23). According to the second account Jesus was born at Bethlehem during a journey which his parents had to make on the

---

[1] ED. MEYER: II, p. 423, n. 1. WELLHAUSEN (*Iraelitische und jüdische Geschichte*, Berlin, 1897, p. 266, n. 2), who concludes from a comparison of Matt. xxvi. 69 with xxvi. 71 that "Galilean" and "Nazarene" are synonymous terms, has suggested that Nazareth may have been a term applied to the whole of Galilee which recurs in the form *Gennesar* (*Garden of Nesar*) (1 Macc. xi. 67, Matt. xiv. 34, and Mark vi. 53 in D). It is an ingenious hypothesis. We hesitate, however, to accept it, for the identification which it proposes has never been proved. It has also been suggested that Nazareth may have been a district in Peraea, or it has been identified with Chorazin (CONYBEARE, BURKITT, quoted by GUIGNEBERT: *Vie cachée de Jésus*, p. 190). These suggestions are pure conjectures.

[2] Quoted by EUSEBIUS: *Eccl. Hist.*, I, 7, 14.

[3] WEINEL: *Ist das liberale Jesusbild widerlegt?* Tübingen, 1910, p. 97.

occasion of the census of Quirinius (Luke ii. 1). Both try to show that the prophecy of the birth at Bethlehem was fulfilled in the Galilean Jesus. Christian tradition would hardly have created a fact which was to cause it so much embarrassment—the fact, namely, that Jesus came from Nazareth.[1]

The problem of Nazareth is rendered more complicated by the fact that in the New Testament we find the two forms Nazarene (*Ναζαρηνός*) and Nazoraean (*Ναζωραῖος*),[2] which are not equivalent terms, since they differ not merely in termination, but also in the quantity of the second syllable. If the form Nazarene is correctly derived from Nazareth, the same cannot be said for the term Nazoraean, which must have a different meaning and a different origin.[3] The Gospel of Matthew, after having related how the parents of Jesus went to Nazareth in Galilee and settled down there, says: "that it might be fulfilled which was spoken by the prophets, He shall be called a Nazarene"[4] (ii. 23). The passage in Isa. xi. 1, to which many exegetes[5] have thought that Matthew was alluding, and in which the Messiah is called *Netzer* (Rod of Jesse), scarcely explains this passage. Nor can we seek an explanation in the idea of the Naziriteship, for Christian tradition has kept a very clear recollection that Jesus was not

---

[1] John vii. 41 shows that the Galilean origin of Jesus was an objection raised by the Jews against his Messiahship.

[2] The form *Ναζαρηνός* is found in Mark i. 24, x. 47, xiv. 67, xvi. 6; Luke iv. 34, xxiv. 19. The form *Ναζωραῖος* in Mark ii. 23, xvi. 71; Luke xviii. 37; John xviii. 5–7, xix. 19; Acts ii. 22, iii. 4, iv. 10, vi. 14, xxii. 8, xxiv. 5, xxvi. 9. There is a certain fluctuation in the manuscripts; thus *Ναζωραῖος* is found in Mark x. 47, in ‎א A. C., in Luke xxiv. 19, in A. D. N. The form *Ναζαρηνός* in Luke xviii. 27 and in John xviii. 5, in D. The dual form is, however, certain, and the evidence in Acts shows that the form *Ναζωραῖος* prevailed. Alongside of the form Nazareth, we find in the New Testament the forms Nazara, Nazarat, Nazaret, etc. The forms vary a good deal, and even in the most ancient MSS. there is no uniformity in the spelling.

[3] MARK LIDZBARDSKI: *Mandäische Liturgien*, Berlin, 1920, pp. xvi ff. *Nazoraios, Z. f. Semitistik*, 1922, pp. 230–233. GINZA: *Der Schatz oder das grosse Buch der Mandäer übersetzt und erklärt*, Göttingen, Leipzig, 1925, pp. ix. ff. ZIMMERN: *Nazoräer-Nazarener, Z. d. deutsch. morgenl. Ges.*, 1920, pp. 429–438, *id.*; 1922, pp. 45 ff.

[4] (Or, as some render it: a *Nazoraean*).—TRANSLATOR.

[5] For example, H. J. HOLTZMANN: *Die Synoptiker*[3], Leipzig, 1901, p. 194. F. NICOLARDOT: *Les procédés de rédaction des trois premiers évangélistes*, p. 31.

an ascetic of the type of John the Baptist (Mark ii. 18–20*; Matt. xi. 18–19*).

Others, like Guignebert[1] point to the passage in Deut. xxxiii. 16, where the dying Moses says: "the goodwill of him that dwelt in the bush: let the blessing come upon the head of Joseph, and upon the top of the head of him who was separated from his brethren."[2] This explanation is not tenable unless we can admit, as has been suggested, that the name Ναζωραῖος is related to the Syriac *naçōrā*, which means prophet, singer of hymns, and that it is a name which was invented in order to glorify Jesus; in any case this hypothesis cannot be accepted as the primitive meaning of the epithet since it was first used by the enemies of Jesus.

Others again, like Loisy,[3] point to Judges xiii. 5 (LXX), where it is said of Samson "he shall be a Nazirite unto the Lord." The idea of consecration to God is also implied in the term "saints," which was one of the most ancient terms used to describe Christians. Salvatorelli has suggested that possibly, in the time of Jesus, the Nazirites formed a group in which the Messianic Hope was strong, and that both John the Baptist and Jesus may have originally belonged to this community. In Hellenic circles, the term Nazirite would be replaced by the word "saint," which was easier to understand. In the East, however, it would still be used. For several reasons I find it impossible to accept this hypothesis. The first is this: the word Nazirite might have given birth to a word like *Naziraios*, but not to *Nazôraios*, and still less to *Nazarènos*. Further, we have no evidence that the Naziriteship was still in existence at the time of Jesus in the form in which it is described in the classic passages in the Old Testament.[4] Nor is it proved that there was any connexion between the Naziriteship and Messianism. Finally, and this is still more

---

[1] GUIGNEBERT: *Vie cachée de Jésus*, p. 183.

[2] Literally the crown. Heb. *nazir*, LXX: Δοξασθείς; Vulg.: *Nazoraei*.

[3] LOISY: *Syn.*, I, p. 376. This is also the theory of SALVATORELLI, *op. cit.*

[4] The accounts which relate to John the Baptist and to James are suspect because they betray the direct influence of passages of the Old Testament. Those which relate to a vow of the apostle Paul or more probably of Aquila, at Cenchrea (Acts xviii. 18), or to the four men who had made a vow whom Paul joins at Jerusalem (Acts xxi. 23), do not refer to the life-long Naziriteship.

important, on those who witnessed his life Jesus produced an impression entirely different from that of an ascetic; indeed, his enemies said that "he came eating and drinking."

Strack-Billerbeck[1] have shown that the idea that the same prophecy may be uttered in different terms by various prophets frequently occurs in the Talmud, and they emphasize the fact that in Matt. ii. 23 the expression used is not, "by the prophet," but "by the prophets." They are thinking not only of Isa. xi. 1, where the Messiah is called *Netzer*, but of the idea of the Messiah as a "shoot" (*tsemach*), which is found in Jer. xxiii. 5, xxxiii. 15, and in Zech. iii. 9, vi. 12; all these references are to passages to which the synagogue had given a Messianic interpretation. It does, however, seem strange that Matthew, who loves to adorn his narrative with quotations from the Old Testament, should not have quoted any passage in this connexion. The connexion between it or the passages of which he might be thinking and the epithet of *Nazarene* cannot be very direct. Under these conditions it may be that it was the term *Nazarene* which suggested the allusion to a prophecy, perhaps intentionally vague.

The explanation of the word Nazarene must therefore be sought outside the pages of the Old Testament.

The Mandaeans, who, on very doubtful grounds,[2] claim that they are spiritual descendants of John the Baptist, call themselves Naṣaraeans. From this we may conjecture that the followers of John the Baptist were called by this name,[3] and, since Jesus began his ministry in connexion with them, he may have been called a Nazarene by his enemies who thus wished to describe him as a renegade from the community of the followers of John. This would also explain why the Christians were called Nazoraeans, or Nazarenes, although it might have seemed unnatural to call them after Nazareth simply because their master originally belonged to this village.[4]

[1] STRACK-BILLERBECK: I, p. 92.

[2] On this point see the remarks in my *Jean-Baptiste*, pp. 113 ff.

[3] It does not much matter what was the real origin of this term, which we might be tempted to attach to the idea of the Naziriteship.

[4] WETTER: *L'arrière-plan historique du christianisme primitif*, *R.h.p.r.*, II, 1922, p. 115. WELLHAUSEN: *Mt.*, p. 142. SCHWEN: *Nazareth und Nazoräer*, *Z.f.wis. Th.*, 1912, p. 37, has noted other cases where two independent sects have

The hypothesis according to which the term Nazoraean was applied originally to the disciples of John the Baptist, is, in any case, more plausible than that of B. W. Smith,[1] who, starting from the root NSR, which means "protector" or "guardian,"[2] suggests that there may have been a pre-Christian sect called Nazoraeans; the proofs by which he tries to justify this thesis are absolutely inconsistent.[3] There is first of all the Hymn of the Naassenes,[4] which might be taken as evidence for a celestial Jesus, but there is nothing which would justify us in regarding this passage as belonging to the pre-Christian era. The Naassene doctrine shows unmistakable traces of the influence of Christian ideas.[5] As for the hymn itself, we cannot be certain whether it was originally placed in the mouth of Jesus. The text of the formula of introduction, "Then Jesus said," is not certain, and noting that at the beginning of the hymn, the first hypostasis is stated to be *Nous* with Chaos and the soul to be saved alongside of it, Bousset has suggested the very probable hypothesis that instead of $Εἶπεν$ $δέ$ $Ιησους$ the original reading was: $Εἶπεν$ $δέ$ $ὁ$ $Νοῦς$. Among the Jewish heresies Epiphanius mentions (*Haer.*, 18) a sect of the Nazoraeans. As he gives no hint that this sect was in any way connected with Christianity or was a Judaeo-Christian sect, B. Smith[6] regards it as pre-Christian, and

borne the same name. In the days of the Maccabees, the patriotic Jewish party bore the name of Chassidim. The same name was given to the partisans of the wonder-working rabbi of Poland, Baal-Schem, in the eighteenth century. The followers of Novatian on the one hand, and the Albigenses on the other, perhaps also the Essenes, according to certain authors, took the name of "Cathari" or the Pure. Two groups also bore the name of Luciferians: the followers of the anti-Arian Bishop, Lucifer of Cagliari, in the fourth century, and a medieval, antinomian sect named after Lucifer, the Prince of Darkness.

[1] B. SMITH: *Der vorch. Jesus*, pp. 36, 42 ff.

[2] This occurs sixty-three times in the Old Testament and already seven times (under the form Na-su-ru) in the Code of Hammurabi.

[3] Let us note in passing, for it is not an isolated phenomenon, that the mythologues are usually as severe in their criticism of the Christian tradition as they are lenient towards the theories which they substitute for it, and by which they try to explain the origin of Christianity.

[4] Preserved by HIPPOLYTUS: *Philosophoumena*, V, 10, 2.

[5] HILGENFELD: *Die Ketzergeschichte des Urchristentums*, Leipzig, 1884, p. 262. REITZENSTEIN: *Poimandres*, pp. 81 ff.

[6] B. SMITH: *Der vorch. Jesus*, pp. 56 f., 64.

explains the silence of other heresiologists concerning it by the fact that, less naïve or less honest than Epiphanius, they saw the danger of the existence of these pre-Christian Nazoraeans to the official doctrine of the Church.

Is this interpretation sufficient to support such a daring argument? Epiphanius was not always well informed, and he was not always judicious in the use he made of the information which was at his disposal.[1] He knew the Jewish Nazoraeans only by name. If he had known that they worshipped Jesus, he would have forthwith called them Christians. There may very well be some confusion in what he says. Schmidtke[2] has proved that all that the Fathers of the Church say about a Jewish-Christian sect of Nazarenes comes from Apollinarius of Laodicea, and the information which Ephiphanius gives about them in his chapter xxix is worthy of credence, but that what he says about the Nazoraeans[3] is simply characteristic of the Ebonites, with the specifically Christian element omitted. On this point he is depending on a list of Jewish sects in which the Christians figured under the name of "Nazarenes."[4] As Bousset rightly says, "the pre-Christian Nazoraeans of Epiphanius may be definitely relegated to the category of errors and mistakes."[5]

The men of Ephesus, who were instructed "in that which concerns Jesus," but who did not know that there was any other baptism than that of John, and who had not received the Holy Spirit (Acts xviii. 24–26, xix. 1–8)[6] may have been, according to Smith,[7] pre-Christians who knew nothing about

[1] "His criticism is not very reliable; as soon as he leaves the ground of contemporary happenings his information needs to be checked, for it is confused and inaccurate." TIXERONT: *Patrologie*, Paris, 1918, p. 253.

[2] SCHMIDTKE: *Neue Fragm. und Unters. zu den judenchrist. Evang.*

[3] He writes the name with a sigma and not with a zeta, in order to distinguish them from the Christian Nazarenes.

[4] The twelfth petition of the *Schemonè Esrè* contains this formula, in the text discovered in the *genizah* of the synagogue at Cairo: "That there may be no hope for the apostates. . . . That the Christians (*nosrim*) and the heretics (*minim*) may be suddenly destroyed. . . ." (STRACK, pp. 66 ff.).

[5] BOUSSET: *Noch einmal der vorchristliche Jesus*, T.R., 1911, p. 381.

[6] For the interpretation of these passages see my book *Jean-Baptiste*, pp. 99 ff.

[7] SMITH: *Der vorch. Jesus*, pp. 7 ff.

the earthly history of Jesus. His interpretation is based upon the idea that Christian baptism is an element which is so essential to the story of Jesus that those who did not know this baptism, could not know the Gospel story. Nevertheless the Gospel tradition has preserved the recollection that Jesus did not institute baptism, and, in spite of its eagerness to make the rites of the Church depend upon the commands of the Master, it has not attributed to the Risen Jesus more than the command to "baptize all nations" (Matt. xxviii. 19). At what moment and under what influence was the practice of baptism introduced? It is improbable that this took place in the very early days of the life of the Church, and that the observance of baptism immediately became a widespread practice in all the groups affected by Christianity. There may have been a form of preaching which was directly connected with the ministry of Jesus, and supported by personal recollections of his life, which knew no other form of baptism than that of John. The "disciples of Ephesus" are witnesses, not of a pre-Christianity which is supposed to have known nothing of an historical Jesus, but of an archaic form of Christianity, previous to the introduction, or the general and widespread practice of baptism in the Church.

Placing himself at an angle of opinion which differs entirely from all those which we have considered hitherto, Albert Bayet[1] has championed the argument in favour of the non-historicity of Jesus by a theory which is presented in the form of a syllogism: all morality which expresses the thought of a real person is coherent, and free from inconsistencies and contradictions. The ethic of the Gospel is not of this character. Therefore it is not that of an individual. But is it certain that a moralist always gives his teaching in a perfectly homogeneous form, above all when he is a man whose outlook is remote from all abstract and theoretical interests and who gives counsel and precepts adapted to particular circumstances? The character of Jesus' audiences varied a good deal, and their situations also varied; this explains why it is that the counsels which he gave not only differed at various times, but

[1] *Les morales de l'Évangile.*

that sometimes they seemed inconsistent. In moral teaching like that of Jesus, we must distinguish between the inspiration and the practical circumstances for which a practical rule is deduced from this inspiration. The diversity of circumstances and conditions affects that of the formulated precepts. Everyday experience shows that apparent neutrality may mean either hostility or friendliness. Thus one day Jesus would say, "He that is not with me is against me" (Matt. xii. 30*), while at another time, in different circumstances, he would declare that "He who is not against us is on our side" (Mark ix. 40*). Would any moralist ever find that his teaching would pass the examination to which Bayet would submit the Gospels?

At the basis of his argument there lies an error which reproduces an old theological conception; modern criticism has had a great deal of trouble to free the history of Christian origins from the idea that the identification of the morality of the Gospels and the morality of Jesus is so evident that it seems as though we were faced with this dilemma: are we to regard the Gospels as direct documents, a faithful summary of the story of Jesus, an unaltered echo of his teaching, or as legend pure and simple? From the point of view of their construction the Gospels are not a unity, and Albert Bayet has not even tried to discover whether the differing moral ideas which he thinks he can discern, even when they are contradictory, belong to the same layer of tradition.

On the preliminary question which the historians of Jesus cannot, under the present circumstances, evade—that is, is Jesus a figure in history or is he the hero of a myth?—my conclusion is quite clear. For several reasons I am obliged to admit that Jesus belongs to the realm of history. On the other hand, the study of the myth theories shows that they will not bear a close examination, and that they raise difficulties infinitely more difficult to solve than those which they claim to avoid. Without any hesitation I affirm the historical character of the person of Jesus.

II. The Historical and the Religious Problem of Jesus

The fact that Jesus lived a human life does not imply that his story can be known. Many critics at the present day—like Loisy and Bultmann, for instance—believe that all that can be known about Jesus practically amounts to nothing, yet at the same time they are very insistent that his story is no myth.

It is, however, quite clear that we cannot find, directly, a *Life of Jesus* in the Gospels; it is not even implied in the conditions from which it would be the sole business of the historian to disengage it. All that can be done is to construct something as well as one can. Is it possible thus to reconstruct the story without falling into the error of being arbitrary?

We ought not to expect the story of Jesus to give us that absolute certainty which does not belong to the realm of history, but to that of religious intuition and faith; all that is needed is to attain that degree of certainty, of probability, in our conjecture, if we prefer to put it so, to which it is possible to attain in other realms of history. When we read the statements of certain critics who are theologians rather than historians, of Bertram for example,[1] we are tempted to enquire: if we were to be as exacting about historical accuracy in other spheres as these critics claim we ought to be about the life of Jesus, how would it ever have been possible to write any history at all? and especially a history of the ancient world?[2]

There is here a dangerous confusion between two domains which ought to be kept quite distinct. The person of Jesus raises two problems, one in the realm of history and the other in the realm of religion.[3]

[1] See especially his brochure: *Neues Testament und historische Methode*, Tübingen, 1928.

[2] Eisler (I, p. xiv) sees, rightly, in this hyper-criticism (which is unknown in other domains), which is manifested at the present time in the criticism of the Gospels, a reaction against the infallibility which used to be attributed to the witness of the Bible at an earlier period.

[3] On this point see my study, *Le Jésus de l'histoire et le Christ de la foi, R.h.p.r.*, IX, 1929, pp. 115–139. English translation by C. J. Wright, in *The Modern Churchman*, XX, 1930, pp. 69–73, 156–165, 227–235.

Confronted by the fact of Jesus, our first questions should be: What was the history of this man? What were the facts of his life, his teaching, the influence which he exercised, the part which, directly or indirectly, he has played in the rise of the Christian religion? These are problems which may be compared with those which an historian who knew nothing about Islam or Buddhism would have to deal, in studying the lives of Muhammad or Buddha. These problems ought to be treated in the same spirit, without any bias at all, whether for or against Christianity, or any of its forms.

The Christian believer, however, feels that although this way of regarding the problem may be legitimate, it does not exhaust it. To him Jesus represents a spiritual and religious value. Christian thought thus regards the person of Jesus as belonging to two different categories at the same time: to the category of humanity, on account of his earthly life, his teaching, his death, and the posthumous influence which he has exerted, and to that of transcendent reality, because of what he means to the collective faith of the Church and to the personal faith of individuals.

The historical problem of Jesus is not merely a religious problem, mainly of interest to convinced Christians within the Church; it also concerns everyone who is interested in the history of the past, and who wishes to understand how the spiritual atmosphere in which he lives came into being, for if Christianity is not the only source of our culture, it is certainly one of the most important.

To all who are Christians by conviction (whether they have remained loyal to the traditional formulae or have liberated themselves from them), on the other hand, the Christ is also a theological and religious problem. This question is raised by the value which the Church attaches to him, and by the necessity of making our conception of him an integral part of a general conception. This problem can only be solved by means of a philosophical and religious conception.

The actual name of Jesus Christ symbolizes the existence of this double problem; this name is quite different from double-barrelled names like Saul-Paul or Joseph-Barnabas, which were so frequent at the beginning of the Christian era.[1] In the expression "Jesus Christ," a proper name, formerly in frequent use among the Jews, is coupled with an official title of a transcendent character.

To say that each of these two problems, belonging to two different levels, may and should be developed according to its own laws and methods may be true, but it is inadequate. There are no water-tight compartments in the human spirit. There are, doubtless, instances where we feel as though we held in our hands the two ends of a chain without seeing how they will ever meet. But this question is different, because here we are dealing with one fact alone, a fact which cannot present contradictory aspects as it is envisaged from different points of view. The time has passed when a thesis could be held to be true in theology and false in philosophy.

To make one consideration subordinate to the other is impossible, for history deals with judgments of fact, and religion and theology with value-judgments. They cannot be reduced to a single equation. A judgment of fact or of existence may remain perfectly indifferent to the consideration of value, but the opposite is not true. Every judgment value implies a judgment of fact. Religious speculation about Christ necessarily presupposes judgments of fact relative to the life of Jesus.

We ought to be able to study the historical problem of the life of Jesus with absolute philosophical and religious detachment, as Strauss believed he was able to do, thanks to the Hegelian philosophy. Is a religious detachment of this kind possible? We believe that it is, at least if we admit that the principle of all philosophy ought to be absolute respect for the truth, that is to say, not only the firm resolution to pay homage to the truth which impresses us almost involuntarily, but the resolve to seek the truth with all our might, in the realm of the facts of history as well as in every other sphere of life. If our conceptions or our philosophical or religious opinions are contradicted by the facts, the facts must not be altered or camouflaged in order to secure agreement, but our opinions must be either abandoned or corrected.

We will not demand an absolute certitude from a *Life of Jesus*.

[1] DEISSMANN: *Bibelstudien*, Marburg, 1895, pp. 181 ff.

Our ambition will be more modest. All we ask is this: is it possible to attain, in all that concerns the life of Jesus, that degree of certitude comparable to that which we are able to attain in other spheres of ancient history?

Two questions connected, but distinct, are raised at this point. Can we base our researches on solid material? And can we organize this material otherwise than in an arbitrary manner?

III. The Criticism of the Material

As we have already seen, the Gospel tradition was enlarged and altered. This was inevitable, since it was so closely mingled with the life of the groups of the first Christian believers. Thus we cannot use it for the purposes of historical criticism unless we possess a criterion which will enable us to distinguish between the primitive and the secondary elements in the narrative. Does such a criterion exist?

The problem is dominated by three facts:

(i) The material of the Gospel tradition was inserted into a general construction dominated by certain dogmatic ideas borrowed from theology and faith about the year 70;

(ii) These materials were adapted to the needs and the functions of the life of the Church;

(iii) Some forty years elapsed between the birth and the establishment of the Gospel tradition. This period of time is short if, for instance, (as is done constantly), we compare the Gospel tradition with the traditions of Genesis, but it is none the less considerable if we think of the changes which Christianity underwent during the first half-century of its existence. The evolution which the Gospel tradition underwent is the resultant of two antagonistic forces: preservation and transformation.

The critics of the nineteenth century, who were not greatly concerned with the problem of tradition, had too much confidence in a purely literary type of criticism; they were too ready to believe that the most ancient records were the most historical. To-day such an illusion is no longer possible; nevertheless literary criticism lies at the root of all historical work.

First of all it is absolutely necessary to begin with a classification of the material according to the stratum of tradition to which it belongs. In order to do this we need to take into account not only the comparison of the parallel narratives but also to make an internal analysis, consider the links in the story, and try to re-constitute the supposed situations; this procedure often shows up the artificial character of certain links in the narrative, and makes it possible to discover different sources in a section which at first sight appeared to have been written by one hand and at one time.

Likewise, it is also necessary to consider carefully the adaptation of each section, both to the general setting of the Gospel and to the particular part of the Gospel in which it is placed. Here again, the lack of coherence, the existence not only of formal contradictions, but sometimes of a simple hiatus, permits us to distinguish different sources and different traditions, that is to say, to get back to a stage earlier than the redaction of our Gospels.

The analysis of the sources, that is to say the unravelling of the different strands in the development of the tradition, is only a preliminary stage in the scientific process. When it has been accomplished we are confronted with a mass of material analysed (so far as that is possible) into the successive strata to which they belong. The next thing to be done is to estimate and establish the value of this material; we have to begin by eliminating that part of the material in which we can discover creations due to the action of those forces of which we spoke in the previous chapter on the development of the Gospel tradition. Here is a typical example: thus we would dismiss as non-historical the account given by Matthew (xxvii. 62–66) of the guard placed at the door of the sepulchre, because it is alien to the primitive tradition, and is evidently inserted in order to reply to a Jewish objection. Usually, however, the situation is not so clear. The influences to which the Gospel tradition has been exposed are so complex that, very often, they can only be discovered when a particular indication like some inconsistency or hiatus makes it possible to detect the action of the causes of alteration in the very act.

It would, however, be a dangerous illusion to imagine that

once this work of elimination has been completed we are then in possession of a tradition which is absolutely primitive, and absolutely reliable. In order to estimate the value of that which has been discovered it is absolutely necessary to use positive criteria. A Gospel incident cannot be considered authentic simply because there is no direct reason for believing it to have been created by tradition; on the contrary, we must be quite sure that there are positive reasons which make it impossible to think that it could have been created by it.

The most ancient Christian theology implies a certain conception of the Gospel history and of the teaching and work of Jesus. A rudimentary creed was composed very early, for it was formulated before the Christianity of the Jerusalem group, represented by the Twelve, and Hellenic Christianity, represented by the Apostle Paul, had been differentiated. This formula, which expresses the common basis of Christianity, is familiar to us from 1 Cor. xv. 3-4: "Christ died for our sins according to the Scriptures; and he was buried, and he rose again the third day, according to the Scriptures." As time went on, however—for instance, in the creed known as the Apostles' Creed—this formula was defined more clearly and developed; it has never been substantially modified. Hence we may lay down the principle that every incident or word which suggests different conceptions from those which we find in 1 Cor. xv. 3-4 belongs to an archaic tradition, earlier than the period which preceded the separation between the Christianity of Jerusalem and the Christianity of Paul. This takes us back so far that we have the right to say that such conceptions may be considered practically as primitive traditions. For the same reason, every time that we find, attributed to Jesus or recommended by him, an attitude which is contrary to that which is current in the very earliest form of the Church, there is room to suppose that we are in the presence of an historical fact.

Let us define more clearly how this criterion is applied. In Matt. ix. 35-x. 40, we find the instructions which Jesus gives to his disciples whom he is sending out on a mission. If there is any passage which would be likely to be changed it would be this one, for in the instructions given by Jesus the Church saw the charter of Christian missionaries, and she would naturally be tempted to adapt them to the actual situation in which the Christian mission was placed at the time of the redaction of the Logia and the Gospels. And indeed, this is what did take place. Now, Jesus says to his disciples: "Go not into the way of the Gentiles, and into any city of the Samaritans enter ye not" (x. 5). The preaching of the Gospel to the heathen and to the Samaritans is as old as the Christian mission itself; an exhortation which prohibits it cannot be a creation of the Church, but must belong to an older tradition. We have here a saying of Jesus whose authenticity is guaranteed by the fact that it is opposed to the practice of the early Christian mission.

The saying of Jesus before the Sanhedrin: "Ye shall see the Son of Man sitting on the right hand of power,[1] and coming in the clouds of heaven" (Mark xiv. 62) is authentic, because it contains no allusion to the resurrection, although primitive Christianity was only able to retain its faith in the *parousia* because it had the assurance that by his resurrection Jesus had triumphed over death.

We might make similar remarks about the statement reported in Luke xvii. 24–25: "For as the lightning, that lighteneth out of the one part under heaven, shineth unto the other part under heaven; so shall also the Son of Man be in his day. But first must he suffer many things, and be rejected of this generation." Here there is no mention either of death or of resurrection. If this were a creation of Christian tradition it would be inexplicable.

Thus, in certain cases at least, we have at our disposal a criterion which permits us to establish the authenticity of some of the sayings of Jesus. Doubtless the number of these is limited. The words of Jesus of whose authenticity we can be quite sure cannot, however, be measured in the same way. The principle which has been laid down cannot be used in the opposite sense, and we have no right to affirm that every word or saying of Jesus which is in harmony with the conceptions of the Christianity of the Apostolic age is not authentic.

The sayings of Jesus whose authenticity can be established can, in their turn, serve as a touchstone for estimating the

[1] That is, of God.

authenticity of other sayings, which are either in connexion with, or in complete harmony with them. The sayings which are admitted to be authentic become centres of crystallization, around which gather the other reliable elements of tradition.

To this criterion of the basis we may add another of form. It is not absolute, and it cannot always be used. However, its application, although a delicate matter, ought not to be neglected. The sayings of Jesus are very original in form, not at all Greek, but rather Hebrew, characterized by parable, by the use of images, and, in the aphorisms, by a construction which may appear learned, but which is quite spontaneous, and consists in a series of short statements which are repeated, urged, or contrasted. The Gospel tradition did not recognize this originality in the form of the teaching of Jesus.[1] At any rate it did not attach much importance to it, since when we compare parallel passages from the Logia we find that the original structure of the words of Jesus has often been broken and this quite as much by Matthew as by Luke. Thus it cannot have been created by tradition. This form, on the other hand, certainly belongs to a period earlier than that when the tradition was transplanted to Hellenistic soil. Now this transfer was made very early, under the influence of the missionary work of the Early Church, and in order to meet the needs of the Christian groups speaking the Greek language. Whenever we can recognize the typical form of the words of Jesus we are confronted by ancient material. The consideration of the form is not a decisive criterion, but the fact that it can create an·assumption of authenticity means that it is worth noting.

IV. The Organization of the Material

The application of the critical method may furnish some isolated fragments of material, but, properly speaking, it cannot produce a *Life of Jesus*. We may apply to history what Henri Poincaré says about science in general: "Science is composed of facts as we build a house with stones; but an

---

[1] See further on, pp. 300 ff.

accumulation of facts is no more a science than a heap of stones is a house."[1] A collection of the authentic sayings of Jesus, and a series of episodes—which are absolutely historical —in which he plays a part, do not constitute a *Life of Jesus*. After the labour of the critics, which is the indispensable basis of research, comes the work of the historian, whose aim it is to set in order the facts which have been accepted as reliable, from the threefold point of view of chronology, geography, and psychology, to link them together, and to explain one set of facts in the light of another. In other words, to use the celebrated passage in Ezekiel, it is the business of the historian to "breathe upon these dry bones that they may live."

From the very beginning research into the facts of the life of Jesus has been carried on in the critical sense, impelled by the desire to clear the ground, and to gain liberty for research. This spirit has survived, although the reasons which gave it birth no longer exist. The problem of the life of Jesus is dominated by a tradition which has behind it the privilege of a long past, the veneration of which it was the object, and the religious authority which is attributed to it. First of all it was necessary to gain full liberty of movement for the scientific spirit. This has given rise to a spirit which, if not exactly hostile, is at least suspicious of tradition, and is not favourable to historical work. The preponderance of critical and negative considerations has also been encouraged by the manner in which the problem was stated not so long ago, when the sole aim of criticism was to determine which of the four Gospels gave the account which was nearest to primitive tradition. Once this question was settled it was thought that all we had to do was to bring to the narrative which was retained the additions and alterations suggested by comparison with the other Gospels, bearing in mind, at the same time, the suggestion that in some of the narratives the imagination of the narrators, and the current ideas of their time, may have coloured their accounts of the miracles. While this method predominated, the work of the historian was reduced to something secondary; all he had to do was to comment, to illuminate, at certain points to purify, the text,

[1] HENRI POINCARÉ: *La science et l'hypothèse*, p. 168.

and to show the connexion between facts which are simply
placed side by side.

At the present time the situation is quite different, but the
change in the position of the problem has not been accompanied by a corresponding renewal in method. It is time to
attack, in a more broadly historical spirit, the problem of the
arrangement of the material of the life of Jesus which can
be retained as authentic. In order to do this we need a method
which will be both supple and varied, which seeks to seize
the significance of the internal relation of the facts to each
other, which tries to understand them (if one may put it like
this) from the inside, by entering into the psychology of those
who have been the actors in the story, by an attempt to revive
their state of mind through an effort of intelligent sympathy
and understanding. A religious history, less than any other
kind, cannot be reduced to a simple record of facts set down
in succession; it needs psychology and intuition. This does
not mean the construction of an ideal and unreal story, it
does not mean supposing or imagining facts, but only the
interpretation of those which have been verified, the effort to
understand them and to relate them to each other. This cannot
be done, doubtless, save by conjecture, but conjecture of this
kind is lawful, if it confines itself to those ideas and sentiments
which are verified by the passages concerned.

V. The General Setting of the Life of Jesus

In a very general way the framework of the life of Jesus is
supplied by the fact that he first appears on the scene in
connexion with John the Baptist, then goes into Galilee to
preach; after that he quits that province for Judaea; at Jerusalem he is sentenced to death, for political reasons no doubt,
at least in part, since it is a Roman tribunal which sends him
to the Cross, but only after he had announced his return on
the clouds of heaven before the Sanhedrin.

The principal effort of the historian should be directed,
naturally, towards what may be called the crises of the Gospel
story: the return into Galilee, the journey to Judaea, the
Passion. It cannot be denied that external circumstances

played an important part in these crises. The hostility of Herod, for example, forced Jesus to leave Galilee, and when Pilate sentenced Jesus to death he was moved by the determination to preserve public order in the province which he governed. Nevertheless, the crises which occurred in the ministry of Jesus were due chiefly to psychological causes; they were occasioned by the reaction caused by his preaching and the development of his thought, under the influence of his own experiences, and by the deepening of his religious life.

Thus there is a direct relation between the thought of Jesus and the exterior events of his life. This relation is complex, for it was the teaching of Jesus which roused the political authorities and the representatives of the religious tradition of Judaism against him, and on the other hand, the hostility of which he was the object meant that Jesus was faced by two alternatives: either he must give up his work, or he must think out what measures he must take—first of all an itinerating ministry and then leaving Galilee—in order to be able to continue. The reflection imposed upon Jesus by circumstances led to a deepening of his thought and of his convictions, and in a certain sense also to a transformation of his ideas, since pressure of events forced him to incorporate the ideas of suffering and defeat into the conception of his work, ideas which, in any case, did not play such a large part at the beginning as at the end of his ministry. Thus we may say without paradox that the history of Jesus is the history of his thought, and as this thought was simply the direct result of his religious experience it was a religious history. It is thus, by the contact which the facts present with the various aspects and factors of the thought of Jesus, that they can be classed between the two extremes of the Gospel narrative: the connexion of Jesus with the movement initiated by John the Baptist, and the crucifixion of Jesus at Jerusalem.

From the outset we can see that in the first and in the last, at least, of the three crises of the ministry of Jesus, that is to say: in the separation from John the Baptist and in the Passion, it was interior motives and states of soul which played the decisive part. It was a different conception of the conditions of salvation which made Jesus decide to cease being simply a disciple and an associate of John, and although exterior causes, the hostility of the Jews and the hesitations of Pilate, played a part in the drama of the Passion, they do not explain it, for Jesus was perfectly aware of the perils to which he was exposed in coming to Jerusalem and in staying there; he might quite well have stayed in some remote place, and if he had consented to renounce his message and deny his own claims before the Sanhedrin and before Pilate probably he could have saved his life. The fact that he died was due to his loyalty to his vocation. The deep explanation of the Passion, therefore, must be sought first of all in the interior life of Jesus. Although perhaps less evident at the first glance, it is also in the soul of Jesus that we must seek for the explanation of his departure from Galilee, for if he had left it simply on account of the threats of Herod, he would not have gone to Jerusalem to expose himself to dangers far greater than those from which he fled.

Paradoxical as it may seem, the thought of Jesus is more accessible than his life. A man like Rudolf Bultmann, who thinks that it is impossible to have any certainty about the events in the life of Jesus, save that he lived and that he died, has yet felt able to give a picture of his teaching.[1] The faith of the Early Church in the resurrection of Jesus, and the interpretation of the drama of the Passion, which was elaborated under the influence of this faith, have given to the religious and theological thought of primitive Christianity a unique, definite, and precise character. In the words attributed to Jesus it is not difficult to discern those which are only a projection into the past of the faith of the Church. The thought of Jesus, further, is peculiarly simple and coherent in character; it is in direct relation with a religious experience which doubtless we are not in a position to understand in its depth, but of which we are able to perceive the dominant features. This is a great help in analysing and reconstructing his thought,

---

[1] BULTMANN: *Jesus*. It is true that Bultmann (p. 17) says that nothing in his book would be changed if the proper name Jesus were understood as representing the thought of the first Christian generation. The account he gives of the thought of Jesus is, however, so connected, and represents so personal a way of thinking, that it is difficult to see how it could be understood as a collective way of thought.

but it is only of use, I need scarcely point out, for the fundamental elements and the leading ideas, and not for the details, particularly where applications of principles are concerned. Although the spirit of the moral teaching of Jesus, for instance, cannot be confused with anything else, there are in the Gospels some precepts of which we can never say with certainty whether they have been formulated by Jesus, or whether they are only applications of his teaching made by his disciples.

VI. WHAT A "LIFE OF JESUS" MAY BE

We must resign ourselves to remain ignorant of many things about Jesus which we would like to know, and we must be content to do without the complete and detailed account which we would so much like to possess. In any sketch which may be attempted large blanks will remain. During the whole of his youth, the whole of that important period during which the personality is being formed and the foundations are being laid for the future work of a human being, we know absolutely nothing, and all *Lives of Jesus* will lack that solid scaffolding of chronological information which supports and holds together the effort to read the story of the past. Although it is possible to fix the date of the death of Jesus with a precision which is not always attained in chronological estimates of ancient history, it is impossible to calculate, other than by conjectures, the total length of his ministry and of its various periods.

For the historian who seeks not only to state the facts but to understand them, the main lines of the life of Jesus are clear. He sees the facts becoming coherent and orderly, although when they are regarded solely from the critical point of view, that is to say, from the exterior, they are, or appear, so much like *membra disjecta* that at first one has the impression that it would be utterly useless to try to gather them into a coherent whole.

But, some may object, a *Life of Jesus* on the lines you suggest will contain a large element of conjecture?[1] This cannot be

[1] Cf. this remark of CAMILLE JULLIAN: "The duty of the historian is not to forbid himself to make conjectures; they are a necessity to him if he is to connect with each other the rare details which remain from the past.

denied, but in historical science this is inevitable. Even when the circumstances seem so favourable that all the historian has to do is to arrange the material at his disposal, after he has proved that it is reliable, it is impossible to attain an objective certainty like that which can be given by a mathematical experiment. The value of the documentary evidence, the competence and the good faith of witnesses, can never be proved in an absolutely rigid manner.[1] As in the case of all historical reconstruction, in the last resort every attempt to understand the life of Jesus must be based upon psychology. This method has its dangers; this becomes evident when we recall the anachronisms implied in the interpretations of some thinkers whose subtle speculations ignore the realism of the view of the future by which Jesus lived, picturing him as a modern man, and even as the ideal of the religious man. The moment we enter the realm of psychological interpretation the danger of falling into subjectivism and arbitrary modernization is great. But, as Wernle remarks,[1] the science of criticism is there precisely to guard against this danger. This it does first of all by showing how far the mentality of a Palestinian of the first century differs from that of a European of the twentieth century, and this will save us from attributing to Jesus our own ways of thinking and feeling. Also this warns us to keep the text in mind all the time, in order that we may add nothing to it of our own, and may only use psychological methods in order to understand the text, but not in order to supplement or alter it. One point, however, must be made quite clear: although we thus give an important place to psychological interpretation, and even to intuition, in the study of the problem of the life of Jesus, we do not leave the ground of history, for although, in principle, the historical method is one, it must still be adapted to the object which it is studying. We do not study the history of a war in the same way that we examine the history of a social movement, nor the history of science like that of art. A religious movement —and is the life of Jesus anything other than a religious move-

But it is equally his duty, both as a scholar and a man, to say plainly which ideas are his own and which are based on the documents" (*Les précurseurs de Clovis, Revue de Paris*, August 15, 1928, p. 752).

[1] WERNLE: *Jesus*, p. vi.

ment?—can only be understood with the aid of psychology. A religion cannot be grasped externally like a mathematical formula. In order to understand something of its intimate life, the study must be approached in a spirit of sympathy and comprehension. In order to understand Buddhism we must look through the eyes of a Buddhist, in order to understand Islam we must look through the eyes of a Muslim, and in order to understand the thought of Jesus we must have or we must acquire the spirit of a Christian. Erudition is indispensable, but where there is nothing else, an essential element is lacking.[1] The Jesus whom it will paint will not be the real Jesus. As Wernle says, in order to understand Jesus, the historian ought to have in himself something that is like Jesus (*etwas Jesuaehnliches*).[2] And perhaps it is for that reason that in the last resort it is possible, for instance, to outline some features in the personality of Jesus, to perceive some elements in his history, but not to make a complete portrait of him nor to compose a detailed biography.

In addition there is at our disposal a method of verification which, until now, has not been used as much as it might have been. The life of Jesus has been studied far too much in isolation, and people have forgotten that it is only the first chapter of Christianity. By separating the story of Jesus from the story of the development which ensued we have lost the aid of much valuable material which would throw a great deal of light on the Gospel history itself. Indeed, in my opinion, it is evident that no conception of the teaching and the life of Jesus can be regarded as valid unless it can fit naturally into a wider narrative. Hence, having set forth my views concerning Jesus and his work in this first volume, I hope to publish a second volume which will explain how the growth of Christianity, in its essential elements, is, in my opinion, connected with his work, and indeed, springs directly from it.

---

[1] Cf. this opinion of Louis BERTRAND: "Hence comes, in matters of religious history, the superiority of a Renan to the ordinary devotees of learning and of what is called positive science. He is strong with the force which comes to him from his whole Breton and Catholic ancestry, and above all from his clerical education" (*Revue des Deux-Mondes*, December 1, 1926, p. 484).
[2] *Jesus*, p. vii.

VII. THE QUESTION OF MIRACLE

At this point it is impossible to avoid a discussion of a question which, although it may seem to be philosophical in character, has pressed very heavily on all research connected with the life of Jesus: the question of miracle; at least I must explain why I consider that it lies outside the sphere of this study.

First of all, let us define more exactly the meaning of a term which is usually used as though its meaning were so clear and obvious that misunderstanding is impossible. The current meaning of miracle is that of a fact which differs from the ordinary course of events, a fact which does not seem to be explained by the play of natural forces, but is the result of supernatural forces. Thus an element of subjective appreciation enters into the description of a fact as "miraculous." Facts are not miracles because their miraculous character has been proved, but certain facts are, for a time at least, unexplained, and some people therefore regard these facts as miraculous. A fact could not be described objectively as a miracle save by someone who knew all the laws of nature and all the multiplicity of their possible combinations.

There are two principal causes which may lead us to describe a fact as miraculous: the first is that it presents the observer with something unusual and inexplicable; the second is that the person who performs the miracle shall appear to be an unusual and impressive person, whose influence is so strong that people begin to think that he may possess supernatural powers.

Renan has said that "the first principle of criticism is that miracle has no place in the fabric of human affairs, any more than it has in the order of the facts of nature."[1] Some theologians, like Père Pinard de la Boullaye, reply that the *a priori* denial of the possibility of certain facts is an unlawful prejudice, and that it is in reality non-scientific. In natural science, no seeker would systematically deny a fact simply and solely because he was unable to explain it by the laws which he knows. To do this, in the name of a science in process of

[1] RENAN: *Études d'histoire religieuse*, Paris, 1859, p. vii.

formation, would be to eliminate the documents and facts which it needs for its own progress.[1] What right have we to adopt a different attitude in history and to deny the facts whose causes escape us? We must acknowledge that P. de la Boullaye is right to this extent, that Gospel historians have sometimes adopted an attitude towards the question of miracle which can be explained from the philosophical point of view rather than from that of considerations of method, and that their position would have been stronger if they had remained upon the ground of facts, and had simply tried to register those which seemed to be established without trying to explain them all. In practice, however, it is difficult to maintain this position quite strictly, although in theory it is unassailable. In certain instances it seems impossible to avoid using the criterion of credibility.

In order to show the position of the question, let us take an extreme example. The Gospel of Pseudo-Matthew, the Proto-Gospel of James, tells how when Jesus was a child, having amused himself with making some birds out of clay, he breathed upon them, and they came alive and flew away (27).[2] Let us suppose that this story has been reported in an ancient Gospel, and that it was presented to us with all the external guarantees that could be desired, would we accept it, or would we ask ourselves a preliminary question? Here we must make a distinction. In the hypothesis which we are considering, we cannot refuse to admit the following facts: that Jesus did model the birds, that these clay birds may have disappeared, and that some living birds were seen flying near by. The element on which we suspend judgment is the explanation given in the text: namely, that Jesus breathed life into the birds. An attitude of this kind would be more scientific than that of denying the fact because those who reported it gave it an interpretation which to us seems inadmissible.

Let us see further how the question of miracle actually presents itself in practice. First of all, it is clear that a part, and perhaps

---

[1] H. PINARD DE LA BOULLAYE: *L'étude comparée des religions*, II, *Des méthodes*, Paris, 1925, pp. 27 f.

[2] TISCHENDORF: *Evangelia apocrypha*, Leipzig, 1853, p. 89.

a large part, of the element of the marvellous which the Gospel records contain, must be put down to the account of tradition. We have not, however, the right to affirm that the primitive tradition did not contain any miracles, that is to say, any fact in which it might have seen something different from the play of natural forces. To people of the first century the miraculous did not seem in any way abnormal or extraordinary. The mentality of the time, being on this point what it was, it is not surprising that the events of the life of Jesus were considered and related as being of a miraculous order; it would be far more extraordinary if the Gospels contained nothing marvellous at all, and the striking element in the Gospel tradition is its sobriety and the discretion with which the miraculous element is introduced; this would be far more evident than it is at present if we were to compare the Gospels with certain recent apocryphal works or with the *Life of Apollonius of Tyana* by Philostratus.[1]

Each record of a miracle ought to be studied by itself. It goes without saying that first of all we must eliminate every miraculous incident reported in conditions such that we would not hesitate to set it aside if we were dealing with a natural phenomenon. For instance, we do not need to ask whether Jesus possessed a natural or supernatural gift of healing a wounded ear, since it is Luke alone who tells us how he healed the ear of the servant of the High Priest (xxii. 51), and the other evangelists would not have omitted this detail if they had known of its existence.

There is a whole group of miracles which should be placed in a separate category: these are those which are in the nature

[1] On the idea of miracle and belief in miracle in antiquity see R. REITZEN-STEIN: *Hellenistische Wundererzählungen*, Leipzig, 1906. O. WEINREICH: *Antike Heilungswunder. Untersuchungen zum Wunderglauben der Griechen und Römer*, Giessen, 1909. P. FIEBIG: *Jüdische Wundergeschichten des neutestamentlichen Zeitalters*, Tübingen, 1911. *Antike Wundergeschichten zum Studium der Wunder des Neuen Testaments zusammengestellt*, Bonn, 1911. To mention only one detail among many others, we know from the Talmud that some rabbis were supposed to possess the power of raising the dead. See A. WUENSCHE: *Neue Beiträge zur Erläuterung der Evangelien aus Talmud und Midrasch*, Göttingen, 1878, p. 373. STRACK-BILLERBECK: I, p. 560.

of a theological explanation. The accounts of the Virgin birth, the Transfiguration, and, at least, to some extent, of the Resurrection, belong to this category. Miracles of this type, although they are of primary importance in the history of Christian thought, mean nothing in the actual record of the life of Jesus.

Mark (viii. 11, 12) reports that on one occasion the Pharisees asked Jesus for "a sign from heaven," that is to say, a marvel which would serve as his credentials as the Sent One of God; he replied: "There shall no sign be given unto this generation." This saying is certainly authentic, for it could not have been created by primitive Christianity which attached a great importance to the miracles of Jesus, and indeed regarded its very life as based wholly upon the Resurrection of the Lord, that is to say, on the greatest of the miracles. This leads us to think that Jesus did not want to work marvels, that is to say, acts of pure display.[1]

In this respect the accounts of the Temptation are also very significant. The Evangelists represent Jesus repulsing the suggestions of Satan in a categoric manner, who suggested that he should turn stones into bread, or cast himself down from the pinnacle of the Temple (Matt. iv. 3–7). Therefore we see that they did not consider Jesus a mere wonder-worker. Even if he did do works which made the impression of the marvellous, he did not consider them essential. They were not at the centre of his work, but on the circumference, and even on the fringe.[2]

Stories like those of Jesus stilling the storm (Mark iv. 35–41) or walking on the water (Mark vi. 45–52) are thus extremely doubtful, for they seem to have issued from the imagination of their narrators. The records of miracles contained in the Gospels should be used only with extreme caution. Are we to see in them the product of a pious imagination? or, as has

[1] We will show further on (pp. 371 ff.) another possible interpretation of this refusal. In any case the word of Jesus has been understood by Mark as the refusal to work a miracle.
[2] On the appreciation of miracles in primitive Christianity see the suggestive but slightly paradoxical book of A. FRIDRICHSEN: *Le problème du miracle dans le Christianisme primitif*, Strasbourg, 1925.

been suggested by some, are we to think that they arose in the interpretation given of certain natural facts or of certain coincidences which impressed the spectators as marvellous? It is impossible to pronounce definitely in favour of either explanation.

Though the stories of Jesus raising the dead and healing the sick may belong to a secondary stage in the evolution of the tradition, there can be no doubt that Jesus did heal the sick, or, according to the interpretation which was given of sickness in the setting in which he lived, that he did cast out demons.[1]

We must note, with regard to the healings accomplished by Jesus, that we possess two accounts in which the attitude of Jesus looks far more like that of a doctor who is proceeding towards a cure, than like that of a wonder-worker whose voice alone sets in motion supernatural forces. These two accounts are given by Mark (vii. 31–37, viii. 22–26). Matthew, who at this point in the story follows the record of Mark very closely, has not reproduced them. But he took care to replace the first by a general statement about healings (xv. 29–31), and he has given a quantitative equivalent of the second by saying that on his departure from Jericho Jesus cured two blind men (xx. 29–31), while Mark spoke only of the healing of Bartimaeus (x. 46–52).

In the first of these stories of which we are speaking, a deaf man, whose speech was also affected, is brought to Jesus. Jesus takes him aside and puts his fingers in the ears of the deaf man, touches his tongue with saliva, then, looking up to heaven, Jesus sighs and says, " 'Ephphatha,' that is, 'be opened.' And straightway his ears were opened, and the string of his tongue was loosed and he spake plain." In the second incident Jesus also takes the patient by the hand, leads him out of the village, spits upon his eyes,[2] and lays his hands upon him.

---

[1] There is no need to distinguish between the healing of the sick and the casting out of demons, for according to the ideas of the time sickness was caused by the action of demons.

[2] Cf. with this fact the manner in which, according to John ix. 6–7, Jesus cures the man born blind. He spits on the ground, makes clay with his saliva, and puts this on the eyes of the patient, whom he then sends off immediately to go and wash in the pool of Siloam.

Then he asks the blind man if he can see anything. The man replies, "I see men as trees, walking." "After that he put his hands again upon his eyes, and made him look up, and he was restored and saw every man clearly."

These two incidents, which are a curious mixture of medical procedure and of religious practices, like that of the laying on of hands and the word of command, justify us in thinking that most of the narratives which have been transmitted to us have undergone a process of simplification, and that in reality, in the healings accomplished by Jesus, it is impossible to distinguish quite clearly between the activity of the healer and the activity of the prophet or the Messiah. This is impossible, not only because the psycho-physiological mechanism of healings of this kind is unknown to us, but also because the distinction between these two elements was not made by the narrators, nor, in all probability, was it made by Jesus himself.

Another detail preserved by Mark only confirms this conclusion. We know that, according to the Gospel records, the disciples of Jesus, when they were sent out on their mission by their master, were in possession of the powers which he also possessed: powers of healing the sick and casting out demons. Now Mark, in telling of the activity of the messengers of Jesus, expresses himself thus: "And they went out, and preached that men should repent; and they cast out many devils, and anointed with oil many that were sick, and healed them" (vi. 12–13). The mention of the anointing with oil, which is not mentioned elsewhere, is also a confirmation of the medical element in the healings recorded in the Gospels. On the other hand, the fact that Jesus could not accomplish healings at Nazareth because of the unbelief of his fellow-townsmen,[1] shows that the attitude of mind of those who came to him for healing played a decisive part in the process of healing, and this confirms the idea that the psychological factor must have played a large part in them. Historians must confine themselves to the facts; it is for the doctors and psychiatrists to give the interpretation.

None the less it is true that these healings were regarded as miracles both by Jesus himself and by those who were the

[1] See pp. 173 ff.

recipients of his bounty, or the witnesses of these incidents, and that the hostile Pharisees did not cast any doubt on the fact that they had been produced by a supernatural power (Mark iii. 22). Thus it was as miracles that these healings were regarded, both by those who witnessed them and by those who saw in them the confirmation of the idea that Jesus had received a divine mission; finally, they deepened the sense of vocation in Jesus himself.

CHAPTER VII

THE CHRONOLOGY OF THE GOSPEL NARRATIVE

THE only direct indication which we possess concerning the chronology of the Gospel narrative occurs at the beginning of the Third Gospel. Wishing to write as an historian, Luke follows the model given by Thucydides at the beginning of the history of the Peloponnesian War (II, 2); he has also been influenced by the way in which the call of Jeremiah is dated (Jeremiah i. 2–3), so he expresses himself thus: "Now, in the fifteenth year of the reign of Tiberius Caesar, Pontius Pilate being governor of Judaea,[1] and Herod being tetrarch of Galilee,[2] and his brother Philip tetrarch of Iturea and of the region of Trachonitis,[3] and Lysanias the tetrarch of Abilene,[4] Annas and Caiaphas being the high priests,[5] the word of God

[1] Pilate was Procurator of Judaea from 26 to 36. The attempt made by Eisler to prove that his period of rule began in the year 21 is based on hazardous conjectures, and forces us to correct the text in a very arbitrary manner. On this point, see my article *R.h.*, CLXII, 1929, pp. 245 f., and above, pp. 80 ff.

[2] Herod Antipas was Tetrarch of Galilee and of Peraea from 4 B.C. till A.D. 39.

[3] Philip was Tetrarch of Iturea and of Trachonitis from 4 B.C. till A.D. 34.

[4] There was a certain Lysanias, Tetrarch of Abilene, who was put to death in 34 B.C. WELLHAUSEN (*Lc.*, p. 4) and SCHWARTZ (*Die Aeren von Gerasa und Eleutheropolis, Nachrichten der Goet. Ges. der Wiss.*, 1906, pp. 371 ff.) think that it is to him that Luke alludes. But it is known from an inscription (*C.I.G.*, 4521. Cf. SCHÜRER, I, pp. 718 f., ED. MEYER, I, p. 48), that there was another Lysanias who lived, at the earliest, in the time of Tiberius, and at the latest in the days of Nero.

[5] Lit. "Under the chief priest Annas and Caiaphas." Some miniscules and versions only have or imply the plural, which is an evident correction. Luke cannot certainly have believed that there could have been two high priests who were in office at the same time; thus usually the passage is taken to mean that it is an allusion to the influence that Annas had preserved after his deposition in 15 and during the term of office of his son-in-law Caiaphas (18–36). In support of this interpretation a passage from Josephus (V, 38, ¶ 193) is quoted which speaks of the "high priests Ananios and Jesus son of Gamaliel" (Ananios was high priest for three months in 62. Jesus, son of Gamaliel, his second successor, was in office from 63 to 65). This explanation does not take note of the singular ἐπὶ ἀρχιερέως. In my opinion it would be better to admit that the original text had the name

came unto John the son of Zacharias in the wilderness" (iii. 1–2).

One only of these indications of date gives us any precise information, namely, the first one: "the fifteenth year of Tiberius." As Tiberius ascended the throne on the 19th of August, A.D. 14, Luke seems to suggest a date between the 19th of August in the year 28 and the 18th of August in the year 29, or, rather, if we accept a very probable theory of Cichorius,[1] between the 1st of October, 27, and the 30th of September, 28.

This chronological note is connected with the call of John the Baptist. How long was this before the beginning of the ministry of Jesus? This does not greatly matter, for the important point here is the way in which Luke represents the chronological connexion between John the Baptist and Jesus. At the moment of writing, John the Baptist already formed an integral part of the Gospel story; by this time his part was reduced to that of a mere forerunner; also Luke doubtless felt that the date which he gave for John would apply equally well to Jesus, perhaps even, as some have supposed,[2] not only to the baptism but also to his death, since Luke represents the whole length of the ministry of Jesus as less than one year. Otherwise it is difficult to understand why Luke (who was far less interested in John the Baptist than in Jesus) should have given a chronological note about John but not about

of Caiaphas only, and that the name of Annas was added later, on account of the part assigned to him in the trial of Jesus by John (xviii. 13).

[1] CICHORIUS (*Chronologisches zum Leben Jesu*, *Z.N.T.W.*, XXII, 1923, pp. 16–20), taking into account the fact that the Gospel of Luke appears to have been written at Antioch, and that, in Syria, from the beginning of the Empire until the end of the first century, the years of the reign were combined with the Syrian calendar by counting as one year the time which had elapsed between the coming of the Emperor and the following September 30th, has proposed to call the period from October 1, 27, to September 30, 28, the fifteenth year of Tiberius. Some authors (for instance, JOH. WEISS: *Die Ev. des Markus und Lukas, Comm. of Meyer*, I, 2, Göttingen, 1892, p. 319) count the years of Tiberius not from his accession but from his association with the Empire (11–12). This system was not followed by Josephus nor by the Roman historians, and there is no reason to follow it now.

[2] LOISY: *L'Évangile de Luc*, Paris, 1924, p. 133. E. CAVAIGNAC: *Chronologie*, Paris, 1925, pp. 197 ff.

Jesus; also it seems strange that he should have given a date for the beginning of his ministry only, and not for his death, which, however, to the Christians was the culminating point of his work, and the fact of his life which, on the whole, ought to be the most easy to date.

What value can we assign to the date provided by Luke? The fact that Mark gives no date proves nothing, in itself, save that the Gospel tradition did not contain, in this respect, any indication, direct or indirect, or that the Christians were not able to collect other than conjectural information about the chronology of the Gospel story. Nor does John give any chronological data. We may, however, take it as certain that he knew the text of Luke. We have no right, however, to lay down the principle that Luke was only able to give the date of the fifteenth year of Tiberius on the authority of arbitrary combinations. The fact is, we are not in a position either to reject or to confirm this date directly, although when we remember the period in which it appeared we realize that it ought to be confirmed if we are to make use of it.

At whatever moment John the Baptist began to preach repentance, his death, in any case, took place before that of Jesus; this we know from the fact that people were asking whether Jesus might not be John the Baptist risen from the dead (Mark vi. 14–16*, viii. 27–28*). Keim[1] claims to be able to fix the date of the death of John the Baptist in the following manner: according to the Gospels (Mark vi. 17 ff.; Luke iii. 19–20), Herod Antipas is said to have imprisoned John the Baptist, then put him to death, because of the way he reproached him for his marriage with Herodias. According to Josephus (*Ant.*, XVIII, 5, 1–2, ¶¶ 116–119), the reasons for which the prophet was executed were political. Antipas is said to have been disquieted by John's influence over the people. The two reasons are perfectly easy to reconcile. The fact that, according to Josephus, the defeat inflicted on Herod by Aretas is regarded as a punishment for the murder of John the Baptist, would be still more intelligible if there had been some connexion between the matrimonial affairs of the

---

[1] Keim, I, pp. 621 f.; III, pp. 484 f.

Tetrarch and the measures taken by him against John the Baptist.[1]

The marriage of Herod with Herodias led to a rupture between the Tetrarch and the king of the Nabataeans, Aretas IV, whose daughter he had married. In the year 36 Aretas inflicted a crushing defeat on the troops of his former son-in-law. Keim thinks that Aretas waged war against Antipas as soon as the latter had dissolved his marriage. This argument is not at all conclusive; Josephus says explicitly that the second marriage of Antipas was "the beginning of the hatred" ($\dot{a}\rho\chi\dot{\eta}$ $\ddot{\epsilon}\chi\theta\rho\alpha s$) between Aretas and himself. This would have been differently expressed if the two enemies had come to blows immediately. Aretas would have had to wait for a favourable occasion to revenge himself on Antipas. Such an occasion arose in the year 36 when the Romans were occupied with the war against Artabanus III, the King of the Parthians.[2] Under these conditions it is not possible to draw a definite conclusion concerning the date of the death of John the Baptist from the defeat of 36, and hence concerning the *terminus a quo* of that of Jesus.

According to the Gospels, Jesus was crucified on a Friday, which, according to John, was the 14th of Nisan, and, according to the Synoptists, the 15th of the same month, that is to say, the day of, or the day after, the spring full moon in one year during the administration of Pilate, somewhere between 26 and 36; thus it seems as though we could determine the date, or the probable date, of his death by calculating in which years between 26 and 36 the spring full moon occurred on a Thursday or a Friday. Calculations which have been made on this basis suggest that the date may have been the 7th of April, A.D. 30, according to the Synoptists, or the 3rd of April, A.D. 33, according to John.[3]

---

[1] On these questions, see my book *Jean-Baptiste*, pp. 18 ff.

[2] OTTO: *Herodes, Beiträge zur Geschichte des letzten jüdischen Königshauses*, Stuttgart, 1913, col. 192.

[3] ACHELIS: *Ein Versuch den Karfreitag zu datieren, Nachr. d. Goett. Ges. der. Wiss.*, 1902. Cf. PREUSCHEN: *Todesjahr und Todestag Jesu, Z.N.T.W.*, V, 1904, pp. 1–17. The date of April 7, 30, had already been given by CHAVANNES: *Essai sur la détermination de quelques dates de l'histoire évangélique, Revue de théologie*, 1863, p. 228.

In spite of its apparent precision, this method can only yield results tainted with such an element of uncertainty that they are devoid of all value. The Jews had a lunar-solar calendar, that is to say, one in which the months were determined by the phases of the moon. The length of the lunar revolution being 29 days, 12 hours, 44 minutes, 3 seconds, the length of the months was alternately 29 days and 30 days. On the other hand, the lunar year (354 days, 8 hours, 48 minutes, 36 seconds) is shorter than the solar year (365 days, 5 hours, 48 minutes, 11 seconds) by 10 days, 20 hours, 59 minutes, 35 seconds, whence the necessity for a correction aiming at securing the agreement of the calendar with the march of the seasons. This correction was made, at the end of the year, whenever it was considered necessary, by intercalating a supplementary month which doubled the month of Adar and was called Veadar (second Adar). The alternation between the two kinds of months and the intercalation of the supplementary month were not fixed by any definite rule, but were decided in a quite empirical manner by the Sanhedrin, according to their knowledge of the phases of the moon. Thus there is an element of uncertainty in the Jewish calendar which cancels its apparent agreement with the solar calendar.

A passage in the Fourth Gospel furnishes a chronological indication which is all the more valuable because the narrator did not realize the significance of his remark from this point of view. After the Cleansing of the Temple, when the Jews asked Jesus for a sign (that is to say, a proof) that he had the right to act as he had done, he said to them: "Destroy this temple and in three days I will raise it up." The Jews did not understand, says the evangelist, that Jesus was speaking of his body and of the resurrection, and they reply to him: τεσσεράκοντα καὶ ἒξ ἔτεσιν οἰκοδομήθη ὁ ναὸς οὗτος (ii. 20). The Temple of Herod not having been completed, according to Josephus (A.J., XX, 9, 7, ¶ 219), until during the administration of Albinus (62–64), the meaning of this saying is not "It took 46 years to build this Temple," but "For 46 years this Temple has been a-building."

According to Josephus (A.J., XV, xi, 1, ¶ 380), Herod began

the construction of the Temple in the 18th year of his reign, either in 20 or 19 B.C. (734–735 of Rome), the year when the Emperor came to Syria.[1] According to Dion Cassius (54, 7), this journey took place in the year 734 of Rome (20 B.C.), thus the building of the Temple was begun in the second part of the year 734 of Rome (20 B.C.). The phrase with which we are concerned having been uttered a little before the Passover, this Passover must have been that of 28 or 27, that is, it depends on whether we admit that the 46 years were wholly accomplished, or whether there were still some months to elapse before they ended.

John connects the saying of Jesus about the Temple with the Cleansing of the Temple, which he places at the beginning of the activity of Jesus. But he displaced this incident because, admitting that Jesus had been several times to Jerusalem, it seemed strange to him that on his last visit he should have experienced an outburst of indignation when he saw the sellers installed in the Temple, when, as John thought, Jesus must have seen this sight many times already. Further, the saying of Jesus about the Temple played an important part in his trial; it ought, therefore, to date from the end, and not from the beginning of his ministry. This seems to us to establish the fact that Jesus died during the Passover of the year 27 or 28.

If we admit that the indication of Luke iii. 2 refers to the story of Jesus as a whole, which it places entirely between the 1st of October, 27, and the 30th of September, 28, we may then claim that, by entirely different ways, we have arrived at the same result, which permits us, so we believe, to consider it as an established fact that Jesus died during the Passover of the year 28.

This date is in closer agreement with the most certain facts in the Pauline chronology[2] than other later dates which have often been suggested. The second journey of Paul to Jerusalem, of which he speaks in Gal. ii. 1 f., must be placed, at the latest, during the early months of the year 44, since we know from Acts xi. 30–xii. 1 that Paul made his second visit to Rome at

---

[1] A different note, given elsewhere by JOSEPHUS (*J.W.*, I, 21, 1, ¶ 401), seems to refer to the establishment of the project.

[2] On the Pauline chronology, see *Intr.*, IV, 1, pp. 81 ff.

the time when Agrippa I was persecuting the Church, and the latter died at the beginning of the year 44.[1] Paul says that he went to Jerusalem for the first time three years after his conversion, and a second time fourteen years later (Gal. i. 18, ii. 1), but he does not say whether it was fourteen years after his conversion or after his first journey. The expressions which he uses ought not to be interpreted too rigidly as though he intended to say exactly after three times or fourteen times 365 days. The three years and the fourteen years might mean 3 years or 14 years less some months. In the first case, the sense is more than two years and less than four; in the second, more than 13 and less than 15.

If the starting-point of the fourteen years, after which the visit at the beginning of 44 is placed, was Paul's conversion, then this must have taken place approximately between the spring of 29 and the end of 30. If the fourteen years are reckoned from his first visit to Jerusalem we ought to push the date back to somewhere between the end of 24 and the middle of 28. The impossibility of fitting this in to any system forces us to regard Paul's conversion as the starting-point for the fourteen years, and, in consequence, to conclude that his conversion must be placed between the spring of 29 and the end of 30; this means that the period between the conversion of Paul and the death of Jesus covered a period of time which lies somewhere between one year and two years and a half. Now, there is in existence a tradition which seems to confirm this fact. We know that Paul considered that the manifestation of Christ which he saw on the road to Damascus was of exactly the same type as those which the other disciples had seen, and that it was the last of the series (1 Cor. xv. 5–8; cf. ix. 1). If we were sure of the length of time that the Early Church considered was occupied by these appearances we would then have a very valuable indication concerning the date of the conversion of Paul in relation to the death of Jesus. Among the various traditions which have been held on this point there is one to which we ought to pay special attention. This is the one which attributes to this period a length of eighteen months.[2]

[1] JOSEPHUS: *A.J.*, XIX, 8, 2, ¶¶ 343–352; *J.W.*, II, 11, 6, ¶¶ 218–219.
[2] HARNACK: *Chronologische Berechnung des "Tags von Damaskus," Sitzber. Berl. Ak. der Wiss.*, 1912, pp. 673–682.

Irenaeus (*Adv. haer.*, I, 30, 14; cf. 3, 2) asserts that this view was current among the Ophites and among the disciples of Ptolemaeus, the Valentinian. It occurs also in the *Ascension of Isaiah*, which is not an heretical book but an ecclesiastical work of the second century.[1] Doubtless, the passages which support the tradition of eighteen months are of comparatively early date. Nevertheless, the fact that this tradition is met with both in the Church at large and among the Gnostics means that we must find the date farther back than that which marks the real separation of the Gnostics from the Church. These indications are not sufficient for us to regard the tradition of the eighteen months as historical, but they are sufficient to make us regard the notion as not entirely devoid of value, above all, if we admit that we do not see how it could be explained by reasons of an allegorical or theological character. If it were well founded—which is, to say the least, not impossible—it would prove an interesting confirmation of the conclusions at which we have arrived.

In the Early Church there existed a different tradition concerning the length of the life of Jesus and the date of his death. Irenaeus,[2] basing his theory on the tradition of the elders who knew John, that is to say, without doubt, on the testimony of Papias, and on the Fourth Gospel, says that Jesus died, not at the age of thirty but at fifty. The *Acta Pilati*[3] say that he died under Claudius (41–54).[4] Irenaeus was too conscious of

---

[1] 9, 16. "And when he (the Son of Man) shall have defeated the angel of death, he will rise again the third day and will remain in this world for 545 days" (1 year (365 days) + 6 months (6 × 30 = 180) = 545 days).

[2] *Adv. haer.*, II, 22, 5. Cf. *Dém. de la prédic. apost.*, 74.

[3] Ch. 29 (TISCHENDORF: *Ev. apocr.*, p. 392 f.).

[4] Cf. also HIPPOLYTUS: *Comm. on Daniel*, IV, 23, 3. SALOMON REINACH (*A propos de la curiosité de Tibère, C.M.R.*, IV, p. 22) also quotes the fact that, in a whole series of the works of Christian art, of which some may even go back as far as the fourth century, John baptizing Jesus is represented as a man of about fifty years of age and Jesus like a boy between ten and twelve. If John was baptizing about the year 30, Jesus would thus have been born between 18 and 20, and, if he died at the age of 30, he would have been crucified about the year 50. This tradition, if it really is a tradition, cannot be connected with the one supported by Irenaeus, since, according to it, Jesus would have died at thirty and not at fifty years of age. It is, however, very uncertain whether we are here dealing with a genuine

the value of the Canon of the four Gospels to have accepted a tradition which differed from them. Corssen[1] has remarked that, in the passage where the statement with which we are dealing occurs, Irenaeus says that after his baptism Jesus went three times to Jerusalem for the Passover. Here he follows the testimony of John and is flagrantly inconsistent with himself. The tradition that Jesus died at the age of fifty, in Irenaeus or others who held the same view, seems to have had a double origin, which on the one hand was speculative: it was felt necessary that Jesus should have reached the age at which it was believed that man attains the fullness of his development, that is to say, the age of fifty,[2] and also exegetical: based on John ii. 20 ff., where the Jews say that forty-six years have gone to the building of the Temple, while, according to the evangelist, Jesus was thinking of his body when he spoke of the Temple; and on John viii. 57, where the Jews said to him: "Thou art not yet fifty years old"; from this Irenaeus has drawn the conclusion that Jesus attained the age of fifty during his ministry. The tradition that he was crucified during the reign of Claudius probably arose out of this exegesis.

Luke, who places the beginning of the ministry of Jesus between the 1st of October, 27, and the 30th of September, 28, gives to the whole of his ministry a maximum of six months; as we shall see, this is not long enough. Luke must have made some error in the combinations which have led him to speak of the fifteenth year of Tiberius, or, what is possibly more likely, has attributed to the ministry of Jesus a shorter time than it seems to have covered in reality. According to Luke (iii. 23), at the moment when Jesus began his ministry he was

tradition at all. At the time to which the works of art which we are considering belong, the authority of the Canonical Gospels had been established, and was not challenged. Thus we must explain these works of art by the freedom accorded to artists, and that, in order to represent the baptism of Jesus, the artist took suggestions from what he knew Christian baptism to be in his own day. On this point, see *Jean-Baptiste*, pp. 205 f.

[1] *Warum ist das vierte Evangelium für das Werk des Apostels Johannes erklärt worden?* *Z.N.T.W.*, II, 1901, p. 216.

[2] HIPPOCRATES, according to *Pseud. Philo, De opificio mundi*, 105. Cf. Num. iv. 3, 30, 39, viii. 25. IRENAEUS (*Adv. Haer.*, II, 22, 4; cf. 18, 7) says that Jesus has hallowed all the stages of human life.

about thirty years old. Meyer[1] has observed that in the ancient world it was difficult to estimate the age of people exactly and that obituary notices are always given in round numbers with formulas like *circiter*, *plus*, *minus*. Hence the suggestion in Luke cannot be used as material upon which it is possible to base an exact date of Christ's birth.[2] It is, however, the most certain date upon which we can depend, since the Gospels of the Infancy are legendary in character. The most we might add to this is a detail which occurs both in Matthew and in Luke, although their accounts are entirely independent of each other, namely, the fact that Jesus was born during the reign of Herod the Great. It is impossible to understand for what theological purpose this tradition could have been created. Thus there is some likelihood that it is historical. Herod died in the year 750 of Rome (4 B.C.) a little before the Passover—that is to say, in the month of March or April.[3] The birth of Jesus seems to have taken place before that date.[4]

[1] ED. MEYER: III, p. 171, n.

[2] It may be that the age of thirty was suggested, as is thought by TURNER (art. *Chronology of the New Testament* in *Hastings's Dict. of the Bible*, I, col. 405), by the fact that, according to Num. iv. 3, 47, it was that which was needed to be attained for the exercise of priestly functions.

[3] For the date of the death of Herod, see SCHÜRER, I, p. 415, n. 167.

[4] This result—that Jesus was born, at the latest, in 4 B.C.—depends on admitting that an error was made by the monk Denis the Little, who, in 525, was charged by the Pope, John I, to calculate the Paschal date at the moment when the close of the period 437–531 was approaching for which it had been fixed by Cyril of Alexandria. For the era then in use (the era of Diocletian which the Christians called the era of the Martyrs) Denis substituted a new era, that of the Incarnation. Denis fixed the Incarnation on March 25, 754, of Rome, and the birth of Jesus December 25, 754. Thus the year 754 of Rome became the year 1 in the Christian era. We do not know on what principle Denis made his calculations. CAVAIGNAC (*Chronologie*, p. 14) thinks that he began with an idea of a Paschal cycle of 532 years and that he fixed the date of the Passion for the 25th of March. Assuming that in the year 563 of the new era (279 of the era of the martyrs) Easter would fall on March 25th, he would have thus concluded that it fell on the same date in 31, and he would have fixed the birth of Jesus as having taken place thirty-one years before, by adding one year for the ministry of Jesus to the thirty years mentioned by Luke (iii. 23).

CHAPTER VIII

THE LENGTH OF THE MINISTRY OF JESUS AND ITS SETTING

THE question of the length of the ministry of Jesus is usually stated in such a way that it simply becomes one aspect of the problem of the Synoptics versus the Fourth Gospel.

The Synoptic Gospels only mention one Feast of the Passover, namely, the one which was being celebrated at the moment when Jesus was crucified; according to them, his ministry must have lasted at the most a little less than a year. This is a minimum estimate, since the incident of the disciples plucking the ears of corn (Mark ii. 23 ff.*) must be placed before the time of harvest, which so far as the barley harvest is concerned, would be reaped a short time before the Passover; the wheat harvest is a little later[1] and would take place after the Passover.

In the Fourth Gospel the ministry of Jesus is represented as certainly longer than in the Synoptic Gospels. After his meeting with John the Baptist in Peraea and the miracle of Cana, Jesus spends some days in Capernaum; then, a feast of the Passover being near (the first of those which John mentions), he goes up to Jerusalem (ii. 3). Thus the narrative begins some weeks before the Passover. After staying in Jerusalem, and then on the banks of the Jordan with John the Baptist, Jesus returns to Galilee by way of Samaria.[2] At the

---

[1] BENZINGER: art. *Ackerbau bei den Israeliten*, *R.E.*, I, p. 137. R. KÖPPEL (*Palästina*, Tübingen, 1930, p. 41) suggests the month of May. There might, of course, be a variation of some weeks, according to the position of the fields. According to BENZINGER (p. 136) certain fields, which were particularly well irrigated, could produce two harvests a year; but this would only occur rarely, and cannot be taken into the reckoning here.

[2] The phrase: "You say, there are yet four months and then cometh the harvest" (iv. 35), is interpreted by certain authors in a literal sense. According to them these words must have been uttered in December or January. But the words of Jesus seem to be spoken in an allegorical sense (cf. Matt. ix. 37*). JEAN RÉVILLE (*Q.Év.*, p. 152) has suggested, with much probability, that this was a proverb. For a detailed discussion see *Intr.*, II, p. 263, n. 1.

beginning of chapter 5 another festival is the occasion for
another journey to Jerusalem. But we are not told what
feast it was.[1] It cannot have been a Passover or surely John
would have mentioned the fact. Jesus then goes to the eastern
shore of the Lake of Gennesaret. At this moment "the Passover, the Feast of the Jews, was at hand" (vi. 4). This is the
second Passover. Jesus stays in Galilee until the time of the
Feast of Tabernacles (September–October); he arrives in
Jerusalem in the middle of this festival (vii. 14); he is still
there on the Feast of the Dedication, in December (x. 22);
then follows a visit to Peraea (x. 40–42) and a sojourn in
Ephraim (xi. 54–57), separated by a visit to Bethany for the
Raising of Lazarus (xi. 1–53). Jesus returns to Jerusalem on
the eve of the Passover (xi. 55), and then the drama of the
Passion takes place. Thus, according to John, the ministry
of Jesus did not last one year but, at the very least, two.

The critics are divided between these two systems: some on
general grounds reject the evidence of John as entirely devoid of
value, while others, arguing from the data given in the Synoptic
Gospels themselves, try to prove that the activity of Jesus at
Jerusalem must have lasted longer than they say, and even
that it may have been repeated several times. A sentence like
this: "O Jerusalem, Jerusalem . . . how often would I have
gathered thy children together . . ." (Matt. xxiii. 37*) is
difficult to understand if Jesus had only spent a few days in
the Holy City. The tears which Jesus shed over Jerusalem on
his arrival, according to the account in (Luke xix, 41–42), and
the commentary on them in this sentence: "If thou hadst
known, even thou, at least in this thy day, the things which belong unto thy peace! but now they are hid from thine eyes,"
suggests the idea of several rebuffs. These passages force us to
make a considerable enlargement in the setting which the
Synoptic Gospels give, or seem to give, to the Jerusalem
ministry of Jesus. They do not prove or even suggest that

---

[1] We retain here the text of MSS. A. B. D. W. Θ., "a feast." Other MSS.
(ℵ. C. L., etc.) read, "the feast," which seems to refer to the Passover.
This is what the MS. Λ says plainly: "the feast of unleavened bread."
MS. 131 has "the feast of Tabernacles." The least definite text is probably
the most ancient. It is also the one for which there is most evidence.

Jesus went up to Jerusalem from Galilee several times. Some have suggested that there is a trace of an earlier journey in the incident of Jesus in the home of Martha and Mary reported by Luke (x. 38–42). Interpreting this story in the light of the Johannine story of the Anointing (xi. 1–2, xii. 1–11), it is usually localized at Bethany, at the gates of Jerusalem. But though it is evident that there is some connexion between the two narratives in which Mary sits at the feet of Jesus during a meal, and is defended by him against a charge brought against her because of her attitude, it is not legitimate to conclude from this that the tradition followed by Luke agrees with John in localizing the incident at the gates of Jerusalem. The third evangelist seems to have received the story of Martha and Mary in the form of an isolated incident. He does not connect it in any way either with what precedes it or with what follows.[1]

The problem of the setting of the Gospel story is more complex than it used to appear, since it is now established that the plans of the four Gospels, that of the Synoptics as much as that of John, are artificial creations, designed to group together into a coherent whole traditions which formerly had an independent existence.

So far as the Johannine record is concerned, in particular, it must be added that its framework, which seems to be so clear and definite, is in reality empty. The evangelist does not take the trouble to fill in the interval which separates two consecutive feasts with general statements. Thus, for the first year (ii. 13–vi. 4) he only mentions one visit to Jerusalem, which common sense forbids us to imagine to have lasted any longer than the usual sojourn of the pilgrims. Two incidents alone are described: the first is the Cleansing of the Temple; normally this should be placed at the arrival of Jesus in the

[1] Other indications of several journeys to Jerusalem which SABATIER (art. *Jésus-Christ, Enc. Lichtenberger*, VII, pp. 360 f.) has distinguished in the Synoptic tradition are still less conclusive. To give one instance only, in Mark iii. 7–8, crowds who come from Jerusalem are mentioned. Sabatier thinks that this proves that Jesus had been there. But this phrase is one which may very likely be an editorial addition, of which it would be very unwise to make much.

city (ii. 13–22). Together with the discourse which is attached to it, at the most the whole would not occupy more than half a day. The second incident is the conversation with Nicodemus (iii. 1–21). The visit to John the Baptist (as the evangelist presents it) cannot have been very long, for the success of Jesus must have been remarkably swift to have provoked the jealousy of the disciples of John. The journey through Samaria only takes two days more than the usual time allowed for the journey (iv. 2–43). In Galilee, the healing of the nobleman's son would not take more than two days (iv. 46–54). The story of the healing of the impotent man at Bethesda in chapter v would not take more than one day. Thus for the first year[1] there is scarcely sufficient material to fill six to ten weeks with the incidents which are described, even on the broadest reckoning.

For the second year nothing is narrated between the feeding of the multitude and the discourse uttered the next morning in the synagogue at Capernaum, which took place at a time when the Passover was near (vi. 1), and the departure for Jerusalem for the Feast of Tabernacles (vii. 1). Thus the period between April and September remains absolutely empty.

The mention of the feasts which mark the stages in the narrative is stereotyped[2] and mechanical, which suggests that it is simply an editorial proceeding.

The form of the narrative is not merely empty and artificial; it is actually incoherent. Two examples will show this: the accounts of the miracle at Cana (ii. 1–12) and of the healing of the nobleman's son (iv. 43–54) are closely connected with each other. In both of them Cana is the centre of the activity of Jesus, and both are followed by statements which obviously have the same origin and which mark their order. The writer of these statements ignores the miracles accomplished at Jerusalem to which allusion is made in iv. 45, since he regards them as valueless. The transition between chapter v, where Jesus is at Jerusalem, and chapter vi, where it is said that he goes to the eastern shore of the Lake of Gennesaret, is also very unsatisfactory. The expression used would only be

[1] Or for the first two years, if the feast of v. 1 is a Passover.
[2] ii. 13, v. 1, vi. 4, vii. 2, xi. 55.

natural were he then leaving the western shore, whereas at the end of chapter v he was at Jerusalem, and there is no suggestion that he was then preparing to leave Judaea.[1]

The Fourth Gospel is a collection of fragments, each of which could really stand by itself; the author has placed these fragments alongside of one another with no concern for the final impression which this would create. His framework cannot be retained any more than that of the Synoptists.

In order to try to solve the problem of the length of the ministry of Jesus, we must see whether it is possible to discover some data from the incidents considered in themselves, apart from their context.

So far as the Synoptic Gospels are concerned, it will be useful to examine, on the one hand, the meaning and the bearing of the indications contained in the Galilean incidents, and, on the other, the significance of the indications relating to the importance of the activity of Jesus at Jerusalem.

In the story of the plucking of the ears of corn (Mark ii. 33 f.) the ripeness of the ears is not an accessory detail which may be considered merely as an embellishment of the narrative;[2] thus the incident took place about the time of the Feast of the Passover;[3] the Synoptic Gospels place it at the beginning of

[1] It has been proposed that the events of the narrative would run more smoothly if the order of chapters v and vi were inverted. But then, at the beginning of chapter vii, it would be related, or, rather, implied, that Jesus returned into Galilee only to leave it again immediately.

[2] As "the green grass" upon which the hearers of Jesus were seated at the moment of the feeding of the multitudes may be (Mark vi. 39). The grass is dried up in Palestine from the moment the spring is over, hence sometimes this detail has been used to prove that the feeding of the multitudes took place in the spring. But the detail of the green grass is not essential enough to be certain that it belongs to the original source, especially since it is not found in Matthew, nor in Luke. We must also take into account the fact that the grass would remain green in the neighbourhood of water, and that it would be natural to suppose that Jesus chose the bank of some water-course or the neighbourhood of a spring to speak to the people and to feed them.

[3] We can infer nothing from the expression "the sabbath second-first" of Luke vi. 1, for we do not know what it means; the most plausible conjecture is that it is due to an error in transcription.

the ministry of Jesus, immediately after the first day at Capernaum, but since it is inserted in a series of incidents which are grouped together because they have certain elements in common,[1] we cannot be sure that it really belongs to the beginning of the ministry of Jesus. All that we can affirm is that Jesus began his public activity, at the latest, a little less than a year before the moment when it ended.

The incident of the Temple Tax (Matt. xvii. 24–27) which had to be paid in the month Adar is too doubtful to be used. If we can retain anything of it (which is very uncertain, as it is so closely connected with a question which was of moment to Judaeo-Christians) in any case, it would have to be dissociated from the miracle of the tribute-money, and then nothing would be left which would permit us to localize it in Galilee rather than in Judaea.

These data are certainly meagre. They lead us to the negative conclusion that there is nothing in the Synoptic Gospels which would lead us to suppose that the ministry of Jesus lasted more than one year.

In my opinion, however, we can arrive at more definite conclusions with regard to the Jerusalem ministry.

In Mark, Jesus arrives at Jerusalem, makes a solemn entry into the city, visits the Temple, and in the evening returns to Bethany with the Twelve (xi. 1–10). The following day, as he is walking into Jerusalem, he curses a fig tree upon which he can find no fruit (xi. 12–14), then he goes to the Temple, expels the sellers of merchandise, and in the evening goes out of the city (xi. 15–19). The third day, passing by the fig-tree, he sees that it has dried up (xi. 20–25). He again visits the Temple, where a good deal of teaching and discussion takes place, which is ended by some severe words addressed to the Pharisees (xi. 27–xii. 40) and by the episode of the widow's mite (xii. 41–44). When Jesus leaves the Temple he announces its destruction to his disciples (xiii. 1–4), and, in response to a question which they ask him about the moment when this

---

[1] The grouping of the conflicts (ii. 1–iii. 6) is earlier than Mark, as is proved by the conclusion of iii. 6, which gives a note which is neither repeated nor utilized in the following course of the narrative.

prophecy will be fulfilled, he pronounces a great eschatological discourse (xiii. 5–37).

Then begins the story of the Passion, which opens, so we are told, two days before the Passover, that is, on the 12th of Nisan. Jesus is still at Bethany, where the Anointing[1] takes place—the chronological indication of xiv. 1 does not tell us the exact moment when this takes place.

Three points strike us in this narrative, apart from any comparison with the parallel passages—the first is that the three days of the activity of Jesus at Jerusalem are filled in a very unequal manner; the first two days are almost empty, save for the entry into the city, on the one hand, and the Cleansing of the Temple on the other, while the third day is filled with a whole accumulation of discourses and controversies. The second fact is that the indications relating to the division into days are in very close connexion with the two elements in the story of the fig-tree. It is not even said that Jesus returns to Bethany, on the evening of the last day; he is there, however, at the moment of the Anointing (xiv. 3). The third, finally, is this: that the two occasions on which Jesus returns to Bethany which are directly reported, separate incidents which seem to be organically connected. The first is inserted between the entry into Jerusalem and the Cleansing of the Temple in such a way that the triumphal or quasi-triumphal march of Jesus breaks off suddenly, and finishes like any other traveller's visit to the Temple: "And . . . Jesus entered into the Temple and when he had looked round about upon all things, and now the eventide was come, he went out into Bethany with the Twelve" (xi. 11). In Matthew and Luke the record is quite different: here the entry into Jerusalem serves as an introduction to the account of the Cleansing of the Temple. Likewise, the second return to Bethany and the conversation about the fig-tree which withered away (xi. 19–25) separates, most unfortunately, two incidents (the Cleansing of the Temple and the question of authority) which may well have been formerly very closely related to each other; for it would have been, at the very least, interesting to hear the question put to Jesus: "By what authority do you

[1] I do not go into this in further detail here as the subject recurs in connexion with the Last Supper, and the question of the day on which Jesus died.

do these things?" (xi. 28) not as a sort of general and rather theoretical question, but as a sort of challenge addressed to Jesus, urging him to justify what he had just done in the Temple.

The account of the Jerusalem ministry in Matthew covers only two days. The first is occupied with the entry into Jerusalem and the Cleansing of the Temple, after which Jesus returns to Bethany, to spend the night there (xxi. 1–17). The episode of the fig-tree (xxi. 18–22), which is not, as in Mark, broken up into two elements, takes place the next morning, as Jesus is on his way to Jerusalem. The second day is still fuller than the third day in Mark, for, in addition to all the elements given by Mark (with the exception of the story of the widow's mite), Matthew gives several more (between xxi. 28 and xxv. 46). The chronological indications of the story of the Passion are the same as in Mark.

Luke's account includes very nearly the same elements as that of Mark, but it does not contain the cursing of the fig-tree, nor the division into days; at the end of the narrative only he has a little note which says that Jesus spent his days teaching in the Temple, and that in the evening he went out of the city and passed the night on the Mount of Olives (xxi. 37). Neither in this remark, nor elsewhere, does Luke provide any direct indication of the length of the visit of Jesus to Jerusalem. His account gives the definite impression, however, that this visit, without being very long, was longer than the two days of Matthew and the three of Mark.

A comparison of these three accounts shows that from the episode of the fig-tree onwards the chronological order is the same. If this incident is not historical, the division into days automatically disappears.

Some exegetes think that the incident of the fig-tree is only another rendering of the parable of the barren fig-tree (Luke xiii. 6–9)[1] completed by some instructions on prayer, drawn from the Logia.[2] The characteristic element in the parable, however,

---

[1] JOH. WEISS: *Aelt. Ev.*, p. 381. LOISY: *Syn.*, II, pp. 28 f.

[2] The instructions concerning prayer are only connected with the incident of the fig-tree in an artificial way. They seem to come from the Logia, as is proved by two facts: (*a*) Mark xi. 25 has a parallel not in Matt. xxi, but in Matt. vi. 14; (*b*) Mark xi. 22–23, and Matt. xxi. 21, have a parallel

is the idea of a delay granted to the fig-tree, and in the incident related by Mark and Matthew there is no trace of this feature. Hence the agreement between the two passages is too imperfect for us to regard it as in any way proved that there is a literary connexion between them.

It is difficult to be sure of the meaning of the incident. The explanation which seems most probable is that which has been suggested by Schwartz,[1] who regards this as an etiological story. The suggestion is this: on the road from Bethany to Jerusalem there may have been a withered fig-tree of which it was said that it would become green again at the moment of the *parousia*.[2] Embroidering this theme the Christians are supposed to have added that the tree was dry, because Jesus had cursed it because it had no figs. In any case, the incident is non-historical; it is a typical example of a miracle for purposes of display only.

The division into days is in close connexion with the idea that Jesus passed the night at Bethany. Luke does not mention this, nor does he report the Anointing at Bethany. Now, the story of the Anointing, in the form given by Mark, is a secondary element. Bethany is not mentioned in the most ancient tradition about the Passion. If Jesus had been in the habit of spending the night at Bethany until then, how would Judas have known on the night of the arrest that he would find Jesus in the Garden of Gethsemane? We arrive, therefore, at this conclusion: that the primitive tradition gave no precise indications about the stay of Jesus in Jerusalem. None the less, if we look at the record of Luke (which on this point seems to have preserved the most exact details), the reader gains the impression that this sojourn was brief. We have already seen that the words of Jesus about Jerusalem oblige us to expand the chronological framework which tradition seems to give us. But examination of the Synoptic Gospels alone does not help us to see to what extent this should be carried out.

(doublet in Matthew), in Matt. xvii. 20=Luke xvii. 6. This latter saying, which speaks of a mountain being cast into the sea, must be Galilean. This shows the artificial character of the combination.

[1] SCHWARTZ: *Der verfluchte Feigenbaum, Z.N.T.W.*, V, 1904, pp. 80–84.

[2] There may be a trace of this legend in Mark xiii. 28–29. But this passage may have given birth to the legend.

In the Johannine account, the Galilean activity of Jesus has, in proportion, less importance than it has in the Synoptic Gospels; three incidents only are reported: the changing of the water into wine at the wedding at Cana (ii. 1–11), the healing of the nobleman's son (iv. 43–54), and the feeding of the multitudes, coupled with the discourse at Capernaum which was connected with it (chap. vi). These three incidents, separated from one another by two visits to Jerusalem, form a solid block; this impression is confirmed by a close examination of the Jerusalem incidents by which the three Galilean fragments are separated from each other. In the first section, apart from the episode of the Cleansing of the Temple (ii. 14–22) (which should, in reality, be placed in the last period of the activity of Jesus) and the story of the meeting with John the Baptist in Judaea (iii. 22–iv. 3) (which belongs to the time which preceded the opening of his ministry), we only find two narratives. One, the conversation with Nicodemus (iii. 1–21) is a purely theological statement, for which the enquiry of the person who comes by night to see Jesus serves simply as a pretext; the other, the conversation with the Samaritan woman (iv. 4–42), taken in itself, does not necessarily imply a sojourn in Judaea. The historicity of the incident is also very doubtful because it is inconsistent with the principle laid down by Jesus that the Gospel must not be preached to the Samaritans (Matt. x. 5). It reflects a situation—the abolition of the Jewish cult and of the Samaritan cult—which did not exist until after the year 70, and we find in it also a series of ideas and expressions which are characteristic of Johannine theology.

There is therefore nothing historically consistent in the Johannine narrative of the first sojourn of Jesus at Jerusalem, nothing which can be retained in order to establish the actuality of a journey of which the Synoptists did not know, or did not relate.

The second visit to Jerusalem includes only one incident, the healing of an impotent man on the Sabbath day, at the pool of Bethesda (v. 1–13), with the discussion which it provokes (v. 14–47), which, starting with the question of the Sabbath, glides immediately into Christological questions which reflect the controversies between Jews and Christians current at the period when the Gospel was being composed. The account of the healing contains some topographical indications[1] in which it is impossible to discover any allegorical significance, which must be derived from one source; they present certain obscurities which cannot be explained save on the supposition that they are due to the mechanical copying of a passage which the editor has not wholly understood because he did not know the places perfectly himself.[2] The word of Jesus to the impotent man: "Rise, take up thy bed, and go to thy house" (v. 8), is exactly the same as that which we find in Mark in the story of the healing of the paralytic (ii. 11). The remark that the healing took place on the Sabbath day is a kind of postscript, that is to say, it occupies a position which is not very natural (v. 9).[3] It shows that the whole passage v. 9–16 is editorial in character and is designed to introduce the discussion with the Jews (v. 17–47). But the connexion between the healing and the discussion it is supposed to provoke is most inadequate. The charge against Jesus is not that he healed the man but that he bade him carry his bed. Further, the discussion only touches slightly on the question of the Sabbath, and then passes on at once to the divinity of Jesus and his relation to the Father.

Hence the only element in chapter v which is derived from tradition is a story of healing, localized at Jerusalem, and perhaps influenced by a story from the Synoptics, but which does not seem to be the same incident in another form. There is nothing to justify the opinion that the localization at Jerusalem is not a primitive element in the narrative, but there is also nothing to indicate that this incident should be placed in relation with any other visit to Jerusalem than that which is mentioned in the Synoptic Gospels. The fact that they do not mention any healing being accomplished at Jerusalem can

---

[1] For these indications see G. DALMAN: *Les itinéraires de Jésus, Topographie des Évangiles*, trad. *Jacques Marty*, Paris, 1930, pp. 402 f.

[2] The existence of a previous tradition is confirmed by the fact that the text does not express the idea which is necessary to make the incident intelligible, that a miraculous power was attached to the pool of Bethesda for the first sick person who would plunge into the water after it had been troubled by the angel. Several copyists have filled in this gap by adding 3*b* to 4 from the received text.

[3] The same indication occupies a similar place in the story of the healing of the man born blind (ix. 14).

be explained by the fact that, from their point of view, all the activity of Jesus in the Holy City had no other object than to bring to a head the fundamental disagreement which existed between himself and the Jewish authorities, in such a way as to provoke the drama of the Passion. There are, however, several suggestions (we shall have occasion to mention several in the course of this book) which show that the Jerusalem ministry of Jesus was not exclusively of this character.

The third arrival at Jerusalem, described in chapter vii, corresponds to the one and only journey of which the Synoptists speak, in the sense that it mentions a definite departure from Galilee. But the Synoptic Gospels, without mentioning the precise moment of this departure, do not seem to have supposed that it took place much before the time of the Passover; John, on the contrary, places it before the Feast of Tabernacles (September–October) and says, further—a point which the Synoptic account ignores completely—that the stay of Jesus at Jerusalem was interrupted from the Feast of the Dedication in December until a few days before the Passover.

At the beginning of chapter vii in John we recognize the utilization of a source which certain inconsistencies in the story permit us to disentangle, at least in part.[1] Jesus is remaining in Galilee, owing to the hostility of the Judaeans.[2] It is the eve of the Feast of Tabernacles. His brothers, who, it is explicitly stated, do not believe in him, advise him to go to Jerusalem in order that the disciples who are there may also see his works. Here the contradiction is manifest. Jesus is supposed to have abstained from going up to Jerusalem because he had not yet done any "mighty works" there, yet some disciples are already there. In ii. 23, the evangelist had alluded to the miracles which Jesus had worked at Jerusalem, and in chapter v he had narrated the healing of the impotent man at the pool of Bethesda. The conception of the evangelist, according to which Jesus had already been at Jerusalem and

---

[1] On this question see my study: *Notes d'histoire évangélique*, III, *La venue de Jésus à Jérusalem pour la fête des Tabernacles*, R.h.r., LXXXIII, 1921, pp. 123–162.
[2] I believe that here, as in other passages in the Fourth Gospel, the word 'Ιουδαῖοι does not mean Jews in general, but the inhabitants of Judaea.

had gained some disciples, is added to that of the source, according to which he was advised to go to Jerusalem in order to make disciples there also.

It is not certain that, in the source, the advice to Jesus to go to Jerusalem was really given by his brethren who did not believe on him. Apart from this passage the brothers of Jesus are only mentioned in the incident at Cana (ii. 12); the story which relates that Jesus gave his mother into the care of the beloved disciple (xix. 26–27) seems to assume that his death would leave Mary alone and desolate; therefore the implication is that she had no other sons. In xx. 17, the "brethren" of Jesus means his disciples, and this may have been the original meaning of ii. 12.[1] If this were the meaning of the term "brother" in vii. 4, the advice to go to Jerusalem would not have been given to Jesus in a hostile or ironical spirit; it would have been dictated by the desire to see his work extended.

Jesus gives a very decided refusal to this request. He says that his time has not yet come, while it is always the time of those who are not exposed to the hatred of the world (vii. 6–9). The notion of the "time" ($\kappa\alpha\iota\rho\acute{o}s$) gives a very definite indication of the utilization of the source. It is distinct from that of the "hour" ($\overset{\circ}{\omega}\rho\alpha$), which means that of the death, or, as the evangelist says, of the glorification of Christ, the very end for which he was born into this world (xii. 23–27, xiii. 1, xvii. 1). This "hour" will come at the moment appointed by God, without which the hostility of men cannot anticipate it (vii. 30, viii. 20). The "time," on the contrary, means the moment favourable for a public manifestation. The hatred of the world hinders it from coming. There is here a conception of the work of Jesus which is very different from that which is revealed in the idea of the "hour," and it is much less dogmatic. The idea of a moment which might be favourable for a manifestation of Jesus implies the idea that he did not come to this earth solely to die, at the hour appointed by God, but, if

---

[1] In ii. 1, at the arrival at Cana, the following are named: Jesus, his mother, and his disciples. At the departure (ii. 12) the brothers of Jesus are added. We may suppose that originally, in ii. 12, there were only the brothers and that the disciples were added later by a scribe who, not realizing that the term "brother" applied to the disciples, thought that their departure ought to be mentioned as their arrival had been.

possible, to act, in order to win his people, in spite of the hostility with which he was confronted.'

Thus a primary and important element in the source has been brought out clearly. The disciples of Jesus ask him to pursue his work by giving it, through the transference to Jerusalem, a new character. Jesus, judging that the moment is not opportune, refuses, and allows the pilgrims to depart.

After their departure, Jesus also starts out for Jerusalem, but he goes secretly (vii. 10). In the narrative the contradiction is blatant, for there is no explanation of this sudden change on the part of Jesus. His secret departure cannot be explained by suggesting that he wished to prevent his enemies from knowing of his presence in Jerusalem since the moment he arrived he began to teach publicly in the Temple. All becomes clear if we conjecture that in the original source Jesus did not refuse to go to Jerusalem but that he refused to go there in order to incite the people to a Messianic demonstration.

Another trace of the source can be found in verses 14–15. While Jesus is teaching in the Temple, the Jews ask how a man who has never studied can speak as he does. This suggests that Jesus was a new-comer to Jerusalem, and cannot be attributed to the evangelist, who has also mentioned several times that he was teaching in the Temple. According to verses 11–13, people are asking each other at Jerusalem, whether he will come up to the Feast. This suggests that he was so well known that no one would be astonished at the fact that he could teach.

The words placed in the mouth of Jesus at this point are concerned with theological themes which really belong to the evangelist himself. Only now and again can one perceive a sort of distant resemblance to the source, which comes out in some details, which do not seem very relevant to this setting. In verse 32 it is said that the Pharisees send men to arrest Jesus. At this moment the Feast is at its height; it is the day when Jesus had first appeared in the Temple. Verse 37 takes us to the very last day of the Feast, and it is only later mentioned that, as they listened to Jesus, the people were divided, that some wanted to arrest him but that no one dared lay hands on him, doubtless because they feared that his supporters would fight for him. Then we are told how the messengers of the Pharisees return without having arrested Jesus, because, as they say, "Never man spake like this man!" (43–46). Furious, the Pharisees take counsel together and it is then that one of them remarks that the Law does not permit a man to be sentenced without a hearing. To which others reply that no prophet can come out of Galilee (47–52). This account contains several confusing statements, which can only be due to the fact that some fragments of the source are mingled with the record of the evangelist. We recognize also certain ideas which cannot be attributed to the evangelist, especially that of Jesus being welcomed by the crowd with an enthusiasm which neutralizes the hostility of the authorities and hinders them from taking action against him. It would be rash to attempt a reconstruction of the source. We can only gather that, according to it, the people listened to Jesus with approval, and that his enemies sought to thwart his activity, but did not, however, dare to push things to such a point that they would come into conflict with the crowds.

We may also attribute to the source the words of viii. 20ᵃ: "These words spake Jesus in the treasury, as he taught in the Temple," because of the curious position of this indication in the midst of a course of teaching. We find another trace of it in viii. 30: "As he spake these words, many believed on him." This detail does not seem to have much obvious connexion with the preceding words, where it is said that the Jews do not and cannot understand what Jesus is saying to them. It is still less connected with what follows, where Jesus does nothing but emphasize the irreconcilable differences which exist between himself and the Jews. In viii. 59 it is said that the Jews took up stones to stone Jesus but that he escaped from them. As it is not stated that this was because his hour is not yet come, this may be derived from the source.

The healing of the man born blind (ix. 1–41) is indeed localized at Jerusalem, but this story does not contain anything which permits us to place it more at one moment in the ministry of Jesus than at another.[1] As for the allegory of the

---

[1] The episode betrays at least a considerable amount of editorial intervention, on account of the symbolical character of the miracle, the teaching which is attached to it, the unnatural way in which the detail relating to the sabbath is introduced, and, finally, because the Jewish authorities

shepherd which follows,[1] it is a fragment which has no special connexion with the Jerusalem ministry.[2]

Perhaps we find another trace of the source in x. 19–21, where it is said that the words of Jesus produce divisions among the Jews, some saying that he is possessed with a demon, the others objecting that no demoniac can speak as he does. The utilization of a source is more evident in x. 22. The scenes which precede it, from verses 7 to 14, have taken place at Jerusalem without any indication of a change of place, save the mention in viii. 59 of the departure from the Temple. Here we are anew in the Temple, in Solomon's Porch. One change of time only has been indicated. In vii. 14 we were in the middle, and at vii. 37 at the last day of the Feast of Tabernacles. Verse 22 of chapter x runs thus: "And it was at Jerusalem, the Feast of the Dedication, and it was winter. And Jesus walked in the Temple in Solomon's Porch." This phrase is too loosely connected with the preceding verses to be derived from the evangelist. It comes from a source, but not from that whose traces we have already noted from chapter vii onwards, for it is the beginning and not the close of a story which relates to Jesus at Jerusalem. The substance of that which follows ought to be assigned to the same source. The Jews surround Jesus and say to him: "How long dost thou make us to doubt? If thou be the Christ, tell us plainly!" This challenge implies teaching quite different from that which the evangelist has reported, and which evidently turned entirely upon the question of Christology. We must assume that

inflict a penalty upon the man who had been born blind, namely, that of exclusion from the synagogue, which implies a situation which could only have existed after the destruction of the Temple.

[1] The two sections are simply placed side by side; the allegory of the shepherd is addressed to the disciples, whereas at the end of chapter ix Jesus is speaking to hostile Jews. No change of situation is indicated between the two sections.

[2] The intervention of the evangelist can be seen in the allegory of the shepherd—in the way in which the idea of the efficacity of the death of Christ is developed, and other elements also, such as the idea of the sheep who are not of this fold. Nevertheless, the section as a whole cannot come from the evangelist himself. When he is left to himself John is very poor in imagery (in the First Epistle of John there is not a single image). The theme developed by the evangelist seems to have been drawn from a saying or a group of sayings of Jesus.

in it the Messiahship had been implied but not directly stated. The reply of Jesus, on the contrary, takes up again the subject of the controversies which were taking place at the time when the Gospel was being compiled. Only verse 31, where it is said that the Jews took up stones to stone Jesus, and verse 39, which says that they tried to arrest him but that he escaped, can be derived from the source.

The section x. 40–42 is very important. Jesus goes to the other side of the Jordan, to the place where John at first baptized.[1] He stays there, and many people go out to him from Jerusalem in order to see him. They believe in him, and declare that although John the Baptist did no miracles, all that he said of Jesus was true. The allusion to the account in chapter i, the rôle assigned to miracles, and the very clear distinction which is made in this respect between Jesus and John the Baptist, are indications by which we recognize the intervention of the evangelist, but the fragment as a whole cannot be attributed to him because it is based on the idea that during his stay in Jerusalem Jesus made disciples and gained followers, whereas the general theme of the evangelist is this: that the Jews rejected the message of Jesus. What is assumed here is in direct connexion with what is indicated in the source behind chapter vii. Thus we may conclude that in x. 40–42 we have yet another fragment of this first source. This shows us a very characteristic situation. Jesus has withdrawn to Peraea, but he is still in contact with his followers in Jerusalem. He seems ready to resume his activity there as soon as circumstances will permit. There is here something quite similar to that which the source indicated at the beginning of chapter vii, when Jesus was waiting for a favourable moment to make a public manifestation.

The story of the Raising of Lazarus is not an element in the original Gospel. Therefore we need not concern ourselves with

[1] This points to the note in i. 28, about Bethany in Peraea. It has been impossible to identify this locality. A conjecture which is earlier than Origen substitutes Bethabara for Bethany. DALMAN (*Itin.*, pp. 124 f.) remarks that the Aramaic expressions for "Bethany of the Jordan" (bêt 'anyâ'ibrêh deyardenâ) and for "Bethabara of the Jordan" (bêt 'aberâ deyardenâ), which we find in the MSS. of Palestinian origin, are so close to one another that it would be very easy to cause confusion between them. He also thinks that the locality in question may have had two names.

it here. The situation which existed at the end of chapter x, and which was interrupted by the departure of Jesus for Bethany, is re-established at the end of chapter xi (45–54), where it is said that the Jewish authorities, moved by the impression produced by the miracle, come to the decision that Jesus must be killed, and this causes him to withdraw into a town called Ephraim, close to the desert. It would be quite in order to enquire whether, in this conclusion of chapter xi, we are not faced with some elements which come from the source. Especially in the content of verses 47–53 and 55–57 is this the case. We shall have to return to this question.[1]

Six days before the Passover, Jesus comes to Jerusalem (xii. 1), and, from this moment, the course of events is practically that described in the Synoptic Gospels; the differences which are found are such that we can safely ignore them as of no account, as we are here simply dealing with the general framework of the Gospel narrative.

When we compare the data provided by the sources which we have disentangled from chapters vii to xi of the Fourth Gospel with the Synoptic tradition, we discover a certain contradiction between them, the origin of which it is easy to recognize, but which might possibly be resolved. The two traditions are agreed on two points: first of all that Jesus did not return to Galilee after having left it in order to go to Jerusalem, and next, that he arrived at the Holy City a very short time before he was arrested. The Synoptics alone, considering, if we may put it like this, the Judaean ministry from the Galilean point of view, have neglected or ignored the fact that it was broken by a retreat at some distance from Jerusalem; they have placed the arrival of Jesus in the Holy City at the moment when, in reality, he was returning to it. Thus they have arrived at the idea of a very brief ministry in Jerusalem, an idea which, as we have seen, contradicts many of the indications which they themselves give.

The combination of our two sources permits us, so we believe, to arrive at a precise conception of the chronological framework of the Jerusalem ministry of Jesus. He left Galilee at the moment of the Feast of Tabernacles, somewhere in September

[1] See pp. 476 f.

or October; he stayed in Jerusalem until the Feast of the Dedication in December; then he left the city in order to withdraw to a remote place on the other side of the Jordan. He returned to Jerusalem on the eve of the Feast of the Passover. Then events moved swiftly. Jesus was arrested, and a few hours later crucified.

The chronology of the Galilean ministry cannot be fixed with so much precision. One incident, the plucking of the ears of corn, took place in springtime, a little while before the harvest. But, how long had the ministry of Jesus then been going on? For weeks? or for months? We might be tempted, in order to answer this question, to bring into play considerations of two kinds from which we may draw very different conclusions. Taking into account the fact that there is no reliable evidence for a Passover during the Galilean period, we might assume that Jesus only began his activity after the Feast. But, on the other hand, does not the incident of the plucking of the ears of corn reveal a condition of the thought and the teaching of Jesus which it would be difficult to place at the beginning of his ministry? Neither of these two suggestions can, we believe, lead to definite conclusions. The nature of the tradition concerning the Galilean ministry is not such that if it had included a Passover this would of necessity have to be mentioned. If it is true, on the other hand, that in the incident of the plucking of the ears of corn Jesus manifests a certain independence towards the Law, how can we estimate the time it needed for him to free himself from the idea of a literal observance of legal rules? We shall see, also, that the new conception of obedience to God which is implied in the attitude taken up by Jesus with regard to the Law is in direct relation with that which led him to separate from John the Baptist. This leads us to think that, in a certain sense, the process of evolution by which Jesus was freed from the Law should be placed, at least to a large extent, in the period which preceded the beginning of his actual ministry.

There is therefore no reason to make the ministry of Jesus begin more than one year before the moment in which it terminated so tragically. We must add, however, that there is also no reason to refuse to entertain the idea that it may have begun earlier.

Before the Galilean ministry comes the period of contact with John the Baptist. Here it is impossible to give a chronological estimate. The Synoptic tradition has distorted the perspective of the story by reducing the relations between Jesus and John the Baptist to the brief moment of the Baptism. Some weeks at least, perhaps some months, are necessary, if we are to understand the influence exerted by John on Jesus and the psychological process through which Jesus was able to free himself from it.

It seems therefore that we can, though doubtless not with absolute certainty (seeing that the nature of the documents at our disposal does not permit this), at least with a great deal of probability, fix the chronological framework of the ministry of Jesus thus: At the close of the year 26, or at the beginning of the year 27, he is with John the Baptist in the neighbourhood of the Jordan. In the spring of 27 he leaves John the Baptist and returns into Galilee where he begins his actual ministry. This he carries on till the month of September. At this moment he definitely leaves Galilee and comes to work in Jerusalem. He stays there till the month of December, then he retires to a solitary place some distance from Jerusalem, while he remains in contact with the disciples he has gained in Jerusalem. On the eve of the Passover of 28 he returns to Jerusalem and there meets his death.

CHAPTER IX

THE ORIGIN OF JESUS

THE stories in the two first chapters of Matthew and Luke are too manifestly legendary in character to enable us to extract any reliable historical data from them. They bring out certain aspects of the development of Christian piety and doctrine during the first century, and from this point of view they are documents which ought not to be neglected. But they afford no assistance to anyone who desires to attempt to construct a biography of Jesus.

It is even impossible to gain from them any reliable information about the place of his birth; the two accounts (which are independent of each other and impossible to reconcile), by means of which Matthew and Luke explain that Jesus passed for a Galilean and was supposed to belong to Nazareth,[1] although he was born at Bethlehem, in reality prove the very opposite of that which they claim to prove, and make it plain that Jesus did not belong to Judaea. How then did it come to pass that although the birth at Bethlehem, the city of David, was an article of the Jewish Messianic dogmatic belief, a tradition arose which claimed that Jesus was born in a despised semi-Gentile province like Galilee?[2]

Apart from his birth in Galilee, and, as it seems in all probability, at Nazareth, we know nothing about the life of Jesus until the moment when, having arrived at man's estate, he appears before us in the circle surrounding John the Baptist. The only incident of his childhood of which the Gospel has preserved any recollection—Jesus at twelve years old staying behind in the Temple after the departure of his parents (Luke ii. 41–52)—is too isolated to enable us to form any definite opinion upon it.[3] It is sometimes said that Luke may

[1] On Nazareth see pp. 192 ff.
[2] Two passages in the Fourth Gospel (i. 46, vii. 52) prove that the Jews raised an objection to his Messiahship from the fact that Jesus came originally from Nazareth.
[3] The episode reported by Luke is very different from the stories of Jesus as a child which are contained in the Apocryphal Gospels. It belongs to a much more ancient stage of the tradition, but this does not prove that it is historical.

have received it directly or indirectly from the mouth of Mary. This is a hypothesis which is not only arbitrary but improbable. If Luke had been able to draw upon a source of information of this kind, he would not have given an account of the birth of Jesus as legendary as that with which his Gospel opens. What we know of the conditions in which Jesus began his ministryprevents us alsofrom supposing that before he separated from John the Baptist he could have had the sense of being called to be the Son of God, in the absolute meaning of the word.

Some authors, in order to supplement, to some extent, our ignorance of that period which Catholic theologians call the "hidden life" of Jesus,[1] have tried to construct an imaginary picture of the probable education of a Galilean child in a humble religious family.[2] It is better not to try to hide our ignorance under a mask of this kind.

Houston St. Chamberlain[3] has argued that Jesus was of Aryan stock. This theory, which is suggested by philosophical and political considerations, rather than by historical reasons, is based upon certain arguments of which all that can be said of them is that they represent a bare possibility. The very name of *Galil-ha-goïm*, Galilee, literally, "circle of pagans" ($Γαλιλαία$ $ἀλλοφύλων$) in Es. viii. 23 and in I Macc. v. 15, shows, apart from anything else, that Galilee was full of Gentile influences.[4] At the time of the Maccabees the purely Jewish element in the population only consisted of a small and weak

[1] The term has been taken up again by GUIGNEBERT: *La vie cachée de Jésus.* It is not a happy expression, because it leads to misunderstanding.

[2] See, for instance, STAPFER: *Jésus Christ avant son ministère.*

[3] HOUSTON ST. CHAMBERLAIN: *Die Grundlagen des neunzehnten Jahrhunderts*, Stuttgart, 1900, pp. 210–219. Chamberlain's theory has been adopted by a certain number of writers like LAFONT: *Aryens de Galilée et les origines de christianisme*, Paris, 1902. A. MÜLLER: *Jesus ein Arier*, Leipzig, 1904. E. BOSC: *La vie ésotérique de Jésus-Christ*, Paris, 1902. P. HAUPT: *Die arische Abkunft Jesu und seiner Jünger*, Orient. Litzg., 1908, pp. 237 ff., etc.

[4] W. BAUER (*Jesus der Galiläer*, in the *Festgabe Ad. Jülicher*, Tübingen, 1927, pp. 16–34) has tried to prove that the Galilean origin of Jesus explains his thought, especially his apparent lack of attachment to the Temple worship. In *R.h.p.r.*, VII, 1927, pp. 243 ff., I have given my reasons for hesitating to accept this theory.

minority. Simon Maccabaeus organized an expedition to come to its assistance. He defeated the Gentiles and killed three thousand of them, but, since he did not feel strong enough to occupy the province properly, and the Jewish inhabitants were not sufficiently numerous to defend themselves, he carried them away and settled them in Judaea, with their wives, their children, and all their goods (1 Macc. v. 23). During the course of the first century before our era[1] Galilee was reconquered and Judaized. These facts seem to make it very clear that the population of Galilee was a mixed race.[2] It is not absolutely impossible that Jesus was not entirely of Jewish descent. But even if this were more than a bare possibility, it would still fail to prove that he did not belong to the Semitic race. In order to assign him an Aryan origin it is necessary to resort to so many conjectures that we may conclude we have the right to ignore this hypothesis.[3] The question of the race of Jesus ought to be answered without hesitation in the traditional sense if we could accept it as an established fact that he was descended from, or believed to be descended from David. The fact that his parents lived in Galilee and occupied a very humble position does not constitute a valid objection to this claim.

Paul, in the Epistle to the Romans (i. 3), affirms categorically the Davidic origin of Jesus.[4] This idea is thus considerably

[1] At the time of Aristobulus (104–103), according to SCHÜRER (I, p. 276); already in the days of John Hyrcanus (135–104), according to DALMAN (*Die Worte Jesu*, Leipzig, 1908, I, p. 7) and G. A. SMITH (*The Historical Geography of the Holy Land*, London, 1901, p. 414).

[2] One could also bring forward certain peculiarities of dialect, attested by the Talmud (see the passages collected by STRACK-BILLERBECK: I, p. 157), but it is very difficult to estimate their exact significance.

[3] KLAUSNER (p. 233) opposes the theory that Jesus was an Aryan: (i) because in the New Testament there is not the very slightest hint that Jesus had a drop of Gentile blood in his veins, although universalists like Paul and Luke would have been glad to emphasize a fact of this kind; (ii) because the character and manner of Jesus were essentially Jewish. These two arguments do not seem to us decisive. To the first we may reply: Paul never denies the privileged position of the Jewish people, but only affirms that the coming of Christ means the abrogation of the Law; we may reply to the second that the character of a man depends at least as much on the education he has received as on the race to which he belongs.

[4] The same assertion also occurs in 2 Tim. ii. 8, and is suggested in Rev. iii. 7, v. 5, xxii. 16.

earlier than the stories of the infancy in the Gospels. It is important to note the facts exactly, because they show that, more and more, tradition insisted on this descent. Blind Bartimaeus calls on Jesus by the name of "Son of David" (Mark x. 47–48*). In the story of the healing of the blind men of Jericho, Matthew reports the same invocation (xx. 30–31). He gives it also in the story of the healing of two blind men peculiar to his Gospel, which seems as though it may be a doublet of the Jericho incident (ix. 27–31). After Jesus had cast out the demon (whose healing calls forth the accusation of "possession" which is brought against him), Matthew says that the spectators, beside themselves with astonishment, said to one another: "Is not this the Son of David?" (xii. 23). Luke, in the corresponding story, xi. 14, does not give this remark. Thus the first evangelist attached a special importance to the fact of the descent of Jesus from David. This is confirmed by the fact that in the story of the Canaanitish woman (which he has in common with Mark), he alone mentions the fact that the woman calls Jesus: "Lord, Son of David" (xv. 22). Similarly, in the account of the ovation which Jesus received at his entry into Jerusalem, although in Mark we read: "Hosanna, blessed is he that cometh in the name of the Lord! Blessed be the Kingdom of our father David, that cometh in the name of the Lord: Hosanna in the highest" (xi. 9–10) and Luke has: "Blessed be the king that cometh in the name of the Lord: peace in heaven and glory in the highest" (xix. 38), Matthew's version reads: "Hosanna to the Son of David! Blessed is he that cometh in the name of the Lord; Hosanna in the highest" (xxi. 9).

The Fourth Gospel seems to admit that Jesus was not descended from David, since it indicates no reply to the objection raised by the Jews (invoking Micah v. 1), against the Messiahship of Jesus, based on the fact that being a Galilean he did not belong to the race of David, and did not come from Bethlehem (vii. 41–42).

The idea of the Davidic descent of Jesus, postulated by Jewish Messianic theology, was very early so widespread, and was regarded as so important, that it is impossible to imagine that John did not know of it. The question therefore arises: what is the reason for this denial of the Davidic descent?—

(which is what the section in vii. 41–42 practically means)— is it part of an authorized tradition, according to which Jesus was not considered to have been the Son of David? or should we explain it by the desire of the Fourth evangelist to detach the Christians of his day from Jewish ideas?

One fact seems to favour the former of these two interpretations, and that is that the Synoptic tradition has preserved an incident in which (if, at least, we accept the interpretation which seems to us the most likely) Jesus denies that the Messiah must be descended from David. The scene takes place in the Temple. Jesus has just answered several insidious questions which have been addressed to him. Then, taking the offensive, he asks questions in his turn. "How," he asks, "say the Scribes that Christ is the Son of David? For David himself said by the Holy Ghost, The Lord said to my Lord, Sit thou on my right hand, till I make thine enemies thy footstool (Ps. cx. 1). David therefore himself calleth him Lord, and whence is he then his son?" (Mark xii. 35–37*).

To the evangelists the question of Jesus was only an argument *ad hominem*, a problem which Jesus proposes to his adversaries in order to disconcert them. Conservative exegetes like Zahn and Wohlenberg, for instance, think that this is the real meaning of the passage.[1] But this question was also embarrassing for the Christians, and it is difficult to understand why there is no suggestion of a solution from the point of view of belief in the Davidic descent. The text before us sets up an antinomy between the idea of the Davidic descent and that of a transcendent Messiah in the sense that he is above all that is human. It does not show how this question can be solved. Here, too, Jesus is using a conception which is entirely different from that of the Messiah of Davidic origin. It is true, of course, that Jesus might have been Son of David, and yet not have considered that this made him the Messiah. Hence we cannot claim that the question which he asks excludes the actual descent from David.[2] There is, however,

---

[1] ZAHN: *Das Evang. des Matth.*, Leipzig, 1903, p. 638. WOHLENBERG: *Das Ev. des Markus*, Leipzig, 1910, p. 323.
[2] J. WEISS (*Schriften*, I, p. 189), LAGRANGE (*Évangile selon St. Marc²*, Paris, 1910, pp. 303 ff.), and others think that the statement of Jesus only shows that he did not attach a great deal of importance to his Davidic descent.

I

still the consideration that the polemic of Jesus against the idea of a Davidic Messiah is better understood if the fact that he was not descended from David was an objection over which he triumphed before he arrived at the conclusion that he was the Messiah; this is why the interpretation in which the passage with which we are dealing would be taken to mean that Jesus was not of Davidic descent seems to us the most probable.[1]

Is the saying of Jesus reported by Mark authentic? Bousset and Bultmann[2] claim that it is not, because, they say, if Jesus had spoken as the Synoptic Gospels say he did, the conception of the Messiah as the Son of David would not have been able to arise. However, the idea became well established that Jesus was born at Bethlehem, although a reliable tradition represented him as a Galilean. Bousset inclines to the idea that the denial of the Davidic descent was a consequence of the transfer of the Christian faith to Hellenic soil, and of the substitution of the idea of the *Kurios*, the heavenly Lord, for that of the Messsiah. But, in reality, Hellenistic Christianity was not opposed to Palestinian Christianity; Greek Christianity did not substitute new conceptions for those which were more ancient. All it did was to add some new elements to the traditional views. It is in a Hellenistic document, the Epistle to the Romans, that we find for the first time the idea of Jesus, Son of David. We must, therefore (so it seems to me), see in the appearance of this idea, in spite of the saying of Jesus which denies it, a result of the influence exerted by Jewish Messianic theology on the development of Christian Christology.

We know very little about the parents of Jesus; in fact, nothing beyond their names, Joseph,[3] and Mary.[4] We cannot use any

---

[1] It is admitted, for instance, by WREDE (*Jesus als Davidssohn, Vorträge und Studien*, Tübingen, 1907, pp. 147–177), WELLHAUSEN (*Mk.*, p. 104), and LOISY (*Syn.*, II, pp. 362 ff.).

[2] BOUSSET: *Kyrios Christos*[2], p. 43. BULTMANN: *Syn. Tr.*, p. 83[2], pp. 145 ff.

[3] Outside the Gospel records of the infancy, and the genealogies, the name of Joseph is found in Luke iv. 22; John i. 45, vi. 42.

[4] Outside the Gospel records of the infancy we find the name of Mary in Matt. xiii. 55; Mark vi. 3; Luke ii. 34; Acts i. 14. In Mark iii. 31 ff., the mother of Jesus is mentioned without her name being given. The same takes place regularly in the Fourth Gospel (ii. 1 ff., vi. 42, xix. 25). It

information contained in MSS. dating from the period when the legend, and perhaps even the worship, of Mary had already begun to develop.

Joseph does not appear again in the story, not even when the family of Jesus come and try to take him home (Mark iii. 20–21*), nor when Jesus comes to Nazareth (Mark vi. 1–6a*). It has been thought that he died before the ministry of Jesus began; this conjecture may very well be true. According to Mark vi. 3 and Matt. xiii. 55, Joseph was an artisan, a carpenter,[1] or a mason, or both at once. Thus the family of Jesus belonged to a humble class in society. According to a fairly plausible conjecture which is based on the comparison of the mention of the women at the Cross, a sister of the mother of Jesus was called Salome, and she may have been the mother of James and John. According to Luke's Gospel of the infancy Mary was the cousin of Elizabeth, the mother of John the Baptist (i. 36). We cannot build on this argument, however, owing to the character of the record in which it occurs, and also because it agrees with the fundamental concern of the Gospel records in relation to John the Baptist, namely, to make him an integral part of the Gospel story.

That Jesus had brothers seems to be certain from Luke ii. 7, where Jesus is called "the firstborn son" of Mary. The sisters of Jesus are mentioned in the scene in the synagogue at Nazareth, but we are not told how many there were nor what they were called. On the other hand, four brothers of Jesus

would, however, be rash to conclude from this that the oldest form of tradition did not know the name of Mary. In any case it had no direct interest in her.

[1] According to Mark vi. 3 (א. B. D.), Jesus carried on the same trade as his father. JUSTIN (*Dial.*, 88) says that he made ploughs and yokes. Similar traditions have been preserved in the *Arab Gospel of the Infancy*, ch. 38 (TISCHENDORF: *Ev. Apocr.*, p. 193), and in the *Gospel of Thomas*, ch. 13 (TISCHENDORF: *Ev. Apocr.*, p. 45). The Talmud (*Ab. Zar. 3 b, J. Jebamot*, VIII, 2) calls Jesus "the carpenter, the son of the carpenter." However, the reading ὁ τέκτων of Mark vi. 3, is not certain. Some miniscules (xiii. 33, 69, etc.) and some MSS. of the ancient Latin version read or suggest ὁ τοῦ τέκτονος υἱός, and this reading is supported by the authority of Origen, who says that nowhere in the Gospels is Jesus called the carpenter. (*Contra Celsum*, VI, 36.) The reading of א. B. D. might well come from a correction made under the influence of belief in the Virgin Birth.

are named: James, Joses or Joseph,[1] Jude, and Simon (Mark vi. 3).

We do not need to concern ourselves here with the dogmatic reasons which prevent Catholic theologians from admitting that Jesus could have had any brothers, which lead them to argue that those who are called his "brothers" in the Gospels were either half-brothers by a previous marriage of Joseph, or cousins. It is unnecessary to give the history of these theories.[2] The chief argument by which they are defended is the absence in Hebrew and in Aramaic of a word expressing a near relationship, such as that which exists between cousins or between an uncle and nephew.[3] The word "brothers" employed in the Gospels may have arisen from a misunderstanding, the Aramaic term having been heard by the Greek translators who rendered it by ἀδελφοί in a more precise sense than it had in Aramaic. It is impossible to admit that this confusion exists, for, in all probability, the transition from the Aramaic form to the Greek form of the tradition took place in bilingual places like the community at Antioch. The Greek translators, who were most careful, would not have used the word ἀδελφοί, but, for example, the word ἀνεψιοί which means "cousins," and is found in Col. iv. 10, if James, Jude, Simon, and Joses had not been regarded as the real brothers of Jesus in Aramaic-speaking circles.

From the historical point of view the question of the brothers of Jesus is not a problem; it is a problem in Catholic dogma only.[4]

[1] There is a little uncertainty about this name. The form Ἰωσῆς seems the best attested in Mark (B. D. Δ. Θ. syr.ˢᶜ), it is not strongly supported in Matthew (K. L. W. Δ.). It is given in Mark by א. 121, 278, b. e. f., etc. In Mark also there is found the form Ἰωσῆ (A. C. W., etc., syˢ), which seems to be explained by the desire not to pronounce judgment on the two preceding ones. Finally, in Matthew, א*. D. read Ἰωάννης, a form which may be explained by supposing that the letters ΙΩΣ have been used as an abbreviation.

[2] See, for instance, PRAT: La parenté de Jésus, Rech. de science relig., XVII, 1927, pp. 127–138.

[3] In Gen. xiii. 8, Abraham says to his nephew, Lot: "We are brethren." Laban says the same of Jacob (xxix. 15). In 1 Chron. xxiii. 21–22 the word "brother" is used in the sense of "cousin."

[4] It is useless to discuss the theory of G. M. DE LA GARENNE: Le problème des frères du Seigneur, Paris, 1928, who imagines that Jesus was really the son of Cleopas, legally the son of Joseph, Cleopas, brother of Joseph, having

The evangelists give a religious meaning to the name of Jesus. Matthew places these words in the mouth of the angel who announces the birth of Jesus to Joseph: "Thou shall call his name JESUS, for he shall save his people from their sins" (i. 21). This is a pure coincidence, and it is quite unnecessary to suggest, as Guignebert does,[1] that the fact of bearing a name so charged with religious significance may have suggested to Jesus the idea of his vocation. Proper names, whatever their original significance may have been, very quickly become commonplace.[2]

What language did Jesus speak? At the beginning of the present era Hebrew was a religious and learnéd language only. The reading of the Law and the Prophets in the synagogue, in order to be understood, had to be accompanied by a translation into the vulgar tongue. Tradition asserts that Jesus had not been taught by the Rabbis (Mark vi. 2; John vii. 15) and there is no reason to doubt its testimony on this point. Thus he would not know Hebrew, or, at the most, he would only have learned a few words from hearing it read aloud in the synagogue. It is very doubtful whether he ever knew Greek. There were, it is true, a good many people in Galilee who spoke Greek; but they were mostly minor officials and shopkeepers as well as the inhabitants of the larger towns like Tiberias or Sepphoris; but Jesus did not frequent such places. He preached in the villages and in the open country. There, Aramaic was the usual language,[3] so it is in Aramaic that a few sayings are reported in the Gospels in which the

married Mary, in accordance with the legal ordinances of the levirate; that James and Joseph were born of a previous marriage of Cleopas; and, finally, that Jude, Simon, and their sisters were really and legally the children of Cleopas and Mary. We have expounded our objections against this theory in *R.h.r.*, XCVIII, 1928, pp. 120–125.

[1] GUIGNEBERT: *Vie cachée*, p. 22.

[2] A characteristic fact of this kind is the heathen name of Isidore which has been borne by so many Jews.

[3] On the particular dialect spoken by Jesus, see ARNOLD MEYER: *Jesu Muttersprache*, Freiburg im Br., Leipzig, 1896. DALMAN: *Die Worte Jesu*; *Jesus-Jeschua*, *Die drei Sprachen Jesu*, Leipzig, 1922. F. SCHULTHESS: *Das Problem der Sprache Jesu*, Zurich, 1917; *Zur Sprache der Evangelien*, *Z.N.T.W.*, XXI, 1922, pp. 216–236, 241–258.

evangelist seemed to be anxious to preserve the *ipsissima verba* of Jesus.[1]

If Jesus did not know Greek, the hypothesis of the influence of Hellenic culture upon him can only be admitted to this extent: the Palestinian Judaism of his day was partially Hellenized, and its influence, though felt, would not be strong.

As for the religious sphere in which Jesus grew up, although as a whole the record of the Gospel stories of the infancy is unreliable, it seems clear that this society must have been characterized by the ardent and simple piety of the "quiet in the land,"[2] whose aspirations are expressed in the *Magnificat* and in the hymn of Zacharias; the aged Simeon and Anna, the prophetess, were typical members of this group.[3] The families which formed these circles belonged to the ranks of the people; they were steeped in the thought of the Old Testament, above all in that of the Psalms and the Prophets, and also the apocalyptic writings; this group was chiefly a religious society, in which the moral and not the political aspect of Messianism predominated. Luke (ii. 25) describes it exactly when he says that it was composed of people who "were waiting for the deliverance of Israel." We do not deny the originality of Jesus when we admit that this social setting must have exerted a profound influence upon him.

It would be interesting to be able to determine whether, before his ministry began, Jesus had come under the influence (whether positive or negative) of the Pharisees and Sadducees. But there is no evidence one way or the other, and the attitude adopted by Jesus towards the two great Jewish parties during the course of his ministry is quite intelligible even if he had not come into touch with them before he began to preach his gospel.

On the question of the possible influence of the Essenes we can arrive at more definite conclusions.[4] Jesus came into

---

[1] Mark v. 41, vii. 34, xiv. 36, xv. 34.

[2] A. CAUSSE: *Les Pauvres d'Israël*, Paris, Strasbourg, 1922.

[3] It matters little whether Anna and Simeon were real persons or ideal figures.

[4] STAPFER: *L'essénisme et le christianisme primitif, Leçon d'ouverture de la Faculté de théologie protestante de Paris*, Paris, 1900.

contact with it as a system at more than one point; these instances, such as the prohibition of swearing, opposition to divorce, and a certain indifference to the cult of sacrifice, are not unimportant. Taken in themselves such similarities prove nothing, especially when they are accompanied by important differences. Among the Essenes the criticism of the sacrificial cult remained negative, while with Jesus it was connected with a new conception of duty towards God. The Essenes were mainly concerned about ritual purity; to the observance of rites prescribed by the Law they used to add the practice of special ablutions, repeated several times a day. They were ascetics who retired from the world without seeking to influence it at all. The attitude of Jesus was quite different. Finally, in him there is nothing which corresponds to the Essene practices which denote extra-Jewish influences and seem to have been survivals of a solar cult.

Thus, under these conditions, even if Jesus had heard of the Essenes, it would be impossible to admit that they had influenced him to any appreciable extent.

CHAPTER X

JESUS AND JOHN THE BAPTIST[1]

THE three Synoptic Gospels open with statements about John the Baptist which serve as an introduction to the account of the baptism of Jesus, and through this, to the Gospel story in general.[2] Christian tradition has represented John the Baptist as the Forerunner, and has reduced the part he had to play to that of announcing the advent of the one "who is greater than he," that is to say, of Jesus himself. Mark has expressed this sentiment, and has incorporated John the Baptist completely into the Gospel story by making his statement about John the "beginning of the Gospel of Jesus Christ" (i. 1).

This point of view is theoretical rather than historical. It grew out of a concern for apologetics, and was developed with the aim of defining the relation between the Christian Church and the group composed of the disciples of John the Baptist. This simple fact shows conclusively that Jesus appears in the light of history for the first time as a member of the circle which surrounded John the Baptist, and that it was from him that he received his first impulse to action.

Our information about John the Baptist is drawn from Flavius Josephus (*A.J.*, XVIII, 5, 2. ¶¶ 117–119) and from the Gospels (Matt. iii. 1–12*; Mark vi. 17–29*). Neither from one side nor the other do we receive our information in an absolutely objective and disinterested manner.

While the evangelists wished to represent John simply as the Forerunner of the Messiah, Josephus, on the other hand, took care to ignore the Messianic character of his teaching so completely that his readers should know nothing about Jewish Messianism, which was in its very essence anti-Roman. Never-

[1] For further details about John the Baptist, and for the justification of the views which are expounded in this chapter, I would refer the reader to my book *Jean-Baptiste*.

[2] The statement about John the Baptist and the account of the baptism of Jesus are not derived from the same source. The former is derived from the point of view of John, and seems to come from the circle of his disciples. The same cannot be said of the second point.

theless, when we compare the material drawn from these two different sources—different both in their nature and in their tendencies—we are able to paint a picture of the prophet, which, although it may not be complete, is at least accurate.

Josephus speaks of John the Baptist in connexion with the defeat inflicted on the Tetrarch Herod Antipas by the King of the Nabataeans, Aretas, whose daughter he had married and then deserted in order to contract a union with Herodias, the wife of his half-brother Herod.[1] She was the granddaughter of Herod the Great and therefore his niece. Josephus reports that among the people this defeat was regarded by some as the chastisement for the crime which Antipas had committed in putting John the Baptist to death. Josephus expresses himself thus:[2]

Now some of the Jews thought that the army of Herod had perished because it was the Divine will and a just retribution for (the wrong done to) John, surnamed the Baptist. For, indeed, he had had him killed, although this (John) was a good man, and he incited the Jews to practise virtue, to be just towards one another, and pious towards God. He invited them to unite themselves by a baptism.[3] For it is on this condition that God regarded baptism with favour, if it served not only for the remission of certain faults, but also to purify the body after the soul had already been purified by justice. Some people were assembled round him, for they were greatly moved when they heard him speak. Herod feared that such a power of persuasion might lead to a revolt, the masses seeming ready to follow the counsel of this man in everything. Hence he (Herod) preferred to lay hands on him before he caused any trouble, than to have to repent, later on, if a movement had taken

---

[1] And not, as the Gospels say (Mark vi. 17*), the wife of Philip. Philip married Salome, the daughter of Herodias. The personal name of this Herod is not known. We only know that he was the son of Marianne II, the third wife of Herod the Great.

[2] The French version here follows the translation of G. MATHIEU and L. HERMANN (Œuvres de Flavius Josèphe, ed. THÉODORE REINACH, IV, p. 155), altering it only at one point, which is mentioned in the following note.

[3] G. MATHIEU and L. HERMANN translate "in order to receive baptism." We have indicated (Jean-Baptiste, p. 16, n. 1) the reasons for which the expression βαπτισμῷ συνιέναι should be, in our opinion, otherwise translated.

place, that he had exposed himself to such dangers. On account of these suspicions of Herod, John was sent to Machaerus, the fortress which we mentioned above, and there he was killed. The Jews believed that it was in order to avenge him that disaster fell upon the army; thus God punished Herod.

There is no valid reason to suspect the validity of this passage, which is given by all the manuscripts without any important variant and was known by Eusebius and even by Origen.[1] It contains no contradiction nor obscurity, and cannot be drawn from the Christian tradition because it does not mention the Messianic preaching of John nor the testimony rendered by him to Jesus.

But the portrait of John which Josephus outlines is certainly incomplete. How, indeed, 'did it come to pass that a simple message of virtue and piety should enkindle among the people such a spirit of excitement that the political authorities considered it to be dangerous? Evidently the intention of Josephus is to represent John merely as a moralist, but it is easy to see that his activity must have been something more than this. The expression "to unite oneself by a baptism" implies the idea of the constitution of a group, without giving any indication of its character. Josephus only assigns a very minor importance to the baptism of John, and in addition his description of it makes it very difficult to understand its character. He represents it as the washing away of the stains of the body after the soul has been purified by justice, but it does not procure pardon for faults which have already been committed. A purely corporal and ritual purification seems to harmonize badly with a purely moral teaching. Thus Josephus has given an inaccurate or incomplete idea of the thought of John. This may be due to ignorance, but it seems more probable that his evidence has been influenced and altered by his preconceived purpose to be silent on the subject of Messianism.

The Synoptic Gospels agree with Josephus on the essential points. They also represent John as a popular preacher who gave moral teaching of a high and rigorous kind and who

---

[1] EUSEBIUS: *Eccl. Hist.*, I, 11, 4–6; *Dem. evang.*, IX, 5, 15. ORIGEN: *Cont. Celsum*, I, 47.

issued a vigorous call to repentance. They also witness to the fact that the preaching of John was most successful and attracted great crowds; they say that John baptized those who wished to be his disciples, and that finally he fell a victim to Herod.[1]

The Gospels give some complementary information on the life of John which sounds very likely to be true: they say that his life was that of an ascetic (Mark i. 6*; Matt. xi. 18*); they speak of the habits of fasting practised by him and followed by his disciples (Mark ii. 18*) and allude to a prayer which he is said to have taught them (Luke xi. 1).

In the Gospels we also find some definite details concerning his teaching. They present his preaching as a summons to repentance motivated by the nearness of the coming of the Kingdom of God and the advent of the Messiah, who will "baptize with the Holy Ghost and with fire," that is to say, will exercise judgment which will separate the good from the bad, those who (following the image which he uses) will be the "wheat" the Messiah will "gather into his garner," but those who are destined to be the chaff "he will burn up . . . with unquenchable fire" (Matt. iii. 11–12).[2] This idea of the imminence of the advent of the Messiah and of the nearness of the Judgment were current in Jewish Apocalyptic writings; but the distinctive element in the message of John the Baptist was this: that in this Judgment the fact that one does or does not belong to the Chosen People will play no part at all. If God wills he can "raise up children unto Abraham" out of the very stones of the desert (Matt. iii. 9*). Judgment will be pronounced solely on the way in which men have obeyed

[1] According to Josephus, John the Baptist was put to death for political reasons. According to the Gospels, this took place because John reproached Antipas for his marriage with Herodias. The two motives are not irreconcilable. The account of the death of John in the Synoptic Gospels bears the marks of a popular legend; the scene in which John reproaches Herod may very well be non-historical. The Tetrarch might only (and not without reason) have interpreted the preaching of John as a personal accusation and as an attempt to undermine his authority. As for the scene of the death of John and the story of the feast (Mark vi. 17–29*), it teems with improbabilities.

[2] Mark (i. 8) has mutilated the text of the source, and has substituted the baptism of the Spirit, that is to say, Christian baptism, for the baptism of the Messianic Judgment.

the Law of God, hence the necessity for repentance of which baptism is the seal, and perhaps something more if we relate the expression used by Josephus (βαπτισμῷ συνίεναι) to the fact that the disciples of John the Baptist constituted an organized group. This leads us to the conclusion that the baptism of John had a twofold character: on the one hand, it was a rite of purification, of the same type as certain Jewish ablutions, legal and extra-legal, especially the ablutions of the Essenes, which were in any case inspired by the same ideas; on the other hand, it was also a rite of admission, which constituted a veritable confraternity of penitents, who were waiting and preparing for the Kingdom of God. Of all this Josephus says nothing, but it cannot all have been created by the Christian tradition, which did not try to bring out the originality of John the Baptist in any particular way, but, on the contrary, tried to efface him and represent him simply as the herald of Jesus. All this, too, is necessary in order to explain not only what the Gospels say, but Josephus himself, about the baptism of John, of the success of his preaching, and of the anxiety which this roused in the mind of Herod.

The development of the thought of John the Baptist can only be described in a very general way. According to Luke (i. 5 ff.) he came of a priestly family, but it would not be fitting to build much on an account in which the legendary and poetical element, to say the least, plays a very large part. Even if this information be correct it has no great significance, for in all that we know about John there is nothing which would lead us to suppose that he had any concern, positive or negative, with the ritual of worship or with the Temple.

Because he laid so much emphasis upon baptism some have thought that John was an Essene, or at least that at some time in his life he had belonged to this sect.[1] But his disciples were only baptized once, whereas the ablutions of the Essenes were repeated several times a day; also John's baptism does not seem to have been of a purely ritual character, but to have been inseparable from repentance. None of the characteristic features of the life of the Essenes, such as the worship of angels,

[1] GRAETZ: *Geschichte der Juden*, III3, Leipzig, 1898, p. 293. RUBINSTEIN: *Rev. des Études juives*, Juillet, 1927, pp. 66–70.

or the prayer at sunrise, are adopted by John, and his costume differed so far as it is possible to imagine from the white robe of the Essenes. Nor do we know anything which would lead us to suppose that among the Essenes the idea of the Messiah and the expectation of Judgment assumed an importance which would explain the part these ideas played in the teaching of John.

John's connexion lay rather in the direction of those popular groups which were characterized by a very simple and living piety, steeped in the spirit of the Prophets and the Psalms, who, according to the expression used by Luke, were "waiting for the consolation of Israel" (ii. 25).

On account of his manner of life it has been suggested that John was a Nazirite; but we do not find in him that concern for ritual purity which predominates in such men. It seems almost certain, as well, that at the beginning of the Christian era the Naziriteship for life no longer existed. On the other hand, John was entirely independent of the Zealot movement. He was concerned simply and solely with religious questions; he had no interest in politics, because he did not expect the Messiah to come and punish the oppressors of Israel, but to judge each man according to his work, and in this judgment the privilege of being a child of Abraham played no part at all. At the same time, in so doing he separated from the Apocalyptic movement, to which from other points of view he belonged.

Thus the diverse influences which we can discern or imagine do not entirely explain the personality of John and the formation of his ideas. As in the case of all who have exercised an influence on the course of history, there is in him something which defies historical analysis, the mystery of his personality.

It is impossible to doubt that Jesus was in contact with John and that he received baptism at his hands. The evangelists (Mark i. 9–11*) bear witness to this fact, which was a source of great embarrassment to Christian thought. For at his baptism, the relation of Jesus to John the Baptist seems to be, if not that of an inferior towards a superior, at least that of a disciple towards his master. Tradition has tried to efface this impression by insisting on the celestial manifestations which took place when Jesus was baptized, the opened heavens, the descent of the Spirit, the heavenly voice.[1] But this has not always been sufficient by itself, as is shown by the fact that the Fourth Gospel omits the account of the baptism altogether,[2] and that Matthew found it necessary to introduce it with a dialogue between Jesus and John, in which the latter protests against the idea of baptizing Jesus, declaring that he himself needed rather to be baptized by him; to which Jesus replies: "thus it becometh us to fulfil all righteousness" (Matt. iii. 14–15), which means, righteousness being that which is in conformity with the will of God, the baptism of Jesus is in conformity with a higher demand, which man is unable to understand.

Although the fact of the baptism of Jesus by John is an established fact, the accounts of it which we have in the Gospels are not thereby rendered historical. They are theological explanations. Mark's account has a double meaning: on the one hand, the Holy Spirit descending upon Jesus, makes him the Son of God, the Messiah; this is an explanation of the Messiahship of Jesus and of its origin; on the other hand, the baptism is the manifestation of Jesus as Messiah to John the Baptist and those around him. The second point alone is retained by Matthew and by Luke. To these two evangelists the Messiahship of Jesus could no longer be explained by the Spirit of God descending on him at the moment of his baptism, since he was already Messiah by virtue of the Virgin Birth.

The idea that Jesus had been publicly proclaimed as the Messiah before the moment when his public activity began cannot be primitive. Even if he had the feeling that he was

---

[1] Later tradition has embroidered this account with the addition of new features: Light and fire (in two MSS. of the ancient Latin version (a, g) in Justin, Tatian, in the Gospel of the Ebionites or of the Twelve Apostles), the presence of angels, thunder, sinking or stirring of the waters of the Jordan, etc. (Cf. *Jean-Baptiste*, pp. 184 ff.)

[2] It is sometimes said that all he does is to omit this story, but it is impossible to see where, in John i. 29–39, the baptism could be placed. John knew the Synoptic account, for he gives two very clear indications of this. First, in i. 29, this phrase: "The next morning John seeth Jesus coming unto him," which is not followed by any account of a meeting between John and Jesus. Further, in i. 32 f., John sees the Spirit descending on Jesus like a dove.

the Messiah, or, to put it more accurately, to be destined to
be manifested as Messiah at the moment of the coming of the
Kingdom of God, he never spoke openly about his Messiahship, and only revealed it, or allowed it to be divined by his
intimates, save at the very close of his life, when, before the
Sanhedrin, he confessed that he was the Son of Man, justifying
his statement by announcing his coming on the clouds of
heaven (Mark xiv. 62*).

The proclamation of the Messiahship of Jesus at his baptism
should then be regarded as the projection into the past of a
much later idea; from a very early date, however, it became
evident that this idea had been present from the very beginning,
and that in a manner which was evident to all unless they were
blinded by preconceived hostility.

The Synoptic Gospels limit the contact between Jesus and
John the Baptist to the brief moment of the baptism of Jesus.
Jesus comes to the Jordan to be baptized by John (Mark i. 9);
immediately after the baptism, the Spirit impels him to go
away into the desert and there he is tempted of the devil
(Mark i. 12). But, in the Synoptic Gospels themselves, certain
details occur which it is not easy to harmonize with the idea
of such a brief contact. First of all there is the profound impression which John the Baptist made upon Jesus, which is borne
out by the numerous occasions on which Jesus speaks of John.
Then there is the indication of Mark (i. 14) which connects
the return of Jesus to Galilee, and the beginning of his ministry
proper, with the imprisonment of John. This touch in the story
seems to suggest that until then Jesus had been staying near
John the Baptist. In thus reducing to a minimum the relation
between Jesus and John the aim of the Synoptic Gospels was
to prevent people from thinking that Jesus owed the substance
of his teaching to John.

In his first chapter, the fourth evangelist goes so far as to
omit all reference to any direct contact between Jesus and
John. He reduces the part of the Forerunner to that of a
testimony given to a personage whom he did not know in
advance, who, at a given moment, was made known to him
by the sign of the Spirit which descends on him like a
dove (i. 29–34). But, in chapters iii. 22–iv. 3 the fourth
evangelist gives the account of that which he regards as a

second meeting between Jesus and John the Baptist, and this story, we believe, is derived from a source which we can to a large extent reconstitute, one which has preserved material of very great value and interest.

After his first visit to Jerusalem, says the Fourth Gospel, Jesus stays in Judaea and there baptizes. At this moment John is staying at Aenon, near to Salim, "because there was much water there." He also was baptizing, for, as the evangelist notes especially, "John was not yet cast into prison." A dispute, or a discussion (ζήτησις) arises between the disciples of John and a Jew or a Judaean[1] on the subject of purification. The disciples of John then come and tell their master that "he that was with thee beyond Jordan, to whom thou barest witness, the same baptizeth, and all men come unto him." John replies by saying: "A man can receive nothing, except it be given him from heaven," which means that the success of Jesus shows that he has been sent by God. John reminds his disciples that he did not call himself the Messiah but only his herald, and he sums up his own attitude in the words: "He must increase, but I must decrease." A section of an abstract character follows, which seems to belong to the words spoken by John, but which at bottom is an exposition of the personal reflections of the evangelist. He speaks of the testimony brought by him who comes from heaven, a testimony which men do not accept. The account closes with these words: "When therefore the Lord knew how the Pharisees had heard that Jesus made and baptized more disciples than John (though Jesus himself baptized not, but his disciples), he left Judaea, and departed again into Galilee."

This story cannot have been written by one hand; the confusion of certain phrases, especially of the last phrase, reveals the marks of revision and editing. Thus alone can we explain the obscurities and contradictions in the passage. The narrator, after having represented John the Baptist as baptizing freely, notes that at that moment he was not in prison. A dispute between a Judaean or Jew and the disciples of John leads to a complaint of the latter against Jesus. The disciples of John are scandalized at the success of a man whom their master, nevertheless, had formally declared to be greater than

[1] The word Ἰουδαῖος is used in the Fourth Gospel in both senses.

he. Some Pharisees emerge unexpectedly from nowhere at the end of the story, and it is on their account that Jesus goes away. The inconsistencies are no less striking than the obscurities. Jesus has more disciples than John (iii. 26; iv. 1) and yet no one receives his testimony (iii. 32). He baptizes (iii. 22; iv. 1) and he does not baptize (iv. 2). We are here dealing with something quite different from editorial incompetence. There is here the use of a source which the evangelist has modified and to which he has added material in order to adapt it to his ideas and to incorporate it into his story. In order to clear this up we must first of all eliminate all that obviously comes from the evangelist himself. Thus, first of all, following the order of the narrative, we must exclude the remark that John was not yet cast into prison. The evangelist realized that his account contradicted that of the Synoptists, according to which Jesus did not begin his ministry until after John had been put in prison. He has emphasized the contradiction[1] in order that people should not think it was due to any confusion or error on his part. This means that he wished to show that he had very good reasons for differing from his predecessors on this point.

We ought also to consider as additions of the evangelist to his source the allusions to the account in the first chapter, for the idea of an activity of Jesus parallel with that of John is not compatible with the conception according to which John recognized in Jesus, with whom he was not in direct contact, a person who was on an entirely different level from himself.

Verses 31-36 deal with a series of ideas[2] in close connexion with the theological thought of the evangelist. Thus these verses also should be assigned to him.

Finally, the touch in iv. 2 (though Jesus himself baptized not but his disciples) almost automatically betrays its character as a secondary element. This statement directly contradicts the data of the source in trying to adapt it (which, indeed, it does rather badly) to the current idea,

[1] As he does in another place in connexion with the date of the death of Jesus (xiii. 1, xviii. 28, xix. 14). Cf. *Intr.*, II, p. 520.
[2] For instance, the ideas of him who cometh from heaven, the witness which he gives and which men do not receive.

which is also that of the evangelist, that Jesus himself did not baptize.[1]

When these additions have been eliminated we still do not find the primitive text of the source. There, where we might suppose that he would follow it, the evangelist has made certain alterations which are easy to perceive, although it is still not possible to reconstitute the original text.

First of all what was this dispute between the disciples of John and a Jew or a Judaean? For a long time it has been suspected that in the text of the source material the reading was probably "with those of Jesus"[2] or "with Jesus."[3] The actual reading of the text before us may be due to a scribe's error, or, as is still more likely, to the evangelist, who concluded that a discussion between the disciples of John and of Jesus would be incompatible with the testimony of the Forerunner reported in chapter i. The recourse to John seems to be derived from the source, as may be also the beginning of his reply, at least in its present form.

Even when it has been freed from the parenthesis of verse 2, the conclusion of iv. 1–3 is still so confused that we must regard it as an adaptation. The allusion to the Pharisees must have been introduced in order to give a different motive for Jesus's departure for Galilee than that of the discussion with the disciples of John. The only words belonging to the original source will then be: "When therefore the Lord knew . . . he left Judaea and departed again into Galilee." Can we guess, from the source, what it was that the Lord thus knew, which caused him to leave Judaea? This cannot be the dispute itself, since he was evidently directly involved in it. It can only mean either: the fact that John had heard of the dispute, or, the remarks which John made on the subject. We are thus confronted with two hypotheses: either that Jesus withdrew and went away to exercise his ministry elsewhere because he did not wish to be, or even appear to be, a rival of John, or that the statement of John the Baptist was differently worded

---

[1] This appears to be true of at least the greater part of his ministry.

[2] O. HOLTZMANN: *Das Johannesevangelium*, Darmstadt, 1889, p. 210.

[3] An old conjecture of BENTLEY and SEMLER, which was taken up afresh by BALDENSPERGER (*Der Prolog des vierten Evangeliums, sein polemisch-apologetischer Zweck*, Freiburg im Br., Leipzig, Tübingen, 1898, p. 66).

in the original source. In that case it would be equivalent to a disavowal of Jesus by John the Baptist. In leaving and going elsewhere Jesus would thus have only drawn the logical conclusion from this statement. At a later stage we shall have to inquire whether it is possible to choose between these two explanations.

At the beginning of this passage we are told that Jesus is in Judaea and that John is at Aenon, near to Salim (iii. 23–32). Jesus is certainly at the same place. The precise indication, however, is only given with reference to John, although the narrative mentions Jesus first of all. From this we may infer that the source was mainly concerned with John, and hence that it emanated from a Baptist group.

Reduced to its essential elements, this passage teaches us that Jesus, after working on lines similar to those of the Baptist, separated from him as a result of a dispute or a discussion, due to a difference of opinion about purification or the question of baptism.

The data provided by this document do not agree with the manner in which the relation between Jesus and John is represented, both in the Synoptic Gospels and in the Fourth Gospel; it is therefore impossible to regard them as traditional. The corrections which the evangelist has made on this document prevent us, on the other hand, from attributing it actually to him. Thus we are forced to regard the source as an ancient document, which is independent of the Christian tradition. The main thing to note about this document is that it bears witness to a very important fact: that Jesus began by preaching and baptizing in the same way and in the same spirit as John; that he then severed his connexion with John because he had changed his views on the question of purification; that is to say, about the efficacy of baptism.

Although Jesus left John, and although his Gospel was thus more than a prolongation of the teaching of the Baptist, the influence of John on Jesus was not wholly negative. The very fact of being obliged to admit a difference of opinion led Jesus to clarify and formulate his own thought. Thus, in this way, John's influence on Jesus was positive and direct. Although Jesus felt that the message of John the Baptist was incomplete and therefore ineffective, nevertheless, he never ceased to regard him as a prophet sent by God. John came "in the way of righteousness" (Matt. xxi. 32), and those who accepted his message and received his baptism "justified God," that is to say, they acted in conformity with His will; those who refused to listen to it "rejected the counsel of God" (Luke vii. 29–30). John the Baptist is the greatest among the prophets (Matt. xi. 9–11*), in the next breath Jesus makes one important reservation by adding that the least in the Kingdom of God is greater than he. This places John outside the new order; he belongs to that of the Law and the Prophets and the close of the old dispensation (Matt. xi. 12–13).

From the Gospels, too, we learn that Jesus compared John with Elijah, who, according to a widespread Jewish belief, was to return as the forerunner of the Messiah.[1]

Mark (ix. 9–13) relates that as they came down from the Mount of Transfiguration the disciples reminded Jesus of the teaching of the scribes about the return of Elijah. Jesus repeated their phrase and then asked: "How then is it written of the Son of Man that he should suffer and be despised?" But, he continues, "Elias is come already, but they have done unto him whatsoever they listed, as it is written of him."[2]

This fragment is composed of contradictory elements. The first saying of Jesus shows the evident contradiction between the necessity for the sufferings and the humiliation of the Son of Man, and the idea of the re-establishment of order in the world through the ministry of Elias. For, indeed, in a world

---

[1] On this doctrine see Mal. iii. 23 f.; Ecclus. xlviii. 10–11; *Or, syb*, V, 187–189; 4 Esdras vi. 26 ff. Cf. SCHÜRER, II, pp. 524 ff. LAGRANGE: *Le Messianisme chez les Juifs*, Paris, 1909, pp. 210–213. BOUSSET-GRESSMANN: *Die Religion des Judentums*[3], Tübingen, 1926, pp. 232 ff. KLAUSNER, pp. 244 ff. STRACK-BILLERBECK, IV, pp. 780 ff., etc.

[2] Matthew (xvii. 9–13) has the same story with some variants which are not very important. The most notable is a conclusion in which he formulates that which Mark had only implied: "Then the disciples understood that he spake unto them of John the Baptist." Luke has no equivalent of this section. This does not prove that he did not know of it. The purely Jewish doctrine of the return of Elijah was of no interest for his readers who were Gentile-Christians, and it was scarcely intelligible to them. This is why Luke has allowed this passage to fall out of his narrative.

ruled by the principles of order the Son of Man would be welcomed with enthusiasm.

This first statement is certainly authentic, since it speaks of the sufferings and the humiliation of the Son of Man and not of his death. Jesus thus rejected the doctrine of the return of Elijah because he regarded it as opposed to the method of the ministry of the Son of Man, as he conceived it.

The second saying of Jesus maintains, on the contrary, the doctrine of the return of Elijah, although, it is true, it is emptied of all positive content; it seems, therefore, to be an editorial addition, designed to re-introduce the doctrine of the return of Elijah, which proved a satisfying interpretation of the position of John the Baptist in relation to Jesus in Christian thought. It might, however, be based upon an authentic saying similar to that which is preserved in Matt. xi. 14, where Jesus says that John the Baptist was the Elijah who was to come. Thus it belongs to the first part of the ministry of Jesus, to that in which Jesus had not yet seen the necessity for the Suffering Messiah.[1]

If this be the true version of the story we would have here a typical example of the way in which Jesus gradually freed himself from certain traditional doctrines.

While, on the one hand, Jesus said: "The Law and the Prophets . . . until John," he also said: "Since John the Gospel is preached (or forced),"[2] thus he felt that John marked the

---

[1] This is also the opinion of DIBELIUS: *Urchr. Ueberl. üb. Joh. d. T.*, p. 32.

[2] This saying is somewhat obscure. It is differently rendered in Matthew and in Luke. Matthew (xi. 12–13) reads thus: "And from the days of John the Baptist until now the kingdom of heaven suffereth violence (?) ($\beta\iota\acute{a}\zeta\varepsilon\tau\alpha\iota$) and the violent take it by force. For all the prophets and the Law prophesied until John." Luke (xvi. 16) has: "The law and the prophets were until John: since that time the kingdom of God is preached ($\varepsilon\mathring{v}\alpha\gamma\gamma\varepsilon\lambda\acute{\iota}\zeta\varepsilon\tau\alpha\iota$) and every man presseth into it." It is Luke who seems to have preserved the original form of that part of the phrase about the prophets until John, for the verb "have prophesied," which can be applied only with difficulty to the Law, seems to have been added by Matthew in order to explain the somewhat obscure formula given by Luke, and also to assert the solidarity of the Gospel with the religion of the Old Testament. The interpretation of the phrase about the Kingdom of God is especially difficult. It seems very probable that the verb $\varepsilon\mathring{v}\alpha\gamma\gamma\varepsilon\lambda\acute{\iota}\zeta\varepsilon\tau\alpha\iota$ has been substituted by Luke for the obscure $\beta\iota\acute{a}\zeta\varepsilon\tau\alpha\iota$ of Matthew. But the meaning varies considerably, according as one reads as a middle (the Kingdom

end of an era, that of the Law and the Prophets, and that a new era was about to open. Hence he saw in John the fore-runner, if not of the Messiah, at least of the Messianic era.

It would also be interesting to know the verdict of John the Baptist on Jesus. On the evidence of chapter iii in the Fourth Gospel it seems unlikely that he did not know him at all, and that on the day of his baptism Jesus was just one of the many pilgrims who pressed round him on the banks of the Jordan.[1] How could John not have known of Jesus, who, after being his disciple, afterwards separated from him? Matthew (xi. 2–6) and Luke (vii. 18–23) relate an incident which to some extent provides an answer to the question which has been raised. From his prison John, who had heard rumours of the activity of Jesus, sent to him two of his disciples, who, on the part of their master, asked him this question: "Art thou he that should come, or look we for another?" Jesus replied by pointing to the miracles which he had worked, and to his preaching of the Gospel, that is to say, to the fulfilment of the Messianic programme which is found in the Book of Isaiah (xxix. 1–19, xxxv. 5, lxi. 1). He concludes with these words: "Blessed is he who is not offended in me," which seems to suggest that in the thought of the evangelists John was not satisfied with the reply of Jesus.[2] We cannot, however, come to a definite conclusion on this point. This shows that the interest of the story centres in Jesus and not in John the Baptist. This seems to suggest that the incident is not authentic, for an historical account would not have been so completely

of God arrives with force) or as a passive (it is forced violently, one tries hard to make it come by violent means, which might be a point against the Zealots). The meaning also varies a good deal according to whether we regard what is said about the violent men as blame or approval. Probably the evangelists did not understand very well the meaning of this *logion* because they were ignorant of the circumstances in which it was uttered. This creates a likelihood of its authenticity, because tradition would not have created a saying whose meaning it could not understand.

[1] E. PETERSEN: *Urchristentum und Mandäismus*, *Z.N.T.W.*, XXVII, 1928, pp. 88 f.

[2] The discourse on John the Baptist which follows and in which Jesus says that the least in the Kingdom of God is greater than John (Matt. xi. 11*) confirms this impression.

detached from the conclusion to which it seemed to be tending. What is still more conclusive is that the question which is supposed to have been put to Jesus is conceived from the Christian point of view, and not from the point of view of John the Baptist, who expected a transcendent Messiah and could not imagine that the Messiah might be a figure in history whose coming he had himself announced.

The way in which Matthew and Luke relate the sending of the disciples of John to Jesus seems to imply that, in the mind of the narrators, John was not convinced. If the tradition had thought the opposite, the evangelists would not have failed to say that after having rendered the homage of a prophet to Jesus John would have rendered it a second time, founded this time upon the work which had been accomplished.

Thus John persisted in his point of view. After Jesus had left him John only saw in him an unfaithful disciple and almost a renegade.

CHAPTER XI

THE FORM OF THE TEACHING OF JESUS

THE apostolic age was less interested in what Jesus thought and taught than in what he was, in his life, his death, and his resurrection. The supreme object of its faith and meditation was the heavenly and glorified Christ. To the extent in which the Church adhered to a doctrine at all, it was not to that which Jesus had taught but to that in which his person and his work formed both the content and the object.[1] This feeling of the Early Church is, on the whole, in harmony with that of Jesus himself. He never said: "I am come to teach," but "I am come to kindle a fire upon earth . . . I have a baptism to be baptized with" (Luke xii. 49).

I. THE GENERAL CHARACTER OF THE TEACHING OF JESUS

However, Jesus did teach, and his teaching must have been remarkably powerful and original, since a tradition which was not particularly concerned with it has preserved a careful and accurate record of it.

The evangelists testify to the impression produced by the preaching of Jesus: "He taught," says Mark, "as one having authority, and not as do the Scribes." (Mark i. 22*; cf. Matt. vii. 29.) His hearers were struck by the contrast between the teaching of Jesus, who spoke directly in the name of God, and with the authority which his sense of prophetic vocation gave him, and that of the rabbis, which was confined to commenting on the text of Scripture and to quoting and discussing the opinion of the teachers of the past and the data provided by tradition.

Of the teaching of Jesus it may be said that the wealth of its content has caused the originality of the form to be ignored. Attention has been concentrated, very rightly, on the actual truths which Jesus uttered, but this means that very often the

[1] This was the case even when, as in the Epistle to the Hebrews (ii. 3, iii. 1), it was believed that Jesus himself had taught the doctrine professed by the Church.

way in which they were said was overlooked more than was just or right. The words and discourses of Jesus, however, would bear comparison with the most finished products of the human mind, and ought to be ranked among the masterpieces of world literature.

In the words of Weidel: "The form of the teaching of Jesus, the way in which he clothes his interior life in words, indubitably possesses an artistic character. The wealth of the style is remarkable. Jesus could tell a story in a very living, simple, and arresting way; he knew how to stir the minds of his hearers with vigour; if necessary he could pour forth scorn with unmistakable energy, he could console with gentleness, humiliate with biting sarcasm, blame with bitterness, be indignant with intense vigour, and rejoice intensely. Everywhere he manifests his creative originality. Everything is brief, every word hits the target, all is concrete. There is never a word too much. His words always give the impression that they are self-evident. They seem as though they could never be any different from what they are, and this proves that they have issued from within in a living and spontaneous manner."[1]

The art in the words and sayings of Jesus is wholly instinctive. It is not the result of an artificial method. There is no striving after effect. Jesus does not try to dazzle his hearers by the brilliance of his eloquence. In him the style is so marvellously adapted to the content that it does not attract attention. His words are only the supple and transparent garment of his thought. With him simplicity never becomes banal. It is the result of a spontaneous capacity for finding the most living, direct, and simple expression for the richest ideas.

[1] K. WEIDEL: *Jesu Persönlichkeit*, pp. 71 ff. Cf. also this opinion of H. H. WENDT: "All his art and all his force expresses itself in his popular and spontaneous eloquence. There is nothing of the pedant about him as a teacher, nor does he use any of the hairsplitting refinements of the speech of the schools. Jesus did not use new forms. He used the usual methods of popular language with all its spontaneity, but he used it with ease and sureness, with restraint and with taste. His great originality came from the wealth of his imagination and the penetration of his judgment. His imagination was always providing him with fresh material. Always he goes straight to the essential, and he presses it home in the most arresting language he can find" (*Die Lehre Jesu*[2], Göttingen, 1901, p. 137).

None of the images used by Jesus—image, comparison, parable, allegory, antithesis, repetition—are absolutely new. They occur in the Prophets, in the Wisdom literature, and among the rabbis. But although, from this point of view, Jesus may have created nothing new, the form of his teaching still remains original; he never used traditional methods in a mechanical way. Never before had any teacher achieved this perfect adaptation of the form to the content, this elasticity, and at the same time accuracy of expression which, from the point of view of form, make the teaching of Jesus something quite unique.

The fact that there is nothing of the dilettante about him, no striving after effect, that nothing comes between him and his hearers, means that each of his sayings permits us to see right into his soul. Each phrase is like a window which opens into his soul, a revelation of his personality. This is why, although his personality remains the most mysterious in history, it is also the most transparent.

There is nothing esoteric about the teaching of Jesus. Properly speaking, the term "teaching" does not describe his words very well. It would be better to call it "preaching," although in this instance the usual sense in which this word is used might lead to misunderstanding. Jesus appeals to the will rather than to the intelligence. If he tries to persuade he does so in order to obtain obedience. He is not aiming at securing an intellectual consent. This is why his words are also acts, and cannot be separated from his person.

In his teaching Jesus did not follow any preconceived plan. The subjects with which he dealt were suggested to him as he went along by the circumstances and the thousand-and-one little happenings of daily life, by the questions of his hearers, or by the objections which some of them raised. With most of his sayings, at least, this must have been the case, even when they have been preserved in the form of aphorisms, without any indication of the circumstances in which they were uttered.

None of his sayings gives the impression of being a fragment detached from a whole, an element in a system. There is no theoretical definition, not even of the ideas which are most essential for his line of thought, as, for instance, those of the Kingdom of God or of the Son of Man.

Cuvier could reconstruct a skeleton from a few bones. We might be tempted to try to do the same in trying to reconstruct the system of thought of Jesus by using the known elements in his teaching. An undertaking of this kind would be useless and unnecessary, since each one of the sayings of Jesus is the overflow of a personality throbbing with life.[1]

The simplicity of the teaching of Jesus strikes us still more when we compare it with the complicated character of the teaching of the rabbis. Even with questions of a most transparent character, their treatment was full of subtle definitions and distinctions, recalling differing opinions on some trifling point of detail, and the most improbable hypotheses. In the teaching of Jesus, on the contrary, everything is concentrated on the essential point, without ever losing touch with reality, and also without any concern to establish logical principles with a theoretical abstract value. On one occasion Jesus will say: "He that is not against us is for us" (Mark ix. 40*); on another occasion he says: "He who is not with me is against me" (Matt. xii. 30*). Neither of these two sayings is an abstract principle. The first refers to men who cast out demons in the name of Jesus without having joined the group of the disciples. The second refers to some Pharisees who accuse him of being inspired by Beelzebub.

This also explains the paradoxes of Jesus. They are not the invention of an ingenious mind bent, at all costs, on creating an original expression. They are only the consequence of his concentration of thought on an essential point thrown into high relief, the ideas with which it is connected being either left in the background or else entirely ignored. This gives the mind a kind of shock and thus prepares people to understand what Jesus is wanting to say. Nothing could be more absurd than to interpret these paradoxes as rational formulae, which, conceived as a programme of life, would prove impossible to realize, and would force us to admit that the teaching of Jesus is visionary in character.

Although the speech of Jesus is essentially spontaneous it

[1] On this point, see the judicious remarks of H. J. HOLTZMANN: *Neut. Theol.*, I², pp. 177 ff.

reveals great dialectical ability, an ability which is entirely instinctive, and possibly due less to his innate gifts than to his habit of mind, which always went straight to the heart of any matter, ignoring all that is non-essential. In discussions with his enemies, Jesus is able equally to escape from the toils of the insidious questions in which they tried to entangle him, such as the question of paying tribute to Caesar (Mark xii. 13–17*), or of the resurrection (Mark xii. 18–27*), or of divorce (Mark x. 1–12*), for instance, or to place his enemies in an embarrassing position himself, by setting the Old Testament over against their law of Corban (Mark vii. 9–13*), or by asking them questions no less cunning than their own, and to which they could not reply, like the subject of the Davidic ancestry of the Messiah (Mark xi. 35–37*), or the origin of the baptism of John (Mark xi. 29–33*). There are several reasons for the superiority of Jesus to his enemies in this respect. He possessed an innate aptitude for seizing the weak point in an argument, thus involving his adversary in contradictory statements and exposing him to ridicule. But, above all, he does not remain on the surface, but goes straight to the essence of the matter, thanks to his profound sense of spiritual reality, and to the fact that his mind is literally steeped in the Scriptures, which to him are not, as they are to rabbis, an arsenal of texts and arguments, but a perennial fountain of living inspiration.

II. The Methods

There is no contradiction, after having emphasized the spontaneity of the teaching of Jesus, in trying to describe the methods which he used most frequently to express his thoughts; the word "method" is, of course, here used in its usual sense, meaning the method which Jesus used most frequently to express his thought and to bring its meaning home to the minds of his hearers with the utmost simplicity and absence of artifice. If we use the term "method" rather than that of "literary form" or "style," which might perhaps convey the meaning better, this is because the expression "literary form" cannot be applied to anything except written work; now what we call "literature" was alien to the method of Jesus, but when he spoke he certainly meant to be understood.

Jesus never starts from formulas or from abstract or theoretical definitions, but the wealth of imagery which he uses gives a very concrete character to all that he says. Everything is presented pictorially. Is he asked a question about one's duty to one's neighbour? He replies by telling the Parable of the Good Samaritan (Luke x. 29–37). Do the disciples dispute for the first place? He sets a little child in the midst (Mark ix. 33–37). Does he wish to show the vanity of riches, in which men place their confidence? He tells the story of a man who is preparing to pull down his barns and build others large enough to hold his abundant harvests, who dies at the very moment when he thinks he has heaped enough wealth to last him for many years to come (Luke xii. 16–21). Or does he wish to show up pride in its true colours, and show that God is gracious to those whose hearts are humble? He gives a picture of a Pharisee and a Publican in the Temple (Luke xviii. 9–14). These are not so much parables as illustrations of a truth by a concrete example. When Jesus wishes to give advice he does so in concrete terms. He does not confine himself to saying that we ought not to resist the wicked, but he adds: "Whosoever shall smite thee on thy right cheek, turn to him the other also . . . and whosoever shall compel thee to go a mile, go with him twain. Give to him that asketh thee, and from him that would borrow of thee turn not thou away" (Matt. v. 38–42*).

Sometimes the image is replaced by an act and a word by a gesture, as when Jesus places a child before his disciples as a model (Mark ix. 36*), or when, during the course of the Last Supper, he passes round the Cup to remind them of the cup which he will drink with them in the Kingdom of Heaven, and bread, as the symbol of the way he gives his life to his own (Mark xiv. 22–25*). His whole manner of life—his itinerating ministry, the discomforts he endured as he went round Galilee preaching the Gospel or when he was obliged to flee from the menacing hostility of Herod—forms part of this teaching by the example which it gives to his own followers.

Now let us examine a little more closely the images which are used by Jesus.[1] In this respect no teacher has ever used more

[1] Cf. WEINEL: *Die Bildersprache Jesu in ihrer Bedeutung für die Erforschung seines inneren Lebens*, Giessen, 1900.

rich and varied language. The images which he employs are drawn from many different sources, from the daily life of the countryside, of the village, of the lake, and also from that of the merchant, from public life and from war. Those of the latter group are, it is true, a little obvious and show a limited knowledge of the sphere from which they are drawn. This is true of images like that of the merchant who sells all that he has in order to buy a pearl of great price or a field which contains a hidden treasure (Matt. xiii. 44–46), or that of the king who sits down to calculate the chances of winning a victory over an enemy whose numbers are superior to his own (Luke xiv. 31), or again, of the man who goes into a far country to take possession of a kingdom (Luke xix. 12), or of the father who divides his possessions between his sons (Luke xv. 12). But, most frequently, the images are drawn from that which Jesus knew directly. The following instances all belong to this category: the sower in his field, the fisherman in the boat with his nets, the father of the family whose children come to ask him for fish or bread, who rules his household, gives orders to his servants, and supervises his steward, the man who wakes his neighbour in order to borrow some bread, the shepherd who takes care of his sheep and counts them, the peasant whose ox or ass has fallen into a well, the woman who sweeps the house, the children who play in the market-place, and the workmen who wait there to be hired, the rich landlord with his cares and his fear of thieves, the judge whom one is obliged to importune in order to obtain justice, the sheep who stray because they have no shepherd. In all these images there is no false accent like those which disfigure the parable of the olive-tree in Paul,[1] or those which make the pictures of the author of the Book of Revelation so confusing. The images of Jesus reveal a gift of keen and accurate observation. Jesus finds material for comparisons which are simple and yet arresting in the very common sights which so many people see without seeing, such as the hen who gathers her chickens under her

[1] Rom. xi. 17–23. Paul speaks of branches of wild olive being grafted into a cultivated olive-tree, and of branches which, after being cut off and thrown out, are regrafted into a "good olive-tree." This picture has not been visualized; it has been laboriously constructed, and the language sounds like algebra. This is the very opposite of the imagery used by Jesus.

wings, the lightning which flashes across the sky, the sheep in the midst of wolves.

It is difficult to understand how some people can have thought that Jesus did not care for nature, because, with views like those of Hermon, Tabor, Carmel, the Lake of Galilee all around him, he never mentions them.[1] First of all our sources are too fragmentary for us to draw any certain conclusions from that which they do not contain. And, above all, we must not forget that feeling for nature, in the sense of the admiration of natural scenery, was a sentiment unknown to the ancient world. Jesus speaks of the birds of heaven (Matt. vi. 26, viii. 20, x. 29) and of the splendour of the flowers (Matt. vi. 28–30) in a way which is sufficient to prove that he is not without a feeling for nature. But what interests him in nature most of all is the living world around him. He speaks of the life of men, of animals, and plants, because in this sphere he finds comparisons to illustrate the moral life. In this sense he could draw nothing from natural scenery. The only occasion on which he spoke of inanimate things was to say that if his disciples were forced to be silent the very stones would cry out (Luke xix. 40). The images of Jesus are never mere ornaments of a discourse. They are means by which it is easier to understand a thought which is wholly practical in its aim. Perhaps it would be better to call them metaphors and comparisons rather than images. If we feel some classification is here required we might arrange the images which Jesus used in two groups. There are first of all those which illustrate a principle and give it a concrete character: for instance, that of the birds which do not fall to the ground without the permission of the Heavenly Father (Matt. x. 29). In a second group we would place those which, although they are very briefly described, really contain a whole story. In reality these are condensed parables.

Jesus did not create the parable; it is a usual literary form in the East, and was frequently used by the rabbis,[2] but as a rule the characters they introduce are shadowy and lifeless figures.

[1] P. W. Schmidt: Geschichte Jesu, I, p. 54.
[2] Fiebig: Altjüdische Gleichnisse und die Gleichnisse Jesu, Tübingen, 1904; Die Gleichnissreden Jesu im Lichte des rabbinischen Zeitalters, Tübingen, 1912.

Frequently the thought is complicated—everything is mean, doctrinaire, artificial. The use made of the parable before the time of Jesus is, however, important, because it was sufficiently frequent to have established certain features and certain characteristics of this literary device in such a way that we can use them in the interpretation of the parables of Jesus. Thus Merx has shown that a parable always contains all it needs for its own explanation, hence there is no need to interpret it in the light of some other idea outside its own sphere of reference. On the other hand, in the parables there are often some features and details whose function is simply that of making the picture more distinct and concrete, and of which there is no need to give an explanation.[1] The parable, as we meet it on nearly every page of the Gospels,[2] is the illustration and demonstration of a truth of a religious order by a story, in which there is set forth a principle or a statement of the same order in the sphere of material life, in the life of nature, in that of the relations of men with one another, etc. A parable is distinguished from a comparison first of all because the truth which is to be demonstrated is most often not directly formulated, and then because instead of being grafted on to a process of development, it forms a whole, which is self-sufficient.

Parable has sometimes been confused with allegory. Jülicher has made a clear and wise distinction between these two literary forms, although possibly his distinction is too rigid and academic. Allegory is a literary device in which a group or a system of ideas is expressed by an entirely different system of ideas. In allegory the agreement between the sign and the thing signified is carried out to the very smallest detail. It is a kind of algebraical language. In the parable, the truth of an idea or of a principle is made evident and tangible by a story which draws its material from a quite different sphere. The

[1] AD. MERX: *Die vier kanonischen Evangelien nach ihrem aeltesten bekannten Text*, Berlin, 1897–1911, II, 1, p. 291.

[2] The standard work on the parables is that of A. JÜLICHER: *Die Gleichnissreden Jesu*, Freiburg im Br., Tübingen, Leipzig, I, 1888, ²1899; II, 1899. See also BUGGE: *Die Hauptparabeln Jesu ausgelegt*, Giessen, 1903. H. WEINEL: *Die Gleichnisse Jesu*, Leipzig, 1910. BUZY: *Introduction aux paraboles évangéliques*, Paris, 1912.

allegorical interpretation of a parable would not merely try to discover the central idea which Jesus wants to bring out, but it would also try to define the meaning of each detail, without realizing that several of these details may have been introduced into the story for no other reason than that of making the story more living and concrete.

Here is an example which will illustrate what I mean. Let us take the Parable of the Prodigal Son. If we regard it as an allegory we must try to interpret it into rational language. Then we would say: the father means God; the prodigal son is the sinner, and an exact meaning will be found for all the other elements in the story: the husks, the robe, the sandals, the ring, and the fatted calf. Allegorical exegesis has expended a wealth of ingenious explanation along this line.[1] Tertullian, for instance, interprets the fortune squandered by the young man as the natural knowledge of God. Eucherius takes the robe to mean baptism and faith; while Olshausen interprets the ring (which he imagines has a seal) as the seal of the Holy Spirit, and the sandals, capacity to walk in the ways of God. Thiersch thinks the fatted calf means the Eucharist. In the husks, St. Augustine sees the *doctrinae saeculares*, and some of the Fathers, on account of the taste of these fruits which are both sweet and bitter, the passions of the world which attract men but only leave them with bitter memories.[2]

If, on the contrary, the story of Jesus is regarded as a parable, we would simply say: the attitude of God towards the sinner who returns to Him is like that of a father who welcomes his sinful and penitent child.

The theory of Jülicher which we have just summarized

---

[1] On this see JÜLICHER, I, p. 219.

[2] Hilary of Poitiers (cf. JÜLICHER, I, p. 226) explains the Parable of the Grain of Mustard Seed in the same way, saying that the branches of the tree are the Apostles of Christ whose preaching covers the world, and the birds which take refuge in the branches are the pagans who seek refuge in the Church in the midst of the tempests stirred up by the spirit of the devil. Some of the Fathers (cf. J. WEISS: *Evang. des Markus und Lukas*, pp. 462 ff.) say that the inn to which the Good Samaritan led the man who fell among thieves is the Church which takes in fallen humanity; the inn-keeper is the bishop, and the two denarii which he receives are the Old and the New Testaments. In some cathedral windows the Fall of Man and the Parable of the Good Samaritan are associated.

K

represents a salutary reaction from all the complicated subtle-
ties of allegorical interpretation.[1] We must not, however,
use it in too absolute a sense. The teaching of Jesus is too
living, and therefore too complex, for us to be able to lay down
as a principle that it contains no element of allegory at all,
and claim that every time a parable is presented as an allegory
it must have been altered in this sense by a later tradition.
Some of the parables, like those of the sower, or the labourers
in the vineyard, for instance, are really allegories and indeed
very transparent allegories.

Jülicher's theory does not harmonize with the fact that
although several of the parables are represented in the Gospels
as replies of Jesus to questions which have been addressed to
him, and hence as illustrations of truths which might have run
the risk of being imperfectly understood if they had been
presented in an abstract form, there are others whose real
meaning can only be understood by the initiated, who—
because the mystery of the Kingdom of God has been given
unto them—receive, in private, explanations which serve as a
key to the parables. For those who are without, the parable,
far from illuminating the thought of Jesus, makes it more
obscure; the hearer believes that he has understood when he
has not, in such instances the parable only serves to dull the
mind and harden the heart of the hearer. This system is set
forth by Mark (iv. 10–12) in the clearest possible manner.

In order to grasp the exact significance of the fragment in
which this theory is expounded we need to realize the position
it occupies. In an earlier group of stories (i. 14–45), Mark
gives a picture of the activity of Jesus, and depicts the enthusiastic welcome which he receives from the crowd. In a
second section (ii. 1–iii. 6) he presents (evidently intentionally)
an accumulation of conflicts which arise between Jesus and
his enemies; this arrangement is obviously dictated more by
the desire to express the idea of the evangelist concerning the
course and connexion of the narrative, and as an explanation
of the story, than by the intention of telling a straightforward
story in the simplest way. Thus in this section he shows the

[1] It is true that the exegesis of the nineteenth century has rarely pushed
this method to ridiculous extremes.

growth of the opposition to Jesus, implies the defeat which is in store, and allows us to guess at the drama which is being prepared, since he shows us the Pharisees and the Herodians discussing together how they can get Jesus put to death. A third section (iii. 7–19) shows Jesus, who, without allowing himself to be discouraged by these unfavourable signs, prepares for the future by the institution of the apostolate. In a fourth section the conflict becomes more acute, the family of Jesus declares that he has become mentally unhinged, and the Pharisees proclaim that he is possessed by Beelzebub (iii. 20–35). It is at this point that the group of parables is placed, with its accompanying theory. After Jesus has told the parable of the Sower (iv. 1–9), his disciples, when they are alone with him, ask him to explain the meaning of the parables (ἠρώτων τὰς παραβολάς) (iv. 10). The answer of Jesus is composed of two elements which are not very well connected with each other. The first element is what we might call the general theory of the parable, the second is the explanation of the parable of the Sower. Jesus says first of all: "Unto you it is given to know the mystery of the Kingdom of God: but unto them that are without, all these things are done in parables: That seeing they may see and not perceive, and hearing they may hear and not understand; lest at any time they should be converted, and their sins should be forgiven them" [1] (iv. 11–12). Hubert Pernot [2] has argued that here ἵνα ought not to be translated "in order that," but "so that." Certainly it cannot be denied that from the philological point of view this interpretation is possible.[3] The reason which Pernot gives for adopting this rendering is this: that if we here give a final meaning to ἵνα, the thought expressed would be in contradiction with the declaration reported a little further on by Mark himself: "If any man have ears to hear, let him hear" (iv. 23). In my opinion this argument does not seem at all conclusive, for

[1] These last words have been drawn from Isa. vi. 9–10 (LXX).
[2] H. PERNOT: *Pages choisies des Évangiles*, Paris, 1925, p. 113. *Études sur la langue des Évangiles*, Paris, 1927, pp. 90 f.
[3] Pernot quotes a certain number of typical passages, especially a passage from the grammarian APOLLONIUS DYSCOLE (second century A.D.), who gives this meaning. See also J. VITEAU: *Étude sur le grec du Nouveau Testament. Le Verbe, Syntaxe des propositions*, Paris, 1893, p. 74, n. 1. ABEL: *Grammaire du grec biblique*, Paris, 1927, ¶¶ 64, 69, *h.k.* 79, *e.f.* BAUER: col. 589.

Mark might very well have thought that "those who have ears to hear" are precisely those to whom it is given to know the mysteries of the Kingdom of God. Although the order of chapter iv in Mark is not very clear, with its alternation of parables addressed to the crowd, and of sayings addressed to the disciples only, it seems, all the same, as if it were to the latter only that the words were addressed: "If any man have ears to hear, let him hear." Pernot could have strengthened his argument still further by saying that although Jesus was speaking to the multitude, and did all that was possible to reach a large circle of hearers, this cannot have been with the intention of not being understood by them. If he wished to reserve his teaching for a restricted circle, nothing would have been easier for him than to instruct them in private. It is difficult to see what could have made him wish to reach the crowd. Pernot also remarks, in favour of the interpretation of ἵνα in the sense of ὅτι, that, in the parallel passages, whereas Luke (viii. 10) has ἵνα like Mark, Matthew (xiii. 13) reads ὅτι. But this argument contradicts the thesis in support of which it has been invoked, for if Matthew has replaced ἵνα by ὅτι it is because, to him, the two conjunctions do not bear exactly the same meaning, and the idea contained in the passage in Mark would have shocked him greatly. Bauer[1] also remarks, very justly, that the two meanings of ἵνα cannot be absolutely distinguished from one another, seeing that the consequence can very easily be confused with the intention, above all when we realize that the evangelists do not admit that the action of Jesus can have any other result than that which is willed by God.

The rendering suggested by Pernot alters the meaning of the passage less profoundly than he seems to think it will, and we cannot say, as he does, that its obscurity "is not due to theological reasons at all, but is simply grammatical." If Jesus presents his teaching in parables to people who are quite unable to understand what he has to say to them, does this really mean that he has given up all hope of ever being understood by them? The fact is, the difficulty of interpretation is neither theological nor grammatical but historical. If we consider the arrangement of the parable chapter as a whole,

---

[1] BAUER: *sub voce ἵνα.* Cf. MOULTON-MILLIGAN, *sub voce ἵνα.*

we see its artificial character, and we see that Mark is trying to explain, in his own way, the reason for the failure of the preaching of Jesus, and to show that this does not undermine the reality of his divine mission because it was willed by God Himself. We might add, for this comes out in the whole of the arrangement of the book of Mark, that, in his mind, this defeat was necessary, in order to bring about the drama of the Passion by which the redemption of the world was to be effected.

After having related the story of the Parable of the Sower, from a boat in which he was sitting, to the crowd assembled on the shore of the lake (iv. 1–9), Jesus converses with the disciples alone. This conversation is introduced by the words: "And when he was alone they that were about him with the twelve [1] asked of him the parable" (iv. 10). This passage implies that the multitude has dispersed after having listened to Jesus, and that the latter has left the boat. However, in the following verses (iv. 26–32) Jesus again addresses the crowd from the boat, since in iv. 35–36 we read: "And the same day when the even was come he saith unto them, Let us pass over unto the other side. And when they had sent away the multitude, they took him even as he was in the ship." All the conversation with the disciples, therefore, has been added to the original tradition by Mark, who has not noticed the confusion which he has thus introduced into the narrative. [2]

Jesus' reply to the disciples' question, a question which was concerned with the general subject of teaching by parables, is, as we have seen, composed of two elements. After the exposition of the reasons for which Jesus used parables (iv. 11–12), comes the explanation of the Parable of the Sower, understood as an allegory (iv. 13–20). It is introduced with the phrase: "Know ye not this parable? and how then will ye know all parables?" The first section assumes that the disciples understand the parables, whereas the people in general do not. The phrase: "they asked him about the parables" is a question

---

[1] Two traditions have here been superimposed, one upon another: the one spoke only of the companions of Jesus, whereas the other works with the idea of a closed circle of twelve men.

[2] Luke seems to have noticed it; he makes this disappear by omitting the idea of Jesus teaching from the boat.

about the use of the parable as a method, and not about the meaning of the Parable of the Sower. The interpretation of this parable in iv. 14–20 implies, on the contrary, that the disciples need explanations if they are to understand. The two sections therefore must belong to different editorial strata.

We can thus perceive three stages in the evolution of the theory. In the first stage the parables are sufficient as they stand. In the second they are accompanied by explanations which serve as commentaries, which inaugurate the methods of allegorical interpretation. Thus the centre of gravity tends to alter and to pass from the parable itself to its explanation. From being the accessory element, which it had been originally, it tends to become the essential. At a third stage, finally, it came to be thought that the parables, bereft of explanations reserved to intimates remained incomprehensible, and that Jesus only used them in speaking to the crowds with the intention of not being understood by them.

The birth of this theory, which is actually an entire misconstruction of the essence of the parable method, has been facilitated by the fact that at the moment when it was constituted, a different problem was occupying the mind of the Christian community. How did it come about, they were asking themselves, that, seeing that Jesus was the messenger and the Son of God, his preaching was not received by those to whom it was addressed, and apparently only led to defeat? The theory of the parable, as a method employed by Jesus to conceal his thoughts from the uninitiated, provided an answer to this question. Jesus was not understood because it was not ordained that he should be understood, because he could not and would not be understood, in order that the drama of his redemptive death might take place.[1]

Various classifications of the parables have been suggested. All of them have one serious defect: they introduce a theoretical element into something which is in no sense a system. We cannot attach a great deal of importance to the fact that certain parables, like that of the Good Samaritan (Luke x. 29–37), and the Pharisee and the Publican (Luke xviii. 9–14), for

---

[1] This theory is similar, in some respects, to that which is outlined in Rom. ix.–xi. where the unbelief of the mass of the Jews is represented as necessary that the Gentiles may be called to salvation.

instance, are not so much images as illustrations of a moral principle by an appropriate comparison, nor to the fact that others, instead of being developed, are merely suggested, nor, finally, to the fact that their introductory phrases vary a good deal.

If we wished to give a classification of the parables, it would be far better to do so on the principle of the images which are employed. A distinction might then be made between the parables which draw their comparisons from the ordinary relations of human beings to each other, from the nature of things, or from some particular fact.

The parables are frequently presented in pairs (the Leaven and the Mustard Seed, Matt. xiii. 31–33; the Pearl and the Hidden Treasure, Matt. xiii. 44–46; the Lost Sheep and the Lost Coin, Luke xv. 1–10). Tradition seems often to have separated two parables which were originally associated.[1] The association of two similar parables is in harmony with a habit of the oriental mind which loves to repeat the same thing in two different ways which differ very slightly from each other. The second form of a couple of parables generally simply reproduces the first with a simple difference in the image, without adding anything to the actual parable. This is the case, for instance, in the parables of the lost sheep and the lost coin. Sometimes, however, the second contains something more than the first, as in Mark ii. 21–22, the parable of the leather bottle is not a mere doublet of the parable of the piece of new cloth on an old garment; it adds the idea that the new element, also, is compromised by its association with the old.

We may regard some of the gestures of Jesus as acted parables, as, for instance, the setting of a child in the midst as a model to the disciples, or the distribution of the bread and the wine at the Last Supper.

---

[1] Thus Mark (iv. 30–32) has the Parable of the Grain of Mustard Seed, but not that of the Leaven; Matthew separates the Parable of the Tares (xiii. 24–30) from that of the Net (xiii. 47–50).

III. The Style

If poetry consists in seeing and thinking in images, and in perceiving connexions which are not seen by those whose outlook is prosaic, it cannot be denied that Jesus was richly endowed with poetic gifts. In poetry there is also an element of form. The true poet pours his thought into a mould which varies with its elements and according to the language in which it is written, but which can always be distinguished from prose.

In this respect also Jesus was a poet. His language, in most cases, is not ordinary prose. This is a fact which comes out even in translation, but it is impossible to analyse it with any precision. When we try to examine this question of the rhythm of the words and sayings of Jesus more closely, however, we are confronted by a preliminary difficulty. The only documents at our disposal are doubly uncertain. We are only dealing with the Greek translation of the Aramaic words of Jesus; inevitably, however, this often means that in passing from one language to another the original rhythm is broken and altered; in addition, the words of Jesus have had to undergo, at the hands of tradition, a process of adaptation which cared still less about rhythmical and strophic construction, since evidently the evangelists did not feel it worth while to preserve it. Nevertheless, the mere reading of many of the sayings of Jesus gives us an impression of rhythm, even to those who regard Père Jousse's theory [1]—(to which Loisy has subscribed,[2] from which, however, he draws very different conclusions)—as a sweeping and, in any case, premature generalization.

In a general way, this kind of rhythm uses the same methods as those employed in Hebrew poetry, that is to say, those of repetition, balance, and antithesis.[3] Sometimes we find con-

---

[1] M. Jousse: *Le style oral rythmique et mnémotechnique chez les verbomoteurs. Études de psychologie linguistique*, Paris, 1925.

[2] Loisy: *Revue critique*, 1923, p. 402. *Mémoires pour servir à l'histoire religieuse de notre temps*, Paris, 1930–1931, III, pp. 473 ff.

[3] Typical examples of the use of these methods by the rabbis are given in the book of P. M. Jousse: *Étude sur la psychologie du geste. Les Rabbis d'Israël. Les récitatifs parallèles, I, Genre de la maxime*, Paris, 1930.

structions which we might describe as strophical, if it were legitimate to employ this term for groupings which do not seem to follow any very precise law. Here, therefore, a few general remarks will suffice.

The first method to note, and the one in most frequent use, is that of the doublet. A typical example is furnished by the instances of the double parables of which we have already spoken. We might add several others, like "the salt of the earth and the light of the world" (Matt. v. 13–14*), "the cup and the baptism" (Mark x. 38–39*), "the dens of the foxes and the nests of the birds" (Matt. viii. 20*). Sometimes we find not a doublet but a triplet. Thus, in the saying preserved in Mark ix. 43–48: "If thy hand offend thee . . . If thy foot . . . If thine eye . . .", or in the warning of Matt. v. 22: "Whosoever is angry with his brother . . . whosoever shall say to his brother *Raca* . . . whosoever shall say, Thou fool. . . ."
The enumeration may also be of more than three terms. There are, for instance, four in Matt. v. 34–36: "Swear not at all; neither by heaven . . . nor by the earth . . . neither by Jerusalem . . . neither by thy head. . . ." There are five in Matt. v. 39–42: "Whosoever shall smite thee on thy right cheek. . . . If any man will sue thee at the law. . . whosoever shall compel thee . . . whosoever shall ask of thee . . . whosoever shall borrow of thee. . . ."

Antithesis, which is one of the most usual methods employed in Hebrew poetry, often occurs in the words of Jesus. It may be simple, as in the contrast between the house built on the rock and the house built on the sand (Matt. vii. 24–27)*, in the Parable of the Two Debtors (Luke vii. 41–43) or in that of the Two Sons (Matt. xxi. 28–32), or each term may undergo a slight process of development, for instance, in the instruction on the Law, in Matt. v. 19: "Whosoever shall break one of these least commandments, and shall teach men so, he shall be called the least in the kingdom of heaven: but whosoever shall do and teach them the same shall be called great in the kingdom of heaven." Sometimes the antithesis is doubled or trebled, as in Matt. vi. 2–18: "When thou doest thine alms, do not sound a trumpet before thee as the hypocrites do. . . .

K*

When thou doest alms, let not thy left hand know what thy right hand doeth. . . . When thou prayest, thou shalt not be as the hypocrites. . . . Thou, when thou prayest, enter into thy chamber, and . . . shut thy door. . . . When thou fastest, anoint thine head and wash thy face."

In certain instances one only of the terms of the antithesis is repeated two or three times. Thus John the Baptist is neither a reed shaken by the wind nor a man clad in effeminate garments, but a prophet (Matt. xi. 7–9). In the Parable of the Sower (Mark iv. 1–9*) some grains fall on the path, some among the thorns and on the rocky ground, and, in contrast to all this, some fall into the good ground.

In Matthew (vii. 13–14) we have an example of repetition and antithesis in association:

> Enter ye in at the strait gate,
> For wide is the gate and broad is the way that leadeth to destruction;
> And many there be that go in thereat.
> Strait is the gate and narrow is the way which leadeth unto life;
> And few there be that find it.

In Mark iv. 21–22 (Luke viii. 16–17) the grouping is a little more complex:

> Is a candle brought
> To be put under a bushel
> Or under a bed?
>
> Is it not brought to be set on a candlestick?
> There is nothing hid
> Which shall not be manifested;
> Neither was anything kept secret
> But that it should come abroad.

(Cf. also Matt. x. 26–27. Luke xii. 2–3.)

The construction is more complex still in a section like Matt. vii. 7–11*, where there is a veritable strophic arrangement, in which, however, the rhythm is far more evident in the grouping of the ideas than in that of the actual clauses:

> Ask, and it shall be given you.
> Seek, and ye shall find.
> Knock, and it shall be opened unto you.
> For everyone that asketh, receiveth.
> He that seeketh, findeth.
> To him that knocketh it shall be opened.
> Or what man is there of you, whom if his son ask bread,
> Will he give him a stone?
> Or if he ask a fish,
> Will he give him a serpent?
> If ye then, being evil,
> Know how to give good gifts unto your children,
> How much more shall your Father which is in Heaven
> Give good things to them that ask him?[1]

A slightly different example of a complex antithesis is furnished by Matt. vi. 19–21. (Cf. Luke xii. 33–34) :

> Lay not up for yourselves treasures upon earth,
> Where moth and rust doth corrupt,
> And where thieves break through and steal.[2]
> Lay up for yourselves treasures in heaven,
> Where neither moth nor rust doth corrupt,
> Where thieves do not break through nor steal.
> For where your treasure is,
> There will your heart be also.

The antithesis may also be associated with a question and an answer, as in Mark ii. 19–20* :

Can the children of the bridechamber fast while the bridegroom is with them?
As long as they have the bridegroom with them they cannot fast.
The days will come when the bridegroom shall be taken away from them,
Then shall they fast in those days.

---

[1] It should be noted, in what may be called the fourth strophe, the use of reasoning *a fortiori*, which is a form of argument definitely employed by the rabbis (*Qal vakhomer*, easy and difficult). The use of this kind of reasoning is frequent in the New Testament.

[2] The balance should be noted, introduced into the phrase by the fact that in one there are two subjects and one verb, and in the other two verbs and one subject.

A rather usual type is that which occurs, for instance, in Matt. vi. 24. It ought to be closely analysed.

The first phrase announces the thesis:

> No man can serve two masters.

Then this subject is demonstrated by two equivalent antitheses, the order in which the terms which constitute them not being the same:

> For either he will hate the one
> And love the other;
> Or else he will hold to the one
> And despise the other.

Finally a conclusion takes up again the general principle, but it applies it to the particular case which Jesus has in mind:

> Ye cannot serve God and mammon.

Here is another example of this construction in Mark viii. 34–38:

Thesis

> Whosoever will come after me,
> Let him deny himself,
> And take up his cross,
> And follow me.

Demonstration by antithesis

For whosoever will save his life shall lose it;
Whosoever shall lose his life for my sake and the Gospel's, the same shall save it,
For what shall it profit a man, if he gain the whole world, and lose his own soul?

Conclusion

What shall a man give in exchange for his soul?
Whosoever shall be ashamed of me and of my words
In this adulterous and sinful generation,
  Of him also shall the Son of Man be ashamed
When he cometh in the glory of his Father with the holy angels.

The tradition which has mistaken the character of the parables by regarding them as allegories, which are only intelligible if they are accompanied by a commentary, and which has not always respected the structure of the pairs of parables, has also not perceived the rhythmical character of the sayings of Jesus. Often, where the rhythm can be clearly perceived in one Gospel, it will be broken in the form in which the same saying is given by another Gospel.

As an illustration of this point it will be sufficient to compare Matt. v. 44–48 with Luke vi. 27–35. The text of Matthew reads thus:

Thesis

I say unto you:
Love your enemies,
Pray for them which despitefully use you,
That ye may be the children of your Father which is in heaven;
For he maketh his sun to rise
On the evil and on the good
And sendeth rain
On the just and on the unjust.

Explanation by Example

If ye love them which love you
What reward have ye?
Do not even the publicans so?
Be ye therefore perfect,
As your Father which is in heaven is perfect.

The following is the text of Luke:

Thesis

I say unto you:
Love your enemies;
Do good unto them which hate you;
Bless them that curse you;
Pray for them which despitefully use you.

Repetition of the Thesis

Unto him that smiteth thee on the one cheek,
Offer also the other.
Him that taketh away thy cloak
Forbid not to take thy coat also;

To every man that asketh
Give.
Of him that taketh away thy goods
Ask them not again.

Summary of Thesis

As ye would that men should do to you
Do ye also to them likewise.

Demonstration

If ye love them which love you,
What thank have ye?
Sinners also love those that love them.
If ye do good to them which do good to you.
What thank have ye?
Sinners also do the same.
If ye lend to them of whom ye hope to receive,
What thank have ye?
For sinners also lend to sinners, to receive as much again.

Conclusion

But love ye your enemies;
Do good;
Lend, hoping for nothing again;
Your reward shall be great.

The arrangement of the text of Matthew is certainly original in comparison with that of Luke, in which the primitive construction of the section has been altered by the introduction of other elements.

This example, chosen from among many others, shows that the tradition, and the evangelists afterwards, had no accurate feeling for the rhythm in the sayings of Jesus. Therefore we may conclude that where rhythm does exist it cannot be put down to the account of the evangelists. Further, this rhythm is far more Semitic than Greek. Hence it cannot have been introduced into the Gospel story after the Gospel tradition had passed from the Semitic world to that of Greece.

We might make similar remarks about the imagery. With the exception of the Book of Revelation, where the images are rather algebraical combinations than poetic visions, and the Epistles of St. Paul, in which there is reflected, not the Palestinian countryside, but the Greek world (the army, games in the circus, etc.), the imagery in the New Testament is poor and scanty.[1] Therefore it seems very unlikely that the variety of images in the Gospels can be due to the influence of the evangelists themselves.

The rhythmical form on the one hand, the imagery on the other, provide us with indications which may be taken into account when we have to decide on questions of authenticity. In any case, they provide proofs of a relative antiquity which cannot be overlooked [2] and which constitute at least some presumptive claim to authenticity.

IV. THE HEARERS OF JESUS

Every public speaker adapts what he has to say to the hearers to whom he speaks and to the aim which he has in view. In order to be able to interpret the words of Jesus correctly, we must take into account the people to whom he spoke, and what it was he wished to obtain from them.

Even if we believe that the evangelists themselves suggested the idea that Jesus only revealed his real mind to a circle of initiates, to whom he gave some esoteric teaching, this does not exclude the idea that although he spoke to the crowds which pressed on him, he also gathered round him a circle of intimate disciples, who were destined to become those who understood his mind, and then his fellow-workers in the cause of the Gospel. It is not certain that Jesus asked all, as he did ask some, to leave all in order to follow him. It seems that he did admit that it was possible to be his disciple without accompanying him on his wandering ministry. We shall return to this question later on; at the moment, all that concerns us is to discover whether, from the data at our disposal, we can distinguish and describe the various categories of persons who were addressed by Jesus, and how much this fact means for the interpretation of his words.

[1] An exception should be made of the Epistle of James, in which there is certainly a Palestinian current of thought.
[2] This criterion is not absolute, and cannot be applied without the addition of an element of objective appreciation. BURNEY (*The Poetry of Our Lord*, Oxford, 1922. Cf. the statement of HEMPEL: *Theol. Litzg.*, 1926, cols. 435 ff.) he goes too far in saying that the element of rhythm should serve as a touchstone for the words of Jesus in every case of uncertainty.

A certain number of them, whether by their content only or owing to the circumstances in which they were uttered, are represented as having been addressed to enemies. Some—for instance, the discourse on the expulsion of the demons by Beelzebub (Mark iii. 23–30*)—correspond to attacks of which Jesus is the object. Others are discussions in which he is involved: sometimes they are due to the initiative taken by his enemies (sayings about divorce, Mark x. 1–12*; on the payment of tribute to Caesar, Mark xii. 13–17*; on the resurrection, Mark xii. 18–27): at other times Jesus himself takes the offensive (the question about the baptism of John, Mark xi. 29–33*; the Davidic descent of the Messiah, Mark xii. 35–37). We must take into account, in order to interpret this group of sayings, what they contain of the argument *ad hominem*. Among them there are some whose significance is only negative.

Mark seems to distinguish two phases in the ministry of Jesus: in the first phase, although he gives some private instructions to his disciples, in the main he is speaking to the crowds; in the second phase he is talking only to his intimates, save in a few instructions which for the most part have a controversial aim, and are no longer concerned with the Kingdom of God, but with the Son of Man, with his return and the necessity for his sufferings. It is impossible to discern clearly how these two kinds of teaching, which seem to correspond to two different phases in the ministry of Jesus, are organically connected with each other. In the mind of the evangelist they seem to correspond to a convention of a higher order and to be the fulfilment of a providential plan. Here, however, there is only a general formula with which the material (even that used by Mark) only agrees very imperfectly. From the early part of the Galilean ministry, Mark sometimes represents Jesus talking with the disciples alone, not in order to give them esoteric teaching, but rather in order to prepare them for a special mission, and to make them capable of being associated with his preaching, and to carry it on after him. The fact that Jesus sent his disciples out on a mission (vi. 6–13), that he told them beforehand about his sufferings and his death (viii. 31), and that he insisted on the duty of following and confessing him (viii. 34–ix. 1), supports this interpretation.

Matthew, who, speaking generally, has the same point of view as Mark, has only slightly modified some of the confusion in his narrative.[1] On the other hand, in the first part he has preserved a scene which shows that the circle of the disciples of Jesus included other men besides those who had left all for him. I refer to an incident in which a man who does not follow him is called a disciple (μαθητής) (viii. 21). By enlarging the scope of the discourse of Jesus when he sent the apostles out on their mission, Matthew has also emphasized the idea that there were two concentric circles of disciples.

In the second part of his narrative, Matthew likewise modifies the idea of a teaching reserved for the disciples only. Thus, in xvii. 22, in the general statement about the journey from Galilee into Judaea, in the course of which Jesus announced for the second time his sufferings, his death, and his resurrection, he does not say, as Mark represents him saying (ix. 30), that Jesus took care that no one should recognize him.

Luke gives a picture which is closer to that of Matthew than to that of Mark. He applies the statement about the sufferings which are the appointed lot of disciples not only to the inner circle of intimates but to all (ix. 23 ff.).[2] If some sections of the Lucan narrative give the impression that in the second part of his ministry Jesus addressed himself less exclusively to his intimates than in the narratives of Mark and Matthew, this is due mainly to the fact that after the incident of Caesarea Philippi, with which it opens in Mark and Matthew, (the period of the teaching given to the disciples only), Luke, by an editorial artifice, has inserted a series of scenes which he could not easily place elsewhere in the plot of Mark's narrative, but of which it is not at all certain that they all belong to the second phase of the ministry of Jesus.

---

[1] He combines, for instance, the teaching to the multitude and the teaching to the disciples by saying that the Sermon on the Mount is addressed to both (v. 1 f.); this is shown to be unnatural by the words in vii. 28–29, where the impression made on the crowd is mentioned.

[2] This correction is all the more significant, since, as in Mark and Matthew at the moment when these words are uttered, Jesus is in a solitary place alone with the inner circle of his disciples.

The Fourth Evangelist, at least if we look at those sections in his narrative which are based on ancient sources of tradition, provides some indications which complete, and—so far as the last part of the life of Jesus is concerned, his Jerusalem ministry —define, and even correct those which we can gather from the Synoptic Gospels. The source used by John in chapter vii [1] represents Jesus giving teaching at Jerusalem, which, although it may not be directly Messianic, does at least raise the question of the Messiahship. At the end of chapter x (40 ff.) we find him in Peraea, and also keeping in touch with the disciples whom he has won in Jerusalem; [2] this confirms the idea of a public teaching ministry of Jesus in the last period of his ministry, and allows us to correct the theory of the Synoptics, according to which Jesus never spoke in Jerusalem save to hold discussions with his enemies.

We cannot therefore retain the idea that, in reality, the teaching of Jesus was meant only for those who were ready to give up everything to follow him, not only in the figurative but in the literal sense of the word, and that he had nothing to say to those who did not consent to this entire sacrifice. Nor can we entertain the idea that during the course of his ministry, having begun by speaking to the multitudes, under the influence of defeat, he concentrated his later efforts only on those of his disciples who were directly associated with his ministry and his life.

The two groups of disciples, the large and the small, which we see gathered round Jesus, correspond rather to a difference in the part they were able to play, and called to play, in the preaching of the Kingdom of God, than to a radical difference between those who were the only true and genuine disciples of Jesus, and those who might have been touched and moved by his teaching in a more superficial way, without, however, having been brought to the point of a personal decision which would make them his disciples indeed, and, as such, would have been associated with him in his life and his ministry.

In order to interpret the words and sayings of Jesus we must bear in mind those to whom he spoke: intimate friends who

[1] See pp. 224 ff.
[2] On the disciples of Jesus in Jerusalem, see Chapter XIV.

were called to become veritable fellow-workers, disciples in a less strict sense of the word, occasional hearers who needed to be won, rather than strengthened in a nascent attachment, and, finally, adversaries. But we would be pressing a legitimate distinction too far if we were to make it mean that Jesus employed two forms of teaching: one which was addressed to everyone in general, and another which was reserved solely for an inner circle of intimates.

CHAPTER XII

THE FIRST PART OF THE GALILEAN MINISTRY

I. THE TWO PERIODS OF THE GALILEAN MINISTRY

IN the spring of the year 27, shortly before the time of harvest,[1] Jesus returned to Galilee. He was intending to stay there until the Feast of Tabernacles (September or October) of the same year. This ministry, which lasted for some months, falls into two periods. At first, Jesus met with a measure of success; although he was confronted by a certain amount of hostility, on the whole, the response to his message was encouraging. We see a group of intimate disciples gathering round him who gradually become more deeply devoted to him and to his cause; as time goes on they develop into eager and humble fellow-workers. These are they who will follow him into Judaea, and, after his death, will form the nucleus of the Church in Jerusalem. Then we see a larger group, composed of people whose hearts have been touched and captured by the message of Jesus; these people flock to hear him whenever they have the opportunity, but they do not "follow" him in the literal sense of the word, perhaps because Jesus has not yet called them to do so, or perhaps because there are various circumstances in their lives which prevent them from responding to his appeal.

It was only natural that the representatives of the Jewish religious tradition should not approve of a man who did not belong to their circle, especially as he had not been educated by the rabbis; moreover, in their eyes, although he could read, he was an illiterate person, who, nevertheless, claimed to be able to teach the people. The instinctive distrust which the mere appearance of Jesus as a popular preacher aroused, was inevitably deepened when the authorities noted the liberties he took with regard to the ritual obligations of the Law, as interpreted by tradition. Their fears were aroused particularly by his attitude towards the observance of the Sabbath, and by his way of life, which, instead of being modelled on that

[1] See pp. 251 ff.

of the Pharisees and of those who were supposed to represent the religious élite of the Jewish people, was in closer contact with that of the tax-gatherers, and those whom people generally called "sinners."[1]

At the outset, however, the hostility which he encountered does not appear either to have hindered his work or endangered his life.

During the first period Jesus seems to have used Capernaum as his headquarters. It was to that town that he returned after each preaching tour. We are not able to say whether he confined his preaching activities to the region North-West of the Lake, or whether he went farther afield. The way in which, as Mark (vi. 1) tells us, at a moment which seems to belong to the close of the first period of the Galilean ministry, Jesus went one day to preach at Nazareth, seems to indicate that until then he had not gone very far away from Capernaum.

The second part of the Galilean ministry is in many respects very different from the first. Opposition now becomes more bitter; not only are the Pharisees hostile, but the political authorities also. The Tetrarch, Herod Antipas, disturbed by the influence which he sees this new prophet is gaining over the people, fears lest the danger which he thought he had overcome by putting John the Baptist to death has reappeared. He begins to dream of treating Jesus as he treated John. Jesus, warned of his danger, escapes. His itinerating ministry now develops into a wandering from place to place. Jesus appears no longer in Capernaum and its neighbourhood, save on rare occasions, and then only on flying visits. The greater part of the time he remains in remote and solitary places; sometimes, no doubt because the messengers of Herod dog his footsteps too closely, he flees out of Galilee, and goes to the Eastern shore of the Lake, into Decapolis, to the region of Caesarea Philippi, and even as far as the borders of Tyre. At the close of this period he gives up the attempt to carry on a work in

[1] This does not mean people whose lives were particularly immoral or scandalous, but persons who, owing to circumstances or to their profession, were unable to be strict followers of the Law, and thus lived on the fringe of strict Judaism.

Galilee which has been made impossible by circumstances, and he leaves Galilee for Judaea.

It is not possible to fix, even approximately, at what point this crisis in the Galilean ministry occurred. It would be useless to hazard conjecture on this point.

II. The Thought of Jesus at the Beginning of His Ministry

When Jesus returned from the region of the Jordan, where he had been staying near John the Baptist, the reason for this move was not that which is implied, even if not actually stated, by Mark (i. 14) and Matthew (iv. 12).[1] These two writers suggest that after John had been put in prison Jesus understood that the moment had come for him to begin his own work to which he felt himself called. The real reason, however, was that the ideas and sentiments which had been developing within him during the time that he was staying near the Baptist, either as a disciple or a fellow-worker, had led him to feel that he was out of sympathy with John's point of view, and that he must separate from him.

In order to gain some idea of the sentiments and ideas of Jesus at the time when he returned to Galilee, we must first of all estimate to what extent some elements of John's message have been incorporated into the Gospel. On his first preaching tour the message of Jesus was couched in precisely the same terms as that of John,[2] and, a little later, Jesus declared that "John is a prophet . . . and more than a prophet. Among them that are born of women there hath not arisen a greater than John the Baptist," but that, nevertheless, "he that is least in the kingdom of heaven is greater than he" (Matt. xi. 9–13*); this means that John's message comes from God, and

[1] Luke does not mention the imprisonment of John the Baptist in connexion with the return of Jesus into Galilee. He does mention it, however, in iii. 19–20. It is possible that he knew of the tradition represented in John iii–iv, or a similar tradition which spoke of a simultaneous ministry of John and of Jesus.

[2] Matthew (iv. 17) gives it in exactly the same terms as that of John the Baptist (iii. 2). Mark (i. 15) adds the words: "And believe in the Gospel." This is an addition by which he wished to make a distinction between the teaching of Jesus and the teaching of the Baptist.

consequently is true, but that, nevertheless, it is incomplete. Matthew and Luke[1] have also preserved a phrase of Jesus: "The Law and the prophets until John,"[2] which expresses the idea that the ministry of John marks the end of the old religious order, and that after him there begins something new: obviously, this means that the Messianic era has begun. The words in which the evangelists have expressed the first message of Jesus, ἤγγικεν[3] ἡ βασιλεία τοῦ θεοῦ mean literally, not, as they are usually translated: "The Kingdom of God is near," but: "The Kingdom of God is at hand," that is, that something has happened which has brought it nearer than it was before; this means that either with the ministry of John or after this ministry the closing period of the present era has begun.

Had Jesus this idea quite definitely and clearly in mind when he began his ministry? Although the nature of the documents at our disposal makes it a very delicate matter to attempt to estimate the development of the thought of Jesus,[4] it seems allowable to think that, from the moment he returned into Galilee, he had the feeling, at least in a confused and obscure way, that new times needed new ways. From the earliest days of his ministry he made it quite evident that he did not feel tied by the rules which governed ritual questions to the point of sacrificing for them what he felt to be essential; this means that he regarded the practices of Judaism merely as means to an end. Thus from the very outset there was in the thought of Jesus a germ whose logical development was hastened by perpetual conflict with the representatives of the Jewish tradition, and was to lead eventually to the idea of the abrogation of the religion of Israel.

On one essential point Jesus differed from the majority of

[1] Matthew (xi. 12) gives it in the same context as the saying about John as the greatest among the prophets. Luke places it at a point (xvi. 16) where it has no real organic relation with the context at all. Hence this saying must have been preserved, originally, in an isolated tradition.
[2] On this expression, see above, p. 277, n. 2, and *Jean-Baptiste*, pp. 62 ff.
[3] The perfect tense denotes a fact in the past whose consequences remain.
[4] This is because the evangelists did not imagine that the ideas of Jesus could develop; hence they give no indication which would enable us to follow their development, and they do not trouble to connect the words of Jesus with the occasions on which they were uttered.

his contemporaries. Like John the Baptist, he believed that the privileged position of Israel did not exempt it from the searching judgment of the Messiah. Whereas to the author of the Psalms of Solomon, for instance, the coming of the Messiah would usher in a long-desired deliverance, to Jesus, as to John the Baptist, the Day of the Son of Man is conceived in the spirit of Amos (v. 18–20) and Joel (ii. 1–11), as a terrible Day, a Day to be feared, in which men will be judged according to their deeds. As Jesus felt opposition increasing, his warnings to the unbelieving Jews became more severe; look at the curse on the Galilean towns, for instance, in Matt. xi. 20–24*, or the destiny which he foretells to those who are rich, satisfied, joyful and enjoying a good reputation (Luke vi. 24–26*).

From the very beginning of his ministry Jesus proclaimed the necessity of repentance, and he did so to the end, that is to say: preparation for the advent of the Kingdom of God and for the coming Judgment.

Jesus never defined exactly what he meant by this "Kingdom of God" which was, nevertheless, at the heart of his message; this, however, was due to the fact that this idea had long been current among the Jews. The Kingdom of God means the new order which will be established when the present order comes to an end. A radical change is necessary owing to the fact that in the present world God does not rule, or, at least, his sovereignty is challenged by a hostile power (that of the demons, and their chief, Satan), which influences both men and events. But while the Jews believed that this restoration of the sovereignty of God would place Israel in a dominant position in world politics, Jesus regards it primarily as a fact in the moral order: men will obey God fully. In the expectation of the Kingdom of God there is a combination of pessimism and optimism: pessimism because the present world is hopelessly evil, and optimism because this condition is not destined to last for ever. To Jesus the Kingdom of God is not a spiritual and inward reality to be fulfilled in those who sever themselves from the world and from the power of evil. Nor is it the ideal society of the disciples. His conception is definitely eschatological, but it is not apocalyptic, in this sense, that although Jesus believed that the Kingdom of God was at hand, he made no attempt to estimate when it would appear, nor to describe (as do the Jewish Apocalypses) the signs of its coming. On the contrary, he taught that the coming of the Kingdom could not be foretold, and that it would come with the swiftness of lightning, when perhaps it was least expected; he made it very clear that God alone knew the precise moment of its coming. Jesus had a much less materialistic idea of the Kingdom of God than his contemporaries; he did not conceive it as a condition in which the power of God would be placed at the service of the nationalistic ambitions of Israel or of human desires; in his mind it was characterized by entire obedience towards God, by the realization in the children of the Kingdom of the very perfection of God Himself. The thought of a God of love and mercy is directly reflected in this idea of the Kingdom of God.

Like his contemporaries, Jesus associated the idea of the establishment of the Kingdom of God with the ideas of the manifestation of the Messiah, of resurrection and of judgment. When the Messiah comes, he will exercise the power of judgment by which the enemies of God (demons and rebel human beings) will be annihilated, and the elect will be introduced into the new world which will be established when all opposition to God will have disappeared.

The preaching and the activity of Jesus was not intended to hasten the coming of the Kingdom of God. The Kingdom will come at the moment appointed for it by God; its establishment will be an act of His omnipotence. Men can do nothing in this sphere, but they can realize in themselves such sentiments and live such a life that they will be ready to enter it when it comes. It was to this that Jesus summoned them.

On one essential point, from the very beginning of his ministry, the thought of Jesus differed from that of John the Baptist. He conceives the condition of entrance into the Kingdom of God quite differently from John. To John the Baptist, those who have repented and received baptism, and who afterwards have produced "fruits worthy of repentance," when the Messiah appears will be wheat worthy of being gathered into the garner. Jesus believed this when he was preaching and baptizing alongside of John the Baptist. But at the moment when he returned into Galilee he believed it no longer, since it was on the question of purification that he had severed his connexion with John. Later on, we shall hear him declare that those who have done all that is commanded them ought to regard themselves simply as unprofitable servants (Luke xvii. 10). Jesus appears to believe that man, even when he is entirely obedient, is not capable of acquiring the virtues which will permit him to receive the Kingdom of Gôd as a reward. Thus the Gospel which Jesus preached was a proclamation of the divine pardon; he placed God where, before his time, man used to stand. Hence, since the entry into the Messianic Kingdom depends on divine and not on human initiative, Jesus does not remain in the desert like John the Baptist, and wait for those who feel the need of being guided towards the Kingdom of God to come to him. He mixes with the people, goes up and down the countryside, through the villages and the open spaces to seek for the lost sheep of the house of Israel. This, too, is why he believes that no one, however low he may have fallen, is unable to receive the gift of the love of God, which God is longing to impart; the only condition being that the message shall be received by penitent hearts, with a childlike faith, which does not need to reason or to understand in order to receive a marvellous gift (Mark x. 15). On the other hand, as for those who are satisfied with themselves, and who live in the assurance that they have an infallible right to the Kingdom of God, Jesus has nothing to give them. It is not to them that he addresses his message. "He saith unto them, They that are whole[1] have no need of the physician, but they that are sick: I came not to call the righteous but sinners" (Mark ii. 17*).

The Kingdom of God therefore is doubly transcendent: first of all because it is not a reality of the present world, and can only come from God, and, secondly, because its value is worth infinitely more than man could ever attain. Thus in the thought of Jesus the mercy of God plays the part which repentance played in the thought of John. The nature of the revolution which he had thus initiated permits us to see the

[1] This means people who believe they are in good health and that they are righteous.

causes. They relate to man on the one hand, and to God and His Kingdom on the other. As he explored the idea of repentance, Jesus was led to think that, however complete it may be, it can, strictly speaking, change the present and the future, give to the life of the penitent a new character, but it cannot alter the past, it cannot undo what has been done. Thus even when repentant, man will be a guilty person before the Judgment Seat of the Messiah and he will deserve punishment. If God were the God of a strict and rigid righteousness all men, in spite of their repentance, would be shut out from the Kingdom; thus this Kingdom would never be realized, for it would not exist at all if God ruled over an empty desert. Jesus cannot therefore think that God is moved only by justice, for his faith in the omnipotence of the Heavenly Father was such that he could not believe that His will to reign over a world which would be voluntarily submitted to him, could be held in check permanently by the forces of evil. Thus he is led to think that God's reign will be ushered in by something other than by justice, that this will take place through his mercy and love, and thus that repentance is not a means by which men who deserved to be kept outside the Kingdom of God can by their own efforts make themselves fit to enter. One condition alone must be fulfilled before they can be welcomed. Thus Jesus ceased to think that baptism, the seal of repentance, could be a veritable purification from sins, and he ceased to baptize those who came to him. Apart from the two passages from the Fourth Gospel (iii. 22, iv. 1) which belong to a period before the separation between Jesus and John, it is never stated that Jesus baptized anyone. When we think of the importance which the Early Church attached to the connexion between its practices and the commands or example of Jesus, we ought to see a great deal of significance in the fact that in prescribing the observance of baptism the Early Church thought she was obeying a command of Jesus which was only given after his resurrection (Matt. xxviii. 19).[1] The absolute conception of God which Jesus held may have also helped to modify his ideas about repentance, because it

[1] In fact, the introduction, or the reintroduction, of baptism into the Primitive Church seems to have been connected with ideas proceeding from disciples of John the Baptist.

must have seemed impossible to him that the realization of the purpose of God for His Kingdom could depend, in some measure, on the goodwill displayed by those who had repented of their past ways.

We must not be led astray by the fact that Mark's narrative gives the impression that at the beginning of his Galilean ministry Jesus simply repeated the message of John. Mark himself has the feeling that from the moment Jesus returned into Galilee something new had begun, since he says that Jesus preaches the "Gospel of God," and he does not apply this term to the preaching of John. The same thought is still more clearly expressed in the picture of the early activity of Jesus, a picture which the formula of Mark merely summarizes (i. 15). We find in it three things which distinguish the activity of Jesus from that of John the Baptist. He cures the sick and those who are "possessed" (Mark i. 29–34, 39, etc.),[1] he pardons sins (Mark ii. 3–12), finally he adopts a very free attitude towards the obligations imposed by the Law as it was interpreted by tradition (Mark ii. 13–iii. 5).

Each of these points should be considered separately. The meaning that Jesus gave to the healings and the casting out of demons which he accomplished comes out very plainly in the discussion between himself and the scribes, who accuse him of casting out demons by the power of Beelzebub, the prince of the demons (Mark iii. 22–30*). Jesus begins by showing the absurdity of the accusation: a kingdom divided against itself cannot stand. If Satan were to rise against himself his rule would be practically over. This argument implies the idea (as a self-evident truth) that every time demons are cast out a blow has been dealt to the rule of Satan. Then, by a parable, or rather by an allegory, Jesus explains the meaning of the casting out of demons. "No man," he says, "can enter into a strong man's house and spoil his goods, except he first bind the strong man: and then he will spoil his house." Obviously

[1] There is no need to make a distinction between the casting out of demons and the healing of the sick. According to the thought of that day all sickness was due to demoniac influence. This comes out clearly in Matt. x. 1, where it is said that Jesus had given to his disciples "power over unclean spirits," they can cast out demons and cure all manner of disease.

the "strong man" here means Satan, and if Jesus can despoil him, that is to say, snatch from him those who are "possessed," it is because Satan is conquered.[1] Thus the healing of the demoniacs is the proof that Satan is bound, and, in consequence, that his final destruction is near. Matthew (xii. 28) and Luke (xi. 20) add to the text of Mark this phrase, which doubtless comes from the *Logia*: "If I cast out devils by the Spirit of God (Matt.) or by the finger of God (Luke), then the kingdom of God is come upon you." The fact that Jesus feels that in casting out demons he is acting by a power that comes from God, explains why he declares that the only blasphemy that cannot be forgiven the sons of men is the blasphemy against the Spirit, that is to say, against the divine power which inspires him and by which he acts (Mark iii. 28–30*).[2]

The forgiveness of sins means exactly the same thing as the casting out of demons, seeing that sin means servitude to Satan. The story of the healing of the paralytic (Mark ii. 1–12*) shows that Jesus regarded sickness as the punishment of sin, since the sick man is cured when he receives the pardon of his sins.[3]

[1] The saying which Luke has placed at the moment of the return of the seventy from their mission (x. 18) also expresses the idea of the defeat of Satan: "I beheld Satan as lightning fall from heaven." I believe that here Jesus is using an image and not speaking of a vision, since no vision of Jesus has been reported. But whether it be an allusion to a vision or a simple image, the meaning of the phrase remains the same: it supports the idea of a defeat of Satan.

[2] Here we follow the text of Mark. Matthew (xii. 31–32) distinguishes between the blasphemy against the Spirit which cannot be forgiven and the blasphemy against the Son of Man which can be forgiven. This seems very much out of place here, for it would be very strange to say that what the Pharisees are saying is not a serious sin. Also it is difficult to see how it is possible to make a distinction in this passage between Jesus and the Spirit of God by which he casts out the demons. Luke has, in a different context (xii. 10), a saying which, with merely formal variations, is the exact equivalent of that of Matthew. With him also this phrase is in absolute contradiction to its context, since it is preceded by this statement: "He that denieth me before men shall be denied before the angels of God" (xii. 9). The idea of the blasphemy against the Son of Man which will be pardoned may perhaps come from an unfortunate transposition of the text of Mark iii. 28, about the blasphemies and sins which will be forgiven to the "sons of men," that is to men in general.

[3] Later on, Christian thought considered this idea altogether too simple. John, in the story of the man born blind (ix. 2–3), argues against the

Finally, the freer attitude—at first it did not amount to more than this—of Jesus towards customs and traditions shows that he placed the centre of gravity in the religious life in a quite different place from that of the Jews. In his eyes the value of rites is entirely secondary. This point of view differs greatly from the desire to free himself and his disciples from a yoke which was too heavy to be borne. The sacrifices which Jesus accepted for himself, and required from his disciples, show that he does not dream of minimizing the demands of God. His attitude reveals a new conception of obedience towards God. In the nomistic system of which ritualism is only one aspect, obedience to God is an external matter. The Law expresses the Divine Will in a certain number of formulas, both positive and negative. It defines certain actions which man ought to do, and others which he should refrain from doing. But it leaves outside the moral life all that has not been foreseen and defined by the Law. The obedience which it requires remains exterior. In the mind of Jesus, on the contrary, the commandment, instead of being an end in itself, is merely a means to an end. The end is submission to God, and when it appears quite clear that the Will of God, for instance, in the manifestation of active love towards a sufferer, is in opposition to the rules of the Law, then the rules must be modified. We are here confronted with a new, or a renewed, conception of what obedience to God means. A passive and mechanical conception has been replaced by an active conception which goes behind the Law and seeks to find out what the Law reveals, that is to say, God and His Will. In Judaism God is not known apart from His revelation of Himself in the Law. This revelation is insufficient, if the ideal which Jesus held up to his disciples in the words: "Be ye perfect, as your Father in heaven is perfect" (Matt. v. 48) be the true one. This ideal of realizing the nature of God in one's own life could not, however, be even imagined if God remains inaccessible and unknowable to man, apart from the fragmentary

assumption that sickness is due to the sin of the individual or of his parents. He regards it simply as an opportunity for the manifestation of the power of God. These ideas reveal a complete transformation of thought about the miracles of Jesus. In the earliest form of the tradition Jesus refuses to work any miracle for display (Mark viii. 11–13*).

revelation of Himself in the Law, if God does not reveal Himself directly to His children, if He is simply the God of majesty who spoke in ancient times out of the midst of the thunders and lightnings of Sinai, if He is not also the God who speaks to the conscience, the God who is always present within the hearts of those who desire to serve Him.[1]

Thus when Jesus went into Galilee to begin his ministry the message he brought was neither the teaching of John the Baptist nor a Judaism shorn of a few abuses which had crept into it, and in part perverted its fundamental principle, but it was in reality a new religion, although probably Jesus was not conscious of this himself.

The Messianic idea was not absent from the first message of Jesus. When he said: "The Kingdom of God is at hand," it was the same as though he had said to the Jews: "The Messiah is about to appear," but there is nothing to show that at the outset Jesus had the idea that he would be called to play the part of Messiah.

When he sends his disciples out on a missionary journey he tells them to carry the message which he himself preaches. They are to say that the Kingdom of God is near, and that men must repent (Mark vi. 12*; Matt. x. 7); Jesus is convinced that they will not have finished going through all the towns of Israel before the Son of Man will come (Matt. x. 23),[2] that is to say, before the Kingdom of God will be realized.

---

[1] On Jesus' thought of God, see RENAN, p. 75. E. EHRHARDT: *Le principe de la morale de Jésus*, in *Séance de rentrée de la Faculté de Théologie Protestante de Paris*, Paris, 1896, pp. 17–35. C. A. BERNOUILLI: *Le Dieu-Père de Jésus d'après les Synoptiques*, Actes du Congrès international d'histoire des religions tenu à Paris en Octobre 1923, Paris, 1925, II, p. 222. K. HOLL: *Urchristentum und Religionsgeschichte*, Ges. Aufs., II, pp. 9 ff. MAURICE GOGUEL: *Le Dieu de Jésus*, in *Séance de rentrée de la Faculté libre de Théologie de Paris*, Paris, 1929, pp. 24–44.

[2] This saying occurs in a conclusion to the missionary instructions of Jesus (x. 17–25), which reflects the point of view of apostolic times (see in particular x. 8). Verse 23 does not agree with its context. There only the cities of Israel are mentioned, as in x. 5–6, whereas, according to verses 17–18, the missionaries will have to appear before tribunals; in verse 23 all that is said is that when they are persecuted in one city they are to flee into the next. Verse 14 suggests an element of harmonization, for the missionaries are recommended—and this because the time is short—when

When Jesus tells his disciples to preach, he also gives them the command and the power to heal and to cast out demons (Matt. x. 8; Mark vi. 13); thus their preaching takes on the same character as his own. It is not the announcement of a fact from which each hearer must draw his own conclusions, it is a message of deliverance. The idea that Jesus is this Son of Man who is to come is absent from this message. In this respect the early phase of the thought of Jesus differs from that into which it was to develop later on.

At the outset, the vocation which Jesus felt he possessed was that of a prophet, not that of a Messiah. He feels he possesses a message which comes from God, for it is the development of the idea of God in him, it is the sentiment of communion with God realized by the submission of his own will to that of his Father, who has revealed to him that entrance into the Kingdom of God can only be a gift of God. Jesus certainly did not regard his ideas about the Kingdom of God as a discovery which he had made, but as a revelation of God which he had to give to his people. This feeling was immediately translated into action: by his preaching, by his activity, by the missionary tours which he undertook in order to reach as many souls as possible. It is manifested also in some of his sayings. For instance, after a day in Capernaum, when he had already left the town, his disciples came after him, protesting: "All men seek for thee" (which meant that the people of Capernaum wanted to keep Jesus to themselves), but Jesus replied: "Let us go into the next towns, that I may preach there also, for therefore came I forth" (Mark i. 38).[1] This sense of vocation is not the Messianic consciousness which was to develop later; but it is the germ of this consciousness. Because of the communion with his Father in which he lives,

their preaching is not welcomed in any house or city, not to linger there but to press on. We may suppose that in the source instead of, "When they persecute you in one city . . .," there was, "Whee they do not welcome you . . ." The present text seems to be due to the influence of the context in which persecutions are mentioned. Verse 23 and verses 24–25 are connected with the missionary instructions and not with the editorial conclusion to the discourse.

[1] Luke (iv. 43) makes this more definite by putting these words into the mouth of Jesus, "For therefore am I sent," that is, sent by God.

Jesus feels God near him when he preaches, when he acts, when he casts out demons (Matt. xii. 28*). This sense of being *a* messenger of God was gradually transformed into that of being His messenger *par excellence*, the One who will not only bring the message of the Divine pardon to men, but who will preside at the establishment of the Kingdom of God when it arrives, that is to say, who at that moment will be the Messiah.

One final feature must be mentioned. The activity of Jesus is limited strictly to the Jewish people. It was to remain so to the end, at least in practice, for it seems as though (we shall return to this point later on) during the last days of his life Jesus had begun to despair of the Jewish nation, and that he had come to think that the whole religious economy of the Jews, and, with that, the privileges of Israel upon which she prided herself, would be abolished, but the time was too short for him to act upon this conviction. However that may be, during the whole of his ministry Jesus confined his efforts to the Jewish people. No incident in the Gospel story takes place in any of the large Galilean towns like Tiberias or Sepphoris whose population was largely Gentile; they were indeed Greek rather than Jewish towns. When a Canaanitish woman besought him to heal her daughter he replied: "I am not sent save unto the lost sheep of the house of Israel," and though, finally, he acceded to her request, it was against his will, and because he felt constrained to do so by the faith and entreaties of the poor mother (Mark vii. 24–30*).[1] When he sends the disciples out on a mission he says explicitly that they are "not to go in the way of the Gentiles, nor into any city of the Samaritans . . . but go rather to the lost sheep of the house of Israel" (Matt. x. 5–7).[2] These passages are certainly

---

[1] Matthew (viii. 5–13) and Luke (vii. 1–10) report another miracle worked for the benefit of a pagan, the centurion of Capernaum, but this miracle has an exceptional character, since it is in connexion with faith so great that Jesus had never seen the like in Israel. Luke further makes out the centurion to be almost a semi-Jew, since he says that he loves the Jewish people and has built a synagogue for them.

[2] The promise of Jesus to his disciples that they will judge (that is, that they will govern) the twelve tribes of Israel (Matt. xix. 28*) shows also that he thinks that there will be Jews only in the Kingdom.

authentic,[1] for from the very beginning the Early Church was definitely universalist in outlook and practice, that is, she adopted an attitude which was the direct opposite of that of Jesus, and for the Church to take this line of action, which could not be justified by the example of her Lord, must mean that she felt bound to act thus owing to the clear and definite memories which had been handed on by the early tradition.[2]

The Gospels report that sometimes Jesus left the territory which was actually Jewish, but he never undertook any missionary tour in Gentile country. He only went there for periods of retirement, which seem to have been necessary from time to time in order to escape from the hostility of Herod. Thus his main object in leaving his own land was to find solitude.

Certain kinds of Jewish particularism, however, are quite remote from the spirit of Jesus. No more than John the Baptist could he have made his own the saying in the Wisdom of Solomon: "Even when we sin we are Thine, because we know Thy power" (xv. 2).[3] Jesus thinks, on the contrary, that God

[1] On the authenticity of Matt. x. 5–6, see my article: *Jésus et la tradition religieuse de son peuple*, *R.h.p.r.*, VII, 1927, pp. 167–169.

[2] Matthew (xxviii. 19) represents the command to preach the Gospel to the heathen as having been given by Jesus after his Resurrection. This solved the antithesis between the attitude of Jesus and that of the Church. In the Fourth Gospel, which is both the most universalist in tendency and also takes the most liberties with tradition, there is a very characteristic incident which explains how it was that the Church was universalist when Jesus was not. At the moment when the ministry of Jesus was drawing to a close, Philip speaks to him of some Jews who want to see him (xii. 20–22), and Jesus replies: "The hour is come that the Son of Man should be glorified" (xii. 23). The reply does not seem to correspond with the request, and we might think that xii. 20–22 and xii. 23 represent two fragments of traditions which have been placed by side in an awkward way. But, in reality, John wished to express the idea that the Gospel could not be preached to the Gentiles until Jesus was glorified (cf. MAURICE GOGUEL: *Sources*, pp. 50 ff.). In x. 16 f. the idea of the sheep who belong to another fold (that is to say, non-Jews), who also ought to hear the voice of Jesus, is equally connected with the idea of his death.

[3] Several Rabbinical texts express the same idea. The treatise *Sanhedrin* (X, 1, trad. HÖLSCHER, p. 103) says, for instance: "All Israel will have part in the new world." Other examples may be found in STRACK-BILLERBECK, I, pp. 116 f. As we know, the whole of the beginning of the Epistle to the Romans is taken up with explaining that sin separates the Chosen People from God every whit as much the Gentiles.

will be more severe towards those to whom His call has been more directly addressed, and who have not listened to it. Tyre and Sidon, Sodom and Gomorrah, will be less severely treated in the Day of Judgment than the Galilean towns which did not repent when he brought them the divine summons (Matt. xi. 20–24*). On one occasion Jesus declared that "many shall come from the east and from the west, from the north and from the south, and shall sit down with Abraham and Isaac and Jacob in the kingdom of heaven,[1] but the children of the kingdom (that is, the Jews) shall be cast out into outer darkness" (Matt. viii. 11–12*). In all this, however, there is, at the most, only a germ of universalism. These Gentiles who will be admitted into the Kingdom of God are exceptions, and the words of Jesus sound more like warnings to the Jews than like promises to the Gentiles. It may be, perhaps, that just as the Apostle Paul tells us why he exalts his ministry as the "Apostle of the Gentiles," saying: "If by any means I may provoke to emulation them which are my flesh, and might save some of them" (Rom. xi. 13–14), Jesus also may have been actuated by similar motives.

III. THE FIRST DISCIPLES OF JESUS

According to the account in the Synoptic Gospels, Jesus began preaching before he called his first disciples, Peter and Andrew, James and John. Mark (i. 16–20) and Matthew (iv. 18–22) give a picturesque account of their call, telling how, at the voice of Jesus, they left all—their boats and their nets—and followed him, leaving Zebedee alone with the hired servants.[2]

---

[1] Jesus says here: "to be at table with Abraham, Isaac, and Jacob in the Kingdom of God," and not, as in Luke xxii. 30: "to be at my table in my Kingdom"; this proves that this saying belongs to the earlier period in the life of Jesus, to that in which his Messianic consciousness was not yet developed.

[2] Mark (i. 20) says that his sons leave him "with the hired servants." Matthew (iv. 22) does not mention the servants. It is impossible to decide whether the servants have been added in Mark by some copyist in order that James and John should not appear to have left their father in a difficult situation, or whether Matthew has omitted to mention them in order to make their sacrifice more complete, and on account of texts like Mark x. 29; Matt. x. 37, etc.

This story, simple as it sounds, raises certain difficulties.[1] These men respond to the call of someone whom they do not know, and who does not even tell them what he wants from them. Luke has felt this difficulty. He has placed the incident a little later in the story (v. 1–11) at a moment when the first actions of Jesus have brought him a certain amount of notoriety, and he has placed a striking miracle—the miraculous draught of fishes—before the call to the disciples, which explains the decision taken by Peter and his companions.[2]

The first chapter of John reports that it was from the circles of the followers of John the Baptist that Jesus recruited his first disciples. When John declares that Jesus is the Lamb of God, two of his disciples, Andrew and another, prepare to follow Jesus. Andrew brings his brother Simon. Then Jesus calls Philip, and in his turn, Philip speaks to Nathanael. The latter hesitates at first, thinking that nothing good can ever come out of Nazareth, but his hesitations vanish when Jesus tells him that he saw him under the fig-tree (i. 35–51). This section illustrates two ideas. The first is the value of the testimony rendered to Jesus by his disciples and of the way the Church grew out of this witness. The second relates to the objection raised against the claim of Jesus to the Messiahship owing to the fact that he came from Nazareth. For John this point was important. He deals with the same objection in vii. 41–42. From this we may conclude that this objection was one which the Christians often had to meet. Neither in chapter i nor in chapter vii is it solved in a rational way. Thus the

[1] Let us recall simply what results from the parallelism of the two scenes relating Peter and Andrew and James and John respectively. The fact that two identical scenes are placed side by side, when they are so alike that we might suspect that one is the doublet of the other, may be intentional. Repetition was a device often used in early Christian literature in order to emphasize the importance of an incident. As illustrations of this tendency it will be sufficient to mention the two accounts of the feeding of the multitudes in the Gospels of Mark and Matthew, and the three accounts of the conversion of Paul in the book of the Acts.

[2] It is sufficient to point out in the Lucan account the doublet constituted by the two expressions: "Peter and all those who were with him," and "and so was also James and John, the sons of Zebedee, which were partners with Simon" (v. 9–10). This affords yet another proof of the secondary character of the Lucan narrative.

evangelist evidently thinks that it is sufficient to point to the witness of Christian experience. A story which illustrates these two important ideas may legitimately be suspected of having been created for that express purpose. We cannot, however, adopt this point of view, for several details show that the evangelist is here using source material. In verse 44 it is said that Philip comes from Bethsaida, the town of Andrew and of Peter. This statement, which is of no particular interest for Johannine theology, does not come from the Synoptic Gospels. Thus there must be a source behind this passage. Indeed, it is only by the suggestion of the existence of a source that we can explain the allusion to the scene under the fig-tree (i. 48), an allusion which remains unintelligible because the source has only been reproduced in a fragmentary manner. Thus this section cannot be an invention of the Fourth Evangelist. Further, his account agrees perfectly with the story in the Synoptic narrative, and even makes it intelligible. If it was before his return into Galilee that the first disciples of Jesus had been won, if from time to time they returned to their usual occupations, then, when Jesus calls them (because the moment has come when he has need of them), we understand how it is they can rise up and follow him without needing any explanation of what he wants from them, nor that he should justify his claim to have the right to draw them away from their ordinary calling.

IV. THE SCENE OF THE ACTIVITY OF JESUS

After leaving John the Baptist, Jesus, in order to avoid the slightest suspicion of personal rivalry, seeks a new sphere of activity.[1] It is natural that he should have chosen Galilee, his native country. Why then did he go, not to Nazareth, but to the region round Capernaum,[2] at present

---

[1] This is what is meant by John iv. 1–3, although the text of the source must here have been altered and some additions made to it, to such an extent that it is difficult to understand what it does mean.

[2] According to Luke, Jesus first preached at Nazareth, but was treated there in such a way that he felt compelled to go away from the village (iv. 16–30). Mark (vi. 1–6a) and Matthew (xiii. 53–58) also know of a visit of Jesus to Nazareth, but they place it considerably later in the story. The account of Luke is secondary so far as those of Mark and of Matthew

Tell-Hum?[1] Possibly there may have been some difficulties between him and the members of his family, who may not have approved of the line he took when he left Nazareth in order to go into the region of the Jordan.[2] Perhaps also Jesus considered Capernaum a better centre for his work than Nazareth.

Although Capernaum seems to have been the first scene of the activity of Jesus, and although the larger number of the Galilean incidents which have been preserved and handed down to us seem to be connected with the district of which this town is the centre, and although the journeys of Jesus are all connected with this town, yet Capernaum was not the only scene of his activity. The warnings which he uttered to the Galilean towns which refused to amend their ways apply equally to Capernaum, Chorazin,[3] and Bethsaida.[4] It was

are concerned. The latter would not have omitted the idea that Jesus was fulfilling a prophecy in Isaiah if they had found it in their source. Further, in iv. 23, Luke alludes to miracles accomplished by Jesus at Capernaum when until that moment there had been no mention either of Capernaum or of miracles.

[1] On Capernaum, see DALMAN: *Itin.*, pp. 178 ff. The remains of a synagogue have been discovered at Capernaum which seems to have been a building of some considerable size, and shows the importance of this centre. See ORFALI: *Capharnaüm et ses ruines*, Paris, 1922. The reasons which P. ORFALI (pp. 67 f.) and P. MESTERMANN (*Capharnaüm et Bethsaïda*, Paris, 1921, pp. 163 f.) give to show that this synagogue dates from the Herodian period, and that it was the very one which Jesus frequented and the one which the centurion built, hardly seem quite convincing.

[2] Perhaps there is here a confused recollection transposed from some other part of the narrative of a conflict between Jesus and his family in the story of Jesus at twelve years of age in the Temple (Luke ii. 41–52).

[3] On Chorazin, now called Kerâzeh, two and a half miles from Capernaum, and about 800 feet above the Lake, see DALMAN: *Itin.*, pp. 205 ff.

[4] On Bethsaida, now known as Khirbet el Kanef, see DALMAN: *Itin.*, pp. 215 ff. Bethsaida-Julias was founded by the tetrarch Philip, at the beginning of the present era, on the site of a village which bore the name of Bethsaida (the name Julias was given to the new town in honour of Julia, the daughter of Augustus). Bethsaida-Julias was on the left bank of the Jordan, where it flows into the Lake, hence it was in Gaulonitis and not in Galilee; it is certainly Bethsaida-Julias which is intended in Luke ix. 10. The question which is raised is this: was there, in addition to Bethsaida-Julias, another Bethsaida in Galilee, on the western shore of the Lake, in the plain of Gennesaret? The etymological meaning of Bethsaida (place where fish is caught) (DALMAN: *Itin.*, p. 216) makes this possible. We

from this locality that, according to the Fourth Gospel (i. 44, xii. 21), Simon Peter, Andrew, and Philip[1] came originally.

cannot consider it proved by the expression Bethsaida of Galilee which occurs in John xii. 21, for JOSEPHUS (*A.J.*, XVIII, 1, 1, ¶ 4) and PTOLEMY (*Geog.*, V, 16, 4) use the term Galilee in a broad sense. The rebel Judas was popularly known as Judas the Galilean (JOSEPHUS: *A.J.*, XVIII, 1, 6, ¶ 23; XX, 5, 2, ¶ 102. *G.J.*, II, 8, 1, ¶ 118. Acts v. 37), although he came really from Gamala in Gaulonitis. Nor can we regard as decisive the fact that in Mark viii. 23–26, Bethsaida, where Jesus cured a blind man, is described as a village (κώμη), although Bethsaida-Julias was a town of some importance. The account in Mark vi. 45–53 seems hardly compatible with the existence of Bethsaida-Julias alone. The first feeding of the multitude took place, according to Mark, in a desert place which Jesus reached by boat after leaving Capernaum (vi. 31). Luke (ix. 10) here names Bethsaida (certainly Bethsaida-Julias). After the feeding of the multitudes Jesus urges his disciples to embark quickly to go to the other side of the Lake to Bethsaida (εἰς τὸ πέραν πρὸς Βηθσαϊδάν). The progress of the boat was slow because the wind was contrary. During the night Jesus rejoined his disciples by walking on the water. When the crossing was over they arrived at Gennesaret (53). This passage seems to imply that Bethsaida, whither the disciples were going, was situated in the plain of Gennesaret. Matthew (xiv. 22) says that Jesus sent his disciples from the other side of the Lake, but he does not mention Bethsaida by name. Thus he does not seem to have known of a village called Bethsaida on the western side of the Lake. In any case, it was probably not an important place. DALMAN (*Itin.*, p. 235) suggests that during the course of the crossing there may have been a change of direction owing to the storm. Those who set out for Bethsaida-Julias in the north may have arrived at the plain of Gennesaret in the west. "On the 6th of April, 1908," he writes, "our Institute (the German Archaeological Institute in Jerusalem) had a similar experience on the Lake. We left the western shore below Hippos, we wished to skirt the shore in our boat in the direction of the north in order to go to Bethsaida once more. But towards midday a strong wind arose in the east which prevented us from landing there and drove us towards Capernaum." But it would be very strange if Mark did not mention an incident of this kind. His statement is too isolated to furnish reliable proofs of the existence of a Bethsaida in the plain of Gennesaret; it may also be considered doubtful because it occurs in a section in which the topographical indications are particularly confused. However, it seems to me that this possibility cannot be ignored; in the maledictions pronounced on the towns, Bethsaida is associated with the purely Galilean towns of Capernaum and Chorazin, which seems to me to constitute a very strong likelihood that there may have been a village or a place of the name of Bethsaida in Galilee proper, doubtless in the plain of Gennesaret.

[1] This statement is not necessarily inconsistent with the fact that according to the Synoptists Peter lived in Capernaum, in a house which may have been that of his mother-in-law (Mark i. 29–31).

Jesus worked mainly in the region round the Lake. Must we believe, as Jean Brunhes suggests, that the fishermen of the Lake were by their trade more ready to welcome novelties and to embark on a great spiritual adventure than the small cultivators, with their patient ways, who lived in the rural districts of the interior, men who by their way of life were accustomed to limit their outlook to the walls which enclosed their plot of ground?[1] Without denying that the manner of life of the hearers of Jesus may have prepared some of them for the reception of his message, we cannot accept explanations of this kind save with a great deal of hesitation. Jesus was a landsman, but this did not prevent him from moving out of the narrow setting in which he grew up.

The Fourth Gospel suggests that one of the centres of the activity of Jesus in Galilee was at Cana (now Khirbet-Kana), to the north of Nazareth,[2] a village which is not even mentioned in the Synoptic Gospels. Two incidents took place at Cana. The first is the miracle of the changing of the water into wine (ii. 1–11). Without discussing the daring hypothesis of certain critics who believe they can discern in this story a syncretistic tendency inspired by the cult of Bacchus,[3] we may remark that this incident does not belong to the most reliable part of the Fourth Gospel. Cana is also mentioned in the story of the healing of the nobleman's son of Capernaum: Jesus is at Cana when the officer comes to beseech him to heal his son. Jesus replies: "Go thy way; thy son liveth." The father returns, full of faith; when he reaches his home his servants come to meet him and tell him that his son is healed. He asks at what time the child began to improve, and learns that the fever left him the previous day at the seventh hour, that is, at the very moment when Jesus was speaking with him (iv. 46–54). This statement agrees very well with the respective position of Capernaum and of Cana;[4] the detail

[1] JEAN BRUNHES: *La géographie humaine*[3], Paris, 1925, pp. 800 ff.

[2] DALMAN: *Itin.*, pp. 139 ff.

[3] J. GRILL: *Untersuchungen über die Entstehung des vierten Evangeliums*, II, Tübingen, 1923, pp. 73–95, 107–119. KUNDSIN (*Topologische Überlieferungstoffe im Johannesevangelium*, Göttingen, 1925, p. 22) has rightly remarked (in opposition to Grill) that there is no indication to prove that there had ever been a centre of the Dionysus-cult at Cana.

[4] DALMAN: *Itin.*, p. 145.

comes from someone who knows the neighbourhood. In itself, however, this still does not prove that the mention of Cana comes from a primitive tradition. Matthew (viii. 5–13) and Luke (vii. 1–10) use an older form of the same story.[1] John has exaggerated the miraculous element, since he makes the healing take place at a greater distance than do the Synoptists. This shows very clearly that his narrative is of a secondary character. Why then did John introduce Cana into his narrative? Is it because he was familiar with a tradition which mentioned this village? or, as has been suggested by Kundsin,[2] because Cana played an important part in the history of Galilean Christianity, perhaps because certain members of the family of Jesus had lived there? The indications which Kundsin cites in support of this hypothesis are very weak. Thus it is not impossible that in addition to Capernaum, Bethsaida, and Chorazin, Cana may have been one of the centres of the Galilean activity of Jesus.

V. The Forms of the Activity of Jesus

The Galilean ministry of Jesus was essentially itinerating in character. We might suspect a general statement like that of Mark i. 39, thinking that it had been added by a later hand, were it not that we cannot imagine that the activity of Jesus would differ greatly from the method which he told his disciples to use on their missionary tours. He also "went through all the cities of Israel" (Matt. x. 23). The incidents reported by the Gospels are placed in very varied scenes, sometimes in the house at Capernaum, sometimes on the shores of the Lake, or in a boat, sometimes on a hillside or in the country, and sometimes again in a synagogue, which is not always that of Capernaum. Mark (i. 35–38*) tells us that Jesus would not let himself be detained in Capernaum because he wanted to go farther and preach in the neighbouring villages. Sometimes these incidents were occasioned by a casual meeting, like that of the fishermen with their

---

[1] The most characteristic point is that Matthew speaks of the παῖς of the officer. This word means either child or servant. Luke says the slave, and John the son.

[2] KUNDSIN, p. 23.

boat (Mark i. 16–20*) or of the publican "sitting at the receipt of custom" at the entrance to some village (Mark ii. 13–14*). Sometimes Jesus explains his attitude during a meal at which he is a guest, or when he has just left the house where the meal took place (Mark ii. 15 ff.*, etc.). On one occasion a meeting with a healed leper, who is not yet ritually purified, gives Jesus an opportunity to explain that he does not intend to set his own authority against that which is regularly established, and that the healed leper ought to go to Jerusalem to fulfil the rites which the Law ordains for his readmission into society (Mark i. 40–45*).[1]

The forms of the activity of Jesus are no less varied than the places where we have seen him at work. Mark gives a general description when he says that Jesus preached and cast out demons (i. 39). A large number of healings are recorded, and although the general statements which refer to them (those of Mark iii. 10–12, vi. 53–56; Matt. iv. 24, xv. 29–31, for instance) may be assigned to an editorial hand, and though some of the particular instances—those, for example, of the healing of the leper (Mark i. 40–45*), of the woman with the issue of blood, and the daughter of Jairus (Mark v. 21–43*)—may also contain a considerable element of redaction, it is impossible to doubt that Jesus did work cures. This may be explained, doubtless (if, indeed, in such a realm an explanation can be suggested at all), by the dominant force of the personality of Jesus. On the other hand, these works of healing greatly enhanced his personal influence.

While the Gospels give full accounts of the healings accomplished by Jesus, they say very little about his teaching. "Jesus

[1] According to the evangelists, Jesus began his ministry by healing a leper. But in the account by Mark there is some confusion. At verse 41 Jesus is moved with compassion for the leper, and in verse 43 he is angry with him and sends him away. In the original account, "Thou canst make me clean," would have meant, "Thou canst declare me clean." These words having been understood by Mark to mean "Thou canst heal me," he added verses 41–42, which tell of the cure. Matthew and Luke have got rid of this obscurity by not saying either that Jesus was moved by pity for the leper or that he was angry with him and sent him away. Cf. RAUCH: *Bemerkungen zum Markustext*, *Z.N.T.W.*, III, 1902, pp. 300–303.

taught," "Jesus preached," "Jesus proclaimed the word," they say, but they scarcely tell us what he taught. In this respect Matthew wanted to complete Mark's narrative, and where the teaching of Jesus is mentioned for the first time, he introduces the Sermon on the Mount, which is both a specimen and a summary of the teaching of Jesus. But this device does not really fill the gap, although, at first sight, it appears to do so. The Sermon on the Mount is a compilation of some of the sayings of Jesus, arranged in such a way that they form a rule of life for the Christians of the Apostolic age; the words themselves doubtless belong to different points in the Gospel narrative. The reason why the evangelists give so little room to an exposition of the teaching of Jesus is this: at the time when they wrote, the main interest of the Christian Church was not so much in what Jesus said and did during his earthly ministry as in what he was in his state as the glorified Lord, and in the drama of redemption which he had accomplished. The evangelists seem to have thought, in a naïve kind of way, that the substance of the preaching and teaching of Jesus was contained in the doctrine of the Church of their day.

Mark, however, does give some fragments of a didactic character which belong to the Galilean period. They are of two main types: controversies and parables. The first group is represented chiefly by the series of six conflicts (Mark ii. 1–iii, 6*). So far as their content is concerned, they might belong to any period in the life of Jesus. However, the conclusion (iii. 6) in which the discussion between the Pharisees and the Herodians is mentioned, proves that the source from which Mark has drawn this material belongs to the Galilean period, and even to the beginning of this period, at a moment when the attitude of Herod with regard to Jesus was not yet decided. In these discussions we see how Jesus becomes increasingly aware of the obstacles which separate him from the traditional ideas of Judaism.

The discussion provoked by the remarks of the Pharisees, who say that Jesus casts out demons by the power of Beelzebub, the prince of the demons (Mark iii. 20–30*), is no less significant. Here we see Jesus becoming ever surer that he is acting in the name of God, and that his Gospel means essentially the power to bring deliverance to men, and to defeat the evil powers which hold them in thrall.

The parables seem to furnish more direct indications about the teaching and preaching of Jesus; their interpretation is a delicate matter, because in each one we need to learn how to discriminate between the main truth which Jesus meant it to convey and the elements which are only introduced into the story to make it more vivid and arresting. We must also resist the temptation to try to discover the whole of the thought of Jesus in each parable. The manner in which the parables are grouped in Mark is not natural, and the theoretical instructions which accompany them show that they have been placed in their present position for systematic reasons. There is therefore no guarantee that they belong to the Galilean period. Nor can one attempt a chronological classification of the parables by assigning to the Galilean period all those which mention the country or the Lake, and to the Judaean period those which refer to the Temple or to the road from Jerusalem to Jericho. Jesus may have spoken of a sower to his hearers in Jerusalem and of the Temple to the people of Capernaum. Thus it is wiser not to use the parables to illustrate the thought of Jesus at the beginning of his ministry.

VI. The Welcome Given to Jesus by the People of Galilee

The Gospel narratives frequently mention the profound impression which the preaching of Jesus made on the Galilean people; according to the Gospels, his reputation spread rapidly, and wherever he went crowds gathered round him, eager to hear him speak. His way of speaking and his actions produced that feeling of amazement, of religious terror which one feels when one is in the presence of something which transcends ordinary human power (Mark i. 22, 27, ii. 12*). When Jesus returns to Capernaum it is enough for the people to hear that he is in the house for the crowd to flock into the house and then overflow into the street till the entrance to the house is completely blocked (ii. 1). At another time we read that people thronged him to such an extent that he had no time to eat his meals (Mark iii. 20). One day when he is teaching, in order to be able to carry on at all, he is obliged to get into a boat which is pushed off a little way from the shore (Mark iii. 9*; cf. Luke v. 3). When the members of his own family wish to speak to him they cannot get at him for the crowd, and are obliged to send in a message asking him to come out to them (Mark iii. 31). When Jesus is on his way to the house of Jairus the crowd which goes with him is so dense that the disciples are astonished that he could feel that someone had touched him deliberately (Mark v. 30–31*).

Certain statements of a general character, as, for example, that of Mark iii. 7–9*, according to which people came to hear Jesus not only from Capernaum but from the whole of Galilee, from Judaea, from Jerusalem, from Idumaea, from beyond Jordan, from the country round Tyre and Sidon, are comments on the part of the editor. It is also possible that the mention of the admiration of the spectators in the narratives of healing may be regarded, at least to some extent, as an element of style which also occurs in the accounts of Jewish or Greek miracles. Nevertheless, it is wise to remember that as the tradition developed, it emphasized and amplified the statements about the size of the crowds which surrounded Jesus.[1] But even when all this has been taken into account there are still sufficient integral elements in the story to make us certain that Jesus exercised an influence over the people which went far beyond arousing a simple curiosity, that, indeed, he did really attract them to himself. It would be possible to assert this without any other evidence at all, simply by noting the opposition which confronted Jesus as much from the Pharisees as from Herod. The fact that people opposed him so virulently proves that they thought he was a dangerous enemy; this he would not have been if his preaching had been ineffective, and if he had not exercised a real influence over his hearers.

In order to get into true perspective what is said about the way the people crowded round Jesus we must note some details which show that in the idea of Jesus being warmly

[1] Perhaps it is not unnecessary to observe that when we remember the kind of house Peter would have at Capernaum a few score of people would suffice to fill it in the way it is said to have been filled in Mark ii. 1 and iii. 20.

welcomed by the crowd, but opposed by the representatives
of the religious tradition, there may be a reflection of a situation which must have often occurred during the history of the
missionary work of the Church.

It is not to the scribes and the Pharisees that Matthew and
Luke make Jesus address this saying: "The Son of Man came
eating and drinking, and ye say: Behold a man gluttonous and
a winebibber, a friend of publicans and sinners" (Matt. xi.
19*).[1] The family of Jesus accused him of madness and tried
to carry him off (Mark iii. 21), and although he took care
to refute the accusation of the scribes who said he was possessed by Beelzebub, this was certainly less in the hope of
convincing them than because he felt that the crowd, and
possibly the disciples themselves, were inclined to be influenced
by these accusations. At Nazareth Jesus met with an atmosphere of unbelief which is not entirely explained by saying
that his fellow-townsmen were disappointed that they had not
actually seen him working miracles like those of which they
had heard.[2]

Jesus himself has stated that the Galilean towns did not listen
to his summons to repentance (Matt. xi. 20–24*). Thus if the
hearers of Jesus were impressed by his teaching, it was in
general, and in a superficial way, which did not lead them
to the acts of decision which he demanded from them.

VII. The Disciples of Jesus

What were the conditions of discipleship which Jesus felt to
be absolutely essential? How are we to understand his appeals
to follow him? in a literal or in a figurative sense?

In order to answer these questions we must examine the
meaning of the term "disciple"; the best way of doing this

[1] We must, however, notice that those who spoke like this were people
who earlier had said of John the Baptist, He hath a demon (Matt. xi. 18*).
Now we know from Matt. xxi. 32* that John was well received by the
people and by the tax-gatherers, whereas the Pharisees and scribes refused
to listen to him. It may be, therefore, that in spite of the clear note at the
beginning of this section, the saying with which we are dealing may have
been addressed to the Pharisees.

[2] On the original forms of the conclusion of Mark vi. 5–6a, see pp. 173 ff.

is to examine the constitution of that group of disciples who accompanied Jesus from the days of the Galilean ministry until the moment of his arrest, those men whom tradition represents as the twelve apostles, chosen and set apart by Jesus himself.

Several stories in the Gospels show how Jesus called certain men to follow him, and how they instantly left all and followed him, some leaving their boats and their nets, and another his office (Mark i. 16–20*, ii. 14*). These narratives are doctrinaire in character. They do not show under what conditions Jesus taught these men what he expected from them, nor how he won their allegiance. The aim of these narratives is not to illustrate the motives which lead to a decision, nor to show how faith is born in the soul. They are really stories of vocation, in which we see how men (who doubtless knew Jesus already and had been convinced by his preaching) decide that they will give up everything in order to be entirely at his disposal and the service of his cause. And since it is legitimate to conclude that the evangelists were thinking of the situation of the Church of their own time, we may enquire whether, when they edited these stories, they were not influenced by the desire to present these men as examples to those of their contemporaries who felt themselves called to place their lives at the service of the missionary work of the Christian Church.

This interpretation is confirmed—concerning those who are mentioned in Mark i. 16–20—by the Johannine evidence; according to John, Simon and Andrew and others were won by Jesus while he was still in the Jordan district near John the Baptist. It is further confirmed in another way by an episode reported by Matthew (viii. 19–22) and by Luke (ix. 57–62). Someone says to Jesus: "Lord, I will follow thee whithersoever Thou goest!" Jesus discourages him with the words: "Foxes have holes, and the birds of the air have nests, but the Son of Man hath not where to lay his head." The man who spoke thus to Jesus was evidently one who had been captured by his teaching, and there is nothing which can make us doubt that his faith was sincere. The reply of Jesus shows that in order to be his disciple, in a special sense (which is indicated in a more precise manner in the two following episodes), it is necessary to be ready to accept the same sacrifices that he has made, and to accompany him on his missionary journeys. To others, Jesus issues a call to follow him. One replies by asking permission first of all to go and bury his father. Jesus replies: "Let the dead bury their dead,[1] but go thou and preach the Kingdom of God."[2] Another asks permission to go home in order to take leave of his relatives. Jesus answers: "No man, having put his hand to the plough, and looking back, is fit for the Kingdom of God." He does not make this call save to those whom he judges fit to respond, and able to bear the sacrifices which the task to which he calls them entails; this also is illustrated by the fact that in the story of the rich man the disciples declare to Jesus that they have left all to follow him, and he admits that they have really given up "house, brethren, sisters, mothers, children, and lands," for his sake and the Gospel's (Mark x. 28–30*).

The special character of such appeals, which were not repeated every time that Jesus preached, at least in the accounts we have in the Gospels, shows that we are here concerned with

[1] In order to explain this expression, which falls a little strangely on our ears, GRESSMANN (*Protestantenblatt*, 1916, p. 281, quoted by KLOSTERMANN: *Das Lukasevangelium*[2], 1929, p. 112) points to certain Egyptian fairy-tales in which the dead bury their own dead. In order that this explanation might be accepted we would need to be certain that these fairy-tales were known in Palestine, and this we do not know. PERLES (*Zwei Übersetzungsfehler im Text der Evangelien*, *Z.N.T.W.*, XIX, 1919–1920, p. 96. *Noch einmal Mt. viii. 20. Lk. ix. 10. Jn. xx. 17*, *Z.N.T.W.*, XXV, 1921, pp. 286 f.) suggests an Aramaic original and a mistake in translation. Thus the original meaning would be: "Leave the dead to the gravediggers." In STRACK-BILLERBECK (I, p. 489) we find serious philological objections to this explanation. Basing his argument on the fact that in the Talmud "dead" is used in a spiritual as well as in a literal sense, STRACK-BILLERBECK suggests this meaning: "Let those who are spiritually dead bury the dead." But this explanation, attractive as it is in itself, breaks down because we have no passage in which Jesus calls those who would not accept his teaching "dead." The best thing to do, so it seems, is to regard this as one of those paradoxical sayings which Jesus was fond of using, and to think that it means: "Do not pay attention to the dead, but to the living."

[2] The fact that the message which is here mentioned is that of announcing the Kingdom of God, and in the incident which follows, of serving it, but not of proclaiming or serving Jesus, shows that these sections belong to that period in the ministry of Jesus in which his Messianic consciousness was not yet developed.

something special. The preaching of Jesus was not designed to gather a band of men who would leave all to follow him, in the literal sense of the word, but the necessity of spreading everywhere the news of the imminence of the Kingdom and of preparing men for its coming, led Jesus to demand from some of his disciples renunciations which are not required from all, and to associate them with his own way of life. On this point the activity of Jesus is clearly quite different from that of the Messianic agitators of whom Josephus speaks, who tended to gather large groups of men who lived on the fringe of ordinary life, and were preparing to fight against the power of Rome or of the Herods, since they did not represent the true national sovereignty.

The evangelists have given definite form to the idea that some men were specially called by Jesus to work with him in the proclamation of the Kingdom of God. This they have done by their theory of the institution of the apostolate.[1] Matthew does not say this directly, but in his account of the disciples' mission, he says that Jesus calls the Twelve and gives them power over unclean spirits, then sends them out provided with his instructions (x. 1 ff.). In a kind of parenthesis he says: "Now the names of the twelve apostles are these" (x. 2). Mark (iii. 13–19), followed by Luke (vi. 12–16), places the institution of the apostolate after the series of conflicts. By this he shows that opposition does not discourage Jesus, who, far from giving up his work, takes steps to strengthen it. Mark tells how, after having cured a number of sick persons, Jesus climbs a hill (iii. 7–12). He calls whom he will, that is, among those who have declared themselves his disciples he chooses some. He picks out twelve[2] to be with him and in order that he may send them forth with the power to cast out demons.

[1] On the question of the apostolate, see H. MONNIER: *La notion de l'apostolat*, Paris, 1903, where there are many bibliographical details. Here we are only concerned with the problem of the apostolate from the point of view of the life of Jesus.

[2] Certain passages (א. B. C*. *Δ. Θ.* 13, 69, etc.) add: "whom he called apostles." The evidence for this phrase is strong. Its authenticity, however, remains in doubt, because, owing to the fact that it occurs in the text of Luke, it is suspected of being a gloss introduced to harmonize the passage, and it is difficult to see why this clause was omitted.

The names of the Twelve follow,[1] and there is a note on the surnames which he gives to three of them.[2]

In the way in which Mark defines the function of an apostle, "to be with Jesus," and, "to be sent forth by him," there is a contradiction which can only be resolved by concluding that these two remarks do not belong to the same moment. "To be with Jesus," that is the part of the apostles during the ministry of Jesus;[3] "to be sent forth by him," that is to be their function after the Resurrection. This shows that already the conception of the apostolate, in the Marcan narrative, has a theoretical character. It contradicts the statement in which it is said that during his lifetime Jesus gave the disciples a charge to preach, and, on the other hand, it introduces the idea of the missionary work of the Church as it existed in primitive Christianity.

The manner in which Mark's account is presented to us shows that in the tradition the institution of the apostolate is not connected with the circumstances of which a definite recollection had been preserved. This does not prove that the record in Mark has no value; it is, however, enough to arouse in us a certain hesitation, and to make us feel that we should regard it with great reserve.

[1] The list of iii. 16–19 is added to the account of the institution. The words "and he ordained twelve," of verse 14, are taken up in verse 15: "and he ordained the Twelve." The list itself is not from one hand. It begins thus: "And he gave Simon the name of Peter." The eleven other names follow in the accusative with, in a parenthesis, the note on the name of Boanerges (sons of thunder) given to James and John. Thus this section must have been formed gradually. First of all, it was not meant to include the names of the apostles, then someone added the name of Simon (which, like the others, ought to be in the accusative); this, however, has been replaced by a phrase borrowed from another tradition: "He gave Simon the name of Peter." Luke has made the whole incident homogeneous.

[2] Commentaries note the interpretations suggested of the surnames given by Jesus to some of his apostles. They are too conjectural to supply us with reliable data. The presence of two Simons and two of the name of James in the group of the Twelve suggests that possibly Jesus was using surnames which the disciples had borne already. The name Boanerges might originally have been borne only by James.

[3] This idea of the apostolate is very clearly indicated in Acts i. 21–22, where it is said that the man who will be called to replace Judas in the apostolic charge which he had deserted must be one who had been with Jesus as a disciple from the baptism by John until the day of the Ascension.

In addition to the three lists of apostles given by the Synoptists there is a fourth in the book of the Acts of the Apostles (i. 13) and a fragment of a fifth at the beginning of chapter xxi in John. These lists have certain differences which are, however, not of great significance. The order in which the apostles are named is not always the same.[1]

John mentions among the intimate disciples a person called Nathanael whom the Synoptists ignore completely. We have seen[2] that the use of a source in the passage in which he is mentioned prevents us from regarding him as a fictitious personage. Thus at the outset the tradition concerning the composition of the body of the apostles was not homogeneous. The idea of its institution is not, in any case, connected with

[1] They all begin with Simon Peter; immediately after him come, in Mark and the Acts, the names of the sons of Zebedee (in the Acts John appears before James, doubtless a consequence of the part which in this book John plays as the head and the representative of the Church in Jerusalem). Matthew and Luke place Andrew immediately after his brother Peter; Philip has the fifth place in all the lists. Bartholomew comes sixth in the Gospels, and seventh in the Acts, where the sixth place is taken by Thomas, who only takes the eighth place on the list in Mark and Luke after Matthew. Matthew's name occurs in the inverse order: Thomas, Matthew. All the lists give as the ninth name James, son of Alphaeus. A Simon who is not Simon Peter also figures in the four lists at the eleventh place in Mark and Matthew, at the tenth in Luke and the Acts. This Simon is called ὁ Κavavaoῖς (Mark, Matthew) or ὁ ζηλωτής (Luke, Acts); the two terms are equivalent, the one being the transcription and the other the translation of the Aramaic word which means "the Zealot" (member of a political party which was violently opposed to the Roman suzerainty). Finally, all the lists place at the end the name of Judas Iscariot (for the meaning of this term see further on p. 495, n. 1). The only case where these lists do not tally is in one name: at the tenth place, Mark mentions Thaddaeus and Matthew Lebbaeus. Luke and the Acts place Judas in the eleventh place (Judas, the son of James). It is rather arbitrary to suggest, as is often done, that Thaddaeus and Lebbaeus are two different forms of the same name. We might rather enquire whether the presence of these two names in Mark and Matthew, where in Luke we find Judas son of James, may not arise from the fact that they did not wish an apostle to bear the name dishonoured by the traitor. The Fourth Gospel, at the beginning of chapter xxi, names Simon Peter, Thomas, Nathanael, the sons of Zebedee, and mentions two unnamed disciples whom it would be possible to identify as Andrew and Levi Matthew, who are named in the last phrase in the Gospel of Peter. He also names Philip (i. 44 f., vi. 53, xii. 21 f., xiv. 8 f.) and the two Judases (xiv. 22, vi. 71, xiii. 2 f., xviii. 2 f.).

[2] See p. 324.

the knowledge of a definite group of persons who are said to have composed it.

In order to describe those who formed the circle of intimate friends of Jesus and who to him were more than occasional hearers, the evangelists employ the term "the disciples" (μαθηταί), "the apostles," and "the Twelve."

Apart from the accounts relating the institution of the apostolate and the sending out of the disciples on their mission, the term "apostle" does not appear in Mark, Matthew, or John. Luke uses it three times (xvii. 5, xxii. 14, xxiv. 10), but when we compare these passages and their parallels[1] we find that the term "apostle" is not used either there or in the sources. The entirely exceptional nature of the use of this word in the Gospels is unfavourable to the historicity of the institution of the apostolate by Jesus.

The term "the Twelve"[2] may be explained as possibly due to Jesus himself, who for symbolic reasons, which are quite transparent, chose twelve men to be specially associated with his work, or possibly it may be simply due to an accident; that is, that after various changes the most intimate group of the disciples may finally have found itself to be composed of twelve men. The appeals to follow him and preach with him the Kingdom of God which Jesus addressed to the man who wished to bury his father, and to the man who wished to go home and take leave of his relatives (Matt. viii. 21–22*), indicate that if he could have done so, Jesus would have enlarged the circle of his collaborators. Thus the number twelve had no particularly sacred character in his eyes. One passage, however, seems to contradict this opinion, it is this saying of Jesus: "Ye which have followed me, in the regeneration when the Son of Man shall sit on the throne of his glory, ye also shall sit upon twelve thrones, judging[3] the twelve

---

[1] The first in Matt. xvii. 20; the second in Mark xiv. 17; Matt. xxvi. 20; the third in Matt. xxviii. 8.

[2] The expression "the twelve apostles" only occurs in Matt. x. 2. The word "disciple" is used far more frequently than the term "apostle." Where "the Twelve" are mentioned we ought to read "the twelve disciples" rather than "the twelve apostles." The expression is used nine times by Matthew, twelve times by Mark, seven times by Luke, four times by John.

[3] To judge here means to govern.

tribes of Israel" (Matt. xix. 28). In any case this saying is archaic because it assumes that there will be none but Jews in the Kingdom of God. It contains a symbolic element: Matthew would certainly not have represented Judas as seated on a throne in the Messianic kingdom. The promise is not made to these men because they have been chosen by Jesus and elevated to the dignity of apostles, but because they have followed him. Luke (xxii. 30) says: "That ye may . . . sit on thrones judging the twelve tribes of Israel." Thus it is not certain whether the agreement between the twelve apostles and the twelve tribes of Israel is a primitive element. Probably it increased rather than diminished with the passage of time. The idea of a closed circle of twelve disciples is therefore a secondary idea. In one passage in Mark we see clearly that it has been added: "And when he was alone they that were about him with the Twelve asked of him the parable" (iv. 10). It is impossible to find a connexion between these two groups. If those who surrounded Jesus had formed two concentric groups, "the Twelve," since it was the more intimate of the two groups, would have been mentioned first. The words, "with the Twelve," are secondary in character,[1] and they have here been added in order to introduce the idea of the circle of the apostles.

The term "disciples" is frequently employed to describe the group of intimates expressly distinguished from the mass of the hearers of Jesus, even in cases where there is nothing to show that these hearers are animated by hostile sentiments. The first feeding of the multitudes and the episode which follows furnish a typical example of this use of the word "disciples." The people who came to join Jesus from the region which extended from Capernaum to Bethsaida-Julias are clearly distinguished from the group of intimates with whom Jesus had retired into a desert place apart (Mark vi. 30–31*) and who play a definite part in the incident (vi. 35–44*). The distinction between the two groups is still more clearly defined in that which follows: Jesus insists on his disciples getting into a boat and pushing off while he sends the multitudes away (vi. 45–46*). It seems as though

---

[1] In the parallel passages, Matthew (xiii. 10) and Luke (viii. 9) have simply "the disciples."

he is anxious to avoid too long a contact between the two groups.[1]

In certain instances the term "disciples" is used in a wider sense. Matthew (viii. 21) mentions a "disciple" who, before he followed Jesus, asked permission to go and bury his father, and who therefore was not one of those who accompanied Jesus. He speaks also of the reward promised to him who will give a cup of cold water to one of these little ones in the name of a disciple (x. 42) in a way which makes it seem at least possible that he is not thinking only of those who helped him during his missionary journeys. When the relatives of Jesus send a message to him, with the intention of calling him away from his work (Mark iii. 21), Jesus replies that his true relatives are those who do the will of God (Mark iii. 35*), and, as he says this, he looks at those who are sitting round him in a circle, that is, not only at his intimate friends, but also at the crowd.

When we look at the apostolate from the point of view of the Early Church we realize that the earliest conception was that of the apostle Paul. The apostle is one who has received a commission from the glorified Christ and from God to preach the Gospel (Gal. i. 1). Such an idea could not have originated at a moment when the theory of an apostolate, instituted by Jesus during his ministry, was already in existence.[2]

Several stories suggest that some of the disciples of Jesus formed a specially intimate group. On the occasion of the Raising of Jairus' daughter Jesus only allowed Peter, James,

[1] On this point see pp. 373 ff.
[2] In 1 Cor. xv. 5 Paul speaks of an appearance to the Twelve (this is the text of ℵ. B. A., etc.), which is certainly primitive; the reading "to the Eleven" of D. G. lat., etc., being a correction due to this reflection that the defection of Judas had reduced the number of the apostles chosen by Jesus to eleven. If we hesitate to regard the term used by Paul merely as an unfortunate expression, there may be in the term the proof that originally the Twelve were not a group of men chosen by Jesus but the original nucleus of the Church. The idea of the apostolate of the Twelve would then spring out of the fact that these men, who were originally, like Paul himself, apostles in his sense of the word, would insist on the authority which they had gained from the fact that they had followed Jesus during his ministry. We shall have occasion to return to the idea of the apostolate in connexion with the history of the Primitive Church.

and John to enter the room with him (Mark v. 37*). These are the same disciples who were with him on the Mount of Transfiguration (ix. 2*), and who, in Gethsemane, went with him further than the rest (xiv. 33*). It is to them, and to Andrew as well, that the Synoptic Apocalypse is addressed (Mark xiii. 3). Two of these four sections do not belong to the primitive tradition. The Transfiguration was originally a manifestation of the Risen Christ,[1] and the great discourse of chapter xiii is a small Apocalypse, a little earlier than the year 70.[2] In the incident in Gethsemane the detail that three intimate disciples were taken further than their companions might quite well not be primitive, since, when Jesus returns to the place where he had left them, it is not said that together they return to the eight others, and yet the eleven seem to be there at the moment of the arrest. The episode of Jairus is not enough on which to settle the question of the existence of a group of three intimates. The idea of this group might be the reflection of the part played by Peter, James,[3] and John in the Primitive Church.[4]

VIII. THE CONFLICTS BETWEEN JESUS AND THE PHARISEES

Although during his ministry in Jerusalem Jesus was confronted by the opposition of the Sadducees as well as of the Pharisees, and although, in the intrigues which incited Pilate to take action against him, the former seem to have taken a greater part than the latter, it was only with the Pharisees[5]

[1] MAURICE GOGUEL: *Notes d'histoire évangélique, II, Esquisse d'une interprétation du récit de la transfiguration, R.h.r.,* LXXXI, 1920, pp. 145–157.
[2] See further on pp. 425 ff.
[3] There may be some confusion here with James, the brother of Jesus.
[4] It seems as though the idea of the three intimate friends of Jesus may have served as an explanation of the fact that for so long tradition ignored the story of the Transfiguration and the Synoptic Apocalypse.
[5] The evangelists seem to treat the terms Pharisees and scribes as though they were interchangeable. They use now one and now the other, and often they use them together. In reality they are not synonymous. Although the majority of the scribes, that is to say, of those who gave themselves to the study of the Law, belonged to the Pharisee party, it was possible to be a Pharisee without being a scribe.

that Jesus had to do during the period of his Galilean ministry.[1] The Gospels represent them as the born enemies and typical adversaries of Jesus. They represent them as fundamentally hypocritical, proud, caring only for the esteem of others, full of contempt for the people, for all who are not of their party, or who do not live in accordance with the demands of the Law. The Pharisees watch Jesus with ill-will, lay traps for him, are unceasingly on the watch for anything which may compromise him, thwart his designs, and cause his ruin. According to the evangelists, Jesus was under no delusion about their feelings towards him; from the beginning to the end of his ministry he is represented as being in open conflict with them.

This conception is rather arbitrary. Jesus opposed the Pharisees on questions touching the tradition whose observance they claimed to have the right to impose; he reproached them for their pride, for all that was extreme and ostentatious in their piety, he criticized them on other points as well, but what he opposed was not the fundamental element in Pharisaism itself. Jesus was not against the Pharisees root and branch; he saw in them (what they really were) the religious élite of Israel, and he would have liked to have gained their support.[2] On two of the points on which they differed from the Sadducees he agreed with them. Like them he believed in the future life, and his concern, like theirs, was essentially religious, and in no way political or materialistic. On one point only was Jesus on the side of the Sadducees against the Pharisees. Like them he did not admit the authority of the tradition to which the Pharisees attributed a value equal to that of the Law. But the significance of this agreement is singularly diminished by the fact that the attitude of Jesus and that of the Sadducees was actuated by entirely different motives. The Sadducees rejected the tradition solely for juridical reasons. Jesus was moved by moral and religious reasons only.

Several times Luke represents Jesus at a meal in a Pharisee's house (vii. 36 ff., xi. 37, xiv. 1); he shows the Pharisees warning him of the designs of Herod (xiii. 31–33), and others asking

---

[1] During the Galilean period the Sadducees are not mentioned, excepting in Matthew (xvi. 1, 6 ff.). See pp. 348 ff.
[2] Cf. ED. MEYER, II, pp. 425 ff.

him a question about the coming of the Kingdom of God which reveals no hostility (xvii. 30).

According to Mark, at the outset there were some scribes and Pharisees amongst the disciples of Jesus.[1] They only left him when they saw him taking certain liberties with the legal observances, and in particular when they saw him sitting down to table with the tax-gatherers and people who did not observe the Law (Mark ii. 16* ff.). It is Matthew, doubtless, who, in the discussion about the washing of hands, introduces this remark of the disciples to Jesus: "Knowest thou that the Pharisees were offended after they heard this saying?" (xv. 12), but in this he has exactly expressed the impression that the attitude of Jesus must have made on the Pharisees. Thus the Pharisees were alienated from Jesus by scruples which were undoubtedly sincere, and from their point of view legitimate.

All the accounts which represent Jesus in conflict with the Pharisees are not of the same character. There are some in which the Pharisees ask Jesus questions on subjects which were subjects of controversy among the learned men of the day, as, for instance, on the question of divorce (Mark x. 1–12*).[2] In questioning him they desired, at the most, to put his knowledge and sagacity to the test.

[1] Mark ii. 15–16, according to ℵ. L. Δ. 33, etc. "Many of the people followed him, even some of the scribes of the Pharisees. Seeing . . ." The other MSS. (for instance A. B. C.) read: "Many people followed him. And the scribes of the Pharisees (A. C.: the scribes and the Pharisees) seeing . . ." Although the first form of the text is less well supported than the second, it ought to be preferred, because the passage from the first text to the second is easier to imagine than a development in the other direction.

[2] The text of Mark seems to be slightly transposed. The question put to Jesus was not meant to question whether divorce were legitimate or not, since the principle was admitted in Deut. xxiv. 1 ff., where it is said that when a man finds something shameful in his wife he may give her a letter of divorce. The school of Shammai interpreted this passage in a rigid sense, and considered that it only applied in a case of adultery; the school of Hillel gave it a wider interpretation, saying, for instance, that a husband had the right to divorce his wife if she had burnt his dinner. R. Akiba (c. 135) would say he might do this even if he saw a woman who was more beautiful than his own wife. See the passages in STRACK-BILLERBECK, I, pp. 313 ff. The reply of Jesus goes beyond the limits of the question which is addressed to him.

Other interventions are of a different character. When the Pharisees asked Jesus to give them a sign from heaven (Mark viii. 11, 13*), or when they challenged him to tell them by what authority he could justify his conduct in casting out the sellers and money-changers from the Temple (Mark xi. 27–33*), their intention was to place him in an embarrassing position and to destroy his influence.

Their hostility is still more evident when they accuse Jesus of blasphemy, because he says to the paralytic that his sins are forgiven (Mark ii. 1–12*), when they reproach him with breaking the Sabbath (Mark iii. 1–5*) or permitting his disciples to break it (Mark ii. 23–28*), still more clearly when they accuse him of casting out demons by Beelzebub (Mark iii. 22* ff.).

The hostility of the Pharisees, or, rather, of certain Pharisees, against Jesus was due to religious motives. They opposed him because to them his teaching seemed scandalous. Was their opposition purely theoretical, at least, during the Galilean period? Directly, the Pharisees could do nothing against Jesus; allied with the Herodians they had the power to become dangerous enemies. The alliance was not difficult to form, and this is what actually took place.

IX. THE ATTITUDE OF HEROD TOWARDS JESUS

Herod, as we know from Josephus (*A. J.*, XVIII, 5, 2, ¶¶ 117–119), had caused John the Baptist to be put to death, not, or not only, as the Gospels say, on account of the resentment of Herodias, but also because he feared the result of John's influence over the people, and dreaded the possibility of a revolt. It was therefore only natural that when he heard that a new prophet had arisen, he should be prejudiced against him. It seems probable that a confused recollection of Herod's hostility to Jesus lies behind the story of Jesus being taken before Herod (Luke xxiii. 7–12; cf. Acts iv. 27).

At the outset, when (apart from those who had come into direct touch with him) it was still possible not to know how Jesus conceived this Kingdom of God whose imminent advent he proclaimed, Herod seems to have tried to discover his attitude towards the political authorities. This is the meaning of the question about the payment of tribute-money put to him by the Pharisees and the Herodians.[1] The Gospels place this incident during the Jerusalem ministry, but the mention of the Herodians proves that it must certainly belong to the period of the Galilean ministry; it is impossible to imagine that Mark could have introduced the Herodians into the story of his own accord, and it would be difficult to explain their presence at Jerusalem. The question they put to Jesus about the lawfulness of paying tribute to Caesar was not a mere academic question, designed to put him in an awkward position, or to test his wisdom and astuteness; it was one on which the minds of many were much exercised at that moment.[2] The men who questioned Jesus were emissaries of the Tetrarch; their business was to discover the attitude of Jesus towards Herod as well as towards the Emperor, whose vassal the Tetrarch was. By his reply: "Render to Caesar that which is Caesar's," Jesus destroyed any excuse for immediate action on Herod's part, yet his answer did not finally allay Herod's fears.

The Herodians appear a second time at the conclusion of the series of conflicts between Jesus and his enemies. After Jesus had cured a man, whose hand was paralysed, on the Sabbath Day: "the Pharisees went forth and straightway took counsel with the Herodians against him, how they might destroy him"[3]

[1] The term Herodians occurs three times, always in conjunction with that of the Pharisees (Mark iii. 6, xii. 13; Matt. xxii. 16). The Herodians can scarcely have been members of the family of Herod; it is difficult to tell who they were; whether they were supporters of the *statu quo*, hostile on principle to everything new which might disturb the settled order of things, or hangers-on of Herod, or even his officials. In my opinion the last suggestion seems the most likely.

[2] According to Josephus, one of the motives for the revolt of Judas of Gamala was the refusal to pay the tribute money (*A.J.*, XVIII, 1, 1, ¶¶ 4 ff. *G.J.*, II, 8, 1, ¶ 118). Among those who paid it many were still much exercised in their minds. It was quite natural that as Jesus announced the nearness of the Kingdom of God people should have asked for his views on this question.

[3] We might also translate: "The Pharisees, going out with the Herodians, took counsel . . ."

(Mark iii. 6). Here Mark alone mentions the Herodians.[1] A discussion of this kind which led to nothing could not very well have been imagined by him. This phrase seems like a stray block of alien matter, a foreign body, or a relic of an older tradition which Mark may have copied without thinking from the source in which the story of the various conflicts is recorded. Originally, something must have happened as a result of the conversation of the enemies of Jesus. Some measures must have been taken against him, and perhaps the primitive narrator reported this in order to explain the departure of Jesus from Galilee.

It is not difficult to understand why the evangelists have not mentioned these measures. At the time when they wrote the Gospel story was conceived in terms of a divine plan. Hence it was impossible to explain it in terms of actual circumstances. No longer could they admit that the departure of Jesus for Jerusalem had been determined by the measures taken against him by Herod.

The saying of Jesus about the "leaven of the Pharisees" and "the leaven of Herod" is also a proof of the hostility of Herod towards Jesus. After the second feeding of the multitudes (having refused to show the Pharisees a sign from heaven), Jesus embarked with his disciples in order to cross to the eastern side of the Lake; after they had started his friends discovered that they had forgotten to take bread with them; it was on this occasion that Jesus said to them: "Take heed, beware of the leaven of the Pharisees and the leaven of Herod." His disciples thought this was a gentle reproach to them for their carelessness. Jesus saw what they were thinking, and asked them if they remembered the two miracles of the multiplication of the loaves, concluding by saying: "Have ye not yet understood?" (Mark viii. 14–21). Matthew (xvi. 5–12) follows the narrative of Mark, but instead of the Herodians he mentions the Sadducees; he also introduces other varia-

[1] Luke (vi. 11) modifies considerably the text of Mark. He says: "Filled with fury they asked one another what they might do to Jesus." The text of Mark is certainly primitive. The omission of the mention of the Herodians in Matthew and in Luke is explained by the reasons which have caused the remembrance of the hostility shown by Herod towards Jesus to be almost entirely effaced.

tions which, as is often the case, give to his narrative an air of greater brevity and concentration. He also adds a closing phrase which says plainly that Jesus was alluding to the doctrine of the Pharisees and the Sadducees. Luke, who does not give the group of incidents which separate the first feeding of the multitudes from the Confession of Peter, gives (xii. 1) the words about the leaven in another place, but he does not mention that they had been misconstrued. In his account, Jesus is speaking to the disciples in the presence of the crowd, but the account of the incident appears to be wholly unrelated to the context. Thus it would seem that this saying was preserved first of all as an isolated *logion*; the fact that it was combined later with the crossing of the Lake, and the fact that the disciples forgot to take bread with them, are therefore secondary elements.[1]

Although neither Mark nor Luke defines the meaning of the warning given by Jesus, it seems evident that they, like Matthew, understood it to apply to the teaching of the Pharisees. This, however, cannot have been its original meaning. This explanation does not agree with the mention of the Herodians, for they did not constitute a religious party, and therefore had no doctrine. Luke left the Herodians out of this story and Matthew substituted the Sadducees instead; both evangelists did this because they could not understand the allusion. The saying about the leaven was originally a warning of Jesus to his disciples about the dangers which threatened him, dangers which possibly threatened them as much as himself. These words belong to a period when the hostility of Herod had not yet been declared openly, but when Jesus had already guessed or foreseen it.

A time came, however, when the attitude of Herod became quite clear. On this point Luke (xiii. 31–33) has preserved a very valuable tradition:[2]

[1] These words must have been uttered some time before the feeding of the multitudes, for, as we shall see, at that time Jesus felt that Herod's attitude was very threatening.

[2] Where it is now placed it has no organic connexion with the section which precedes it (xiii. 22–30), in which Jesus is represented as being already *en route* for Jerusalem (22), nor with that which follows (the prophecy over Jerusalem whose children Jesus has tried in vain to gather

The same day there came certain of the Pharisees, saying unto him, Get thee out, and depart hence: for Herod will kill thee. And he said unto them, Go ye and tell that fox, Behold I cast out devils, and I do cures to-day and to-morrow, [and the third day I shall be perfected].[1] Nevertheless I must walk [to-day and to-morrow and] the day following, for it cannot be that a prophet perish out of Jerusalem.

The part played by the Pharisees in this incident is so contrary to the usual idea of them fostered by tradition that we can be sure we are here dealing with a fact of history. The authenticity of the reply of Jesus is less evident; Wellhausen[2] suggests that it has been altered by the unfortunate introduction of the words which we have placed within brackets. It is also rendered rather suspicious by the dogmatic idea that the departure of Jesus for Jerusalem has been determined by the sense of a higher fitness that he shall die at Jerusalem. The warning of the Pharisees shows that at a given moment Herod, who until then had been hesitating, made the decision to have Jesus put to death.

This fact illuminates the meaning of an incident relating to Herod which appears in the three Synoptic Gospels under rather peculiar conditions. This is the account of the feelings of Herod when he hears people talking about Jesus (Mark vi. 14–16*).

In the preceding section, Mark has told how the disciples went about preaching and healing in accordance with the instructions and the powers given to them by Jesus (vi. 6–13). He continues thus:

And king[3] Herod heard of him (for his name was spread

together (34–35)), a saying which could only have been uttered at the close of his Jerusalem ministry.

[1] The text may mean, "and then I shall have finished," that is to say, "I shall have finished the ministry which I wish to accomplish in Galilee," or "that will be the end of me." As in point of fact Jesus leaves Galilee after this warning, the former meaning is to be preferred.

[2] WELLHAUSEN: *Lk.*, pp. 75 ff.

[3] In reality Herod only possessed the title of Tetrarch, but it is possible that usually people called him by the title of King, which he bitterly regretted he did not actually possess. On this point Matthew and Luke have corrected the slight inaccuracy in the text of Mark.

abroad,[1]) and he said: That John the Baptist was risen from the dead, and therefore mighty works do shew themselves forth in him. Others said, That it is Elias. And others said, That it is a prophet or as one of the prophets.[2] But when Herod heard thereof he said, It is John, whom I beheaded: he is risen from the dead.

Compared with Mark the text of Matthew presents some variations; it will be sufficient to mention the chief ones. Matthew has tried to connect his account more naturally with what precedes it. He begins less abruptly: "At that time Herod . . . said." Matthew reports only the first declaration of the Tetrarch, and leaves out the other opinions which were current among the people.

Luke's account differs more widely from that of Mark than from that of Matthew. According to Luke, Herod is uneasy because he has heard it said that John the Baptist is risen from the dead; others say that Elijah has reappeared amongst men;[3] others, again, that some other ancient prophet has come to life once more. As for himself, he declares: "As for John, I beheaded him! Who, then, is this man of whom I hear all these things?" Luke has a conclusion which is peculiar to his narrative: "and he sought to see him."[4]

The theme of the diverse hypotheses suggested concerning Jesus reappears in the incident of Peter's Confession (Mark viii. 27–28*):

. . . by the way he asked his disciples, saying unto them: Whom do men say that I am? And they answered, John the Baptist; but some say, Elias, and others, One of the prophets (is returned).

---

[1] This clause is an awkward attempt to conceal the absence of a complement which is, however, indispensable. Matthew and Luke felt this and they tried to fill in the gap by a vague term, "the renown of Jesus" (Matthew), "all that had taken place" (Luke).

[2] Literally, "a prophet like one of the prophets."

[3] According to Jewish ideas, Elijah was to come as a forerunner of the Messiah. See pp. 276 ff.

[4] In the incident of the appearance of Jesus before Herod, Luke says that for a long time past Herod had desired to see Jesus because he heard of him and desired to see him work some miracle (xxiii. 8). The agreement between the two passages is only apparent, for in ix. 9 Herod desires to see Jesus because all that he hears about him disturbs him, not because he wants to see him work a miracle.

These two developments of the same theme cannot be independent of one another. In the way in which Jesus is identified with John the Baptist risen from the dead, as presented by Mark vi. 14, and Matt. xiv. 2, there is something which does not reappear in the episode of Caesarea Philippi, and that is, the idea that this explanation is suggested or confirmed by the miracles of Jesus. This may seem an argument in favour of the form in which the theme is presented in the episode of Herod,[1] but it is difficult to see for what reason Mark could have avoided speaking of the miracles in the account of the Confession of Peter. And, if we consider the true character of the idea of miracles accomplished by a person risen from the dead, we are led to consider this element in the narrative as secondary. The idea that a person who has died and come back to this life possesses supernatural powers is fairly easy to understand. However, in spite of many researches into this question, it has been, until now, impossible to find a single Jewish or pagan author who expresses this idea. The accounts of the raising of the dead which we find in the Gospels (of the daughter of Jairus, the young man of Nain, and Lazarus), do not contain anything to suggest that these persons were any different after the miracle than they were before. The idea of a supernatural power with which a person raised from the dead would be endowed is thus absolutely characteristic of this passage. Its origin should be sought, therefore, very probably, in the cycle of ideas and beliefs which gather round the Resurrection of Jesus, especially in the idea that the Risen Jesus possesses certain powers which he did not possess during his earthly ministry. He can, for instance, appear and disappear suddenly, and enter into a room where the doors are shut (cf., for instance, Luke xxiv. 15, 31, 36; John xx. 19).[2] We can easily understand why this feature has been introduced into the episode of Herod and not into the story of Peter's Confession. In the first section it was natural that the identification of Jesus with John the Baptist risen from the dead should be suggested since it is the leading idea

---

[1] This view is suggested in *Jean-Baptiste*, pp. 46 ff.
[2] It is easy to understand why it was that the Christians of the primitive period did not represent the life of the Risen Jesus like that of the daughter of Jairus, the young man of Nain, or Lazarus. These people did not finally escape death. Although it is not explicitly stated, it is assumed that each of them will have to die, when the time comes, later on. For them it meant only that all that was premature in their death was abolished. On the contrary it was believed that the return of Jesus from death was a victory gained over death, an anticipation of the general resurrection which was to take place at the *parousia*.

to which Herod returns, after putting aside certain explanations which had been suggested to him. On the other hand, in the story of the Confession of Peter the central idea is that Jesus is the Messiah. The other interpretations of his person which are mentioned are only there in order to throw this fact into relief. There was thus no reason for the narrator to suggest the identification of Jesus with John the Baptist any more than with Elijah.

Thus it is not possible to say that because the theme of the various hypotheses about Jesus is more fully developed in the episode of Herod, it is therefore a primitive element, whereas in the conversation of Jesus with his disciples near Caesarea Philippi it could only be a secondary element.

In the story of the Confession of Peter, the theme of the different hypotheses is organically connected with the sentiment which Peter, the mouthpiece of the apostles, expresses concerning Jesus. This opinion and those which were current among the people have this in common: they express the idea that Jesus was not an ordinary person. It is otherwise in the incident relating to Herod, which does not seem to lead to any definite conclusion.

We must examine the text of Luke with special care. In Mark the uneasiness of Herod is caused by the fact that he believes Jesus is John the Baptist risen from the dead, risen, as he thinks, in order to revenge himself upon him by the supernatural power which he now enjoys. His companions try to reassure him by suggesting other explanations which would be less terrifying, but he persists in holding to his previous opinion.[1] In Luke's account two reasons are suggested for Herod's uneasiness: On the one hand, some say that John the Baptist is risen, and this disturbs Herod. Thus he considers the identification of Jesus with John the Baptist, risen from the dead, as at least a possibility. At the conclusion of the narrative, on the other hand, Herod absolutely rejects this hypothesis and says: "I had John beheaded. Who then is this man about whom I hear all these things?" This contradictory statement proves that here an editor has tried to combine the elements of two accounts. Behind Luke's account

[1] We cannot draw any conclusion from the fact that Matthew reports only the opinion of Herod, but does not speak of the other hypotheses concerning Jesus, because it seems probable that he wished to avoid the doublet which occurs in Mark with the Confession of Peter; hence he has reproduced the beginning of the story only.

M

we can discern a tradition which said simply that when Herod heard Jesus mentioned he asked who this new prophet was who had emerged after John the Baptist had been beheaded? The absence of a complement to the word ἤκουσεν in Mark vi. 14, and the vagueness of the words with which Matthew (xiv. 1) and Luke (ix. 7) have tried to fill in, or, to be more accurate, to conceal this gap, show that the incident is not organically connected with that which precedes it. Nor is it any more closely connected with that which follows. In Mark and in Matthew it is the retrospective account of the death of John the Baptist,[1] which thus constitutes a parenthesis, then comes the mention of the return of the disciples (vi. 30), which is in organic connexion with the account of their mission (vi. 6–13). In the Gospels in their present form, the two sections which relate the perplexity of Herod about the reports concerning Jesus, and the death of John the Baptist, are really in the margin.[2]

In Mark and in Matthew the account of the perplexity of Herod leads to nothing. It is only said that the Tetrarch thinks that Jesus is John the Baptist risen from the dead, but nothing indicates any possible or actual results to which this opinion might lead. In Luke (ix. 9) the story has a conclusion: Herod tries to see Jesus. Martin Dibelius[3] sees in this desire of Herod a direct menace to Jesus. If the Tetrarch wants to see him, it cannot be out of mere curiosity, it must mean that he has made up his mind that he will make it impossible for him to continue his activity. Dibelius is certainly right in thinking that in the primitive tradition the episode relating to Herod should lead to a positive conclusion, directly connected with

[1] Matthew (xi. 12–13) has tried, but awkwardly enough, to hide the fact. He says, like Mark (vi. 29), that the disciples of John came to take away his body in order to bury it, and he adds that they then went to Jesus to tell him what had happened, and that when he heard of the death of the forerunner Jesus went away with his disciples into a desert place. In giving this ending to the story of the death of John he had forgotten that this event had already taken place some time ago, at the moment when the account of it is being given.

[2] In Luke, the episode of the perplexity of Herod is followed by the return of the disciples (ix. 10), as it is in Mark by the account of the death of John the Baptist.

[3] MARTIN DIBELIUS: *Urchr. Überl. üb. Joh. den Täufer*, p. 82.

the story of Jesus. But he has not gone far enough, and has too easily resigned himself simply to reading this menace between the lines of the narrative.[1] He has rightly observed that the story of the death of John serves the purpose of concealing the fact that there is no conclusion. It is, however, impossible to see for what reason Mark and Matthew would have insisted on the omission of anything so vague as Luke's ending to the story; we must conclude, therefore, that, in its primitive form, the episode ended differently. In my opinion, probably in the original MS. the writer stated not that Herod desired to see Jesus, but that he wanted to put him to death.[2]

All these points: the introduction of the theme of the various opinions concerning Jesus into the narrative, the omission of the conclusion by Mark and Matthew, and its correction by Luke, lead in the same direction. Instead of representing Herod as a prey to an uneasy curiosity, we see him taking a fateful decision, a decision which inevitably must have directly influenced the course of events in the life of Jesus.

In Mark and in Matthew the character of the primitive tradition is so largely altered that if we had nothing but their text we might at the very most merely suspect that the position of this episode was originally different from that which it now occupies: on the fringe of the Gospel story; it would, however, have been quite impossible to make any conjecture about the part which it had really played in the narrative.

It is now possible to return to a point which has not been settled. The original narrative must have reported what Herod had heard which decided him to take measures against Jesus.

---

[1] MARTIN DIBELIUS: *Urchr. Überl. üb. Joh. den Täufer*, p. 83.

[2] This conjecture has been suggested, but not formally proposed, by WELLHAUSEN (*Mk.*, p. 51). Wellhausen has not noticed that the text of Luke cannot here be understood as the resultant of a correction of that of Mark; he thinks that Luke was quite right to omit the account of the death of John the Baptist and to give the conclusion, "and he wished to see him," to the Herod episode; he considers that in this Luke shows that the reflections of the Tetrarch contained something menacing to Jesus. He adds: "It would be more accurate to say: 'He sought to have him killed.'" The criticism that SPITTA (*Streitfragen der Geschichte Jesu*, Göttingen 1907, pp. 94 ff.) has made of the interpretation of Wellhausen does not seem justifiable.

The evangelists have omitted this point, but the resultant text still bears traces of the adaptation it has undergone, in the artificial confused character of the Marcan narrative, and the vagueness of Matthew and Luke. Since the narrative concerning Herod is traditional, and, in its primitive form, must have formed an integral part of the Gospel narrative, it is probable that the modification which the beginning of the story has undergone was intended to sever the connexion between it and its context, that is, very probably, with the story of the mission of the disciples.[1]

The instructions which accompany it cannot have been created by tradition, for the following reasons: they imply a message which is limited to the preaching of repentance and the announcement of the imminent manifestation of the Kingdom of God and the Messiah; they do not proclaim that his coming must be preceded by a crisis; they do not link the idea of the fulfilment of the Kingdom with the Person of Jesus; finally, they apply to a mission which is strictly limited to the towns of Israel.

By placing the sending out of the disciples after the defeat of Jesus at Nazareth, and by assuming that Jesus remained inactive while his messengers were away on their preaching tour, Mark seems to suggest that Jesus sent his disciples on a mission in order to prepare them for their future task, but that, although not exactly discouraged, he himself was under the conviction that his own work of preaching would be unsuccessful, and that only by his death on the Cross would the task which God had given him to do be accomplished. In reality, however, it was a feeling of optimism which determined Jesus to associate his disciples with him in the work

[1] This is the incident which precedes our section in Mark and Luke. In Matthew the story of Herod follows the rejection of Jesus at Nazareth. Evidently it cannot have been due to the knowledge that Jesus was harshly treated at Nazareth that Herod was uneasy. It is possible that Matthew placed the mission of the disciples earlier than Mark does, because he wished to omit the connexion between the mission of the disciples and the decision taken by Herod against Jesus. In any case it is not possible to come to any certain conclusion in this matter, for the reasons for which Matthew altered the order in which Mark gave the account of the first part of the activity of Jesus in Galilee seem to have been rather complicated.

of preaching. The time is short, the Messiah is about to appear; the matter is urgent. The experience which Jesus had already gained would doubtless help him to realize that the message of his disciples would not be accepted everywhere. Nevertheless, the power which he gave them to cast out demons shows that at that moment his sentiments were not at all those of a man who feels he has failed; this idea is confirmed by the terms in which Mark (vi. 12–13) speaks of the manner in which the disciples carried out their task. The same may be said, still more definitely, about Luke's account of the mission of the Seventy (or seventy-two) disciples (which is manifestly only a doublet of the mission of the Twelve). It is at this moment that he places the triumphant exclamation: "I saw Satan as lightning fall from heaven!" Obviously, it was the fresh impetus given to the new movement by the preaching of the disciples of Jesus that attracted Herod's attention and made him determined to take measures to thwart it. Although behind the account of the mission of the disciples and the incident of Herod we may be able to discern an ancient tradition which connected these incidents, and thus explained why it was that Herod decided to kill Jesus, it does not follow, inevitably, that this was what actually took place. All that the tradition knew was that it was after the mission of the Twelve that Herod definitely ranged himself against Jesus, but the scene in which he came to this decision in conversation with his confidential companions can only be imaginary. The incident has been presented in a condensed and somewhat dramatic form. We have mentioned the indications which show that Herod had been watching Jesus for some time before making a definite decision. Thus Herod did not hear Jesus mentioned for the first time at the moment of the mission of the disciples, as the tradition followed by the Synoptic Gospels seems to have believed, but it was at the time when he saw how the movement was spreading, which he was already watching, that he made the decision (which till then he had not felt it necessary to make) to put Jesus to death. Some Pharisees who knew of this project warned Jesus in time, and thus Herod was not able to carry out his purpose.

X. Conclusion

We can now gain some idea of the first period of the Galilean ministry of Jesus as a whole. Returning from the Jordan with the certainty that he had received from God the mission to announce to the Jews that God willed, by a free gift of His love, to open to repentant men the gates of the coming Kingdom, Jesus went forth to proclaim this Kingdom whose members would obey God wholly, and would realize the divine perfection in their own lives. He did not pose either as an enemy or as a reformer of the ancient tradition, but his wholly spiritual conception of the Kingdom, the way in which he conceived the nature of obedience towards God, led him to adopt a free and progressive attitude towards the tradition and the Law, an attitude which roused the Pharisees against him. At first the latter received him with a certain amount of sympathy. So long as he did not offend their theological prejudices his activity was not thwarted to any appreciable extent. He continued to gather around him a large number of listeners who were impressed by the healings which he accomplished, in which the crowd was disposed to see the foreshadowing of the defeat of Satan and of the establishment of the Kingdom of God.

Herod did not remain indifferent to the popular movement which seemed to be forming in the Capernaum district. First of all he kept a watch on the movements of Jesus; then, as he saw that his influence was growing, he decided to take vigorous action, and intended to kill him.

CHAPTER XIII

THE CRISIS IN GALILEE

I. The Record in the Gospels

HEROD's decision to kill Jesus makes a break in the story of the Galilean ministry. From that time forward Jesus was obliged to flee from place to place and sometimes to conceal himself altogether. This explains the comings and goings which Mark reports from vi. 30 onwards. The evangelist does not explain them, but the actual situation to which the story refers becomes plain when we examine its structure in detail, and compare it with the parallel passages in Luke.

The first fact which strikes us when we read the group of stories which extends from the return of the disciples to the Messianic confession of Peter, is that in this section we find two stories of a miraculous feeding of the multitudes (Mark vi. 30–44, viii. 1–9). They are so close to one another and reveal such typical similarities that it is impossible to regard them as two independent stories of the same incident; nor can we regard them as distinct though similar incidents. They are two variants of the same story;[1] indeed, we may even say that Mark has placed two parallel cycles of tradition side by side, since there are some very striking analogies in the arrangement of the episodes which follow the two stories of the feeding of the multitudes.[2] In the Fourth Gospel the feeding of the

[1] When we compare the two accounts we gain the impression that chapter vi is the more recent. It is fuller, and it gives the highest number of figures.

[2] The parallel passages are arranged thus:

vi. 30–44. The feeding of the multitude.	viii. 1–9. The feeding of the multitude.
vi. 45–56. Return to the western shore.	viii. 10. Return to the western shore.
vii. 1–23. Dispute with the Pharisees (washing of hands).	viii. 11–13. Dispute with the Pharisees (request for a sign from heaven).
	viii. 14–21. Leaven of the Pharisees.
vii. 24–30. The Canaanitish woman.	viii. 22–26. Cure of the blind man of Bethsaida.
vii. 31–37. Cure of a deaf-mute.	[Continued overleaf

five thousand (vi. 1–15) is followed, as in Mark, by a return of Jesus to the western side of the Lake (vi. 16–21), then by a discourse which causes opposition to break out between the Jews and himself (vi. 22–66). The fact that the Johannine narrative contains some important elements, to which we shall have to return presently, which are not found in Mark, prevents us from thinking that here John is directly dependent on the Synoptic tradition.

The three stories of the feeding of the people, of the crossing of the Lake, and of the conflict which ensued, must therefore, before Mark's time, have been grouped together in a tradition which was very widespread, since we have two forms of the story in Mark and a third in John.

Luke has not preserved any trace of this grouping. According to his account, when the disciples returned from their missionary tour, Jesus takes them to Bethsaida (ix. 10), where they are joined by the crowd. It is there that the feeding of the multitudes takes place (ix. 11–17). The account in Luke's Gospel, when it is compared with that of the first feeding of the multitudes in Mark, only gives a few variations, which, save in one instance,[1] are only of secondary importance. In it we find none of the details which belong to the story of the second feeding of the multitudes. Thus here Luke is using Mark as his source; like him, he groups the series of incidents

[Footnote continued from previous page

In Matthew the arrangement is the same, save that instead of the healing of the deaf-mute there is a general statement about several healings, and the cure of the blind man of Bethsaida is omitted (on the other hand, further on, at the arrival at Jericho, where Mark (x. 46–52) places the healing of the blind man Bartimaeus, he reports the cure of two blind men (xx. 29–34)). The two accounts of Mark (vii. 31–37, and viii. 22–26) are fairly circumstantial, in the sense that instead of saying that Jesus healed by a word he heals by a gesture, and that instead of being instantaneous cures, they are gradual and, we might even say, a little laboured. It is doubtless for this reason that Matthew has not reproduced these incidents, but has given the numerical equivalent instead.

[1] This concerns the localization of the incident in the region round Bethsaida (Luke ix. 10). This detail may have been in the primitive tradition and have been omitted by Mark because he tells how after the people had been fed Jesus and his disciples left for Bethsaida. On this, see page 326, n. 4.

together: the sending of the disciples out on their mission, the perplexity of Herod, the return of the disciples, the departure of Jesus with them for the eastern shore of the Lake, and the feeding of the multitudes. When he reaches this point he leaves the thread of Mark's narrative behind, in order to narrate immediately the incident of Peter's Confession; this account differs very slightly from the account given by Mark; there are a few insignificant variant readings and the introduction and setting are different (ix. 19 ff.). Has Luke omitted, as a whole, the group of stories which in Mark separate the first feeding of the crowds from the Confession of Peter? or has he been influenced, as Spitta suggests,[1] by a source which would establish an organic connexion between the return of the disciples and Peter's Confession?

He might easily have recognized that the two stories of the feeding of the people referred to the same incident; in that case the fact that he only reports one version of this incident might be assigned to critical reasons. But this theory does not take into account the omission of all the stories which follow the first feeding of the multitudes.

In Mark's account of the feeding of the multitudes the geographical indications are very obscure. Jesus is rejoined by his disciples at a place which must have been on the western shore of the Lake, probably at Capernaum or in its neighbourhood; then he goes with them[2] into a desert place, very probably in the direction of Bethsaida (vi. 31).[3] After the feeding of the multitudes, instead of letting his disciples have a rest as he had intended, Jesus makes them embark in haste, and then he sets out with them on a period of wandering which was to prove very full of movement and change. This leads us to wonder whether after all Jesus had really taken his disciples to the eastern side of the Lake for rest at all? Mark does not usually give the motives for the changes from place to place which Jesus makes. Although in this instance he gives the reasons for which Jesus had left Capernaum, reasons which, as we have seen, do not correspond with the reality

[1] See pp. 381 ff.
[2] In a boat, since the boat is mentioned in iv. 22. Cf. Mark vi. 32.
[3] See p. 326, n. 4.

M*

of the situation, we may infer that he did so in order to replace something else which was in the source, which he did not reproduce because it did not harmonize with his own view of the course of events. After the feeding of the people, Jesus returns in passing to the plain of Gennesaret[1] (vi. 53–56). Then a discussion arises between him and the Pharisees on the question of eating with unwashen hands (vii. 1–23). Then he goes away secretly into the far north, into the region of Tyre.[2] It is at this point that the incident takes place of the Canaanitish woman who comes to Jesus and beseeches him to heal her daughter. At first he refuses her request because he has only been sent to the "lost sheep of the house of Israel," then, yielding to the persistence of the unhappy mother, he grants her what she asks (vii. 24–30). This incident shows that Jesus did not go into the region round Tyre in order to preach the Gospel, but solely in order to get away from Galilee. At the end of a certain period of time (to the length of which the story gives no clue) Jesus comes back from the region of Tyre, through Sidon[3] into Decapolis by the Sea of Galilee (vii. 31).[4]

[1] Concerning the coming of Jesus into the plain of Gennesaret there is a considerable difference between the accounts of Matthew (xiv. 34–36) and of Mark (vi. 53–56). Matthew tells how people hastily gathered the sick of the district together that Jesus might heal them. This assumes that there was something exceptional in his presence in the district. Mark (vi. 56a) adds that wherever Jesus went, into villages or towns or rural districts or market-places, the sick were brought to him that he might heal them, which suggests that at that moment he was engaged on a missionary tour. This note, which betrays by its character (which is quite general) its editorial origin, directly contradicts the beginning of the story where it is said, as in Matthew, that people were hastily gathering together the sick of the district. In verse 56b, therefore, we have reason to believe that there is a secondary addition from the hand of Mark.

[2] Matthew (xv. 21) mentions Tyre and Sidon. We shall have to return to this point a little further on.

[3] We follow the text of the MSS. א. B. D., etc. Others (A. N. X.) read "of the country of Tyre and Sidon," which is evidently a correction.

[4] This note is curious. Sidon is about twenty miles north of Tyre in the opposite direction from the road which leads towards the Sea of Galilee. Matthew (xv. 29) seems to have noticed this difficulty, for he says that Jesus returns to the Sea of Galilee. It is probably owing to the mention of Sidon by Mark that this town is mentioned in xv. 21. WELLHAUSEN (*Einl.*[1], p. 38) has suggested that in the Aramaic source there was בצידן,

The second incident of the feeding of the multitudes which is then described (viii. 1–9*) takes place—we do not know where—on the eastern shore of the Lake. After he has sent the multitudes away, Jesus enters the boat[1] with his disciples and returns to Galilee at a spot which Mark (viii. 10) calls Dalmanutha and Matthew (xv. 39) Magadan.[2] There Jesus has a brief encounter with the Pharisees to whom he refuses to show a sign from heaven (viii. 11–12*); then he again crosses the Lake (viii. 14–21*) and arrives at Bethsaida, where he cures a blind man (viii. 22–26). Thence he goes towards the North, in the direction of Caesarea Philippi, and it was during this journey that the Confession of Peter took place (viii. 27* ff.).

These perpetual changes of place can only be explained for two reasons. Either we have before us a series of independent incidents which Mark has placed side by side for editorial reasons, without taking into account the geographical confusion to which this might lead, or Mark (or the tradition which he follows) has preserved the recollection of the comings and goings of Jesus, but was ignorant of or did not mention the circumstances which would explain them.

The second hypothesis seems the more convincing of the two. In the only incidents which are said to have taken place on the western side of the Lake, Jesus is represented as one

which was translated by $\delta\iota\grave{\alpha}$ $\Sigma\iota\delta\tilde{\omega}\nu o\varsigma$ (by way of Sidon), when it should have been translated by $B\eta\sigma\sigma\alpha\iota\delta\grave{\alpha}\nu$ (at Bessaïda). This form, which Wellhausen regards as primitive, is found in Mark vi. 45, in MS. D. This hypothesis, which is quite attractive in itself, and which would have the additional advantage of making the first cycle of the feeding of the people occur at the same place as the second, breaks down at one point, the difficulty, namely, that Bethsaida is not a city of the Decapolis. Whatever we may think about this detail, the story itself places Jesus on the eastern shore of the Lake of Gennesaret.

[1] The mention of the boat, at a place where Jesus arrives, coming from Tyre, shows the artificial character of the link by which the two stories of the feeding of the crowds have been attached to one another.

[2] Neither of these two places can be identified. It seems probable that Matthew has substituted Magadan, a name which he might know, for Dalmanutha, which he did not know. It is possible that the name which was originally in the text of Mark or in the source may have been altered by the mistake of some scribe in copying the MS.

who is making a hurried journey. At Gennesaret the sick
are brought to him in haste, as if people had a feeling that
this was an opportunity which might never occur again. The
second time he passes that way is just after his refusal to give
the Pharisees the satisfaction of seeing him work a sign from
heaven; immediately after this he embarked for the other
side of the Lake; his saying about the "leaven of the Pharisees
and the Herodians"[1] shows that he is dominated by the
thought of the dangers which menace him. It is because he
feels himself a hunted man that Jesus only appears again in
Galilee as a passer-by and leads a wandering life. This leads
us to think that Luke, who did not understand the reason for
all these comings and goings, gave up the attempt to disentangle the geographical confusion of this part of the story,
and has omitted all that followed the first feeding of the
multitudes. This has made his narrative very coherent.

In Mark's account there is no organic connexion between
the cycle of the feeding of the multitudes and the conversation
of Jesus with his disciples on the subject of the various opinions
abroad among the people concerning the riddle of his personality. Nor is there any link in the Fourth Gospel, where
the opposition aroused by the discourse at Capernaum on
the Bread from heaven leads many of those who have followed
Jesus up to that time to leave him and "go no more with
him"; this leads Jesus to ask those who remain whether they
also wish to go away. Peter then declares, in the name of the
Twelve: "Lord, to whom shall we go? Thou hast the words
of eternal life; and we believe and are sure that thou art that
Christ, the Son of the living God" (John vi. 66–69). This is
the equivalent of the Messianic Confession of Peter as it is
reported in the Synoptic Gospels. In John's account, the
feeding of the multitudes provokes a crisis, at the close of
which the Twelve, by the mouth of Peter, declare that they
wish to remain loyal to Jesus. Has John here used a tradition
of the real course of events? or is there here only an ingenious
combination of incidents? It will not be possible to examine
this question in a useful way until later.

[1] See pp. 349 ff.

II. The Feeding of the Multitudes

The episode of Gennesaret (Mark vi. 53–56*) shows that at the moment when, after the first feeding of the multitudes, Jesus appears in Galilee, his appearance there was regarded as quite exceptional and an occasion of which full advantage should be taken. The accounts of the feeding of the multitudes give the same impression. It is not easy to understand why those who wished to hear Jesus made such efforts to rejoin him in the neighbourhood of Bethsaida, unless they had the feeling that he would not return to them. The crowd therefore had understood that Jesus had not gone away simply on a preaching tour, as he had often done before, after which he would return to them, but that he had gone away for a quite different reason.

There is one statement which appears to belong to the same period (in its present position it does not harmonize with its context): this is the conclusion to the story of the healing of the leper as it is given in the Marcan narrative. At the close of this story, it is said that Jesus told the leper to speak to no one, but to go and show himself to the priest, and thus to accomplish the rites prescribed by the Law of Moses for the readmission of lepers into society (i. 44). The positive command which accompanies the prohibition of all publicity makes it clear that Jesus does not wish him to depart from the rules of the Law. In i. 45 Mark says that the leper goes away and begins to talk about the matter so much and so widely that Jesus can no longer enter publicly into any town or village but that he "was without in desert places; and they came to him from every quarter." This conclusion does not agree with what precedes it. The subject of the ritual purification of the leper, to which Jesus wished the healed man to submit, seems to have dropped out of the story, and the expression "to speak to no one" has come to mean something quite different from its original meaning in the story itself. It implies that Jesus wanted to keep the healing of the man a secret. It is the transposition of an entirely different idea, which we find, for instance, in Mark iii. 11–12 and Luke iv. 41. There it is said that the demons, when they saw Jesus, prostrated themselves before him, crying out: "Thou art the Son of God," but Jesus forbids them to make him known (cf. Mark i. 23-24). The evangelist thinks that the demons see and know that which is hidden from men. When they see Jesus they perceive that he is the Messiah. But Jesus, who does not wish to be presented to the masses as the Messiah, tells them to hold their peace. Wrede,[1] who believes that Jesus did not feel he was the Messiah, regards the theory of the Messianic secret as an artifice intended to reconcile the Messianic faith of Primitive Christianity with the fact that Jesus was not the Messiah. We shall see that there are very solid reasons for thinking that, in one sense at least, Jesus did believe that he was the Messiah. But, save when he was before the Sanhedrin, he never openly proclaimed his Messiahship. He only allowed it to be divined by his intimate friends. Wrede's theory, however, contains a great deal of truth, for this reserve of Jesus did constitute a problem for the Early Church, a problem which she solved by the idea that it was only the Resurrection which proclaimed publicly the Messiahship of Jesus. The discreet character of the Messianic affirmations reported in the Gospels may be explained by the fact that Jesus possessed the conviction, not that he was actually the Messiah, but that he was destined to be manifested as Messiah, at the moment of the establishment of the Kingdom of God.[2] Further, the term "Messiah" aroused in the minds of the majority of his hearers, and even, doubtless, in the minds of his most intimate disciples, a world of ideas and feelings which Jesus did not himself share, and which he felt he ought to discourage as definitely as possible. This is why he was so restrained in his statements about the Messiahship, and why he seems to have preferred to use the term "Son of Man," which was of more recent origin, at least in Jewish circles; this term, which was not burdened with a long history, still preserved a certain elasticity. Thus the transference of the commandment to keep silence, originally addressed to the demons, to the healings, is a secondary phenomenon.[3] In the

[1] WREDE: *Messiasgeheimnis.*
[2] Again, he did not have this feeling from the beginning of his ministry.
[3] A typical example of this is furnished by Matt. xii. 15-16, that is, in the passage parallel with Mark iii. 11-12, where the sick are mentioned, and not the demoniacs, as in Mark.

particular instance before us we ought to add that a command given by Jesus to keep secret the healing that had just been accomplished, would have been in direct opposition to his intention (to which this story bears witness), which was this: by telling the leper to go and show himself to the priest he made it quite clear that he had no intention of rebelling against the legal regulations. The conclusion of the episode of the healing of the leper is not connected with the narrative; further, it does not say merely that the healing which had been accomplished is known, but that Jesus can no longer show himself in any town, and has to remain in desert places. As it is also stated that people come to see him from all quarters, this retreat cannot be explained by the fear that his presence would provoke a movement which would soon get beyond his control. The situation which is here assumed is quite different; it is similar to that which lies behind the stories of the feeding of the multitudes: Jesus cannot show himself in public any longer because if he were to do so Herod's emissaries would immediately arrest him. His influence over the people is still strong, since they flock to him, whether he is in desert places or even outside Galilean territory.

At first, the hostility of Herod, far from injuring the influence of Jesus over the people, may have even strengthened it. Since the development of events had brought Jesus into opposition to the semi-pagan Tetrarch, people may have thought that this was the sign that Jesus was the One whom God had ordained to restore the pure theocracy. They may have hoped that he would prove to be a second Maccabaeus, who would defeat another Antiochus.

Thoughts like these may have been seething, in a confused way, in the minds of the people, when Jesus fled from Capernaum to take refuge in the neighbourhood of Bethsaida. This was why they set out to find him. It is impossible to estimate, even approximately, the importance of the group which gathered there. The records speak of three thousand men or of five thousand; one account even adds that these figures do not include the women or the children. These variations show how easily the numbers may have been exaggerated by tradition.

The story in the Gospel is too well known to be repeated in detail. Having made the people sit down, Jesus takes some bread, breaks it, pronounces a blessing upon it,[1] then gives it to the disciples to distribute to the crowd. Everyone is satisfied, and after the meal several baskets are filled with the broken fragments which are left.

What exactly did take place? Are we to suppose, as a good many interpreters have suggested, that Jesus, by distributing the few provisions which he possessed, gave such an example of faith and confidence that all those who had their food with them imitated his example, and shared what they had with others who had not thought of bringing food with them? This explanation is plausible, but it is a mere hypothesis. In any case, the evangelists themselves regard the incident as a miracle; and it seems extremely probable that those who helped to serve, and those who partook of the meal, and Jesus himself, felt the same. But the narrators have not laid a great deal of emphasis upon the actual miraculous element. In their minds the central point of interest in the story was not the multiplication of the food but its distribution.

The story is repeated twice by Mark and Matthew; it occurs also in John; hence in the eyes of the early tradition it was of particular importance. The Early Church interpreted it in the sense of the Eucharist.[2] This interpretation occurs first of all in the Fourth Gospel, as is shown very plainly in the discourse on the Bread of Life which Jesus gave on the following day (vi. 25–59). This interpretation of the incident is quite natural. People would spontaneously link the meal at Bethsaida with that which Jesus took with his disciples some hours before his arrest. The Last Supper of Jesus—even if it had been no more than that—was, through the words which accompanied the distribution of the Cup, an evocation and an anticipation of the Messianic Feast. The idea of this Feast was so widespread in the Judaism of that day[3] that it is quite natural to think that Jesus may have had it in mind when he invited the multitude, to whom he had just been speaking about the Kingdom of God, to sit down to this meal. To him also the

[1] The one which the Jews pronounced every time they took food.
[2] On this point, see MAURICE GOGUEL: L'Évangile de Marc, Paris, 1909, p. 160, n. 1; Eucharistie, p. 285, n. 1.   [3] See Eucharistie, pp. 54 ff.

distribution of the loaves was a symbol of the Messianic Feast. By such a gesture, made at the very moment when Herod's attitude threatens to interrupt his activity, Jesus proclaims that he is neither discouraged nor defeated, that his faith in the speedy realization of the Kingdom of God is inviolate. By the frugal impromptu repast taken together in a desert place, he suggests the splendours of the Messianic Feast. His thought seems to become more definite. By presiding over the meal in the desert, does he not mean that he also will preside at the Messianic Feast?

The purely conjectural element in this interpretation soon disappears when we consider what followed the feeding of the multitudes.

As we read the Synoptic narrative we feel that something must have happened at this point which Mark has not mentioned, and that this unknown element has exercised a direct influence on the following course of events. After the feeding of the multitudes, according to Mark, Jesus seems to have turned away from the masses. Although he may have spent some further time in Galilee, under conditions which it is impossible to define more closely, most of the time he went about alone with his disciples, and spoke to them of the lot which would befall the Son of Man, and of the sufferings which they themselves would have to undergo. In the mind of the evangelists the change was more on the side of the disciples than on the side of Jesus. The allusion to the days when the bridegroom will no longer be with his friends (Mark ii. 20) in an incident which the evangelist places at the very beginning of the ministry of Jesus, shows that although, according to their account, Jesus did not speak of the necessity for his death from the outset of his ministry, this was because the disciples were not yet prepared to understand what he had to tell them. It was not until the moment of the Messianic Confession of Peter, when they understood that Jesus was the Christ,[1] that he was able to reveal to them the destiny which awaited the Son of Man.

[1] Matthew (xvi. 17) brings out the nature of this Confession of Peter as a revelation more clearly than Mark by the declaration of Jesus to Peter: "Flesh and blood hath not revealed it unto thee, but my Father which is in heaven."

This theory of the Gospel story does not correspond with the facts. The disciples were so little ready to receive teaching about the sufferings of the Son of Man that, according to the evangelists themselves, every time that Jesus spoke to them on this subject they did not understand what he meant. They were so little prepared for the events of the Passion that they were absolutely dumbfounded when their Master was arrested.

Thus the fact that after the Galilean crisis Jesus set his mind in a fresh direction cannot be explained by saying that from this time forward Jesus had a group of people round him who, at least in part, could understand ideas which until that time they had been unable to grasp.

The Marcan narrative also suggests that after the feeding of the multitudes, Jesus preached the Gospel to the people less regularly than before, although he did not give it up entirely. A critical analysis of the narrative suggests that a certain number of the scenes in the second part of the Marcan narrative, which place Jesus in the presence of the people, may have been inserted in the story at this point because, in the sources from which they were taken, they were connected with sections which reported some private teaching given by Jesus to his closest friends among the disciples.

The Gospel tradition has preserved a somewhat confused recollection of a conflict which took place between Jesus and the Jews after the feeding of the multitudes. This comes out quite plainly in the Johannine narrative, where it is said that after the discourse in Capernaum Jesus was abandoned by a section of his followers who until then had stood by him (vi. 66). We must make a distinction between the fact to which the record bears witness and the explanation, given by the evangelist, of the fact. According to John, many of the disciples of Jesus, after they had heard the discourse on the Divine Bread, said: "This is an hard saying: who can bear it?" To those to whom this discourse was addressed, however, "hard" scarcely seems the right word to use to describe their sensations. It seems far more likely that they found the whole discourse unintelligible. This disharmony between the fact and its explanation leads us to believe that here the evangelist has been tempted to explain, in his own way, a fact which had been handed down by tradition.

In Mark's account, after each incident of the feeding of the multitudes, we find an account of a conflict between Jesus and the representatives of the Jewish religious tradition. After the first of these incidents comes the dispute about the washing of hands (vii. 1–23): Mark here introduces the intervention of the Pharisees and scribes who had come from Jerusalem, as in iii. 22. We ought not to accept, save with the very greatest caution, the idea that during the Galilean ministry of Jesus the religious authorities at Jerusalem were concerned with his doings in the North, or that they would have sent a delegation of Pharisees and Scribes to investigate his activity and discuss certain questions with him. This, however, gives still more point to the detail recorded by the evangelists. It shows that in their opinion this was not one of those occasional controversies which arose constantly between rabbis of different schools of thought. In their minds this was actually a challenge thrown down by the Jews to Jesus, and an assertion that the difference between them is irreconcilable. Certain differences of form and arrangement in the text of Matthew and Mark lead us to think that Matthew has not only retouched the text of Mark, but that he has also used the source from which Mark drew his material. This fact, combined with the character of the section, justifies us in seeking for its origin in the Logia. The fact that Luke has omitted this fragment is due to the fact that he was writing for Gentile-Christian readers, for whom the discussion about ceremonial purity would have no interest.

The refusal to give a sign from heaven (Mark viii. 11–13*) also comes from the Logia, since this saying also occurs in Matthew (xii. 38–39) and in Luke (xi. 29). Mark gives this section in a more primitive form than the other evangelists, since in his text the refusal of Jesus is more absolute.[1]

Mark may here have followed the tradition of the Logia more faithfully than Matthew and Luke, or he may have known a more ancient version, but it is also possible that the whole section means something other than would appear at

[1] See p. 219.

a first reading. This is suggested by a passage in the *Jewish Antiquities* relating to Theudas.

Josephus says that "While Fadus was Procurator of Judaea, a magician named Theudas persuaded a great multitude of people to follow him, carrying their goods down to the Jordan, which, said he, at his command would divide and allow them to pass over dry shod. By these sayings he led many astray. But Fadus did not leave them to their folly. He sent out a detachment of cavalry against them, who surprised them, killed many, and captured many prisoners. As for Theudas, having taken him prisoner, the soldiers cut off his head and brought it to Jerusalem" (*A.J.*, XX, 5, 1, ¶¶ 97–99).

The intervention of Fadus shows that Theudas was not a magician but an aspirant to the Messiahship. The miracle which he had promised to work was doubtless to be the proof of his divine mission, and the sign for the opening of a campaign against Rome.

May we not then suppose that the miracle asked from Jesus[1] may also have been the sign for the rallying of his followers and the signal for the beginning of a Messianic revolt? This would explain the formal refusal of Jesus, which was unaccompanied by any explanation or instruction, even for the use of the disciples, and that immediately after it had been formulated Jesus left the place which he had only just reached, as if the fact of having been the object of such a request made his activity in Galilee either useless or impossible.

It is not difficult to discern the thought that Mark wished to express by his arrangement of the double cycle of the feeding of the multitudes. In his mind, the event that happened in the solitary place where Jesus was alone with the multitudes constitutes the culminating point in his preaching of the Kingdom of God. At this critical moment, when Jesus is threatened by Herod, and when the question is whether he will yield to the menaces of the Tetrarch and give up his work, his gesture is an evocation and anticipation of the

---

[1] In that case he would not have been asked for this by Pharisees who wished to entrap him, but by his own followers, who wanted to see him lead them against Herod. The mention of the Pharisees would be determined by the meaning given to the episode by the Gospel tradition.

Messianic Feast. It is thus a proclamation of the Kingdom of God, so living, so direct, and so earnest, that if those who heard it remain untouched, this means that the work of Jesus cannot be fulfilled by preaching, and he will have to tread another road, a road which will lead to Calvary. The fact that Mark places an incident which shows Jesus in conflict with the Pharisees after each account of the feeding of the multitudes shows that he wants to emphasize the failure of the Galilean ministry.

Here, as in the Johannine narrative, we must make a distinction between the fact which Mark knew by tradition and his explanation, an explanation whose artificial character is the result of the combination of materials (whose origin was different) by which it is expressed.

In the narrative which follows the first feeding of the multitudes there is a detail which is organically connected with it, a detail which needs to be examined very closely. Immediately after the people had been fed, Jesus urged his disciples to get into the boat and go off before him to Bethsaida where he was to rejoin them. He waited behind to send the people away, and then he went up into the mountain to pray (Mark vi. 45–46*). Thus Jesus seems to have been anxious that there should be no prolongation of the contact between the people and his disciples. It is not forcing the meaning too much to suggest that Jesus may have had some difficulty in persuading the people to depart, since, once they had gone, he went away to renew his strength in solitary prayer. Mark is remarkably restrained in all he says about the interior life of Jesus. He does not speak of his meditations and reflexions and rarely mentions his prayers. The fact is not at all surprising; in the mind of the evangelist, it is not possible to regard Jesus as a man whose mental evolution can be studied, or whose actions can be explained by examining the interior movements of his soul. Jesus is the bearer of a divine message, the agent of divine action; this message and this action can no more be explained than we can explain God Himself. Hence the rare occasions on which Mark does mention the prayers of Jesus are all the more significant. He does this in three places only. The first time is when, after the long day in Capernaum (related in chapter i), Jesus leaves the town very early in order to go away and pray in a solitary place. Simon and his companions search for him; when they find Jesus they tell him that everyone is looking for him. He replies that he must go on to the neighbouring towns, and that this is why he went forth (i. 35–38). Mark also records the prayer in Gethsemane (xiv. 32–42). These two prayers form a kind of framework for the whole of the active ministry of Jesus. The first prepares Jesus for his work of preaching; in the second he is preparing himself for his Passion. Is it audacious to suggest that when Mark shows us Jesus in prayer on the night after the feeding of the multitudes he wished to make it plain that this day had marked a turning-point in his ministry? But what had actually happened Mark does not say.

The information which Mark does not disclose we find in John, who expresses himself thus:

Then those men, when they had seen the miracle which Jesus did, said, This is of a truth that prophet which should come into the world.[1] When Jesus therefore perceived that they would come and take him by force, to make him a king, he departed again into a mountain by himself alone. And when even was now come, his disciples went down unto the sea, and entered into a ship, and went over the sea toward Capernaum (John vi. 14–17).

After this, as in Mark, Jesus rejoins his disciples by walking on the water. Just when they were prepared to receive him into the boat they reached the place to which they wished to go (vi. 18–21). At this point John's narrative is rather confused; he says that the crowds, having looked for Jesus in vain, decide to go to Capernaum by water, some boats having just arrived, very opportunely, from Tiberias (vi. 22–24). The confusion of the narrative, the improbability of transporting a crowd of five thousand men to Capernaum in a few boats, shows that we are here dealing with an editorial combination of a rather unfortunate kind.

Having returned to Capernaum the crowd continues to search for Jesus; finally, they find him in the synagogue[2] and ask him: "Rabbi, when camest thou hither?" (vi. 25); Jesus

[1] That is, the Messiah.
[2] This detail is not given in vi. 24; it comes from vi. 59.

replies with a long discourse on the Bread of Life (vi. 25–59). This discourse reflects the theology of a much later period; it is most important for an analysis of Johannine thought, but it does not help us to understand the thought of Jesus. All we can learn from it is the way in which the evangelist interpreted the feeding of the multitudes. At first Jesus reproaches his hearers for seeking him merely because they have seen a miracle, and have been satisfied by the loaves with which he has fed them. He urges them to seek rather for the food which abides unto life eternal, which the Son of Man will give them (vi. 26–27). In answer to a question, he says that to work the works of God is to believe on Him who sent him (vi. 28–29). Then they ask for a "sign," that is, a miracle which would support this faith which he demands: "What sign showest thou then? . . . Our fathers did eat manna in the desert" (vi. 30–31). This request, when Jesus had actually just worked a miracle which had filled the people with enthusiasm, and also a miracle which is exactly like the one which they suggest as an example, shows that in writing out the discourse at Capernaum the evangelist has lost sight of the circumstances, which, according to his story, were the occasion of this discourse. All the rest of the discourse may be summed up in this formula, which Jesus uses after the Jews have declared that his words are too hard for them, and that they cannot bear them: "It is the spirit that quickeneth; the flesh profiteth nothing." This means that the distribution of the loaves to the multitudes is the symbol of the gift which by his death Jesus will make of himself to his own, and through which they will have life. The Jews, who have been merely impressed by the miracle and want to see others like it, have not understood the true meaning of the feeding of the multitudes. In this act, which was intended to show them the doctrine of the gift of his life, they have merely seen something marvellous. To John the feeding of the multitudes is the occasion which brings to light a latent misunderstanding between Jesus and the people, and shows that the Jews were incapable of understanding the gift of life through Christ.

This is a theological explanation, but it points to a fact which was supported by tradition. Alongside of this explanation we find another, or at least an attempt at another. The way in which, after the feeding of the people, Jesus evades a Messianic demonstration on the part of the crowd explains the cooling of the popular enthusiasm quite differently from the discourse in Capernaum; it also explains the fact that Jesus was deserted by those who had seemed disposed to follow him if he would have consented to be their leader. The evangelist shows that he has not understood that the disappointment of the people explains the rejection of Jesus, since by giving the discourse at Capernaum he has suggested a quite different reason for the defection of the people. What is said of the attitude of the people after Jesus went away from them has been altered and explained in such a way that the text has become almost unintelligible, so that it now conveys only a general sense of its meaning. This is what usually happens when an editor uses a tradition which he does not understand or in which he thinks or wishes to find something other than what it says. This also explains why the conclusion of the story has disappeared. The crowd always returns to Capernaum to look for Jesus (vi. 29). The fact that Jesus had evaded a Messianic ovation on the previous evening would not have been sufficient to cause the popular enthusiasm to cool down. In this narrative, however, all traces of popular enthusiasm have disappeared, and at Capernaum Jesus is faced by an audience of people who want to see him work marvels, but who are quite persuaded that in the religion handed down to them by their fathers they possess the truth, and nothing but the truth. Thus the fragment which speaks of the intention of the people to take Jesus by force and make him a king cannot have been invented by the evangelist.

There is no trace in the Synoptic Gospels of this detail which is preserved by the Johannine record. It must, however, have been present in the source which Mark used, and the reason why the second evangelist has not introduced it must be either because he did not understand how an enthusiasm which was so ardent could have faded so swiftly or, still more probably, because, in order to avoid creating difficulties for Christian missionaries among loyal Roman subjects, and also because he considered that such a thing was impossible, he did not wish to say that Jesus, at a certain point in his career, was on the point of being proclaimed King by his followers; that is, he wished to avoid representing Jesus as in any way an enemy of Rome. It is obvious that there is a gap in the Marcan narrative because it does not explain why Jesus is so anxious to separate his disciples from the crowd as quickly as possible. The tradition reported by John fills this gap exactly. It is because he dreads that the disciples may become infected with the enthusiasm of a political Messianism that Jesus makes them embark so hastily. In the second cycle the refusal of Jesus to accept the ideas of political Messianism has left a trace in the section on the "sign from heaven," to which Mark has given a very different meaning from that which it seems to have had originally.

It is now possible to reconstruct what took place at the moment of the feeding of the multitudes. The Galilean masses, which until then had been greatly impressed by Jesus and his preaching, and were expecting the imminent advent of the Kingdom of God, then began to wonder how Jesus would act now that he was in open conflict with Herod. Would he go away and give up his preaching? or would he take up the challenge, throw himself into the struggle, and gather his followers around him in order to lead a campaign against the Tetrarch? The teaching Jesus gave to the crowds when they sought him outside the borders of Galilee convinced them that he would not give up his work. Through all his utterances there rings more clearly than ever his certainty of the speedy realization of the Kingdom of God. At once the mind of the people turns more and more in the direction of the expectation of a political movement. In their eyes there are only two possible ways out of the situation: either to give up and retire altogether from the scene or to fight. The refusal of Jesus to accept the title of king, and to use the force supplied by his followers, coupled with the supernatural power which God would give him to overthrow the Tetrarch, led to the immediate collapse of his influence over the masses. At the beginning he was regarded as a prophet, circumstances forced him to play the part of Messiah. This he refused to do. To the masses of the people this was a confession of impotence, and they turned their backs upon him in disgust.

III. The Conversation at Caesarea Philippi

At the moment when the Messianic enthusiasm of the masses was at its height the primary concern of Jesus had been to preserve his disciples from the contagion; hence he must have known or believed that they were open to the seductions of political Messianism. For them also Herod's hostility to Jesus ushered in a critical period. In which direction would they go? Would they be discouraged and return to their boats and their nets? or to the office, or to their fields or their homes? Or would their aggressive spirit awaken and would they attempt to drag Jesus into a Messianic armed revolt? Or, finally, were they sufficiently permeated by his spirit to follow him along the obscure path which he must now follow, when the vision of the realization of the Kingdom of God, without becoming less certain, receded and gave way to dark views of the future? Jesus had to ask his disciples some questions in order to find out where they stood.

Two independent accounts have been preserved of his conversation with them on this subject, one from the Synoptic Gospels and the other from John. The Synoptists certainly regarded the conversation at Caesarea Philippi as very important. It was directly after it, and in close connexion with it, that there appeared the necessity for the sufferings of the Son of Man, an idea which was henceforth to dominate the Gospel story to the very end.

The conversation itself (Mark viii. 27–30*) is presented in the Synoptic Gospels in the same way. Here is the text of Mark:

And by the way he asked his disciples, saying unto them, Whom do men say that I am? And they answered, John the Baptist: but some say Elias, and others, One of the prophets. And he saith unto them, But whom say ye that I am? And Peter answereth and saith unto him, Thou art the Christ. And he charged them that they should tell no man of him.[1]

---

[1] The chief features peculiar to the account in Matthew are the following: First of all, Jesus does not ask, "Whom do men say that I am?" but, "Whom do men say that I the Son of Man am?" which destroys in advance all the interest of Peter's statement. Then the words which in verse 28 in

The narrative which follows is also arranged in the same way in the three Synoptic Gospels. After Peter's Confession comes the first announcement of the sufferings (Mark viii. 31–32*) which is logically attached to it, for the statement that the Son of Man must suffer can only mean something to the disciples when they have understood that their master is the Messiah, the Son of Man. Luke says nothing of the effect produced by the declaration of Jesus. Mark (viii. 32b–33) and Matthew (xvi. 22–23) place here a protest of Peter which Jesus repels as a suggestion of Satan. The severity of the rebuke addressed to the apostle explains why it is omitted in the Third Gospel.

The section which follows (Mark viii. 34–ix. 1*) is directly connected with the idea of the sufferings of the Son of Man, since it deals with the sufferings which the disciples will have to undergo, and the reward which is promised to those who sacrifice their lives.[1] Then comes the account of the Trans-

Mark we have placed within brackets, and which are implied in his narrative, are expressed in Matthew, which makes the passage clearer. To the hypotheses reported by Mark, Matthew adds another: some say that Jesus is Jeremiah. In the reply of Peter, instead of, "Thou art the Christ," Matthew reads, "Thou art the Christ, the Son of the Living God." Finally, the last admonition of Jesus is more precise in Matthew: Jesus does not forbid his disciples to mention him, but to "tell no man that he was Jesus the Christ." As a reminder, we should recall the fact that Matthew mentions a special declaration to Peter: "Blessed art thou, Simon Bar-Jona: for flesh and blood hath not revealed it unto thee, but my Father which is in heaven; and I say unto thee that thou art Peter, and upon this rock I will build my church . . ." The text of Matthew is certainly secondary to that of Mark. There are only three peculiarities in the text of Luke which need be mentioned. They make the passage clearer and more precise. Instead of "one of the prophets" Luke has: "that one of the old prophets was risen again." Instead of "the Christ" he has "the Christ of God"; and in the conclusion Jesus forbids his disciples to tell this to anyone. On this last point Luke departs from the text of Mark in the same direction as Matthew, but as he does not do it in the same way, and as he and Matthew have in common only one word which is also in Mark, there must be here two corrections independent of each other.

[1] Logical though the connexion may be, it does not, however, come from the source; it has been realized by Mark because, in his account and in that of Luke (Matthew omits this detail), the words about the sufferings of the disciples are addressed to the multitude as well as to the disciples, while the preceding section was placed at a moment when Jesus was alone on the road with his disciples.

figuration (Mark ix. 2–8*), which to the evangelists is the divine confirmation of the Messianic Confession of Peter.[1] This grouping of incidents shows that, in the view of the evangelists, the conversation at Caesarea Philippi marks the moment when the Messiahship of Jesus becomes more definite and clear to the disciples, making them able to receive fresh teaching from the lips of Jesus.

The linking up of this episode with that which precedes it is less clear in Luke; above all, it is rather different from the arrangement in Mark and Matthew.

In Mark, after Jesus has cured a blind man at Bethsaida, he turns his steps, with his disciples, towards the villages of Caesarea Philippi, that is, doubtless, towards the villages situated in the neighbourhood of that town. It is while they are on the road that Jesus asks them what the people are saying about him (viii. 27).[2] He is seeking a refuge outside Galilee, in the territory of the Tetrarch Philip. Nowhere else in the Gospels is Caesarea Philippi mentioned, and it is difficult to see what interest there could be for Mark to introduce the name of this town to which no particular memories are attached. From the geographical point of view this incident connects very well with that section in the narrative which deals with the feeding of the multitudes. The fact that Caesarea Philippi is mentioned may, therefore, be regarded as a proof that it belongs to the primitive tradition.

In Luke, the conversation with the disciples follows the feeding of the multitudes, and ought to be placed, like it, at

[1] For the origin and the real character of this incident, see above, p. 343, n. 1.

[2] In Matthew it is almost the same, but the expression is simpler. The conversation is placed at the moment when Jesus has arrived in the country round Caesarea Philippi (xvi. 13). In Matthew the connexion with that which precedes it is less satisfactory than in Mark. In xvi. 5 it is said that after having refused to give a sign from heaven, Jesus embarks in order to cross over the Lake. Between the embarkation and the arrival in the region of Caesarea Philippi, which is far from the Lake, something is missing; we ought to have been told that Jesus disembarked and then set out for Caesarea. This gap may be explained by noting that Matthew has omitted the archaic account of the healing of the blind man of Bethsaida because it contained features which were too much opposed to his way of conceiving the healings of Jesus.

Bethsaida. There is no suggestion of Caesarea Philippi. Luke says that one day, while Jesus was praying alone, his disciples gathered round him, and it was then that he questioned them (ix. 22). Spitta[1] argues, with much ingenuity, that Luke has here reproduced, with more exactitude than Mark, the fundamental common source of the Synoptic Gospels (*Grundschrift*), and that if Mark has substituted Caesarea Philippi for Bethsaida, this is because, having added the secondary account of the healing of the blind man, in which it is said that Jesus was "going out of the village," he had to give the incident which followed a local habitation and a name in a different district. Spitta thinks that the account of the feeding of the multitudes was not included in the *Grundschrift*. In ix. 10 it is said that Jesus "went aside privately (that is, far from Galilee) into a desert place belonging to the city called Bethsaida"; now, Spitta thinks that it is as impossible to localize the feeding of the multitudes in a town as to take "at Bethsaida" to mean "in the neighbourhood of Bethsaida." In order to express this idea Luke had at his disposal the usual expression in the Gospels: εἰς τὰ μέρη Βηθσαιδά, "in the region of Bethsaida."[2] In his opinion, in the *Grundschrift*, Peter's Confession was directly connected with the journey of Jesus to the eastern shore of the Lake, after the return of the disciples, at the moment when Herod had just declared his hostility towards Jesus. This leads Spitta to interpret this incident in a manner which differs greatly from the usual point of view. His suggestion is this: Jesus, rendered uneasy by the threats of the Tetrarch, is anxious to know what the people are saying about him. He asks his disciples what they have heard in their wanderings amongst the villages of Galilee; then he asks them what they themselves have said about him, and urges them

[1] SPITTA: *Das Gespräch Jesu mit seinen Jüngern in Bethsaïda*, in *Streitfragen der Geschichte Jesu*, pp. 85–143. *Die synoptische Grundschrift in ihrer Ueberlieferung durch das Lukasevangelium*, Liepzig, 1912, pp. 214–228.

[2] In order to buttress his point of view, Spitta asserts that it is that of numerous scribes, who, instead of the most certain reading, "in a town named Bethsaida," have placed something else, as, for example, "at the gate of a town called Bethsaida" (sy[s].). "In a desert place" (‭א‬ 69, etc.), "in the desert place of a town called Bethsaida" (A. C. D.), "in a desert place which is Bethsaida (lat.), "in a village called Bethsaida, in a desert place" (Θ.).

henceforth to tell no one that he is the Messiah. The silence which he imposes on them thus becomes a measure of precaution. If Herod came to hear that Jesus called himself the Messiah, and was represented as such by his disciples, his enmity would only be increased.

There are some conclusive objections to Spitta's reconstruction of the *Grundschrift*. If Luke had known of the existence of a connexion between the menace of the attitude of Herod towards Jesus and the questions he was asking his disciples about what people were saying about him and about what they themselves had said in their preaching, it is difficult to understand why he should have interposed the feeding of the multitudes between the two sections, or why he should have given such an insignificant ending to the section on Herod, by saying simply that the Tetrarch wanted to see Jesus. This simple curiosity does not seem to fit well with the idea that, after Herod began to notice him, Jesus should have taken the precaution to leave Galilee, and have charged his disciples to conceal the fact that he is the Christ. Hence we must conclude: either Luke knew that the *Grundschrift* (in the sense in which it is reconstituted by Spitta) was right in establishing an organic relation between the episode of Herod and the conversation of Jesus with his disciples, and if this is right we cannot understand why he has weakened the ending of the Herod episode as he has done, or he did not know it; and then we do not understand why he has only added to the content of the *Grundschrift* the first feeding of the multitudes, and not all the other sections which follow it in Mark.

Spitta is right in thinking that the feeding of the multitudes cannot be localized at Bethsaida, but the text of Luke does not say this. It says that Jesus comes to Bethsaida, that the crowds follow him, and that after he had welcomed them he spoke to them of the Kingdom of God, and that after he had healed some sick folk he fed the multitudes who had followed him; there is nothing to indicate that Jesus stayed at Bethsaida from the moment he reached it until he fed the hungry people. Even if Jesus had been rejoined by the crowds at Bethsaida he would have had to take them aside in order to be able to speak to them privately, which he could not do in a pagan city. This is so obvious that it would be useless to say so explicitly, especially as the evangelists took no trouble to place the incidents which they narrated in their right setting. If the account of the feeding of the multitudes is not a section foreign to the *Grundschrift*, and even if we admit, contrary to our previous conclusions, that Luke has preserved the primitive arrangement of the source in not bringing Jesus back into Galilee after the feeding of the people, the link which Spitta has thought he could perceive between the return of the disciples and the question which Jesus addressed to them becomes so slight that it practically disappears. If Jesus had been dominated by the preoccupation which Spitta suggests, how is it that while they were crossing the Lake, or before the arrival of the crowd, Jesus did not make an opportunity to sound them on this subject? Further, what we know of the first preaching of Jesus, and of the instructions he gave his disciples, does not allow us to believe that they could have had the idea of presenting their master as the Messiah.

The introduction to the account of this conversation is as unnatural in Luke as it is natural in Mark and in Matthew. At a moment when Jesus is alone in prayer his disciples gather round him (ix. 18). This would seem to suggest that the disciples were about to ask Jesus a question and make some request of him. On the contrary, it is he who questions them. Thus evidently this introduction is purely editorial. Further, Luke has not composed it entirely himself, and this is why it does not blend very well with the narrative. He has reproduced material which, in the source which he was using, belonged to another section. Here it is, in xi. 1–2 :

And it came to pass that, as he was praying in a certain place, when he ceased, one of his disciples said unto him, Lord, teach us to pray, as John also taught his disciples. And he said unto them, When ye pray, say, Father . . .[1]

This introduction to the teaching of the Lord's Prayer is as suitable as it is unsuitable as an introduction to the conver-

[1] The care which has been taken by tradition to avoid anything which would make Jesus look like a disciple of John the Baptist, and to declare his complete independence, guarantees the historicity of an incident in which Jesus is represented as consciously imitating an example given by John.

sation with the disciples. Thus we must reject the theory of Spitta, and admit that, in the source which Mark followed, the conversation at Caesarea Philippi followed the cycle of the feeding of the multitudes, and that Luke, who does not give this group of incidents, has been obliged to invent an artificial introduction to the account of Peter's Confession.

Although the preceding observations make it seem probable that in the source which Mark followed the conversation at Caesarea Philippi was placed after the cycle of the feeding of the multitudes, and even that this interview may be placed in the period which followed immediately that of the feeding of the multitudes, still this does not prove that there is an organic connexion between the two incidents. In the Johannine record this connexion comes out quite clearly. After Jesus had uttered in the synagogue at Capernaum the discourse which had offended the Jews, the evangelist says:

From that time many of his disciples went back, and walked no more with him. Then said Jesus unto the Twelve, will ye also go away? Then Simon Peter answered him, Lord, to whom shall we go? Thou hast the words of eternal life. And we believe and are sure that Thou art that Christ, the Holy One of God (vi. 66–69).[1]

There is a direct connexion between this passage and the Synoptic narrative. Even when we allow for such Johannine expressions as "words of eternal life" or "we have believed and are sure," it is impossible to admit that the Johannine passage is derived from the Synoptic narrative. It is impossible to understand why the Fourth Gospel should not have reproduced the term "Christ," which it found in its source, in such a way that the Christological statement of its text would remain rather nearer to the Synoptic Gospels, nor why it

---

[1] Instead of "the Holy One of God," which is the best attested reading (‎‎אּ. B. C*. D. L.), the received text has: "the Christ, the Son of God" (C3. *Γ*. *Δ*. *Λ*., etc.); sy²., vg., arm., eth., etc. Tertullian confirms the reading "Christ"; *b* and syᶜ have "The Son of God." All the secondary readings may be explained by the desire to bring the passage in John into agreement with the statement of Peter in the Synoptic Gospels, as well as with the usual formulas of the Christian faith.

should have sacrificed the antithesis between the faith of the Twelve and the opinions which were current among the people on the subject of Jesus, and should have reduced it to a simple opposition between those who remained faithful to Jesus and those who deserted him. Thus in John vi. 66–69 we have a tradition which is independent of the Synoptic record of Peter's Confession, but is parallel to it and refers to the same incident. Thus the declaration which the apostle makes in the name of the Twelve, while it appears to be a statement of belief in Jesus, is really and mainly a declaration of personal attachment and loyalty. So at the very moment when Jesus is being pursued by Herod, and deserted by many of his disciples, Peter proclaims the undying attachment and loyalty of the Twelve. Thus the result of the Galilean crisis was that Jesus was left with a very small group of loyal and faithful disciples.

IV. THE INFLUENCE OF THE GALILEAN CRISIS ON THE THOUGHT OF JESUS

The declaration of Peter permits us to assume that a process of evolution has taken place in the thought of Jesus since the moment when he sent his disciples out on their first missionary journey. He now asks for attachment to his person, and not only for the acceptance of his message.

A message like that of Jesus could not have an effect on the souls of the hearers save in so far as the personality of the preacher inspired confidence. The more such a message penetrates into the hearts of those who hear, the greater is the influence of the messenger. From the very beginning of his ministry people were forced to regard Jesus in one of two ways. He might be regarded as a dreamer, a visionary, or an impostor, whose word commanded no respect, or, if people recognized in his word a divine message, they would have to admit that he was a messenger of God, at the very least a prophet. Those who gathered round him must have become quite as attached to his person as to his message. Then when Jesus called certain men to follow him, with the idea that he would make them co-workers in his cause and preachers of the Gospel, the impossibility of distinguishing clearly between

N

attachment to his message and attachment to his person was merely increased. As time went on circumstances strengthened the link between Jesus and the Gospel. When he became the object of the opposition of the Pharisees, to accept or to refuse his message meant deciding for or against him, and when Herod wished to kill him this necessity became still more evident. Thus it was no longer a question of taking a side in a theological controversy but of throwing oneself wholly on the side of Jesus or of denying him. Hence from that moment Jesus laid great emphasis on the importance of confessing him before men, and the seriousness of denying him (Matt. x. 32–33; Luke xii. 8–9; Mark viii. 38*). This also is why he felt that his ministry brought division among the people. Luke has preserved this saying:

I am come to send fire on the earth; and what will I, if it be already kindled? But I have a baptism to be baptized with; and how am I straitened till it be accomplished! Suppose ye that I am come to give peace on the earth? I tell you, Nay, but rather division: For from henceforth there shall be five in one house divided, three against two, and two against three. The father shall be divided against the son, and the son against the father; the mother against the daughter, and the daughter against the mother; the mother-in-law against her daughter-in-law, and the daughter-in-law against her mother-in-law (xii. 49–53).

Matthew gives the same passage in a rather more condensed form:

Think not that I am come to send peace on the earth: I came not to send peace, but a sword. For I am come to set a man at variance against his father, and the daughter against her mother, and the daughter-in-law against her mother-in-law. And a man's foes shall be those of his own household (x. 34–36).[1]

The phrase about baptism is peculiar to Luke and is suspect, especially if it be compared with the expression about baptism

---

[1] In Luke this declaration occurs in a group of sayings which have no obvious connexion with each other. In Matthew they form part of the missionary instructions, which, as we know, are considerably more developed in the first Gospel than in the others. It may come from the Logia, which would doubtless have preserved it as an isolated saying.

referring to the Passion in Mark x. 38. It seems to be an editorial addition. But verse 49 in Luke: "I am come to send fire on the earth . . ." seems to be primitive, for it is necessary in order to explain the expression, which sounds a little strange at first, about "not peace but a sword" in Matthew. We might therefore reconstruct this passage thus, which seems as though it may very well be authentic:

I am come to cast fire upon the earth and much I wish it were already alight. Do not think I am come to cast peace on the earth. I am come not to cast peace but the sword. . . .

This saying refers to the situation which arose at the moment that the determination of Herod to kill Jesus forced his disciples to be opposed if necessary even to the members of their own families.

Jesus said: "He that loveth father or mother more than me is not worthy of me: and he that loveth son or daughter more than me is not worthy of me" (Matt. x. 37). In speaking thus, Jesus was not condemning natural feeling. Could one who, in order to express the infinite love of God, could find no better image than that of the heavenly Father, have asked his disciples to kill their human affections? What Jesus meant to say, in a paradoxical form perhaps,[1] was that in the present crisis they must be ready to sacrifice all for him, or else they must leave him altogether.

We must therefore conclude that when Jesus required his followers to sacrifice everything for his sake, his own sense of vocation must have been not merely maintained but deepened during this crisis in his life. External circumstances alone do not explain how it was that Jesus came to place his own person in the very centre of the Gospel, and to declare that at his glorious advent the Son of Man would treat people according to their attitude towards himself, denying before

[1] Luke (xiv. 26) gives this saying in this form: "If any man come to me, and hate not his father, and mother, and wife, and children, and brethren, and sisters, yea, and his own life also, he cannot be my disciple." We cannot tell whether he has forced the terms which Jesus used or whether he has preserved the paradoxical form which Matthew may have weakened.

God those who were ashamed of him, and on the other hand confessing those who had confessed him before men (Matt. x. 32–33*; Mark viii. 38*). The link thus established between the Son of Man and Jesus implies, even if it does not directly state it, the feeling that Jesus knows that he is the Messiah for whom men were waiting. These words seem most relevant if we assume that they belong to a moment when Jesus is being pursued, and when, as a result, it compromises anyone to declare himself on his side; that is, the moment of the Galilean crisis.

A religious feeling (and the Messianic consciousness of Jesus is, in the highest degree, a religious feeling) may be encouraged or thwarted by circumstances, but in its essence it can only be explained by the existence of an interior energy; it issues from the deepest and most hidden sources of human personality, from those depths of consciousness of which the individual himself is often unconscious, in which the personality grows and takes shape. Whether such forces may be explained as the phenomena of auto-suggestion, or as the expression of the aspirations of the human conscience, or as intuitions which lie outside the usual ways of feeling and thinking, or again, as phenomena which can only be explained by that witness of the Spirit of God to the spirit of man of which the Epistle to the Romans speaks (viii. 16), is not a matter of great moment, for this question lies outside the province of the historian. We must leave the task of its solution to the psychologists and philosophers, although it is doubtful whether they can do this in a purely objective manner. All we can do here is to try to understand what took place in the soul of Jesus.

At the very beginning the Gospel brought with it a discovery of a moral order. The Kingdom of God, the condition in which the sovereignty of God will be unhindered by any obstacle, either in men or in things, is so precious that no one, even by the most thorough and logical repentance, could ever earn the right of admission. The entrance to the Kingdom can only be a gift of the love of this God whom Jesus conceives—without in any way denying or weakening in any degree his holiness and righteousness—in such a way that his most essential attributes are those of love and mercy. Jesus feels that he has been sent to bring the message of divine forgiveness to the lost sheep of the house of Israel. In order that men may receive this forgiveness they must repent and look for the Kingdom by realizing, henceforth, in their lives the divine perfection. At the outset, Jesus evidently thought that this liberating message, accompanied as it was by a display of saving power (like that of casting out the demons), would be welcomed with enthusiasm; the way in which he was welcomed at the beginning of his ministry encouraged this expectation. But soon difficulties arose, opposition began to gather strength, and even among those who had been attracted and won by his message he had to admit that the spirit of the Kingdom of God was very far from being the dominant factor. This experience reinforced and accentuated his sense of vocation and led him to think that his vocation was unique. As he watched his disciples he had to admit that even the best and the most convinced of them was not wholly dominated by the desire to obey God. People whose ideals are high are sometimes tempted to see reality only in the light of these ideals. But it was not so with Jesus. This idealist, who conceived human life as a realization of the divine perfection, was also a realist. He saw men as they were and judged them without leniency. He saw that evil lay not in external circumstances, but in the heart of man, whence come all sins and evil thoughts (Mark vii. 21–23). Yet in his own heart Jesus could find nothing of this kind. In his words there is nothing which could possibly be interpreted as a sense of sin or repentance. It is, of course, true that from the historical point of view we cannot assert the holiness of Jesus, primarily because this would not be a statement of fact but an affirmation of principle. Also we must remember that all the documents which we possess were compiled by men who believed in the holiness of Jesus. It is, however, significant that, although on some other points the words of Jesus present certain inconsistencies, in none of those which have come down to us can we find anything at all which can be construed as an expression of a sense of sin or penitence. When we remember that the moral consciousness of Jesus was extremely fine and sensitive, this statement assumes a very special importance. It is impossible that Jesus could not have known of the moral superiority which he possessed. This sense of moral purity must have helped him to believe in his unique vocation; and this must have led him to feel that he was not merely one of the children and messengers of God among many others, but that in a more absolute sense he was His Son and His messenger. This seems to be the first germ of his Messianic consciousness. Although the forms which it adopted and the formulas by which it was expressed may have been conditioned and determined by the ideas and conceptions of the time, it did nevertheless issue from the depths of his soul.

Although Jesus realized that he was not the only one to will the Kingdom of God, he felt that he alone willed it absolutely, accepting all the conditions it imposed, and that he alone subordinated everything else to it. When circumstances showed him that he could not for ever evade his enemies, and that the sufferings which formed part of his ministry were perhaps only the prelude and presage of sufferings far greater still, his faith in himself and his confidence in the fulfilment of the Kingdom of God were not diminished. He then realized that he could not attain his end as he had still believed he would when he sent out his disciples on their first mission, and he knew in the depths of his soul that he himself must pass through a period of desertion, humiliation, and suffering. Though we may have to admit that the triple announcement of the suffering, death, and resurrection of the Son of Man, which forms the outline of the second section of the Gospel story, has a certain theological bias, the declaration of Jesus in which, after having spoken of the Day of the Son of Man, he says: "But first must he suffer many things, and be rejected of this generation" (Luke xvii. 25), falls into an entirely different category. This saying cannot have been invented by tradition, for it does not mention death or resurrection. We do not know when it was uttered, but it does not seem probable that it could have been pronounced before the Galilean crisis. It expresses the result of the meditations of Jesus on the experience which began at the moment when he was hunted down by Herod, and deserted by many of his disciples. To regard this statement as something theoretical and purely ideological would be a very serious misunderstanding of the nature of the thought of Jesus. All that it affirms is that his sufferings will be efficacious. This statement is not an explanation like "The Son of Man is not come to be ministered unto, but to minister, and to give his life a ransom for many" (Mark x. 45*), or the giving of the broken bread as the symbol of the body of Jesus (Mark xiv. 22*). We have no right to introduce at this point doctrines of redemption which were only developed much later, from the point of view of belief in the Resurrection. Either we must regard these passages as non-authentic, which would be an arbitrary proceeding, or we must regard them simply as figures of speech.

The affirmation of the necessity for the sufferings of the Son of Man is a statement of fact and not of principle; this is why it is not accompanied by any kind of explanation. At the beginning of his ministry Jesus did not think that he would have to suffer and die. It was only during the course of the last evening, and at Gethsemane, that death, which many a time, doubtless, he had looked in the face, appeared inevitable. When he met suffering in the course of his life he accepted it from the hand of God. He did not believe that anything could happen apart from His will. Believing, as he did, that the hairs of our heads are all numbered, and that not a sparrow can fall to the ground apart from the Will of God (Matt. x. 29-30), he was still more sure that if *he* had to suffer, he, the Son of God, it was because God Himself willed it so. To him acceptance of suffering was an act of that obedience to God which summed up his whole conception of religion. At the same time, however, Jesus believed in the absolute wisdom of God, and, without knowing how, and even without needing to try to imagine it, he had the assurance that his sufferings formed part of the plan which God, in his infinite wisdom, had designed for the establishment of his Kingdom. This is something very different from a doctrine of redemption; this is not a theological system but simply a directly religious affirmation. Jesus might have evaded persecution and death. It would have been enough for him to retire to some remote village and keep quiet. This he did not do because he desired to remain faithful to his mission and to obey God.

Thus the sacrifice which Jesus accepted out of fidelity to his vocation reinforced the sense of vocation itself. So long as he believed that to be Messiah simply meant presiding over the glorious establishment of the Kingdom of God, he did not claim the title of Messiah. But from the moment when he realized that the Messiah must suffer, be humiliated, and rejected, he claimed the title of the Son of Man. The only honour he desired was that of being the suffering Messiah. Thus in his mind the mystery of the Messiahship and the mystery of suffering were indissolubly connected.

It is not difficult to understand why this was so. At the outset, when Jesus did not foresee that a tragic crisis would precede the coming of the Kingdom of God, he simply felt that he was called to prepare men for its coming; he did not realize that he himself was called to work for its coming. When obstacles began to block his way and he realized that it was part of his mission to be rejected, he did not despair of the fulfilment of God's purpose; he did not think that it would be realized in spite of his failure and in spite of his rejection, but by his sufferings and by his rejection. This was a direct result of his faith in the omnipotence of God.

Through the idea that his sufferings were necessary for the coming of the Kingdom of God, Jesus was led beyond the sense of a simple prophetic vocation and to regard himself, no longer simply as the herald of the Kingdom of God, but as the one who was to realize it himself, who, after having been humiliated and rejected, would appear as the glorious Son of Man. Thus this Messianic consciousness of Jesus appears as the triumph of faith over experience, of the ideal over reality; it was a faith which surged up from the depths of his being. This is why, as the human outlook became darker, this consciousness increased in force and certainty; this is why he declared it publicly and unequivocally before the Sanhedrin at the very moment when it was evident that his position was desperate. Jesus did not believe that he was the Messiah *although* he had to suffer; he believed that he was the Messiah *because* he had to suffer. This is the great paradox, the great originality, of his Gospel.

V. THE DEPARTURE FOR JERUSALEM

The Synoptic Gospels do not give a clear account of the conditions under which Jesus left Galilee in order to go to

Judaea. This is not due to the fact that the tradition has not preserved some clear recollection of this detail. Luke, in the central section peculiar to his Gospel, mentions this departure several times. But, very early, these memories became, if not effaced, at least confused and scattered, under the influence of the idea that Jesus went up to Jerusalem in order to accomplish the divine plan of his death. Even in Luke's time there was no homogeneous tradition, for the accounts which we find in his record of the departure of Jesus for Judaea are scattered throughout the narrative, and it is impossible to weld them into a coherent unity.

We must gather up these relics of the ancient tradition before we analyse the manner in which the evangelists represented to themselves the coming of Jesus to Jerusalem.

In Luke ix. 51–53 we read:

And it came to pass, when the time was come that he should be received up,[1] he steadfastly set his face to go to Jerusalem, and sent messengers before his face: and they went, and entered into a village of the Samaritans, to make ready for him. And they did not receive him, because his face was as though he would go to Jerusalem.

We must make a distinction between the incident itself and the way in which it is introduced. The latter is obviously due to the work of an editor; it gives a dogmatic reason for the journey to Jerusalem. The episode which is narrated implies that Jesus was going up to Jerusalem by way of Samaria. He is alone with his disciples, and the journey is not in the nature of a missionary tour. This aspect is not due to Luke himself, who considers—(the incidents which follow show this[2]) —that Jesus had not then given up, even for a time, the work

---

[1] That is to say, the moment when, according to the Divine plan, Jesus must die, was approaching.

[2] These are, first of all, the episodes relating to the disciple who wished to follow Jesus, but whom he rejected as being incapable of bearing the sacrifices which this vocation involves, and also to those whom Jesus called but who found excuses for refusing to obey (ix. 57–62). Then follows the sending out of the Seventy (x. 1–16). These two sections come from the Logia. The first has a parallel in Matt. viii. 19–22, the second is a doublet of the sending of the Twelve.

of preaching the Gospel, and was to be accompanied, up to the moment of his arrival in Jerusalem, by a crowd of hearers. His passage through Samaria does not seem to contradict the principle to which Jesus seems to have remained faithful to the very end of his ministry—that his message was addressed solely to Jews—because he is only passing through the country without stopping to work there. Jesus may have done this because if he had remained in Peraea he would have been exposed to the enmity of Herod.

Further on (xiii. 31–32) there comes an incident which has already been mentioned,[1] that of the Pharisees who counsel Jesus to depart because Herod intends to kill him. When he received this warning, Jesus was carrying on his ministry in Galilee; Luke has forgotten that he has already mentioned his departure for Jerusalem, due, as he says, to the fact that the time of his death was drawing near.

Is it perhaps possible that Luke has not quite caught the meaning of this incident? It looks rather like it, for he gives it in a series of incidents which show Jesus peacefully pursuing his ministry in Galilee, without any hint of danger or of the need for precaution. It is only in chapter xvii, in the account of the healing of the ten lepers (xvii. 11–19), that he seems to be once more on the road towards Jerusalem, but it is not certain that at that moment he had definitely left Galilee; he seems to be only on the borders of that province and of Samaria, and nearer Galilee than Samaria, since, of the lepers who were healed, there were nine Jews and only one Samaritan.

Luke does not seem to have considered the departure for Jerusalem (mentioned at the beginning of the account of the healing of the ten lepers) to be very important, since, directly afterwards, in xvii. 20 ff., he represents Jesus in conversation with the Pharisees. The incident might just as well have taken place in Judaea as in Galilee; it would have been impossible during the journey through Samaria.

Finally, at the beginning of the third prophecy of suffering, after he has taken up the thread of Mark's narrative once more, Luke reports this word of Jesus to his disciples: "Behold, we go up to Jerusalem" (xviii. 31).

Thus Luke knew some narratives which related either to

[1] See p. 350 ff.

the departure from Galilee or to the journey from Galilee to Jerusalem, through Samaria, but he has taken no trouble to connect them with each other. What he has preserved, however, is valuable, because it gives us some idea of the state of the early tradition before the Gospels were compiled.

The section of Mark's narrative which refers to the period in which Jesus left Galilee represents a grouping of incidents arranged in accordance with the system in the mind of the editor. We have already noted this fact in connexion with the way in which (in viii. 34) Jesus addresses the multitude, when he is supposed to be alone with his disciples on the road to Caesarea Philippi. After speaking to the crowd comes the incident of the Transfiguration (ix. 2–8), which, in order to be inserted at this point, has been detached from a cycle of incidents enclosed within a definite chronological setting. Although a return of Jesus into Galilee has not been reported since the moment when he was in the region of Caesarea Philippi, the healing of the boy who was possessed with an unclean spirit (ix. 14–29) is scarcely conceivable save in Galilee, at a spot where Jesus was carrying on a settled work. There follows a very brief allusion to a journey in Galilee, in the course of which Jesus did not wish to be recognized (ix. 30). What follows does not suggest a wandering ministry; here, therefore, this element is not due to the hand of an editor. The situation which is implied by this statement is exactly that which we found at the close of the cycle of the feeding of the multitudes, at the moment when Jesus was in danger owing to Herod's threats against his life.

After the second prophecy of suffering, Mark brings Jesus back to Capernaum (ix. 33) and reports a series of teachings which show that there he exercised a ministry of some duration. He tells of his departure, in verse 1 of chapter x, in the following terms:

And he arose from thence, and cometh into the coasts of Judaea by the farther side of Jordan:[1] and the people resort unto him again; and, as he was wont, he taught them again.

---

[1] We follow the reading of א. C., etc. The received text reads, with A. N. X., and the majority of the MSS.: "by the other bank of Jordan," thus Jesus

The contrast is striking between ix. 30, where Jesus is travelling about in Galilee, taking care that he should not be recognized, and this solemn departure for Judaea escorted by a large crowd, among whom there are also some Pharisees, who question him on the subject of divorce. As they go along, the group, composed of Jesus and his followers, attracts attention. Children are brought to him to be blessed (x. 13). A rich man comes, and, kneeling down before him, asks what he shall do that he may gain eternal life (x. 17). As Jesus enters Jericho, a blind man hears that "Jesus of Nazareth is passing by" and he begins to cry out: "Son of David! Jesus! have mercy upon me!" and Jesus heals him (x. 46–52);[1] finally the entry into Jerusalem, amid the shouts of those who accompanied him, assumes the character, if not exactly of a triumphal entry, at least of a Messianic entry (xi. 1–10); Jesus goes into the Temple, and acts with authority by casting out the people who sold and bought therein (xi. 15–19).

In the midst of this narrative comes the third prophecy of suffering, with its undertone of disaster. Mark (x. 32) introduces it thus:

And they were in the way going up to Jerusalem; and Jesus went before them: and they were amazed; and as they followed, they were afraid. And he took again the twelve, and began to tell them what things should happen unto him.

---

would have avoided Samaria and have passed by way of Peraea. The reading of the received text is a correction of that of ℵ. C., etc., which is difficult to understand, since it seems to place Judaea on the left bank of the Jordan. WELLHAUSEN (*Mk.*, p. 83) retains the reading of C². D. G. W. Δ. Θ., which have: "the Judaea of the other side of the Jordan," and thinks that this may be a description of the Peraea. But this expression does not occur elsewhere. Doubtless the text has been altered. It is probable that in a form which we cannot now reconstruct, Peraea was named in connexion with the departure of Jesus for Judaea. Jesus must, indeed, have reached Jerusalem by way of Peraea, since he passes through Jericho and Bethany.

[1] This feature is still more accentuated in the Lucan narrative. Luke places the healing of the blind man at the arrival at Jericho, and at the moment when Jesus leaves the town he places the story of Zacchaeus, who, because he was a short man and the crowd was dense, had to climb up into a sycamore-tree in order to see Jesus (xix. 3–4).

Here the journey up to Jerusalem is represented as a march to execution.

Thus through the narrative in the Synoptic Gospels we can trace three layers of tradition.

According to the first tradition, in order to escape more quickly from Herod, Jesus, in spite of the reserve which he exercised towards those who were not Jews, went through Samaria.[1] While he thought that it would be sufficient for him to leave Galilee for a short time he was able to find a refuge in the regions of the North. Then, when he knew that his native province was definitely closed to him, he felt that he must go to Judaea, in order to preach the Gospel in another district.

Another tradition represents Jesus as leaving Galilee without being forced to do so, simply because he wishes to extend his work.

A third tradition, finally, represents him as going up to Jerusalem to die, because it thus became him to fulfil the plan of God. Thus he went thither freely of his own accord to meet the destiny which he knew in advance would be his lot.

Alongside of these traditions we must place that which is attested by the source followed by John in chapter vii.:[2] Jesus, who is asked to go up to Jerusalem in order to make a Messianic demonstration, refuses, but goes up to Jerusalem later, in secret, οὐ φανερῶς ἀλλὰ ὡς ἐν κρυπτῷ, says the text, which does not mean concealing himself, since, although he left after the pilgrims who were going up to the Feast of Tabernacles, the moment he arrived in Jerusalem he began to preach in the Temple.

In the Johannine narrative, the departure for Judaea is not connected with the crisis provoked by the feeding of the multitudes. Although, according to John (who on this point

[1] There is no irreconcilable difficulty between the passage by Samaria mentioned by Luke (ix. 52) and the arrival in Peraea implied by him (xviii. 35), as by the two other Synoptists (Mark x. 46*). Jesus, dogged by the agents of Herod, may have gone into the Samaritan territory and then have passed along the left bank of the Jordan after he had thrown his pursuers off the scent. Mark may have omitted the passing through Samaria, which gave to the departure of Jesus the air of a flight, and not of a proceeding undertaken deliberately, of his own free will.

[2] See pp. 233 ff.

does not seem to have exactly understood what the source has said), the suggestion to go and work miracles at Jerusalem was made to Jesus by people who did not believe in his divine mission, this could only have taken place at a moment when Jesus had achieved a measure of success. Otherwise why should he be told that he cannot go on manifesting himself in secret, that is, in a remote province, but that he ought to go to Jerusalem in order that the disciples who are there may see the works which he does? But in the source the account of the departure of Jesus for Jerusalem may have been of a quite different character. The proposal to go to Jerusalem may have been made, not in a spirit of ironic hostility, but with the desire to see his work extended, and to summon him to a brilliant manifestation at Jerusalem which would efface the sense of defeat, or partial defeat, caused by his experience in Galilee. Understood in this sense, the content of the source would connect well with the situation created by the feeding of the multitudes and the events which followed. The handful of disciples which has remained faithful to Jesus has been somewhat affected by the events which have taken place. Peter and his companions are not beyond being attracted by the ideal of a victorious Messianism. Jesus knew this, since, at the moment when, after the feeding of the multitudes, the popular enthusiasm rose to fever heat, his first care was to send them away. Disappointed by the defeat suffered by their master, they desired to be reassured and confirmed in the confidence which they had in him, by a triumphant manifestation which they could no longer expect in Galilee but which they might yet hope to see in Jerusalem.

The source followed by John expresses definitely the idea that although Jesus obeyed, or appeared to obey, the suggestion which had been made to him, the reasons which caused him to accept this suggestion were quite different from those which had been put forward by the disciples. Jesus went up to Jerusalem, not in order to arouse a striking public manifestation, but simply in order to teach. The account in John says nothing more than that. In the phrase, "He went up . . . not openly, but as it were in secret" (vii. 10), we may perhaps recognize the relic of a tradition which had already been transposed in the source which John used. Originally Jesus may have had to leave secretly for the reasons which forced him to go away or conceal himself many a time during the last part of his ministry in Galilee when he was being hunted down by Herod.

A comparison of the various data which we have tried to discover by the analysis of the Gospel narratives relating to the departure of Jesus from Galilee enables us to discover the development of tradition on this point. Originally, people thought that Jesus had left Galilee owing to the hostility of Herod, and because the precautions which he had taken in order to be able to carry on his work proved insufficient. Soon, however, the Early Church could not be satisfied with this manner of presenting events; the Christians felt that something as important as going up to Jerusalem could not have been imposed upon Jesus by external constraint, and they felt uneasy at the suggestion that he had yielded to the threats of Herod. So they came to the conclusion that Jesus went up to Jerusalem either in order to continue his work of preaching in a more important sphere (this is John's account), or, in order to give himself up to a Messianic manifestation, to make a triumphal entry into the city, and to be welcomed there as the One who "cometh in the Name of the Lord." At the third stage, finally, it seemed that, in going up to Jerusalem, Jesus could not have been ignorant of what was going to happen there. Thus he left Galilee knowing that he would meet the Cross in the Holy City, and in consequence that in going up to Judaea he would fulfil the divine purpose. The triumphal march was then transformed into a march to execution; at the same time, all the details in the story which represent him as hoping that his message would win the hearts of the people of Jerusalem, or even as fleeing from Herod, have not been entirely effaced from the record.

CHAPTER XIV

THE JERUSALEM MINISTRY

As we have seen,[1] Jesus did not enter Jerusalem a few days before the Passover but at the Feast of Tabernacles, in the month of September or October; he stayed there till the Feast of the Dedication, in December. Then he went away into retirement in Peraea; at the same time he remained in touch with his disciples in Jerusalem; he did not return to the capital until a short time before the Passover, "six days before," says John (xii. 1), that is to say, about the same time as his arrival is placed by the Synoptists.[2]

The fact that the Synoptic Gospels have reduced the length of Jesus' ministry at Jerusalem almost to a minimum is due, doubtless, to the fact that they have confused the arrival of Jesus at Jerusalem with his return to the city. The consequence is that they have represented the activity of Jesus at Jerusalem as consisting almost entirely of a preparation for his Passion.

I. THE SYNOPTIC ACCOUNT OF THE JERUSALEM MINISTRY

Apart from the division into days, and the incident of the barren fig-tree, which are secondary elements, the Marcan narrative falls into three parts. Jesus begins his activity at Jerusalem by a public demonstration. He makes a solemn entry into the city and expels the sellers of merchandise from the Temple. These actions provoke the chief priests, the scribes, and the elders to make a protest; they ask him by what authority he has acted thus? Jesus replies by a question which puts his questioners in an embarrassing position (Mark xi. 1-33), then comes a series of fragments of a controversial character which explain how the conflict—provoked

[1] See Chapter VIII.

[2] According to Mark, the ministry of Jesus lasted three days; according to Matthew, two. To this two or three days we must add the day spent at Bethany (day of the Anointing). Luke does not give the division into days. His narrative, however, leaves the impression of a brief ministry in Jerusalem, though less brief than that of Matthew and Mark.

by the first acts of Jesus at Jerusalem—immediately becomes
so acute that the Jewish authorities decide to arrest him
(xii. 1–47*).[1] Here, as a sort of intermediate incident, stands
the story of the widow's mite (xii. 41–44),[2] given at this point
because it took place in the Temple.

The third part of the narrative is very different in character.
Jesus leaves the Temple; his public activity is over, and he is
alone with his disciples, to whom he announces the destruction
of the Temple (xiii. 1–4*), and speaks of the last things.
The discourse which he pronounces on this subject is known
by the name of the Synoptic Apocalypse (xiii. 5–37*).[3]

The construction of this narrative is unnatural. The accumulation of fragments of the same type reveals the work of a
compiler. The discussions, which serve to explain the rapidity
with which the drama of the Passion developed, do not all
actually belong to the period in Jerusalem.[4] Among them are
some which were originally included, not so much in order to
represent Jesus in conflict with the Jewish authorities, as to
show that although he had not received the instruction which
was given to educated rabbis he was able to hold his own in a

---

[1] Parable of the Husbandmen (xii. 1–12*), questions addressed to Jesus
on the payment of tribute money (xii. 13–17*), on the resurrection (xii.
18–27*), on the greatest commandment of all (xii. 28–34*), a question
put by Jesus himself on the Davidic ancestry of the Messiah (xii. 35–37*),
warnings against the Pharisees (xii. 38–40*). Matthew adds the parable of
the Two Sons (xxi. 28–32), and that of the Marriage Feast (xxii. 1–14),
which includes, in his Gospel, that of the Husbandmen. He also develops
further the warnings against the Pharisees (xxiii. 1–36).

[2] It is reproduced by Luke, but not by Matthew.

[3] In the form of a conclusion, Matthew adds here a series of fragments
which are peculiar to his Gospel, such as the parable of the Ten Virgins
(xxv. 1–13), and that of the Last Judgment (xxv. 31–46), and others
which have equivalents in Luke but at a different place: words about the
days of Noah (xxiv. 37–41; cf. Luke xvii. 26–27, 34–35), parables of the
master of the house who keeps watch (xxiv. 42–44; cf. Luke xii. 39–40),
of the good and bad servants (xxiv. 45–51; cf. Luke xii. 42–46), of the
talents (xxv. 14–30; cf. the parable of the pounds in Luke xix. 12–27).

[4] The question of the tribute money, on account of the part which the
Herodians play in it. Perhaps also the questions of the greatest commandment, which Luke, who has an earlier form of the passage, places at a
different point in the narrative.

discussion with the doctors of the Law, and that the most difficult questions could not embarrass him.[1]

The Synoptic Gospels represent Jesus in conflict with the Pharisees in Jerusalem; this is shown by the kind of teaching he gives which is emphasized still more by the use of invective directed against the Pharisees. The doublet in Luke, where these same invectives already appear in chapter xi, and the wider development which Matthew gives to this section, show that it comes from the Logia, and that originally it had been transmitted without any indication of time or place. Although, under these conditions, it is not possible to attach a great deal of importance to the words which serve as an introduction to this section: "and he said in his teaching" (xii. 38), we may note that they do not agree very well with the idea that Jesus did not actually teach at Jerusalem, but that he only answered questions which were put to him. The little incident of the widow's mite also shows that Jesus wished to teach and preach in Jerusalem and not merely to engage in controversy with the representatives of traditional Judaism.

In the last of the three parts which we have been able to distinguish in the narrative of the ministry at Jerusalem, the Synoptic Apocalypse is certainly non-authentic; it is also very awkwardly connected with the prophecy of the destruction of the Temple which serves as an introduction to it, since it is not a reply to the disciples' question: "When will this prophecy be fulfilled?" but to a quite different question: "What will be the signs which will announce the Coming of the Son of Man?"[2]

The announcement of the destruction of the Temple is not a prophecy *ex eventu*, since it is described as a destruction by some natural catastrophe like an earthquake, whereas in the year 70 the Temple was burnt. We cannot explain these words by supposing that Jesus had foreseen that a desperate conflict of a fatal character would break out between Rome and Jerusalem, and, knowing that the weight of physical force would be on the side of Rome, that the only possible end would be the defeat of the Jews, to whom the destruction of

---

[1] Discussions about the tribute money, the Resurrection, and the greatest commandment of all.

[2] See the Appendix to this chapter, pp. 425 ff.

their national sanctuary would be both the consequence and the symbol of this defeat. Jesus moved in a realm of thought which was too remote from political life for us to suppose that he would have foreseen all this. Besides, if he had done so, would he not have believed that the issue of the struggle depended wholly on the will of God? The announcement of the destruction of the Temple is not that of a disaster but of a chastisement. If the Temple must be destroyed, this is because it no longer serves its real purpose. Thus the announcement of the destruction of the Temple reveals a very great change in the thought of Jesus: his outlook is now quite different from that which inspired him when he protested against the profanation of the Temple courts by the presence of the sellers of merchandise. Then Jesus desired to see a reform which would restore the Temple to its true purpose; it is evidently because this appeal was not regarded that, despairing of his own nation, he announces the destruction of the Temple. The purification of the sanctuary with which the activity of Jesus in Jerusalem opens in the Synoptic narrative, and the announcement of its destruction by which it ends, are the two extremities of one line. The narrative does not explain how they are linked together, nor how it was that Jesus came to realize that the Jewish people would not listen to his appeal.

Matthew (xxiii. 37–39) and Luke (xiii. 34–35), the former at the moment when Jesus leaves the Temple for the last time, and the latter at a moment when he had not yet set foot in Jerusalem, have preserved this saying of Jesus:

O Jerusalem, Jerusalem, which killest the prophets, and stonest them that are sent unto thee; how often would I have gathered thy children together, as a hen doth gather her brood under her wings, and ye would not! Behold, your house is left unto you desolate: and verily I say unto you, Ye shall not see me until the time come when ye shall say, Blessed is he that cometh in the name of the Lord.

These words would be unintelligible if Jesus had not carried on a ministry of some length in Jerusalem, or if he had confined his efforts to discussion with the religious leaders. This passage alone is sufficient to show the artificial character of the Synoptic account of the Jerusalem ministry.

Further, the narrators seem to have had the feeling, even if they have only touched on it very lightly, that Jesus did give some regular teaching in Jerusalem. The final statement in Luke is couched in the following terms:

And in the day-time he was teaching in the Temple; and at night he went out, and abode in the mount that is called the mount of Olives. And all the people came early in the morning to him in the Temple, for to hear him (xxi. 37–38).

This statement comes from a source, for it is not really connected with that which precedes it. The idea that the crowd listened gladly to Jesus also occurs in Mark and in Matthew. After the account of the Cleansing of the Temple Mark says: "And the scribes and chief priests heard it,[1] and sought how they might destroy him: for they feared him, because all the people were astonished at his doctrine" (xi. 18).[2]

The idea that Jesus was so popular with the masses that the authorities were obliged to be very careful how they took action against him, occurs again in the story of the Passion; this explains why Jesus was arrested at night. This idea cannot be assigned to the editors, since the assumption underlying their narrative is that it was the cries of hatred from the people which drew from Pilate the condemnation of Jesus.[3] This suggestion comes from a tradition which is too solidly established to be eliminated. Further, apart from the idea of a ministry of teaching which had made a good deal of impression, it would be difficult to understand how it was that Jesus was

---

[1] The saying: "My house shall be called a house of prayer for all peoples, and you have made it a den of thieves."

[2] Matthew has omitted this saying, which led to the same result as the conclusion of the parable of the Vineyard (Mark xii. 12*). Luke has developed the remark, which in the second Gospel served as the conclusion to the incident of the cleansing of the Temple: "And he taught daily in the Temple. But the chief priests and the scribes and the chief of the people sought to destroy him. And could not find what they might do: for all the people were very attentive to hear him."

[3] This idea is not contradicted, in the whole story of the Passion, save by two small fragments in Luke (xxiii. 27–31, 48), which are awkwardly inserted in their context. On this, see further on pp. 470, 532 f.

able to find someone in Jerusalem who was ready to lend him the upper room for his last evening with his disciples (Mark xiv. 12 ff.*), or how it was that, at the moment of his arrest, there was in the Garden of Gethsemane a young man who did not belong to the group of the Twelve, and who was nearly arrested at the same time as Jesus (Mark xiv. 51–52); how also could the tradition have been formed which we find in Luke (xxiii. 27–31, 48), according to which the people as a whole regarded the death of Jesus as a great disaster? Finally, if the author or the editor of Acts had not known of a tradition which reported a period of teaching carried on by Jesus at Jerusalem, we cannot explain how he could say that immediately after the death of Jesus his disciples formed a group of about one hundred and twenty persons (i. 15).

The picture of the activity of Jesus at Jerusalem has been perverted in the Synoptic narratives, partly under the influence of the idea that Jesus only went up to Jerusalem to die and partly owing to the confusion by which Mark has reduced the length of the stay of Jesus in Jerusalem to a few days; this prevented him from conceiving the idea of an actual ministry of preaching, and led him to regard the time in Jerusalem simply as a period of preparation for the Passion.

II. The Johannine Narrative of the Jerusalem Ministry

The point of view regarding the ministry of Jesus in Jerusalem to which we are led by the analysis and criticism of the Synoptic narrative is confirmed by the data of the source which we have been able to discern behind chapter vii and the following chapters in the Gospel of John.[1] Here we see that before he entered Jerusalem, a few days before the Passover, Jesus had spent the closing months of the year 27 in the Holy City; even after he had gone away he remained in touch with the disciples whom he had gained during his brief ministry. According to this source his activity, in Jerusalem had some measure of success. Although it roused the hostility of the Jewish authorities, it also gained a certain number of disciples, and, so far as the masses of the people were concerned, he had

[1] See pp. 233 ff.

gained their sympathy to such an extent that the Pharisees and the scribes were obliged to take note of it, and this hindered them, even though they wished to do so, from taking violent measures against him.

In x. 22 we read: "And it was at Jerusalem, the feast of the Dedication, and it was winter. And Jesus walked in the Temple in Solomon's Porch." The detail "at Jerusalem" cannot come from the evangelist, nor from the source, both of which imply that Jesus has been at Jerusalem for three months past. Here, then, we are confronted with another tradition.

Nor can that which follows be assigned to the evangelist. The Jews surround Jesus, saying: "How long dost thou make us to doubt? If thou be the Christ, tell us plainly!" It is difficult to understand the point of this question after all the explicit Christological statements which have filled the preceding chapters. We are here confronted by a tradition according to which Jesus did not state his Messiahship directly, but acted and spoke in such a way that it led his hearers to ask themselves whether, after all, he might not be the Messiah?

The following points must also be assigned to the same source (or that which we have discovered in chapter vii), the attempt to stone Jesus mentioned in x. 31, and the attempt to arrest him in x. 39; Jesus escaped both these dangers. Verse 39 in particular: "Therefore they sought again to take him, but he escaped out of their hand," is necessary, in order to explain what is described in x. 40–42: Jesus went away to the other side of the Jordan, to the place where John at first used to baptize. Many people went out to him and believed in him; they said: "John did no miracle: but all things that John spake of this man were true" (x. 40–42). It is impossible to say that this is simply a literary artifice designed to place the arrival of Jesus at Jerusalem at the time of the Passover in order to be consistent with the Synoptic narrative. Indeed, we cannot charge John with the desire to make his narrative agree with that of the Synoptic Gospels, since he does not mention the public activity of Jesus between his solemn entry into the city and his arrest. When Jesus leaves Jerusalem it is on account of the hostility of the Jewish authorities, but he stays near the city, in contact with his friends within the walls, and he is evidently ready to resume his work there as soon as the atmosphere is sufficiently clear. This idea is in flagrant contradiction with the conception of the evangelist, according to which the life of Jesus follows a plan ordained by God. It is equally opposed to the idea of the Synoptic narrative. Thus it must come from a source early enough to be free from the domination of a theological idea.

III. The Johannine Narrative of the Last Visit of Jesus to Jerusalem

Although John, like the Synoptists, records that Jesus enters Jerusalem a few days before the Passover, he represents the situation in a totally different light. According to the Synoptic Gospels, Jesus is still unknown when he enters Jerusalem. The Cleansing of the Temple, the discussions which he holds with the representatives and leaders of traditional Judaism, the invective which he hurls at the Pharisees, cause the Jewish authorities to determine to take action against him; they decide to do this after the public activity of Jesus in Jerusalem is over (Mark xiv. 1–2). John also mentions a council (xi. 45–53), but, according to his narrative, this takes place before the return of Jesus to Jerusalem.

The Johannine account of the entry of Jesus into Jerusalem (xii. 12–19) is more restrained than that of the Synoptic Gospels. It is the crowd which, on its own initiative, gives Jesus an ovation, and makes him ride upon an ass, without any remembrance, at the moment, that in so doing the prophecy of Zechariah is being fulfilled.

When Jesus is thus welcomed to Jerusalem, the Pharisees say to one another: "Perceive ye how ye prevail nothing? Behold, the world is gone after him!" (xii. 19). This does not tally with the final decision of the authorities, nor with the order which had been issued for his arrest, mentioned in xi. 57; rather it implies that until that moment the efforts of the authorities had been confined merely to making some attempt to counteract the influence of Jesus. The presence of this statement in the narrative confirms us in thinking that the idea of a fixed decision to kill Jesus does not come from the evangelist himself, but that he has taken it from some original source.

The end of chapter xii is composed of material in which the editorial element has a large place. Some passages, however, come from earlier traditions. The section xii. 27–30, for instance, is certainly a transposition of the episode of Gethsemane as it is told in the Synoptic Gospels, adapted, however, to the special form of Christology peculiar to the fourth evangelist.

The incident of the Greeks who wished to see Jesus, which leads him to make a statement about the imminence and the fruitfulness of his death (xii. 20–26), is an expression of John's idea that the Gospel can only be preached outside Palestine after the Lord has been glorified. It is, however, possible that in order to construct this narrative John may have used a fragment of a tradition in which Jesus may have met some of the Jews of the Dispersion in Jerusalem. But in any case this early tradition is not clear enough to be very positive or to justify us in using it.

Save for the entry into the city, in which it is not Jesus who gives it the character of a Messianic demonstration, John does not report any public act of Jesus between his return to Jerusalem and his death. The incident of the Greeks seems even to indicate that in the mind of the evangelist the public activity of Jesus was already over.

The artificial character of this narrative is obvious. There is a contradiction between the decision taken by the Pharisees to arrest Jesus and the fact that he can stay at Bethany where "a great crowd of Jews went to see him" without any attempt being made to lay hands on him. It would be no less difficult to reconcile what is said about the design of the Jews with the entry into Jerusalem and with what is said at the close of the narrative about the remarks of the Pharisees, who admit that they are powerless to hinder the masses from following Jesus.

These confusing statements may be explained by the fact that the Johannine narrative combines the Synoptic tradition with another tradition, according to which Jesus was arrested the moment he returned to Jerusalem.

IV. The Nature of the Jerusalem Ministry of Jesus

In order to determine the nature of the ministry of Jesus in Jerusalem, we are not obliged to solve a problem. Neither the Synoptic narrative nor the Johannine narrative can be regarded, just as they are, as historical. Seeing that Jesus went twice to Jerusalem (during his public life), to which of these visits can we assign the solemn entry into the city, the Cleansing of the Temple, and the announcement of the future destruction of the Temple? Did the Jewish authorities decide to take action against Jesus before or after his return to Jerusalem? We cannot deal with these questions until we have tried to estimate the meaning and the value of the narratives in question.

In the Synoptic Gospels the entry into Jerusalem is the crowning event in those elements of the previous narrative which present the coming of Jesus into Judaea as the triumphant march of an aspirant to the Messiahship. When Jesus, escorted by his disciples, arrives in the neighbourhood of Jerusalem, at a point of which the tradition does not seem to have preserved an accurate recollection,[1] he sends two of his disciples into a village near at hand—none of the evangelists mention the name—telling them to bring an ass to him, and giving them the words with which they can tell the owners of the animal why they are taking it away, if they are asked. When the animal is brought, the disciples throw their garments upon it and then Jesus seats himself upon the animal's back. The evangelists seem to have seen a miracle in the fact that everything fell out exactly as Jesus had said it would. Thus in their

---

[1] The text of Mark is given in two different forms: (a) "When they approached from Jerusalem and from Bethany towards the Mount of Olives" (D. 700. a. b. c. ff. i. k. vg. Or.). (b) "When they approached from Jerusalem, from Bethphage, and from Bethany, towards the Mount of Olives" (א. A. B. C. D. Θ. min. sy^s. f. l. q.). The second reading has the most support, but it contains a geographical inconsistency: Bethany is situated about 15 stadii, or about 2½ miles from Jerusalem, whereas Bethphage, according to the Talmud, was at the gates of the city. Thus text (a) should be retained; the addition of the words "from Bethphage" can be explained by the influence of the text of Matthew, which only mentions Bethphage, and the text of Luke, which mentions Bethphage and Bethany.

minds the entry into Jerusalem was the fulfilment of a divine
plan. Many of the people spread their garments on the ground
as he passes by, and others strew branches before him which
they have torn down from the trees by the side of the road.
Those who go before Jesus and those who follow cry: "Hosanna!
Blessed be he that cometh in the name of the Lord! Blessed
be the kingdom of our father David, that cometh in the name
of the Lord: Hosanna in the highest!" This is a Messianic
demonstration in which Matthew and Luke make the meaning
still more clear by the words: "Hosanna to the Son of David!"
(Matt.), and "Blessed be he that cometh in the name of the
Lord!" (Luke); these ascriptions bring out the fact that it is
not only the Messianic kingdom which is being acclaimed, but
the Messianic King himself (Mark xi. 1-10*).

According to Matthew (xxi. 10-11), the whole city is agitated;
people ask: Who is this? And the crowd replies: "This is the
prophet Jesus, from Galilee." Luke (xix. 39-40) emphasizes
the significance of the episode in another way. Some Pharisees
who are in the crowd say to Jesus: "Master, rebuke thy
disciples!" Jesus replies: "I tell you that if these should hold
their peace, the stones would immediately cry out!" As is
explicitly stated by Matthew (xxi. 4-5), and suggested also by
John (xii. 14-16), tradition saw in this episode the fulfilment
of this prophecy of Zechariah ix. 9:

> Behold, thy King cometh unto thee:
> He is just and having salvation:
> Lowly, and riding upon an ass,
> And upon a colt, the foal of an ass.[1]

This correspondence with the prophecy does not prove that
the narrative was forged, because Jesus may have been inspired
by the passage in Zechariah to make his Messianic entry into
Jerusalem in this manner.

The Synoptic narrative is possibly not absolutely homogeneous; the details concerning the ass may have been added

---

[1] Matthew has emphasized, in a mechanical and awkward manner, the
agreement between the prophecy and the event by interpreting literally
the double expression: "the ass, the foal of that which bears the yoke,"
which is in the text of Zechariah, by saying that the disciples brought to
Jesus an ass and her colt and that he rode upon them.

later in order to explain—what an earlier form of the narrative may have not been concerned about at all—how it was that just at the moment when he needed it Jesus was able to procure the use of an ass. The contradictions and the vagueness of the narratives about the place where Jesus makes the start and the absence of any equivalent indication in John are favourable to this interpretation.

The people who acclaim Jesus appear to be those who have come up with him from Galilee. This is how Luke understands it: he makes the Pharisees say to Jesus: "Master, rebuke thy disciples!" Matthew has emphasized the significance of the incident by saying that when he entered Jerusalem, "all the city was moved, saying, 'Who is this?'" If this had been an actual triumphal entry this demonstration would not have been without result. Neither the Jewish authorities nor the Roman administration could have regarded it with unconcern. In point of fact, it did not spur them to take any kind of action; Jesus was not immediately arrested, and during his trial, neither before the Sanhedrin nor before Pilate was he ever charged with pretensions to the kingship manifested by his entry into Jerusalem. If the narrative has an historical foundation—and there does not seem to be any conclusive reason for doubting it—tradition has greatly accentuated its character; the manifestation to which Jesus allowed himself to be subjected must have passed unperceived in the midst of the crowd of pilgrims who were going up to Jerusalem. It had significance only for the disciples of Jesus; it confirmed them in their belief that Jesus was indeed returning to Jerusalem as the Messiah, but as a lowly and humble Messiah who laid no stress on outward prestige, but who, nevertheless, did not despair of making himself known.

John's account (xii. 12–19) is simpler than that of the Synoptists. Those who demonstrate are not those who had accompanied Jesus from Galilee; the initiative of this Messianic entry is not attributed to Jesus but to the crowd, which without realizing it fulfils a prophecy; this the disciples only discover later on. The crowd, which has heard that Jesus meant to come in from Bethany, takes palm branches and goes out to meet him, crying: "Hosanna! Blessed is the King of Israel that cometh in the name of the Lord!" "And Jesus, when he had found a young ass, sat thereon." The whole crowd proclaims that he has raised Lazarus from the dead. The Pharisees, as they witness the popularity of Jesus with the masses, state that all that they have done to check his influence has been entirely ineffective.

Since the story of Lazarus was not included in the earliest form of the Gospel, we must admit an editorial element in the explanation of the ovation received by Jesus. The secondary character of the allusion made to the Raising of Lazarus comes out in the place it occupies, which is right at the end of the narrative. It is superfluous, since it gives a double motive for the enthusiasm of the people. The reason why the entry into Jerusalem is told more briefly by John, and is represented as a spontaneous ovation, is because, according to John, Jesus did not act publicly at Jerusalem after the moment when he had left the city in order to retire into Peraea.[1]

In representing the ovation offered to Jesus as quite spontaneous, and by saying that its meaning was only perceived later, John seems to have transformed the tradition in order to make it agree with his idea that Jesus only returned to Jerusalem on the eve of the Passover in order to die and not to act. This fact permits him to place the ovation at the moment when he returns to the Holy City after his time of retirement in Peraea.[2]

In the narratives of Matthew and of Luke the entry into Jerusalem serves as a direct introduction to the incident of the Cleansing of the Temple. This is not the case in Mark, owing to the introduction of the first part of the episode of the fig-tree. The narrative, in its present form, is cut short,

[1] This transposition seems difficult to understand on the part of a later editor. This is the reason which prevents me from accepting the theory of WELLHAUSEN (*Das Evangelium Johannis*, Berlin, 1908, p. 56) and of SCHWARTZ (III, p. 176), who believe that the story of the entry into Jerusalem was not found in the original primitive form of the Gospel of John (*Grundschrift*), and that in the present state of the Synoptic narrative it is an interpolation.

[2] In support of this conclusion we can take note of the evidence from the source used in chapter vii in John. The fact that Jesus refused to come and allow himself to be made the hero of a Messianic demonstration in Jerusalem would not agree very well with the idea that his entry into the city was a public Messianic demonstration.

and, as we have said, Jesus enters Jerusalem as the Messiah, and visits the Temple like any other pilgrim. In John, the Cleansing of the Temple is placed at the very beginning of the ministry of Jesus (ii. 13–17) and the entry into Jerusalem at the close. The reasons for this dislocation are easy to grasp. According to the tradition, Jesus's action in driving out the sellers of animals and the money-changers was an outburst of indignation; it would be difficult to understand if Jesus had often seen these men carrying on their traffic in the Temple courts. The fact that John has not moved the account of the entry into Jerusalem to the beginning of the ministry of Jesus, at the same time as the Cleansing of the Temple, is due, doubtless, to the fact that he thought it impossible that Jesus could have been the object of a popular demonstration when he had only just arrived in Jerusalem as an unknown stranger; he would also be influenced by a very early tradition that the Messianic entry of Jesus had taken place a very short time before his death.

Mark (xi. 15–17) and Matthew (xxi. 12–13) give accounts of the scene in the Temple which, save for one or two details, are practically the same.

Mark says: "And Jesus went into the Temple, and began to cast out them that sold and bought in the Temple, and overthrew the tables of the money-changers, and the seats of them that sold doves;[1] and would not suffer that any man should carry any vessel through the Temple.[2] And he taught, saying unto them, Is it not written, My house shall be called of all nations the house of prayer? but ye have made it a den of thieves."

The arrangement of this narrative is not natural: the gesture of Jesus, and the words of comment on it, are separated by the

[1] The money-changers gave the pilgrims Tyrian money in exchange for their own coinage, as this was the only kind of money which was permitted to be placed in the Temple coffers (SCHÜRER, II, p. 259).

[2] The Sadducees, who were the masters of the Temple, allowed people to carry burdens through the Temple courts in order to avoid going a long way round. The Pharisees seem to have condemned this habit (see the passages cited by STRACK-BILLERBECK, II, p. 27). This detail does not occur in Matthew; he has omitted it, either because he considered that it broke up the story too much by separating the gesture of Jesus from the comment upon it, or because, not knowing the topography very well, he did not understand it.

remark that he forbade anyone to pass through the Temple carrying burdens. This detail, which is in itself perfectly comprehensible, and which betrays the same anxiety as the protest against the commerce in the Temple courts, breaks the organic connexion of the narrative. If it had been added later, it would have been placed either after the comment of Jesus or after his gesture of expulsion. The place which it occupies shows that the link between the gesture and the comment are not primitive; there must have been a tradition which told simply how Jesus drove the buyers and sellers out of the Temple, and also said that he prevented people from using the Temple simply as a right of way. The saying of Jesus, preserved at first by itself, may have been added later to the account of the action taken by Jesus against the traffic in the Temple courts.[1]

Matthew and Luke have connected the elements of the narrative better by omitting the remark referring to the use of the Temple as a right of way. Matthew has attached the saying more closely to the gesture by giving it a simpler introduction: "and he said unto them" (xxi. 13). Luke has combined the two elements and makes the saying a direct commentary on the gesture by condensing the account of the actual "Cleansing" itself. "And he began . . . to cast out them that sold therein and them that bought, saying unto them: It is written . . ." (xix. 45-46).

In John's account (ii. 14-16) the gesture of Jesus is more fully described; the saying is shorter:

And Jesus . . . found in the Temple those that sold oxen and sheep and doves, and the changers of money sitting; and when he had made a scourge of small cords, he drove them all out of the Temple, and the sheep and the oxen; and poured out the changers' money, and overthrew the tables; and said unto them that sold doves, Take these things hence; make not my Father's house an house of merchandise.

_____

[1] This conclusion is confirmed by the fact that the saying is introduced by a formula ("and he taught them and said unto them"), which fits in better with an independent saying than with the explanation of a gesture which has just been mentioned. Nor can we see clearly to whom Jesus is supposed to be speaking.

The central point in the incident, which in the Synoptic account oscillates between the gesture and the saying, is here concentrated on the gesture. The development of the account is, to some extent, artificial. If the detail of the scourge of small cords had been in the source Mark would have had no reason for omitting it. Thus John has embroidered the primitive story by speaking of the oxen and sheep, for, although we know that doves could be bought in the Temple, sheep and oxen could not be sold there.[1]

At the outset the record must have been a great deal simpler than it is now. Originally it would have said that Jesus protested against the presence of the sellers of merchandise and money-changers in the Temple. Quite naturally the saying of Jesus was transformed into an incident, and, at a third stage of development, the saying and the story to which it had given rise were combined.

If this be the right interpretation, if the only element in the story which can be regarded as historical is a saying of Jesus protesting against the profanation of the Temple, there is no reason why this saying should have been uttered at the very end of the ministry of Jesus, and the link which, in the Synoptic narrative, is established between the Messianic entry into Jerusalem and the condemnation of the trading in the Temple seems to be artificial. This conclusion explains why the Synoptists and John have been able to place the Cleansing of the Temple at two different moments in the ministry of Jesus.

According to John, when Jesus had driven out the sellers and buyers the Jews say to him: "What sign shewest thou unto us, seeing that thou doest these things?" and Jesus answers: "Destroy this temple, and in three days I will raise it up" (ii. 18–19). This saying, as we shall see later on,[2] was not imagined by the evangelists, but, originally, it meant something quite different from a veiled prophecy of the Resurrection.

There is a certain agreement between this request for a sign and a dialogue which the Synoptists have placed after

---

[1] DALMAN: *Itin.*, p. 382. The passages which STRACK-BILLERBECK (I, pp. 851 ff.) quote in order to prove the contrary are far from conclusive.
[2] See pp. 507 ff.

the account of the Cleansing of the Temple, without, however, connecting it organically with it. The chief priests, the scribes and the elders come to Jesus in the Temple and ask him :"By whose authority are you acting thus? Who gave you authority to do this?" Jesus replies by a question. He will answer them, he says, if they will first of all tell him what was the origin of the baptism of John. Jesus knows very well that this will place them in an awkward position, for they cannot attribute the baptism of John to either a divine or a human origin. In the first case, Jesus would reproach them with not having listened to the preaching of the Baptist, and in the second they would anger the masses, who regarded John as a prophet.

It seems, at first sight, as though the connexion established by John between the Cleansing of the Temple and the question put to Jesus occurs also in the Synoptic Gospels, although veiled in Mark and in Matthew, by being placed between the two sections of the return to Bethany and the episode of the fig-tree;[1] there is, however, no such connexion. In Mark the account of the Cleansing of the Temple has a conclusion :

And the scribes and the chief priests heard it,[2] and sought how they might destroy him : for they feared him, because all the people was astonished at his doctrine (xi. 18).

If Mark had known of a discussion about the Cleansing of the Temple, it is at this point that he would have reported it. Luke says almost the same thing, but he begins with this phrase : "He was teaching each day in the Temple."[3] Thus the beginning of the incident is presented also by him under conditions which prove that this incident had been transmitted to him as an isolated fragment :

And it came to pass that on one of those days, as he taught the people in the Temple, and preached the Gospel, the chief priests and the scribes came upon him, with the elders (xx. 1).

---

[1] In Mark only by the second part of the incident of the fig-tree.

[2] The saying of Jesus about the house of prayer being turned into a den of thieves.

[3] Luke has added this phrase in order to explain how it was that the people were able to admire some of the teaching of Jesus which had not been mentioned in Mark.

Thus the Cleansing of the Temple and the question addressed to Jesus are not organically connected, but are simply placed side by side.

The Synoptic Gospels and the Fourth Gospel do not present the reply of Jesus in the same way. If the Synoptic account here reproduces the primitive tradition, it is difficult to understand why John, instead of saying that Jesus had refused to answer, should have transposed an authentic saying by giving it a different meaning from that which it actually possessed. Can it be that he is here following an earlier tradition? The hypothesis would be presented in the following manner: the question addressed to Jesus would have referred to his teaching in general and to the mission which he said he had received from God. It would have been like that mentioned in John x.22 :

On the day of the Feast of the Dedication the Jews surrounded Jesus, asking him: "How long dost thou make us to doubt? If thou be the Christ, tell us plainly."

To the question addressed to him concerning the authority by which, and in the name of which, he acts, Jesus would have replied: "I will destroy the Temple, and I will rebuild it again in three days." The meaning of this reply would have been that the course of events, the collapse of Judaism and the coming, not merely of a new form of worship, but of the Kingdom of God, would be a brilliant manifestation of the divine origin and divine character of his mission. Very early this saying would have shocked the Christians, who could not believe that Jesus could ever have uttered it at all.[1] Under the influence of this sentiment, John would have given it a symbolical meaning which destroyed the point of the saying, and the Synoptists simply said that Jesus evaded the necessity for a reply, thus reducing a dialogue of primary importance to the level of a simple controversial discussion in which Jesus displays a dialectical skill which is greater than that of his opponents.

If Jesus had announced the destruction of the Temple and its reconstruction, that is to say, the destruction of Judaism and the coming of a new religious order, would not this saying have been, from the point of view of the Jews, a blasphemy?

[1] This will be proved later, pp. 507 ff.

o

Would it not have meant that Jesus would have immediately been arrested? The reading of the narratives of Mark and Matthew concerning the appearance of Jesus before the Sanhedrin gives the impression that the witnesses—or the false witnesses—who report the sayings of Jesus concerning the destruction of the Temple are making public a statement which had been made in private. This last objection has very little weight, since Mark and Matthew are convinced that this saying has only been attributed to Jesus by false witnesses. As for the fact that Jesus was not immediately arrested, this can be explained for a reason which is often mentioned in the Gospels, and in which it is impossible to see merely a suggestion of the later editor, and that is that Jesus was so popular with the masses that an attempt to arrest him might have provoked such an outburst on the part of the people that the Jewish authorities felt they must avoid it at all costs.

If the entry into Jerusalem was only a Messianic demonstration to the disciples of Jesus, if the Cleansing of the Temple was simply a protest against the traffic in the Temple, and if the question addressed to Jesus about the authority by which he acted is independent of the episodes which precede it in the Synoptic narrative, the connexion which has been supposed to exist between these three incidents exists only in the minds of the narrators. This raises the question: at what moment, when Jesus was questioned by his enemies, did he utter the saying which was to lead to his condemnation? This saying amounted to a declaration of war upon Judaism; after he had uttered it, it was impossible for Jesus to carry on his public ministry in Jerusalem any longer. He may have uttered it at the close of his first visit, just before he went to Peraea for solitude, or at the moment of his return, and it would then have led to his arrest. The analogy between the question put to Jesus according to the Synoptic Gospels and that which is reported by John x. 22 makes us lean towards the former hypothesis. The two questions: "If thou be the Christ, tell us plainly!" and "By what authority do you do these things?" are only variants of the same question. Jesus is questioned about his mission. According to the Synoptic Gospels he replies by making an appeal to the revelation which the future will bring. The final drama which is imminent will be the proof of his mission. According to John he invokes the testimony of his works (x. 25). Here we can perceive a theological idea of the evangelist who could not invoke the final drama since he spiritualizes and in actual fact eliminates the eschatology. In reality, Jesus could not give a more direct answer, since he did not feel that he was the Messiah but simply that he ought to be the Messiah in the future.

We still have to examine the prophecy of the destruction of the Temple reported in Mark xiii. 1-2*. We have seen that it cannot be considered as a prophecy *ex eventu*, and that it is not the foreshadowing of a disaster but the announcement of a chastisement. It expresses the same idea as the saying about the destruction of the Temple, with this difference, however, that Jesus does not assign to himself any part in the disappearance of the Temple. The attitude which he adopts may be compared with that of the peasant who was called Jesus, son of Ananias, who, four years before the beginning of the war, that is, in 62, while the city was still at peace, appeared in the Temple at the Feast of Tabernacles and began to cry aloud: "Voice of the East! Voice of the West! Voice of the four winds! Voice against Jerusalem and against the sanctuary! Voice against husbands and wives! Voice against all the people!" As he repeated his warnings night and day, in the end he was taken before the Procurator, who was then a man named Albinus. The latter had him cruelly scourged without being able to extract from him a tear or a plea for mercy. At each blow he repeated: "Woe to Jerusalem!" Albinus, convinced that the man was mad, set him at liberty, and Jesus, son of Ananias, again began to pour out his maledictions, and from that time forward no one disturbed him.[1] We can see from this example that to announce a disaster which would come upon Jerusalem was neither a blasphemy nor a crime. A person who uttered such a prophecy might be considered tiresome. If he were too insistent he might be accused of disturbing public order, but even then he would not be treated as a blasphemer, but simply handed over to the Roman tribunal.

[1] JOSEPHUS: *J.W.*, VI, 5, 3, ¶¶ 300 ff.

The particular point in this saying for which his enemies condemned him was his declaration that it was he who would destroy the Temple. The parallelism between this saying and the prophecy of Mark xiii. 1-2, which might very well be simply a modified variant of the declaration of Jesus that he would destroy the Temple, is therefore only apparent.

The account of the Jerusalem ministry of Jesus has therefore undergone a good deal of alteration in John, because the theological ideas of the evangelist replace the teaching given by Jesus; in the Synoptic Gospels, because (the perspective of the stay of Jesus in the city having been foreshortened and the ministry thus reduced to a few days) the sojourn in Jerusalem is conceived solely as a period of preparation for the Passion. Under these conditions it is not possible to give, properly speaking, an account of what took place in Jerusalem. All that we can do is to try to outline the main course of events, and to estimate their significance and their results.

When Jesus had been forced to leave Galilee, owing to the hostility of Herod, his faith in his mission was undisturbed, his certainty of the near fulfilment of the Kingdom of God had not been in any way modified, but he had realized that the difficulties and obstacles which he would meet would be greater than he had at first foreseen. He was forced to admit that not only were the political authorities unfriendly, especially at such a critical period of change and transition, towards those who gained any kind of influence over the masses, but on the other hand his experiences connected with the feeding of the multitudes had shown him that the masses were still strongly attached to the ideals of political Messianism, to the hope and expectation of a Jewish kingdom which would be achieved by violence and the crushing defeat of the enemies of Israel. The new order which they expected, and to which they gave the name of the Kingdom of God, was not new, save in the sense that it was conceived as a reversal of a situation in which the power would pass from the hands of the oppressors into those of the oppressed. To the mind of Jesus such a Kingdom, even if it had been realized, would still have been merely the perpetuation of the old order; he regarded the old order as bad, and he condemned it, because so long as it continued to be dominant it meant that the relations of men with each other would continue to be dominated by violence. Jesus was obliged to admit that among his disciples there were few who were really open to the idea of a revolution which would change men's hearts; this, he felt, was the only real way of revolution, since the heart is the central point in the life of man; if this central kernel, now the source of all kinds of sin and impurity, were cleansed and filled with the ideal of a perfect obedience to God which would make them able to accept every kind of sacrifice, then the Kingdom of God would truly come.

It was certainly with the sense of the difficulties of his task and the personal dangers to which he would be exposed that Jesus set out for Judaea, escorted by the small group of his disciples and a few women. He did not go up to Jerusalem to die, but he knew that his own life was the pledge of the group, which had enlisted under his leadership, in conditions which, if not desperate, were at least very menacing. He had already offered his life in advance. He knew that before his glorious day of triumph would arrive the Son of Man must suffer many things and that he would be rejected by this generation (Luke xvii. 25). He anticipated that the inhabitants of Jerusalem would remain deaf to his words just as the contemporaries of Noah had allowed themselves to be suddenly overtaken by the Flood in spite of the warnings of the patriarch.

At Jerusalem, which he reached at the beginning of the Feast of Tabernacles, the preaching of Jesus produced effects similar to those which it had had in Galilee. The people were impressed; they regarded Jesus as a prophet. When he spoke in the Temple, the people crowded to hear him. Very soon Jesus became popular. But this success was not exactly what he desired or sought, for Jerusalem had not been really captured by his teaching. He did not feel that he had been able to "gather his children as a hen gathereth her chickens under her wings."

Incomplete though it was, however, the success of Jesus aroused the hostility of the traditional representatives of Judaism, both that of the Sadducee priests, whom he accused of profaning the Temple whose sanctity they ought to have preserved, and that of the doctors of the Law, the Pharisees, whom he did not spare in his preaching, denouncing both the hypocrisy and inconsistency of their conduct, and that superstitious veneration of the letter of the Law and of the tradition which made them misunderstand the clearest teaching of the Scriptures.

At the outset, doubtless, the adversaries of Jesus thought that they would soon get the better of him, and that they would find it easy to worst him completely in argument owing to their dialectical skill and the superiority of their theological training. Under the pretence of deferring to his authority as a teacher inspired by God, they submitted delicate questions to him which the rabbis were accustomed to discuss at great length. They thought that he would reply in such a way that they would be able to confute him by showing that he had not foreseen all the possible difficulties which might arise, nor make all the distinctions in which the subtlety of the rabbis excelled. They thought also that his replies would appear rather weak because he would not know how to buttress them with opinions drawn from the teaching of venerated rabbis. Though Jesus had not been educated by the rabbis, he had a sense of spiritual reality, a gift of going straight to the heart of a situation, and a natural good sense, which enabled him to discern the intentions of his questioners and to frustrate their purposes. Among the controversial dialogues which tradition has preserved for us there may be some unequal elements. If we compare Luke x. 25–28 with Mark xii. 28–34, we can see that here a wise saying of a scribe has been attributed to Jesus, and it is not impossible that this may have happened in other instances where the material at our disposal does not enable us to discern this. Nevertheless, the fact remains that, on the level of dialectical discussion, although he used different weapons from those of his enemies, Jesus succeeded in frustrating their attempts and in discrediting them in the eyes of the people.

The hostility of the Pharisees and Sadducees to Jesus was not due merely to low and interested motives. They did not oppose him simply as a rival. The sincerity of their sentiments in opposing him ought not to be doubted. What he said about the tradition, for instance, or the way of observing the commandments, seemed to them scandalous, and the way in which he spoke of God and invoked His authority in order to justify his teaching was in their eyes a blasphemy. If Jesus really cast out demons, cured the sick, pardoned sinners, welcomed publicans and people of immoral life at Jerusalem as he did in Galilee—which in our opinion there is no doubt he did—this also must have shocked the Pharisees and the Sadducees, and they must have had the feeling that it was their duty to oppose him with all their might. This explains why it was that Jesus was perpetually being watched, and that when his enemies were quite sure that he really was a heretic, they resolved to nail him down, and extract from him a statement which would show them definitely what position they ought to take towards him. This is why they asked him whether he were the Messiah, or (this comes to the same thing) by what authority he spoke and acted as he did. It was then that Jesus is said to have stated that he would destroy the Temple and rebuild it in three days, that is, that Judaism had had its day and that all that yet remained for it was to wait for the judgment of God and the new order which would follow. Perhaps Jesus may already have expressed beforehand (by the parable of the labourers in the vineyard (Mark xii. 1–12)) the idea that Judaism was spiritually hopeless. It is probably not a pure chance that in the Synoptic Gospels this parable follows immediately after the episode of the question put to Jesus. In its present form it is a transparent allegory of the death of Jesus, of the preaching of the Gospel to the heathen, and of the destruction of Jerusalem. It went through an editor's hands after the year 70, but its basic idea may be due to Jesus; the fact that it expresses the same ideas as the saying about the destruction of the Temple and its rebuilding is one reason for thinking thus.

Thus the ministry of Jesus in Jerusalem culminated in a rupture with Judaism. When this had occurred there was nothing for it but to leave the city as speedily as possible and take refuge in Peraea. It was doubtless at the moment when he was leaving the city that, as Luke tells us, he wept over it (xix. 41), and that he uttered these words: "O Jerusalem, Jerusalem, thou that killest the prophets, and stonest them which are sent unto thee,[1] how often would I have gathered thy children together, even as a hen gathereth her chickens under her wings, and ye would not!" (Matt. xxiii. 37*).

The words of Jesus over Jerusalem terminate in Matthew and in Luke with these words: "I say unto you, Ye shall not see me henceforth till ye shall say, Blessed is he that cometh in the name of the Lord" (Matt. xxiii. 39*). In the thought of the evangelists this Day is that of the *parousia*. But this was not the original meaning, for in the mind of Jesus the *parousia* was a menace to unbelievers, and Jerusalem was unbelieving. There is a striking similarity between the words: "Ye shall say: Blessed is he that cometh in the name of the Lord," and the Messianic demonstration at the return of Jesus to Jerusalem. It seems fairly clear that a form of tradition must have existed in which this saying was an announcement of the return of Jesus to Jerusalem. Thus at the very moment when he was leaving Jerusalem he intended to return as soon as circumstances should seem favourable. He hoped that the masses of the people, already influenced by his preaching, would come out boldly for him, and that, supported by the popular enthusiasm, he would be able to brave the opposition of the authorities.

Jesus chose the time of the Passover to make his supreme attempt; perhaps he hoped that the great numbers of pilgrims and the presence of his disciples from Galilee would aid in

[1] According to John (x. 31), when Jesus had replied to the question: "If thou be the Messiah tell us plainly?" the Jews took up stones to stone him, then they tried to arrest him, but he managed to escape (x. 39). Another attempt to stone him is mentioned in viii. 59. These two points in the Fourth Gospel are not sufficiently circumstantial for us to rely on them with any certainty. The thwarting of the attempts against the life of Jesus illustrates one of the apostle's favourite ideas, namely, that the death of Jesus was not due to the hatred of his enemies, but was the fulfilment of the Divine design. It took place at the appointed hour; all previous attempts were abortive. These reasons are sufficiently strong for us to conclude that we cannot regard it as certain that people did try to stone Jesus. They are not sufficient to prove, however, that the idea of these attempts is simply a creation of John himself. If one of these attempts did actually take place, the words, "that stonest them that are sent unto thee," in the lament of Jesus over Jerusalem, would have a very concrete significance.

bringing this popular movement into being, and that a change of feeling would take place in his favour. He organized his arrival in Jerusalem in such a way that it formed a fulfilment of the prophecy of Zechariah. Thus, in his own eyes, as in those of his disciples, this entry into the Holy City was the act of a future Messiah. But in the midst of the thronging crowds the demonstration passed almost unobserved. Did Jesus then intend to resume his work of preaching and teaching? This would not have been impossible, but we have no light on this point. In any case, even if, on the day after his entry into Jerusalem, Jesus had intended to resume his work of preaching, he could not even begin to carry out this intention. The story of the Last Supper implies a situation in which Jesus knew that no further activity was possible. At that moment his enemies had closed in on him in a circle, from which, he felt sure, it would be impossible to escape. During his absence they had not been idle. Under conditions of which the details are beyond our knowledge, but whose main outline it is not difficult to reconstruct, they had gained the ear of Pilate. By representing Jesus as the possible leader of a popular movement, they succeeded in persuading Pilate to take action against him. Only a day or two after his return to Jerusalem, during the night, Jesus was arrested on the Mount of Olives, in the Garden of Gethsemane. The swiftness with which events then moved proves that, although there was a semblance of a legal trial, his doom had already been sealed.

Appendix. The Synoptic Apocalypse

While the authentic words of Jesus reported in Luke xvii. 20 ff. represent the day of the Son of Man as coming suddenly and instantaneously like a flash of lightning, in a way which it would be impossible to foresee, the Synoptic Apocalypse (Mark xiii. 3–37*) describes a series of signs which would be the forerunners of the *parousia*, which is thus represented as the conclusion of a whole drama. This fact, taken by itself, would not force us to regard the Synoptic Apocalypse as non-authentic, for the thought of Jesus may have oscillated between an apocalyptic conception and one which was not apocalyptic. Or it may have evolved in such a way that it could either free itself from the apocalyptic idea or return to it. The artificial character of the connexion between the announcement of the destruction of the Temple and the eschatological discourse does not prove, either, that of the two sections one must necessarily be non-authentic. They may both be authentic, but they may have been linked together by an editor. We must estimate the authenticity of this fragment from an entirely different point of view.[1]

In Mark xiii. 14 the fact which is to mark the culminating point of the crisis, the fact which will determine the faithful to flee as swiftly as possible from Jerusalem and from Judaea, is described in these terms: "the abomination of desolation . . . standing where it ought not." Matthew (xxiv. 15) uses the same expression, and adds further that it is that of which the prophet Daniel has spoken, and instead of "where it ought not," he has: "in the Holy Place." Luke's version (xxi. 20) is quite different: "And when ye shall see Jerusalem compassed with armies, then know that the desolation thereof is nigh." Then follows, as in Mark, the advice to flee from Jerusalem (21-23); at the end of the section is a prophecy which is linked very closely to the announcement of the siege: "And they shall fall by the edge of the sword, and shall be led away captive into all nations, and Jerusalem shall be trodden down of the Gentiles, until the times of the Gentiles be fulfilled" (24). These lines can only have been written between the year 66, —at the moment when the revolt broke out, when it might have been foreseen that, sooner or later, the Romans would bring up their troops and force Jerusalem to surrender—and the spring of the year 70, that is, the moment when the preparations for the siege were beginning, but when it was still possible for those who were inside the city to leave it. If this passage were written after the year 70, it would have mentioned the total destruction, and not a temporary occupation of Jerusalem by the Gentiles. Nor would an author writing considerably after 70 have been able to establish an organic connexion between the siege of Jerusalem and the *parousia* of the Son of Man. This conclusion, of course, only applies to Luke's version. If it were primitive, we would be obliged to conclude that Mark's version had been adapted during a

[1] See *Intr.*, I, pp. 301 ff.

period when sufficient time had elapsed to enable Christians to admit that the fall of Jerusalem was not the "sign" which preceded the *parousia*. Matthew may have used a copy worked over by Mark, and Luke may have used a copy of his earlier form.[1] If this were so, the non-authenticity of the Synoptic Apocalypse would be proved. But another hypothesis is possible: namely, that under the impression of the events of the year 70, Luke, in writing his Gospel, may have replaced "the abomination of desolation" by an allusion to the siege. In this case the question of the authenticity of the passage would remain open. Piganiol[2] is in favour of this second hypothesis. He understands the expression, "the abomination of desolation," in the concrete sense in which it is employed in the passage in the Book of Daniel (xii. 11), where it is used for the first time. There it refers to the statue of Zeus which Antiochus Epiphanes had erected in the Temple. In the Synoptic Apocalypse Piganiol relates it to the statue of Caligula which in the year 40 the legate of Syria, Petronius, had received instructions to erect in the Temple of Jerusalem. We know that the affair did not materialize. The Jews protested so violently that Petronius consented to allow a delay, and to refer the matter to the Emperor, who did not withdraw his instructions. Then came the death of Caligula and the project was abandoned.[3] It is to this unexpected deliverance that these words are believed to refer in the passage in Mark: "And except that the Lord had shortened those days, no flesh could be saved: but for the elect's sake whom he hath chosen, he hath shortened the days" (xiii. 20). The link which Piganiol believes he has discovered does not exist. In the year 40 there was no crisis provoked by the profanation of the Temple; there was some danger of a crisis, but this was dispelled, first of all by the decision of Petronius to refer the matter to Rome, and finally by the death of the Emperor. The text of Mark,

[1] The conclusions to which we have come concerning the incident of the barren fig-tree, the anointing and the division of the Jerusalem ministry into days are favourable to this hypothesis.

[2] A. PIGANIOL: *Observations de la date de l'Apocalypse synoptique, R.h.p.r.,* IV, 1924, pp. 245–249.

[3] On this matter, see JOSEPHUS: *A.J.*, XVIII, 8, 2–9, 261–309. *G.J.*, II, 10, 1–5, 184–203. PHILO: *Legatio ad Cajum*, 30–43 (ed. MANGEY, II, pp. 575–595).

on the contrary, refers to something positive. There is thus no concrete fact with which it is possible to identify the abomination of desolation of which Mark speaks; we must therefore regard it simply as an apocalyptic idea which had become traditional under the influence of the text of Daniel.

There are several reasons for regarding the formula of Mark as an adaptation of the primitive text preserved by Luke. It is easy to understand that a passage which was originally conceived from the Jewish point of view (which is the case in that of Luke) may have been altered in such a way that it would acquire a more general significance (which is the case in Mark) where "all flesh" is mentioned (xiii. 20). Further, there is in Mark a preoccupation which does not appear in Luke and which characterizes a comparatively late period, i.e. that which is meant to calm the impatience of the readers. Mark says that the beginning of the sufferings is not yet the end (xiii. 7). In xiii. 21-23 he puts the Christians on their guard against the false Christs and false prophets who will exploit the sentiment of the faithful that the end is near. In his conclusion, finally, Mark has this characteristic expression: "But of that day and that hour knoweth no man, no, not the angels which are in heaven, neither the Son, but the Father" (Mark xiii. 32).

Thus the earliest form of the Synoptic Apocalypse is found in Luke, and this form dates from the period which preceded the siege of Jerusalem. It has been suggested that this may be the prophecy mentioned by Eusebius (*Eccl. Hist.*, III, 5, 3) on the authority of which the Christians left Jerusalem at the beginning of the war in order to take refuge outside Jewish territory, at Pella in Peraea, which enabled them to remain outside the conflict between the Jews and the Romans. This hypothesis is ingenious, but it breaks down at two points. The first objection is this: that in the Synoptic Apocalypse there is nothing which refers to the relations of the Christians with the Jews. The second is: that if we leave out the sections which, occurring as they do only in one or two of the three versions we possess, are strongly suspected of being additions made under the influence of the Logia, there is nothing specifically Christian in the Apocalypse at all, which inclines us to think that it may be of Jewish origin.

CHAPTER XV

THE DAY OF THE LAST SUPPER AND THE DATE OF THE DEATH OF JESUS

ACCORDING to the Synoptic Gospels (Mark xiv. 12–16*), on the eve of his death Jesus is said to have given two of his disciples instructions to prepare the Paschal Feast which he desired to celebrate that evening.[1] This would mean that he was crucified on the 15th of Nisan. According to the Fourth Gospel, the Jews who led Jesus to Pilate did not enter the Praetorium lest they should be defiled and therefore unable to eat the Passover (xviii. 28). This implies that the trial of Jesus took place not on the 15th but on the 14th of Nisan. Few chronological problems have been more ardently discussed than this one, which is caused by the apparent discrepancy between these two accounts. It would be easy to fill a large volume with an account of all the theories which have been proposed and discussed in the attempt to reconcile these two pieces of conflicting evidence.

First of all, let us define clearly the meaning and the character of the two pieces of evidence before us.

The day on which Jesus sends two disciples to Bethany in order to prepare the meal is described by Mark as the first day of unleavened bread, the day on which the Passover lamb is sacrificed. This is the 14th of Nisan. This meal should be taken on the evening of the first day, that is to say (since the Jews reckoned the beginning of the day from the appearance of the first star), at the beginning of the 15th of Nisan. At the end of the day of the 14th, Jesus arrives and sits down to

---

[1] Jesus tells them to follow a man whom they will meet carrying a pitcher of water. In the mind of Mark this seems to be a miraculous encounter. Matthew did not understand it thus; he makes Jesus say: "Go . . . to such a man." There is a striking parallelism, extending even to the actual words, between the sending of the disciples who were told to prepare the Last Supper and the sending of those who, in xi. 2–3, are to lead to Jesus the ass on which he will make his entry into Jerusalem. This fact makes it probable that we are here confronted with an editorial element.

table with his disciples. Judging from the hour at which this meal is taken it ought to be the Paschal Feast; however, in the account given by Mark and Matthew there is not a single feature which refers to the ritual of the Passover; there is no mention of a lamb, and, during the meal, Jesus distributes to his disciples some bread, which, since it is described by the ordinary word for bread, cannot have been unleavened bread,[1] the only kind which was allowed to be eaten at the Passover Feast and on the following days of the Festival.[2]

In Luke's Gospel, at the moment when he sat down to table, Jesus said to his disciples:

With desire I have desired to eat this Passover with you before I suffer: for I say unto you, I will not any more eat thereof, until it be fulfilled in the Kingdom of God (xxii. 15–16).

The majority of exegetes, interpreting this saying in the light of the preceding section, take this to mean that the Passover which Jesus is about to celebrate will not be followed by any other. But the negative phrase in verse 16 is absolute. Jesus does not say: "I will not eat another," but "I will not any more eat thereof," and this phrase would have no meaning if, after it had been uttered, Jesus had immediately contradicted it.[3]

Further, in the record of the events which follow the Supper,

---

[1] The word ἄρτος being a general term might, in theory, be used to describe all kinds of bread, including bread that has not been leavened. It would, however, be surprising, and more than that, if in an account of a Paschal Feast the technical term of ἄζυμα were not employed, since the evangelists knew it, and took for granted that it was known by their readers, since when they use it they do not give any explanation.

[2] Mark (xiv. 26) and Matthew (xxvi. 30) say that before leaving the upper room Jesus and his disciples sang together. It has been suggested that this would be the last part of the song of Hallel (Psa. cxiii–cxviii) by which the Paschal Feast was concluded. Although BEER (ed. and trans. of the treatise *Pesachim*, Giessen, 1912, p. 99) objects that in the LXX the verb *hallal* is translated by αἰνεῖν and not by ὑμνεῖν (the term which occurs in Mark and Matthew), the interpretation which sees here the Song of Hallel cannot be excluded, but it may refer to any other psalm, and it would be very extraordinary if Jesus and his disciples did not sing the psalms on any other occasion than on that of the Passover.

[3] BURKITT and BROOKE: *St. Luke xxii. 15–16. What is the general meaning?* *Journal of Theological Studies*, July 1908, pp. 569 ff.

there is no direct chronological indication in any one of the three Synoptic Gospels; it is, however, difficult to imagine that the comings and goings of the Jewish authorities (which the narrative of the trial of Jesus implies) could have taken place on the 15th of Nisan, the great day of the Feast, which was celebrated by a Sabbath observance of the strictest kind.

From the introduction to the account of the burial we conclude that, according to the Synoptic Gospels, Jesus died on a Friday, the day of the Preparation (*paraskeuè*), which is the eve of the Sabbath (Mark xv. 42).[1]

Finally, the Synoptic Gospels all agree in making the discovery of the empty tomb, which took place on the third day, happen on the first day of the week, that is to say, on the second day after the death of Jesus.

Thus the Synoptic Gospels present clear and united evidence in support of that tradition that the death of Jesus occurred on a Friday; the evidence for the day of the month is not so clear. Regarded as a whole, the narrative seems to suggest that Jesus did not die on a Feast day. On the other hand, the episode of the preparation of the Last Supper, which gives the repast a Paschàl character, implies that Jesus died on the 15th of Nisan, the great day of the Feast, the first day of unleavened bread.

The evidence of the Fourth Gospel for the date of the death of Jesus is more homogeneous. At the beginning of the account of the last evening John says: "Before the Feast of the Passover" (xiii. 1). This evening, therefore, is not that on which the 15th of Nisan began.

In the account of the trial of Jesus, it is said that the members of the Sanhedrin did not enter into the Praetorium in order that they might not be defiled, but might be able to eat the Passover (xviii. 28). In order to achieve agreement it has sometimes been claimed that here the word Passover does not

---

[1] Luke (xxiii. 54) gives the same indication at the end of the account of the burial. Matthew does not mention the day at this point, but in the incident which follows he says: "The next day, that followed the day of the preparation (*paraskeuè*)." This variety of ways of introducing the time of the burial, which is characteristic of the three Synoptic Gospels, suggests that it may only have been introduced as a secondary element.

mean the Paschal Lamb but the *Chagiga*, that is to say, the sacrifice which was offered during the whole course of the Feast of Unleavened Bread and especially on the 15th of Nisan. In Deut. xvi. 2 and 2 Chron. xxxv. 7, the word *pesah* is actually used in connexion with all the sacrifices offered during the Paschal period. But, in these two passages, the sense is clearly indicated by the context, and, as Strack-Billerbeck have observed (II, p. 839), in a book like the Fourth Gospel, which was written for Gentile Christians, the word Passover, without any explanation, could only be applied to the lamb or to the Paschal Feast. Therefore John xviii. 28 shows clearly that Jesus died before the 15th of Nisan.

A more precise indication is found in xix. 14. When Pilate presents Jesus to the Jews as their king, the evangelist notes that it was the eve (*paraskeuè, παρασκευή*) of the Passover, about the sixth hour (noon).

The term *paraskeuè* occurs again in xix. 31, but there in the sense of the eve of the Sabbath. Thus, according to John, the year that Jesus died, the 15th of Nisan fell on a Sabbath Day (xix. 42, xx. 1, 19).

Thus we are here confronted with two traditions; both say that Jesus died on a Friday, but according to the one, he celebrated the Paschal Feast on the evening preceding his death, according to the other, this repast was celebrated on the following day.

We will not enumerate the many attempts which have been made to harmonize these two traditions;[1] to give some idea of their content, it will be sufficient to discuss briefly those which have been suggested with great ingenuity and erudition by Chwolson[2] and, more recently, by Billerbeck.[3] These two

---

[1] See MAURICE GOGUEL: *Sources*, pp. 15 ff.

[2] CHWOLSON: *Das Letzte Passamahl Jesu-Christi und der Tag seines Todes nach den in Uebereinstimmung gebrachten Berichten der Synoptiker und des Evangeliums Johannis*, St. Petersburg, 1892.

[3] STRACK-BILLERBECK: *Exkurs: Der Todestag Jesu*, II, pp. 812–853. BILLERBECK thus expresses himself: "A real divergence of view in the tradition concerning the day of the death of Jesus in the earliest form of Christianity seems to us incredible (*will uns undenkbar scheinen*). A solution must be found (*Es muss sich eine Lösung finden lassen*) which will lead to this result: we

authors admit that, in certain instances when the 15th of Nisan fell on a Sabbath Day (Chwolson), or when there were differences of opinion as to the day on which the month began (Billerbeck), the Pharisees and the Sadducees did not celebrate the Passover on the same day. It is suggested that Jesus may have accepted the theory of the Pharisees and may have celebrated the Paschal Feast on the Thursday. The members of the Sanhedrin who accused him before Pilate, and who belonged to the Sadducee party, would not celebrate the Feast until the Friday. Even if we could be sure that these different theories were already developed in the time of Jesus, the system of the Sadducees alone had any practical value. They were the masters of the Temple, and they controlled all that had to do with the sacrifices of lambs or kids at the Passover. Even if the Pharisees had considered that the Passover ought to be celebrated on a different day from that which had been fixed by the Sadducees, they would not have been allowed to follow their convictions. They would have been obliged to celebrate the Passover like the Sadducees, or else they would have been forced to abstain from celebrating it altogether, which they certainly would not have done.

Thus it is impossible to reconcile the traditions represented by the Synoptic Gospels on the one hand, and by the Fourth Gospel on the other. We cannot harmonize them; we must, therefore, choose one or the other. Two reasons have convinced me that I ought to regard the tradition which fixes the death of Jesus on the 14th of Nisan as the earlier of the two. The first reason is this: that the other tradition is only represented by one passage, in which one of the essential elements, the account of the preparation of the Passover, is suspect on account of the parallelism which it presents with the sending of the disciples with instructions to fetch the ass. The second, which is more conclusive, is that it is very easy to understand how it was that the last meal of Jesus came to be regarded as a

must interpret John in the light of the Synoptic Gospels, not the Synoptics in the light of John; but the Synoptic Gospels are right, and John is right" (p. 845). One could not find a more ingenuous way of revealing the fact that one is approaching the problem with preconceived ideas about its solution, and that one is dominated by a theological principle.

Paschal Feast. Very early, Christian thought tried to find a theological interpretation of the death of Christ, and in so doing it was led to regard it as a sacrifice. Owing to the time of year at which it took place it was only natural that it should have been assimilated to the Paschal sacrifice. Paul himself says: "Christ our Passover is sacrificed for us" (1 Cor. v. 7). This is only a figure of speech, for nowhere, so far as we know, has the apostle developed a theory on this point. However, the Corinthians, who were nearly all of Gentile origin, would not have understood the exhortation of the apostle if his teaching had not already rendered them familiar with the idea of Christ as the Paschal Lamb.

This idea recurs in the Fourth Gospel in the incident in which, after Jesus had died, the soldiers did not break his legs as they did those of his companions in suffering; they merely pierced his side with a lance; John says that this took place, "that the scripture should be fulfilled, 'A bone of him shall not be broken'" (xix. 36). The text which is here quoted (Exod. xii. 46; cf. Num. ix. 12) refers to the Paschal Lamb.[1]

The Eucharistic bread representing the body of the Lord, and the assimilation of the death of Christ to the sacrifice of the Paschal lamb, would lead to the assimilation of the Christian rite of Communion to the Paschal feast; the history of the liturgy shows that this assimilation took place. Since it was felt that the Communion Service repeated what took place at the Last Supper of Jesus, it was quite natural to arrive at the idea that this Last Supper was Paschal in character. Thus the idea grew up that Jesus had celebrated the Passover with his disciples before he died, although tradition had preserved the recollection that he had died on the 14th of Nisan.

According to the four Gospels, Jesus died on a Friday, a day of *paraskeuè*. This explains the haste with which the body was laid in the tomb. According to John, this *paraskeuè* was the eve of the Passover and also a Sabbath day. The year that

---

[1] The assimilation of the death of Jesus to the immolation of the Paschal Lamb is not related to a theological conception peculiar to the fourth evangelist, since, in his mind, the redemptive significance of the death of Christ is not connected with the idea of sacrifice, but with that of the return of the Lord in heavenly glory.

Jesus died, the 14th of Nisan may have been a Friday, but the idea that the day of the death of Jesus was both a *paraskeuè* of the Sabbath and of the Passover may have been created in the Synoptic tradition in order to reconcile the death of Jesus on the 15th of Nisan with the fact that the following day was a day of Sabbath rest. Thus the idea of the death of Jesus on a Friday may have passed into the Fourth Gospel from the Synoptic accounts of the Burial and the Resurrection.

This idea seems to be confirmed by the tradition which has placed the Resurrection on the third day, the morning of the first day of the week. The two statements are actually closely connected. The questions of the growth of the tradition of the third day and the real origin of the Christian Sunday are extremely obscure. Here it is enough to observe that although the tradition relating to the third day may be early, since it is confirmed by its mention in 1 Cor. xv. 4, it is not primitive. In the expression "after three days," which occurs in Mark (viii. 31, ix. 31, x. 34), and, still more clearly, in the phrase preserved by Matthew: "For as Jonas was three days and three nights in the whale's belly; so shall the Son of Man be three days and three nights in the heart of the earth" (Matt. xii. 40), there is a more archaic conception, according to which the body of Jesus remained in the tomb longer than from the Friday evening to the Sunday morning. This statement takes away all value from the confirmation of the death of Jesus on a Friday which seemed, at first sight, to provide the tradition of the third day. On the contrary, it suggests that the idea of fixing the date of the death of Jesus on a Friday may have been deduced from two ideas whose origin remains shrouded in much obscurity: these are, the fixing of the Resurrection of Jesus on the morning of the third day and its commemoration on the first day of the week.

Can we at least regard it as settled that Jesus died on the 14th of Nisan? This fact is not attested directly save in the Fourth Gospel. The idea of the Synoptic narrative, that the day after the death of Jesus was a day of Sabbath repose, may have been created in order to explain why the women did not go to the tomb of Jesus on the next day, but only on the day after that, as is required by the theory of the

Resurrection on the third day; and the haste with which the burial of Jesus had taken place might be justified on the score of the anxiety which the disciples felt lest they should transgress the rule laid down in Deuteronomy (xxiv. 15), which forbids the sun to set on the body of one who has been executed. This explanation cannot be pressed, but the simple fact that it is possible is sufficient to prove that the idea that Jesus died on the 14th of Nisan cannot be accepted with any certainty of accuracy. All that seems actually certain is that Jesus died about the time of the Feast of the Passover.

How can this conclusion be reconciled with the chronological data of the statement by which the account of the Passion is opened in the Synoptic Gospels? "The Passover," says Mark, "and the feast of unleavened bread was after two days." The Jewish authorities assembled in council and decided that Jesus must die, but they wished to take him by stratagem and not to allow him to die during the Feast lest this should lead to an outbreak among the people (Mark xiv. 1–2*). This brings us to a point two days before the Passover, that is, therefore, the 13th of Nisan. The intention of the Jews not to kill Jesus during the festival may be understood in two ways: either he must be killed before the festival or they must wait until it is over. It is possible to imagine that some unforeseen circumstance having arisen, such as, in this particular case, the offer made by Judas to betray his master into their hands, the Jewish authorities may have modified their original intention, and, in order that he should not escape out of their hands, they may have decided to kill him during the festival. This hypothesis, however, must be rejected, since although it is said that the proposal of Judas made the Jewish authorities glad (Mark xiv. 11), we do not learn that it led them to modify their plans. The person who edited Mark xiv. 1–2 thought that Jesus did not die during the Feast. As it is not said that he died later, his statement confirms our conclusion that the tradition which was followed by the Synoptists, save in the account of the preparation of the Last Supper, represented the death of Jesus as having taken place before the 15th of Nisan.

Can we regard the tradition from which the statement in

Mark xiv. 1–2 has been drawn as absolutely reliable from the chronological point of view? This seems doubtful. Apart from the fact (to which we will return later) that the Fourth Gospel places the decision to kill Jesus considerably earlier, we must note that in the Synoptic Gospels there is only the mention of one project, whose realization depends on the conjunction of favourable circumstances, since the Jewish authorities seem to be very anxious to prevent a popular outbreak at all costs. In Mark xiv. 11 it is said, likewise, that from the moment that Judas came to terms with the Jewish authorities he sought a favourable moment to betray him. This cannot be reconciled very easily with the idea that the execution took place immediately after the sentence, and leads us to assign to the editor these words: "The Passover and the feast of unleavened bread were after two days." When these words are omitted, which the evangelist introduced in order to establish a logical chronological scheme of three days[1] leading to the death on the 15th of Nisan, the statement of Mark xiv. 1–2 merely tells us that Jesus died before the Festival, but without saying on which day.

[1] First day, 13 Nisan: council meeting of the authorities. Judas's offer. Anointing at Bethany. Second day, 14 Nisan: preparation of the Paschal Feast. Third day, 15 Nisan: the Last Supper. Arrest. Trial. Execution.

CHAPTER XVI

THE LAST EVENING IN THE LIFE OF JESUS

At the moment when he returned to Jerusalem after his retreat in Peraea, Jesus still hoped that the people would range themselves on his side, and that thus he would be able to resume his preaching, in spite of the opposition of the Jewish authorities. This hope was not fulfilled. The Messianic entry into Jerusalem was scarcely observed, and only meant something to the little group of disciples who accompanied him, and to the disciples whom he had already won in Jerusalem, with whom, according to John (x. 41), he remained in contact during his retreat in Peraea. Jesus, however, did not go far away from Jerusalem, but simply remained outside the city: at Bethany, according to the tradition which has been followed by Mark, Matthew, and John,[1] on the Mount of Olives, according to that followed by Luke (xxi. 37); the latter seems the more reliable tradition, since not only does Luke say (xxii. 39) that Jesus often slept out on this hill, but John also says that Jesus and his disciples often went there together (xviii. 3).

I. The Last Meeting of Jesus with His Disciples

A few hours before he was arrested, Jesus returned to Jerusalem, taking care, however, that he should not be recognized.[2] Bertram[3] wonders whether, after all, the last meeting of Jesus with his disciples may not have taken place at Bethany, and suggests that a trace of this fact may still remain in the incident of the Anointing (Mark xiv. 3–9*). The transfer of the meal to Jerusalem would be made when it was regarded as a Paschal Feast; this would take place later, since the Passover could be

---

[1] Perhaps, as KUNDSIN (pp. 46 ff.) suggests, because Bethany had become a Christian centre of some importance.

[2] We may infer this from the account of the preparations for the meal (Mark xiv. 12–16*), although, as a whole, this passage may be due to the hand of an editor.

[3] BERTRAM: *Leidensgeschichte*, p. 16.

celebrated nowhere save in Jerusalem itself. There are several reasons which make it impossible to accept this hypothesis. The story of the Anointing is completely isolated, and it seems difficult to base any theory upon it.[1] Further, if Jesus had been in the habit of spending the evenings at Bethany it would be difficult to understand how it was that he was arrested during the night at the gates of Jerusalem. It seems that Jesus returned to Jerusalem in order that he might meet his disciples who lived in the city, with whom he had arranged a trysting-place in an upper room placed at his disposal by one of them.[2]

The Gospel narrative implies, it is true, that the Twelve[3] alone

[1] See further on, Appendix I, pp. 454 ff.

[2] The Gospels say absolutely nothing about the part of Jerusalem in which this house was situated. Evidently they are not interested in identifying the house where the Last Supper was held, which proves that at the time when they were writing, this question was not considered particularly important. Later tradition was less detached (see, on this point, ABEL, II, pp. 421 ff., 441 ff. DALMAN: *Itin.*, pp. 412 ff.). Perhaps from the beginning of the fourth century, but very probably only from the sixth century, it was identified with the Cenacle, which at first seems to have been regarded as the place where the apostles assembled after the Ascension (Acts i. 13), with the upper room of the Last Supper, although the term used in the Acts (ὑπερῷον) differs from that used in the Gospels (ἀνάγαιον). The Vulgate renders these two words by *coenaculum*. Tradition has claimed to have discovered the site of the Cenacle on the south-west of the city, on the western hill, at a place which was within the walls of Jerusalem at the time of Jesus, but which was left outside the walls of the Aelia Capitolina. There was erected the Church of Holy Zion, surnamed the mother of churches, erected between 337 and 347 by the Bishop Maximus. According to Epiphanius (*De mensuris et ponderibus*, 14) a little church stood there which had survived the destruction of the year 70. Later, the Cenacle was identified with the house of the Apostle John, in which he had received the Virgin Mary (John xix. 27). It is there that she is said to have died; also the Church of Holy Zion was also called the *Dormitio Beatae Virginis*. It is easy to see how these traditions have developed. The identification of the upper room with that of the apostles led to its being regarded as the house in which Mary lived, the mother of John-Mark, in which the Church in Jerusalem was assembled at the time of the miraculous deliverance of Peter (Acts xii. 12). This house, in its turn, was confused with that of the Apostle John, in which he is said to have received the Virgin Mary. There is here such a tangle of hypotheses that it is impossible to base any theory upon them.

[3] According to the Synoptic Gospels, Judas also was present (Mark xiv. 17*). However, in Gethsemane he arrives at the head of the band which

were present at the Last Supper, but there are some hints in
the tradition which permit us to assume that the limitation
of the number of the participants at the Last Supper to the
Twelve reflects the idea that members of the Church alone
may receive the Eucharist.[1] Cleopas, who is not one of the
Twelve, recognizes Jesus when he breaks bread at Emmaus
(Luke xxiv. 30–31; cf. 18). This incident can only have been
composed at a moment when the idea existed that it was
not only the apostles who were there when Jesus distributed
the elements at the institution of the Communion rite. It is
also possible—we shall return to this point later—that the
young man who, according to Mark (xiv. 50–51), fled at the
moment when Jesus was arrested, leaving his garment in the
hands of the soldiers, may have followed Jesus from the upper
room. According to the Apostolic Constitutions,[2] Martha and
Mary were there also. The part assigned to the women at the
moment of the burial of Jesus and of the discovery of the empty
tomb permits us to suppose that here too there is the echo
of a very early tradition. Finally, we may remember that a
fragment of the Gospel of the Hebrews preserved by Saint
Jerome (*De viris inll.*, 2) implies the presence of James, the
brother of Jesus, at the Last Supper.

According to Mark and Matthew, at the beginning of the meal
Jesus began by saying that one of his disciples would betray
him. Luke and John, who report the same incident, place it,
the one after the distribution of the bread and the wine, the
other after the washing of the feet of the disciples, which takes
the place of the Communion in the Johannine narrative.

According to Mark (xiv. 18–21), Jesus declared to his disciples
that one of them, who was sharing the meal with him, would

comes to arrest Jesus (Mark xiv. 43*). John has dispelled this inconsistency
by saying that Judas went out after Jesus had given him the sop (xiii. 30).
The uncertainty on this point makes us think that the earliest tradition
was inaccurate, and this is not favourable to the idea that the Twelve alone
were present at the Last Supper.

[1] This comes out very clearly in JUSTIN MARTYR (*Apol.*, I, 66), who says
that Jesus gave the bread and the wine to the apostles only; this, however,
does not exclude the possibility, but rather implies it, that there were also
other people present.

[2] HARNACK: *Die Lehre der Zwölf Apostel* (*T.U.*, II, 2), Leipzig, 1889, p. 236.

betray him. One after the other the disciples say: "Is it I?" and Jesus replies: "It is one that dippeth with me in the dish." There is no indication of the impression produced by the prophecy, whether on the disciples in general or, in particular, upon the one to whom it refers, hence the expression "he that dippeth with me in the dish" cannot refer to a gesture being made at that moment. Thus Jesus does not answer the disciples' question. He simply repeats his prophecy in another form. Thus the primitive tradition can only have preserved a saying of Jesus proclaiming that one of his own comrades would betray him. The language used leads us to think that this saying was pronounced during the course of a meal.

The account in Luke (xxii. 21–23), which is more condensed than that of Mark, also contains only one announcement of the betrayal. Matthew (xxvi. 21–25) follows the narrative of Mark fairly closely, but adds a conclusion which changes its character. Judas asks: "Master, is it I?" and Jesus replies: "Thou hast said." John (xiii. 18–30) seems to have known the two traditions, and he has reconciled them by placing the precise designation of the traitor in an aside. The beloved disciple alone, and perhaps Peter, at whose suggestion he has questioned Jesus, know that the remark is aimed at Judas. In John, the announcement of the treachery is made by quoting this verse from Psalm xli: "He that eateth bread with me hath lifted up his heel against me" (Psa. xli. 9). The Synoptic Gospels also mention a prophecy, but without making a definite quotation.

Originally the tradition of the announcement of the treachery of Judas seems to have been simply a sentence of Jesus saying that one of those who ate habitually with him would betray him; the image used was taken literally, and the incident was said to have taken place at a certain meal. This would probably be the source of the text of Mark and Luke, which John also would have followed in xiii. 18–22, while the idea that the destiny of the Son of Man had been announced beforehand was made more definite by using a quotation from the Old Testament. Matthew would have added the detail concerning the traitor, and finally, John, in order to combine the two ideas of the announcement of the betrayal and the disclosure of the name of the traitor, may have invented an aside in which Jesus was able to reveal to the beloved disciple the name of the traitor (xiii. 23–30). The fact that Jesus was betrayed by one of his own disciples may have given birth to the story of the announcement of the treachery. This hypothesis would be convincing if we were dealing with some event which could not be foreseen, but this is not the case. An act like that of Judas is the result of a long preparatory process, and in the attitude of the hesitating and disappointed disciple Jesus would have been able to note signs which would have roused his suspicions. Perhaps the absence of Judas from the upper room revealed to him that the act which he feared might take place had been accomplished.

Was it at the beginning of the meal, as is suggested by Mark and Matthew, or a little later, as Luke and John say, that, according to the most ancient tradition, Jesus spoke of the treachery of one of his own disciples? The order suggested by Mark is the one to be preferred. Although the distribution of the bread and the wine shows that Jesus is very conscious that his death is imminent, this is not directly stated. The disciples could not understand the state of mind of their master until they knew what was in his mind. It is easy to understand the reasons for which Luke and John have placed the announcement of the treachery after the distribution of the bread and the wine, or after the washing of the disciples' feet. Luke may have wished to place the Supper in relief by placing it at the beginning of the narrative because, in the account of the meal in the upper room, he reported incidents that Mark and Matthew do not mention (the saying about the two swords), or that they give elsewhere (the dispute about precedence, the announcement of the scattering of the disciples and of the denial of Peter); if it had kept the position it occupies in Mark it might have run the risk of being merely one incident among several others. In John the announcement of the treachery, which ends with the departure of Judas, has been put at the beginning of the account in order that during the washing of the feet and the last supreme words of teaching Jesus should have none save his faithful disciples with him.

II. THE LAST SUPPER[1]

In the view of the Synoptists the distribution of bread and wine by Jesus constitutes the culminating point in the story of the last evening. We have three testimonies to this fact,[2] those of Mark (xiv. 22–55), of Luke (xxii. 15–20),[3] and of Paul (1 Cor. xi. 23–25).[4] The Fourth Gospel does not report the distribution of the bread and the wine, but it has a kind of equivalent in the scene of the washing of the feet of the disciples by Jesus.[5]

Bultmann and Bertram[6] have argued that originally the narrative of the Last Supper was an independent fragment. It is

---

[1] We are studying the question of the Communion simply from the point of view of the life of Jesus, reserving for Vol. II the study of the relation between the Last Supper and the Eucharist in the Early Church. In reality the two problems are inseparable, and one aspect of the justification for my conclusions can only be given later. Meanwhile, I would refer the reader to the works which I have already published on this question: *L'eucharistie. La relation du dernier repas de Jésus dans 1 Cor. xi et la tradition historique chez l'apôtre Paul, R.h.p.r.*, X, 1930, pp. 61–69.

[2] We shall not take into consideration those of Matthew (xxvi. 26–29) and of Justin (*Apol.*, I, 66, 3). The first is only the reproduction of the text of Mark, with some variants, clearly secondary in character, of which the following are the principal: instead of saying, like Mark, that all the disciples drink, Matthew puts into the mouth of Jesus the words: "Drink ye all of it," which makes a more complete parallelism with the command "Take, eat," which accompanies the distribution of the bread. To the words "the blood of the new covenant shed for many" Matthew adds an explanation, "for the remission of sins." Mark would certainly not have omitted these words, which are in harmony most certainly with his line of thought, if they had been found in the source which he used. The text of Justin is merely a summary of the Gospel narratives. He also refers explicitly to the "recollections of the apostles which are called Gospels."

[3] On the passage in the text of Luke, see Appendix II, pp. 458 ff.

[4] LOISY (*Les origines de la cène eucharistique, Congrès*, I, pp. 77–95) has uttered some doubts on the authenticity of 1 Cor. xi. 23–25, and has suggested that this passage may be a later interpolation. In support of this hypothesis he only brings forward subjective impressions. For the discussion on this point I would refer the reader to the article quoted on p. 443, n. 1. In my opinion, the text of Paul is authentic. So far as I know at present, no critic has been found to support the theory of Loisy.

[5] For the incident of the washing of the disciples' feet, see Appendix III, pp. 464 ff.

[6] BULTMANN: *Syn. Trad.*, p. 169. BERTRAM: *Leidensgeschichte*, p. 29.

indeed only placed alongside of that of the announcement of the treachery of Judas, and we cannot connect it—in addition to the preparation for the Last Supper whose editorial character we have seen—with the assembly of the Jewish authorities (Mark xiv. 1–2*) or with the treachery of Judas (Mark xiv. 10–11*), which are narratives of a quite different character. But it fits in with the account of Gethsemane and of the arrest, and, although it may not seem to be connected with what precedes it, this is because, as we have seen in the Synoptic records, the perspective of the ministry of Jesus in Jerusalem has been perverted, and they do not contain any direct recollection of the real situation on the eve of the Passion. In Paul, who is only interested in the actual story of the Last Supper, the words by which he opens the narrative: "The Lord Jesus, the night in which he was betrayed," shows that the episode related by the apostle has been detached from a more complete narrative.

The account of the Last Supper is etiological in character; it is meant to explain a ritual custom, and at the same time to define its character, and determine the manner in which it should be observed. An etiological narrative is not necessarily secondary with reference to the custom with which it is connected. The narratives have been influenced by the liturgical practice, but this does not mean that the facts themselves did not give birth to the practice. The connexion between the practice and the narratives is complex: there is action and reaction. Just as there is no liturgical development which was not determined by the account of the facts,[1] so there has been no literary development which is not to some extent the reflection of the development of the liturgy.

---

[1] The method proposed by H. LIETZMANN (*Messe und Abendmahl. Eine Studie zur Geschichte der Liturgie*, Bonn, 1920) and by G. P. WETTER (*Altchristliche Liturgien, I, Das christliche Mysterium, II, Das christliche Opfer. Studien und neue Studien zur Geschichte des Abendmahls*, Göttingen, 1921–1922) is thus based upon an arbitrary postulate when it claims to be able to discover the nature of the Last Supper of Jesus by an analysis of liturgical development. A similar method, but which takes its point of departure only in the Eucharist as it was at the time of Justin, has been followed by JEAN RÉVILLE: *Les origines de l'eucharistie, Messe, Sainte Cène*, Paris, 1908.

When we compare the text of the narratives of Mark and of Paul there seems to be some reason to assume that the tradition preserved by Paul is to be preferred, since the First Epistle to the Corinthians was composed from fifteen to twenty years, at least, before the Gospel of Mark. But the date of the composition of a passage does not fix the age of the tradition to which it is assigned, and, after the year 70, Mark may have reproduced an older form of tradition than that which is given in the First Epistle to the Corinthians. Did Paul, however, intend to record an historical tradition? His account begins with the words: "For I have received of the Lord (᾽Εγὼ γὰρ παρέλαβον ἀπὸ τοῦ κυρίου) that which also I delivered unto you. . . ." Couchoud and Alfaric[1] consider that this proves that here Paul is not repeating what he has heard directly, or indirectly, from those who actually took part in the Last Supper with Jesus, but that he is making known the content of a vision or a revelation. If we look at the text of Paul only, the theory of Couchoud and Alfaric cannot be justified. It is not the only possible interpretation, nor is it the most probable. The parallelism made by the words: "I have received," and "I delivered unto you," would be impossible to understand if the conditions in which Paul had received the tradition had been fundamentally different from those in which he transmitted it to the Corinthians. The expression, "I have received of the Lord," does not exclude the possibility that it was mediated through others, between the Lord and Paul; it only marks that the tradition which it represents goes back to the Lord himself, that is to say, that it does represent what the Lord did and said during the Last Supper with his friends, with the intention that the memory of it should be kept green and fresh. When, in the Epistle to the Galatians, Paul wishes to affirm that his apostleship comes directly from Christ and from God, he says that he is an apostle "not of men, neither by man," οὐκ ἀπ᾽ἀνθρώπων, οὐδε δι᾽ ἀνθρώπου (Gal. i. 1). Thus it would be possible to conceive of an apostleship coming from God but mediated through man. Thus when Paul says that he has received of the Lord the tradition of the Last Supper, he does not mean that it may not have reached him through human intermediaries.

[1] COUCHOUD: Le mystère, pp. 146 ff. ALFARIC: Congrès, II, pp. 89 f.

There are three differences between the text of Mark and of Paul:

(i) To the words: "This is my body," Mark does not add, as Paul does, "for you."

(ii) Paul gives the same value to the Cup as to the Bread; he omits the eschatological significance which it has in Mark (or at least which it gained afterwards) through these words: "Verily I say unto you, I will drink no more of the fruit of the vine, until that day that I drink it new in the Kingdom of God" (Mark xiv. 25).

(iii) In the Pauline narrative, after Jesus has distributed the bread and the wine, he says: "This do in remembrance of me." The Marcan narrative does not mention any command to repeat this gesture.

These three points make it clear that Paul's account belongs to a stage in the evolution of the tradition which is later than that of the Second Gospel. Mark would not have had any reason to omit the words "for you" if he had found them in the source he was using. The second and the third points, however, are of decisive significance. Paul was aware of the eschatological character of the Communion service, for in the commentary which accompanies the remainder of the tradition, he says: "For as often as ye eat this bread, and drink this cup, ye do shew[1] the Lord's death till he come" (1 Cor. xi. 26). The elimination of the eschatological meaning from the Cup in the First Epistle to the Corinthians is not due to the fading of the eschatological hope. It can only be explained by the tendency to place the two constituent elements of the Communion in exact parallelism, in order to make of them two expressions of the same ideas and the same sentiments. Thus it represents a secondary element. The same must be said about the introduction of the command to repeat the rite. Since the Early Church believed that it was obeying the will of the Lord in celebrating the Communion, the suppression by Mark of a command to repeat the rite which he found in the source would be unintelligible. In introducing it Paul was not conscious that he had altered the tradition. Perhaps, without realizing it, he was only making explicit something which was already implicit. Therefore we may conclude that

[1] Or "announce," in the imperative mood.

Paul's version is derived from the tradition accepted by Mark, and we need not discuss this question any further.

Thus we now have two passages before us, those of Mark and Luke:

Mark xiv. 22–25 : And as they did eat, Jesus took bread, and blessed, and brake it, and gave to them, and said, Take, eat: this is my body. And he took the cup, and when he had given thanks, he gave it to them: and they all drank of it.[1] And he said unto them, This is my blood of the new testament, which is shed for many. Verily I say unto you, I will drink no more of the fruit of the vine until that day that I drink it anew[2] in the Kingdom of God.

Luke xxii. 15–20: And he said unto them, With desire I have desired to eat this Passover with you before I suffer: for I say unto you, I will not any more eat thereof, until it be fulfilled in the Kingdom of God. And he took the cup and gave thanks,' and said, Take this, and divide it among yourselves: For I say unto you, I will not drink of the fruit of the vine, until the kingdom of God shall come. And he took bread and gave thanks and brake it, and gave unto them, saying, This is my body which is given for you: this do in remembrance of me. Likewise also the cup after supper, saying, This cup is the new testament in my blood, which is shed for you.

The fact that Luke's version contains a command to repeat the rite means that we may apply to it the same observations which we applied to the similar command in Paul's version.

A more important difference is that Mark speaks of one cup only, a cup which is both the cup of the new covenant and the cup of the tryst, whereas Luke mentions two, of which the former is the trysting cup and the second the cup of the covenant. It does not seem natural that Jesus should have attached two different meanings to the same gesture. It is all the more difficult to admit that he may have done so, since the idea of a tryst implies that he drank of the cup with his

---

[1] In STRACK-BILLERBECK (IV, 1, pp. 58 ff.) there are passages which show that the account means that each disciple filled his own cup from the large cup which was handed round the table, and did not drink from the one cup.

[2] Matthew defines this further by saying "with you" (Matt. xxvi. 29).

disciples, whereas the symbol of the new covenant makes this very unlikely.

The idea expressed by the trysting cup is clear and natural. It is absolutely fitting at a moment when Jesus feels that he is going to be separated from his disciples. We cannot say so much for the idea of the covenant in the shed blood. This idea originated in the Old Testament. It refers to a new covenant which was to replace that which God had made with Abraham. We meet with it in the Pauline writings (2 Cor. iii. 6–14; Gal. iv. 24), but it is, above all, the author of the Epistle to the Hebrews who has developed it by insisting on the idea that the blood of Christ was necessary in order to establish the new covenant (in particular ix. 15 ff.). The saying about the cup of the covenant expresses the same idea. The death of Christ is represented as a sacrifice which establishes a new alliance between God and the elect. Jesus may have had an idea of this kind; to some extent it would be in line with the thought expressed in the saying about the destruction and reconstruction of the Temple, that is to say, about the establishment of a new religious order. There are, however, serious reasons for doubting the authenticity of the saying about the covenant. First of all, no other saying of Jesus in our possession deals with the idea of sacrifice. Nor is the idea of the covenant represented in any authentic saying of Jesus. These two observations have all the more weight because in the Communion Service the idea of a covenant is rather implied than explained.

Thus there is no need to think that Mark has combined into one the idea of two cups, with two different meanings, or that Luke has mentioned the one cup twice, with a double meaning attached to it. We may therefore assume that originally the tradition only mentioned one cup, the cup with an eschatological significance. The cup of the covenant owes its origin to the tendency, which arose very early, to establish a parallelism between the two elements in the Communion rite. In Mark the eschatological meaning has been maintained in an accessory sense, while in Paul's version it has been eliminated.

We must therefore regard as doubtful the unity of the tradition represented by Luke. The third evangelist has followed a source which only mentioned the trysting cup, but he was sufficiently under the influence of Mark to add a second interpretation in the sense of the new covenant.

Luke has not only taken the idea of the first cup from the tradition which is peculiar to his Gospel. In this tradition, verse 19 leaves us in no doubt on this point, for the cup was mentioned at the beginning of the narrative. There is no reason to suppose that this tradition did not mention the bread. In any case we must admit that the command to repeat the rite formed part of it. The place which it occupies in Luke's version should be noted. It is placed between the distribution of the bread and that of the first cup. If Luke himself had introduced this element, he would not have placed it in its present position. Either, like Paul, he would have placed a command to repeat the rite in relation to each element in the meal, or, if he had only given it once, he would have placed it at the close, in such a way that it would refer to the whole. The command to repeat the rite comes, therefore, from the particular tradition which was followed by Luke. This tradition is represented by verses 15–19. Verse 20 is an addition which Luke has made in harmony with the Marcan narrative.

In the tradition followed by Luke, the cup was offered before the bread; the other traditions reverse this order. This may appear more normal, since the symbolism which makes the broken bread represent the broken body may seem more natural than the symbolism of the cup with its suggestion of the outpoured blood. But if we restore the original meaning to the cup the sense is quite different. The distribution of the bread as the symbol of the body of Jesus and as the announcement of his death is not intelligible save from the point of view of the imminence of his death, but it does not express this idea directly. The Supper began with the distribution of the eschatological cup, with the statement that Jesus would not celebrate the approaching Passover, and that he would drink wine no more: this at once gives direct meaning to the distribution of the bread. On the other hand, after the statement of the death which is implied by the distribution of the bread, the declaration of Jesus that he will no longer drink wine becomes a meaningless repetition. The order which

P

places the cup before the bread in the tradition followed by Luke makes an entirely satisfying arrangement. Jesus begins by announcing the imminent separation, he will not celebrate the Passover which is at hand, nor will he drink wine any more. But his death, the thought of which broods over the whole gathering, will not be a defeat. A day will come when he will be reunited with his own disciples in the fulfilled Kingdom of God. Then Jesus explains that the death which he accepts is a gift which he makes to his own.

Loisy[1] has conjectured that the primitive tradition had undergone another and a more important transformation. He suggests that originally the saying about the bread did not refer to the body of Jesus, but that it was parallel to that which accompanies the distribution of the eschatological cup. Jesus spoke of the bread which he would never eat again, just as he spoke of the cup from which he would not drink. The conjecture is ingenious, but it is arbitrary to suppose that the two elements in the act were originally strictly equivalent to each other, as they have been in the later tradition and in Sacramentarian theology. These two elements may very well have been complementary instead of parallel.

Now let us picture to ourselves what actually happened during the Last Supper. Jesus seats himself at the table oppressed by the sense of an impending disaster; perhaps the absence of ths disciple whose fidelity he had begun to doubt helps to make these fears more definite. The death which he now feels very near appears to him as the crown of the humiliations and sufferings which have marked the different stages of his ministry. It will be the definite rejection of the Son of Man by this generation. This Jesus accepts, just as fully as he had accepted the sufferings which led up to it, and which he does not separate from it, because he is sure that this is the will of God. He has accepted this mysterious law without needing to know how his death could be the condition of the fulfilment of the Kingdom of God and of his coming as the glorious Messiah. This is why he feels that, although the disaster is inevitable, it is not a defeat. The separation from his own will be followed by a reunion in the Kingdom of God.

[1] Loisy: *Les origines de la cène eucharistique, Congrès*, I, p. 80.

In order to express this twofold confidence, first of all he takes a cup and drinks from it, with his disciples, saying to them that he will not drink of it henceforth until he is united with them in the great Messianic banquet. Then, having announced the coming catastrophe, he defines its meaning by a second gesture. If he had not felt called to be the Son of Man, and if he had not willed to remain faithful to the end to the mission which he had received from God, he might have escaped from death. All he needed to do was to remain in retirement in Peraea, or, after he had discovered that the people would not support him, it might have been sufficient if he had simply left Jerusalem. Thus his death was something quite different from an inevitable disaster. He accepted it, and it became a voluntary sacrifice. By consenting to die, Jesus gave himself up for his own, and for all those to whom he had preached the Gospel of the Kingdom of God, just as he had already given himself for them in all the renunciations and sufferings which he had accepted from the beginning of his ministry. And this is what Jesus expresses in the symbol of the broken bread. There is here no dogmatic theory, no sacramental idea, but something very different, the symbolic expression (or parabolic, if we prefer to call it so) of the idea which had dominated the thought of Jesus during the whole of the second part of his ministry: of the Son of Man who must suffer and be rejected, but who will later return in glory.

III. The Episodes Reported by Luke

Luke has developed the account of the last evening still further by adding to it three elements: the dispute about precedence (xxii. 24–30), the announcement of the denial of Peter (xxii. 31–34), and the saying about the two swords (xxii. 35–38). The second is given also by Mark and by Matthew, but after Jesus and his disciples had left the upper room in order to go to Gethsemane. We will deal with this later. Here we will simply examine the two others.

The dispute about precedence, placed by Luke in the last evening (xxii. 24–30), is merely the transposition of an incident, the discussion provoked by the request for the first places in the Messianic Kingdom by the sons of Zebedee, which Mark (x. 35–45) places quite differently, and which Luke has not reproduced because it did not seem to him compatible with the dignity of the martyr apostles, James and John. Matthew (xx. 20) has evidently felt the same, since he attributes the request not to James and John, but to their mother, which is evidently a secondary idea, since the other disciples were indignant with the two brothers, and it was to them that Jesus made his reply. The secondary character of the account in Luke is confirmed still more by the fact that, in his narrative, the dispute about precedence at the Last Supper constitutes a doublet with that which he gives in ix. 46–48 after Mark ix. 33 ff. Further, the account of xxii. 24–30 is composed of two fragments which have not the same origin. The one comes from the tradition of Mark (xxii. 24–27=Mark x. 42–45), the other from the Logia (xxii. 28–30=Matt. xix. 28).

The saying about the two swords is much more obscure:

Luke xxii. 35–38: And he said unto them, When I sent you without purse, and scrip, and shoes, lacked ye anything? And they said: Nothing. Then he said unto them: But now, he that hath a purse, let him take it, and likewise his scrip: and he that hath no sword, let him sell his garment and buy one. For I say unto you, that this that is written must yet be accomplished in me, And he was reckoned among the transgressors (Isa. liii. 12): for the things concerning me have an end.[1] And they said, Lord, behold here are two swords. And he said unto them, It is enough.

Some exegetes[2] have seen in this passage a relic of a tradition that at one moment Jesus thought of resisting his enemies by force. But for a group of a dozen men or so two swords would have been ridiculously insufficient.[3] Others[4] think that by

---

[1] That is to say, the prophecies which have not yet been fulfilled are now going to be accomplished.

[2] This interpretation is given by RENAN (p. 403), LOISY (*Syn.*, II, pp. 555 ff.; *Év. de Luc*, pp. 521 ff.), WINDISCH (*Der messianische Krieg und das Urchristentum*, Tübingen, 1909, pp. 28 ff.), and ED. MEYER (I, p. 182).

[3] It is not merely forcing the text, but making it say something quite different from that which it does say, to read: "They presented him with two swords, naturally, each of them two," as EISLER reads in II, p. 268.

[4] KEIM, III, p. 294. REUSS: *Hist. évang.*, p. 645. ZAHN: *Das Evangelium Lukas*, Leipzig, 1913, pp. 685 ff. HARNACK (*Militia Christi, die christliche*

these words Jesus wishes to make his disciples understand that
the period of difficulty was beginning. They, taking what he
says quite literally, presented him with two swords, some of
them being armed,[1] or possibly they may have found the
swords in the upper room. Jesus, discouraged by their lack
of understanding, dropped the subject. If we were to accept
this interpretation, the attitude of Jesus would be incomprehensible. How could he have failed to try to dissipate the
misunderstanding which his words had raised? Salomon
Reinach[2] suggests that in speaking of the two swords the source
from which Luke drew his material was alluding to the passage
in the Book of Judges (vii. 21) in which two swords are mentioned: the sword of Jahweh and the sword of Gideon, by
which the Midianites were defeated. This hypothesis could
only be accepted if the passage from the Book of Judges were
quoted, which is not the case. Wellhausen[3] thinks that the
fragment is composed of several elements, and he would retain
the idea that the disciples possessed two swords as coming
from an old tradition. It is the incident of the servant of the
high priest who was struck by a sword at the moment when
Jesus was arrested (Mark xiv. 17*) which makes him consider
that these facts are historical. But neither Mark, nor Matthew,
nor John felt any need to explain that the disciples, or even
some of them, were armed.

Having rejected all these interpretations, we must now propose one in our turn. At a moment when Jesus—perhaps, as
Luke suggests, on the last evening—felt his life was in danger,
when he knows or suspects that the order for his arrest has
already been given, he uttered a saying full of bitter irony.
Inspired, as Luke says, by the text in Isa. liii. 12, or, more

Religion und der Soldatenstand in den ersten drei Jahrhunderten, Tübingen, 1905,
p. 4, n. 1) accepts a similar interpretation, but he admits that it is not
entirely satisfactory.

[1] At the moment when Jesus was arrested one of his disciples was armed.
We know from JOSEPHUS (*G.J.*, II, 8, 4, ¶ 125) that the country was so
unsafe that the peaceful Essenes did not travel without weapons. As the
bearing of arms seems to have been forbidden to the Jews (see EISLER,
II, p. 268, n. 6), it may be that the "swords" were really daggers, which
were easy to hide under one's clothes.

[2] S. REINACH, *C.M.R.*, IV, pp. 167–173.

[3] WELLHAUSEN: *Lk.*, pp. 125 ff.

simply, seeing the situation just as it was, he said to his
disciples: "Since we are being treated as brigands, let us play
the part of brigands! Let us lead the lives of brigands and
arm ourselves!" The disciples, bewildered, show him the two
solitary swords (or daggers) which they possess. A fine band
of brigands indeed! who, in order to fall upon the passers-by
and resist armed force, can only produce two swords and had
therewith to be content!

APPENDIX I. THE ANOINTING AT BETHANY

Mark and Matthew report an incident which happened on
the eve of the Passion at Bethany, where, according to them,
Jesus passed the night; it is that of the Anointing (Mark xiv.
3-9; Matt. xxvi. 6-13). Their accounts cannot be distinguished
from each other save by some insignificant differences.[1] Without giving any precise indication of time, we are told that Jesus
being at table in Bethany in the house of Simon the leper,
a woman brings to him an alabaster cruse full of precious
perfume, and, having broken it, she pours the contents over
the head of Jesus. Some of the people who were present
deplored the useless waste when the perfume might have been
sold for three hundred denarii and given to the poor. Jesus
reproaches these critics for hurting the feelings of the woman
who has done this act: "Ye have the poor with you always,"
he says, "and whensoever ye will ye may do them good: but
me ye have not always. She hath done what she could: she
is come aforehand to anoint my body for the burying. Verily
I say unto you, Wheresoever this Gospel shall be preached
throughout the whole world, this also that she hath done shall
be spoken of for a memorial of her."

John (xii. 1-8) places the same scene before the entry into

[1] For instance, Matthew speaks only of a very precious ointment, and
Mark says that it was an ointment of spikenard or pure nard (or perfume
of the pistachio nut); the meaning of the word is uncertain. Matthew
does not say that the woman broke the vase. In his version it is the disciples
who grumble; they say that the perfume might have been sold for a great
deal of money; Mark, who is more exact, says: "for more than 300 denarii."

Jerusalem. The feast takes place six days before the Passover, probably, though it is not explicitly stated, in the home of Lazarus and his sisters. Lazarus is one of the guests, Martha serves at table, and it is Mary who anoints Jesus. She takes a pound of oil of pure nard (or perfume from the pistachio nut), anoints the feet of Jesus and wipes them with her hair. Judas protests, the evangelist remarking that he did not care for the poor, but that he had charge of the common purse, and that he would have converted to his own use the three hundred denarii, which was the value of the perfume if it had been sold. Jesus replies: "Let her alone: against the day of my burying hath she kept this. For the poor always ye have with you; but me ye have not always."

Luke (vii. 36–50) reports a similar incident, but he gives it at an entirely different point in the story: he makes it take place in Galilee, in the house of a Pharisee named Simon who has invited Jesus to a meal; this is one of the elements which constitute the section vi. 20–viii. 3, which has no equivalent in Mark, and of which the first is the Sermon on the Plain. In Luke, the woman who anoints the feet of Jesus is a notorious sinner. Having entered the banqueting-room, she kneels at the feet of Jesus, washes them with her tears, kisses them and anoints them with oil. The Pharisee who has invited Jesus says to himself: "If this man were a prophet, he would know what kind of woman this is who is touching him; he would know that she is a sinner." Jesus, who has divined his thoughts, replies by telling the parable of the Two Debtors, and he adds: "I say unto thee, her sins which were many are forgiven; that is why she loves much.[1] But he to whom little is forgiven the same loveth little." Then he turns to the woman and says to her: "Thy sins are forgiven thee; thy faith hath saved thee, go in peace."

---

[1] The preposition ὅτι which Luke uses can be taken in the causative sense (because she has loved much) or in the consecutive sense (this is why she has loved much); this second meaning is postulated by the parallelism of the phrase which follows it: "to whom little is forgiven the same loveth little," as well as by the parable of the two debtors, where love for the merciful creditor is in proportion to the amount of the debt which he has remitted.

It is impossible to say that there is no connexion between these three narratives, but this relation is complex, for they are too different for us to suppose that they are directly derived from one another.

In the account in John there are some features which are clearly secondary with reference to that of Mark, for example, the mention of Lazarus, the pointedness of the designation of the personality of the woman who anoints Jesus, the attribution of the protest to Judas and the explanation of his motives. The protest itself is intelligible in the Marcan narrative, where the whole content of the vase of alabaster has been poured out; it is not in place in that of John, where some drops only have been poured out, since Jesus says that Mary must keep the perfume for the day of his burial. This fact should be noted. The anticipated anointing which is reported by Mark is perhaps an allusion to the fact that Jesus will be placed in the tomb in haste without time to anoint his body. In John's narrative, where Nicodemus brings one hundred pounds of a mixture of myrrh and aloes (xix. 39), and where the body, before it is placed in the tomb, is enveloped in linen cloths and spices (xix. 40), the anticipation of an anointing has no point. This is why the evangelist has only spoken of a foreshadowing of the anointing, in spite of the contradiction to which this led, since Mary would not actually participate in the anointing until the body of Jesus was laid in the grave.[1] In the Marcan narrative the gesture of the woman is not explained; in John it is described as a manifestation of the gratitude of Mary to Jesus for raising her brother to life. This also is a secondary element.

The Johannine narrative, on the other hand, has been affected by that of Luke. In John, as in Luke, the woman anoints the feet of Jesus and wipes them with her hair, and this is described in the same words (cf. Luke vii. 38, and John xii. 3). The gesture of the woman who wipes the feet of Jesus with her hair is intelligible in Luke's version, where she has wetted them with her tears; it has no meaning in John's account, where only a few drops of the perfume have been poured on them. Finally, we must connect the episode

[1] Schwartz, III, pp. 178 f.

reported by Luke in x. 38–42 with John's narrative. In a village (whose name is not mentioned) a woman named Martha serves Jesus at table, while her sister Mary remains seated at his feet. The names and the attitude of the two sisters are the same in both instances. This cannot be a mere coincidence.

In the account of Mark and of Matthew, the solemn statement of Jesus that the story of this anointing will be told wherever the Gospel will be preached throughout the world, might possibly be a justification for the presence of the incident in the Gospel, and, in consequence, the evidence, or at least the recollection, that it had not always been there.

Bertram[1] regards the story of the anointing as a justification of the worship of Christ, in opposition to the view of those who thought that the essential function of the Church lay in the service of the poor. But we know absolutely nothing of any conflict in the Early Church between the tendency to exalt worship and the tendency to place moral duties in the foreground. Further, it is not clear that the gesture of the woman is to be regarded as an act of adoration in the precise sense of the word. There is only one meaning which can be read into the incident, and that is, that it is a solemn prophecy of the burial of Jesus. The protests of those who were present is only inserted in order to lead up to the statement of Jesus. The incident is reported in order to show that Jesus knew perfectly well the destiny which awaited him, even while his enemies still kept their decision secret. Thus it is related to the triple prophecy of the sufferings, death, and resurrection of the Son of Man, and thus it appears to be definitely a secondary element.

In Luke the meaning of the narrative is clear: the story of the woman who was a sinner illustrates the idea of the gratitude and love which follow the sense of forgiveness; it also illustrates the idea of the welcome given by Jesus to people whom the Pharisees crushed with their contempt. The anecdote is thus related to some of the features which are most clearly traced in the Gospel portrait of Jesus. The story, what-

[1] BERTRAM: *Leidensgeschichte*, p. 16.

P*

ever may be the embellishments which it may have undergone,[1] is not the product of a complex process of evolution. The accounts of Luke and of Mark are not independent; however, they cannot be regarded as being derived from each other. Behind them we must assume the existence of a simpler archetype. The preceding observations show that it is Luke's version which keeps closest to the original form of the story. There is no reason to think that the story of the Anointing was originally recorded in connexion with the story of the Passion.

APPENDIX II. THE TEXT OF LUKE XXII. 15–20

The text of Luke appears in the manuscripts under six different forms, which are divided into two groups. The first (I) given by the MSS. ℵ. A. B. C., etc., is characterized by the distribution of a cup at the beginning of the meal, accompanied by a saying concerning a future tryst, and at the end by that of a second cup presented as the new covenant. In the texts of the second group (II) only one cup is mentioned, but in different ways: (a) in the manuscripts D. a. d. ff². i. l. the second cup is absent; (b) in the Syriac-Sinaitic version there is only one cup at the end of the supper, but the distribution of this cup is accompanied by the same words as those of the first and the second in the text I; (c) in the manuscripts b. e., and in the Curetonian-Syriac there is no mention of the first cup, the second is accompanied only by the words which apply to the first cup in the text I; (d) the Peshitto version mentions the first cup only; (e) Marcion does not mention any cup at all, but between the word of introduction and the distribution of the bread he gives the declaration of Jesus that he will no more drink of the fruit of the wine until the Kingdom of God shall come. As illustrations we reproduce below the translations of texts I and II a and b.[2]

---

[1] BULTMANN (*Syn. Trad.*, p. 36) has observed that the story of the woman who was a sinner contains one improbable feature. A Pharisee would not have allowed a woman of the kind implied by the story to enter his house at all. See also BULTMANN², p. 70.

[2] We print in italics, in text I, the material which does not occur in text IIa, and in the text IIb those elements which are common to both books are placed in a different position.

I (ℵ. B. C.) : And he said unto them : "I have greatly desired to eat this Passover with you before I suffer, for I say unto you, I will eat it no more until it be fulfilled in the Kindom of God." And taking a cup, having pronounced the blessing, he said : "Take this and share it among yourselves, for I declare unto you, I will no more drink of the fruit of the vine until the Kingdom of God be come." And taking bread, having given thanks, he brake it and gave it to them, saying : "This is my body *given for you*; *do this in remembrance of Me*," and (*with*) *the cup* (*he did*) *the same after supper*, *saying* : "*This cup* (*is*) *the new covenant in my blood which is shed for you.*"

II*a* (D. a. d. ff². i. l.) : And he said unto them : "I have greatly desired to eat this Passover with you before I suffer, for I say unto you, I will eat of it no more until it be fulfilled in the Kingdom of God." And taking a cup, having pronounced the blessing, he said : "Take this and divide it among yourselves, for I say unto you, I will no more drink of the fruit of the vine until the Kingdom of God be come." And taking bread, having given thanks, he brake it and gave it unto them, saying : "This is my body."

II*b* (Syriac-Sinaitic version) : He said unto them : "I have greatly desired to eat the Passover with you before I suffer, for, I say unto you, henceforth I will not eat of it until the Kingdom of God be come." And taking (the) bread, having given thanks over it, he brake it and gave unto them, saying : "This is my body which I give for you, do this in remembrance of Me." And, after supper, *holding* (*taking*) *the cup and having given thanks over it, he said* : "*Take this and divide it among yourselves. This is my blood, the new covenant. I say unto you, indeed, henceforth I will no more drink of this fruit until the Kingdom of God be come.*"

II*a*, *b*, *c*, *d*, *e*, by various methods, displacements, or omissions, reduce to unity the two cups of the text I ; thus they make the narrative agree with the other accounts in the New Testament and with the liturgical practice. This is one reason for regarding text I as primitive.

To this conclusion we might oppose that to which we have been led by the analysis of the text of Luke. The tradition which we see Luke has followed agrees in fact with the text II*a*, with the one exception of the command to repeat the rite, which, in any case, we must regard as a secondary addition.

Here there seems to be an argument favourable to the primitive character of the text II*a*, which is admitted by editors like Westcott and Hort, B. Weiss, Blass, and by a large number of critics (as, for instance, Johannes Weiss, Nestle, Zahn, Wellhausen, Loisy, Lietzmann, etc.). The verses 19*b*–20 would then have been added under the influence of the text of the First Epistle to the Corinthians. Although the fact that in Luke the command to repeat the rite is absent with reference to the cup constitutes a difficulty, we would doubtless have accepted this interpretation if the evidence had been confined to the texts I and II*a*. But in my opinion the existence of the texts II*b*, *c*, *d*, *e*, constitutes a decisive objection. Actually these texts can only be explained by starting from text I. The hypothesis which would have to be constructed in order to derive text I from II*a*, then the texts *b*, *c*, *d*, *e*, from I, would be too complicated to be probable, and the date to which we would have to assign the composition of the text I would scarcely agree with the secondary character which we must assign to it. For further details on the discussion of text II, see *Eucharistie*, pp. 108–117.

APPENDIX III. THE ABSENCE OF AN ACCOUNT OF THE LAST SUPPER IN THE FOURTH GOSPEL[1]

The Fourth Gospel does not contain an account of the Last Supper, although the narrative of the last evening of Jesus is more developed than that of the Synoptic Gospels, and although John certainly had views concerning the Eucharist which were similar to those of the earlier evangelists. The way in which he makes Jesus insist that in order to have life it is absolutely necessary to eat the flesh of the Son of Man and to drink his blood (vi. 48–58) is typical in this respect. The absence of an account of the Last Supper cannot be explained by[2] the accidental loss of a page, since there is no trace of a join or

---

[1] MAURICE GOGUEL: *Sources*, pp. 55 f.

[2] As has been suggested by SPITTA: *Z. Gesch. u. Lit. d. Urch.*, I, Göttingen, 1893, pp. 187 ff. Since then Spitta has rejected this explanation, but he has not suggested another to take its place (*Das Johannes-Evangelium als Quelle der Geschichte Jesu*, Göttingen, 1910, pp. 341 ff.).

of a gap in the narrative of John, and the place where the account of the Communion should be found is not empty, but is occupied by the incident of Jesus washing the feet of the disciples (xiii. 1–11). Certain critics[1] have thought that John had said enough about the Eucharist in chapter vi, and that therefore he did not feel it necessary to return to the subject in the account of the last evening of Jesus on earth. But the problem is raised precisely because he mentions it in chapter vi and not in chapter xiii. Bernhard Weiss and Zahn[2] suggest that John may have felt that the accounts of the Synoptic Gospels and of Paul were sufficient. But if this were so, why did they not also simply omit the whole story of the Passion? Bruno Bauer, and after him Heitmüller,[3] have seen in the silence of John a protest against the chronology of the Synoptic Gospels, but this hypothesis cannot be maintained unless there were in the Synoptic narrative some details giving to the meal a Paschal character, which, as we have seen, is not the case.

The incident of the washing of the feet (xiii. 1–11) is a representation or an allegory of the Communion. It is an artificial account which is only the translation into action of the saying which Luke attributes to Jesus during the course of the last evening: "I am among you as one that serveth" (xxii. 27). The statements of Jesus about the importance of the act which he is doing, and the command to repeat it with which it is accompanied, have not given birth in the Church to a veritable sacrament of the washing of the feet, but only to a liturgical custom.[4] The statement of Jesus that they will not understand his gesture until later shows that it has a mysterious meaning: the washing of the feet is a purification which is complementary to that of baptism. All this leads us

---

[1] RENAN, pp. 302, 387. OSKAR HOLTZMANN: *Leben Jesu*, p. 67. JEAN RÉVILLE: *Q.E.*, p. 237.

[2] B. WEISS: *Johev.* (MEYER, II[8]), Göttingen, 1893, p. 469. ZAHN: *Ev. d. Joh.*, Leipzig, 1908, p. 566.

[3] B. BAUER: *Kritik der Evangelien und Geschichte ihres Ursprungs*, III, p. 195. HEITMÜLLER: *Schr.*, IV, p. 143.

[4] Saint Augustine seems to have been familiar with a custom of the feet-washing on Good Friday (cf. TSCHACKERT: art. *Fusswaschung, R.E.*, VI, p. 325), but the custom does not appear formally until the second half of the eighth century in the Mozarabic Liturgy (cf. DOM LECLERQ: art. *Lavement des pieds, D.A.C.L.*, VIII, c. 2004 ff.).

to think that it represents the Eucharist. This substitution has been made because, in the mind of the fourth evangelist, the glorification of the Christ is the condition of his redemptive action. This is the meaning of the episode of xix. 34, where after he has died there flow forth from his side blood and water, symbols of the Eucharist and of Baptism. For the evangelist this episode has evidently a special significance, since he insists on the veracity of the witness who reports it. We may compare with this the passage in the First Epistle of John, which insists on the fact that Jesus came by water and by blood (1 John v. 6–7).

CHAPTER XVII

THE STORY OF THE PASSION

I. The Character of the Passion Narrative

ORIGINALLY the Passion narrative was complete in itself. It seems probable that it was the first section of the Gospel story to be committed to writing, on account of its importance for the faith and for the proclamation of the Christian message.[1] It opens with a chronological note: "After two days was the Feast of the Passover and of unleavened bread" (Mark xiv. 1). This statement is not directly connected with anything which precedes it.[2]

The fact that the Passion narrative is more logical and coherent than the other parts of the Gospel story is not because its author was concerned with matters of history, but simply because the elements which form the narrative are not isolated incidents (like a parable, or an account of a healing, or a discourse) but parts of a whole, whose significance is absolutely dependent on their relation to the whole. No part of the Gospel narrative has been more influenced by the doctrine of the Church than the story of the Passion. The early Christians could not and did not even attempt to make a distinction between the fact of the death of Jesus and its religious significance; instinctively, when they told the story of the death

---

[1] Cf. Gal. iii. 1.

[2] Matthew (xxvi. 1–2) has tried to combine the narrative of the Jerusalem ministry and that of the Passion by giving to the latter an introduction peculiar to this Gospel: "And it came to pass, when Jesus had finished all these sayings, he said unto his disciples, Ye know that after two days is the feast of the Passover and the Son of Man is betrayed to.be crucified." Then follows the account of the council of the Jewish authorities. In John, the beginning of chapter xiii is also definitely a beginning: "Now before the feast of the Passover, when Jesus knew that his hour was come that he should depart out of this world unto the Father . . ." However, the indications given in xi. 55 (the Passover of the Jews being near), and in xii. 1 (six days before the Passover), reveal the writer's desire to connect the story of the Passion with that which precedes it.

of Jesus[1] they tended to express their own faith. They also took infinite pains to prove that the death of Jesus had been foretold in the Old Testament. In no other part of the New Testament has the interpretation of prophecy exerted a deeper influence than in the story of the Passion.[2]

II. JEWS AND ROMANS

Many factors have influenced the Gospel story; in the case of the Passion narrative, however, another element—which has little or no influence on the rest of the Gospel story—must be taken into account. When we compare the four records of the trial of Jesus we see that one idea which is definitely suggested in Mark is emphasized far more strongly in Matthew and in Luke, and above all in John.[3] The idea is this: that although it is true that Pilate passed sentence on Jesus and actually carried it out, it was the Jews who were responsible for his death, that it was they who forced the Procurator to condemn him to death; indeed, that Pilate would have released him if his hand had not been forced by the Jewish authorities and by the angry mob which they had stirred up by their suggestions. Mark mentions Pilate's effort to give Jesus the benefit of the special pardon granted to some criminal at the time of the Passover (Mark xv. 6 f.); he notes that Pilate knew that the Jews had delivered him up "for envy" (xv. 10). Luke emphasizes this point and makes Pilate declare to the high priest: "I find no fault in this man" (xxiii. 4), and in the episode of Barabbas he says quite plainly that Pilate wished

---

[1] The influence of the form of worship upon the narratives of the Passion has been studied by G. BERTRAM: *Leidensgeschichte*. His theory contains a good deal of truth, but it is developed in too systematic a manner, and on many points it assumes that the form of worship has influenced the narrative at a time when we do not know what was the form of Christian worship then in use; also it does not take into account sufficiently the direct influence that the narrative, or rather the remembrance of the facts which they relate, has had upon the cult itself.

[2] On this point, see the studies of K. FEIGEL and K. WEIDEL, quoted above (p. 175, n. 1).

[3] On this, see my study: *Juifs et Romains dans l'histoire de la passion, R.h.r.*, LXII, 1910, pp. 165–182, 295–322.

to release Jesus (xxiii. 20). When the Jews refused to listen to this proposal, he makes Pilate reiterate his declaration of the innocence of Jesus: "Why, what evil hath he done? I have found no cause of death in him" (xxiii. 22). In the account in Matthew, Pilate's wife sends him an urgent warning even while he is actually on the judgment seat: "Have thou nothing to do with that just man: for I have suffered many things this day in a dream because of him" (xxvii. 19); and when the Procurator pronounces the sentence he washes his hands before the people, saying: "I am innocent of the blood of this just person: see ye to it." To which the crowd replies: "His blood be on us and on our children" (xxvii. 24–25). In John, Pilate formally declares twice over the innocence of Jesus (xviii. 38, xix. 6), and it is still more evident than in the Synoptic narrative that in condemning Jesus to death he is yielding to the pressure of the people, and to the fears that he might be accused at Rome for not being "Caesar's friend," because he had released an aspirant to the royal power (xix. 12).

As time went on this tendency increased. In the Gospel of Peter Pilate washes his hands, just as in the Gospel of Matthew, but it is added that neither Herod nor the Jews washed their hands, and that it was Herod who pronounced and carried out the sentence (1–2). The narrator emphasizes these details by saying that when Joseph of Arimathea went to ask for the body of Jesus, Pilate sent him on to Herod (3–4).

Later, still more weight was laid upon the testimony given by Pilate to the innocence of Jesus. Tertullian says that he was *jam pro sua conscientia christianus* (*Apol.*, XXI); Origen (*Contra Celsum*, II, 34) asserts that it was the Jewish authorities rather than Pilate who sentenced Jesus to death, and in the *De Principiis* (IV, 8) he uses this phrase: "The Jews nailed him to the cross." The Epistle of Barnabas, Melito of Sardis, Aristides, Irenaeus, and others[1] use terms which, although they do not actually say that it was the Jews who condemned and crucified Jesus, at least suggest that they were entirely responsible for his death.

---

[1] See the passages collected by W. BAUER: *L.J., nt. Ap.*, pp. 199 ff.

There are several reasons for the growth of this tendency to absolve the Romans and Pilate of the responsibility for the death of Jesus, and to throw the entire blame for it upon the Jews. First of all, it reflects the fact that the real cause of the Passion was the hostility of the Jewish authorities towards Jesus; it is also due, however, to the opposition which existed, from the very earliest days of the life of the Church, between Jews and Christians. Very naturally, the Christians would think that as the Jews were their sworn foes, they must also have been the enemies of their Master; on the other hand, they would naturally conceive the Roman attitude towards Jesus to have been the one to which they were accustomed: a somewhat contemptuous indifference.[1] They would also see an analogy between the rejection of the Gospel by the Jews and the rejection of Jesus himself. From another point of view, the tendency to relieve the Romans of responsibility was due to a necessity of apologetics. The One whom the Christians presented to the world as the messenger of God and the Saviour had been sentenced to death by a Roman tribunal. This fact created difficulties for the preaching of the Gospel in the Roman world, for it might give the impression that to be converted to the Christian Faith meant taking the side of a rebel, and therefore to be in revolt against the Imperial authority. Hence the Christians were anxious to prove that the Procurator who had sent Jesus to execution had been convinced of his innocence, and that he had publicly announced that he had been forced to yield to the irresistible pressure of the populace and of the Jewish authorities. Christianity was not always in conflict with the Roman Empire. Before the moment when the conflict broke out of which the Johannine Apocalypse (Book of Revelation) remains the typical document (especially in its thirteenth chapter), a conflict which was to last until the time of Constantine, there was a period in which Christianity was definitely loyal to the Empire, and regarded the Roman power as a power established

---

[1] This was naturally only in the very early days, while Christianity was still, in the Empire, confounded with Judaism, and enjoyed the privilege of being treated as a *religio licita*. There was no persecution of the Christians until the Jews, by their complaints, had succeeded in persuading the Roman authorities that Christianity was not a Jewish sect.

by God in order to maintain order in the world. (Cf. Rom. xiii. 1–7.[1])

The existence of a friendly attitude towards the Romans within primitive Christianity explains some of the modifications in detail to which the Passion narrative was subjected from Mark to John and even to pseudo-Peter. The question therefore must be faced: was this influence already present in the Marcan narrative? And can it be that all the other passages which mention the part played by the Jews and Romans respectively have been altered by this idea? Careful examination of this question is all the more necessary because the manner in which the Gospel narratives present the part played by the Sanhedrin and by Pilate in the trial of Jesus are not free from inconsistencies and obscurities, and do not seem to be in accord with the legal administration of Palestine under the government of the Procurators.

The main theme of the Gospel record is this: Jesus is arrested on the initiative of the Jewish authorities. It is they who decide to take action against him (Mark xiv. 1–2*), who receive with joy the proposal of Judas, which will make it easier for them to carry out their plans (Mark xiv. 10–11*). It is they who send to Gethsemane a band of men armed with swords and staves (Mark xiv. 43*). When Jesus is arrested, he is brought before the high priest. The Sanhedrin assembles, interrogates Jesus, and after it has extracted a declaration from him, the members of the Council declare unanimously that he is worthy of death (Mark xiv. 53, 55–64*). In the mind of the narrator this amounts to a death sentence. Immediately after the sitting of the Sanhedrin Jesus is actually treated not as an accused person, but as a condemned criminal. This is manifested in the scene of the outrages which he suffers at the hands of the agents of the Sanhedrin and the servants of the high priest (Mark xiv. 65*). The Synoptic Gospels do not say why the sentence which has just been pronounced is not carried out immediately. It does not seem doubtful that the reason why the Roman trial follows the Jewish trial is,

[1] On this point compare my study entitled: *Les Chrétiens et l'Empire romain à l'époque du Nouveau Testament*, Paris, 1908.

according to them, that which is suggested by the Fourth Gospel, when the Jews say to Pilate (who advises them to try Jesus themselves): "It is not lawful for us to put any man to death" (John xviii. 31). It seems strange that the Jews need to remind the Procurator of the limits which the Roman power has placed to their rights; it is no less strange that the Synoptic Gospels do not explain clearly the necessity for the second trial, when we cannot suppose that they were writing for readers who were familiar with Palestine affairs. Thus the source followed by Mark may have presented the report of the two trials in a different way from that in which the evangelists understood it, or it may not have explained it at all. In any case, so far as the evangelists are concerned, their theory is pure conjecture.

When Jesus appears before Pilate, the Jewish authorities, the chief priests, and the elders of the people play the part of accusers, and, supported by the fanatical crowd, force the Procurator to pass the sentence of death (Mark xv. 1-15*).

This arrangement of the Gospel records raises two questions. First of all, is it a unity? that is, can it contain all the elements of the story? Further, does it agree with what we know about the legal administration of Palestine in the time of the Procurators?

In John's account of the arrest of Jesus, both at the beginning and at the end, he mentions the presence of the cohort and of the centurion. "Judas, taking the cohort and the agents of the chief priest and the Pharisees . . ." (xviii. 3).[1] "The cohort, the centurion and the agents of the Jews seized Jesus, bound him, and led him away" (xviii. 12). The philo-Roman tendency being still stronger in the Fourth Gospel than in the Synoptic Gospels, it is impossible to suppose that the cohort and the centurion have been introduced into the narrative by John.[2]

[1] The English version (A.V.) reads: "Judas then, having received a band *of men* and officers from the chief priests and Pharisees . . ." (xviii. 3). "Then the band and the captain and officers of the Jews took Jesus, and bound him . . ." (xviii. 12).—(TRANSLATOR.)
[2] Several attempts have been made to suppress or reduce the contradiction which seems to exist on this point between the Johannine evidence and

Thus we must admit that he is here following a source which mentioned a collaboration between the Jews and the Romans, or which may have mentioned the Romans only. The Jews will have been added by the evangelist under the influence of the Synoptic narratives.

We shall have to return to these hypotheses later. *A priori*, however, it seems very unlikely that the Jews and the Romans would have co-operated to arrest Jesus. Whether that be so or not, if the Romans did proceed to arrest Jesus, or if they merely collaborated, the initiative, or at least part of the initiative, must be assigned to them. In consequence, the Gospel narrative which attributes this initiative wholly to the Jews is a biassed perversion of the primitive tradition.

If the trial before Pilate had taken place under the conditions described by the evangelists, it would have been of a very special character. Pilate would not have had to condemn or acquit Jesus, but merely either to ratify the sentence passed by the Sanhedrin or to forbid its being carried out. Now, in the whole account of the Roman trial there is no allusion whatever to the Jewish trial, nor to its conclusion. In the two instances the accusation is not the same. Before the Sanhedrin Jesus is accused of blasphemy, which is a religious crime; before Pilate he is charged with wishing to make himself king of the Jews. It is of course true that the two

that of the Synoptic Gospels. ZAHN (*Ev. Joh.*, p. 609), for instance, thinks that the cohort did not take part in the arrest, but that it only came to the place in order to intervene if necessary. There is nothing to show that this was so, and besides, if this theory were correct, then it would imply that the Jews had already come to an understanding with Pilate before Jesus was brought before the Roman tribunal. LOISY (*Quatr. Év.*², p. 453) argues against the historicity of John's remark by saying that a cohort would be a very large detachment of men to be sent to arrest one man, even though he was surrounded by some of his disciples, and that if Jesus had been arrested by the cohort he would have been brought before Pilate at once, and not before the Sanhedrin. But John may have said "the cohort" when he really meant "a detachment of the cohort." For the second point, see further on, pp. 481 f., 511 f. Loisy (cf. also SPITTA: *D. Johev.*, p. 361) explains the Johannine text by the anxiety of the chronicler to bring into the narrative of the arrest of Jesus all the earthly powers ranged against him (an idea which we meet in Acts iv. 27). But that would go right against the tendency which was so strongly marked in him, to insist that Pilate was well disposed towards Jesus.

accusations are not wholly unconnected. The second, however, might be understood as a transposition of the first into
language intelligible to a Roman. But in the hypothesis before
us there seems no necessity for such a transposition. If the
course of events was such as is here described, Pilate would
not have needed to enquire whether Jesus had committed
acts which could be punished by Roman law; all he would
have had to do would have been to find out whether he had
really committed offences which were punishable under the
Jewish law, and then see that they were correctly applied.
In this case, however, there is no question of a Jewish sentence
sanctioned by the Roman authority, but both the sentence
and the execution were carried out by the Romans in accordance with Roman Law.

One of the leading ideas in the Gospel story of the Roman
trial is the passionate clamour of the Jewish populace for the
death of Jesus. In the Gospel of Luke, however, there is a
trace of a tradition which contradicts this idea. When Jesus is
being led away to be crucified, Luke says:

And there followed him a great company of people, and of women,
which also bewailed and lamented him. But Jesus turning unto
them said, Daughters of Jerusalem, weep not for me, but weep for
yourselves and for your children.

This is followed by a prophecy of the destruction of Jerusalem
which ends thus:

If they do these things in a green tree, what shall be done in the
dry? (Luke xxiii. 27–32).

After Jesus has drawn his last breath, again Luke says:

And all the people that came together to that sight, beholding the
things which were done, smote their breasts and returned (Luke
xxiii. 48).[1]

Thus a tradition existed according to which the death of
Jesus was felt by the people as a disaster. Thus the general

[1] We should also note that Luke does not say, like Matthew and Mark,
that the crucified Jesus was insulted by the passers-by.

scheme of the narrative, which seems to have been that of the evangelists, is not developed in a logical manner; here and there in their record we can discern elements which imply differing traditions about the trial of Jesus.

Does the theory of the two trials harmonize with what we know of the legal administration in the time of the Procurators? Mommsen[1] says quite definitely "Yes." He believes that, in essentials, the Marcan narrative is accurate (*kaum betrübt*). In his opinion Jesus was sentenced by the Sanhedrin in regular order, but that he had to appear before Pilate because, although in accordance with the principles of their policy in dealing with conquered peoples they had allowed the Jewish legal system to remain in existence, the Romans, in order to avoid the Sanhedrin becoming the tool of an anti-Roman policy, had reserved to themselves a right of control by taking away from them the right to pass capital sentences without the approval of the Procurator.

In the work *Sanhedrin* (I, 18a, 37. STRACK-BILLERBECK, I, p. 1027), an anonymous *baraïta* says that "forty years[2] before the destruction of the Temple the right of pronouncing capital sentences was taken away from Israel."[3] It does not seem necessary to take this piece of evidence quite literally.[4] The

---

[1] MOMMSEN: *Die Pilatus-Acten, Z.N.T.W.*, III, 1902, pp. 199 f. LIETZMANN (*Bemerkungen zum Prozess Jesu*, II, *Z.N.T.W.*, XXXI, 1932, pp. 81 ff.) admits that, although it may seem very improbable, we cannot entirely reject the view of Schlatter and of Joachim Jeremias, namely, that the priest's daughter may have been executed during the reign of Agrippa I (41–44).

[2] This figure must be regarded as approximate only.

[3] The Talmudists connect this fact with what is said in *Sanhedrin*, 41a, and other passages (cf. STRACK-BILLERBECK, I, p. 1000), who say that forty years before the destruction of the Temple the Sanhedrin ceased to meet in the Temple and that it held its sittings in the bazaars. "This means," says R. Izchak, "that the members of the Sanhedrin no longer gave sentence in criminal cases."

[4] Did those who edited the passages with which we are dealing feel concerned to show that a Jewish tribunal could not be made responsible for the death of Jesus? We note that, by forty years before the destruction of the Temple, an epoch is suggested which corresponds approximately to that of the trial of Jesus. I hesitate to regard the statement about the right of pronouncing judgment in criminal cases as dictated by apologetic considerations, since in the same work, *Sanhedrin* (see above, p. 72), it is said that before the sentence passed on Jesus was carried out the sentence

right which had been taken away from the Sanhedrin was not the right of passing capital sentences but that of carrying them out without a preliminary approval by the Romans. Until the eve of the war, instances occurred in which Jewish sentences were pronounced and carried out. Rabbi Eliezer ben Zadok, who died before 130 of our era, tells that when he was a child he was present at the execution of the daughter of a priest, who was burned alive because she had been convicted of adultery (*Sanh.*, 7, 2, 52*b*).[1] Josephus (*G.J.* II, xi. 6, ¶ 220) says that until Cuspius Fadus and Tiberius Alexander, that is to say, until the year 48, the Procurators did not disturb the Jewish customs. After that date the Roman administrators did not alter the legal system itself, but from time to time they would interfere, and irritate the feelings of their subjects.

Regnault[2] has opposed the theory of Mommsen by dwelling on the difficulties which would have been introduced by the system of having two trials in direct succession, in cases where the Jewish law and the Roman law did not impose the same penalty, or did not agree on the nature of a crime or a misdemeanour. From this he concludes that when the administration of the Procurators was established the jurisdiction of the Sanhedrin must have been forbidden in the sphere of criminal law.

This objection would carry weight only if the control of the Procurator could be conceived solely in the form of a Roman trial, independent of the Jewish trial, and following it. But this system would have led to the actual suppression of national Jewish institutions, and this would have been contrary to the policy of the Roman Empire. The Procurator simply had to assure himself that the rules of the Jewish Law were being correctly applied, and to see that the Sanhedrin

was made known publicly, and plenty of time was allowed for evidence in defence of the prisoner to be procured. In this passage, which is designed to exculpate the Jewish judges, it is not said that they had no right to pronounce a capital sentence, or that it was Pilate who sentenced Jesus to death.

[1] Quoted by JUSTER: *Les Juifs dans l'Empire romain*, Paris, 1914, II, p. 138, n. 1.

[2] REGNAULT: *Une province procuratorienne au début de l'Empire romain. Le procès de Jésus-Christ*, Paris, 1909, pp. 64 ff.

did not use the power which had been left in its hands as a weapon against the Roman administration.

To the argument from theory Regnault adds an argument from fact. Josephus (*A.J.*, XX, 9, 1, ¶¶ 200–203) reports that in 62, between the death of Festus and the arrival of his successor Albinus, the high priest Ananias assembled the Sanhedrin and brought before it James the brother of Jesus and some other individuals, who were condemned to death and executed. Certain Jews went to meet Albinus and accused the high priest of having acted illegally, and the Procurator admitted that their complaint was well founded. Regnault concludes from this that the Sanhedrin could not be assembled without the consent of the Procurator, and that therefore it was no longer an independent tribunal. But, as Juster, in particular, has proved,[1] the narrative of Josephus contains certain inaccuracies. Between the death of Festus and the arrival of his successor there cannot have been a real lapse of the Roman authority in Jerusalem. If it had really been illegal to call the Sanhedrin together, Albinus (knowing what we do of his character) would most certainly have exercised his prerogative and have imposed certain penalties. Probably all that he said was that it would have been more fitting to await his arrival instead of hurrying the matter through with the approval of the sentence of the Sanhedrin by the acting-governor.

No one would dispute the fact that until the destruction of Jerusalem the Sanhedrin remained the competent authority in all matters of secondary importance. It cannot always have been easy to see in advance whether a case was going to be sufficiently serious for the Sanhedrin to know whether the penalty it would inflict would be within its powers or not. There is only one possible and logical solution, and it is this: that the Sanhedrin had preserved intact the right to judge a case, but that the capital sentences which it might pronounce could not be carried out before they had received the approval of the governor.

The approval necessary for the carrying out of the sentence imposed by the Sanhedrin did not mean that a Roman trial had to follow a Jewish trial, or that a Roman penalty was

[1] JUSTER: *Les Juifs dans l'Empire romain*, II, pp. 141 ff.

added to the Jewish penalty; the case of James and that of the priest's daughter, reported in the work entitled *Sanhedrin*, prove this.[1] Thus Mommsen's theory about the legal system in Palestine in the time of the Procurators seems to be well founded. The condemnation of Jesus by the Sanhedrin, followed by the approval of the Procurator, seems to have been theoretically possible. There are, however, two reasons which prevent us from thinking that this was the actual course of the trial of Jesus. The first is this: the Roman trial, as it is described in the Gospels, is not represented as the control of the Jewish trial but as a second trial, quite independent of the first one, on an entirely different charge. The second is that the penalty inflicted is Roman and not Jewish.

Although the Sanhedrin was competent to try Jews who did not possess the rights of Roman citizenship, its jurisdiction did not annul or limit the *jus gladii*, which was one of the prerogatives of the Procurators.[2] The governor retained the right to prosecute, to try, and to execute whom he would. The trial of Jesus could have been conducted solely under the orders of the Procurator, on his own initiative, without any intervention on the part of the Sanhedrin at all, or with a merely semi-official consultation with this tribunal or with some of its members.[3]

It may be of interest to enquire in what way Christian tradition outside the Gospels[4] represented the circumstances of the death of Jesus.

[1] We do not take into account here the stoning of Stephen, for it is not clear whether Stephen was stoned at the end of an official trial or during an outbreak of popular violence.

[2] JOSEPHUS: *G.J.*, II, 8, 1, ¶ 117. MOMMSEN: *Röm. Staatsrecht*, I, 3, pp. 136–161; III, pp. 127 ff.

[3] The possibility of such a consultation is established by the account in Acts (xxii. 30 f.), according to which the tribune Claudius Lysias, after he had arrested Paul at Jerusalem, called the Sanhedrin together in order to gather information from it which he needed in order to send in his report to Felix.

[4] We are only mentioning here the Christian tradition, for the non-Christian evidence about Jesus is too general to give us any real information. Tacitus, for instance, says that Pilate crucified Jesus, but that does not give us any definite information regarding the authority which pronounced the sentence on Jesus. We do not know whether it was Pilate who

In the First Epistle to the Thessalonians (ii. 14–16), referring to the difficulties and annoyances which the Christians had to undergo at the hands of their heathen compatriots, the apostle Paul expresses himself thus:

For ye, brethren, became followers of the churches of God which in Judaea are in Christ Jesus: for ye also have suffered like things of your own countrymen, even as they have of the Jews: who both killed the Lord Jesus and their own prophets, and have persecuted us; and they please not God, and are contrary to all men: Forbidding us to speak to the Gentiles that they might be saved, to fill up their sins alway: for the wrath is come upon them to the uttermost.

The words: "The Jews killed the Lord Jesus," cannot be taken quite literally, since the penalty of crucifixion was a Roman form of execution. Paul is not giving an account of the facts, but he brings a charge against the Jews simply from the point of view of their moral responsibility. He cannot have meant, actually, that the Jews hindered him from preaching the Gospel; he must be thinking of the difficulties and hindrances which they have placed in his way by their intrigues.

In the First Epistle to the Corinthians (ii. 6–8) Paul speaks of the crucifixion of Christ by "the princes of this world," that is, by the spiritual powers which inspire earthly authorities. This passage, taken by itself, can be reconciled just as well with the hypothesis of the crucifixion of Jesus by the Romans as with that which says that he was put to death by the Jews.

The passage in the First Epistle to Timothy (vi. 13), which speaks of the "good confession witnessed by Christ Jesus before Pontius Pilate," gives an example to the Christians who are summoned before a pagan tribunal, rather than an exact account of the conditions under which Jesus appeared before Pilate. Finally, in the book of Revelation, with reference to the *parousia* of the Lord, these words occur: "Every eye shall see him, and they also which pierced him: and all kindreds of the earth shall wail because of him" (i. 7). Here there is the idea of the Christ appearing at the end of time to confound all those who were responsible for his death, that is, all the

passed the sentence or whether he simply carried out the sentence passed by the Sanhedrin.

tribes of the earth. This is not an historical tradition but a dogmatic opinion.

In the book of the Acts, in general the Jews are held responsible for the death of Jesus, and some very definite statements (if they might or could be taken literally) would seem to indicate that it was they who crucified Jesus.[1] But other passages, belonging to the same stage of tradition, show that the author of the Acts is only thinking of their moral responsibility, as, for instance, in this phrase in a sermon by Peter: "God . . . hath glorified this Jesus whom ye delivered up, and denied him in the presence of Pilate, when he was determined to let him go" (iii. 13–15; cf. vii. 52).

The examination of the Christian tradition outside the Gospels brings out the fact that it is far more interested in the question of the moral responsibility for the death of Jesus than in that of the circumstances under which this sentence was passed. This explains why the evangelists did not attempt to give a very exact record of the actual events.

III. Who Took the Initiative in the Proceedings Against Jesus?

The Synoptic Gospels and the Fourth Gospel both mention the conditions in which the Jewish authorities make the final decision to kill Jesus.

After two days [says Mark] was the feast of the Passover, and of unleavened bread. And the chief priests and the scribes sought how they might take him by craft, and put him to death. But they said, Not on the feast day, lest there be an uproar of the people (xiv. 1–2).[2]

---

[1] For instance, iv. 10: "Jesus the Nazarene, whom ye crucified"; v. 30: "Jesus, whom ye slew and hanged on a tree."

[2] Matthew (xxvi. 1–5) develops the brief statement of Mark somewhat further. He begins his narrative by a declaration of Jesus about the proximity of the Passover and the necessity for the crucifixion of the Son of Man at that moment, and he transforms what in Mark seems to be a simple conversation into a council which is held in the court of the high priest. The text of Luke (xxii. 1–2) does not mention the desire to act without the knowledge of the people. Luke has omitted this detail, because it did not

The chronological note with which this statement begins is difficult to reconcile with that which follows, and must be assigned to the editor. Further, the words, "they sought," do not refer to any precise moment, and only show the state of mind of the Jewish authorities. Matthew has made his account more definite by alluding to a meeting at the house of the high priest. In its most ancient form this tradition bore witness only to the intention of the Jewish authorities to kill Jesus and to their resolve to avoid doing anything which might lead to a riot.

The statement of John (xi. 47–53, 57) is more detailed. When the Pharisees learn of the Raising of Lazarus and of the impression which this has produced upon the Jews, they call the Sanhedrin together. The question before them is this: "This man doeth many miracles. If we let him thus alone, all men will believe on him, then, they said, the Romans will come and take away both our place and nation." Caiaphas, the high priest for that year,[1] declares that it would be better that "one man should die for the people . . . that the whole nation perish not." The evangelist notes that this declaration was really inspired by the Holy Spirit, due to his official position as the high priest that year, but that in reality Jesus did not die only for the people, but "that he should gather together in one the children of God that were scattered abroad." Thus the decision is taken to have Jesus killed.

The following verses tell that Jesus could no longer show himself in public, but that he went to Ephraim near to the wilderness until the time when the Feast of the Passover was nigh; people were asking: Will he come up to the Feast or not? for, says verse 57, "both the chief priests and the Pharisees had given a commandment, that if any man knew where he were, he should show it, that they might take him."

seem to him possible to reconcile it with the *rôle* attributed to popular pressure in the account of the Roman trial. Luke certainly knew the text of Mark, of which in his narrative there still exists a relic in the words: "for they feared the people," which do not actually belong to the phrase.

[1] It is not permissible to translate τοῦ ἐνιαυτοῦ ἐκείνου by "at that moment," in order to make the text agree with the fact that the high priest was not elected for a year, but, in principle at least, for life.

There is an appreciable difference between verse 53 and verse 57. In verse 53 the decision is only taken in principle. With verse 57 we are in the presence of a first attempt to carry it out, with an order of arrest issued against Jesus. The difference is not so great that it would be impossible to assign verses 46–53 and 57 to the same tradition. The measure to which allusion is made in verse 57 has its natural place as the result of the decision in principle mentioned in verse 53.

Without waiting to discuss the fact that in this statement there are elements which do not show a very exact knowledge of the organization of the Sanhedrin, we must call attention to the obscurities it contains. The Jews admit that Jesus works miracles which give him a great influence over the masses. How then can they dream of treating him as though he did not possess great supernatural power? It is also surprising that a series of miracles is mentioned when all that has just been described is the Raising of Lazarus. The allusion to the miracles must be assigned to the evangelist. Probably the source only mentioned the popularity of Jesus, but, as the evangelist implies that the teaching of Jesus has been misunderstood and rejected, he has to bring in the miracles to explain why the people were so greatly attached to Jesus.

According to John, the members of the Sanhedrin were not only anxious because they were afraid that the influence of Jesus might endanger their own, but also because they feared lest his popularity should become the cause of the pretext for an intervention on the part of the Romans. What are we to think of this suggestion? There is some agreement with that which is reported in vi. 15. After the feeding of the multitudes the enthusiastic crowds wanted to take Jesus by force and make him king. Is it possible that something similar may have happened in Judaea? Can we imagine that at Jerusalem, as in Galilee, the disciples of Jesus had dreamed of seeing him set at the head of a Messianic movement, and had perhaps tried to force him into it? The conjecture would be plausible, for Jesus may have been misunderstood in Jerusalem as well as in Galilee. But this hypothesis is not necessary. The Jews may have been afraid that if they allowed the influence of Jesus to increase, a moment might come when he would take advantage of the tide of popular feeling and place himself at the head of a political movement which was not yet even on the horizon. On the other hand, there may be a far simpler explanation: they may have feared lest the Procurator should become alarmed by the growing authority of a prophet and that he might intervene with measures which might involve others than those who were directly implicated, of which in any case it would be impossible to foresee the consequences. They may have also been afraid that, quite unjustly, they would be held responsible for a popularity which they had vainly tried to prevent. Their fears were certainly not futile. To be convinced of this we have only to remember how, when the preaching of John the Baptist had been merely apocalyptic and in no way Messianic in the political sense, the mere fact that he exercised a real influence over the people was enough to make Herod decide to have him killed. No more than this was needed to call forth the intervention of the Procurator. It would have been quite enough for him to think that Jesus might prove dangerous, for him to give orders to put him out of the way. In the eyes of Pilate the life of a Jew was not of great importance. The Sanhedrin may have feared, or feigned to fear, that the authority of Jesus would increase, and that Pilate would be led to take action against him which might recoil upon the Jewish authorities themselves. Thus they may have decided to take the initiative, and either to take action against Jesus themselves or to provoke the Procurator to take action against him.

The preceding observations do not make it certain that this was the actual course of events; they only prove that there is no impossibility in assuming that the account given in John may be reliable, or, at least, that the original form of the narrative which forms the basis of this story may be reliable.

The evangelist, who insists frequently on the settled hostility of the Jewish authorities towards Jesus, cannot have invented the idea that they decided to act against him in the interests of the people as a whole. The tradition from which this idea is drawn reveals a tendency which is not mentioned elsewhere, and is one which especially contradicts the dominant character of the Johannine narrative: that of exonerating the Jews to some extent, by pointing out that they did not wish to act save in the higher interests of the people. Such a tradition must be archaic; we cannot imagine that it would have been created before the time when the establishment of the mission to the Gentiles made it necessary to place the Romans outside the whole incident as far as possible. The account of the council of the authorities therefore cannot be regarded as a simple development of the shorter statement in Mark. In reality the two statements are very different. In John there is a council and the decision is made. The tradition followed by Mark merely states the hostility of the Jewish authorities towards Jesus and their intention to manipulate the feelings of the people. The Johannine account explains—although possibly in a rather incomplete way—the events which followed; in Mark's account the explanation is more apparent than real.

The fourth evangelist places the decision of the Jewish authorities before the moment of Jesus' return to Jerusalem, on the eve of the Passover. This would explain the swift development of subsequent events.

We have seen how, at the close of the stay of Jesus in Jerusalem, a bitter conflict broke out between him and the Jewish authorities, provoked by the position which he had adopted towards Judaism. At that moment the opposition of the authorities seems to have been due to reasons of a religious and theological order. In the account in chapter xi there is no mention of such reasons. Does this fact shake one or other of the two theses which we have tried to discern? We do not think so. The Jewish authorities may quite well have had a double motive in taking action against Jesus, or the members of the Sanhedrin, while determined to act against Jesus because they saw in him a blasphemer, may have put forward a different motive in order to be more certain of attaining their end.

The Sanhedrin may have feared that if they condemned Jesus as a blasphemer, they would not easily obtain the ratification of the Procurator, or that, by the steps they would be obliged to take, they might provoke the partisans of Jesus to intervene, and thus cause a disturbance among the people, eventualities which it was in their own interest to avoid. Thus the Jews may have decided to give their action a different motive.

There is a positive reason for thinking that this was the actual course of events. We can only touch upon this here by anticipating what will be said in the following chapters. From the very outset the proceedings against Jesus were not purely Jewish in character, since the Roman cohort was present when Jesus was arrested. Thus Jesus was not arrested for blasphemy but as an agitator, or as a person who might furnish a pretext for, or become the occasion of, a political agitation. Thus the account in John does not wholly explain why Jesus was arrested. The tradition recorded by him may have been invented in order to conceal the real reason for the arrest. We shall see that the narrative of his appearance before the Sanhedrin cannot be regarded as fictitious. Jesus did actually appear before the Jewish authorities and was judged by the Sanhedrin to be guilty of blasphemy and worthy of death. The only possible way to reconcile the data, which we are led to retain as historical, consists in admitting that the arrest ordered by Pilate was provoked by the Jews, but that Pilate, who was on bad terms with the Jewish authorities, was able to insist, although he followed their suggestions, that they should not lead him into a trap, and that after they had forced him to condemn Jesus to death he took care that they should not incite the people to rise against him, or that they would not go to Rome to accuse him of having shed the blood of an innocent man. In order to be reassured he insisted on an explicit statement from the Sanhedrin.

This hypothesis assumes that the decision taken by the Jewish authorities to kill Jesus was not followed (as John says it was (xi. 57)) by the order to arrest him as soon as they knew the place of his retreat, but by conferences with the Procurator. There is at least an indirect trace of these conferences in the fact that, according to Mark (xv. 2), when Jesus was led before Pilate the latter questioned him without the Jewish authorities having given him an account of the matter or having formulated any charge against him.[1] If

[1] Luke (xxiii. 2) has evidently felt this to be curious, and he has added a little introduction in which he says that the members of the Sanhedrin accuse Jesus of stirring up the people, of hindering them from paying tribute to Caesar, and of declaring himself the Messiah, that is, the King.

tradition has not preserved any direct recollection of an understanding between the Jewish authorities and Pilate, this may be explained, on the one hand, by the tendency of the tradition to reduce the part of Pilate to a minimum, and, on the other, also by the fact that the conferences between the Sanhedrin and Pilate must have taken place in secret. The Christians may have suspected this when they noticed how the course of events developed. If they did not guess it, this would be because their thoughts about the story of the Passion were not concerned with discovering the actual course of the events themselves, but with their desire to discover their meaning. They were not concerned to probe into the immediate causes of these events, but to discover their moral causes. These they found in the opposition provoked by the teaching of Jesus among the Jewish authorities, and in the hatred they bore him. Christian tradition has not been deceived in seeing in their hostility the cause of the arrest of Jesus, of his trial and the sentence of death. It has only overlooked one detail, which it has not perhaps even perceived, of which in any case it has not seen the part it played in the story, and that is that they found the instrument which they needed to accomplish their end in the susceptibilities of the Roman authorities, the instrument which they needed, if they were to attain their end.

CHAPTER XVIII

THE NIGHT OF THE ARREST

I. Jesus and His Disciples

During the course of the evening, after supper, Jesus left the upper room to go to the Mount of Olives. At that moment his mind was obsessed by the thought of the dangers which menaced him, and his trouble was increased by the feeling that he could not be absolutely certain of the loyalty of his disciples. On the way through the city he said to them:[1] "All ye shall be offended (that is, you will cease to believe in me) because of me this night, for it is written: I will smite the shepherd and the sheep shall be scattered" (Zech. xiii. 7), then, following a rhythm which often occurs in the Gospel story, when, after the announcement of a defeat there comes the announcement of a compensation, he adds: "But after that I am risen I will go before you into Galilee."[2] Peter protested that even if all the others were disloyal he would remain faithful. "And Jesus saith unto him, Verily I say unto thee, That this day, even in this night, before the cock crow twice,[3] thou shalt deny me thrice." Peter protested all the more vehemently that even if he had to die with him he would not deny him. "Likewise also said they all" (Mark xiv. 26–31*).

In this account we can distinguish the following elements:

(i) An announcement that the disciples would be scattered, in which it is not certain whether it was presented originally as the fulfilment of a prophecy;

(ii) A saying about a return into Galilee, conceived in the present version as a prophecy of the Resurrection;

(iii) An announcement of the denial of Peter, made in response to a presumptuous assertion of the apostle.

[1] Luke (xxii. 31–34) places the equivalent of these words before the moment when Jesus leaves the upper room.
[2] The word προάξω may mean: "I will go before you," or, "I will gather you together by going before you as your leader." The allusion to this word in xvi. 7 shows that Mark understood it in the former sense.
[3] Matthew does not mention that the cock crowed twice.

These three elements appear to be logically connected; this, however, is not sufficient to convince us that their connexion may not be due to an editorial combination.

The announcement that the disciples will be scattered is perfectly intelligible during the course of the last evening. It is not directly essential to the way in which the flight is narrated further on, hence it is not necessary to regard it as a prophecy which was introduced into the narrative later on. The quotation from the Old Testament which accompanies it reveals the intention of modifying the guilt of the apostles by showing that their scattering formed part of the divine plan.[1] At this point, then, we can see that an editor has intervened.

Johannes Weiss[2] has suggested that the phrase about returning to Galilee may be a relic of a tradition which said that Jesus foresaw a crisis, after which, he promised, he would gather his disciples together in Galilee. From the philological point of view this interpretation is possible, but in the present state of the documentary evidence it seems impossible to imagine a situation in which such words could have been uttered, with the meaning which Weiss suggests. This does not prove, of course, that such a situation could not have existed. But it would be more than strange if the recollection of this situation had been so completely ousted by an entirely different view of the Jerusalem ministry that a relic of it should have subsisted in the supposition that Jesus would return to Galilee as the leader of his disciples. Hence it is impossible to explain this saying in any other sense than that given in Mark, not to regard it as anything more than an editorial element intended to prepare the way for the account of an appearance of Jesus in Galilee.

[1] The same tendency is visible in Luke, who does not directly mention the flight, and in John, who covers it by a saying of Jesus to those who are arresting him: "if therefore ye seek me, let these go their way," and John adds: "That the saying might be fulfilled which he spake, Of them which thou gavest me have I lost none" (xviii. 8–9).
[2] JOH. WEISS: Das Urchristentum, Göttingen, 1919, p. 12.

The character and the origin of the announcement of Peter's denial raise a more delicate question, which must be examined later.

According to Luke (xxii. 31-34), it is to Peter only that Jesus speaks: "Simon, Simon, behold, Satan hath desired to have you, that he may sift you as wheat: But I have prayed for thee, that thy faith fail not, and when thou art converted, strengthen thy brethren." The mention of the denial is connected with Peter's declaration that he is ready to go with Jesus to prison and to death.

This story is not a unity. The words of Jesus addressed to Peter are an exhortation to vigilance, not an assertion that Peter will deny him, and it is strange that the prayer of Jesus for Peter that his faith should not fail should be immediately followed by the statement that his faith will fail. The contradiction is modified by the allusion to the part which Peter will play later on, but it is not concealed, and it is possible to trace, behind the text of Luke, a tradition according to which Jesus, speaking of the crisis which was about to begin, told Peter that, sustained by the prayer of his master, he would be able to strengthen his brethren.

In Luke the only trace which remains of an allusion to the scattering of the disciples is in the fact that Jesus says: "Satan . . . desired to have *you*," whereas he appears to be addressing Peter only.

In the account of the arrest, Luke does not say, like the other evangelists, that the disciples leave Jesus and flee. He does not ignore this fact, however, since from the moment of the arrest the only disciple whom he mentions is Peter, in the story of the denial.

In the Fourth Gospel, as in Luke, Jesus foretells Peter's denial (xiii. 33-38) during the course of the Last Supper. Jesus tells his disciples that he is going to leave them. "Whither I go ye cannot follow me now." Then Peter asks: "Whither goest thou?" and Jesus replies: "Whither I go thou canst not follow me now, but thou shalt follow me afterwards." This allusion to Peter's martyrdom is intended to diminish the guilt of the apostle. In its present form the Johannine narrative could only have been composed at a rather late date. Peter replies: "Lord, why cannot I follow thee now? I will lay down my life for thy sake." It is then that Jesus says: "Wilt thou lay down thy life for my sake? Verily, verily, I say unto thee, the cock shall not crow till thou hast denied me thrice."

Corssen [1] has observed that in this instance the disciples know that Jesus is alluding to his death, whereas later on, when Thomas says: "Lord, we know not whither thou goest" (xiv. 5), they seem to have entirely failed to grasp this. John must, therefore, be depending on an earlier tradition, which is, in any case, very similar to that of Mark.

Thus in this narrative two strands of different traditions are mingled: on the one hand, there is the tradition represented by Mark, in which, in response to a presumptuous assertion of Peter, Jesus tells him plainly that he will deny him; on the other hand, there is the tradition of which Luke has retained some elements, combined with an account which is inspired by Mark, in which Jesus announces to the apostle that he will have to strengthen his brethren. Obviously these two traditions refer to the very same situation; hence it is impossible to retain both by saying that they belong to different points in the narrative. We must choose between them. The tradition peculiar to Luke is so clearly the reflection of the part which Peter actually played that its formation can be explained without difficulty.

The agreement between the words of Jesus announcing Peter's denial and the incident which is described immediately afterwards, is so complete that from the literary point of view the two sections cannot be regarded as independent of each other. Either the denial was described because Jesus had foretold it or it has been put into the mouth of Jesus because it actually happened. At first sight this second explanation seems to have the most to recommend it, for it is difficult to conceive that tradition could have invented a story in which the leader of the group of the Twelve would appear in such an unfavourable light; thus the majority of critics consider that this settles the question. The matter is, however, not so simple as it appears.

[1] CORSSEN: *Die Abschiedsreden Jesu im vierten Evangelium*, *Z.N.T.W.*, VIII, 1907, p. 142.

The second hypothesis does not suggest that the story is a pure invention, since it argues that the story of the denial arose out of a saying of Jesus.

The episode is incorporated into the story of the appearance of Jesus before the Sanhedrin; the way in which this is done is far from natural. It raises many difficulties, psychological as well as textual; indeed, it is hard to understand how it was that the primitive tradition could have preserved the recollection of such a tragic incident without feeling any need to explain the fact that, after such a terrible fall, Peter was able to play such a leading part during the period which immediately followed the death of Jesus. The whole question bristles with difficulties which need to be examined in detail.[1]

According to the three Synoptic Gospels (Mark xiv. 54, 66–72*), when Jesus is led away by those who have arrested him, Peter follows at a distance, and then enters the court of the high priest where he seats himself by the fire with the high priest's servants. Thus Mark and Matthew introduce a story without narrating its conclusion; this they do later on, after they have described the appearance of Jesus before the Sanhedrin, and the scene of the insults offered to him; they do not say definitely when the incident happened, and they introduce it very abruptly into the narrative. Luke narrates the whole story at once. He could not do otherwise, since he places the session of the Sanhedrin in the morning. His dependence on the tradition of Mark is shown by the fact that he also does not place Peter's first denial at his entry into the courtyard, but later, at a moment which is not specified. A woman servant charges Peter with having been in the company of Jesus; he gives an evasive reply (Mark, Matt.), or a denial (Luke). After that, Mark and Matthew say that Peter goes off into the entrance to the courtyard, into the προαύλιον.[2] It is there that, according to the first two Gospels, the second denial took place. According to the narrative in Mark, the same woman servant says to those who were standing round: "This is one of them!" that is to say: "He belongs to this group of the followers of Jesus," an expression which is slightly

---

[1] For further details, see my study: *Did Peter Deny His Lord? A Conjecture. The Harvard Theological Review*, XXV, 1932, pp. 1–27.

[2] Mark adds that at this moment the cock crows.

surprising, since Jesus alone is prosecuted. Peter denies the fact, though it is not said what words he used. Here, therefore, there is no distinct development in the story. In Matthew, it is a different servant who interferes and says: "This fellow was also with Jesus of Nazareth!" Here Peter's denial is more explicitly stated. "He began to curse and to swear, saying, I know not the man."

According to Luke, the second scene takes place at the same spot, and in the presence of the same spectators as the first. Doubtless Luke thought it curious that Peter, after he had been in the entrance to the courtyard, should be found later on in the central court. Here it is a man who says: "Thou art also of them," and the apostle replies: "Man, I am not."

According to Mark and Matthew the third denial takes place immediately after the two first; an hour later, in Luke's account. In Luke's narrative the story begins at the moment when Peter enters the courtyard; it cannot be ended, however, until the cock crows. Mark and Matthew do not say definitely where the third denial took place. Peter is questioned by the spectators, or, according to Luke, by one of them only. This time the charge is made in a more assured manner and is supported by the fact that the man who accuses Peter sees that he is a Galilean. In the narratives of Matthew and Mark, Peter asserts with oaths that he does not know Jesus. In Luke he merely says: "Man, I know not what thou sayest." Just after Peter has said this, the cock crows ("for the second time," says Mark).[1] Peter then remembers the words of Jesus, and he goes out and weeps bitterly.

In John (xviii. 15–18, 25–27), as in Matthew and Mark, the story is cut into two parts, which form the setting of the questioning of Jesus by the high priest. The incident is described far more clearly: Peter follows at some distance with another disciple whose name is not given.[2] This disciple is a friend of the high priest; he has freedom of access to the house. He goes into the courtyard and then asks the portress to allow him to admit his friend Peter as well. It is at this moment that the portress says to Peter: "Art thou not also one of this man's

---

[1] Luke adds that the Lord Jesus turned and looked at Peter.
[2] It seems clear that in the mind of the evangelist this is John.

disciples?" and Peter replies: "I am not." After Jesus has been questioned before the Sanhedrin the story is continued as abruptly as in Mark. The two other denials are briefly narrated. Someone says to Peter: "Art not thou also one of his disciples?" and he denies it saying: "I am not." Then another man looks at Peter curiously—this time the questioner is a relative of the man whose ear Peter had cut off in the Garden of Gethsemane —and says: "Did I not see thee in the garden with him?" Peter again denies the accusation, and "immediately the cock crew."

The Johannine narrative is thus more coherent and more natural than those of the Synoptic Gospels; why is this? Is it due to the fact that John was able to draw upon a tradition which Mark either did not know at all, or which he only knew in a different form?[1] Or, can it be that he was very conscious of the confusions in the Synoptic narrative, and that he was trying to eliminate them? This hypothesis seems most improbable, for John does not usually take any trouble to see whether his narrative is coherent or not. John has a different aim than that of making the story more clear. He assumes, and this is certainly not historical, that a disciple of Jesus stood at the foot of the cross (xix. 26), and this fact is for him of primary importance, because it makes it possible for him to introduce the witness to the water and the blood, symbols of Baptism and the Eucharist, which broke forth from the side of Jesus (xix. 34–35) when it was pierced by the soldier's lance. The idea that this disciple was a friend of the high priest may be designed to explain the presence of this disciple.

The difficulty which seems to be cleared away by the intervention of this anonymous disciple may very well be only apparent; we do not know to what extent the gate to the courtyard of the high priest was guarded, or whether it may have been possible for someone who was neither a Temple servant nor a servant of the high priest to have slipped into the courtyard without being observed, under cover of the excitement caused by the arrest of Jesus.

The nameless disciple and Peter also appear together in the account of the visit to the tomb after Mary Magdalene has

---

[1] As JOH. WEISS believes (*Aelt. Ev.*, p. 307), and as I have said myself: *Sources*, pp. 82 ff.

found it empty (xx. 3–10). It is said of "that other disciple" that "he saw and believed." The same is not said of Peter; thus the sight of the empty tomb was not sufficient to convince him of the reality of the Resurrection. This suggests that in this respect the nameless disciple is superior to Peter. The introduction of this figure into the story of the night at the palace of the high priest may have been suggested by the same consideration.

The fact that John's narrative, like that of Mark, is cut into two parts establishes a direct relation between them. In John's narrative the division takes place after, and not before, the first denial. If Mark had known of this arrangement he would not have reduced the first part of the story to the level of an introduction which has neither meaning nor interest in itself. The fact that Luke gives a unified account does not prove that his story was based on a different source from that of Mark, for the idea of uniting the two elements of the narrative in the second Gospel was one which might very easily occur to the mind. Further, Luke was obliged to do this, because he places the appearance before the Sanhedrin in the early morning and not during the night.

There is therefore no trace of a form of tradition in which the account of Peter's denial was not already combined with that of the appearance of Jesus before the Sanhedrin. But the connexion between the two sections is artificial. They are related to each other by a method which is identical with that which Mark uses in chapter iii (20–35) to connect two sections of a different origin: the accusation of madness launched against Jesus by his own relatives, and the statement of the Pharisees that he casts out demons by Beelzebub, the prince of the demons. We may therefore assume that Mark— or the author of the Passion narrative which follows—knew the story of the denial of Peter as an isolated fragment, and that he tried to insert it into the story of the events of the night in the palace of the high priest.

The story of Peter's denial raises various psychological and textual difficulties. It is difficult to understand how it was that Peter, after he realized that he had already been very indiscreet, stayed in the courtyard instead of going away at once. The fact that after the first denial Peter goes out into the vestibule also seems to suggest that he was about to leave the building. This difficulty might be resolved by assuming another and earlier tradition which might have contained only one denial. The two others might then be explained as due to the existence of several parallel traditions which maintained a separate existence instead of being fused into one. Another and more serious difficulty, however, has still to be faced: Peter is supposed to have denied his Master, and the tears which he shed on leaving the courtyard of the high priest's palace are supposed to have been sufficient to abolish the consequences of this fault and this lie.[1] No one is astonished, apparently, that the very moment the group of the disciples of Jesus is reconstituted, Peter plays a leading part in it. At a time when discipline was so strict that it was believed that the deceitful couple, Ananias and Sapphira, were punished with death (Acts v. 1-11), no one seems to have thought that the cowardice and lying of Peter might have disqualified him for leadership. Also, would not Paul, in whose interest it was to weaken Peter's authority in the eyes of the Galatians, in their hesitating state of mind, and who speaks out very plainly about what he calls (unjustly) his hypocrisy at Antioch (Gal. ii. 11 f.), have laid stress on the weakness of the apostle whom the Judaizing missionaries set up against him?

Thus there are serious difficulties in the way of accepting the story of the denial as historical. They are not counter-balanced by those which assume that tradition created a legend attributing to the leader of the Twelve such an unfortunate attitude. There must be something, therefore, to account for the formation of the story. This "something" is a saying of Jesus blaming Peter for his presumption, and, if not announc-

___

[1] It is true that commentators, with rare exceptions (for instance, SPITTA: *Die Auferstehung Jesu*, Göttingen, 1918, p. 18) believe that in reporting the interview between the Risen Jesus and Peter, after which the Master confides to his disciple the mission to feed his sheep (John xxi. 15-17), the author of chapter xxi of John (without doubt the editor of the Gospel) intended to convey the rehabilitation of Peter. But the story contains no allusion either to the denial or to any forfeiture of confidence as the result of it. In the conclusion, Jesus does not give to Peter the apostolic authority which he is supposed to have lost, but he confides to him a special mission, that of governing the Church.

ing it positively, at least hinting at a defection on his part. It would be impossible for tradition to believe that anything which Jesus foresaw could not have been fulfilled; thus there grew up the idea that Peter denied his Master. Once this idea was established, it is not astonishing that a story should have been invented relating in what circumstances and in what way this incident took place.

Under these conditions, the historicity of the saying of Jesus may be retained, and that of the denial rejected.

II. GETHSEMANE

When Jesus left the upper room, he set out for the Mount of Olives. John (xviii. 1–2) says that he stopped at the foot of the hill, on the other side of the brook Cedron, in a garden to which he often went with his disciples. Luke speaks more definitely of his habit of spending the night on the Mount of Olives (xxii. 39; cf. xxi. 37). Mark (xiv. 32) and Matthew (xxvi. 36) alone mention the name of Gethsemane. It has no symbolical or allegorical significance.[1] It cannot be assumed that it belongs to a secondary stage of tradition, since at this point in the story the evangelists would take the utmost care to say at what precise spot the scenes of the Agony and the arrest of Jesus took place. Indeed, it was not until the fourth century that there was any interest in this question at all. Thus the name of Gethsemane must have been present in the primitive tradition. Luke does not mention it because he was writing for readers outside Palestine; possibly John omitted it because the scene of the Agony did not harmonize with his Christology.

According to Mark (xiv. 32–42) and Matthew (xxvi. 36–46), whose accounts do not differ much, save for some slight variations in style, when Jesus arrived at the garden of Geth-

---

[1] Various derivations have been suggested for this name. The choice may lie between "press of the signals" (which would refer to the custom to which the Talmud bears witness of giving the signal for the new moon by lighting fires on the Mount of Olives) or "oil-press." For the discussion of this subject, as well as of the traditions relating to the site of Gethsemane, see ABEL. II, pp. 301 ff. DALMAN: *Itin.*, pp. 420 ff.

semane he took with him Peter and James and John, and asked them to watch with him. Passing through a moment of anguish and despair he went further on, fell on his knees and prayed: "Father, if it be possible, remove this cup from me. Nevertheless, not what I will, but what Thou wilt." Then he came back to Peter and his companions and found them asleep. He reproached Peter for being unable to watch one hour with him. The same scene is repeated a second and a third time. Then Jesus wakened his disciples, saying to them ironically: "Sleep on now and take your rest. It is enough, the hour is come; behold, the Son of Man is betrayed into the hands of sinners. Rise up, let us go; lo, he that betrayeth me is at hand."

In Luke (xxii. 40–46) the arrangement of the story is simpler. Jesus leaves all his disciples together when he goes away to pray. His prayer does not remain without response. An angel appears from heaven to strengthen him. Being in an agony, he prays more earnestly, till his sweat is like drops of blood falling upon the ground;[1] then he rises from the ground and goes to his disciples, whom he urges to pray in order that they may not fall into temptation.

It is not necessary to assume that Luke knew the episode in Gethsemane in a different tradition from that used by Mark. The fact that Jesus leaves all his disciples together when he goes away to pray eliminates a confusing statement in the

[1] Verses 43–44 (the appearance of the angel and the bloody sweat) are lacking in several cases in the textual evidence (א. A. B. N. R. T. W. 13–69, 124, 788–826, 579 f. sys. sa. bo. Cyril, Athanasius, Ambrose). Among critics opinion about the authenticity of these two verses is greatly divided. Keim, Tischendorf, Blass, Holtzmann, Pfleiderer, Harnack, W. Bauer, are in favour of their authenticity. On the contrary, Westcott and Hort, Bernh. Weiss, Merx, Gregory, Wellhausen, reject it. In my opinion these verses are genuine, for at a comparatively late period, when the idea of the divinity of Christ was definitely established, Jesus would not have been represented as being overwhelmed to the point of needing to be strengthened by an angel. One section of the evidence for the text (without verses 43–44) is Egyptian, and would date from the time of the Athanasian orthodoxy; it may have been under the influence of this orthodoxy that these verses were omitted. Their authenticity is confirmed by the fact that John knew the incident of Gethsemane and the angel (see p. 494).

Marcan narrative, in which it is said that Jesus rejoins his three intimate friends but not the eight others. The episode of the angel is intended to show that the prayer of Jesus was not left unanswered. It expresses something which was implicit in the Marcan narrative, where there is a great contrast, which is certainly intentional, between the anguish in Gethsemane and the fortitude which Jesus reveals at the moment of his arrest. This detail having been introduced, however, the story could not be prolonged; the mention of a second and a third prayer would only have weakened it.

John has regarded the incident of Gethsemane as incompatible with his Christology. But he must have known of it. At the moment of his arrest Jesus exclaims: "The cup which my Father hath given me, shall I not drink it?" (xviii. 11). A still more direct trace of the incident appears in the section xii. 27-30: Jesus, after he has spoken of the necessity for and the fruitfulness of his death, exclaims: "Now is my soul troubled." This is a direct allusion to the language used by Mark, but John does not admit that Jesus asked to be delivered; he makes him say: "What shall I say? 'Father, save me from this hour?' But for this cause came I unto this hour. 'Father, glorify Thy name.' " Here Jesus does not need to struggle in order to accept death. And the story closes with a feature in which it is easy to recognize the transposition of the story of the angel. A celestial voice declares: "I have both glorified it, and I will glorify it again." Those who stood by were divided in their opinion when they heard this sound. Some said that it had thundered; others, that an angel had spoken to Jesus. He himself explains it thus: "This voice came not because of me, but for your sakes."

It is impossible to discuss the historicity of a scene whose only witnesses were men who were at some distance and were asleep. This does not mean, however, that the incident of Gethsemane loses its value. The striking contrast between the trouble and the anguish of Jesus and the serenity which he is said to have manifested from the moment he was arrested prove that this tradition could only have been formed at a time when his friends still knew that when Jesus realized that he was caught in a net from which it was impossible to escape, he passed through an experience of positive agony, and that he had to struggle in order to be able to accept what he believed to be the will of God. Although this incident cannot be regarded as literally accurate, on a higher plane it is true. In an admirable allegory it expresses what took place in the soul of Jesus.

III. JUDAS

The four Gospels are agreed in saying that Judas,[1] one of the Twelve, served as a guide to those who went forth to arrest Jesus. Thus he must have revealed to his enemies the place of his nocturnal retreat.

Very early, legend became busy about the figure of Judas.[2] Even in the New Testament we have two versions of the story of his death which cannot be reconciled with each other (Matt. xxvii. 3–10 and Acts i. 18–19),[3] and we find attempts at a psychological explanation of his act which shows that it was not understood. The Synoptic Gospels say (Mark xiv. 10–11*) that he betrayed Jesus for the sake of a reward in

---

[1] The surname Iscariot is obscure. It is given in different forms, in different passages, and in different MSS. It may have been given to Judas during the ministry of Jesus in order to distinguish him from another apostle, Judas, son of James. The reading of MS. D. in John xii. 40 indicates that it means the man from Kerioth, a town or village to the south of Judaea (BUHL: *Geographie des alten Palästina*, Freiburg im Br., Leipzig, Tübingen, 1896, p. 182). SCHULTHESS (*Die Sprache der Evangelien*, *Z.N.T.W.*, XXI, 1922, pp. 250 ff.) declares this statement impossible from the philological point of view. Adopting a suggestion already given by WELLHAUSEN (*Mk.*, p. 25), he reads "the *sicaire*," that is "the assassin." He thinks also that Iscariot might mean "man of Sychar," that is, a Samaritan, or "the man of Issachar" (because of the *Testament of the Twelve Patriarchs, Issachar*, I: "Because of the salary I have been named Issachar"). CHEYNE (art. *Judas, E.B.*, II, c. 2623) suggests tentatively that Iscariot may be a corruption of Ἰεριχώτης, the man of Jericho. We may conclude, with HEITMÜLLER (art. *Judas, R.G.G.*, III, col. 795), that it is impossible to find any satisfactory meaning for the name Iscariot.

[2] WREDE: *Judas Ischariot in der urchristlichen Ueberlieferung*, in *Vorträge und Studien*, pp. 127–146.

[3] They are not, however, absolutely independent of each other, since in both there is mention of a field acquired with the price of the betrayal which bears the name "field of blood."

money, and Matthew, basing his story on a phrase in Zech. xi. 12, states that the price of the treachery was thirty pieces of silver. John (xii. 6) alludes to the same explanation, but at the same time he suggests another: at the moment when Jesus hands the sop to Judas Satan enters into him (xiii. 27). These explanations of the evangelists are only conjectures, for the motives of the act of Judas remain unknown, and the interviews which must have taken place between him and the Jewish authorities must have been secret.

For various reasons the historicity of the betrayal has sometimes been doubted.[1]

The first reason is this: the impossibility of coming to a definite conclusion about the nature of the betrayal. This consideration, however, is one which ought rather to constitute a reason for maintaining the historicity of the incident. If it had been fictitious the whole incident would have been presented in a more concrete manner. The obscurity of the narrative is due to the fact that the events of the close of the ministry of Jesus are presented in the Gospels in a light which does not exactly correspond with the actual course of events. If the decision to arrest Jesus had been made without preparation, at a moment when Jesus was carrying on his public activity, it is difficult to understand in what way the intervention of Judas would have been either necessary or useful. It would have been sufficient to arrange to have Jesus followed by a few police officials in order to have him seized during the night. This would not be the case, however, if Jesus had been in hiding near the city, and if he only returned to it for the Last Supper, with a great many precautions.

Another argument which is often used is this: outside the Gospels and the Acts the treachery of Judas is not mentioned

---

[1] For instance, VOLKMAR: *Die Religion Jesu und ihre erste geschichtliche Entwickelung*, Leipzig, 1857, pp. 260 ff. WEIDEL: *St. u. Kr.*, 1912, pp. 167 ff. G. MARQUARDT: *Der Verrat des Judas Ischariot, eine Sage*, München, 1900. G. SCHLÄGER: *Die Ungeschichtlichkeit des Verrats des Judas*, *Z.N.T.W.*, XV, 1914, pp. 50–59. MARG. PLATH: *Warum hat die urchristliche Gemeinde auf die Ueberlieferung der Judaerzählungen Wert gelegt?* *Z.N.T.W.*, XVII, 1916, pp. 178–188,

in the New Testament.[1] He is always mentioned as one of the Twelve (for instance, 1 Cor. xv. 5;[2] Rev. xxi. 12–14), as though their circle had not been broken by the defection of one of them. Doubtless the editor of the Acts has tried to clear up the difficulty (i. 15–26) by recording the incident of the election of Matthias in place of Judas. But this is a later narrative, which only shows that the fact upon which the critics have insisted was already perceived in the Early Church. This objection does not seem to be any more conclusive than the previous one, seeing that the idea of a group of twelve apostles is a later one, which, under the influence of the conflicts between the Pauline apostolate and the Jerusalem apostolate, was projected into the story of the life of Jesus.[3]

It is difficult to conceive how the tradition of the betrayal could have been invented without any historical basis. Weidel has suggested that it may have originated in the words of Psa. xli. 9: "Mine own familiar friend . . . which did eat of my bread, hath lifted up his heel against me." But in this passage there is only the idea of hostility, not of treachery. Further, it is only in John's account that this verse of the Psalm is quoted. Volkmar thinks that the legend of Judas was created in order to diminish the authority of the Twelve, and to make a breach in their circle, in order to allow the apostolate of Paul to be asserted. But the story of Judas has never been used against the Twelve, and although Paul claimed an authority equal to that of the apostles of Jerusalem, he did not demand a place in their group.

The treachery of Judas has raised a problem for Christian thought which it has found very difficult and perplexing. How could one reconcile the foreknowledge attributed to Jesus with the fact that he admitted to the intimate circle of his friends one who was to betray him? In primitive Christianity the story of Judas was a terrible scandal.[4] It was only

[1] In 1 Cor. xi. 23 Paul speaks of the night in which the Lord was delivered up. This may be an allusion to the betrayal. It is not certain, however, for it may also mean "in which he was delivered by God into the hands of his enemies."

[2] Certain MSS. D. F. A. 464 lat. have corrected "to the Twelve" into "to the Eleven." [3] See pp. 342 ff.

[4] And not only to Primitive Christianity, as is evidenced by this statement of KEIM: "It would lift a very heavy burden from the heart of Christianity

included in the story because there were solid reasons for believing that it actually happened.

We know too little to attempt a psychological explanation of this fact. The explanation suggested by the Gospels, that Judas betrayed Jesus for some personal advantage of his own, is hardly plausible. If Judas had been essentially a self-centred miser, would he have ever begun to follow Jesus at all? It has been suggested that he may have been deceived in his hopes by seeing that Jesus refused to enter on the path of political Messianism.[1] We might also assume that he wished to drive Jesus to the necessity for working some striking miracle. All these theories are mere conjectures, whose basis is so uncertain that it is not worth while spending time in discussing them.

IV. The Arrest

Mark (xiv. 43) and Matthew (xxvi. 47) relate that at the moment when Jesus went to rouse his disciples from slumber Judas appeared with a crowd armed with staves and swords, sent by the Jewish authorities. They imply, therefore, that these were Temple police, reinforced perhaps by some other men enlisted and armed in haste. Luke (xxii. 47) uses a term which is more vague, "a crowd" ($\check{o}\chi\lambda os$). John (xviii. 3; cf. xviii. 12) speaks of "the cohort," or, more exactly, of a detachment of the cohort which proceeded to the arrest of Jesus.[2]

According to the Synoptic Gospels (Mark xiv. 44–45), Judas had arranged beforehand with the soldiers that he would give them a sign to show them the person they were to take into custody. So he approached Jesus to give him the kiss of friendship; at once the soldiers laid hands on Jesus.

John, instead of giving the account of the treacherous kiss, sketches a little picture which is most characteristic. When

if it could be proved that the betrayal of Judas did not take place, and that it is the product of the Christian imagination. Unfortunately," he concludes, "this cannot be proved" (III, pp. 242 f.).

[1] WINDISCH: *Der messianische Krieg und das Urchristentum*, pp. 36 ff.

[2] P. 467 (n. 1 of p. 466).

Jesus sees the band of soldiers and Temple police approaching, he steps forward to meet them and says: "Whom seek ye?" They reply: "Jesus of Nazareth." "I am he," says Jesus. At once the men fall back and fall on the ground. Jesus repeats his question, and then he says: "I have told you that I am he: if therefore ye seek me, let these go their way" (xviii. 4–9). The aim of the evangelist is to show that Jesus gave himself up willingly into the hands of his enemies rather than that he was arrested by them against his will. The initiative belongs to him alone. If he only needed to speak, and the men fell to the ground, it would have been very easy for him to escape.

One of the spectators draws his sword and strikes the servant of the high priest such a heavy blow that he cuts off his ear (Mark xiv. 47); Luke adds the detail that it was the right ear (xxii. 50). John says that the man who struck the blow was Peter, and that the name of the servant was Malchus (xviii. 10–11). According to Mark, the disciple's action does not provoke any reaction on the part of Jesus. Matthew (xxvi. 52–54),[1] Luke (xxii. 51), and John (xviii. 11) say that Jesus checks this show of resistance, and Luke adds that he cures the man who was wounded. We are here confronted with a typical example of the rapid evolution of tradition. The result of its development is not merely the introduction of fresh details into the story, but a more complete integration of the episode into the narrative as a whole. Matthew and Mark are content to place facts simply alongside of one another, and they place this detail at the moment when Jesus is already in the hands of the soldiers, that is to say, when it is too late to attempt to resist. Luke and John have transposed it, and have placed it before the actual moment of arrest. These facts make us doubt whether the incident of the blow with the sword was included in the tradition which was followed by Mark in the story of the arrest. It is a relic of a tradition which we are not able to reconstitute as a whole, and of which it is impossible to say whether it is based upon history or not.

[1] Matthew (xxvi. 53–54) adds that Jesus declares that he could call on his Father who would send to his assistance more than twelve legions of angels, but that the Scriptures must be fulfilled.

There is reason to doubt the historicity of the reproach which, according to the Synoptic Gospels (Mark xiv. 48–49*), Jesus addresses to those who arrest him: "Are ye come out as against a thief, with swords and with staves, to take me? I was daily with you in the Temple teaching, and ye took me not: but the scriptures must be fulfilled."[1] This saying assumes the conception of the Jerusalem ministry which is outlined by the Synoptists, a conception which, as we have already seen, does not agree with the facts. The narrative of this part of the story ends both in Mark (xiv. 50) and in Matthew (xxvi. 56) with the flight of the disciples.

Mark (xiv. 51–52) adds another detail: A young man was following Jesus clad only in a linen cloth.[2] The soldiers caught hold of him. But he left the cloth in the hands of the soldiers and fled from them naked.

The words "followed with"[3] which the text uses, without saying with whom the young man followed, shows that the incident is drawn from a different version than that used by Mark.

Some writers[4] have connected this detail with the words of Amos ii. 16: "And he that is courageous among the mighty shall flee away[5] in that day, saith the Lord." This interpretation is, however, untenable, because there is no quotation

---

[1] In the Lucan narrative (xxii. 52) Jesus addresses his words to the chief priests, the Temple authorities, and the elders of the people. Their presence at the moment of the arrest is not mentioned at the beginning of the account. Thus we may regard this as improbable.

[2] The text of the printed editions reads, in the majority of the MSS., περιβεβλημένος σινδόνα ἐπὶ γυμνοῦ, literally, "wrapped in a piece of material round a naked body." The MSS. Θ. 13–69–346, 565 eth. sy^p read, or imply, instead of ἐπὶ γυμνοῦ, γυμνός, "clothed with a piece of stuff, naked," which is hardly satisfactory. W. 1–118, 209, sy^s· c. k. sah. read, or imply, simply: "clad in a piece of stuff." It is this text which we regard as primitive. The word γυμνός, afterwards corrected to ἐπὶ γυμνοῦ, must be due to some error in copying, which has confused this with verse 52.

[3] συνηκολούθει (א. B. C. L.) or συνηκολούθησεν (Δ) (followed with) is corrected to ἠχολούθει (followed) by D. I., etc., and to ἠκολούθησεν by A. N., etc.

[4] For instance, KEIM, III, pp. 318 f. S. REINACH: C.M.R., IV, p. 168. LOISY: Syn., II, p. 679. KLOSTERMANN: Mk., p. 171.

[5] Text of Lucian; the others have "will be pursued."

to indicate it, and also because, if the writer was thinking of the most courageous of Jesus' followers, he would have mentioned the disciple who tried to defend Jesus with his sword.

Many interpreters, as for instance Fr. Abel and Fr. Vincent,[1] think that this was a young man who had been sleeping out in the Garden of Gethsemane, and who rose in haste on hearing the sudden commotion. Some suggest that, although no name is given, this may be the evangelist himself, John-Mark, the son of Mary.[2] This conjecture breaks down because the account of the arrest of Jesus is not that of an eye-witness. We are mistaken if we admit, on the basis of the most widespread version of the text, that the young man was clad merely in a piece of linen. The word γυμνός sometimes means "an undergarment," that is to say, "without a cloak" (ἱμάτιον),[3] and it is probably the fact that some scribes have misunderstood the meaning of γυμνός in verse 52, which explains why they have introduced γυμνὸς or ἐπὶ γυμνοῦ in verse 51. Thus it is impossible to draw the inference from the scanty costume of this person that he had risen in haste and had appeared from nowhere. In this incident we must see a fragment of a tradition—perhaps of that from which the episode of the blow with the sword is drawn—according to which the friends of Jesus tried to prevent his arrest. It is not the tradition which has created the idea of resistance, since it tries to show that Jesus accepted his fate without making any effort to escape. If the aim of the writer was simply to defend the apostles by showing that they did not flee until they had perceived that resistance was useless, the blow with the sword would not have been first of all attributed to some nameless individual, and it would not have been suggested that it was a young man, who did not belong to the circle of the Twelve, who was very nearly arrested with Jesus.

---

[1] ABEL, II, p. 303.
[2] ZAHN: *Einleitung in das Neue Testament*, II, Leipzig, 1900, pp. 243 f. SWETE: *The Gospel according to Saint Mark*[2], London, 1905, pp. LXV, 354.
[3] *P. Magd.*, 6, 7. A passage in the Talmud (*Menachot*, 44a) quoted by STRACK-BILLERBECK (II, p. 51) calls a person naked who was without his mantle, though still clad in his robe with the regulation tassels.

V. Jesus Before the High Priest [1]

Immediately after his arrest Jesus is led before the high priest. At that time the high priest was Caiaphas. Matthew (xxvi. 3, 57) alone gives his name. According to the Synoptic narrative Jesus was led to the palace of Caiaphas [2] itself. The detail is probable, although we cannot be absolutely sure of the facts of the case, since this part of the narrative belongs to the section which includes the story of Peter's denial, which, as we have seen, cannot be retained as historical.

According to Mark (xiv. 55) and Matthew (xxvi. 59), the Sanhedrin assembled immediately. Although this is not explicitly stated, the narrative seems to imply that it was already assembled, waiting for Jesus to be brought before it. According to Luke (xxii. 66), the Sanhedrin did not assemble till the early morning. John (xviii. 19–24) [3] does not mention

[1] The question of the trial of Jesus, and especially of the Jewish trial, has just been taken up by H. Lietzmann: *Der Prozess Jesu S. B. A.*, 1931, XIV, pp. 310–322 (we quote from the special edition). Cf. Martin Dibelius: *Das historische Problem der Leidensgeschichte*, *Z.N.T.W.*, XXX, 1931, pp. 193–201. Büchsel: *Die Blutsgerichtbarkeit des Synedrions*, *Z.N.T.W.*, XXX, 1931, pp. 202–210. Lietzmann: *Bemerkungen zum Prozess Jesu*, I, *Z.N.T.W.*, XXX, 1931, pp. 211–215; II, *Z.N.T.W.*, XXXI, 1932, pp. 78–84. I have indicated (*A propos du procès de Jésus*, *Z.N.T.W.*, XXXI, 1932, pp. 289–301) the reasons for which the remarks made in the course of the discussion do not seem to me of a nature to cause me to modify my conclusions.

[2] According to Josephus (*G.J.*, 17, 6, ¶ 426) the house of the high priest was in the upper part of the city. In 383 this house was shown (Pèlerin de Bordeaux, P. Geyer: *Itineraria hierosolymitana*, Vindobonae, 1898, p. 22). In the sixth century there was on the supposed site of the palace of Caiaphas a church in which was shown the pillar of the scourging with the marks of the breast, the arms, and the hands of Jesus. On this point, see Abel, II, p. 484. Dalman: *Itin.*, pp. 429 ff.

[3] We follow the Greek text. It is arranged thus: (i) Jesus is led to Annas, the father-in-law of the high priest Caiaphas (12–14); (ii) Peter and the nameless disciple, who follow Jesus at a distance, enter the court of the high priest, the first denial (15–18); (iii) Jesus is questioned by the high priest (19–23); (iv) Annas sends Jesus bound to Caiaphas (24); (v) second and third denials (25–27); (vi) at break of day Jesus is led to the Praetorium. In this passage there are certain inconsistencies and obscurities. Led to Annas, Jesus is questioned by Caiaphas, then sent by Annas to Caiaphas. Peter and the nameless disciple who follow Jesus arrive at the courtyard of the high priest when Jesus has been led to Annas. P. Abel

the Sanhedrin; he says that Jesus was led before Annas, the father-in-law of the high priest Caiaphas, and that there he underwent a process of questioning on the part of the high priest. There is not a single phrase which makes any allusion to the presence of the members of the Sanhedrin. After this questioning Annas sends Jesus away, bound, to Caiaphas. Mark and Matthew mention two sittings of the Sanhedrin: one took place immediately after the arrest, the other in the morning (Mark xv. 1*), before Jesus was led before Pilate. Luke and John only mention one appearance of Jesus before the Sanhedrin, the former places this in the early morning; the latter does not say definitely when it took place, but seems to imply that it happened at the moment when Jesus was brought into the palace of the high priest.[1]

In Mark (xiv. 55–64) the account of the appearance of Jesus

(II, p. 483), taking up afresh an opinion which had already been suggested in very early days by Euthymius Zigadenus (cf. ZAHN: *Johev.*, p. 626), has suggested that possibly Annas and Caiaphas lived in two main buildings opening on to a common courtyard. The hypothesis is ingenious, but, in addition to the fact that it is a pure conjecture, it still does not explain the *rôle* attributed to Annas. The Syriac-Sinaitic version arranges the account quite differently. It intercalates verse 24 (Annas sends Jesus to Caiaphas) between verses 13 and 14. Thus Jesus, led to Annas, is immediately sent on to Caiaphas, and it places verses 15–18 (the entrance of the nameless disciple and Peter into the courtyard and the first denial) immediately before verses 25–27. Thus the denial is told as one connected story. This may be due to the influence of the Lucan narrative, but it does not give a satisfactory arrangement, since it does not explain how it was that the disciples did not arrive sooner. WELLHAUSEN (*Das. Ev. Joh.*, pp. 81 f.) and BLASS (*Ev. sec. Joh.*, Leipzig, p. 91) think that, at least so far as the position of verse 24 is concerned, the Syriac-Sinaitic version has preserved the original text. But, as has been noted by JEAN RÉVILLE, for instance (*Q.É.*, p. 267, n. 2), and SCHWARTZ (I, p. 350 f.), although it is easy to imagine that tradition may have displaced verse 24 in order to obtain a more connected story, the transference of this verse to the place where we find it in the Greek text would be inexplicable if it had been originally between verses 13 and 14. In my opinion the explanation of the text seems to be provided in this instance rather by literary than by textual criticism.

[1] LIETZMANN (*S.B.A.*, XXXI, 1931, XIV, pp. 9 ff.) gives a proof that the account of the first appearance does not occur in the original tradition. We have expounded the reasons which prevent us from accepting this opinion in *Z.N.T.W.*, XXXI, 1932, pp. 293 f., 296 ff.

before the Sanhedrin falls naturally into four parts, of which the first three seem to be simply placed alongside of one another.

(i) (55–56). The chief priests and all the members of the Sanhedrin make vain attempts to find evidence on which they could convict Jesus of some crime; false witnesses appear, but their evidence does not agree, and it cannot be used against the prisoner.

(ii) (57–61a). The false witnesses report that they heard Jesus say: "I will destroy this Temple that is made with hands, and within three days I will build another made without hands." But their witness does not agree together, doubtless on questions of time and place. Although, under these conditions, the accusation cannot be maintained, the high priest asks Jesus whether he has anything to say to the charges brought against him. But Jesus does not reply.

It is difficult to understand why, if this were an actual instance of false evidence, the narrator should enter into details which he does not give in connexion with the charges mentioned in the beginning of the narrative, nor why the high priest questions Jesus about a charge which, from the legal point of view, does not exist.

(iii) (61b–62). The high priest gives a new turn to the trial. He asks Jesus whether he is the Messiah, the son of the Blessed, and Jesus replies: "I am: and ye shall see the Son of Man sitting on the right hand of power (that is, of God), and coming in the clouds of heaven." [1]

(iv) (63–64). The high priest, when he hears the statement of Jesus, rends his garments and says: "What need we any further witnesses?" All present decide that Jesus deserves to be put to death. It should be noted that it is not stated that the judges pronounce a sentence of death, but only that they declare that Jesus is "guilty of death."

The narrative in Matthew (xxvi. 59–66) only differs from that of Mark on a few points. We will only examine those which are more than mere variations in expression.

The two statements are not simply placed side by side; the meaning is this: "The proof that I am he is this, that you will see the Son of Man, whom I am, coming on the clouds of heaven."

After he has mentioned the false witnesses whose evidence was not accepted, Matthew says: "At the last came two" (xxvi. 60). He does not say, like Mark, that they are false witnesses, nor that their evidence does not agree. The words put into the mouth of Jesus are in a different form from those quoted in Mark. The contrast between "made and not made by the hands of man" is not brought out at all, and Jesus is reputed to have said, not "I will destroy this Temple," but "I am able to destroy it."

Some of the points raised by the reply of Jesus should be noted. Instead of saying, "I am," Jesus replies, "Thou hast said." This formula seems more in keeping with the general attitude of Jesus, to whom the Messiahship is a mystery which ought not to be published abroad. In the second place, the two elements in the reply of Jesus, simply set side by side in Mark, are connected by the phrase: "Nevertheless I say unto you." Instead of the declaration in Mark which refers to the *parousia*, Matthew has: "Hereafter shall ye see the Son of Man sitting on the right hand of power, and coming in the clouds of heaven." Thus Matthew substitutes the idea of glorification for that of the return, but in an incomplete way, since the idea of the return is retained. This makes the text of Matthew confused, since it places an assertion relating to a state which will be seen "henceforth" (it is not said how), by an act which will take place in the future, and will only last for a moment. Here there has evidently been some manipulation of the text.

Luke's account (xxii. 66–71) seems, at first sight, very different from that of Mark. Here there is no mention of any desire to find witnesses. The members of the Sanhedrin ask Jesus immediately: "Art thou the Christ? tell us." He replies: "If I tell you, ye will not believe: and if I also ask you, ye will not answer me." After this sentence, which seems to suggest that he will not reply, he declares: "Hereafter shall the Son of Man sit on the right hand of the power of God." Then the members of the Sanhedrin ask: "Art thou then the Son of God?" Jesus replies: "Ye say that I am." [1] So far as the main

---

[1] Literally, "You say that I am he," which might be regarded as an evasive reply. Luke certainly does not give this meaning to it.

point is concerned the conclusion is the same as in Matthew and Mark: "What need we any further witnesses?" say the members of the Sanhedrin, "for we ourselves have heard[1] of his own mouth." Nor is there here any actual sentence of death, in the usual meaning of the phrase. The council is then adjourned, and Jesus is led away to Pilate.

Luke's narrative is not as independent of that of Mark as would appear at first sight. A very clear trace of an allusion to the search for witnesses in the source employed by Luke persists in the words of the conclusion: "What need we any further witnesses?" The doubling of the question concerning the Messiahship adds nothing to the story; the fact that in the first reply of Jesus an evasive statement and a formal declaration are placed close together can only be explained if we assume that Luke knew that two questions were put to Jesus, and that he had refused to answer the first of them.

The narrative in the Fourth Gospel (xviii. 19–23) is far more vague, and this seems particularly strange, seeing that in John the tendency is to throw a great deal of guilt on to the Jews. The high priest questions Jesus about his disciples and about his teaching. Jesus replies: "I spake openly to the world; I ever taught in the synagogue, and in the Temple, whither the Jews always resort, and in secret have I said nothing. Why askest thou me? Ask them which heard me, what I have said unto them: behold they know what I said." One of the Temple police who was standing by struck Jesus with the palm of his hand, saying: "Answerest thou the high priest so?" Jesus replies: "If I have spoken evil, bear witness of the evil: but if well, why smitest thou me?"

This version is very vague. Either John knew neither the Synoptic narrative nor any other tradition about the appearance of Jesus before the Sanhedrin, or possibly there was something in the Marcan narrative which he did not wish to reproduce. He knew the saying of Jesus about the Temple (ii. 19), but he gives it an allegorical interpretation. He could not find a place for it in the account of the trial. How could he have imagined that Jesus, who had declared that neither on Mount Gerizim nor in Jerusalem would men worship the Father (iv. 21),

---

[1] That is to say, we have heard the confession or the blasphemy.

would be concerned about the fate of the Temple and its eventual rebuilding? How, on the other hand, could he who had spiritualized the eschatology of Jesus, and had substituted the sending of the Paraclete for the *parousia*, have made Jesus speak of his coming on the clouds of heaven?

We cannot be absolutely certain that John knew the Synoptic narrative, but we can see that it would [have been impossible for him to reproduce it; in any case he knew no other. However, he knew and insisted on saying that Jesus had been questioned by the high priest.[1]

In order to determine what connexion exists between the narrative of Mark and that of John, we must first of all examine the value of the tradition relating to the two sayings of Jesus which are reported by Mark. The saying about the Temple expresses the feeling which Jesus had reached as the result of his ministry, that there was nothing more to hope from Israel. The boldness of this saying frightened the first generations of Christians who were still greatly attached to Judaism; some of them thought that Jesus could never have said such a thing, and they believed that the words were only suggested by the false witnesses.

Mark and Matthew did not merely try to proclaim that the words are inauthentic; they also tried to modify them in two ways: Mark by introducing the contrast between "made and not made by the hands of man," Matthew by replacing the summary statement, "I will destroy," by a simple possibility, "I am able to destroy." Thus in two ways the attempt was made to dispel the difficulties raised by this saying for Christians who were still attached to Judaism: on the one hand, by weakening the force of the saying, and on the other, by declaring that it was not authentic.

[1] If the Johannine narrative thus appears to be shorn of its value, and has, as it seems, no other source than that of Mark, an enigma remains. How are we to explain the mention of Annas, the father-in-law of Caiaphas? Did John know a tradition in which Jesus was questioned by Annas? In the tradition there may have been some confusion caused by the fact that the words "high priest" are frequently used in the Gospels in two different senses: one, the precise sense, meaning the leading priest who offers sacrifice, and, in the wider sense, of a member of one of the great priestly families.

Mark (xv. 29–30) and Matthew (xxvii. 39–40) tell how while Jesus hung in agony on the cross the passers-by mocked him, saying: "Ah, thou that destroyest the Temple, and buildest it in three days, Save thyself, and come down from the cross." This detail, whether it be historical or not, proves at least the existence of a tradition according to which Jesus is said to have been condemned to death because he proclaimed that he would destroy the Temple, while, according to Mark and Matthew, this charge was recognized as inconsistent and was abandoned.

The Fourth Gospel also reports this saying. It places it at the beginning of the ministry of Jesus, at the moment of the Cleansing of the Temple. The Jews asked Jesus for a sign which would show that he had the right to act as he had just done, and he declared: "Destroy this Temple, and in three days I will raise it up" (ii. 19). The dialogue which follows shows that the evangelist gives this saying an allegorical meaning, and makes it refer to the death and resurrection of Jesus.

According to the Book of the Acts of the Apostles (vi. 14), Stephen is accused of having said that "Jesus of Nazareth shall destroy this place, and shall change the customs which Moses delivered us." It is of course true that the editor of the Acts is speaking of false witnesses, but, in what he has preserved of Stephen's discourse, in spite of the additions and modifications which he has introduced into it, there is no protest against the ideas which are put into the mouth of Stephen, but the whole form of Jewish worship, from the days of the Tabernacle in the wilderness, is represented as one long course of idolatry. The conclusion must be that Jesus will put an end to all this.[1]

Thus we ought not to regard this saying of Jesus about the Temple simply as a calumnious charge against Jesus, with no foundation in fact,[2] nor an authentic saying which has been

---

[1] In this there may be a distant allusion to the charge brought against Jesus in the passage in the Gospel of Peter (26), which says that the disciples hid themselves because they were being tracked down as evil-doers who wanted to burn the Temple.

[2] BRANDT: *Ev. Gesch.*, p. 67. SPITTA: *Das Johev.*, p. 77; *Syn. Grundschrift*, p. 397.

altered and changed in meaning,[1] but a fully authentic saying in the form in which it is given by Mark, with the exception of the expression: "made, or not made by the hands of man."[2]

The Messianic declaration of Jesus is also absolutely authentic. It cannot have been invented either by Jews or Christians. The former would have been the last to place in the mouth of Jesus words which would justify the claims made by his disciples. The latter, if they had wished to express their faith in a declaration attributed to their master, would not have simply affirmed their expectation of the *parousia*, but would also have expressed their faith in the certainty of the resurrection, which was its guarantee.[3]

The two essential elements in the account of the appearance before the Sanhedrin therefore being admitted to be authentic, we cannot lay any weight on the objection which is sometimes raised against the Marcan narrative, based on the fact that it seems to have been certain that none of the disciples of Jesus were actually present while he was being examined by the

---

[1] HOLTZMANN: *H.C.I.*, I, 1³, p. 102. SWETE: *The Gospel according to St. Mark*, p. 359. ZAHN: *Matthev.*, p. 694. WOHLENBERG: *Mkev.*, p. 362. HOFFMANN: *Das Wort Jesu von der Zerstörung und Wiederaufbau des Tempels, Neutestamentliche Studien* HEINRICI dargebracht, Leipzig, 1914, p. 153. LAGRANGE: *Mk.*, p. 374, etc.

[2] This is the opinion of WREDE: *Messiasgeh.*, pp. 74 f. JOH. WEISS: *Aelt. Ev.*, p. 313. WELLHAUSEN: *Mk.*, p. 131. LOISY: *Syn.*, II, p. 396. NORDEN: *Agnostos Theos*, Leipzig, Berlin, 1913, pp. 195 f. BULTMANN: *Syn. Trad.*, p. 73. BERTRAM: *Leidensgesch.*, p. 56. LIETZMANN (*S.B.A.*, 1931, XIV, pp. 5 ff.) thinks that the accusation concerning the Temple is only a transposition of that which was really brought against Stephen. The analogy between the two instances is certainly striking; but I believe that the reason for this is that Stephen adopted the thought of Jesus, and in so doing provoked the same reaction among the Jews. Cf. my remarks in *Z.N.T.W.*, XXXI, 1932, p. 299, and my article, *Jésus et les origines de l'universalisme chrétien*, *R.h.p.r.*, XXI, 1932, pp. 193–211.

[3] LIETZMANN (*S.B.A.*, XIV, 1931, p. 6) brings it as an argument against the authenticity of this saying that the idea of the Messiah as Son of God is Greek and not Jewish. The remark is quite sound, but it only touches the form in which the saying of the high priest has been handed down; it does not touch the substance of the statement of Jesus.

members of the Sanhedrin.[1] The proclamation of the Messiahship of Jesus and the affirmation of his Resurrection provoked
the opposition of the Jews, who would certainly not refrain
from saying that the one whom Peter and his companions
preached had really been a blasphemer, and that this could be
proved from his own statements.

When he said that he would destroy the Temple, Jesus was
not dreaming of any acts of iconoclasm in the actual sanctuary.
He believed that the Temple, since it no longer served its
purpose, was doomed to perish. But as, on the other hand, he
did not conceive of a religion without a form of worship,[2] he
was obliged to point forward to the establishment of a new
sanctuary in the Messianic period. This is all the more probable
since the idea, if not of a new Temple, at least of the restoration
of the Temple to a fresh splendour in the Messianic era, was
widespread among the Jews.[3] From this idea to that of the
re-establishment of the Temple by the Messiah is only a step,
and it is easy to understand why the statement of Jesus that
he would destroy and rebuild the Temple was considered by
the high priest as a Messianic declaration, and why he then
asked Jesus if he believed that he was the Messiah.

Thus there is a logical connexion between the two questions
of the high priest. Mark, however, was unable to see this,
because he regarded the saying about the Temple as non-
authentic. That is why he represents the second question as
leading in a new direction.

Thus we can restore the tradition followed by Mark in the
following form:[4]

"And there arose certain and bare this witness against him,
saying: 'We heard him say: I will destroy this Temple . . .
and in three days I will build another. . . .' And the high
priest stood up, and asked Jesus, saying: 'Art thou the Christ,

[1] This objection has been taken up by LIETZMANN (*S.B.A.*, 1931, XIV, p. 5).
The fact that we know the origin of evidence is certainly not without
interest. But the absence of this guarantee does not force us to reject the
evidence. It is the question of the basis which is decisive.

[2] Cf. the saying about the celebration of the Passover in the Kingdom
of God (Luke xxii. 16).

[3] STRACK-BILLERBECK, I, pp. 1003 f.

[4] The dots indicate where words have been omitted.

the Son of the Blesséd?' Jesus said: 'I am,[1] and ye shall see the Son of Man sitting on the right hand of power, and coming in the clouds of heaven.' "

To declare that he would destroy the Temple and would rebuild it, to proclaim himself as the Messiah, the Son of the Blesséd, and to announce that he would return seated on the clouds of heaven: did all this constitute a blasphemy sufficiently serious to merit a death sentence? According to the treatise *Sanhedrin* (vii. 7), blasphemy occurs when the Divine Name has been uttered. This is not the case here. We have no guarantee, it is true, that the rules and legal principles formulated in the work entitled *Sanhedrin* were in force at the time of Jesus. It is, however, unlikely that the idea of blasphemy should have been modified to such an extent that it would not include the statement of Jesus if he had really been condemned as a blasphemer.

To claim to be the Messiah does not seem to have been considered blasphemous, for there is no indication which would lead us to suppose that the numerous aspirants to the Messiahship with whom the Procurators had to deal, would have had any quarrel with the Sanhedrin. Nor was it a crime to announce the destruction of the Temple. Josephus (*G.J.*, VI, 5, 3, ¶¶ 300 ff.) relates that at the Feast of Tabernacles, in the year 62, a peasant of the name of Jesus, the son of Ananias, began to prophesy against the city and against the Temple. The Jewish authorities only intervened in order to hand him over to the Romans, who had him scourged, but this penalty did not persuade him to cease from prophesying. The charge against him was that he was a disturber of the peace, not that he was a blasphemer.

Jesus did not say merely that the Temple would be destroyed, but also that it was he who would destroy it; and it was this declaration which brought the long conflict to a head, and must have exasperated the Jewish authorities, and have given them the feeling that Jesus was guilty of death.

In reality, Jesus was not tried by the Sanhedrin. None of the rules of procedure which are laid down in the treatise *Sanhedrin* was observed, and, although there are excellent reasons for

[1] Or: "Thou hast said."

thinking that they did not exist at the time of Jesus as they were formulated in that book, something must have been in existence all the same. There was no trial before the Sanhedrin. At the moment when Jesus appeared before the high priest he was not his prisoner at all, but the prisoner of Pilate, since he had been arrested by the cohort of Roman soldiers. Jesus was taken before the Jewish authorities because the Procurator wished it, and Pilate's motive can only have been that he wished to be quite sure that by urging him to have Jesus killed the Jewish authorities were not leading him into a trap.

The way in which the high priest questioned Jesus makes it seem very unlikely that Jesus appeared before the tribunal twice. Mark (xv. 1) and Matthew (xxvii. 1-2), who imply that the Sanhedrin assembled a second time, in the morning, doubtless imagined that after the Sanhedrin had sentenced Jesus, it had to meet in order to decide on the measures to be taken in order to obtain the ratification of the sentence by Pilate. Mark says nothing about what took place at this session. From his account we might suppose that the decision to hand Jesus over to the Procurator was made at this meeting. In any case, this is how Matthew understood the passage in Mark.

Mark (xiv. 65) and Matthew (xxvi. 67-68) report that after the Sanhedrin had proclaimed Jesus worthy of death, he was insulted by the servants of the Sanhedrin, who spat in his face, struck him, and asked him mockingly, since he was a prophet, to guess who had struck him. Luke records the same incident (xxii. 63-65), but places it before Jesus' appearance before the high priest. In his narrative this could not be placed anywhere else, since, in his account, the moment Jesus left the Sanhedrin he was led to Pilate. John has no equivalent of this scene of insult and mockery; he seems, however, to have known of it, and the blow given to Jesus during his questioning before the high priest (xviii. 22) is a relic of this incident. Considered in itself, the scene is only too likely to have happened. It seems to be a doublet of the mockery and insult endured by Jesus after his sentence at the hands of the Roman soldiers. The two scenes are, however, very far from being exactly parallel. Since, from the literary point of view, the two accounts are independent, the two incidents may both be historical.

CHAPTER XIX

THE SENTENCE

In the morning, the soldiers belonging to the cohort which had arrested Jesus, and who had led him before the high priest, now brought him before Pilate. Where did this scene take place? The Synoptists did not think it necessary to mention this fact. John (xviii. 28) speaks of the Praetorium, and in the course of his narrative he mentions the place where the tribunal was held; he gives the Greek name, "the Pavement" (λιθόστρωτον), and the Hebrew, *Gabbatha* (xix. 13).[1] These terms do not give us any accurate topographical information. The word Praetorium meant the residence of the Governor, but it could also be applied to any place where he chose to sit and try cases. In a town like Jerusalem there must have been some site, near his residence, where he usually sat to try the cases which were brought before him. We know from Josephus (*G.J.*, II, 14, 8, ¶ 301) that the Procurators, when they came to Jerusalem, lived in Herod's palace, which was situated in a prominent position, to the north of the western hill. The trial of Jesus, therefore, must have taken place in that part of the city. In the opinion of some writers, however,[2] during the Feast of the Passover, the Procurator would have resided in the Fortress Antonia to the north of the Temple, whence it was easy to overlook the Temple courts. If this view be the right one, the trial would have been held there. This is only a conjecture, however, and it seems more probable that Jesus was sentenced to death in front of Herod's palace.[3] The Synoptic narrative gives the impression that everything

---

[1] Gabbatha is not the translation of λιθόστρωτον, but a different name referring to a different aspect of the same place. P. Abel (II, p. 564) thinks that the word means "eminence." If so, this would mean some kind of platform, perhaps paved in mosaic, upon which the seat of the Procurator would be placed.

[2] For instance, P. Lagrange : *L'Évangile de Jésus-Christ*, p. 551.

[3] P. Abel (II, pp. 565–571) inclines towards this opinion, although he does not state this formally. On the identifications of the Praetorium made by tradition, see Abel, II, pp. 571 ff., and Dalman : *Itin.*, pp. 438 ff.

took place in the open air.[1] John implies the opposite when he says that the Jews who had led Jesus to the Praetorium did not enter it, lest they should be defiled and thus be unable to eat the Passover (xviii. 28). According to John's narrative, Jesus was led to the interior of the palace or of the Fortress Antonia, and during the course of the trial Pilate went out several times to speak to the Jews. This reading of events sounds rather improbable. If the Procurator had wished to respect the scruples of the Jews he could have conducted the whole of the trial outside. Further, if we remember that, according to xix. 13, the seat of the tribunal was outside the palace, and that several of the scenes which took place within the Praetorium have no equivalent in the Synoptic Gospels, we can only conclude that the idea of a trial which took place partly inside and partly outside the palace is a literary artifice to which the author of the Fourth Gospel has resorted in order to develop the Synoptic narrative without appearing to contradict it.

According to Mark, as soon as Jesus was brought before Pilate, the latter asked him: "Art thou the King of the Jews?" Jesus said: "Thou sayest it," which, taken in conjunction with the context, may be understood as a refusal to reply. As the chief priests heaped up their accusations, Pilate again questioned Jesus without obtaining any reply, which amazed him (Mark xv. 2–5*).

Nothing is said at first about the charge brought against Jesus; this is only mentioned after he has been questioned the first time. These accusations were only formulated in order to prevent Pilate from releasing a prisoner who impressed him as being harmless. Originally the question, "Art thou the King of the Jews?" may not have been asked in the tone of contemptuous irony which is suggested by the Synoptic narrative, and, in the fact that this question is addressed to Jesus before the Jews have had time to tell Pilate what happened during the trial which they had conducted, there is a trace of a tradition which said that the whole affair was

---

[1] See, in particular, Mark xv. 16; Matt. xxvii. 27, where it is said that after the sentence had been pronounced the soldiers made Jesus enter into the interior of the court which is the Praetorium.

in the hands of the Romans. It was on the initiative of the Procurator that Jesus appeared before him. Luke realized that to begin the story like this would contradict the general tendency of the Christian tradition; hence he has introduced the story in his own way by saying that the members of the Sanhedrin declared that they found Jesus stirring up the people, preventing them from paying tribute to Caesar, and claiming to be the Messiah, the King (Luke xxiii. 2); this is a secondary addition.

Luke has also brought out the meaning of the first questioning more definitely than Mark and Matthew, by saying that Pilate, after he has heard the reply of Jesus, declares to the priests and the crowd that he finds no fault in this man; they insist, saying that Jesus has been stirring up the people by his teaching all over the country, from Galilee to Judaea (xxiii. 4–5).[1]

Here there occurs an incident which gives a new character to the whole affair. It is no longer a question of whether Jesus

[1] It is to this mention of Galilee that the account (peculiar to Luke) is attached of the appearance of Jesus before Herod (xxiii. 6–12). When Pilate hears that Jesus comes from Galilee, and is thus a subject of Herod, he sends him to him. Herod is glad, because in the hope of seeing some miracle performed he had for a long time been anxious to see Jesus. Herod questions Jesus, but receives no answer at all, and, after he and his soldiers have mocked him, he sends him back to Pilate, dressed (in ridicule) in a purple garment. This incident cannot be historical. The idea that Pilate would recognize that a prince of the family of the Herods could have the right to exercise a legal function at Jerusalem is highly improbable. The episode does not add anything to the story; it has no point; the trial continues before Pilate just as if it had never taken place. This legend is based, no doubt, upon a confused recollection that Herod had been hostile to Jesus during the Galilean ministry; it may also have been suggested by the idea expressed in Acts iv. 27, that all the powers of this world were arrayed against Jesus. Later, if the trial of Jesus took place before the palace of Herod, a confusion could have crept into the story which would have given rise to the idea that Herod played some part in the trial. After the episode of Herod, Luke, by means of a fragment which is peculiar to his narrative, takes up the thread of the narrative again. Pilate summons the priests and the people and declares to them that neither he nor Herod has found any fault in Jesus. So he proposes to release him after he has had him punished, that is, scourged (xxiii. 13–16). The legendary character of the appearance before Herod is admitted by a number of critics, among others by DIBELIUS: *Herodes und Pilatus*, *Z.N.T.W.*, XVI, 1915, pp. 113–126, and by LIETZMANN, *S.B.A.*, XIV, 1931, p. 4.

is innocent or guilty, that is to say, whether he should be released or condemned, but of deciding between Barabbas and Jesus, which should die and which should be released.

According to Mark, at each festival the Governor was accustomed to release one prisoner, one chosen by the Jewish people themselves. Now at that moment there was in prison, with some other rebels, a man named Barabbas, who had committed murder in the course of a riot. The people come before the judgment seat in order to ask from the Procurator the favour which he usually grants them. Pilate knows that the chief priests have delivered Jesus "for envy," and he proposes to release the King of the Jews. But the priests persuade the crowd to clamour for Barabbas. Pilate then asks: "What will ye then that I shall do unto him whom ye call the King of the Jews?" A great cry goes up: "Crucify him!" Pilate insists: "Why, what evil hath he done?" "And they cry out the more exceedingly: Crucify him!" Then Pilate decides to yield to the clamour of the crowd; he releases Barabbas, and hands Jesus over to the soldiers to be scourged and crucified (xv. 6–15*).

Several remarks show that the story of Barabbas is a fragment of a tradition which was originally independent of the story of Jesus. The name of Jesus-Barabbas which is found in Matthew [1] already proves this. It is said in verse 6: "He released *unto them*" ($\dot{a}\pi\acute{\epsilon}\lambda\upsilon\sigma\epsilon\nu$ $a\dot{\upsilon}\tauo\hat{\iota}\varsigma$). Until now the only

[1] The reading Jesus-Barabbas is given in Matt. xxvi. 16, 17, by some evidence: Θ. 1–118–131–209, 22, 872, 1582, 2193, 2992, syr[s.hl.] arm. In the miniscules 209, 241, 299, a corrector has added the word Jesus. ORIGEN (see the texts in TISCHENDORF's *apparatus criticus*) proves that "Jesus" was found in many MSS., but he thinks that this name was not fitting for a sinful man and he insinuates that it has been added by heretics. The fact that already in the time of Origen he could consider it impossible that a sinful man should have borne the name of Jesus prevents us from thinking that this name had been added, perhaps under the influence of some of the apocryphal writings, as LAGRANGE suggests (*Matthieu*, p. 521). Thus the reading may be regarded as primitive, as it is also regarded by RENAN (p. 406), BAUER (*L.J. nt. Ap.*, pp. 527 ff.), ZAHN (*Mt.*, p. 700), MERX (II, 1, pp. 400–402), BERTRAM (*Leidensgesch.*, p. 67). We must go still further and think, as does KLOSTERMANN (*Das Matthäusevangelium*[2], Tübingen, 1927, p. 345), that Jesus-Barabbas was originally also in Mark, but that it was omitted in most of the manuscripts of Matthew.

people who have been mentioned are the priests and the members of the Sanhedrin; the pronoun, however, cannot refer to them, since they are forced to persuade the crowd to claim the pardon for Barabbas. It is to the people that this grace is granted; it is they who have the right to choose who shall benefit by this relaxation of the rigour of the law. Now, until this moment the people have not been mentioned; they do not appear till verse 8, where it is said that "the multitude crying aloud began to desire him to do as he had ever done unto them." We must also note that it is said that Barabbas and his companions have committed murder, not in the course of *a* rising, but "in *the* insurrection." This detail can only come from a tradition in which the story of this rising has been described. This proves definitely that originally the story of Barabbas was an independent tradition.

In the other Gospels the incident of Barabbas is incorporated more fully into the account of the trial of Jesus than it is in Mark. Instead of saying, "He released unto them," which does not agree with the context, Matthew (xxvii. 15) says: "the governor was wont to release unto the people." He represents Barabbas, or rather Jesus-Barabbas, as a notorious prisoner, but he does not mention either murder or revolt (16). He evades any mention of the crowd, which had not been brought into the story before this point, by the use of a vague term: "when they were gathered together" (17); finally, in his account, it is not the crowd which demands the usual privilege, it is Pilate who proposes to the people that they should choose between Barabbas and Jesus (18).[1]

Luke does not mention the custom of releasing a prisoner at the Passover festival.[2] Doubtless he knows that such a custom never existed. He relates the proposal made by Pilate to release Jesus immediately after he had been scourged. The crowd replies: "Away with this man and release unto us Barabbas" (xxiii. 18). Luke says that Barabbas was in prison

---

[1] After this the narrative in Matthew follows the same course as that in Mark. We only need to note the addition of the dream of Pilate's wife (19) and the incident of Pilate washing his hands (24–25).

[2] At least in the best texts. A certain number of MSS. add (this is verse 17 in the received text): "he was obliged to release a prisoner to them at each festival" (א. W. X. Λ. Θ. lat. (excepting a.) sy[p.ph.] bo.).

on account of a "certain sedition made in the city and for murder." The crowd which, without being urged by the priests, clamours for the release of Barabbas and the execution of Jesus, is supposed to have been present from the beginning of the trial. In Luke, contrary to that which is suggested in Mark and in Matthew, at first the crowd does not seem particularly interested in Barabbas; they only clamour for his release in order to prevent Pilate from allowing Jesus to profit by the Paschal pardon.

Thus the development of the tradition relating to Barabbas from Mark to Luke is very evident. When we compare the three accounts, we see how an incident at first very awkwardly inserted into the story of the trial of Jesus ends by being completely fused with it.

In the Fourth Gospel less significance is attached to the episode of Barabbas; here it is a mere incident. Pilate, after he has questioned Jesus about his kingship and his view of the truth, in the interior of the Praetorium, comes out and says to the Jews: "I find in him no fault at all. But ye have a custom that I should release unto you one at the Passover: will ye therefore that I release unto you the King of the Jews?" Then the crowd cries out again: "Not this man, but Barabbas." "Now," says the evangelist, "Barabbas was a robber" (xviii. 38–40). There is here only a relic of a tradition similar to that of Mark, since it is said that "then cried they all *again*, saying, Not this man, but Barabbas!" although until then Barabbas has not been mentioned.

The introduction of the tradition concerning Barabbas has caused a definite modification of the situation implied at the beginning of the narrative. Pilate has questioned Jesus, he has admitted his innocence, and still he seems to hesitate to draw the logical inferences from this statement, which in the ordinary way he should be ready to do. It is strange that the evangelists do not suggest the reason for his hesitation. This fact proves that their record does not agree with the actual course of events, and casts a doubt on the admission of the innocence of Jesus by Pilate. We gain a very definite impression that the story of Barabbas serves to conceal the fact that Pilate did condemn Jesus, either because he regarded him as guilty, or because he considered that the interests of Rome required that he should die. Instead, we find a story in which the situation is supposed to be this: that Pilate could only avoid passing sentence on Jesus if the people agreed that it was he and not Barabbas who should be given the benefit of the Paschal pardon.

The part of the narrative which refers to Barabbas was originally an independent tradition; it is not certain that in its original form it had any connexion with the story of Jesus; before we examine the disturbance caused by its insertion into this narrative, let us examine the actual story itself.

Nowhere is there the slightest allusion to the custom of granting a free pardon at the Passover whose object should be chosen by the people. Whether we think of an *abolitio privata*, that is to say, of a remission of the penalty granted by the judge at the request of the prosecutors, as Rosadi [1] has done, or of an *indulgentia*,[2] these do not explain the essential elements in this story, such as the bringing of this legal method into play before the sentence is pronounced, the right granted to the people to choose the prisoner who should benefit by this act of clemency, the connexion of the pardon with a festival, and, finally, its limitation to one condemned person, in such a way that the liberation of Barabbas means inevitably the sentence of death on Jesus. From the point of view of Roman legal institutions, the historicity of the incident of Barabbas is in any case very doubtful. Originally the tradition relating to Barabbas must have been of a very different character.[3] Brandt,[4] adopting the form Barabbas given by a scholium of the manuscript S and several miniscules, translates Barabbas

---

[1] Quoted by REGNAULT: *Une province procuratorienne*, p. 130.

[2] The right to grant the *indulgentia* seems to have been limited to the Emperors (REGNAULT, p. 133), but under certain circumstances it could be delegated to some provincial governors, since Pliny seems to have exercised it during his government of Bithynia (*ep.*, X, 40, 41). HIRSCHFELD (*Sitzber. Berl. Ak.*, 1889, p. 439) and SCHÜRER (I, pp. 468 f.) think that this right may have been conceded to the procurator of Judaea.

[3] Numerous hypotheses have been made on this subject. It does not seem necessary to expound or discuss them.

[4] BRANDT: *Ev. Gesch.*, pp. 97 ff.

as "the son of the rabbi"[1] and suggests that at some period a good deal later than that of the Gospel narrative the son of some influential rabbi [2] may have committed some crime, and that the Roman authority, out of regard for his father, and perhaps as a result of the intervention of the Jewish authorities, may not have prosecuted him, or may have treated him leniently. The Christians may have been shocked at this proceeding, and may have made a comparison between the leniency shown to a murderer and the way in which Jesus was treated; then a confusion arose, and people thought that the murderer, the son of the rabbi, had been acquitted at the same time that Jesus was sentenced, and finally it was said that the people had chosen between them. The advantage of this conjecture is that it takes into account all the peculiarities of this account of the incident. It is quite possible that a tradition was in existence which related how Jesus, son of Abbas, had been saved from execution by the intervention of the Jews, who pleaded for him at the very moment when he appeared before the Roman tribunal. This story may have been compared with that of Jesus, and then become fused with it through the idea of a free pardon which could be granted to one prisoner only.

The Barabbas incident, which, in the form in which it is presented in the Gospels, implies the idea that Pilate was well disposed towards Jesus, and that he desired to release him, can only have been introduced into the Passion narrative at a time when this narrative had already been affected by the desire of the Christian community to keep on good terms with Rome.

The combination of the tradition concerning Barabbas with the Passion narrative has altered this narrative to such an extent that it has rendered it quite impossible to reconstitute

---

[1] Barabbas may mean "son of the father." It is not certain that Barabbas is not a symbolical name. The treatise *Berachot* (186, text quoted by STRACK-BILLERBECK, I, p. 1031) reports a story which shows that the name Abbas was used a great deal. Thus Barabbas may simply mean "son of Abbas."

[2] In the light of the fact mentioned in the preceding note, we ought to adapt Brandt's hypothesis, and, instead of speaking of the son of a rabbi, we should call him the son of a popular and influential person named Abbas.

it in its original form. Two elements only of the account of the Roman trial can be retained: first, that the trial began with a question put by Pilate to Jesus about his claims to be a king, a question which showed immediately that he regarded the matter as very serious indeed; and secondly, that it closed with the death sentence preceded by scourging.[1] Before the tradition had been transformed in such a way that the Romans were absolved of responsibility for the death of Jesus, and all the guilt was transferred to the Jews, this may have been the whole extent of the narrative. Our usual conception of the trial of Jesus is influenced by the fact that to us the closing act in the Gospel story, owing to its results, seems to be the most important event in the history of the first century. Pilate did not see things in this light, and, doubtless, he would have been very much surprised if he had been told that the "poor little Jew" who appeared before him that day would cause his own name to be handed down in an immortal story. It may be that Pilate had examined the case of Jesus before he made his decision, and he may have made up his mind beforehand. In asking Jesus, "Art thou the King of the Jews?" he was perhaps less formulating a question than indicating the motive for the sentence which he intended to pronounce, without paying attention to anything the accused might say. The fate of Jesus was sealed not at the Praetorium but at the moment when the Jewish authorities denounced Jesus as an agitator and as an aspirant to the Messiahship, and when the Procurator decided to arrest him.

The incident of the *titulus* confirms the view that Jesus was condemned as an aspirant to royal power, that is to say, as the Messiah. It was a Roman custom to publish abroad the reason for the condemnation by an inscription which was sometimes carried before the condemned person on the way to execution, and sometimes fixed to the instrument of torture itself.[2]

---

[1] This does not mean that Jesus was condemned to a double punishment, for those who were condemned to death were regularly scourged before they were crucified.

[2] SUETONIUS: *Domitian*, 10; *Caligula*, 32. DION CASSIUS, 54, 8. EUSEBIUS: *Eccl. Hist.*, V, 1, 44.

Mark's note about the *titulus* (xv. 26) is very simple and natural; it implies that the evangelist did not attach any special significance to it. First of all he does not speak of *an* inscription, but of *the* inscription. In his mind, therefore, the chief point was the content of the inscription, which was the usual accompaniment of every crucifixion. In his account it was simply this: "The King of the Jews."

Matthew's account does not differ from that of Mark save for a few details of expression (xxvii. 37). Luke (xxiii. 38) speaks of *an* inscription,[1] as though it were something exceptional. As he mentions the inscription after the scene of the insults with the words, "there was also an inscription," he seems to have regarded the inscription as something intended to be deliberately insulting to Jesus.

John (xix. 19–22) has developed the incident of the *titulus* still further. Pilate writes and orders an inscription to be nailed to the cross which reads thus: "JESUS OF NAZARETH, THE KING OF THE JEWS." A great many people read this inscription, which is inscribed in Greek, Latin, and Hebrew (that is, in Aramaic). The chief priests protest. They say to Pilate: "Write not, The King of the Jews; but that he said, I am King of the Jews." Pilate refuses to modify what he has written, and declares: "What I have written, I have written."

The tendency of this account is obvious: the inscription no longer forms part of the usual publicity which accompanies such an execution; it is not by chance, but by a providential arrangement, that Pilate thus proclaims the truth of the royalty of Jesus against which the Jews protest in vain.

In the preceding pages we have been following the Synoptic narrative only. Now let us try to see whether the Johannine narrative may not contain some data which will allow us to confirm, complete, or correct our conclusions. This narrative is more fully developed than that of Mark. Although it contains none of the incidents peculiar to Luke (the appearance before Herod), or Matthew (the dream of Pilate's wife, Pilate washing his hands), and although it condenses the episode of

[1] According to a certain number of MSS. (א*. A. D. N. W., etc.), this inscription was written in Greek, Latin, and Hebrew. This is an addition made according to the text of John.

Barabbas, its length is almost double that of Mark (29 verses instead of 15).

The trial begins at dawn (xviii. 28), but the sentence is not pronounced until about the sixth hour, that is, at noon. Evidently John wished to show that Pilate resisted the pressure of the Jews for a long time.

There first comes an interview between Pilate and the Jews, at which Jesus is not present. Pilate enquires into the charges brought against Jesus, the Jews reply that if he had not been guilty they would not have delivered him up. To which Pilate replies: "Take ye him and judge him according to your law." The Jews remind him that "It is not lawful for them to put any man to death" (xviii. 29–32). John is no better informed than his predecessors concerning the charges which the Jews are supposed to have brought against Jesus before Pilate. The idea that the Jews were forced to remind Pilate that the Roman Government had removed from them the right of trying cases in which the extreme penalty can be pronounced is extremely improbable. Its only point is to stress the fact that Pilate was forced to take up the case of Jesus against his will.

After this first conversation Pilate returns to the Praetorium and asks Jesus: "Art thou the King of the Jews?" This is the same question as the one recorded in the Marcan narrative, and neither here nor there is it explained by that which preceded it. The answer of Jesus is more detailed. Jesus begins by asking Pilate: "Sayest thou this thing of thyself, or did others tell it thee of me?" To which the Procurator replies: "Am I a Jew? Thine own nation and the chief priests have delivered thee unto me. What hast thou done?" Then Jesus declares that his kingdom is not of this world, for "if my kingdom were of this world, then would my servants fight." Pilate repeats his question: "Art thou a king then?" Jesus replies very gravely: "Thou sayest that I am a king. To this end was I born, and for this cause came I into the world, that I should bear witness unto the truth." Pilate asks: "What is truth?" As he goes out without waiting for an answer, we can only regard these words as a contemptuous exclamation (xviii. 33–37). Apart from the question, "Art thou a King then?" which comes from the Synoptic narrative, this fragment must be assigned to the evangelist. We find in it some of his most characteristic ideas, and it reveals his intention to emphasize the spiritual and non-political nature of the royalty of Jesus.

After the enquiry Pilate goes out a second time to speak to the Jews. He declares that he has found no fault in Jesus; hence he proposes to let him take advantage of the Paschal pardon. The people refuse and clamour for Barabbas (xviii. 38–40). This comes directly from the Synoptic Gospels.

Although the sentence has not yet been pronounced, Pilate gives the order for Jesus to be scourged; the soldiers drag him away and ill-treat him (xix. 1–3). The position of this episode is most singular. The torture begins before the trial is over. This is because in the Synoptic narrative the sentence and the scourging take place immediately after the people have refused to allow Jesus to take advantage of the Paschal pardon.

After the scourging and mockery, Pilate takes Jesus and leads him out before the people, saying: "I bring him forth to you that ye may know that I find no fault in him." He presents Jesus to the people wearing the crown of thorns and the purple robe and says: "Behold the man!" which in his mind simply means: "Here is the individual in question." To the evangelist the declaration also means: "Behold! the Son of Man." When they see Jesus, the chief priests and their agents cry out: "Crucify him! Crucify him!" Pilate then says to them: "Take ye him and crucify him, for I find no fault in him." The Jews reply: "We have a Law, and by our Law he ought to die, because he made himself the Son of God" (xix. 4–7). We need not try to discover some historical tradition behind this account. The very fact that Pilate advises the Jews to crucify Jesus apart from his orders proves that this element is not historical.

When Pilate hears the words, "Son of God," he begins to be afraid. Until that moment, thinks the evangelist, he has regarded Jesus as an innocent man; now he has a vague sense that he is possibly in the presence of someone with super-natural powers (xix. 8). He returns to the Praetorium with Jesus and asks him: "Whence art thou?" but Jesus makes no reply. In this silence of Jesus there is a recurrence of a detail which occurs in the beginning of the Marcan narrative, and which John had omitted. Pilate becomes irritated, and reminds

Jesus that he has the power to release him and the power to crucify him. This phrase does not fit in well with the rest of the story, which assumes, on the contrary, that the Procurator can only release Jesus if the Jews are willing that he should do so. The saying of Pilate is only there in order to call forth the response of Jesus: "Thou couldest have no power at all against me, except it were given thee from above: therefore he that delivered me [1] unto thee hath the greater sin" (xix. 9–11). The meaning of this declaration is not quite clear: the fact that Pilate has received his authority from on high does not lessen his responsibility. We must give up the attempt to find a logical connexion between the two propositions, in spite of the words, "this is why," which connects them with each other. They are two affirmations of loyalty to the Roman Government. The authority of the magistrates comes from God (cf. Rom. xiii. 1), and actual responsibility for the death of Jesus must be laid at the door of the Jews.

When Pilate receives this reply he makes another effort to release Jesus, but the Jews cry out: "If thou let this man go, thou art not Caesar's friend: whosoever maketh himself a king speaketh against Caesar" (xix. 12). This fragment does not fit in very well at this point. This scene cannot have taken place in the Praetorium into which the Jews have not entered; and it is only at verse 13 that it is said that Pilate makes Jesus come forth. Here there has been some editorial carelessness.

When, for the last time, Pilate has made Jesus come forth, he seats himself on the judgment seat and says to the Jews: "Behold your King!" They clamour aloud: "Away with him, away with him, crucify him!" "Shall I crucify your King?" says Pilate. The chief priests reply: "We have no king but Caesar." [2] Then Pilate decides to hand Jesus over to them to be crucified.

---

[1] According to xviii. 35, it is the people and the chief priests who delivered Jesus up to Pilate. There is here a slight confusion in the use of the singular. It would disappear if what was meant was that it was Satan who delivered Jesus up to Pilate. This interpretation does not seem probable, assuming that the whole account of the sentence has been arranged in such a way that the guilt is thrown upon the Jews.

[2] In Greek the same word means King and Emperor.

The fact that this scene is localized at the place called "the Pavement" suggests that it comes from a source. It seems strange that the topographical detail should occur at the end of the story. It is also surprising that Pilate should not take his place on the judgment seat till towards the sixth hour, although the trial had begun at break of day. Here John seems to be following a tradition concerning the death of Jesus which is independent of that of the Synoptics, since that did not include any topographical details. But this tradition has been adapted by John, who has used it for the conclusion and the summing up of his narrative. The link between the kingship attributed to Jesus and the sentence of death seems to come from this source, but we must assign to the evangelist the intervention of the crowd, and its declaration, so opposed to all that we know of the sentiments of the Jews: "We have no king but Caesar." Jesus was not crucified because he was, or pretended to be, the King of the Jews, as the account of the trial implies, but precisely because he was accused of wishing to be the King of the Jews.

The alteration of the primitive tradition on the question of the death sentence comes out again in these words: "Then delivered he him therefore unto them to be crucified." The tendentious character of this formula is revealed by the fact that it is contradicted by what follows, where it is not the Jews but the Romans who crucify Jesus.

A study of the Johannine narrative therefore has led to the same conclusion as that of the Marcan narrative. There was no real trial of Jesus before Pilate. The Procurator simply had Jesus brought before him and told him that since he was the King of the Jews he would be crucified.

CHAPTER XX

THE SENTENCE INFLICTED

I. Scourging and Mockery

THE scourging which regularly preceded crucifixion is mentioned very briefly by Mark (xv. 15) and by Matthew (xxvii. 26): "And when he had scourged Jesus, he delivered him to be crucified." Thus the scourging seems to have taken place in the presence of Pilate, at the same place where the sentence had been passed condemning Jesus to death. Jesus was bound to a pillar and then beaten by soldiers armed with *flagella*, that is, with whips of leather whose thongs were knotted and interspersed with pieces of metal.[1] Here, and in the whole account of the tortures to which Jesus was subjected, the narrators exhibit remarkable restraint. They do not seek to stir the feelings of their readers by dwelling on the sufferings of Jesus; on the contrary, the language of their narrative resembles that of an official report. Instinctively they realize that such a story is far more moving if it is told with simplicity.

By placing the scourging and the mockery during the trial John has misrepresented its character. We know why he altered[2] the order of the incidents in this part of the story. Luke does not mention this part of the Passion narrative. The way in which, twice over, he mentions the proposal of Pilate to the people to release Jesus after he has had him scourged (xxiii. 16, 22) seems to indicate that he had not understood that scourging was a penalty which accompanied the penalty of crucifixion; he seems to have thought that at a given moment Pilate had hesitated between two possible choices: should he have Jesus scourged or crucified? Another explanation may also be suggested, namely, that Mark and Matthew do not only mention the scourging inflicted upon Jesus, but, between

---

[1] FULDA: *Das Kreuz, und die Kreuzigung*, Fulda, 1878, pp. 134 f. Scourging covered the backs of those unfortunate people who underwent this punishment with blood. Cf. JOSEPHUS: *G.J.*, VI, 5, 3, ¶ 304.

[2] See p. 524.

the verdict and the departure for the scene of the execution, they also relate the scene of the insults and mockery to which Jesus had to submit within the Praetorium. Luke gives the equivalent after the appearance of Jesus before Herod; this was doubtless in order to suppress an episode which was in itself rather inconsistent, and it is perhaps the alteration of the position of the scene of the mockery which also caused the disappearance of the scene of the scourging. Thus it is not necessary to imagine that Luke and John were acquainted with a tradition according to which, directly the sentence had been passed, Jesus was led away to be crucified.

Mark (xv. 16–20) and Matthew (xxvii. 27–31) describe the scene of the mockery in almost the same way; the difference between their accounts is of very slight significance.

The soldiers lead Jesus to the interior of the court called the Praetorium, and gather the members of the cohort together.[1] They throw a purple robe round the prisoner, place on his head a crown of thorns,[2] and then say: "Hail! King of the Jews!" They strike his face, spit upon him, and kneel before him in mocking homage. Then they remove the purple mantle, give him back his clothes, and lead him away to be crucified. Thus, in derision, Jesus is treated as a king. This also is the significance of the two scenes which Luke and John report at another point in the story: Luke, after Jesus had been brought before Herod (xxiii. 11), and John, in the middle of the trial, when the people have refused to allow Jesus to be pardoned and set free under the special conditions attached to the Passover festival (xix. 5), and a little later when Pilate presents him to the Jews as their King. These three different scenes, which differ in position, and also in those who take part in them, cannot be independent of each other from the literary point of view.

Some critics[3] have compared the scene recorded by Mark

---

[1] That is to say, the detachment of the cohort which, according to whichever hypothesis we adopt, was at the fortress Antonia or at the Palace of Herod, and not the whole of the Jerusalem garrison.

[2] Matthew adds that they placed a reed in his hands as a sceptre.

[3] WENDLAND: *Jesus als Saturnalienkönig*, Hermes, 1898, pp. 175–179. F. CUMONT: *Les Actes de S. Dasius*, Analecta Bollandiana, 1897, pp. 5–16; *Le roi*

with a custom which, varying from a mystery rite to a simple popular custom, centres round the idea of the King of the Carnival, a theme whose primitive idea seems to have been that of the annual sacrifice of a victim who was first of all treated as a king.[1] But in these customs and rites, the hero who was destined to be the victim was treated with the honour due to a real king and not in mockery. The duration (probably very short) of the scene of the mockery, and even its very character, are not in line with these customs. It is probable that the scene recorded by Mark had no special significance: the soldiers, before they led Jesus away to the place of execution, gave free rein to their instincts of cruelty by mocking him who had just been condemned on the charge of aspiring to be King of the Jews. Although the evangelists may have given a symbolic meaning to the incident, this is no argument against its historicity.

The comparison between the scene which took place in the Praetorium and that which took place in the court of the high priest's palace is not sufficiently close for us to argue that the one is derived from the other. One detail, however, should be noted. At the palace of the high priest Jesus is condemned for having believed that he was the Messiah, that is, the Prophet *par excellence*,[2] and it is the Prophet whom the servants of the Sanhedrin treat with contempt. Pilate, in sentencing Jesus to death, was sentencing the King of the Jews, and it was as King of the Jews that the soldiers mocked him. This similarity shows that the two accounts have undergone, to say the least, a good deal of editorial elaboration. It is difficult to say to what extent the editor has carried this process of

des Saturnales, Revue de philologie, 1897, pp. 143–153. FRAZER: *Le bouc émissaire*, trad. P. SAYN, Paris, 1925, pp. 373 f. S. REINACH: *Le Roi supplicié*, C.M.R., I, pp. 332–341. REICH: *Der König mit der Dornenkrone*, Giessen, 1905. VOLLMER: *Jesus und das Sacaenenopfer*, Giessen, 1905. GEFFCKEN: *Die Verhöhnung Christi durch die Kriegsknechte*, Hermes, 1906, pp. 220–229. K. LÜBECK: *Die Dornenkrönung Christi. Eine religionsgeschichtliche Studie*, Regensburg, 1906.
[1] On the meaning and the nature of this rite, see the very suggestive study by J. TOUTAIN: *L'idée religieuse de rédemption et l'un de ses principaux rites dans l'antiquité grecque et romaine*, Annuaire de l'École des Hautes Études, Sciences religieuses, 1916–1917.
[2] In John i. 21, it seems that, if not in the text, then at least in its source, the term prophet should be taken to mean Messiah.

adaptation: has it merely extended to giving a symbolic meaning to the ill-treatment which Jesus underwent before he was led to Pilate, and after he was sentenced to death? or is it the duplication of one incident? or has it actually created the two accounts, which, in the Marcan narrative, are its counterpart?

II. ON THE WAY TO EXECUTION

When the scene of mockery is over the soldiers lead Jesus away to be crucified (Mark xv. 20–21; John xix. 17).

Mark, Matthew, and Luke say that a passer-by, Simon of Cyrene, who had come in from the country,[1] is forced to carry the cross, or, more exactly, the *patibulum*, the cross-beam which every condemned person had to carry to the place of execution.[2] According to John, Jesus himself carried it.[3]

Salomon Reinach[4] considers the fact reported by the Synoptists to be untenable from the historical point of view, and this for three reasons. The first is that there is no other example of soldiers forcing a passer-by to carry the cross of a condemned person, and he asserts that such an act would have been illegal; the second is this, that the bearing of the *patibulum* by the condemned person was an integral part of the penalty, and the third that the episode is only an illustration of the saying of Jesus: "Whosoever will come after me, let him deny himself, and take up his cross, and follow me" (Mark viii. 34*). None

---

[1] Mark says that Simon was the father of Alexander and Rufus. Paul (Rom. xvi. 13) names a Rufus who may have been one of Simon's sons. We know that there are good reasons for thinking that the Gospel of Mark was written at Rome (BACON: *Is Mark a Roman Gospel? Harv. theol. St.*, VII, Cambridge, Mass., 1919). Matthew and Luke do not give the names of the sons of Simon, doubtless because they were not people who would be known to their readers.

[2] On this point, see PLAUTUS: *Miles gloriosus*, 359; *Carbon*, fragm. 3 (WEISE). PLUTARCH: *De sera numinis vindicta*, 9. ARTEMIDORUS: *Oneirocriticon*, I, 56. From the first of these passages we learn that the *patibulum* was placed on the nape of the neck of the condemned person, and that the arms, which were extended, were fastened to it.

[3] Nor is there any mention of Simon carrying the cross in the Gospel of Peter.

[4] SIMON DE CYRÈNE: *C.M.R.*, IV, pp. 183 f.

of these arguments are valid. No legal obligation can overrule a physical impossibility, and there is no word anywhere, in any part of the narrative, to suggest that Simon was asked to carry the cross from motives of pity. It is, of course, true that the Gospels do not say, as do the later legends, that Jesus fell to the ground under the weight of the *patibulum*, and that his guards had to allow him to be relieved of the burden; but it is not improbable that after the torture of the scourging Jesus was actually physically unable to carry the *patibulum*, or at least to carry it all the way. The conjecture is confirmed by the swiftness with which death came to him, for very often those who were crucified lingered a much longer time. When the condemned person was actually unable to carry the *patibulum* someone else had to be found to carry it. The fact that Simon of Cyrene was impressed for this service was illegal, it is true, but the whole history of Judaea under the government of the Procurators teems with annoying and illegal actions. Finally, it is inconceivable that the episode could have been suggested by a saying in which everyone is summoned to carry his own cross, and not that of Jesus, and to do so willingly, and not under compulsion.[1]

Thus there is one objection only against the historicity of the episode of Simon of Cyrene, and that is, the silence of the Fourth Gospel. Many critics, Jean Réville and Salomon Reinach[2] for instance, have thought that the incident was omitted for controversial reasons. The evangelists may have wished to dispose of Docetist attempts to exploit it in a way favourable to their ideas. But there is nothing to justify us in thinking that, at the period when the Fourth Gospel was being composed, the following theory was in existence: that Simon of Cyrene, after he had carried the cross for Jesus, had been crucified in his place and in a form exactly like his own. According to Irenaeus[3] this was a favourite theory of the Docetists. If John had really wished to dispose of an erroneous

[1] The most one could admit—and that would still be only a possibility— is that a feature peculiar to Luke (Simon carrying the cross "after Jesus") might have been suggested by the words: "If any man will come after me," of Luke ix. 23.

[2] JEAN RÉVILLE: *Q.É.*, p. 273. S. REINACH: *C.M.R.*, II, pp. 183 f.

[3] IRENAEUS: *Adv. Haer.*, I, 24, 4.

interpretation of the incident, he would have said that when Calvary was reached the soldiers set Simon free. We prefer the view expressed by Brandt, Bauer, and Loisy:[1] that the evangelist desired to eliminate any element in the story which might seem to diminish the sufferings of Christ; perhaps he had also been influenced by the saying of Jesus that everyone must carry his own cross (Mark viii. 34), and also in addition by the story in the Old Testament in which Isaac himself carries the wood for the sacrifice (Gen. xxii. 6). We must also draw attention to the fact that John has not only omitted the incident of Simon of Cyrene, but several other accessory details of the Passion narrative, as though he wished to concentrate the reader's attention entirely on Jesus himself.

In the account of the walk to the place of execution Luke has a passage which is peculiar to his Gospel:

And there followed him a great company of people, and of women, which also bewailed and lamented him. But Jesus turning unto them said, Daughters of Jerusalem, weep not for me, but weep for yourselves, and for your children. For, behold, the days are coming, in the which they shall say, Blessed are the barren, and the wombs that never bare, and the paps which never gave suck. Then shall they begin to say to the mountains, Fall on us; and to the hills, Cover us. For if they do these things in a green tree, what shall be done in the dry? (xxiii. 27–31).

This great company which had compassion on Jesus is mentioned again at the close of the account of the crucifixion. After Jesus had died:

All the people that came together to that sight, beholding the things which were done, smote their breasts and returned (xxiii. 48).

These two fragments belong to the same tradition. The spirit they describe which animates the crowd is contrasted with that which is described in the account of the trial before Pilate. It is impossible to understand how people who have clamoured for this penalty can now feel it to be a disaster.

---

[1] BRANDT: *Ev. Gesch.*, p. 174. BAUER: *L.J. nt. Ap.*, p. 292. LOISY: *Quatr. Ev*[1]., p. 872; [2] p. 483.

The words of Jesus (in Luke xxiii) do not agree with the idea that it was the Jews who were responsible for his death; here the Romans seem to be regarded as the enemies both of Jesus and of the Jewish people.

This section cannot have been created by Luke. It can only be explained as the survival of an older tradition than that which placed the blame for the death of Jesus upon the Jews. Doubtless it is also due to the influence of this tradition that Luke does not mention the insults hurled at Jesus by the passers-by as he hung on the cross.

III. THE CRUCIFIXION

Calvary, in Aramaic Golgotha, to which the soldiers led Jesus (Mark xv. 22*),[1] was a bare hill, with a distant resemblance to the outline of a skull. Later on this name, which seems originally to have meant the same as the French name *Chaumont* (bare hill), was to serve as a point of departure for all sorts of speculations and legends: Golgotha was at last said to be the place where the skull of Adam had been buried.

In the ancient world executions took place in public; there were no special places reserved for them. Usually they took place near towns, by the roadside or at cross-roads, in order that passers-by might see the gibbet. Apart from all the traditions which have gathered round the question of the site of Calvary, topographical considerations alone lead us to think that very probably the execution of Jesus took place to the north of Jerusalem, since it is the only side of the city from which the ground does not slope away abruptly.

Mark (xv. 23) tells us how before Jesus was crucified he was offered some drugged wine, which he refused to drink. In the Book of Proverbs we read:

Give strong drink unto him that is ready to perish, and wine unto those that be of heavy hearts. Let him drink and forget his poverty, and remember his misery no more (xxxi. 6–7).

---

[1] For the site of Calvary and of the Holy Sepulchre, see the Appendix, pp. 546 ff.

In obedience to this exhortation in the Sacred Books, the women of Jerusalem used to give this "wine of heaviness" to those who were condemned to death by crucifixion.[1] This detail has no particular significance. It formed part of the usual course of an execution. By pointing out that Jesus refused the drink which was offered him, Mark wishes to lay stress on the fact that Jesus bore all the sufferings of the cross to the very end.[2]

The crucifixion is mentioned very briefly—indeed, this brevity of statement is remarkable; a word or two, and that is all. Jesus was crucified, certainly according to the usual methods, which were not fixed rigidly in every detail.

The torture of crucifixion[3] is of eastern origin. From the days of the Punic wars the Romans used it as a punishment for slaves; it was the *servile supplicium par excellence.* According to Josephus the Romans used it a great deal in Palestine. After the Siege of Jerusalem Titus crucified so many Jews that, says Josephus, "there was not enough room for the crosses, nor enough crosses for the condemned" (*G.J.*, V, 11, 2, ¶ 451).

The shape of the cross varied. Sometimes it was simply a stake or a tree to which the victim was fastened by his hands. Sometimes the cross was made of two parts, a cross-beam (*patibulum*) being fixed either above the vertical beam (*crux commissa* or *patibulata*), or a little lower down (*crux immissa* or *captitata,* the Latin cross). The mention of the *titulus* does not prove that Jesus was crucified on a cross of the Latin type. As the arms of the victim could not remain in the horizontal position, an inscription fastened to the *patibulum* itself would have been easily visible on a cross *patibulata.*

[1] Passages which bear witness to this custom will be found in STRACK-BILLERBECK (I, p. 1037).

[2] In Matthew (xxvii. 34) the drugged wine has become wine mingled with gall. Here we can recognize the influence of Psa. lxix. 22 (LXX: lxviii): "They gave me also gall for my meat, and in my thirst they gave me vinegar to drink." Neither Luke nor John has given this detail, doubtless because they thought it would only mean duplicating the incident of the vinegar.

[3] FULDA: *Der Kreuz.* SAGLIO: art. *Croix,* in the *Dictionnaire des Antiquités de Saglio,* I, 2, col. 1573. HITZIG: art. *Crux,* in PAULY-WISSOWA, *Realenc. f. class. Altertumswissenschaft, Neue Bearb.,* IV, pp. 1728–1731. DOM LECLERQ: art. *Croix, D.A.C.L.,* III, 2, col. 3045 ff.

The condemned person, stripped of his clothing, was fastened to the *patibulum*, sometimes (and this seems to have been the most usual way) with cords and sometimes with nails.[1] In this case, after the *patibulum* had been placed in position, the feet were sometimes fastened in the same way.[2] The horizontal beam was placed at such a height that the feet of the victim could not touch the ground; the cross was usually just high enough to make this possible, but no higher.

We can scarcely imagine the sufferings endured by those unfortunate beings who died by crucifixion. "Crucifixion," says Albert Réville, "is one of the most abominable forms of torture that has ever been invented by those whose genius created forms of torture. We may perhaps even regard it as first among the '*crudelissimum teterimumque supplicium*, the most cruel and the most hideous of tortures,' as Cicero says (*In Verrem*, v. 64): In actual fact it represented the acme of the torturer's art: atrocious physical sufferings, length of torment, ignominy, the effect on the crowd gathered to witness the long agony of the crucified. Nothing could be more horrible than the sight of this living body, breathing, seeing, hearing, still able to feel, and yet reduced to the state of a corpse by forced immobility and absolute helplessness. We cannot even say that the crucified person writhed in agony, for it was impossible for him to move. Stripped of his clothing, unable even to brush away the flies which fell upon his wounded flesh, already lacerated by the preliminary scourging, exposed to the insults and curses of people who can always find some sickening pleasure in the sight of the tortures of others, a feeling which is increased and not diminished by the sight of pain—the cross represented miserable humanity reduced to the last degree of impotence, suffering, and degradation. The penalty of crucifixion combined all that the most ardent tormentor could desire: torture, the pillory, degradation, and

[1] It is not at all certain that Jesus was nailed to the cross. The earliest passage which mentions the nails in the hands of Jesus is John xx. 25–27; JUSTIN MARTYR (*Apol.*, I, 35; *Dial.*, 97, 3) is the first to speak of nails in the feet.

[2] Some representations of the torture of the cross seem to suggest that the feet of the victim rested on a support, the *suppedaneum* or *pedale*. The idea of the *suppedaneum* may simply be due to the fact that the artist found it difficult to represent the nailing of the feet.

certain death, distilled slowly drop by drop. It was an ideal form of torture."[1]

The torment of crucifixion could last for many hours. The agony of Jesus, according to the account in Mark (xv. 25, 34), lasted for three hours, from the sixth until the ninth hour (from noon until three o'clock), and, as the evangelist cannot be suspected of any desire to shorten the sufferings of Jesus, this point may be regarded as historical. We do not know what was the actual cause of death on the cross.[2] The torture may have affected both the circulation and the respiration, and thus have led finally to heart failure.

According to the received text of Luke (xxiii. 34), after Jesus was crucified he is represented as saying: "Father, forgive them, for they know not what they do." These words are absent from many important manuscripts.[3] It is easy to conjecture that they may have been added by transposing the precept in the Sermon on the Mount: "Pray for them which persecute you" (Matt. v. 44), and, further, owing to the influence of the prayer of the dying martyr, Stephen: "Lord, lay not this sin to their charge" (Acts vii. 60). This saying may also have been imputed to Jesus under the influence of Isa. liii. 12: "He made intercession for the transgressors." On the contrary, it would be impossible to imagine that this saying could have been omitted by some of the copyists if it had formed part of the original text of Luke, and by Mark and Matthew if it had been present in the primitive tradition.

After the soldiers had crucified Jesus they divided his garments among themselves. It was the custom for the garments of condemned persons to belong to the executioners. This detail is quite natural, and in recording it the Synoptists simply intended to mention a point in the course of the process of crucifixion, just as Mark did in speaking of the drugged wine. Later it was noticed that in verse 18 of Psa. xxii (LXX, xxi) the righteous man who is being persecuted says: "They parted

---

[1] ALBERT RÉVILLE: *Jésus de Nazareth*, II, pp. 405 f.

[2] See, on this subject, P. W. SCHMIDT: *Gesch. Jesu*, II, pp. 409–414.

[3] B. D. W. O. 124–38–435–579–1241 ab. sy^s sa. Someone has corrected the text of ℵ by placing them between brackets.

my garments among them, and for my robe they cast lots."
The first three evangelists did not notice this coincidence, for
if they had noted it they would most certainly have pointed
it out.[1] John did notice it (xix. 23–24), and he has emphasized
the fulfilment of a prophecy by quoting the verse of the Psalm;
and in order to adapt the narrative more fully to the text of
the Psalmist he has made a distinction between the distribution of the clothes and the casting of lots for the tunic.[2]

After speaking of the crucifixion, the *titulus*, and the distribution of the clothing, Mark (xv. 27) adds: "And with him
they crucify two thieves, the one on his right hand and the
other on his left."[3] Matthew (xxvii. 38) modifies what seems
strange in the fact that the crucifixion of the robbers is not
mentioned until now by saying: "Then . . . were crucified. . . ."
Luke mentions the robbers at the arrival at the place of
execution, and, like John, he says that they were crucified at
the same time as Jesus (Luke xxiii. 32–33; John xix. 18). Thus

[1] It is true that in Matt. xxvii. 35 the received text adds with some MSS.
of the western group (*Δ. Θ. Φ.*) and some versions: "in order that it might
be fulfilled which was written by the prophet: 'they have parted my
garments among them and for my vesture did they cast lots.'" This is most
decidedly an addition which has come from John (xix. 24). SALOMON
REINACH (*Le verset 18 du Psaume 22, C.M.R.*, II, pp. 437–442) did not perceive the non-authenticity of this text when he appealed to it to prove that
the division of the garments was a creation of prophetic exegesis.

[2] He explains this procedure by saying that the robe of Jesus was woven
in one piece throughout. This idea may have been suggested to him by
the fact that, according to JOSEPHUS (*A.J.*, III, 7, 4, ¶ 161), the high priest
wore a robe woven in one piece because of Lev. xxi. 10. It is not at all
certain, as has sometimes been supposed, that John attached to this fact
speculations like those of PHILO (*De profugiis*, 20; *De ebrietate*, 21), which
he develops with reference to the robe of the high priest, in which he sees
an image of the Logos. The doubling of the sharing of the garments and
the casting of lots for the robe, as the result of the literal interpretation of
a prophetic expression, have an equivalent in Matt. xxi. 7, where the
evangelist represents Jesus as riding on an ass and on a colt at the same
time because there was a double expression in Zech. ix. 9.

[3] Some MSS. (E. F. G., etc.), the Latin versions, the Peshitto, and some
others, add: "And thus was fulfilled the Scripture which said: 'and he was
numbered with the transgressors'" (verse 28 in the received text). The
verse quoted is from Isa. liii. 2, which Luke had placed in the mouth of
Jesus in xxii. 37. Here again it is the later tradition only which asserts
that this was the fulfilment of a prophecy.

the development of tradition has tended to incorporate the crucifixion of the robbers into the narrative. May this not be an added element, perhaps under the influence of Isa. liii. 2? From the idea of Jesus crucified like a malefactor it would be easy to pass to the idea that Jesus was executed with malefactors. However, since there is no reference in the text to the passage in Isaiah we cannot come to any conclusion on this point.

IV. Mockery and Insult

The mockery to which Jesus was subjected forms one of the main themes in the Passion narrative. It is taken up three times by Mark and by Matthew. First of all it is the passers-by who shake their heads, saying: "Ah, thou that destroyest the temple, and buildest it in three days, Save thyself, and come down from the cross" (Mark xv. 29–30*);[1] then it is the chief priests who say: "He saved others, himself he cannot save. Let Christ the King of Israel descend now from the cross, that we may see and believe" (Mark xv. 31–32a*).[2] Finally, the robbers also revile Jesus (Mark xv. 32b*).

In the Lucan narrative the people simply watch in dumb silence (xxiii. 35a).[3] On the other hand, as though he wished to insist on giving three scenes of mockery, like Mark and Matthew, Luke says that the soldiers mocked Jesus, offering him vinegar and saying: "If thou be the King of the Jews, save thyself" (xxiii. 36–38). This scene is artificial, as we can soon see when we perceive that it is composed of two elements detached from their context in Mark, in one of which the original meaning has been changed. The first element is that the priests and the scribes call Jesus the "King of Israel" (Mark xv. 32), and the second is the incident of the vinegar (Mark xv. 34–36*).

[1] Matthew (xxvii. 40) adds: "If thou be the Son of God."

[2] Matthew (xxvii. 43) adds a phrase borrowed from Psa. xxii. 8, and Wisd. of Sol. ii. 3: "He trusted in God that he would now deliver him, for he said: I am the Son of God."

[3] The omission of the mockery of the passers-by is also the result of the fact that in the account of the trial before the Sanhedrin Luke has omitted all mention of the saying about the destruction and reconstruction of the Temple.

Only one of the robbers, according to Luke (xxiii. 39, 43), insults Jesus by saying to him: "Art not thou the Christ? Save thyself and us!" In order to develop this story out of the simple mention of mockery and insults in Mark and Matthew, Luke has merely utilized a detail already mentioned in connexion with the mockery of the priests and the soldiers. The method which he has used makes it seem very unlikely that in this case he was making use of a private tradition. The other robber reproaches his companion with having no fear of God, although his punishment is well deserved, whereas the one who is crucified with them has done nothing amiss; then he looks at Jesus and asks him to remember him when he comes into his kingdom; and Jesus replies: "Verily I say unto thee, to-day shalt thou be with me in Paradise." This conception is practically the same as that in the parable of Dives and Lazarus (Luke xvi. 19–31), where, immediately after his death, Lazarus is borne by angels into Abraham's bosom. This idea of a salvation realized immediately, at the moment of death, differs materially from that which we find in the earliest forms of Christian thought, according to which salvation would not be fully realized until the *parousia* of the Lord. This is all the more significant since the prayer of the robber is uttered from the point of view of the eschatological hope. If we add to this difficulty the fact of the silence of the other evangelists, it seems impossible to accept the historicity of this incident.

John does not mention the insults addressed to Jesus on the cross. Is this because he has simply ignored the details which he regarded as merely accessory? or did he know of a tradition which did not contain these scenes of mockery and insult?

There are certain resemblances between the accounts of the insults hurled at Jesus by the passers-by in the Synoptic Gospels, and Psa. xxii (LXX, xxi), verses 8 and 9, which make it impossible to reject the idea that the verses from this Psalm may have suggested the scene.[1] If this incident has really

[1] Psa. xxi. 8–9 (LXX). The words of the Psalm which occur in one or other of the Gospel narratives are underlined: Πάντες οἱ θεωροῦντές μὲ ἐξεμυκτήρισαν με, ἐλάλησαν ἐν χείλεσιν, ἐκίνησαν κεφαλήν. Ἤλπισεν ἐπὶ κύριον, ῥυσάσθω αὐτόν σωσάτω αὐτον, ὅτι θέλει αὐτόν.

been created from a passage in Scripture, it is probable that the other scenes of mockery have been modelled on it. These scenes are secondary developments in the narrative.

V. THE DEATH OF JESUS

"And when the sixth hour was come, there was darkness over the whole land until the ninth hour," says Mark (xv. 33*).[1] In the eyes of the evangelists there is no doubt that something supernatural took place at this moment.[2] At the ninth hour Jesus cried out in a loud voice, in Aramaic: "Eloi, Eloi, lama sabacthani,"[3] that is, "My God! my God! why hast thou forsaken me?" This is verse 2 of Psa. xxii. The spectators think that he is calling for Elijah, and one of them, apparently inspired by a sudden feeling of pity, fills a sponge with vinegar (the ordinary beverage of the soldiers),[4] places it on a reed, and hands it to him to drink, saying: "Let alone; let us see whether Elias will come to take him down." Then "Jesus cried with a loud voice and gave up the ghost" (Mark xv. 34–37*).

Luke knew the Marcan account which we have just summarized, for he has included the detail about the

[1] Luke adds: τοῦ ἡλίου ἐκλιπόντος. We need not understand by that that he was referring to an eclipse, for we cannot imagine that the evangelist wished to suggest that an eclipse would take place at the time of the spring full moon. Julius Africanus (cf. above, pp. 91 ff.) reproaches Thallus the Samaritan for having stupidly (ἀλόγως) explained the darkness as due to an eclipse.

[2] Luke places the incident of the rending of the veil of the Temple at the beginning of the time of darkness which Matthew and Mark place at the moment when Jesus breathes his last.

[3] As is only natural, since the words are in a language which the copyists do not know, the transcription of the saying of Jesus varied a good deal according to the MSS. SIDERSKY (La parole suprême de Jésus, R.h.r., CIII, 1931, pp. 151–154) has suggested that the text should read ζαβαχθανι instead of σαβαχθανι and that in this word we have the transcription of זבקתני and not of עזבתני. It would then mean: "Wherefore hast thou sacrificed me?" It is not possible to accept this hypothesis which has no support in the manuscript tradition. Also the ritual idea of sacrifice plays no part in the thought of Jesus.

[4] Matthew doubtless thought that there was a contradiction between the merciful action and the words which accompany it, and he has attributed the words to a second soldier.

vinegar in the incident relating to the mockery of the soldiers which is peculiar to his Gospel. The fact that he has transposed it, and that he does not mention the despairing cry of Jesus, must be due to the fact that in his mind it seemed impossible, as it also seemed impossible to the Fourth Evangelist, that Jesus could have died feeling that God had abandoned him. Both of them have altered the last words of Jesus. Luke, doubtless remembering Stephen's cry, "Lord Jesus, receive my spirit!" places in the mouth of Jesus a verse from another Psalm (xxxi (LXX, xxx) 6): "Father, into thy hands I commit my spirit" (xxiii. 46), thus replacing a cry of despair by a cry of filial confidence. And John makes Jesus say τετέλεσται (xix. 30), a word with a double meaning (a kind of word John likes to use), which means both "It is finished," that is, "I die," and "It is accomplished," that is, "My work is finished, the redemption of the elect is assured."

The fact that both Luke and John felt this difficulty constitutes a very strong reason for believing that the cry of dereliction is authentic.[1] It is in striking contrast with the fact that the Gospels represent Jesus as living always in perfect communion with his heavenly Father, and also, in no less striking a way, with the absolute serenity which characterizes the attitude attributed to him from the moment of his arrest. The Early Church could never have imagined that Jesus felt that he was deserted by God, and the fact that this idea is expressed by Mark and by Matthew shows that they felt themselves bound to relate it on the strength of the tradition they had received. And, indeed, it is not without significance that the earliest account of the Passion has not attempted (as it would have been easy to do) to emphasize the physical torture which Jesus endured, while it has retained so accurate and precise a recollection of his spiritual agony; for the sense of being abandoned by God must have caused unfathomable pain to him whose whole life had been supported by the experience of the presence of God.

The idea of the darkness which accompanies the death of those

[1] The fact that Jesus expressed his sense of desolation by a phrase from a psalm is not at all surprising, for his mind was steeped in the psalms.

who are loved by the gods is so frequent, both in pagan and in Jewish tradition,[1] that it seems unnecessary to search for a natural explanation.[2] Certain passages in the Old Testament may have helped to form this tradition, as, for instance, Amos viii. 9:

> And it shall come to pass in that day, saith the Lord God,
> That I will cause the sun to go down at noon,
> And I will darken the earth in the clear day.[3]

Or Jer. xv. 9:

> She that hath borne seven languisheth:
> She hath given up the ghost;
> Her sun is gone down while it was yet day.

Although the Fourth Evangelist does not mention the darkness at the moment of the death of Jesus, this does not prove

---

[1] For the former, see USENER: *Rheinisches Museum*, 55, p. 286; for the latter, see STRACK-BILLERBECK, I, p. 1041 f. Cf. SAINTYVES: *Essais sur le folklore biblique*, Paris, 1923, pp. 423–463.

[2] My former pupil, ANDRÉ PARROT, has kindly sent me the following note: "On Friday the fifteenth of April, 1927, Good Friday, we observed at Jerusalem an atmospherical phenomenon which illustrated for us the mention of the darkness on the day of the Crucifixion. The sky, which since the preceding Saturday had been very blue and clear (it had rained very heavily from the 4th to the 7th of April), suddenly became covered with heavy clouds, after a night which had been perfectly clear, on the morning of the fifteenth (Good Friday) and about ten o'clock. Without becoming actual 'darkness' the clouds, which remained practically motionless, spread a kind of curtain which lasted so long that on that day we might almost say that it had hastened the sunset and the close of the day. The day was very hot; in fact, it was absolutely oppressive. With only a slight modification the sky remained covered throughout Saturday and did not clear until about eleven o'clock at night. The next morning (Easter Sunday) the sun rose in a cloudless sky. These natural manifestations which so unexpectedly formed such a symbolic setting for the events of the Christian year, have been noted objectively. The cause is easy to see. It was due to the action of the east wind (*khamsin*), which can darken the whole atmosphere and cause literally a kind of 'darkness' compared with the dazzling light of an Eastern sky." J. LEPSIUS (*Das Leben Jesu*, II, pp. 325 ff.) explains the incident of the darkness by a similar story. The hypothesis cannot be declared impossible, but in my opinion it is unnecessary.

[3] IRENAEUS (*Adv. haer.*, IV, 33, 12) has seen in the text of Amos a prophecy of the darkness at the death of Jesus.

that he knew a tradition in which this detail was absent, for in his mind the death of Jesus was his glorification. A manifestation of the sorrow of nature would not have been in keeping with the idea that the Son of God was at that moment passing into heavenly glory.

The episode of the vinegar, which is presented in such a way that at first sight it is difficult to see its point, may be perhaps explained by the belief that the death of a person who is crucified is hastened if something is given him to drink.[1] A glossologist of the fourteenth century, Nicholas of Lyra, writes with reference to John xix. 29: "*Illud (vas) enim portaverunt milites ut darent crucifixis ad bibendum ut per hoc citius morerentur et sic de custodia eorum in cruce expedirentur. Talis enim potatio aceti mortem accelerat, ut dicunt aliqui.*" ("The soldiers brought a vessel (containing vinegar) in order that they might give it to the crucified to drink in order that they should die more quickly, and that they (the soldiers) might be set free the sooner from their watch by the cross. According to certain people the fact of drinking vinegar under these conditions hastens death, so it is said.") A correspondent of Renan in 1863 informed him that in the East there was a very widespread notion that a person who was crucified or impaled would die immediately if something were given him to drink; in support of this idea he quoted the case of Solyman, the assassin of Kleber, who remained alive upon the stake more than four hours. Several times he asked for something to drink; the executioners did not wish to accede to this request, saying that the act of drinking would at once stop the beating of the heart; but when they had retired, a French sentry, moved by pity, gave the unhappy man some water to drink in a vessel attached to the end of his rifle. Solyman had scarcely finished drinking when he breathed his last. Renan also quotes[2] an incident from an English newspaper about a crucifixion in China in which the same idea occurs. If this belief, confirmed in three places, and at three periods, very

---

[1] On this, see RENAN: *Vie de Jésus*[15], p. 439. This does not occur until the thirteenth edition. For the reasons which determined Renan to envisage this explanation, see the communication of JEAN POMMIER to the *Société Ernest Renan*, March 27, 1920, *R.h.r.*, LXXXI, 1920, pp. 204 ff.

[2] According to the *Revue Germanique* of August 1864.

different from each other, existed in the first century, the Marcan narrative would then be very clear. The soldier who gave Jesus something to drink thought he would hasten his end, and the words, "let us see whether Elijah will come to save him," would then mean, "He will die, instead of being the object of an impossible deliverance."

It is possible that the incident of the vinegar may also be due to the influence of the interpretation of prophecy. John says actually that some moments before he died, seeing that all was accomplished, in order that the Scripture might be fulfilled, Jesus said, "I thirst." The soldiers filled a sponge with vinegar, put it upon hyssop and gave it to him. When Jesus had taken the vinegar he died (xix. 28–30). The passage of Scripture to which this alludes is Psa. xxii. 15 (LXX, xxi): "My strength is dried up like a potsherd; and my tongue cleaveth to my jaws," and Psa. lxix. 21 (LXX, lxviii): "In my thirst they gave me vinegar to drink."

Mark (xv. 38) and Matthew (xxvii. 51)[1] say that at the moment when Jesus expired the veil of the Temple was rent in twain from top to bottom. Luke reports the same fact, but, in order to fill up the marvels which accompanied the death of Jesus, he places it at the moment when the darkness began (xxiii. 45). On the testimony of Saint Jerome,[2] the Gospel of the Hebrews reported, not that the veil was rent, but that the lintel of the door of the Temple, which was of a remarkable size, broke. This is a correction of the Synoptic narrative under the influence of Isa. vi. 4 (LXX).

The detail of the rent veil seems as though it should be interpreted as a portent of a symbolic nature. It is a prophecy of the destruction of the Temple.[3]

After Jesus had died the centurion who had watched

---

[1] Matthew adds that there was an earthquake, that the rocks were rent, that the graves were opened, and that many of the saints which were asleep rose from the dead, and that after his Resurrection (the resurrection of Jesus) they entered into the city and were seen by many. It is unnecessary to emphasize the meaning and the character of this development.

[2] *Comm. sur Mt.*, 27, 51. *Ep.*, 120, 8.

[3] Cf. the interpretation of this given in the Epistle to the Hebrews (x. 20).

his agony said: "Truly this man was the Son of God" (Mark xv. 39*).[1]

It is not surprising that very early the narrative of the death of Jesus received all kinds of developments and additions. The sections which have been added are easy to recognize, and when they are eliminated the primitive tradition which remains is very simple. It told how Jesus was taken to Golgotha and crucified, after (according to the usual custom) he had been offered some drugged wine. A *titulus* was placed upon the cross which made known that he had been condemned as King of the Jews, then the soldiers divided his garments among themselves. After a time of agony which was comparatively short, since it lasted only three hours, Jesus, having lamented that God had deserted him, yielded up his spirit.[2]

[1] None of the scenes which are peculiar to the Johannine narrative can be regarded as historical. John tells that at the foot of the cross there stood his mother with other women and the belovéd disciple. Seeing them, Jesus says to his mother: "Woman! behold thy son!" and to his disciple: "Behold thy mother!" "And from that hour that disciple took her unto his own home" (xix. 25–27). He also relates that after Jesus had died, since it was the eve of a very solemn sabbath, the Jews obtained permission from Pilate to break the legs of the condemned men in order to hasten their death, that it might be possible to take down their bodies and bury them before sunset. As Jesus was already dead the soldier simply pierced his side with a lance and there came out blood and water. And the evangelist insists that this fact is well proved by a reliable witness who saw it with his own eyes; this witness is evidently the beloved disciple. In this fact he sees the fulfilment of two passages of Scripture: "A bone of him shall not be broken" (this refers to the Paschal Lamb) (Exod. xii. 46), and: "They shall look on him whom they pierced" (Zech. xii. 10). We have already seen (p. 462) what the blood and water from the side of Jesus meant in the mind of the evangelist (xix. 31–37). These two fragments belong to the earliest parts of the Fourth Gospel. It is impossible to regard what they say as historical. The oldest tradition would not have been able to pass over in silence the presence of the mother of Jesus at the cross and that of one of his disciples.

[2] The study of the traditions relating to the burial of Jesus cannot be separated from the problem of the Resurrection. I deal fully with the questions raised by this problem in *La foi à la résurrection de Jésus dans le christianisme primitif*, Bibliothèque de l'École des Hautes Études, Sciences religieuses, XLVIII, Paris, 1933. The conclusions will be summarized at the beginning of my second volume.

Appendix. The Site of Calvary [1]

A tradition which goes back without a break to the time of Constantine fixes the site of Calvary and the tomb of Jesus on the spot where the Church of the Holy Sepulchre now stands. On the evidence of the New Testament, all we can learn is that Golgotha was outside the city, and probably by the roadside. According to John (xix. 41), the sepulchre where the body of Jesus was laid was close to Calvary; however, the words: "Now in the place where he was crucified there was a garden; and in the garden a new sepulchre, wherein was never man yet laid," need not necessarily be interpreted in the sense that between the cross and the grave there was a very short distance, or one which was practically negligible. It is still less certain that the narrative of John, in which two traditions are combined, attributing the burial of Jesus to Joseph of Arimathea on the one hand, and, on the other, to Nicodemus, can be considered absolutely reliable. Under these conditions it is not permissible to claim that Calvary and the Holy Sepulchre are on exactly the same site, as is assumed by the archaeologists when they discuss this question.

The traditional site of the Holy Sepulchre corresponds very nearly to the conditions which the narratives require, but these conditions are too general in character for this fact to be conclusive. It is on the north of the city, and forms part of the district of Bezatha, which used not to be within the walls, but which would have been included in the enclosure begun by Agrippa in the year 43 to 44.

Are there good reasons for supposing that an unbroken tradition of this kind will carry us back from the moment when,

[1] Of the immense mass of literature dealing with the site of Calvary I will mention only: VINCENT-ABEL, II, pp. 89–300. DALMAN: *Itin.*, pp. 449 ff. VINCENT: *Garden Tomb, Histoire d'un mythe, Revue biblique*, 1925, pp. 401–431. *L'authenticité des Lieux Saints*, Paris, 1932. Cf. my observations, *R.h.p.r.*, XII, 1932. J. JEREMIAS: *Wo lag Golgotha und das heilige Grab? Die Ueberlieferung im Lichte der Formgeschichte, Aggelos*, I, 1925, pp. 161–173. *Golgotha und der heilige Fels, Eine Untersuchung zur Symbolsprache des Neuen Testaments, Ibid.*, II, 1926, pp. 74–128.

under Constantine, what may be called the official recognition of the Holy Places took place, to the period of the Passion of Jesus, in spite of the fact that Jerusalem was destroyed twice, in 70 and in 132? Accurate recollections would only have been preserved if the Christians who were on the spot were also interested in the Holy Places. Schlatter and Joachim Jeremias have demonstrated, in a manner which we may regard as convincing, that there was always a small Christian community at Jerusalem and then at Aelia Capitolina.[1] Thus the first condition is fulfilled. What of the second? Neither before nor after the year 70, until the beginning of the fourth century, do we find a trace of any interest in the Holy Places. In the Gospel of Luke the angel says to the women: "Why seek ye the living among the dead? He is not here" (xxiv. 5). This saying reflects the sentiment of the Early Church, to whom Jesus is not a person who has died, whose memory must be preserved, but the living Lord, present among his own.

In order to prove their interest in the Holy Places, Jeremias[2] has emphasized the prestige which the Church in Jerusalem enjoyed among the other Churches, which was manifested, for example, in the collection which the Apostle Paul organized on its behalf. But the Apostle explains very clearly (Rom. xv. 27) that the Churches of the Diaspora ought to assist the Church of Jerusalem with material things, since they had shared in her spiritual gifts, which means that the Christian missionary enterprise began at Jerusalem. The visits of Paul to Jerusalem were not pilgrimages. They were occasioned by the necessity felt by the apostle to wake and maintain contact with the Christians of Jerusalem, in order to try to resolve the grave conflict which had broken out as the result of the admission of the Gentiles into the Church.

The Passion and the Resurrection narratives contain some topographical considerations, but they are not presented in such a way that they could serve as a guide, even in a very general way, to pilgrims.

[1] SCHLATTER: *Die Tage Trajans und Hadrians*, Guttersloh, 1897. *Die Kirche Jerusalem von 70–130*, Gutersloh, 1928. JEREMIAS: *Aggelos*, I, 1905, pp. 150 ff.
[2] JEREMIAS: *Aggelos*, I, 1925, pp. 150 ff.

Towards 170 Melito of Sardis went to Palestine on pilgrimage. He says in a fragment which Eusebius (*Eccl. Hist.*, IV, 26, 14) has preserved, what he went to see: "Having gone to the East, I sojourned there where that which the Scriptures contain had been announced and accomplished, and I have learned with exactitude which are the books of the Old Testament. I have made a list of them which I am sending to thee." Eusebius, who knew Melito's book, was interested in the Holy Places. If he had found something in it which referred to them he would certainly have quoted it.

Origen went to Palestine when he was driven out of Alexandria, and he was interested in questions of sacred geography, but his interest was that of an exegete, and not that of a pilgrim.

The martyr Pionius of Smyrna also visited Palestine, but what struck him most was the desolate aspect of the Dead Sea, in which he saw a pledge of the fulfilment of the prophecies relating to the Last Judgment.[1]

Jerome speaks (*Ep.*, 46, 9), it is true, of bishops, martyrs, and doctors of the Church, who "from the time of the Ascension went to Jerusalem, believing that they would have less knowledge and religion and an imperfect practice of virtue if they had not worshipped in the very places whence the Gospel first began to radiate out into the world from the Cross"; but these pilgrims are not named, and the phrase is simply a literary one.

Although they are negative, these indications are not unimportant. Although we only possess the relics of the Christian literature before the fourth century, Eusebius knew the greater part of it. He believes in the Holy Sepulchre of Constantine, but he is aware that the proofs for the genuine character of the site are weak. If he had discovered passages in the earlier literature (which he knew better than any man of his own time) relating to the Holy Sepulchre, whether fixing the site of the tomb, or simply stating that the place was known, he would certainly have mentioned it.

The doubts which the preceding observations cannot fail to raise in our minds are far from being dispelled by the examina-

[1] *Mart. S. Pionii*, 4, 18 ff.

tion of the conditions in which, in the fourth century, under Constantine, the site of the Holy Sepulchre was said to have been discovered. On this point we have the testimony of Eusebius in his *Life of Constantine* (III, 25 ff.).[1] Eusebius says that the Emperor undertook to bring to the sight and the veneration of all the blessed place of the Resurrection of the Saviour in Jerusalem. This place had actually been left in obscurity and forgetfulness (σκότῳ καὶ λήθῃ) by impious men, or rather by demons. They had made it invisible (ἀφανές). They had brought earth and had hidden the divine grotto under an embankment and an enormous heap of rubbish (τὸ θεῖον ἄντρον). Above it there had been constructed a vast terrace and a "tomb of souls," a sanctuary of Aphrodite. Constantine, inspired by the Spirit of God, ordered that this sanctuary should be destroyed; he had the ground cleared, and then there reappeared the venerable and very holy witness to the Resurrection of the Saviour (τὸ σεμνὸν καὶ πανάγιον τῆς σωτηρίου ἀναστάσεως μαρτύριον). Thus Constantine restored the Sepulchre which had been forgotten and invisible. He discovered it when there seemed no hope of doing so (παρ᾽ ἐλπίδα πασᾶν ἀνεφαίνετο 28). Would Eusebius have said this if Constantine had been guided by precise indications, and if he had been able to depend upon an unbroken tradition?

It seems very improbable that, before the time of Constantine, it was known that the temple of Aphrodite covered the site of Calvary and the Holy Sepulchre. An intentional profanation of this kind would not have been conceivable unless it had occurred at a place to which pilgrims resorted. The Christians would have felt this blow very painfully; their attachment to the profaned site would have been redoubled, and it would be more than strange if, in the literature of the second and third centuries, Eusebius should not have gathered some echo of their distress and indignation. Thus Constantine was only able to depend, at the most, upon an occult tradition, and in consequence one which was uncontrolled and suspect, or else he acted on intuition, or on guesswork. Eusebius does not say by what Constantine was guided. Dalman[2] thinks that

[1] On the interpretation of this evidence, see K. HOLL: *Über Zeit und Heimat des pseudotertullianischen Gedichtes adv. Marcionem, Ges. Aufs.*, III, pp. 37 ff.
[2] DALMAN: *Itin.*, p. 456.

we have no right to accuse him of taking part in a piece of trickery through his silence. This silence is, however, very disturbing. Tradition has preserved the recollection of a miracle. The monk Alexander (sixth century)[1] tells how the Bishop Macarius, having received orders from Constantine to discover the Holy Places and to make them known, felt himself in a very embarrassing position. He invited those who were with him to pray, and he received a revelation which determined him to excavate on the spot where the temple of Aphrodite stood.

It is not certain that there were very positive reasons for seeking for the Holy Sepulchre in a place which had been defiled. Other explanations seem more probable. Constantine never ordered the systematic destruction of pagan temples. The motive assigned to the destruction of the sanctuary of Aphrodite at Jerusalem was the fact that it profaned the site of Calvary. Would not the Bishop Macarius, in order to obtain permission to have this temple destroyed, whose presence in the Holy City would be especially offensive to him, have had the idea of claiming that this must be the site of Calvary? Ths bishop may have acted in all good faith. Let us try to put ourselves in his place. He is concerned to discover the site of Calvary. He does not imagine that the generations which have preceded him have been anxious to know the actual places where the Passion took place, although this concern was so much alive in his own day. This may have led him to think that since such holy places have not been the object of veneration of the faithful, this must be because men, led astray by demons, have concealed them from their sight and knowledge. Then it would be quite natural to imagine that instead of the tomb of Jesus there had been erected something which was the exact opposite, a "tomb of souls," as Eusebius calls it. The most holy place in Jerusalem had been covered up by the most abominable thing in the city, whence comes the idea of looking for the site of Calvary and the Holy Sepulchre under the Temple of Venus. It is a well-known fact that when we search for relics we find them.

Very early, before the close of the fourth century, the legend

---

[1] *De inventione sanctae crucis, P.G.*, LXXXVII, 3, col. 4045.

of the Invention of the Cross was formed.[1] On the initiative of the Empress Helena, a search, which was conducted on the supposed site of Golgotha, resulted in the discovery of three crosses. That of Christ was recognized either by the *titulus* or by the fact that a corpse was brought back to life when the body was brought into contact with it. This cycle of very living legends was born of the desire to confirm the authenticity of the Holy Places. In order to have recourse to such arguments those of another order must have been insufficient and non-existent.

Jeremias[2] admits the seriousness of this fact. He tries to do away with its consequences by showing (by a series of examples taken from various directions) that a miracle of invention of the same type as that of the discovery of the cross forms part of what he calls the style of the narratives of the foundation of an Oriental sanctuary. There is one serious objection to his argument, and that is, that the account of the Foundation of the Holy Sepulchre arose entirely with Eusebius. The legend of the Invention of the Cross was added to it. This cannot have been for reasons of form; it must have been for fundamental reasons. And these reasons must have been that the authenticity of the site of the Holy Sepulchre was not sufficiently established.

Thus there is no real guarantee of the value of the traditional localization of the Holy Sepulchre and of the site of Calvary. The site which has been considered the right one since the days of Constantine may be that on which the cross was erected. But if the other sites which have been proposed, especially that which Gordon[3] believed he had discovered for reasons of mystical topography, cannot be accepted, this does not constitute a positive argument in favour of the traditional site of Calvary. Its authenticity is possible, but it has not been proved. The Calvary of Gordon is impossible; this does not prove, however, that the traditional Calvary marks the place where Jesus was crucified.

[1] Cf. Dom Leclerq: art. *Croix (Invention de la)*, *D.A.C.L.*, III, 2, col. 3131 ff.
[2] Jeremias: *Aggelos*, I, 1925, pp. 162 ff.
[3] See the incisive and conclusive criticism of P. Vincent: *Revue biblique*, 1925, pp. 401–431.

CHAPTER XXI

THE GOSPEL

THE thought of Jesus cannot be separated from his action, for both mutually condition and explain each other. The Gospel is not a theoretical system which was built up in an abstract way, nor even a static idea whose component parts were gradually perceived as circumstances made it possible. The thought of Jesus varied on points as essential as the following: his own consciousness of the significance of his person and of the part he was called to play in the world; the conditions in which the Kingdom of God would be realized; the time at which the Kingdom would come; and, finally, the privileged position of the Jewish nation. In these oscillations (although this may not be the full explanation) we perceive the reflex action of circumstances on the mind of Jesus. Thus, in following what we know of his story, we have been led to envisage the principal aspects of his thought. We will now proceed to make a brief survey of his thought as a whole.

The first point we notice is that it was developed within the setting of Jewish thought,[1] whose essential elements and structure it preserved intact. Like his contemporaries, Jesus believed that one world-order would be followed by another; he believed that the present world, which was dominated by demons, was destined to disappear in the near future, and that it would be replaced by a new world-order in which God would be supreme. He believed that the transition from the one order to the other would take place at the moment when the Son of Man, the transcendent Messiah, would appear on the clouds of heaven, escorted by hosts of angels; the Messiah would then sit in judgment upon humanity; the final destiny

---

[1] For Judaism in the time of Jesus the reader is referred to the following, among others: SCHÜRER, BALDENSPERGER: *Die messianisch-apokalyptischen Hoffnungen des Judentums*, Strasbourg, 1903. P. VOLZ: *Die jüdische Eschatologie von Daniel bis Akiba*, Tübingen, 1903. LAGRANGE: *Le messianisme chez les juifs*. BOUSSET-GRESSMANN: *Die Religion des Judentums*. MOORE: *Judaism in the First Century of the Christian Era*, Cambridge, Mass., 1927. BONSIRVEN: *Sur les ruines du Temple*, Paris, 1928, etc.

of men will be in his hands; some will be admitted into the Kingdom of God, while the rest are doomed to destruction. On questions like the abstract conception of God, the world, demons, angels, and the revelation of God to Israel, Jesus held the same ideas as his contemporaries. He conceived the problem of religion in exactly the same terms as Judaism. He felt that the one thing that mattered was that men should know and realize the conditions which would ensure their admission into the Kingdom of God at the critical moment of the advent of the Messiah and the Day of Judgment.

A systematic reconstruction of the thought of Jesus, even if it were possible, would only give a very inaccurate picture. Each aspect of his thought is self-contained. In each of his sayings Jesus expresses himself wholly. It would be wasted toil to try to connect the various aspects of his thought by searching for the dialectical links between them. The unity of his thought is of a quite different character. It is not a logical unity; it is a unity of inspiration. We can only perceive it by working back from each saying to the religious conception behind it, or, to be more accurate, to the state of soul which it reveals.

I. The Authority of the Law and the Authority of God

The character of every religious and theological conception is determined by its attitude towards the problem of authority. This rule applies with equal force to the thought of Jesus. His thought does not actually contain any new element, unless we single out his original way of conceiving and realizing in his own life, to the uttermost, the spirit and practice of obedience to the absolute and unique authority of God.

In theory, Jesus shared the views of Judaism about the revelation of God in the Old Testament; in practice, he introduced ideas into this conception which made it wholly new.[1]

In this respect the thought of Jesus has a twofold aspect.

[1] See, on this point, my study: *Jésus et la tradition religieuse de son peuple, R.h.p.r.*, VII, 1927, pp. 154–175, 219–244.

Sometimes Jesus seems to act as a Jew who is entirely loyal to the religious traditions of his people, and even a strict observer of the Law; at other times his attitude towards these traditions appears absolutely revolutionary. This apparent dualism can easily be explained. So far as the Jewish Law was concerned Jesus had no desire for reform. Even when he criticized the rules formulated by the scribes he was careful to add: "All therefore whatsoever they bid you observe, that observe and do; but do not ye after their works, for they say, and do not" (Matt. xxiii. 3, 23). On the other hand, whenever the Law and the tradition seemed to him to be opposed to that which he regarded as the direct revelation of God to his own soul, he rejected them. To Jesus the authority of the Old Testament is absolute. He appeals to it in every discussion (cf. Mark. ii. 25*, vii. 9–13, x. 6*, xii. 35 ff.*); and this was not merely because the Scriptural argument was the one most likely to carry weight with his hearers. When we read the words of Jesus it becomes evident that He was steeped in the Old Testament, and that he regarded it as something very different from an arsenal of texts with which to confute his adversaries. It is typical of his way of using the Old Testament that in a number of instances [1] he criticizes certain customs or ideas based upon the Old Testament in the name of the Old Testament itself. This habit of setting one passage of Scripture against another, as, for instance, the passage in Genesis which says that God created man and woman to be one flesh, against the Mosaic legislation on divorce, is in reality an exercise in discrimination in the interpretation of the Scriptures; by this method Jesus was able to declare that one passage was inspired and another was not; that it was, in fact, merely a concession to human weakness. This implies an authority which judges the Old Testament itself. Henceforth, therefore, the Old Testament ceased to be a code, or a collection of oracles; it is a Word of God addressed to the conscience which becomes the source of a present revelation, hence it does not stifle spontaneity of judgment and the autonomy of conscience. To Jesus God is not merely a reality of the past, belonging to the days when He spoke with Moses

[1] With reference to the Sabbath (Mark ii. 25* f.), to divorce (Mark x. 6*), to the Davidic descent of the Messiah (Mark xii. 36*).

or the prophets; He is, and He remains, a living, present Reality.

Matthew has preserved the following declaration of Jesus: "Think not that I am come to destroy the Law or the Prophets: I am not come to destroy, but to fulfil" (v. 17). From the letter of the Law he goes back to the principle which inspires it, in order to make all its implications explicit; this carries one far beyond the letter of the commandment, and even, if necessary, into opposition to its formula. This comes out very clearly in the concrete examples which serve as a commentary on the principle which has been laid down. Jesus does not condemn murder or adultery only, but still more, and just as much, the thought of hatred and the lustful gaze. A revelation conceived in these terms is not addressed to beings whose only duty it is to yield a passive and mechanical obedience; it assumes that there is an active energy at work in the hearts of men; this force is the conscience, which acts as a living ferment in the soul. This revelation is progressive, and this explains the co-existence of the traditional and the new elements in the thought of Jesus, and reconciles them to each other. Thus, although Jesus does not in any way disparage the Old Testament, he has been able to present his teaching as a new revelation, and to set his "I say unto you" against "Ye have heard that it was said by them of old time" (Matt. v. 21 ff.). This explains what his hearers meant when they said that his teaching was "with authority," that is to say, that it was that of a man who spoke in the name of God, whose Voice he had heard in his own soul; they contrasted it with that of the scribes, which was only a commentary on the tradition, or a discussion and balancing of opinions uttered by the doctors of the law in the past (Mark i. 22*).

Thus we can now understand how it was that the same Jesus who said: "I am not come to destroy the Law and the prophets, but to fulfil," said also: "The Law and the prophets were until John" (Luke xvi. 16; cf. Matt. xi. 13). It is not necessary to suppose that these two sayings were uttered at two different periods in the ministry of Jesus, for, although they seem opposed to each other, they are not contradictory. It is the fulfilment of the Law, that is to say, the development of the principle which inspires it, which leads Jesus to go beyond it, and to discover that the Law and the Prophets—at least in the sense in which it was conceived around him—have had their day, and that a new era has begun in the history of religion.

Ought we to regard this new element in the thought of Jesus as the flowering of the Jewish conception, and hence merely an extension and expansion of it, or is it something wholly new and original? Judaism gives obedience a central place in religion: the will of God is manifested in the Commandments. It is this which constitutes the real Good. It does not reveal an ideal which can exist apart from the will of God; rather, it is the Divine will which creates the ideal; the Good is that which God commands. Obedience to a Law, however complete and detailed, can never be more than a partial fulfilment of the Divine will, for a system of commandments can never foresee and embrace all the complexity and diversity of life. Beyond all that is commanded and all that is prohibited lies the vast domain which contains those actions which, being neither commanded nor forbidden, may be considered to be permitted, that is, they are morally neutral.[1] Inevitably such a conception limits the practice of obedience to God. The attitude of Jesus is entirely different. It is often said—and rightly—that in his commentary on the Commandments in the Sermon on the Mount he substituted the ethic of intention and of the will for that of the act, or, in other words, he made morality an inward thing. Thus he has not merely transformed the moral side of life, but religion itself; the religion of the heart, of inner moral purity, replaces a religion of outward conformity to God's demands. It would, of course, be unjust to Judaism to represent it as a religion of ritual practices alone. It is, however, true that in it God remains external, since he can only be known through an objective and historical reve-

---

[1] This was aggravated still further by the fact that there is a great temptation to extend, through subtle distinctions in interpretation, the domain of that which is permitted to the detriment of that which is commanded and forbidden. The discussions relating to *Corban* (Mark vii. 6–13) or to the oath (Matt. xxiii. 16–22) show that Judaism was not always able to resist this temptation.

lation. To Jesus, on the contrary, God, the object of religion, becomes interior. He is directly perceived by the soul.

Bultmann [1] has seen this very clearly; he emphasizes the fact that in the thought of Jesus the principle which the Commandment contains has been thought out to its ultimate conclusion, and developed logically in all its implications. For Jesus taught that the will of God should control, not merely some of the acts of men, but that it should govern their life as a whole. This implies a revelation quite different from one which can be formulated in a Law, a revelation which is permanent and direct, since it reveals not merely the will of God, but God Himself. The logical conclusion of the principle of obedience towards God, of that fulfilment of the will of God which Jesus made the first object of the prayer he taught his disciples (Matt. vi. 10*), the ideal set before them in all their action, is the formula of the Sermon on the Mount: "Be ye therefore perfect, as your Father in heaven is perfect" (Matt. v. 48).

This ideal which Jesus sets before his disciples, the realization within humanity of the very nature of God, could not even be imagined if God were remote and inaccessible; if, apart from the fragmentary and limited revelation represented by the Law, God did not reveal Himself directly to His children; if He were only the God of majesty who spoke in ancient time out of the midst of the thunders and lightnings of Sinai; if He were not also the God within, the God who reveals Himself to the soul, who speaks directly to the human conscience.

II. THE GOD OF JESUS

Thus Jesus inaugurates an entirely new conception, if not of God, at least of the revelation of God. At the same time we must note that the theoretical idea of God in the thought of Jesus cannot actually be distinguished from that of the Judaism of his day.

Like the Jews of his own time, Jesus believes in a God who is perfect, omnipotent, and omniscient. But—and this is where his originality becomes evident—he places all the emphasis

[1] BULTMANN: *Jesus*, pp. 69 ff.

upon the practical consequences, which are thus specifically religious, of the Divine attributes. He does not insist on a theory of omnipotence and omniscience, but he speaks of the God who counts every hair on the heads of his children, without whose permission not a sparrow can fall to the ground. He does not speculate about the divine perfections, but, by his teaching and by his whole attitude, he makes us feel that he has an incomparable sense of the mercy of God. But above all, the unique originality of Jesus consists in his sense of the presence of God, in that conscious and living communion with God in which he lives. To him God is no abstract idea, but an immediate and living reality; God in him, not a God conceived with the mind, or imagined, or dreamed, but a God who is experienced, felt, known. This has been well expressed by Renan: "Jesus does not have visions, God does not speak to him as someone outside himself. God is in him; he feels that he is in God, and when he speaks of his Father he is speaking from his heart. He lives in the heart of God in continual communion. He does not see Him, but he feels Him." [1]

Usually, when men try to formulate conceptions of God, by a sort of fatality a twofold peril threatens to block their way. On the one hand, they may conceive God to be so transcendent that he can no longer have any contact with man at all; He is thus reduced to a kind of abstract idea, which has no value for actual life. The other danger is this: that in order to maintain contact between man and God, men sacrifice the absolute character and transcendence of God and fall into an anthropomorphism which may be more or less naïve. Jesus has avoided both these pitfalls. In his mind God is absolutely transcendent and absolutely holy, yet at the same time he is a God who is very near to men, not a Judge with an inflexible sense of justice, but a Father.

The moral austerity of Jesus is as strong as that of John the Baptist. His judgment on humanity is very severe. "Ye who

[1] RENAN, p. 75. Cf. C. A. BERNOUILLI: *Le Dieu-Père de Jésus d'après les Synoptiques, Actes du Congrès international d'histoire des religions tenu à Paris en Octobre,* 1923, II, p. 222. K. HOLL: *Urchristentum und Religionsgeschichte, Ges. Aufs.,* II, pp. 9 ff.

are evil," he says to his hearers (Matt. vii. 11); he calls them "a wicked and adulterous generation" (Matt. xvi. 4, xvii. 17, etc.); and he points out that the root of evil is in the very heart of man, to such an extent that it is without excuse and without remedy. "That which cometh out of the man, that defileth the man. For from within, out of the heart of men, proceed evil thoughts, adulteries, fornications, murders, thefts, covetousness ... pride, foolishness ..." (Mark vii. 20–21). The pessimism of Jesus is more radical than that of John the Baptist. He does not say to his hearers: "Repent and bring forth fruits worthy of repentance," that is, "make an effort which will make you worthy to enter the Kingdom of God," but he says: "When ye shall have done all those things which are commanded you, say, We are unprofitable servants" (Luke xvii. 10).

Hence no effort made by man could possibly bridge the gulf which separates him from God; no strenuous act of will could create that state of absolute submission of all creatures to God, which, in Jewish thought—and Jesus is decidedly Jewish on this point—the idea of God postulates absolutely. The Kingdom of God cannot be realized along this path. But Jesus does not believe that it is impossible to realize the Kingdom of God. For the pessimism of Jesus regarding merely human effort is only equalled by his optimism when he turns to God. The idea that God could possibly be finally thwarted and defeated by the powers of evil never even enters his mind. Thus Jesus came to feel that there is only one possible solution: we must admit that justice is not the supreme nor the only attribute of God. Jesus did not reach this conclusion through abstract considerations concerning the conditions which must be fulfilled if the Kingdom of God is to come on earth. All his thought on this subject was controlled and quickened by the fact that in his own experience God had not revealed Himself to him as an inflexible Judge, or a strict Master, but as a Father.

Can we discover the origin of this idea, or rather of this sense of the merciful God who pardons sin and yet remains a just God? Karl Holl [1] has shown that this is the great and para-

---

[1] KARL HOLL: *Urchristentum und Religionsgeschichte, Ges. Aufs.*, II, pp. 9 ff.

doxical new element in the Gospel of Jesus.[1] It is, of course, true that the idea of the Divine mercy was not alien to Jewish thought; it occurs especially and very beautifully in the Psalms, but, as Bultmann has observed,[2] Judaism never attained a logical development of the ideas of sin or of grace. Its emphasis on ritual expiation, on the singular and exceptional clemency manifested by God towards the Chosen People,[3] and on the idea that good works can, to some extent, compensate for the disobedience of man: all this weakens the idea of sin. So far as the idea of grace is concerned, it is conceived as an act of benevolence by which God turns away His eyes from beholding the sin of man: "Remember not the sins of my youth nor my transgressions," cries the Psalmist (Psa. xxv. 7), and another Psalm speaks of the joy of him whose "sin is forgotten" (Psa. xxxii. 1). The grace of God is divorced from His justice and His holiness. Wherever in Jewish thought[4] the ideas of the divine justice and holiness have been fully maintained, there is no room for the idea of pardon. Klausner[5] argues that the God of Jesus is not a just God, and that He is unaware of evil. In his opinion conscience demands that God should be not only the merciful Father but also the Judge. This is why, he concludes, Judaism cannot admit the idea of a God who forgives.

Hellenism is no less opposed to this idea. Plato declares that the most perverse and the most impious of all the impious are those who think that the gods could betray the strict

---

[1] See also E. EHRHARDT: *Le principe de la morale de Jésus*, p. 23.

[2] BULTMANN: *Jesus*, pp. 136 ff.

[3] Cf. Wisd. of Sol. xv. 2: "Even when we sin, we are Thine, for we know Thy power." In Rom. ii the Apostle Paul is seeking to controvert the idea that God judges the sin of the Jews in a different light from that of the Gentiles, and the way in which he does this shows how deeply this idea was rooted in the Jewish consciousness.

[4] In the *Fourth of Esdras* (viii. 34 ff.) the seer thinks with pity of the fate of the damned, and he beseeches God to have mercy on them: "Lord, he says, Thy goodness and Thy justice will be manifested if Thou hast pity on those who have no treasure of good works." The angel of revelation does not grant this request. "You must not torment yourself," he says, "about the destiny which sinners have prepared for themselves; you must simply rejoice in the thought of the blessedness of the just," and the seer sees that the angel is right, and that the treasure of good works is indispensable.

[5] KLAUSNER, pp. 377 f.

justice of which they are the guardians (*Laws*, X, 907). Celsus ridicules the idea of a kingdom promised to sinners. He compares the Christian God with the captain of a robber band who gathers a company of evil-doers around himself.[1] In the thought of Hellenism the divinity only enters into contact with men whose souls are pure. Purification occupies a large place in the Hellenic religions, in the mystery religions in particular, but it is not the consequence of contact with the divinity; it precedes this contact, and is, indeed, the condition on which communion is possible; thus it is not equivalent to a pardon which comes from the divinity.

The conception of the God of Jesus may have been foreshadowed in the Prophets and in the Psalms; nevertheless, in its essence, this idea is new, since it puts all rational and moral conceptions of the relation between man and God entirely out of court. It is not surprising that this view of God should have made the scribes and Pharisees indignant, and it is easy to understand why it was that, in their eyes, Jesus seemed nothing short of a blasphemer. This does not mean, however, as Klausner seems to think it does, that it constitutes a complete denial of the difference between good and evil; it is impossible to regard it as the suppression of morality, for Jesus makes a very high demand on men: nothing less than that they should realize the divine perfection in their own lives. These ideas are not brought together in a purely external way, which would be illogical, since it is precisely on the idea of a God who forgives that his ethic of perfection is based. The story of the "woman who was a sinner" at the feet of Jesus, and the parable of the Two Debtors (which is the commentary on this incident (Luke vii. 36–50)), illustrate the organic connexion which exists, in the thought of Jesus, between Divine pardon and service. The man who is pardoned by God, that is to say, the man who has experienced the Love of God, will love Him, and will therefore be capable of being inspired by His nature. This reverses the apparently normal and rational order of the relation between religion and morality. Usually the faithful can only enter into contact with the divinity if their hearts are pure. The nearer one is to holiness the nearer to God.

[1] ORIGEN: *C. Celsum*, I, 253, 256; III, 59, 62.

In the thought of Jesus, on the contrary, the communion with God which is given with the pardon of sin is the principle of the moral life and its starting-point.

III. The Kingdom of God

This new idea of God brought by Jesus brings with it also a new idea of the Kingdom of God, or at least of the conditions under which it can be realized.

In Israel the expectation of the Kingdom of the transcendent God arose out of the transformation of national hopes. When events had proved that it was no longer possible to hope that the play of political factors would restore national independence to Israel, and, still less, enable it to attain world domination, the undying hopefulness of the Jewish soul took refuge in the transcendental realm. This was because, even when it took on a political form, it had, at bottom, an essentially religious basis. Israel being the people of Yahweh, its final defeat would mean the defeat of Yahweh Himself, but such a scandal could not be imagined. It was thus that the Jews came to expect a judgment of God upon the world which would make the triumph of Israel certain, and would either annihilate or subdue all her enemies. As time went on this hope became more and more transcendental, and finally led to the idea of a new world which would be substituted for the old.[1]

This new world is described by the two equivalent terms of the Kingdom of God and the Kingdom of Heaven which we find in the Gospels.[2] They do not conceal different conceptions, but the use of the second term is due to the scruple felt by the Jews about pronouncing the name of God. The Kingdom of Heaven is not a kingdom which is or will be in heaven, it is the reign of Him who is in heaven. The Kingdom of

---

[1] This development was facilitated by certain ideas from abroad, especially from Persia. See H. Gressmann: *Der Messias*.

[2] Mark and Luke use regularly the term Kingdom of God. Usually Matthew uses the term Kingdom of Heaven. The term Kingdom of God is used by him only three or four times (in xix. 24 the evidence of the MSS. varies). The three passages in which he uses Kingdom of God quite certainly (xx. 1, xxi. 31, 43) are peculiar to Matthew.

God is transcendent in its origin, and not in the sphere where it will be established.[1]

To Jesus also the Kingdom of God is a new order which will be realized by an act of God. In the present world God does not reign, or at least He does not reign in an absolute manner, whether we admit that His action is limited and opposed by that of the demons, or whether we admit that,[2] offended by the sin of man (the result of the revolt of certain spirits), God has handed over the world to the rule of the angels. "The dominion is in the hands of man," says Wellhausen, "that is the actual fact; but it belongs to God, and this is the necessary correction."[3] The establishment of the Kingdom of God will be the translation of this ideal into fact. On this point Jesus is in entire agreement with the views of his contemporaries. The establishment of the Kingdom of God will mean the restoration of the sovereignty of God, thwarted at the moment by the domination of the power of Satan. But whereas, to the Jews, the power of Satan was manifested supremely by the fact that the political supremacy was in the hands of the Gentiles, to Jesus it consisted in the fact of the reign of sin.

In theory, Jesus' idea of the Kingdom of God is the same as that of his contemporaries. He feels the necessity for the rule of God in the world to be re-established. Actually, his idea of what this rule of God should be is something entirely different from the ordinary Jewish idea, and consequently his idea of the conditions in which it could be re-established is also quite different.

The present world is evil, and the violent take it by force (Mark x. 42). The parable of the Unjust Steward (Luke xvi. 1–13) and that of the Unjust Judge (Luke xviii. 1–8), the advice given to those who go to law (Matt. v. 25–26), show that Jesus judged the social organization very severely. The elect, that is the just, are ill-treated in the world since they cry to

---

[1] This is illustrated by the picture in the Book of Revelation, in which the seer contemplates the new Jerusalem which descends from heaven from God (xxi. 10).

[2] This is the theory developed in the Book of Enoch.

[3] WELLHAUSEN: *Einl².*, p. 88.

God day and night to obtain justice (Luke xviii. 7); riches in general, and not only ill-gotten wealth, are called "unrighteous mammon" (Luke xvi. 9). Satan dominates in the world and holds in his power the sick and the possessed (Luke xiii. 16). The Beatitudes, in the primitive form in which they have been preserved by Luke (vi. 20, 23), imply, on the one hand, that there are people who suffer, and on the other those who oppress them, and who do not trouble about the misery of their brethren. The point of view from which things are judged in the world is radically different from the view of God: "for that which is highly esteemed among men is abomination in the sight of God" (Luke xvi. 15). The feeling roused in the heart of Jesus when he beholds the multitudes is that of a profound compassion (Mark vi. 34).

These judgments are exclusively moral in character. They are not inspired by philosophical opinions. Jesus was not an ascetic; he did not practise fasting, and he did not impose these habits upon his disciples (Matt. xi. 18, 19*; Mark ii. 18–22*). Without doubt, he accepted hard renunciations and he asked his disciples also to accept sacrifices. But these necessities are inspired not by a systematic asceticism but by the principle of a hierarchy of values. He is thinking only of sacrifices voluntarily accepted, not because in themselves they have any positive value, but because they open the door to the higher good. "Seek first the Kingdom of God," says Jesus (Matt. vi. 33).

Certain passages, for instance the Beatitudes, in the form in which they are presented by Matthew (v. 3 ff.), seem to represent the Kingdom of God as a reward. We ought to be quite clear about the significance of the idea of reward in the thought of Jesus. His language is conditioned by that which was usual in his own day. A precise statement like that which is reported by Luke (xvii. 10): "When ye shall have done all those things which are commanded you, say, We are unprofitable servants," is enough to show that the passages which mention the subject of reward ought to be taken with a grain of salt, and that all that we can really gather from them is the idea of logical development. Jesus is not speaking of acts which his disciples ought to do in order to deserve to be admitted into the Kingdom of God, but of the conditions which they must fulfil in order to be allowed to enter.

To enter the Kingdom of God, and to enter into life, are interchangeable terms. As their antithesis there is the phrase: "to be cast into Gehenna or into eternal fire," which seems to imply not an everlasting torment but annihilation. The Kingdom of God, from the moment that it is established, will be the only reality. We might define it as the state of being in which the sovereignty of God will be exercised without let or hindrance in men or in things, because all the forces hostile to God will have been either destroyed or subdued.

This eschatological idea of the Kingdom of God has been challenged by some thinkers, but they are wrong. Since the world in which Jesus lived was dominated by the eschatological point of view, if we are to regard the expressions used by Jesus which reflect the ideas of eschatology as purely pictorial, we would need to be convinced that his views were quite different from those which were current in his own day. This is not the case.

It is unnecessary to recall here all the sayings of Jesus which imply an eschatological conception of the Kingdom of God. We only need to remind ourselves of the first petition in the Lord's Prayer: "Thy kingdom come" (Matt. vi. 10), and also to note the way in which the ideas of the coming of the Kingdom of God, of the manifestation of the Messiah, of judgment, and of resurrection, are regarded as equivalent terms.

One passage is often quoted in order to uphold the idea that at least, even if Jesus did think that the full realization, the manifestation of the Kingdom of God should be expected at the end of the present era, this does not exclude the idea of a present existence of the Kingdom of God, in a humble and hidden way, which may be compared with that of the seed which is a reality, although it is not yet the tree into which it will grow. It is suggested that parables like those of the Hidden Treasure and the Pearl of Great Price (Matt. xiii. 44–46) which seem to present the Kingdom as a good which can be acquired even now, or like those of the seed growing secretly (Mark iv. 26–29), or the Grain of Mustard Seed (Mark iv. 30 ff.*) and of the Leaven (Matt. xiii. 33*), which seem to regard it as a germ capable of development, are also a true picture of the thought of Jesus about the Kingdom of Heaven.

So far as the first series of these parables is concerned, we must remember [1] that a parable is not an allegory, and that the main point in these particular parables is that the Kingdom of God is so precious that it is worth all the sacrifices we can make for it.[2] As for the parables of the Leaven and of the Seed, the idea they convey is simply that certain conditions ought to be realized from the present moment if we are to enter into the Kingdom of God. The ancient world had no conception of the idea of organic development which is contained implicitly in the seed. In the thought of that day germination was an act of the power of God which produced the plant after the seed had died (John xii. 24; 1 Cor. xv. 36–38).

It has sometimes been suggested that the idea of a spiritual Kingdom is contained in Luke xvii. 20–21. This passage is somewhat obscure, partly, no doubt, owing to the fact that we do not know the circumstances in which the saying which is here reported was uttered. Jesus is questioned by the Pharisees, who ask him when the Kingdom of God will come. Since there is no controversial point either in the question or in the answer, it seems as though this indication might be retained. The question does not refer to the nature of the Kingdom of God but only to the moment when it will come. This would scarcely be intelligible if Jesus' own idea of the Kingdom of God had been different from that of his questioners. Jesus then declares that "the Kingdom of God cometh not with observation," that is, it does not come in such a way that its coming can be foreseen in advance.[3] This passage contains a

---

[1] See pp. 288 ff.

[2] This interpretation is confirmed by the fact that the parables of the Hid Treasure and of the Pearl of Great Price are placed in the setting of those of the Tares (Matt. xiii. 24–30, 36–43) and of the Net (Matt. xiii. 47–50), which exclude the idea of a present Kingdom, for a state in which the wicked live side by side with the good is a negation of the absolute dominion of God.

[3] Μετὰ παρατηρήσεως. This word is used of the observation of the symptoms of a malady or that of the movements of the stars. From both sides there is the idea of a necessary course of events which one can foresee when the first elements have been observed. This meaning agrees absolutely

controversial point which is opposed to the fundamental idea of apocalyptic thought: that of an immutable plan, known in advance, towards which the final events inevitably move. "Neither shall they say, Lo here! or Lo there!" says Jesus. The Kingdom of God will come suddenly, and not as the final act in a process of development. In the same chapter Luke gives this saying: "And they shall say to you, See here; or, see there: go not after them, nor follow them. For as the lightning, that lighteneth out of one part under heaven, shineth unto the other part under heaven; so shall also the Son of Man be in his day" (xvii. 23–24).[1] Thus the meaning of the first part of verse 20 is clear. Jesus says that we cannot foresee the moment of the realization of the coming of the Kingdom of God in such a way that we can prepare ourselves to take advantage of its coming. After that, Jesus adds, and this is where the difficulty begins: "Behold! the Kingdom of God is within you" (ἐντὸς ὑμῶν ἐστιν). Many interpreters, identifying Jesus with the Kingdom of God, think that this means: The Kingdom is here, in my own person, and is realized by me for those who attach themselves to me. But the text does not say, "in the midst of you" (ἐν μέσῳ ὑμῶν), but "in you."

For the same reason we reject the interpretation of Loisy,[2] who reads: "The Kingdom will be with you as it is elsewhere." That is the meaning of xvii. 23–24, but xvii. 21 says something different.

Since the evangelist gives this saying as addressed to the Pharisees, that is to say, to people whom he usually represents as hostile towards Jesus, he cannot have meant "in you" in the sense of "in your hearts."

In order to discover the meaning of this statement we must remember, so I believe, that all the teaching of Jesus about the Kingdom of God has essentially a practical bearing. In the mouth of Jesus the term the Kingdom of God often conveys a

with our text. Jesus means that the Kingdom of God will not come in such a way that by the observation of premonitory signs we can be sure when it will come.

[1] Luke xvii. 23 ought to be considered as simply placed alongside of xvii. 20, on account of the repetition of "and he said unto his disciples." The logion xvii. 23 has been inserted by Matthew in a slightly different form in the Synoptic Apocalypse (xxiv. 26).

[2] LOISY: *Syn.*, II, pp. 402 ff.; *Évangile de Luc*, p. 430.

meaning which is very nearly equivalent to "the conditions of entrance into the Kingdom of God." If we also take into account the fact that the same form in Aramaic expresses both the present and the future, we are led to think that the meaning of the saying of Jesus is this: "The Kingdom of God, that is, the possibility of entering it, will be in you."

Jesus speaks of the Kingdom of God in the same terms as his contemporaries. His conception, however, seems to have been far less material than theirs. It is true, of course, that he did speak of being at table in the Kingdom of God and of eating and drinking therein (Matt. viii. 11*; Luke xxii. 30), he believed that there would be seats of honour in the Kingdom (Mark x. 40*; Matt. xix. 28*); he speaks of people who enter into it maimed or lame (Mark ix. 43–48*); but, on the other hand, when he is interrogated by the Sadducees about the case of a woman in the Kingdom of God, who in accordance with the Levitical Law had successively married seven brothers, he declares that in the Kingdom of God men would be as the angels in heaven (Mark xii. 25*). When the sons of Zebedee ask for the foremost places in the Kingdom of God, Jesus says to them: "Ye know that they which are accounted to rule over the Gentiles exercise lordship over them; and their great ones exercise authority upon them. But so shall it not be [1] among you: but whosoever will be great among you, shall be your minister: and whosoever of you will be the chiefest, shall be servant of all" (Mark x. 42–44*). How far we are here from the ideal of the Jews who longed for the Kingdom of God in order that they might be able to oppress their enemies!

The first petitions in the Lord's Prayer, according to the version in Matthew's Gospel, are these: "Thy Kingdom come; Thy will be done as in heaven, so on earth" (Matt. vi. 10). These are not two requests but one, since the Kingdom of God is precisely that state in which the will of God is done. Luke (xi. 2) gives one petition only, and there are many reasons for believing that he may be following a primitive text, since it says the same as that of Matthew, only in fewer words. If it is the will of God, that is, as Matthew says, that

[1] Though translated as a future tense, the verb is really in the present; the Aramaic word used by Jesus can have both meanings.

men should be perfect, or as Luke says, that they should be merciful like their Heavenly Father (Matt. v. 48), we may apply to the Kingdom of God what Jesus says about God Himself: thus it will be characterized by kindness, mercy, and love.

There is one point in which the conception of Jesus differs profoundly from that of his contemporaries: it has no political reference at all. It is true that by the very fact that he proclaimed the imminence of the Kingdom of God Jesus announced the collapse of earthly empires, and this explains how it was that the Jews found it easy to rouse Pilate to arrest him and sentence him to death as an aspirant to the Messiahship.

Jesus conceived the Kingdom of God differently from his contemporaries, because he saw in it the fulfilment of the will of God, and not the divine power placed at the service of the hatreds and ambitions of the Jewish people.

IV. ESCHATOLOGY AND APOCALYPTIC

Although the thought of Jesus about the Kingdom of God was definitely eschatological, it was not apocalyptic. The two ideas of eschatology and apocalyptic are often confused, but this should not be. Eschatology is characterized by the idea that the present world should be replaced by a new world, and that the transition from one order to the other is imminent. To this fundamental idea apocalyptic adds the conviction that the coming of the new world will take place according to a plan which is not merely fixed in advance by God, but which also can be known and is revealed to the wise man by the study of and combination of traditions and prophecies. The fundamental idea of apocalyptic is that it is possible to calculate in advance, with precision, the successive phases of the great drama which is about to be played in such a way that when it occurs it will be possible to follow its development, moment by moment, scene by scene. The conception of Jesus was not apocalyptic, for when some Pharisees asked him about the advent of the Kingdom of God, he declared that it would come in such a way that it would be impossible to foretell in advance the precise moment of its arrival (Luke xvii. 20), while to his disciples he said that the day of the Son of Man would come as suddenly as a flash of lightning (Luke xvii. 24). This is the explanation of this apparently paradoxical fact that a habit of thought, dominated by the obsession of the End of the world, is not expressed by descriptions of the events which would mark the End, or at least is not accompanied by pictorial descriptions of a similar character. On yet another point, the thought of Jesus differs very definitely from the apocalyptic conception. The latter is, by its very nature, strictly determinist. An Apocalypse is only indirectly an appeal, and it is then merely an appeal to perseverance which is addressed only to the faithful. To the others the authors of Apocalypses have nothing to say. They do not summon them to conversion: "He that is unjust, let him be unjust still: and he which is filthy, let him be filthy still" (Rev. xxii. 11): that is its principle. It is the exact antithesis of the position taken by Jesus when he says: "I am not come to call the righteous to repentance, but sinners" (Mark ii. 17).

The Gospel is not the revelation of an immutable plan of God. It is an appeal which brings men face to face with a decision which they must make, on which will depend their destiny at the appearance of the Son of Man.

The difference between the conceptions of Jesus and those of apocalyptic come out very clearly on another point. According to a doctrine which was, if not universal in Judaism, at least very widespread, the *rôle* of the Messiah was to be glorious, since his coming was to be preceded by that of Elijah, whose mission it would be to establish order in the world. At first, Jesus may have accepted this conception, but he ultimately rejected it.[1]

The non-apocalyptic character of the thought of Jesus is definitely confirmed by Mark (xiii. 32) and by Matthew (xxiv. 36): "But of that day and that hour knoweth no man, no, not the angels which are in heaven, neither the Son, but the Father." This saying is found in the Synoptic Apocalypse, but, as Luke does not give it, and it is not in agreement with but rather in opposition to the rest of the discourse, it must be regarded as an addition of Mark to the source. By inserting this saying the evangelist has acted in the same way as Matthew, who, in several passages in the Synoptic Apocalypse, has

[1] See, on this point, pp. 276 ff.

introduced sayings which certainly came originally from the Logia, since they have parallels in other places in Luke.[1] But, theoretically, it might also be possible that this saying has been created by Mark, or by the editor who gave to his Gospel the form which we know, in order to modify what might have been difficult for the believers in the fact that events which Jesus had announced as close at hand were not fulfilled. This interpretation, however, does not seem tenable. We have no positive indication which would permit us to conjecture that the progressive modification of the eschatological expectation caused a crisis in the Church, and, if this had been the case, a saying like this would certainly not have helped to allay agitation. The Son does not know the day nor the hour, that is to say the precise moment of the *parousia*, but he is not ignorant of the time, that is of the period, in which it will take place.[2] The saying preserved by Mark xiii. 32 does not contradict the declaration according to which the Son of Man will come before the generation to which he belongs has entirely passed away (Mark ix. 1). When we take into account the fact of the swiftness with which Christology developed, it is difficult to suppose that a statement of ignorance about the moment of the *parousia* by the Son could have been created later than the year 70. Hence this statement may be regarded as historical.

Thus we can distinguish three phases through which the thought of Jesus passed. At the moment of the sending out of the disciples on their mission he believed that the *parousia* was very near. The disciples will not have time to pass through all the towns of Israel in haste before the Son of Man will come (Matt. x. 23). A little later, after the Galilean crisis, he says simply that among his hearers there will be some who will not taste of death until they have seen the coming of the Kingdom of God (Mark ix. 1). The horizon has already

[1] For instance, xxiv. 26–28 (= Luke xvii. 23–24, 37); xxiv. 39–41 (= Luke xxvi. 27, 34–35); xxiv. 42–44 (= Luke xii. 39–40); xxiv. 45–51 (= Luke xii. 42–46); xxv. 14–30 (= Luke xix. 12–27).

[2] The passage 1 Thess. v. 2–3, may serve as an illustration of my point. Paul states that the day of the Lord will come suddenly like a thief in the night, and he adds: "as travail upon a woman with child." The point that she does not know is the exact moment when she will be confined.

receded, since the present generation will only have a few of its members left. In the saying of Mark xiii. 32 the statement of ignorance of the precise moment shows that the expectation was already becoming more distant. If it does not indicate the abandonment of the eschatological conception, at least it indicates that more and more Jesus was opposed to the apocalyptic conception, since the idea of a precise prevision of the moment of the final drama formed an essential element of this idea. The fact that Jesus himself does not know when the precise moment of the End will occur is the logical conclusion to the statement that the *parousia* will be sudden and impossible to foresee. In this idea there is the germ, if not of denial, at least of the weakening of the eschatological conception. This leads us to think that this conception was merely the framework for the thought of Jesus provided by the surroundings in which he lived. He thought in eschatological terms just as he spoke Aramaic, but that which is most intimate and essential in his thought may not be connected any more closely with eschatological thought than with the Aramaic tongue. This explains, to some extent, how it was that Christianity was able, as time went on, to free itself from the eschatological conception without hurt to itself.

V. THE MESSIANIC CONCEPTION

In the thought of Jesus, as in that of contemporary Judaism, the three ideas of the Kingdom of God, the coming of the Messiah, and of the Judgment are closely associated and practically equivalent.

Jesus speaks frequently of the advent of the Messiah and of the coming of the Kingdom in a quite objective manner. The appearance of the Son of Man is imminent (Matt. x. 23; Mark viii. 38–ix. 1). It would not have entered the head of anyone to understand what Jesus says about this in a spiritual sense, and to refer it to the outpouring of the Holy Spirit, or to the establishment of the Church, if people had not been obsessed by the idea that any prophecy uttered by Jesus must necessarily receive its complete fulfilment. The fact that the coming of the Kingdom of God and the manifestation of the Son of Man are regarded as identical is due to the fact that in Luke (xvii. 20, 23–24), with reference to both, Jesus advises people not to listen to those who say "Lo! here! or Lo! there!"

Although during the early part of his ministry Jesus sometimes spoke of the coming of the Kingdom of God and of the coming of the Messiah as though he had no personal part to play in these movements, more often he spoke in such a way that he identified the coming of the Kingdom with the manifestation of his own Messiahship and his glorious return.

The problem of the Messianic consciousness of Jesus is rendered a delicate question by the fact that the evangelists had a very clear conception of the Messiahship of Christ which has reacted on the way in which they have presented the history of Jesus. In the Synoptic Gospels there is a whole dogmatic system concerning the Son of Man who is destined to suffer, be put to death, and be raised on the third day, and this dogma can only have been formed in the Apostolic age. Starting from this point, some critics like Wrede [1] have claimed that the dogmatic perversion has not only determined the form in which the thought of Jesus is presented in the Gospels, but that it has even introduced into it the very idea of the Messiahship itself. Mark and those who followed would thus have given the story a Messianic colouring, when in reality it was not Messianic at all.

An important part of the discussion refers to the expression "Son of Man." According to certain writers [2] the Messianic term of Son of Man was due originally to an error in translation: it is said that the Aramaic expression *bar-anasch*, which corresponds to the Hebrew *ben-adam*, has been literally reproduced. This expression, more frequent in Aramaic than in Hebrew, where it still retains a certain poetical character, describes an individual of the human species, a "man" of some kind. By calling himself by the term of *bar-anasch* Jesus was simply speaking of himself in the third person.

[1] WREDE: *Messiasgeheimnis.*

[2] LEITZMANN: *Der Menschensohn*, Freiburg in Br., Leipzig, 1896. WELLHAUSEN: *Des Menschen Sohn, Skizzen und Vorarbeiten*, VI, Berlin, 1899, pp. 189–215. Lastly, DUPONT: *Le Fils de l'Homme*, Paris, 1924, with full bibliographical notes.

This theory is much less weighty than it appears at first sight. Philologists like Dalman and Fiebig [1] have remarked that what is true of the expressions *ben-adam* and *bar-anasch*, in which the noun "man" is not determined, does not necessarily apply if the word is determined. The Hebrew expression *ben-haadam* and the Aramaic expression *bar-anascha* may perfectly well mean something different from "a man." Thus this is not only a question of philology. Gunkel [2] has also observed, very justly, that even if "Son of Man" meant originally only "man," the word could very well have taken on a Messianic significance just as in the Apocalyptic of Judaism and primitive Christianity the word "day" has often been used in the sense of "day of Judgment" (cf., for instance, 1 Cor. iii. 13). "Man" may very well have become the abbreviated expression of something like "the man from heaven," or "the first man," or "the typical man," or "the man who comes upon the clouds," and this is all the more likely because the doctrine of the Son of Man is certainly connected with speculations about the first man and his return at the end of the age, which were very widespread wherever the influence of Mazdaism was strong.[3]

If the Messianic expression "Son of Man" was due originally to an error in translation, it would have been on Hellenic soil that it would have been formed; now it is remarkable that in the documents of Hellenic Christianity we do not find it (in the Pauline epistles, the Epistle to the Hebrews, the First Epistle of Peter, the Johannine Epistles, the Acts), or that we only find it in virtue of a survival coming from Palestinian sources (Fourth Gospel).

The term "Son of Man" was in use before the time of Jesus, and it was then already definitely Messianic in meaning. In Dan. vii, after the four beasts, which represent the empires of Babylonia, Media, Persia, and Greece, have been shorn of

[1] DALMAN: *Die Worte Jesu*, I, pp. 191–219. FIEBIG: *Der Menschensohn*, Tübingen, Leipzig, 1901.

[2] GUNKEL: *Aus Wellhausen's neuesten apokalyptischen Forschungen*, *Z. f. wiss. Th.*, 1900, pp. 588 ff. Cf. BOUSSET-GRESSMANN: *Religion des Judentums*, p. 266, n. 1.

[3] Cf. REITZENSTEIN: *Das iranische Erlösungsmysterium*, Bonn, 1921. The Pauline theory of Christ, the second Adam, is explained, in particular, by this influence.

their power, there arrives on the clouds of heaven one "like unto a Son of Man," who receives "a dominion which shall not pass away, and a kingdom which shall not be destroyed" (vii. 13–14). The figure "like a Son of Man" is here not a personal Messiah, but the symbolic figure of the Messianic reign of Israel (vii. 27). In the passage of time the term employed by Daniel was understood to refer to a personal Messiah. This is the case in the Parables of Enoch,[1] a book which was composed during the first century before our present era. In chapter xlvi the seer perceives "the Lord of Spirits,"[2] that is to say, God, and with Him another being whose aspect was that of a man and whose face was full of gracious beauty like one of the holy angels. The angel who conducts Enoch explains:

This is the Son of Man who hath righteousness,
With whom dwelleth righteousness,
And who revealeth the treasures of all that which is hidden,
Because the Lord of Spirits hath chosen him,
And whose lot hath the pre-eminence before the Lord of Spirits
    in uprightness for ever.
And this Son of Man whom thou hast seen
Shall raise up the kings and the mighty from their seats,
    [and the strong from their thrones . . .] (xlvi. 3–4).

(then there follows a description of the Judgment). This Son of Man is pre-existent (xlviii. 3). All men will tremble when they see him seated on the throne of his glory (lxii. 5). He will exercise judgment, and after the Judgment

The Lord of Spirits will abide over them,
And with that Son of Man shall they eat
And lie down and rise up for ever and ever (lxii. 14).
As for the wicked, they shall be condemned,
Their faces shall be filled with shame,
And the darkness shall grow deeper on their faces (lxii. 10).

---

[1] There are other terms for the Messiah in the Book of Enoch, as, for instance, "the Messiah," "the Just One," "the Elect," "the Elect of Justice and Holiness."   [2] Or the "Head of days."

Some authors have supposed [1] that these passages and others which express similar ideas are interpolations. Others think that they are Jewish additions, destined to set the idea of a purely celestial Messiah against that of a Son of Man who would appear under a human form before being manifested on the clouds of heaven. The controversial method must have been very indirect, since the idea of a terrestrial phase of his life is not directly indicated. It is still more difficult to admit the idea of Christian interpolations. Here there is a typical example in a book like the *Ascension of Isaiah*. The Christian editor through whose hands it has passed has introduced into it, without troubling about the confusions to which this led, the ideas of the Virgin Birth, of the Passion, and the Resurrection. A Christian author who had touched up the Book of Enoch would not have described the Messiah without mentioning his existence on the earth and without making allusions to the Cross.

The author of the Book of Enoch always says, "This Son of Man." Thus he is alluding to an earlier conception which was already familiar to his readers. He interprets the impersonal Messiah of the Book of Daniel in a personal sense, and thus he constitutes an intermediate link between Daniel and the Gospels. The fact that Enoch always uses the term "this Son of Man" shows that this term is not a Messianic title which was in current use, but a somewhat mysterious designation, an allusion to a passage in which it was thought there was a reference to the Messiah.

Bousset [2] thinks that the transformation of the idea of the Son of Man which took place between Enoch and Daniel betrays the influence of the Iranian doctrine of the man from heaven. It is indeed difficult to imagine that such an important development can have taken place as the result merely of an error in interpretation.

Thus at the time of Jesus the term "Son of Man" was a rather rare designation of the Messiah envisaged in his *rôle* as Judge. The title was a little mysterious and elastic, which

[1] For instance, P. LAGRANGE (*Messianisme*, pp. 88 f.), who does not give a definite opinion.
[2] BOUSSET-GRESSMANN: *Religion des Judentums*, pp. 265 ff.

made it more suitable than some other terms in current use to express new ideas.

If we try to examine more closely the fact of the Messianic consciousness of Jesus, we must first of all note the Messianic impression which his person and his activity produced on those who were the witnesses of his life, an impression apart from which the genesis of the faith in the Resurrection, and through that the birth and the development of Christianity, would be unintelligible. Let us note also the episode of the request of the sons of Zebedee (Mark x. 35–45*) which, when we recall in what an unflattering light it places the two apostles, one of whom in any case was the first apostle to die the death of a martyr, cannot be regarded as a creation of tradition. We should remember also what we have said about the casting out of demons [1] and the sentiment which is expressed in this saying of Jesus—whether we see in it a simple figure of speech (as I believe we should), or an allusion to some vision which Jesus had experienced—"I saw Satan fall as lightning from heaven" (Luke x. 18). Finally we can recall the entry into Jerusalem, which, as we have seen, was in the nature of a Messianic demonstration.[2]

Jesus declares that "Whosoever therefore shall be ashamed of me and of my words in this adulterous and sinful generation, of him also shall the Son of Man be ashamed, when he cometh in the glory of his Father with the holy angels," and inversely he also says that he will confess before his Father in heaven those who confess him before men (Mark viii. 38*; Matt. x. 32–33; Luke xii. 8–9). These words have no meaning unless they mean that Jesus feels himself to be the Son of Man; more exactly if it is he who is to appear in the part of the Son of Man. Here we would only remind the reader of his declaration before the Sanhedrin, a statement which we have seen to be wholly authentic.[3]

Jesus spoke of himself as "Son of Man" in the future. But, by a quite natural anticipation, even during the course of his ministry, he was already called the Son of Man (Mark ii. 10*;

---

[1] See pp. 316 ff.   [2] See pp. 409 ff.   [3] See pp. 207, 509.

T

Matt. xi. 19*) in a way which was intelligible only to those
who were his intimates and knew his mind.

It is not possible to say at what precise moment Jesus knew
that he was called to be the Son of Man. At the moment when
this idea was fully developed, after the Galilean crisis, it was
so closely connected with the ideas of humiliation and suffering,
that it is difficult to think that there can have only been an
external and occasional link between them. Without being
able to produce actual proof, it seems probable that the two
ideas of the Messiahship and of suffering developed together
alongside of each other. The Messianic consciousness of Jesus
was a synthesis of the optimism which the final success of his
cause inspired in his soul, his faith in the omnipotence of his
heavenly Father, and of the pessimism which was imposed on
him by experience. Thus it was the triumph of the ideal over
the actual.

The fact that Jesus felt he was the Messiah caused him to
take up the line we see in the Gospels, and, instead of asking
men to adopt this or the other system of ideas, or to follow a
certain way of life, he asked them to follow him (Mark i. 16*;
ii. 14*; viii. 34*). It is for his sake that sacrifices and insults
must be accepted (Mark viii. 34*; Matt. v. 11). We cannot
regard this as a retrospective projection of the apostolic faith
into the Gospel, for the object of this faith was not Jesus in
his ministry on earth but the glorified Saviour.

Jesus' consciousness of being the Son of God is not directly
Messianic in character, but it led to the growth of the
Messianic consciousness. Jesus speaks of God as the Father of
all men almost as often as he calls Him his Father, but when he
is speaking of himself he gives to the idea of the Father-God a
very living sense because there is no sin to disturb his relation
with God. In their present condition men are not, in the full
sense of the word, sons of God, but they have to become so
by entire obedience to the Divine Will. For instance, they have
to learn to love their enemies and to pray for those who
persecute them, in order that they may become "sons of their
Father which is in heaven" (Matt. v. 45).

VI. The Preparation of Men for the Kingdom of God

Since the Kingdom of God is definitely transcendent in character, it can only be set up by an act of God. Jesus does not feel that he has been sent to prepare for the Kingdom of God or to hasten its coming. The Kingdom will come at the hour appointed for it by God, which He alone knows. It will come as a thief in the night, or like a master who returns when he is not expected, and surprises his servants. The work of Jesus is not to prepare the way for the Kingdom of God nor to hasten its coming; his mission is to prepare men for it that when it shall come they may be ready to enter in.

At the end of the parable of the Unjust Judge Jesus says that since this Judge finally listened to the persistent widow, men should not doubt that God will see that justice is done to his elect who call upon Him (Luke xviii. 6–8a) and he adds: "nevertheless, when the Son of Man cometh, shall he find faith on the earth?" (xviii. 8b). The meaning of this saying is evident. Men aspire after the coming of the Kingdom as a deliverance, but it will be no deliverance for them unless the Son of Man finds that they have faith in their hearts.[1] What Jesus desires is that his work may create this faith. In order to do this the separation between God and man must be abolished by a free pardon, and while waiting for the Kingdom men must live the kind of life which draws its inspiration from the ideal of this Kingdom. The proclamation of the forgiveness of sins by Jesus corresponds to the first need, and his moral teaching to the second.

The forgiveness of sins is one of the objects of the petitions in the Lord's Prayer. Its condition is repentance and faith in Jesus, but also the one who desires to be forgiven, must be willing to forgive those who may have offended him (Matt. vi. 12,* 14*). Here there is no idea of a bargain. The pardon which is received does not pay for the pardon given; it is due to a sense of guilt, which is necessary in order that the pardon offered by God can be grasped and appropriated by man.

---

[1] Here faith certainly contains the Jewish thought of fidelity to God.

This is the evident meaning of the parable of the Unmerciful Servant (Matt. xviii. 23–35).

For whom is the Kingdom of God intended? Jesus speaks several times of the elect (Mark x. 40*; Matt. xxii. 14,* xxv. 34; Luke xviii. 7) in terms which have seemed to some people to authorize us in believing in a doctrine of predestination. He has declared that many are called but few chosen (Matt. xxii. 14).[1] This is because all those who are called do not listen to the call which is addressed to them, or because they will not accept the sacrifices involved in answering the call. In the allegorical description of the Last Judgment (Matt. xxv. 31–46) the sentence which is pronounced is not due to a divine decree, but to the conduct of those who are the objects of the Judgment; and the words to the Galilean towns which at the day of Judgment will be treated more severely than the Gentile towns (Matt. xi. 20–24*), and on the Gentiles who will be received into the Kingdom of God while the sons of the Kingdom will be shut out (Matt. viii. 11–12), show that we cannot charge Jesus with the doctrine of predestination in the usual theological sense of the word.

VII. The Ethic of Jesus [2]

The ethical teaching of Jesus constitutes the indispensable complement of the proclamation of the Divine pardon. It is this which gives to this pardon a character which is not simply negative.

Jesus did not proclaim a new morality, since to the rich man who asked what he should do to inherit eternal life he replied by quoting the commandments of the Old Testament (Mark x. 19* f.). The principle of the ethic of Jesus does not differ from that of Jewish morality, that is, obedience towards God. But the conception of morality is new, since Jesus con-

---

[1] We might also quote here Luke x. 20, where Jesus says to his disciples that they ought to rejoice because their names are written in heaven. But it is not said that they have been there from all eternity, and that they are there precisely because they are attached to Jesus.

[2] On the ethic of Jesus, see my article: *Quelques remarques sur la morale de Jésus, Revue philosophique*, 1923, pp. 271–284.

ceived of obedience towards God in a way which was entirely different from that of the Judaism of his own day. It is also original in that it is addressed to men who live in the expectation of the Kingdom of God and for whom this Kingdom is the one veritable good.

If we were to make a list of the axioms, aphorisms, maxims, and images which, taken as a whole, make up the moral teaching of Jesus, we would gain a rather confused picture, in which we could distinguish moral axioms whose self-evidence is obvious, and whose truth is independent of the central idea of the Gospel,[1] proverbs and aphorisms of popular wisdom, many of which, doubtless, were drawn by Jesus from the tradition of Jewish morality, and finally, standing out distinctly from the former groups, a series of sayings in which the essential moral ideas of Jesus are expressed. They are in relation with the living centre of his thought, that is, with the idea of the Kingdom of God, and with the part which he himself has to play in establishing it.

The ethic of Jesus is not a system of legislation for the Kingdom of God. The idea of the Kingdom represents an ideal which is sufficiently clear not to need further definition. Those who will be admitted into it will instinctively know the will of God, and will accomplish it without effort. The moral teaching of Jesus is only addressed to men who are living in that period, both tragic and fruitful, which is the last in the history of the world.

The Beatitudes (Matt. v. 3–12*), which are often considered as the charter of the Kingdom of God, have definitely a future reference; they do not proclaim a reversal of values; they do not say that poverty, hunger, thirst, and persecution are good in themselves, but that they are the condition of obtaining the supreme good, which is the Kingdom of God.

Jesus often proclaimed the necessity for renunciation, but he did not require it as something in itself, a sacrifice without an aim, an asceticism which is an end in itself. He demanded

---

[1] For instance, the words about serving two masters (Matt. vi. 24*), the tree and its fruits (Matt. vii. 15–20*), and on the salt of the earth (Matt. v. 13*).

sacrifices for "Himself, or the Gospel, or for the sake of the Kingdom."

Doubtless in the moral teaching of Jesus there are positive moral precepts like those, for instance, to give one example only, which deal with the love of one's neighbour. They express principles which go far beyond the significance of a preparation for the Kingdom of God. But Jesus did not formulate them in order to describe the Kingdom of God, but in order to define an ideal which must be realized before the coming of the Kingdom. It has often been claimed that Jesus taught a double morality (this is the view of Catholic theology). Alongside of precepts obligatory for all men, he is said to have formulated counsels which were intended only for an *élite* which was determined to attain an ideal of superior holiness. According to Matthew (xix. 21), to the rich man who asks what he is to do in order to inherit eternal life, that is, to enter into the Kingdom of God, and who says that he has observed all the commandments from his youth up, Jesus says: "If thou wilt be perfect, go, sell all that thou hast and give to the poor." But this passage cannot be taken into account, for it does not occur in Mark or in Luke, and there are some very clear indications (for instance, the modification of the beginning of the account of the incident),[1] which show that in the section on the danger of riches Matthew has altered the text of Mark.

There is another saying which is interpreted in the same sense. After Jesus has condemned divorce, his disciples say to him:

If the case of the man be so with his wife, it is not good to marry. But he said unto them, All men cannot receive this saying, save they to whom it is given. For there are some eunuchs, which were so born from their mother's womb; and there are some eunuchs, which were made eunuchs of men: and there be eunuchs, which have made themselves eunuchs for the kingdom of heaven's sake. He that is able to receive it, let him receive it (Matt. xix. 10–12).

In Catholic theology, chastity, poverty, and renunciation are said to be required by Jesus from some men but not from

---

[1] Instead of, "Why callest thou me good? there is none good but one, that is, God," Matthew makes Jesus say: "Why do you ask me about that which is good? One alone is good, even God."

all. But the summons to an absolute perfection, since it is
that of God, is addressed without distinction to all those who
wish to be the disciples of Jesus (Matt. v. 48). If we read the
story of the rich man to the end we see that his refusal to sacrifice
that which is asked of him means not that he renounces a
perfection which he might otherwise have attained, but that
he definitely alienates himself, and thus excludes himself,
from the Kingdom of God. The words that Jesus utters after
he has gone away leave us in no manner of doubt on this
point.

The saying about the eunuchs is one of those paradoxes
of Jesus which must not be interpreted too literally. We must
not, however, go too far in the opposite direction. The Sermon
on the Mount contains exhortations which (with regard to
the question of non-resistance, for instance), if taken literally,
seem in absolute opposition to the normal conditions of human
existence, and would lead almost inevitably to the annihilation
of those who would take them absolutely literally. All the
same, it is not enough to regard them merely as an ideal
towards which we must aspire. Such an interpretation would
dishonour the ethic of Jesus and destroy its originality, by
taking from it that heroic element which is one of its most
essential characteristics.

In the words about the eunuchs Jesus speaks of "those to whom
it is given." This introduces a leading idea which is the key
to the moral teaching of Jesus, that is, the idea of vocation.
There is no question here of different degrees of holiness or of
optional duties. Here the idea is of duties which vary from
man to man, according to the gifts each has received and the
situation in which he finds himself. The content of duty is not
the same for all, but its form remains the same, and it is always
absolute.

The way in which Jesus speaks of marriage as indissoluble
and instituted by God, and the terms in which he speaks of
children, show that in his eyes the family has positive value.
He admits, however, and he shows this also by his own
example, by the attitude he adopted towards his mother and
his brothers when they came and tried to hinder him from
carrying out his mission (Mark iii. 31), words like those about

the eunuchs or about the hatred of relatives (Luke xiv. 26), that the renunciation of the joys of family life may be required of some.

It is the same with material possessions. For entrance into the Kingdom wealth is no greater obstacle than anything else. When Jesus says that it is more difficult for a rich man to enter into the Kingdom than for a camel to pass through the eye of a needle, directly afterwards, to the question, "Who then can be saved?" he replies: "To men this is impossible, but not to God, for with God all things are possible" (Mark x. 26–27*). In the incident of Zacchaeus Jesus declares: "To-day is salvation come unto this house" (Luke xix. 9). Yet he had laid no burden on Zacchaeus and the latter had not given away all his goods.

There are some people, however, to whom under special circumstances Jesus addresses a special call to renunciation. This renunciation may have as its object wealth, an easy life, the joys of family life, or life itself. His ethic is essentially an ethic of sacrifice. This sacrifice may go so far as to mean the entire destruction of the individual in question. It is accepted not for any personal end but in a disinterested manner, for the sake of an ideal whose value exceeds that of the individual. Essentially it must be irrational. No law can demand it. It represents in the moral realm the faculty of invention, of newness, of creation. It is an obligation for the one who accomplishes it, and yet it cannot be exacted. This teaching on sacrifice is only the transference into the sphere of morality of the most intimate thought of Jesus about himself and his work. Just as Jesus saw in the acceptance of suffering, humiliation, and death the condition of his manifestation as a glorious Messiah, he saw, in the sacrifice demanded from his disciples, the way which leadeth unto life: "Whosoever will come after me, let him deny himself, and take up his cross, and follow me. For whosoever will save his life shall lose it; but whosoever shall lose his life for my sake . . ., the same shall save it" (Mark viii. 34–35; cf. Matt. x. 38–39; Luke xiv. 27, xvii. 33).

There have been some who have tried to argue that the teaching of Jesus on moral questions lacks originality, and it is not difficult to show that he owes much to the tradition of his people.[1] But a mere similarity does not constitute a conclusive argument. What makes the originality of the moral thought of Jesus is not the amount of new material, whether great or small, which he has brought, it is the way in which he has linked this moral teaching with a new religious conception and a new religious experience.

VIII. CONCLUSION

DID Jesus feel that he was bringing a new religion to his nation? This question did not occur to him. His attitude towards the religious tradition of his people seems to have been modified to the extent in which experience caused the disappearance of the hopes or the illusions which he may have cherished at the outset. But although in the end he may have despaired of his own people, and though he may have thought that the economy of Judaism would have to be abrogated, he did not condemn the religion of the Jews, but the Jews themselves, because, as slaves of the letter, they did not grasp the principles laid down in the Law and the Prophets, and did not attempt to make them bear all the fruit which they might have done. It was through fidelity to the ideal Judaism that Jesus became detached from empirical Judaism and condemned it, and he did not feel that he was the founder of a new religion.

In the volume which will follow the present work we shall see how a religion grew out of the work of Jesus; all that the early founders did, however, was to develop the feelings and experiences which, directly or indirectly, had been implanted in them through the impression made on them by his person and by his teaching.

John tells how on the Cross one last saying is breathed from the lips of Jesus: "τετέλεσται." The evangelist, perhaps without knowing it, thus expresses a great truth. Τετέλεσται. This

[1] For instance, the charge has sometimes been levelled at Jesus that on the question of divorce he was simply following the lead of Shammai and his school, which, in contrast to the school of Hillel, tried to limit the extreme facility of divorce. But Shammai merely gave a more rigid interpretation to the Law, whereas Jesus placed himself far above the Law in order to condemn the very principle of divorce itself.

means: It is finished. Indeed, everything seemed finished. The attempt made by Jesus to lead Judaism beyond itself had failed. Judaism had lost the opportunity of realizing all the latent possibilities and capacities which it possessed. Henceforth it was to be a religion which had survived itself. The Sanhedrin and Pilate think that they have finished with one whom they believe—or pretend to believe—to be a Messianic agitator. The danger which they feared has been definitely dispelled. If at one moment on the shore of the Lake of Galilee the disciples of Jesus had wished to take him by force and make him king, never again would such a thing happen; and when conflicts arose later between the Empire and the Church they had no other cause than the intolerance of the Empire, which disputed with the Church its right to exist by wishing to impose upon its members the duty of participating in the official worship of the Emperor. Christianity was so little hostile to Rome that when the conflict of 66–70 between Jerusalem and Rome broke out, the Christians of Jerusalem, although they were still attached to Judaism, left the city and took refuge at Pella, in order that they might not have to take part in a conflict which they felt did not concern them, for their fatherland was neither in Jerusalem nor in Rome, because it was not of this world (1 Pet. ii. 11).

But τετέλεσται also means: "All is accomplished." The work of Jesus was finished. The faith which he had been able to plant in the hearts of a few men, feeble and hesitating as it was, had roots which were too deep to be ever eradicated. Nothing was finished; in reality, everything had just begun. The faith in the Resurrection was about to be born, and with it that Christianity which was destined to conquer the Ancient World and to march through the centuries.

ADDENDA

WHILE this book was in the press a thesis for the doctorate of the University of Louvain has appeared which should at least be mentioned, since it deals with the question of the Eucharist. This work is entitled, *Les Origines de l'Eucharistie. Sacrement et Sacrifice*, by Werner Goossens, Gembloux, Paris, 1931. It is an important work, remarkably well informed, which contains, among other things, a good survey of the history of the problem of the Eucharist, and a very full bibliography.

Here I will simply note some of the points which show the position of Goossens on this question of the Last Supper of Jesus.

On the question of the text of Luke his views coincide with mine, that is to say, he accepts the authenticity of the Eastern text (pp. 101–109).

With reference to the absence of the account of the Last Supper in the Fourth Gospel, he alludes to the explanation suggested by H. Huber (*Das Herrenmahl im Neuen Testament auf Grund der neuesten Forschungen dargestellt und beurteilt* (*Inaugural Dissertation, Bern*), Leipzig, 1929, p. 92), based upon the existence of the *Arcani Disciplina*. Goossens rightly makes the following objections to this theory:

(i) We have no grounds for assuming that the Secret Discipline was in existence at the period when the Fourth Gospel was being compiled.

(ii) That if this idea of a secret practice of the Sacrament were in existence at that time, it is impossible to understand why John spoke so freely and with so much detail about the Eucharist in chapter vi. Goossens himself inclines towards a view which is similar to that adopted by Renan, Oskar Holtzmann, and Jean Réville (cf. p. 461 n. 1), and thinks that John did not mention the Last Supper because he had said all he had to say about the Eucharist in chapter vi.

Goossens (pp. 110–127) regards the Last Supper as Paschal in character, and, like Billerbeck (cf. p. 432, n. 3) regards it, in principle, as impossible that there can be a real disagreement between the Synoptics and the Fourth Gospel: "A real discrepancy in the ancient tradition concerning the date of

the death of Christ does not seem possible," he writes, on
p. 121.

Finally, he seeks to prove that Jesus did actually institute
the Sacrament of the Eucharist (pp. 372 ff.). In order to prove
this thesis he tries to show the inadequacy of the theories in
which independent critics (this is his own expression) explain
the origin of the doctrine of the Sacrament. In my second
volume, in which I shall deal with the subject of the Eucharist
in the Apostolic age, I shall discuss the theories on this subject
which have been put forward by Goossens and other Catholic
theologians.

INDEX